Michael Müller

The Holy Mass

the sacrifice for the living and the dead, the clean oblation offered up among the nations from the rising to the setting of the sun

Michael Müller

The Holy Mass

the sacrifice for the living and the dead, the clean oblation offered up among the nations from the rising to the setting of the sun

ISBN/EAN: 9783741103193

Manufactured in Europe, USA, Canada, Australia, Japa

Cover: Foto ©Lupo / pixelio.de

Manufactured and distributed by brebook publishing software (www.brebook.com)

Michael Müller

The Holy Mass

THE HOLY MASS:

THE

SACRIFICE FOR THE LIVING AND THE DEAD.

THE CLEAN OBLATION OFFERED UP AMONG THE NATIONS FROM THE RISING TO THE SETTING OF THE SUN.

BY

MICHAEL MÜLLER,

PRIEST OF THE CONGREGATION OF THE MOST HOLY REDEEMER.

FOURTH REVISED EDITION.

NEW YORK: CINCINNATI:
No. 52 Barclay Street.   No. 204 Vine Street.

FR. PUSTET,
PRINTER TO THE HOLY APOSTOLIC SEE.
1875.

TO THE

MOST SACRED AND ADORABLE

HEART OF JESUS

IN THE BLESSED SACRAMENT

THIS

𝕭𝖔𝖔𝖐 𝖎𝖘 𝕳𝖚𝖒𝖇𝖑𝖞 𝕯𝖊𝖉𝖎𝖈𝖆𝖙𝖊𝖉,

IN REPARATION, THANKSGIVING AND LOVE.

CONTENTS.

                 PAGE

CHAPTER I.
Introductory 9

CHAPTER II.
The Wonderful Promise of God................................ 25

CHAPTER III.
The Wonderful Gift of God..................................... 38

CHAPTER IV.
A Wonderful Means of Awakening Faith in the Real Presence... 49

CHAPTER V.
A Wonderful Manifestation of the Real Presence................ 64

CHAPTER VI.
The Wonderful Effects of the Blessed Sacrament in Nicola Aubry. 88

CHAPTER VII.
Further Wonderful Manifestations of the Real Presence.......... 96

CHAPTER VIII.
The Sacrifice before the Coming of Christ....................... 128

CHAPTER IX.
The Sacrifice of the New Law................................... 135

CHAPTER X.
The Sacrifice of the New Law—continued....................... 149

CHAPTER XI.
Mass Applies to us the Merits of Christ.......................... 159

CHAPTER XII.
Mass, the Renewal of the Mysteries of the Life of Christ........ 167

CHAPTER XIII.
Mass, the Renewal of the Incarnation............................. 173

CHAPTER XIV.
Mass, the Renewal of Christ's Life in the Womb of Mary......... 181

CHAPTER XV.
Mass, the Renewal of the Birth of Christ........................ 188

CHAPTER XVI.
Mass, the Renewal of the Life of Christ......................... 197

CHAPTER XVII.
Mass, the Renewal of God's Wondrous Works....................... 205

CHAPTER XVIII.
Mass, the Renewal of Christ's Passion........................... 214

CHAPTER XIX.
Mass, the Renewal of Christ's Passion—continued................. 224

CHAPTER XX.
Mass, the Renewal of Christ's Resurrection...................... 239

CHAPTER XXI.
Mass, the Renewal of Christ's Resurrection—continued............ 246

CHAPTER XXII.
Mass, the Renewal of the Virtues of Christ...................... 255

CHAPTER XXIII.
Mass, a Sacrifice of Adoration and Infinite Praise.............. 263

CONTENTS.

CHAPTER XXIV.
Mass, a Sacrifice of Propitiation.................................. 281

CHAPTER XXV.
Mass, a Sacrifice of Thanksgiving............................... 300

CHAPTER XXVI.
Mass, a Sacrifice of Impetration.................................. 318

CHAPTER XXVII.
Mass, a Sacrifice of Impetration—continued............... 337

CHAPTER XXVIII.
Mass, the Hope of the Dying...................................... 350

CHAPTER XXIX.
Mass Propitiatory for the Dead................................... 361

CHAPTER XXX.
Mass, the Joy of the Blessed Virgin............................. 382

CHAPTER XXXI.
Reverence and Devotion at Mass................................. 395

CHAPTER XXXII.
Why Catholics must Hear Mass.................................. 418

CHAPTER XXXIII.
How to Hear Mass.. 431

CHAPTER XXXIV.
How to Hear several Masses at once............................ 454

CHAPTER XXXV.
The Dignity and Sanctity of the Mass.......................... 463

CHAPTER XXXVI.
Satan's Hatred for the Mass.. 475

CONTENTS.

CHAPTER XXXVII.
Why Mass is celebrated in Latin................................ 500

CHAPTER XXXVIII
The Honorary of Mass... 506

CHAPTER XXXIX.
The Use of Ceremonies.. 510

CHAPTER XL.
The Use of Sacred Vestments................................... 520

CHAPTER XLI.
Low Mass.. 527

CHAPTER XLII.
Low Mass—continued.. 544

CHAPTER XLIII.
Low Mass—concluded.. 560

CHAPTER XLIV.
Solemn High Mass—Lights and Incense......................... 575

CHAPTER XLV.
Music at High Mass... 586

CHAPTER XLVI.
The Use of Holy Water before High Mass....................... 595

CHAPTER XLVII.
How and Why Catholics Build Churches........................ 601

CHAPTER XLVIII.
The Love of God.. 624

THE HOLY SACRIFICE
OF
THE MASS.

CHAPTER I.

INTRODUCTORY.

TOWARDS the middle of the fifth century there lived in the City of Rome a hidden saint named Alexius. He was the son of the Roman senator, Euphemian, a man of great wealth. At an early age he felt inspired by God to leave his home for a strange country. Obedient to this inner voice, he went forth from his father's house, and passed seventeen years in pious pilgrimages in the East, amid many trials and dangers. At length, to show his love for God in a still more striking manner, he resolved to return to his house in the garb of a poor beggar, and spend there the remainder of his days. On arriving at Rome, he met his father, Euphemian, in the street, followed by a train of attendants, as became his high rank. Clad in rags and attenuated by fasts, Alexius was not recognized by his father. So he besought him for charity to give him shelter in his house, and for food, the crumbs that fell from his table.

The nobleman, moved with pity, bade one of his servants to lodge and take care of the poor beggar. The servant conducted him to an obscure apartment under the staircase where, for twenty-two years, he passed a life of suffering and humiliation, because the menials made him a butt for their which he bore with invincible patience. Thus did the life he spent in his father's house become one long-continued prayer, fast, penance, and austerity. At length, when he felt death approaching, he begged one of the servants to bring him writing materials. Then he wrote down on a sheet of paper the story of his whole life, whither he had wandered, what had happened to him, what he had suffered at home and abroad. He stated at the same time that he was Alexius, the son of the house, whom his parents had missed for so many years. This paper he held in his hands until death took him on a Sunday at the time when his parents were at mass. No sooner had his soul taken flight to heaven than all the bells of the churches in Rome began to ring, and a loud voice was heard to say distinctly three times:—" Go to the house of Euphemian to find the great friend of God who hast just died and prays for Rome, and all he asks is granted." Then went the people to find the saint, and Euphemian was the first to enter his house. He went straightway to the room under the staircase, and to his surprise found that the poor beggar had just expired. Seeing the paper, he took it out of his hands, and reading its contents aloud burst into tears, embraced his holy son, hardly able to utter a word. The mother of Alexius was still more deeply affected, and cried out, " O my son, why have I known thee too late! "

The story of Alexius is a good illustration of what often happens in these days to many a Christian. Alexius went back to his father's house as a beggar clad in tatters, the better to disguise his rank and wealth. Our dear Saviour acts in the same manner in the holy Sacrifice of the Mass. There He is, but by no outward sign does He betray His real presence; His heavenly glory and brightness He hides from us; He is there, as one may say, in a poor miserable dress, under the appearances of bread and wine. As the parents of Alexius paid little attention to their son in his state of poverty and subjection, so, in this life, many Christians pay but little attention to Jesus Christ, because He humbly condescends to conceal His glory in the sacrament of His love. But when this life is over and they come to see Him face to face, whom here they possessed in the Holy Eucharist, at the sight of the consolations, of the beauty, and of the riches that they failed to recognize in time, they will exclaim, with the mother of Alexius, "O, Jesus! dear Saviour, why have we known Thee too late! Ah! had we only known Thee in Thy mystery of love, when alive on earth, we would have allowed no opportunity to escape us of assisting at the celebration of Thy sacred mysteries, of receiving Thee, in holy communion. Not an hour should have passed without a thought of Thee. Thou wouldst have been our whole delight, our whole joy, our whole happiness, the object of all our desires, thoughts and actions. O dear Lord, why have we known Thee too late!"

"Verily Thou art a hidden God, the God of Israel, the Saviour!" cries out the prophet Isaias (xlv. 15). Yes, undoubtedly, God is a more hidden God in the Eucharist than anywhere else. His greatness lies concealed under the littleness of a host, His power under the feeble species, His universality under an atom, His eternity under a moment, His wisdom under an apparent folly. There indeed is He the hidden God; more hidden than in Mary's womb, more hidden than in the crib, more hidden than under the darkness of Calvary, more hidden than in the gloom of the Sepulchre. For here His humanity, His divinity, His glory, His beatitude—all, are hidden. To all unbelievers and heretics He is hidden indeed. To many luke-warm Catholics, nay, even to many of those who stand at His altar and touch His sacred body He is hidden. Alas, that that adorable sacrifice and sacrament of the altar should be to so many a hidden treasure; that there should be so many who have eyes and see not, although to them is granted to behold what kings and prophets, and patriarchs and saints have sighed in vain to gaze on! Alas! that there should be so many who deserve the reproach which our Lord made to his disciples, "I was a stranger, and you received me not." "Your little faith in my presence in the blessed sacrament made Me appear to you a stranger, although quite near. Touching Me, you knew Me not. You are like those disciples of Mine, journeying to Emmaus, to whom I appeared after My resurrection, conversing with them most familiarly, but they knew Me not," saying, "Art thou only a stranger in Jerusalem and hast not known the things that have been done there in these days?" "So long a time have I been with you and have you not known Me?" Three years had Jesus spent in the company of His Apostles. This He calls a long time, in which they certainly should have learned who He was. Yet their faith was not such as He wished it to be. Philip asks of our Lord to show them His Father. Jesus answers, "So long a time have I been with you and have you not as yet known Me? he who sees Me sees also the Father; for the Father is in Me and I am in Him. We cannot be separated." And we? How long have we been with Jesus? We became acquainted with Him in our childhood; we went to Mass at least every Sunday; we received Him over and over again for so many years; and yet the complaint of our Lord, made to His Apostles, applies perhaps more justly to us. "So long a time have you celebrated Mass," says He to many a priest; "So long a time have you assisted at the Holy Sacrifice of Calvary," says He to many a Catholic; "So long a time have you entered into close intimacy with Me in holy communion and yet you seem not to know Me. You know not My Divinity in the sacred Host, or your respect and veneration for it could not be so small; you know not My Body and Soul there present, for you do not imitate the example I gave you on earth and give you in this mystery of love; you know not My love, or it would affect you more; you know not My heart, which is ever open to you, with charity inexhaustible, for you still seem to doubt its goodness and meekness, its tender love and its unbounded mercy. You know not My sanctity or you would not appear at the altar, without gravity, without devotion, and without reverence. You know not My high dignity, or you would not touch Me with such coldness and thoughtlessness, nor would you approach the altar in a state of unworthiness. Indeed were you thoroughly impressed with the thought that in the adorable sacrament of My love you receive *your Lord and your God*, had you a lively conviction of this truth, would you dare approach Me as you do, without preparation, without sorrow, humility, or reverence? Would you presume after having received Me, your Redeemer, to employ the eyes that have contemplated your Lord and God in this adorable mystery, in the indulgence of curiosity, the tongue on which He has reposed, in slander, raillery, or expressions wounding to charity? Would you profane the heart into which He has entered, by inordinate affections, anger, hatred, or envy? Whence is it that you relapse so frequently into habitual failing and draw so little profit from hearing Mass and receiving holy communion? It is because you know Me not in the mystery of My love.

"Every object that is brought in contact with fire experiences its effects; it is either enkindled wholly or at least is heated. What fire more intense than the fire of divine love in the Blessed Sacrament? To receive this divine fire so often into your heart, to be near it every day and yet remain cold, not to burn for Me with that ardent love which consumed the just men of the old Law, in expectation of their Saviour coming! Do you then value the possession of a benefit less than its promise? You are always permitted to enjoy My Presence in the sacred tabernacle, and those patriarchs only asked for the momentary appearance of a Redeemer. Truly the faith of the patriarchs, and their fervent desires will one day rise up in judgment against you. Their desires had no centre upon earth, but you can repose your thoughts and your heart upon Me in this tabernacle, in which abides your God. My love could not suffer you to repeat the complaint of the Prophet 'O my God,

The tabernacle in our churches does not contain, like the ark of the covenant, the perishable records of the past mercies of God. It encloses the living God himself, the creator of heaven and earth. "It is the Lord." The pure eyes of St. John speedily recognised his Divine Master when He appeared to His Apostles after His resurrection. "It is the Lord," he exclaimed. Our Lord is recognized by the beloved disciple because the pure heart easily penetrates those veils which surround His holy and glorious humanity. At the altar it is also the purest and most loving souls that enjoy the most intimate and consoling sense of His Sacred Presence; the outward appearances under which He hides Himself are sufficiently transparent to the eyes of their faith; they touch, they embrace Him in mutual love, and no sooner do they behold the Sacred Host than they exclaim, "It is the Lord."

This earth, which is the abode of the holy Eucharist, would appear a kind of terrestrial paradise, if we were only capable of appreciating that precious treasure. Wonderful and ineffable truth which thrills every Catholic heart! Neither human nor angelic intelligence and imagination combined could ever in their highest flights have conceived the idea of power and love like this. "It is the Lord!" Fervent priests and Catholics, however, are not satisfied with merely knowing our Lord well in the Blessed Sacrament themselves, but consider it their duty to make Him known also to others by whatever means lies in their power; for He is not equally well known to all.

Dark clouds of error and weakness in faith have settled thickly around the throne of our dear Saviour in the sacrifice of the Mass ever since the time of the Reformation. It is the duty of priests especially to scatter those clouds, by speaking on the sublime subject with a lively faith, in language glowing with love for this mystery of love, in words that work miracles; that is in words which create in the mind of the hearers such profound conviction of this great truth of our religion, and which at the same time enkindle in their hearts such great love for our Lord in the Blessed Sacrament as is calculated to make them *run* with a holy joy and delight to assist at the sacrifice and receive the communion. Our Lord upon the altar is silent during Mass, expecting that His priests upon reflecting what He is there for—for them and for all the faithful—and what He has done for them in this mystery, would become inflamed with such love for Him as would put into their mouths words of such burning eloquence whenever they have to speak of His real presence, that every word should be a fiery dart piercing the hearts of their hearers with that divine love, and light of faith, and ardor of devotion, which are burning in their own. This is indeed what Jesus Christ expects from every good priest of His, especially in our time when faith in this great mystery grows weaker every day, not only among the higher classes of society, but even among the common people, especially among the young men and young women. How many are there who regularly attend at Mass without ever entering into the spirit, nay, without ever properly joining in the external ceremonies? How many are present at Mass with so much indifference, as clearly to show, that they either do not value these awful—these most beneficial mysteries, or that they understand little or nothing else than that the priest turns sometimes to the right, sometimes to the left, and is clothed in a motley-colored garment. To them Mass and Vespers, or the performance of the funeral rites are all pretty much the same thing. With great reason, then, did the Council of Trent command all the pastors of congregations frequently to explain the holy sacrifice of the Mass to the faithful, that at least they may not be answerable for any want of respect, devotion and diligence which the people may be guilty of in attending at Mass. The Fathers of the Council were fully convinced that the power and influence of the Church over the hearts of men depended on the efforts which her priests would make to enkindle in souls a lively faith in, and an ardent love for, the Sacred Mysteries. "Many are infirm and weak among you," writes St. Paul to the Corinthians, "and many sleep" in sin and indifference towards God and their own salvation, "because they discern not the Body of the Lord," that is, because they are ignorant of the great treasure of the Mass and holy communion. As Samson was celebrated for his extraordinary bodily strength, so is the Catholic Church noted for her extraordinary spiritual strength. Were she asked like Samson wherefrom she derives all this invincible strength and vitality, she would answer,—"It is from her faith in the holy sacrifice of the Mass; it is from holy communion. Take away the Mass and we are shorn of our strength, weak like the rest of mankind."

This faith is the dove with the olive branch come to proclaim the passing away of the mighty deluge of sin; it rouses the lukewarm from the fatal lethargy that has fallen upon their souls, it brings sinners back to God, it inflames the pious with more ardent love for Jesus Christ, it causes the unbeliever to reflect on the truths of our religion, it dispels the clouds of religious errors, it puts the devil to flight and makes him tremble; it brings down the angels from heaven upon earth to stay with the Christians and defend them against the attacks of Satan; it opens the source of all heavenly benedictions; it brings true peace and joy into the heart. It is this faith that disposes the heart for participating in the plenitude of this divine mystery and makes it easy for the soul to contemplate the Son of God, to approach Him with ardor, and to enjoy Him in peace; that keeps the interior eye of the soul forever fixed, not upon the weak accidents that show themselves to the senses, but on the Son of God, the King of glory. Who veils the splendor of His countenance that she may have easy access to His mercy unawed by the greatness of His Majesty. This is the faith that causes the heart to leap with joy, and give forth acts of every virtue, in order to receive with greater reverence the divine guest who honors it with His presence. This faith fills the soul with hope to approach Him with gladness; with humility to lose herself in profound respect; with charity to embrace Him; with devotion to render Him homage; with obedience to submit herself to His divine will. This is the spirit that concentrates all the powers of the soul in a profound recollection, and banishes from her whatever can interrupt her conversation with her dearly beloved Saviour, Jesus Christ. It introduces her into the true kingdom of God, leading her frequently as it does to the sacred banquet to unite herself with her divine Spouse by means of the Blessed Sacrament.

The learned and the wise ones of this world are often blind to all this; and as they rely too much on their own opinion and judgment, contented to guide themselves only by their own lights, not caring to rise higher than human reason, for want of humility and devotion, so they grovel all their life-time in the littleness of their own ideas and sentiments—a littleness incredible in all that regards the mysteries of the faith and the spiritual direction of souls. So they are vexed at Revelation, and histories of miracles—with an occasional professed exception in favor of those recorded in the Gospel—offend them, just as though the Lord could and would no longer perform a miracle, nor reveal Himself again after His ascension into heaven, forgetful that in the very Gospel they profess to believe, He has told us plainly, "Amen, amen, I say to you, he that believeth in me, the works that I do, he shall do also, and greater than these shall he do;"[*] and he that loveth me, shall be loved by my Father; "and I will love him and will *manifest myself to him.*"[†]

These men do not consider that wonders are in a particular manner the work of God, intended to awaken our attention to His holy Providence, and to move our souls to praise His goodness and power, often also to bear witness to His truth.

[*] John xiv. 12.   [†] Ib. verse 21.

Our fathers in the faith never, as do so many of the wise ones to-day, found it so difficult for Almighty God to work miracles, especially by means of the Blessed Sacrament. Bossuet said: "Why do people wish to make it so laborious a work for the Almighty to cause miraculous effects?" "There are," says a great poet, "more things in heaven and on earth than are dreamed of in your philosophy." That which is considered to be impossible at the present day, was doubtless possible formerly, when the world was younger and more innocent than it now is,—more worthy of the miracles God wrought in it—when angels and saints of heaven loved to commune with its simple and innocent people, whose life was divided between labor and the practice of good works.

"The bad," says St. Alphonsus, "are as ready to deride miracles as the good are to believe them;" and he adds, "as it is weakness to give credit to all things, so, on the other hand, to reject miracles which come to us attested by grave and pious men, either savors of infidelity, which supposes them impossible to God, or of presumption which refuses belief to such a class of authors. We give credit to a Tacitus, a Suetonius, and can we deny it without presumption to Christian authors of learning and piety? There is less risk in believing and receiving what is related with some probability by honest persons and not rejected by the learned, and which serves for the edification of our neighbor, than in rejecting it with a disdainful and presumptuous spirit." "When facts are related that teach and edify us," says St. Francis de Sales, "we should not believe that the proofs upon which they rest are entirely defective and worthless. 'Charity believeth all things,' which is to say, it does not easily believe *that one lies*. And if there be no sign of falsehood in what is represented to her, she makes no difficulty in giving it credence, especially when it relates to anything which exalts and praises the love of God towards men, or the love of men towards God, the more so as Charity, which is the sovereign queen of virtues, takes pleasure after the manner of princes in those things which tend to the glory of her empire and domination. Supposing then, that the narrative be neither so public nor so well attested as the greatness of the wonder would seem to require, it loses not for that its truth; for, as St. Augustine excellently says, ' when a miracle is made known, however striking it may be in the very place where it happened, or even when related by those who witnessed it, it is scarcely believed, but it is not the less true.' " " Though an assent of Catholic faith be not due to them," says Pope Benedict XIV., " yet they deserve a human assent according to the rules of prudence by which they are probable and piously credible."

At the time of St. Bernard, some reverenced the revelations of St. Hildegarde, even those passages which they could not understand; others, on the contrary, condemned them as mere reveries. St. Bernard himself read them with the greatest care, and he was *edified beyond description*. Now as those revelations were differently judged by divers persons, St. Bernard said to his companions, " These revelations are not the work of man; and no mortal will understand them unless love has renewed in his soul the image and likeness of God." However, one of those present observed, that many persons, both learned and ignorant, religious and secular, daily pierced the soul of the handmaid of God, by repeating that her visions were only *hallucinations of the brain*, or deceits of the devil. Upon which St. Bernard replied: " Let us not be surprised, my brethren, that those who are sleeping in their sins should regard revelations from on high as follies, since the Apostle affirms that the animal man cannot comprehend the things of the spirit. Yes, certainly, those who lie buried in pride, in impurity, or in other sins, take the warnings of God for reveries; but if they were vigilant in the fear of God, they would recognize *by sure signs*, the divine work. As to those who believe those visions to be the suggestions of the devil, they show that they have no deep knowledge of divine contemplation; they are like those who said of our Lord and Saviour, Jesus Christ, that He cast out devils through the power of Beelzebub."

Such men, for being in the habit of always thinking first how a tenet or practice or a fact is most presentable to the public, are soon and almost imperceptibly led to profaneness, from a habit producing, as it generally does, the spirit of rationalism in matters of faith. Their too delicate and fastidious taste has too much regard for the feelings of a certain class of people. I am aware that Christian charity, the great queen of virtues, demands of us to have due regard for the feelings of others; and I am thoroughly persuaded, that no one was ever yet converted by harsh means, or abusive language. Charity is, however, not only not incompatible with truth, but it ever demands that the whole truth should be told, especially when its concealment be a cause of error or of perseverance in error and sin, in matters, too, of most deep and vital importance. Hence to judge from the works of our greatest Catholic divines, it would appear that the deeper theologian a man is, the less does he give way to this studious desire of making difficulties easy at any cost short of denying what is positively *de fide*. They seem to handle truth religiously just in the way that God is pleased to give it to us, rather than to see what they can make of it themselves by shaping it for controversy, and so by dint of skilful manipulation squeeze it through a difficulty. Let such men examine themselves well to see whether they are not out of harmony with the mind of the Church and the spirit of the saints, whether their faith is not too feeble, and their distrust of God's wonders too overweening and too bold, whether, in short, for the good of their own soul they may not have the principle of rationalism to unlearn, and the temper of faith—sound, reasonable, masculine, yet childlike faith—to broaden, to heighten and to deepen in themselves by the very contemplation of what may now be in some degree a scandal to them, namely, *Quam mirabilis est Deus in Sanctis suis*, by means of the holy Eucharist.

What difficulty can one pretend to have in believing certain extraordinary graces which we read of in the lives of the saints? He who believes the favor which God conferred on men by making Himself man, ought to find no other incredible and surprising. All the communications which God can make after this are as nothing. God, having given Himself in such a wonderful manner to men, can now refuse them nothing. It is to give them all else, that he gave Himself in the Incarnation and the holy Eucharist. The belief in this truth naturally inclines all good Christians to believe whatever appears to reveal the power, the goodness, and the love of their divine Saviour towards men in the august mystery of the Mass. They appreciate the manifestations of this goodness of the Lord; they bless and thank Him for them, and feel powerfully, yet sweetly, drawn by them towards this centre of all earthly happiness.

It is principally for this reason that, for my own use and for the use of others, I have often wished for such a compilation on the holy sacrifice of the Mass as I now offer to my brethren of the Catholic Communion, a compilation which I have endeavored to write as much as possible in the same manner as the book "The Blessed Eucharist, Our Greatest Treasure," being fully convinced from a long experience that this manner of explaining so sublime a truth is better calculated than any other to convey instruction to the minds of all, especially of the humbler classes, who compose the greater part of the body of the faithful, to enliven their faith and make them relish and practise what they are taught to believe of so stupendous a mystery. A book like this, containing a full, plain, and, I trust, correct explanation of the Mass may be welcome to Catholics in general, but especially to well-disposed and pious souls, whose chief desire and aim in life is to know the will of God, their heavenly Father, and knowing it, to do it.

I am impressed more strongly than ever with a sense of the grandeur and sublimity of the subject. It has always been a matter of considerable difficulty not only to Protestants, but even to most Catholics, nay even to many theologians to form a clear conception of the holy sacrifice of the Mass. Perfectly conscious of my utter incompetency for the task, I could have wished that some one more competent, and more experienced in writing, had engaged in the undertaking. Hence I am ready to charge myself with presumption for venturing on so difficult a task which has occupied the pens of the ablest theologians.

I can find for myself no excuse but in the sincerity with which I have sought to collect, from all the authors at my command, the most select and pithy sentences of the Fathers and theologians, in order to give devout persons an opportunity, with little effort or expense, to become acquainted with the ideas of those great men and saints of God on the subject, that their hearts may be inflamed with greater ardor for the holy sacrifice of the Mass—a fountain so full that the farther it extends, the fuller it becomes; and the fuller it becomes, the farther it extends, which signifies that the holy Mass is a subject so grand and so sublime that the more we say of it, the more there remains to be said. Notwithstanding this sincerity of mine, I am fully sensible that I am far from having done justice to a mystery inaccessible to angels, impenetrable to devils, and totally incomprehensible to human reason, a subject so difficult to handle, so vast in its extent, so sublime in its conceptions, so unspeakable in its blessings, both spiritual and temporal. It is not necessary to urge in my defence any theological embarrassments under which I labored, since that will hardly be an excuse for not doing well what it was not necessary for me to do at all. But I may be permitted to add, that in my book, "The Blessed Eucharist, Our Greatest Treasure," a certain deficiency may have been felt by many a pious reader in the perusal of the first chapter on the Real Presence, and of those chapters treating on the holy sacrifice of the Mass; they may have wished to see in the former still more solid proofs in confirmation of the Real Presence, especially as the belief in this truth forms the basis of our whole conception of the Mass; in the latter they may have desired to see a fuller and more detailed explanation of the treasure of graces we possess in the divine gift of the Mass. To supply this deficiency, the following pages were written during intervals snatched, since last Fall, from my many religious and missionary labors. As to the defects of this undertaking—which unquestionably are many—I hope the sincerity of a good will and the desire of spiritually benefiting my Catholic brethren, will be sufficient to plead my cause with the indulgent and considerate reader. And thus, imperfect as this new production may be, I present it to my brethren of the clergy and laity, confidently hoping that it will induce many souls to betake themselves with greater eagerness and assiduity to the source of all temporal and everlasting happiness—to Jesus Christ, their sweet Saviour and good Shepherd, in the Eucharistic Sacrifice.

Now should my brethren of the clergy and laity, many of whom would have been certainly better qualified than myself for the task, deem this publication ever so little calculated to realize this hope of mine, I would most humbly request them to encourage its circulation to the best of their power. "A willow-tree," says St. Gregory, "bears no fruit, but by supporting as it does the vine together with its grapes, it makes these its own by supporting what is not its own." (Hom. 20, in Evang.) In like manner, he who warmly recommends a book calculated to do much good makes his own all the good that is done by the book.

But as it is only by faith that we can understand what the Lord teaches us in a mystery in which everything is sublime, everything is prodigious, and as it is only by prayer that we can derive profit from it, it is from Him that we must implore the necessary grace to discover the infinite treasures of the divine goodness and mercy which lie so humbly hidden under the outward appearance of bread and wine, saying often;—It is Thyself, O Lord, Who hast accomplished this sublime mystery; of Thee we humbly beg understanding and love, so as to be able to apply to ourselves the fruits of it; and you, holy Mary, Mother of God, and our tender Mother, obtain for us these precious graces, so that a work, whose accomplishment cost so many sorrows to your heart, may not prove sterile to our souls. Intercede particularly for me, I beseech you, that I may relate with benefit the supreme glories—the wonderful works—of your beloved Son, and my Divine Master. May the mysteries which I undertake to explain make a deep impression on our minds and hearts—so that they may shine forth in our whole life,—so that they may be our strength at the hour of death and become the pledge of our everlasting happiness. Beseech your Divine Son to bless these instructions, which I now offer to His people under your patronage, for the glory of Jesus Christ, the sanctification of the faithful and the edification of the Church. In the name of the Father, and of the Son, and of the Holy Ghost.

CHAPTER II.

THE WONDERFUL PROMISE OF GOD.

MANY centuries ago, when King Solomon reigned in Jerusalem, he bent his mind to the gratification of every desire of his heart, seeking for happiness. "I said in my heart, I will go and abound with delights, and enjoy good things; I made me great works; I built me houses, and planted vineyards, I made gardens and orchards, and set them with trees of all kinds, and I made me ponds of water, to water therewith the wood of the young trees. I got me men-servants and maid-servants, and had a great family; and herds of oxen and great flocks of sheep above all that were before me in Jerusalem: I heaped together for myself silver and gold, and the wealth of kings and provinces; I made me singing men and singing women, and the delights of the sons of men; cups and vessels to serve to pour out wine; and I surpassed in riches all that were before me in Jerusalem; my wisdom also remained with me. And whatsoever my eyes desired, I refused them not, and I withheld not my heart from enjoying every pleasure, and delighting itself in the things which I had prepared, and I esteemed my portion, to make use of my own labor."

After such ample enjoyment of all earthly pleasures, might we not think that Solomon was happy indeed? Nevertheless he tells us that his heart was not satisfied, and that he felt himself more miserable than before. "And when I turned myself," he says, "to all the works which my hands had wrought, and to the labors wherein I had labored in vain, I saw in all things *vanity* and vexation of mind, and that nothing was lasting under the sun."*

---

* Eccl. II.

What happened to Solomon, happens still in one shape or form to every man. Here on earth we are never satisfied; we always crave for something more, something higher, something better. Whence comes this continual restlessness that haunts us through life and pursues us even to the grave? It is the home-sickness of the soul, its craving after God. All things were created for man, but man was created to live with God, and to be united with God. Therefore the idea, the essence of all religion may be expressed in one word: "Emmanuel, God with us."

The existence of God among men in some sensible form is a want of the human heart. To satisfy this craving after the Real Presence of God, men made use of unholy means. Blinded by their passions they fell into idolatry, and instead of raising themselves to the true and pure God, they foolishly worshipped what they deemed the divine presence in stones, plants, and animals. It was God Himself who planted in the human heart the desire for the Real Presence, and God Himself also found means to satisfy this desire.

The works of God come to perfection slowly and gradually. This is the case in all, but especially in that most admirable of His works, the Real Presence. He first revealed Himself to man by creation, which is a continual revelation of His presence, although He is hidden therein. The good and pure indeed behold God in creation; they see His power in the storm, in the cataract, in the earthquake. They see His wisdom in the laws that govern the boundless universe, His beauty in the flower, in the sunbeam, and in the many-tinted rainbow. But the wicked and impure use this very creation only to outrage and blaspheme the Creator.

God then made use of a more perfect means to reveal to man His divine presence. This was His word. If a friend visits us at night, and finds us sitting in the dark, he speaks, he makes use of words to show that he is really present. In like manner, God wishing to reveal His Real Presence to man, sitting in the darkness of this life, has addressed him in words. This is the very first article of faith. God spoke to our first parents in the garden of Paradise. He spoke to the Patriarchs, to the Prophets, and finally, as St. Paul assures us, He has spoken for the last time by His only begotten Son.

But merely to hear the voice of a friend is not enough; the heart longs for something more; the eyes yearn to look upon him. God knows this want of the human heart, and He has satisfied it also. The prophets have besought Him again and again to show Himself. "Show us Thy face, O Lord, and we shall be saved." This too was the ardent prayer of Moses. "O Lord, show me Thy glory." *

In the Old Law, God satisfied this desire by manifesting His Real Presence to the Israelites, under the form of a cloud, and of a pillar of fire. He next commanded an ark or tabernacle to be made, and there He manifested His Real Presence by a peculiar, supernatural light, called the Shekinah. But all this did not satisfy either man's heart or God's unbounded love. If we love a person dearly, it will not satisfy us to hear his voice or to see him in disguise; we wish to behold him face to face. God gratified even this desire. He had commanded a tabernacle of wood to be made by the hand of man, and that tabernacle He chose for His dwelling place. But now with His own divine hands He made a living tabernacle, holy and spotless, the Immaculate Virgin Mary; and in that tabernacle He took up His abode. There He formed for Himself a human body and soul. Thence He came forth to live among men and to be as one of them.

In becoming man, God revealed His Real Presence to all our senses. Men saw God, heard God, even touched God. He had already revealed His Real Presence to man's reason in the creation, but man had forgotten Him. He had revealed His Real Presence by His word, and man refused to listen to Him. He had shown Himself face to face to man, and man

---

* Exod. xxxiii. 18.

crucified Him. There was now but one means left for God to reveal His Real Presence, and that was by faith. He hides Himself from our senses, He hides Himself from our reason; He reveals His Presence in a far more perfect manner. He shows Himself to the eyes of faith in the blessed sacrament.

The blessed sacrament, or holy Eucharist, is indeed a great mystery. Our Saviour knew that if He were to teach the Jews and His disciples the new and wonderful doctrine of this mystery without having first prepared them for it, there would be scarcely one found to believe Him. When God intends to do something very extraordinary, He generally prepares men for it by revealing to them beforehand, what He is about to do. Thus we know that, when He intended to destroy the world by the deluge, He made it known through Noah, a hundred years before the event took place. Again, when the Son of God had become man, and was about to make Himself known as the Redeemer of the world, He sent St. John the Baptist to prepare the people for His coming. Finally, when He intended to destroy Jerusalem, He foretold it by the prophets, and Jesus Christ has also described the signs by which men may know when the end of the world is near at hand. God acts thus with men because He does not wish to overwhelm them by His strange and mysterious dealings. Hence, when our divine Saviour was about to tell the people that He intended to give them His flesh and blood as food and drink for their souls, He prepared them for this mysterious doctrine by working an astounding miracle—the feeding of five thousand people with five loaves and two fishes. Those who witnessed this miracle, were so filled with reverence for Jesus Christ, that they wished to take Him by force and make Him their king. But Jesus, perceiving this, fled from them. They found Him again however, on the following day; and then He took occasion, from the impression the miracle had made on them, to introduce the subject of the heavenly food which He was about to give the world. "Amen, I say to you; ye seek

Me, not because you have seen signs, but because you have eaten of the loaves and were filled. Labor not for the meat which perisheth, but for that which endureth to life everlasting, which the Son of man will give you." Here our Lord declares that the food He was to give them would confer eternal life. Their curiosity being excited by these words, they desired to know more about this heavenly food and asked what sign He would give them, and whether the food He spoke of was better than the manna from heaven, which God had given their fathers in the Desert. Before giving any further explanation, our Lord speaks of the absolute necessity of faith in His Divine Person. "This is the work of God that you *believe* in Me as your divine Redeemer. But you have seen Me and you believe not. This is the will of My Father that sent Me; that every one who seeth the Son, and *believeth* in Him, may have life everlasting, and I will raise him up in the last day. Amen, amen I say unto you he that believeth in Me hath life everlasting." [*] In ordinary words Our Lord would say, you must believe that I am your Redeemer and your God, and that, therefore, it is in My power to give you such bread as bestows upon you life everlasting. Then having required of them an unwavering faith, He promises to give them a heavenly bread. He had just given them miraculous bread, a kind of bread far superior to ordinary bread, but the bread from heaven, which He was to give, was something far superior to the miraculous bread, and consequently far more than ordinary bread. The Jews thought that He would perhaps give them something like manna, but Jesus assured them that the heavenly bread, which He intended to give, was far superior even to manna. "Your fathers," He said to them, "did eat manna in the desert, and are dead, but he that eats of the bread that I will give, shall live forever."

Now manna was called bread from heaven, the bread of

---

[*] John xxix. 47.

angels. It was better than the miraculous bread, with which Jesus had fed the Jews, and consequently far better than ordinary bread. But Jesus Christ promises to give us a kind of bread superior even to manna. This He calls the true bread from heaven, to show us, that the manna was but a figure of this heavenly bread. He calls it also the living bread, to show us unmistakably that it is far more than ordinary bread, for ordinary bread is not living. Now what is this bread that Jesus Christ promises to give us? This bread, far superior to ordinary bread, to the miraculous bread, to manna, the bread of the angels, this bread from heaven, this living bread, must indeed be something very extraordinary, something which had never yet been given to man, since before promising it, before telling us what it is, our Lord insists so earnestly upon the necessity of faith. What then is this extraordinary bread? Our Lord no longer conceals it; He tells us in the strongest, clearest language— "I am the bread of life, I am the living bread, which came down from heaven. If any man eat of this bread, he shall live forever; and the bread that I will give, is My flesh for the life of the world."* "The Jews therefore strove among themselves saying: 'How can this man give us his flesh to eat?'" St. Cyril of Alexandria, who lived in the fifth century, asks here: "O Jew, how can you make this question? Let me also ask you, How didst thou go out of Egypt? Tell me how the rod of Moses was turned into a serpent, how was his hand made leprous, and again restored, as it is written? How was water changed into the nature of blood? How didst thou pass through the midst of the sea, as through a dry plain? How was the bitter water of Merrha changed into sweet by a piece of wood? How was water given thee from the bosom of the rocks? How was the manna brought down from heaven for thee? How did the Jordan stand still in its bed? Or how, by a mere shout, did the impregnable

---
* John vi. 48, 51, 52.

wall of Jericho fall? And wilt thou not cease to utter that *how?* Therefore it became thee to believe in Christ's word and to strive to learn the *manner* of the eulogy (Eucharist), rather than say inconsiderately, like men drunk with wine, *How can this man give us His flesh to eat?*

"The Jews understood our Lord as inviting them to a barbarous cruelty. They thought it something horrible to order them to eat flesh and drink blood in an inhuman manner. Hence they thought: How can a human body introduce eternal life into us? How can this body which is of the same nature as ours bestow immortality?

"'It is the Spirit that quickeneth (vivifies),' says our Lord to them; 'The flesh profiteth nothing.' That is to say; there is no absurdity in saying that the flesh is not able to bestow life; the nature of the flesh is such that by itself it cannot vivify in any way. On the contrary, it stands in need of a vivifying power. Now were you to believe that I am your God and Saviour, were you to consider the mystery of the Incarnation, were you to believe that the Divinity is united to My humanity in one person, you would also understand that My flesh is food indeed and that My blood is drink indeed. You would understand that he who eateth My flesh and drinketh My blood, abideth in Me and I in him, and thus hath everlasting life. It is therefore very foolish on your part to be scandalized at my words. If you think that my flesh cannot infuse life into you, how shall it ascend to heaven? And yet this spectacle shall be placed under your own eyes. What will you say then? When you see My flesh ascend to heaven, which, to all seeming, is contrary to its nature, will you still say that My flesh contains no vivifying power? 'Amen, amen, I say to you, he that believeth in Me, hath everlasting life.' You must, then, believe Me to be what I have so often told you. 'The words which I have spoken to you are spirit and life.' My flesh is not flesh only, it is spirit also, because of its being perfectly united to My divinity, and assuming the entire vivifying power of

My Godhead. Although your human body is subjected to death by sin, and forced to yield to corruption, yet if I am in you, by means of My own proper flesh, you shall assuredly rise again. For it is incredible, yea rather, it is impossible, that the life should not vivify those in whom it lives. It is by means of My own flesh, that I wish to hide life within you, and to introduce into you, as it were, a certain seed of incorruption which destroys the whole of the corruptible within you. For receiving within yourselves both My human and divine nature, you will become glorified by becoming partakers of and sharers in that nature which is above all things." It is thus that St. Cyril confounds the Jews for daring to say, "How can this man give us his flesh?"

In the sixteenth century came the Protestants, in their pride and ignorance, to imitate the Jews in contradicting our Saviour, saying that He spoke only figuratively when He promised, and commanded us to eat His flesh. Now such an assertion is as absurd and ridiculous as it is false and blasphemous. In Hebrew, and in all the Oriental languages, the expression, " to eat one's flesh," when taken figuratively, means to backbite, to slander, to persecute, and nothing else. To say, then, that our Saviour spoke only figuratively, would be to say, that He commands us under pain of eternal damnation, to backbite and to slander Him.

When our Lord Jesus Christ had made this extraordinary promise to the Jews, did they really understand Him to say, that He would give them His flesh to eat and His blood to drink? They clearly did understand Him so, and for this reason asked in astonishment; "How can this man give us His flesh to eat?" And some of them said: "This is a hard saying, who can hear it?" And even many of his disciples were so shocked at the idea of eating the flesh of Jesus, and drinking His blood, that they went away from Him altogether, and never went with Him any more. The Jews then did not understand our Lord to have spoken figuratively, for had they done so, there was no reason for being shocked at His words. The whole Jewish religion was made up of types and figures, so that if our Lord had spoken figuratively, it would have been nothing new to them. No, the Jews understood Him to speak of eating His very flesh and drinking His very blood.

But the question is: Did our Saviour wish the Jews to understand Him in this manner? Most certainly He did. Our Lord saw that the Jews understood him to speak of eating His real flesh and drinking His real blood. Instead of contradicting that opinion, He confirmed it again and again, in the strongest and most unmistakable terms. Had His intention been to give them His flesh and blood to eat in a figurative manner only, would He not, and should He not have corrected the mistake of the Jews there and then? He had come on earth to banish falsehood and error and to teach the truth. Must He not then have told the truth at that moment?

Jesus Christ gave Himself to us as a model; we were to learn from Him how to speak the truth with honesty and sincerity. Could He then act as an impostor only to deceive us? Even to think of such a thing would be blasphemous. An impostor usually makes fine promises; he exaggerates the value of what he promises to give; but an honest man will rather underrate than exaggerate the value of what he promises, especially if he sees that his friends really believe his words, and that any exaggeration whatever would be productive of great evils. Suppose you promise a friend of yours, to make him a present of a fine house, but you intend to give him only a picture of the house which you have in your room. You see, however, that your friend believes that you intend giving him a real house; you foresee, moreover, that this misunderstanding of his will be the cause of long and bitter quarrels and law suits. Are you not bound by every sense of honesty, charity, and justice, to inform him that he has misunderstood you, that you intend to give him only a picture of your house? Our Lord promises in the clearest terms to give us His flesh to eat; He sees that the Jews, His disciples, His Apostles, understood His words literally. He sees many already take offence and leave Him; He knows that by leaving Him, they incur eternal damnation. He sees that in aftertimes disputes and quarrels will arise among men as to what is the real meaning of his words; that many will understand them literally, whilst others will take them in another sense. Was it not His most sacred duty to explain beyond doubt the meaning of His words? If He wished to be understood figuratively, should He not have said: My children, you misunderstand Me; I will not give you my real flesh and blood, but only a figure of My flesh. But instead of speaking thus, and correcting the Jews, on the contrary, He confirms what He has said. He repeats at least five times, that He will really give us His flesh to eat. And as our Lord foresaw that there would be many who would refuse to eat His flesh and drink His blood, He solemnly threatens eternal damnation to all those, that refuse. "Unless you eat My flesh and drink My blood, you shall not have life in you." Whilst to all who obey Him, He promises eternal life. "He that eateth My flesh hath life everlasting." He asserts twice that what He has spoken is a literal statement; for the Greek word "alethos," means true and literal. "For My flesh is meat indeed—*i. e.* it can be eaten indeed, and My blood is drink indeed"—*i. e.* it can be drunk in very deed.

Jesus Christ had at first said that He would give us bread from heaven, a living bread, but now, to take away every shadow of doubt, He tells us, that the bread, which He will give, is His flesh; while to convince us that He really intends to give us His flesh, He says: "He that eateth Me, shall live by Me." And to confirm all this and take away every shadow of doubt and of excuse, He swears in the most solemn manner, at least four times, that He will give us His real flesh and blood, that He will give us

Himself to be our food. "Amen, amen, I say unto you . . . ." Now in Hebrew, "amen," when used thus, is equivalent to an oath. Again Jesus swears, by His mission and by His life, that He will give us Himself to be our food. "As the living Father hath sent Me, and as I live by the Father, he that eateth Me . . . ." It is just as if Jesus had said: "I declare to you, as true as the living God has sent Me, and as true as I live by the Father, he that eateth Me . . . ." Now what stronger, what clearer language could our Lord have used, to convince us, that He really intended to give us His flesh and His blood? It is impossible to furnish stronger proofs than these, for any single truth in the whole Christian religion. No wonder that our blessed Lord was filled with sadness when He saw, in spite of all that He had said and done, there would still be many who would be lost for not believing in His words. "What!" said He, turning to the unbelieving Jews, "does this scandalize you? You do not believe that I can give you My flesh to eat? What then will you say when you see the Son of Man ascending to where He was before?" Jesus Christ appeals to the mystery of His ascension, to show us that it is just as easy for Him to give us His sacred body to be our food, as it is for Him to ascend with that body to the right hand of God in heaven. He appeals to His ascension, to convince us that just as certainly as His body is now in heaven, so certain is it that His body is now also in the Blessed Eucharist.

Whenever Jesus Christ had spoken figuratively in public, He always explained Himself in private to His disciples. But here He speaks in private as in public, to show us, that He does not speak figuratively, that He wishes to be understood literally. When He saw that many, even of His own disciples, left Him because they would not believe His words, He turned to the twelve, to His chosen, beloved apostles, and instead of giving them any new explanation, He asked them: "Will you also go away?" As saying: I have told you the truth, I cannot change what I have said;

for it is the truth. If you will not believe Me, you also may go.

Indeed, the Christian, who after so many clear unanswerable proofs sees not the truth, must in very deed be wilfully blind. He is like the owl, that closes its eyes at mid-day, and flaps its wings and says: The sun does not shine, for I do not see it. If Jesus Christ left us His body only in figure, if He left us after all only a piece of bread, why did He use so many precautionary measures, in order to persuade us? why did He insist so much upon the necessity of faith? For faith is to believe in something that we do not see. If Jesus Christ left us only a piece of bread, why did He tell us that it is far superior even to manna? Why did He tell us in so many formal and affirmative propositions that He would really give us His flesh to eat? If He intended only to give us a piece of bread, what need was there to appeal to the great miracle of His ascension? If He intended to give us His body only in figure, why did He suffer the Jews and His own disciples even to go away without modifying a single word of His oft-repeated assertion, that He would really give us His flesh to eat? Jesus, seeing that the Jews and many of His disciples would not believe that He was to give them His flesh and blood as food for their souls, suffered them to go away offended, and when they were gone, He said to the twelve: "Will ye also go away?" Then Simon Peter answered in the name of all: "Lord, to whom shall we go? Thou hast the words of eternal life. And we have believed and have known that Thou art the Christ the Son of God." *

Remark the noble simplicity of faith of the Apostles. They believe the words of their Master without the least hesitation; they receive His words in that sense in which the others had refused to receive them. They accept them in their obvious meaning, as a promise that He would give

---

* V. 68, 70.

them His *real flesh* to eat and His *real blood* to drink; they believe with a full faith, simply because He is " the Christ, the Son of God," too good to deceive and too wise to be deceived, too faithful to make vain promises, and too powerful to find any difficulty in fulfilling them. It was from this time forward that the disciples were constantly expecting that Jesus Christ would fulfil His promise.

CHAPTER III.

THE WONDERFUL GIFT OF GOD.

THE Apostles always remembered the promise which Jesus had made to give them His most holy Flesh and Blood. But the promise was not fulfilled at once.

In Jerusalem there is a hill called Mount Sion. On this hill, near the tomb in which King David was buried, was a house which contained a large dining-room. If you had entered that room the evening before Jesus died on the cross, you would have seen Him sitting at a table with His twelve Apostles. What a sight! To behold the Creator in the midst of His creatures, whom He had made out of the dust of the earth! It was a solemn moment, for He was then about to work the greatest miracle that ever had been, or ever will be wrought. He was going to give Himself away, to give His own most sacred body and blood to be the food of His creatures. To give us heaven and earth, His angels, and His Blessed Mother to watch over us was surely gift enough. It would seem almost too good, what St. Augustine has well called the folly of love to give us Himself. But the love of Jesus for us was boundless, so that nothing seemed to Him too good to do for us.

Let us consider how it was done. The word of God is life-giving and all-powerful. When God created the heavens and the earth, He merely spoke and everything was made. He said: "*Let light be made and light was made.*" For when God speaks, the thing is done, and done directly. Well, let us listen: Jesus is about to speak the word that will change the bread and wine into His Body and His Blood. On that table at which they were sitting, there was bread and wine. First of all, as the Evangelist tells us, "Jesus took bread and blessed and brake, and gave unto His disciples," and said these solemn words: "*Take ye and eat: This is My Body.*" Quicker than a flash of lightning that bread was changed into His Body. Then did all the Apostles eat the most sacred flesh of Jesus.

In like manner He then took the chalice with wine and gave to them saying: "*Drink ye all of this: For this is My Blood* of the New Testament which shall be shed for many unto the remission of sins."* And the wine obeyed the voice of Him whom the winds and the sea obeyed. In that moment the wine was changed into His sacred Blood. "Eat and drink," said Jesus then to His Apostles; it is all your own; do not think of what your senses perceive; it is to your faith, not to your senses that I say, "This is My Body." Remember that it is I who have said this: I and no other: —the Son of God, by whom everything was made, alone could speak thus; for to Me nothing is impossible. The Apostles believed simply; they believed as strongly as our Saviour had spoken, and with as much submission on their part as He had displayed of authority and power. There was in their faith that same simplicity contained in the words of Jesus: "This is My Body, This is My Blood." It is then really His Body under the appearance of bread, and His Blood under the appearance of wine, said and believed the Apostles.

Then did they all receive our Lord's Body, and drank of the most precious Blood of Jesus Christ. An eternity had passed, and the most holy Flesh and Blood of God had never yet been given to any creature. The Apostles were the first to whom this blessing of blessings was given. It was the will of Jesus that from that moment forward, all His poor creatures should everywhere freely eat His Flesh and drink His Blood to make them holy before God. For the good of His creatures, He wished His Body and Blood to

---

* Matt. xxvi. 26-29

be scattered over the earth, like the dew of heaven. But Jesus knew that in about forty days He would be no longer present in the flesh on earth, to give away with His own hands His sacred Body and Blood. For this reason He wished to leave others on earth to perform this office for Him. So He said to His Apostles and priests—" Do this in remembrance of Me;" that is to say, to you I give the power to do what I have done—to change bread and wine into My Flesh and Blood, and to give it to My people. The word of Jesus will never pass away. The sun will shine on the earth until the last day of this world. So the Body and Blood of Jesus Christ will be given by the priests of Jesus Christ to His people, to be the light and strength and joy of their souls to the end of the world. It is therefore an article of Catholic belief, that in the most holy Sacrament of the Eucharist, is truly and really contained the body of Christ, which was delivered for us, and His blood which was shed for the remission of sins; the substance of the bread and wine being, by the power of God, changed into the substance of His blessed body and blood, the species and appearances of bread and wine, by the power of the same God, remaining as they were. This change has been properly called Transubstantiation.

"As Christ our Redeemer," says the Council of Trent, "declared that to be truly His own body, which He offered under the species of bread; therefore has it always been firmly believed in the church of God, and this holy Synod again declares it, that; by the consecration of the bread and wine, a change is made of the whole substance of the bread into the substance of the body of Christ our Lord, and of the whole substance of the wine into the substance of His blood: which change has been aptly and properly called by the holy Catholic Church, Transubstantiation." * Hence—
"If any one shall deny that, in the sacrament of the most Holy Eucharist, there is contained truly, really, and substan-

---

* Sess. xiii. c. iv.

tially, the body and blood together with the soul and divinity of our Lord Jesus Christ, and therefore the whole Christ; but shall say that He is only therein in sign, or figure, or virtue, let him be anathema."

Now Christ is not present in this sacrament, according to his natural way of existence; that is, as bodies naturally exist, but in a manner proper to the character of His exalted and glorified body. His presence then is real and substantial, but sacramental and ineffable, not exposed to the external senses, nor obnoxious to corporal contingencies. Hence the Council of Trent says: "The holy synod openly and plainly professes that in the holy sacrament of the Eucharist, after the consecration of the bread and wine, our Lord Jesus Christ, true God and man, is truly, really, and substantially contained under the species of those sensible objects. For these things are not mutually repugnant: That our Saviour, according to His natural manner of existence, should always be seated in heaven, at the right hand of the Father; and that, nevertheless, He should be present with us, in many other places, sacramentally in His own substance, in that way of existence, which, though in words we can hardly express it, the mind, illumined by faith, can still conceive to be possible to God, and which we are bound most firmly to believe. For so all our ancestors—as many as were in the true Church of Christ—who have written concerning this most holy sacrament, have most openly professed." *

The body of Christ, however, in this holy sacrament, is not separated from His blood, nor is His blood from His body, nor is either of them disjoined from His soul and divinity; but all and the whole living Christ is entirely contained under each species, so that, whoever receives under one kind, becomes truly partaker of the whole sacrament: He is not deprived either of the body or the blood of Christ. "For at all times," says the Council of Trent, "the faith

---

* Sess. xiii. ci.

has been in the Church of God that, immediately after consecration, the true body of our Lord and His true blood, together with His soul and divinity, are present under the species of bread and wine; but the body indeed under the species of bread, and the blood under the species of wine, by virtue of the words (of consecration): moreover, that the body itself *is* under the species of wine, and the blood under the species of bread, and the soul under each, by virtue of that natural connection and concomitance, by which the body and soul of our Lord, who, being now risen from the dead, can die no more, are naturally joined together; the divinity, furthermore, is there, on account of its admirable hypostatic union with the body and soul. Wherefore, it is most true that as much is contained under either species, as under both; for Christ, whole and entire, exists under the species of bread, and under each (divided) particle of that species: and whole under the species of wine, and under its separated parts." *

It is thus that our Lord has redeemed His promise of giving to the world His flesh to eat and His blood to drink. It is thus that we see the truth of what He said to His apostles: "I will not leave you orphans." † I shall indeed withdraw from you My visible presence by ascending into heaven, but I will stay with you in the blessed sacrament to the end of the world.

"When Elias ascended into heaven," says St. John Chrysostom, "he left nothing else behind him to his disciple than his mantle. 'With this,' said he, 'have I wrestled with the devil; take this and arm thyself also with it against him.' Eliseus received that mantle as the greatest inheritance, for indeed it was the greatest inheritance, a more precious one than all gold. And that Elias was now a twofold person, an Elias above and an Elias below. I know that you reckon that just man blessed, and each one of you wishes to be he.

---

* Sess. xiii. clii.   † St. John xiv. 18.

What then if I show you that we have received something else much greater than that which he had? For Elias left a mantle to his disciple, but the Son of God, when ascending to heaven, left unto us His own flesh. Elias indeed having stripped off his covering went up, but Christ left His flesh unto us, and yet retaining it, ascended.

"Parents, indeed, have given their children to others to feed, but 'not so I,' says Jesus Christ, 'but I feed Mine with My flesh; I set Myself before you; My will being that you shall be ennobled, and holding out to you, as regards future things, glad expectations. For He that has given Himself unto you here, much more will He do so in the world to come. I was willing to become your brother; for you I partook of flesh and blood, again do I give to you that same flesh and blood, whereby I became your relative.'

"This blood effects for us that blooming kingly image, this begets beauty unrivalled; this suffers not the soul's dignity to fade away, irrigating and nourishing it continually. For the blood that is formed within us, from our food, does not at once become blood, but something else; but not so this; it at once irrigates the soul and infuses a mighty power. This blood, worthily received, drives away demons, and keeps them far aloof from us, but summons angels to us, and the Lord of angels. For wheresoever they behold the Lord's blood, demons fly, and angels crowd in haste. This blood when poured out washed the whole world. Wherefore, let us not be cast down, nor lament, nor fear the difficulties of the times; for He who refused not to pour out His blood for all, and who has given us to partake of His flesh and of His blood again, what will He refuse to do for our safety?"*

Jesus Christ, the Son of God, has said: "I am the *truth:*" i. e. all words that I speak are true. Now He took bread into His hands and said, "This is My Body;" it is then really His Body under the appearance of bread. He took a cup of

---

* T. ii. Hom. ii. ad PopuL Antioch. n. g.

wine and said: "This is My Blood;" it is then really His Blood under the appearance of wine which He poured into the cup and presented to His Apostles. He who spoke in this manner was the creator of heaven and earth, with Whom to speak and to act are the same thing.

When God works miracles for the relief of bodily necessities, men believe. Now when His immense love for our souls prevails upon Him to change bread and wine into His body and blood for the relief of our spiritual necessities, they refuse to believe. What blindness of the mind! What perverseness of the heart! Had Christ said, "This is not My body, This is not My blood," every one would say that neither His body nor His blood was present in the sacrament, because these words, taken in the natural, literal sense, could convey no dubious idea. But Jesus Christ has said—"This *is* My body, this *is* My blood:" why then shall not those words be held to have equal force in proving that His body and blood are truly and really present in the Blessed Sacrament?

"Since Christ Himself pronounced it," writes St. Cyril of Jerusalem, in the fourth century, "and said '*This is My Body*,' who after that shall dare to doubt of it? And since He says, '*This is My Blood*,' who would dare to say it is not His Blood? He once changed water into wine, and does He not deserve to be believed, when He has changed wine into His blood? With a certainty excluding all manner of doubt, we take the body and blood of Christ; for under the appearance of bread His body is given, and His blood under the appearance of wine."

"Let us, therefore," says St. John Chrysostom, "believe God always, let us never contradict Him, though what He says appears above our reason; for His word cannot deceive us, but our senses may easily be deceived. As, therefore, He said, This is My body, let us believe it without the least hesitation. We are nourished with that flesh which the angels see, and before which they tremble. What shepherd ever fed his flock with his flesh? He nourished us with His own body, He cements and incorporates us with Himself. He makes us His own body, not merely by faith, but in fact and in reality.

St. Isaac, a holy priest of Antioch, in the fifth century, says: "I saw the mingled vessel (cup), and I saw it filled with blood instead of wine; and instead of the bread, I saw the body placed in the middle of the table. I saw the blood and feared; I saw the body and was awed. She, Faith, beckoned, saying, 'Eat and be silent; drink, search not, my child.' She showed me a body slain, of which, placing a portion on my lips, she calmly said, 'See what thou eatest.' She held out to me a reed, and bade me subscribe myself. I took it, wrote and confessed that, This is the Body of God! In like manner taking the chalice I drank, and out of the chalice the odor of that Body which I had eaten smote me. And what I had said of the Body, namely, that it is the Body of God, that also did I say of the chalice, namely, that This is the Blood of our Redeemer!"

We read in the Gospel of St. Matthew * that our Divine Redeemer one day asked His disciples to tell Him whom men said that He was. The disciples answered that some said He was John the Baptist, others that He was Elias, others again that He was Jeremias or one of the prophets. Then Jesus asked, "But whom do you say that I am?" Simon Peter answered, "Thou art Christ, the Son of the living God." And Jesus replied: "Blessed art thou, Simon Barjona, because flesh and blood hath not revealed it to thee, but My Father, Who is in heaven;" that is to say, it is not by your senses, or by any human means, that you know for certain, that I am the Son of God, for your senses behold in Me but an ordinary man, but My heavenly Father has enlightened you to know that I am His Son, God and man at the same time; for this faith of yours, I call you blessed.

---

* xvi. 18–17.

Now, suppose our Lord Jesus Christ should say to Protestants: "Tell Me, what is the consecrated Host?" Some of them would answer: It is but a figure of Thy Body; others, again would reply: It will become Thy Body in the mouth of the recipient; whilst others still would respond otherwise. But were our Lord to ask every one of the two hundred millions of Catholics all over the world, all would at once answer like St. Peter: The consecrated Host is Thy own Body; It is Christ, the Son of the living God, for the simple reason that Thou hast made it, and therefore declared It to be Thy Body. And Jesus Christ then would answer what He said to St. Peter: Blessed are you, because it is not flesh and blood that has revealed it to you: it is not by your senses, that you know the consecrated Host to be really My Body, but by the gift of faith bestowed upon you by My heavenly Father. Most assuredly then, the heavenly Father has not revealed Himself to those who do not believe in His Son in the consecrated Host.

In the beginning of the world, God promised to give Himself to us. But not contented with a promise which had reference only to eternity, He gave us even in this life His divine Son—another and yet Himself in the Institution of the Holy Eucharist. It is therefore in Holy Communion that Jesus is our beatitude begun. He is the Head of His church, of all the faithful on earth, who form His mystic body. Now where the head is, there also should be its body. But since we—the mystic body of Christ—cannot be as yet with Jesus Christ, in heaven, He, our Head vouchsafed to stay with us, His body, on earth, though in a manner invisible to our eyes.

Moreover, Jesus Christ is the Spouse of the Catholic Church; with her He is more inseparably united than man and wife can be. The bond of His union is the immense love of Jesus Christ for His Spouse. St. Paul holds up for imitation to married people this love of Jesus Christ for His Spouse. "Husbands," he writes in his Epistle to the

Ephesians, "love your wives as Christ also loves the church and delivered Himself up for her." *

Now all the faithful are members of this church; they were cleansed from all defilement of sin in Holy Baptism. Hence it is that the love of Jesus Christ for a pure soul—a member of His mystic body—infinitely exceeds that of a bridegroom for his bride. This exceedingly great love of Jesus Christ for His Spouse induced Him to stay with her to the consummation of the world. The reason, however, why our Divine Saviour stays with His Spouse on earth in a hidden manner, is because He is espoused to her in faith: His union with her being spiritual, not carnal, as was foretold by the prophet Osee, "I will espouse thee to Me forever, and I will espouse thee to Me in mercy, in commiserations; and I will *espouse* thee to me in *faith*, and thou shalt know that I am the Lord." †

Since our Lord then is espoused to the church, *in faith*, it was fitting that He should be with her in a hidden manner, in order that her children might find herein a good opportunity to exercise their faith and obtain in heaven the reward promised in the Gospel to those who have not seen, *yet have believed*.

Since the Church then is the Spouse of Jesus Christ, He feels bound in duty, as it were, to provide her with the necessary life-giving food, and to see to her spiritual welfare and prosperity. Now this He does especially by giving Himself as food and drink in the Blessed Eucharist to all the faithful of His church, thus clearly showing that He truly loves His Spouse, the Church, and supplies all her temporal and spiritual wants.

O God, so glorious and yet so intimately united with us, lifted so high above the heavens and yet stooping to the lowliness of Thy creatures, so immense and yet dwelling near us on our altars, so awful and yet so worthy of love! Oh,

---

(* Ephes. v. 25.) († Chap. ii. 19.)

for a voice loud enough to reproach the world with its blindness, coldness, and unbelief: to declare with power all that Thou art: to cover with confusion all those who neither believe in Thy wonderful promise nor in thy wonderful gift! Thou, O Lord, givest me too much, in giving me Thyself, for I am unworthy of so much happiness. Yet wouldst Thou give me too little in giving me anything but Thyself; for everything Thou couldst give me without the gift of Thyself, would be too little for the satisfaction of Thy love, and also insufficient to fill my heart.

May Jesus in the Blessed Sacrament be praised forever.

CHAPTER IV.

A WONDERFUL MEANS OF AWAKENING FAITH IN THE REAL PRESENCE.

Our dear Saviour tells us in the Gospel that He is the Good Shepherd. Jesus is indeed a good Shepherd. He knows His sheep in general and in particular. He instructs them by His word, He strengthens them by his grace, animates them by His spirit, and enriches them with His merits. He does not, like other shepherds, nourish Himself with their flesh, or clothe Himself with their fleece; on the contrary, He gives them His flesh to eat and His blood to drink. He watches over His sheep with a special Providence; He never abandons them; He defends and protects them against the foe who would devour them. When he prowls about the sheepfold and would enter, Jesus comes to their assistance to drive him off and save them.

This Good Shepherd foresaw that Luther and other ravenous wolves, would enter in and carry off many of His sheep: that they would kill them by preventing them from eating the "Bread of Life"—the flesh and blood of Jesus Christ in holy communion. It was Luther's own opinion that in no wise could he hurt the sheep of Jesus Christ more than by undermining their faith in the Real Presence. Jesus had foreseen this. So to prove Himself a Good Shepherd to His flock, He made use of a wonderful means to awaken their faith in the Blessed Sacrament. This means was the institution of the Feast of Corpus Christi.

I need not relate here the wonderful manner in which it was introduced into the Church in the thirteenth century. This may be read in the "Blessed Eucharist, our greatest

Treasure." I only wish here to call attention to the fact, that it was instituted by divine inspiration in order that the Catholic doctrine might be strengthened by the institution of this festival, at a time when the faith of the world was growing cold and heresies were rife. This feast is celebrated with all possible magnificence and pomp. The solemn procession of the Blessed Sacrament is the public recognition by the Catholic world of the Real Presence of Jesus in the Blessed Sacrament; it is a reversal of the judgment that an unbelieving world would pass upon our Lord and a compensation for the outrages which it has inflicted on Him. As He was once in the most ignominious manner led as a malefactor through the streets of Jerusalem from Annas to Caiphas, from Caiphas to Pilate, from Pilate to Herod, from one tribunal to another, on this day He is borne in triumph through the church and open streets, as the spotless Lamb and as man's Highest Good.

As His sufferings had no other witnesses than envious and unworthy Jews, so now, on this day every knee bends in adoration before Him. As the executioner once led Him forth to death, so, in this procession, the great ones of the world mingle with the throng to do Him reverence. As then His ears resounded with the most scornful and outrageous blasphemies, so now, on this great festival, the church greets Him with music and songs of praise. The crown of thorns that once pierced His brow is now exchanged for the wreath of flowers around the remonstrance, while civil magistrates with their insignia and troops of heroes, with glittering arms and waving banners, replace the fierce Roman soldiers, who once kept watch around His dark and silent tomb. The Cross which Jesus bore with sorrow and sweat, up the rugged hill of Calvary, is, on this day of triumph, carried before all as the sign of victory. Jesus Himself, who was lifted up upon it, is now, in the Blessed Sacrament, raised aloft to impart His benediction to His kneeling and adoring people.

It is thus that on this memorable day faith triumphs, hope is enhanced, charity shines, piety exults, our temples re-echo with hymns of exultation, pure souls tremble with holy joy, the faith of the lukewarm is awakened, whilst infidelity and heresy are confounded. It cannot be doubted, therefore, that the institution of this solemn Feast of Corpus Christi, has ever since its first celebration been a most powerful means of awakening the faith in the Real Presence.

However, in spite of the efficacy of this means, it has not always produced the desired effect upon all the faithful. In the sixteenth century especially, many grew lukewarm and indifferent, even towards Jesus Christ in the Blessed Sacrament. They treated their Good Shepherd in this divine mystery as a stranger. It is the lukewarm and indifferent Catholics who have always done the most harm in the Church; for they have lost all relish for God; they are deprived of all consolation; they wander more and more from the ways of Providence; they sin without remorse or fear; they fly from confession and communion; they are sick, but unconscious of their ailing; wicked, but blind to their vices; they are slaves and believe themselves free; they abuse all remedies, reject every inspiration, are impervious to the impressions of grace. Hence it comes that the lukewarm dishonor virtue, cry down devotion, scandalize their neighbors, and become a burden to the Church. They offend against the Holy Ghost, afflict the sacred Heart of Jesus, and by their own stubbornness and sin, compel Him, in a manner, to spurn them, after which they hardly ever return, as that which has been vomited forth is not again eaten.

To rid Him of these sheep and to prevent their communicating their contagion to others; or, to rouse them from their fatal state of lethargy, and make them become better Christians, our divine Shepherd had recourse, as it were, to amputation. If one member of the body endangers the others, the physician, if he may, amputates it in order to save the whole. Jesus Christ, our divine physician, often acts thus. Especially was this the case in the sixteenth century. He permitted Protestantism, one of the greatest evils in the world, to arise. But as the Lord is Infinite Wisdom itself, He knows how to draw good from evil. One good, fervent Catholic is dearer to His Heart than a thousand who are lukewarm and indifferent. Protestantism was the instrument of amputation to separate the lukewarm and dead of the mystic body of Christ from the living members. The former followed Luther, the apostate-monk and great heresiarch of the sixteenth century.

Protestantism has ever been a most bitter antagonist of the Church. It has denied and combated her most vital doctrines, especially that of the Real Presence. There must be scandals, a fatal, though divine warning! There must be storms in nature to purify the air from dangerous elements. In like manner God permits storms—heresies to arise in His church on earth, that the erroneous and impious doctrines of heretics may, by way of contrast, set forth in clearer light the true and holy doctrines of that Church. As is light in the midst of darkness, gold contrasted with lead, the sun among the planets, the wise among the foolish, —so is the Catholic Church among non-Catholics. If two things of different natures, says the wise man, are brought into opposition, the eye perceives their difference at once. "Good is set against evil, and life against death; so also is the sinner against the just man. And so look upon all the works of the Most High. Two and two and one against another."* Christ then permits the storms of heresies to burst upon His church to bring forth into clearer light His divine doctrine and to remove dangerous elements from His mystic Body. In fighting heresies, the Church defines her own doctrines in clear terms, and sets forth solid arguments in confirmation. It is certain that the doctrine on the

---

* Eccle. xxxiii.

Real Presence was never so fiercely attacked by any heretic as by Luther and his companions. The consequence was, that ever since that time the priests of the Catholic Church have been obliged to defend this holy doctrine and uphold it by most convincing and undeniable arguments. It is thus that they increase their own faith in this mystery of love as well as that of the flock of Jesus Christ, and thus has our Lord drawn good from evil, thus has salvation come to His Church,—from the very enemies of our religion.

In order the better to understand this, let us examine the false, absurd and blasphemous assertions of Protestants, and see how, by those very assertions, our faith in the Real Presence of our Lord in the Blessed Sacrament is the more confirmed.

Protestants assert that our Lord spoke only figuratively. Now I would ask them: Did not Jesus Christ foresee that men would dispute and quarrel about the meaning of His words? Assuredly He did, for He is Infinite Wisdom. Did He not wish to tell us the truth? Undoubtedly He did, for He is Truth itself. Was He not able to tell us the truth? Most certainly He was, for He is almighty. Why then, if He wished to give us only a figure of His body, if He wished to give us bread and wine simply, did He not say so? Why did He say: "This is My Body?" Why did He not rather say—"This represents My Body?" There are in the Syro-Chaldaic, the language our Saviour spoke, at least forty-five words which mean, to signify, to represent. Why did He not use one of those words? Why did He say—"This is?" The opinion that our Lord spoke only figuratively at the last Supper is false, absurd and blasphemous.

I would not wish for the world to offend any of my readers, but I must in conscience raise my voice against that lying and impious perversion of the blessed word of God, known as the figurative interpretation. To say that our Lord spoke only figuratively is *absurd*, for bread bears no resemblance to the human body, and consequently never was and never can be a figure of it. I defy any one to show me a single expression, in any language, in which bread is taken as a figure or symbol of the human body.

To say that our Saviour spoke figuratively is false, for our Lord does not say: This bread is My Body, but He says: "This is." Now in Greek, the language in which the Apostles wrote, the demonstrative pronoun "This" is neuter and cannot agree with the word "bread," which is masculine; but with the word "body," which is neuter. It is the same as if our Saviour said: "My Body is this." Now that which is our Lord's Body, cannot at the same time be a piece of bread.

Our divine Saviour came on earth to put an end to the figures of the Old Law and to give us instead their reality. The Paschal lamb was a figure of our Lord's passion and death. To say, therefore, that our Lord left us only bread and wine, is to assert that He substituted one figure for another. Moreover, the Paschal lamb was a very intelligible figure of our Lord's death; not so with bread and wine, which are always symbolical of feasting and joy.

Indeed, to say that our Lord spoke figuratively is *blasphemous*. For according to St. Luke, our Saviour said: "This is My Body, which is given for you;" and according to St. Paul—"This is My Body, which is broken for you." Now the words "given for you," "broken for you," mean, given, broken for your redemption. So that to say that our Saviour gave us only a piece of bread, is to assert that a piece of bread is the cause of our redemption. This is still more clearly to be gathered from the words which our Saviour used in consecrating the chalice. "Take and drink ye all of this, for this is My blood, the blood of the New Testament, that shall be shed for many, for the remission of sins." Now mark well: it was that blood which our Saviour gave to the Apostles, and which they drank, that was to be shed for the remission of sins. If it was only wine, then a cup of wine was the cause of our Redemption.

FAITH IN THE REAL PRESENCE. 55

At the last Supper there are two very important circumstances which should be particularly taken into consideration. The first is, that our Saviour gave a commandment or *law;*—" Do this," He said to the Apostles; *i. e.*, do what I have done. "Do *this* in remembrance of Me." In a law, the words must be always clear, precise, expressive, without metaphor, or figure of any kind, and must always be taken in their natural and literal meaning. Therefore, when our Lord Jesus Christ says: "This is My Body," it must really be His body. Our Saviour made a law and consequently He must have spoken clearly and precisely. Suppose that a lawgiver, instead of expressing his laws in clear and simple language, were to express them in figures and parables, would he not be misunderstood, and consequently disobeyed? And yet there are men so rash and blasphemous as to assert, that when our Lord Jesus Christ commands us to eat His flesh, under pain of eternal damnation, in so important a commandment He speaks only in parables and figures.

In the second place, our Lord made a will or *Testament.* "This chalice is the New Testament in My blood.*" Our Lord calls it the *New* Testament, to distinguish it from the Old Testament, from the covenant He had formerly made with the Jewish people. On that occasion, Moses by the commandment of God sprinkled the people with blood, saying: "This is the blood of the covenant." Now our Saviour makes a new covenant and a New Testament: "This is the blood of the New Testament." The blood which Moses used in the *first* covenant was real blood, and the blood which Jesus used in the new covenant at the last Supper, must also have been *real* blood.

At this last Supper our Saviour made a testament, a *will.* In a testament, as in a law, the words must be clear, expressive, without metaphor of any kind, and must always be taken in their natural and literal meaning. A will or testa-

---

* Luke xxii. 20.

ment, is always written in the simplest and clearest language, for were the language ambiguous or obscure, it would easily give rise to lawsuits or quarrels. In every nation, the last will of a deceased person is held sacred. No one has the right to change it, or to reform it. Every word is respected. It would be a grievous crime to add to it any gloss or explanation. When a will or testament is opened, after the death of the testator, all heirs stand around in silence. Every word is listened to with profound attention, and though the testator is stiff and cold in the grave, yet his last will is respected, his words are received without figure, without explanation, in their literal and obvious meaning. The last will of man is respected, the will of a man cold in the grave; yet the last will and testament of the *living God*, the will and testament of Jesus Christ in heaven is contradicted! Jesus Christ tells us in His last will and testament: "I bequeath to you My body and My blood." He bequeathed His legacy to us in the clearest and most formal manner; nevertheless there are men who dare tell us that Jesus Christ left us only the figure of His body and blood.

Suppose that a relative or friend had in his will bequeathed to you in clear and expressive terms a house. Suppose that when you went to take possession of the house, the administrator were to present you with a picture of it, assuring you that this was all the testator meant to give you in his will. Would you not think that either the administrator or testator was a cheat, and wished to make a fool of you? And yet, O great Jesus, Son of the living God! is it thus that wicked men wish to represent Thee? Thou hast promised with a solemn oath to give us Thy body and blood in Thy testament, and wicked men dare to gainsay Thy living word and assert that Thou hast not left us Thy body and blood, that Thou hast left us only bread and wine. The last will of the lowest man on earth is respected, and the last will of the Son of God is falsified and contradicted. We know that it is a crime punishable by law to change or to insert a single word in the testament of any man, and shall it not be a crime, punishable by the God of heaven, to change the clear words of the testament of Jesus Christ?

The false and absurd grounds of Protestant tenets on this doctrine of faith are made still more apparent from what St. Paul teaches us on the Blessed Eucharist. The Apostles understood our Lord to have really given them His body and blood—to have given them the power to change bread and wine into His body and blood. In the first Epistle of St. Paul to the Corinthians, we find that St. Paul himself and all the Christians of his time really believed that Jesus Christ left us His body and blood. St. Paul asks the Corinthians: "The cup of benediction, which we bless, is it not the partaking of the blood of Christ? And the bread which we break, is it not the partaking of the body of the Lord?" He assures the Christians that our Lord Jesus Christ had appeared to him and instructed him concerning the doctrine of the Eucharist. He then relates the very words that our Lord used in consecrating the bread and wine at the last Supper. And after relating how our Lord gave us His body and blood, he concludes: "Therefore whosoever shall eat of this bread, or drink of this chalice of the Lord unworthily, shall be guilty of the body and blood of the Lord:" *i. e.* guilty of the most grievous offence against the body and the blood of the Lord.

If the Holy Eucharist be merely a piece of bread, how can it be eaten unworthily? How can one become guilty of a grievous crime against the body and blood of Christ by eating it? But it might be objected: The piece of bread is a figure of Christ's body, and it therefore is a crime to receive it unworthily. Let us take then a crucifix, a picture, or an image of Christ. Any one of them would be a better figure of Him than a piece of bread. And yet Protestants, the so-called reformers, dishonored and trampled on such images. But even granting, by impossibility, that a piece of bread be a figure of our Lord's body, how can the recipient of it become guilty of the body and blood of the Lord? Moreover, St. Paul commands the Christians to prove themselves, to examine their conscience before receiving the Holy Eucharist, for he says—" He that eateth and drinketh unworthily, eateth and drinketh his own damnation, because he doth not discern the body of the Lord." * Now, if the Blessed Eucharist be only bread and wine, how can you discern therein the body of the Lord? How can we eat and drink our own damnation, by eating a little bread and wine? How can we incur eternal torment for not discerning the body of Christ, where it does not exist?

But it may be objected, that to believe in transubstantiation is to go against reason, common sense, and the evidence of the senses. Are we then to set up our senses, our reason and common sense, as the infallible standard of our faith? If so, how can we believe in God, God being a pure spirit imperceptible to the senses? How can we believe in the Blessed Trinity—for neither senses, reason, nor common sense can perceive how the three Divine Persons are entirely distinct, yet but one in essence? If the evidence of the senses be our only criterion of faith, then must we deny that there is such a thing as the grace of God, or that there is such a thing as a soul at all. Nay, eternity, hell and heaven must be denied as imperceptible to the senses, and St. Paul assures us that " no eye has seen, no ear has heard, nor heart conceived what heaven is." Can our senses perceive any difference between an unbaptized child and one that has been baptized? Can they perceive the existence of original sin in the soul of a new born babe? Will reason or common sense explain how it is that a child born in 1870 should be charged with the crime of Adam's disobedience committed nearly six thousand years ago? This child could not have consented to the crime of Adam, as he was not then in existence. Now it is against common sense, and against the laws of every civilized country, to charge one man with the

---
* 1 Cor. xi.

guilt of another, whose accomplice he never was and never could have been. And yet you must believe in original sin or deny the necessity of baptism.

But it is asked: How can bread and wine be changed into the body and blood of Christ? The answer is very simple: by the almighty power of God. Transubstantiation in the Holy Eucharist is a stupendous miracle; but a certain kind of transubstantiation, or change of one substance into another, is going on continually in nature. We see it in the woods, in the grass, in the animals, in fact, in everything around us. When we take in food into our bodies that food is changed into flesh and blood. Now if bread and wine, by the operation of nature can become flesh, cannot God, by the power of His almighty word, change bread and wine into His flesh and blood? Transubstantiation, or the change of one substance into another, is nothing new with God. When He created man He performed an act of transubstantiation, for He changed the slime of the earth into the flesh, blood and bones of Adam, and this change was wrought by the word of God acting on matter. Again, God took a hard, bony rib from the side of Adam, which He changed into the flesh and blood of Eve. This change of one substance into another, has been going on continually in nature, ever since the beginning of the world. God has wished thereby to prepare us for the miraculous and infinitely more stupendous change of substance which is wrought in the Holy Eucharist.

But it may be said: God can change one substance into another; but how can man do the like? And the answer is, as God's instrument, when God gives him the power so to do. Moses changed a rod into a serpent and a serpent into a rod; he changed water into blood, and blood into water, by the power of the word of God. If a man in the Old Law changed water into blood by the power of the word of God, cannot a man in the New Law change wine into blood by the same power—the word of God? Is the word of God less powerful now than it then was?

Take a piece of coal; it is hard, heavy, and opaque. Throw it into the furnace of a gasometer and it becomes liquid. Examine it again in the gasometer and it becomes light as air, impalpable, transparent. Examine it in the tube, it is invisible; look at it in the jet, it again becomes visible. We see therefore the same thing, the piece of coal, become visible and invisible, palpable and impalpable, heavy and light, light and darkness, opaque and transparent. Now if a single piece of matter can possess such contradictory properties, is it so difficult to conceive how our Lord Jesus Christ can give His glorified Body any bulk or form of existence He pleases?

To admit the evidence of the senses only is to deny every article of the Creed, every revealed truth; nay, to deny and disown the father and mother who have borne us; for to prove by the evidence of the senses alone who is our father or our mother is impossible. To reject the mystery of transsubstantiation, merely because one cannot understand it, or because the peculiar sect to which a person belongs rejects it, is about as reasonable as if a congregation of frogs were to deny the existence of algebra, astronomy, or photography, merely because some elders of the tribes would neither see nor feel, nor understand the subject.

Are we to limit our belief to what we can understand? If so, then we can never make an act of faith, for faith is precisely the belief in some truth that we do not yet see or understand, but which we nevertheless firmly believe, simply because God has revealed it. Believing only what we can understand, we must deny the fact of creation, because no man can understand how all things were created out of nothing. It is impossible to believe the existence of anything, not even of one's own self, for it is impossible to understand how one exists; we cannot understand even how a blade of grass grows.

Man is progressive. His first state after the fall was the patriarchal religion, the religion of nature. His second state was that of the Jews, a revelation of religion of figures, or types and veils; as Manna, Paschal lamb and the rest. The third state is that of the Christians, who possess God, hidden indeed but really present. Man's fourth state is that of the Blessed in heaven, who possess and see God without veils or figures, face to face. To say that Christ is not present in reality, but only in figure, as He was with the Jews, is to put mankind back two thousand years. You can no more do this than you can cause the sun to turn back its course, or cause an old man to return to childhood. To require that Christ should manifest His Presence here on earth as He does to the Blessed in heaven, is to destroy the present state of time, to hasten the end of the world, to enter upon eternity. Christians here on earth hold a middle state between that of the Jews and that of the Blessed in heaven. Our Lord Jesus Christ came on earth to fulfil the law, to perfect it. In the Old Law God was really present in the midst of His chosen people. He was present with them in the desert, in the ark of the covenant, in the temple. And as the New Law is the fulfilment and perfection of the Old, God must still remain really present on earth in the midst of His chosen people.

This is Catholic belief. We believe most firmly that the Lord of heaven and earth—our dear Saviour and future Judge—dwells amongst us in the Blessed Sacrament on our altars. This was the belief and the doctrine of the Apostles, of all the Councils and Fathers of the Church. For this doctrine, hundreds of popes and bishops and priests fought, and laid down their lives, and most assuredly millions of Catholics are ready to do the same with cheerfulness, at any moment, should God require the sacrifice of their lives in confirmation of this doctrine. And why? It is because Catholics are as infallibly certain and intimately convinced of this truth as they are of any other of their holy religion; they feel as certain of it as Marie Bernard Bauer, a Jewish convert, felt after his conversion to the Catholic faith in 1865.

Marie Bernard Bauer is the son of one of the wealthiest

Jewish families in Vienna. At an early age, the young Jew, fiery and enthusiastic, and gifted already with singular eloquence, threw himself into the ranks of the Revolution, and became one of its most ardent emissaries. At eighteen, he was entrusted with important missions, and considered a rising Freemason. But during his travels he became acquainted with a young Frenchman, a zealous Catholic, whose influence and friendship laid the foundations of his conversion. He visited his friends and his mother also, who by her example more even than by her exhortations contributed to the work of grace begun in his soul by her son's solicitations. Bauer wore, at the request of these two, a medal of the Immaculate Conception. After being fully instructed in the faith, he required nothing but grace to believe. While at Lyons with several worldly acquaintances, he happened to be standing on a balcony, on the Feast of Corpus Christi; the procession of the Blessed Sacrament was to pass below, and they, with cigars in their mouths, and mockery in their hearts, were watching for the pageant. No change came over the young Jew until the canopy under which the priest carried the Divine Host was close beneath the balcony. The change at that moment was lightning-like. Faith entered his heart, or rather—as he himself afterwards declared—a conviction of the real presence of our Lord in the Blessed Sacrament so absolute that it made itself felt throughout his whole being.

It was by means of this light of faith, that he saw our Lord in the Blessed Sacrament more distinctly than if our Lord had appeared to him in some sensible manner. The same *knowledge*, so to speak, returned to him many times since while consecrating at Mass, and he said he could not *believe* merely, in a matter of which he was so blissfully and unerringly certain. As Jesus passed, Bauer threw himself on his knees and professed himself a Christian.

It was in consequence of this most intimate conviction that he concluded one of his discourses in Paris, as follows:

"And Thou, Lord Jesus, Who art the Truth 'that enlighteneth every man that cometh into the world' (John i.), let it not come to pass that one soul out of this great assemblage should return this day from the foot of this pulpit to the common turmoil of the world without bearing within itself the ineffable wound of a dawning conviction. And if, O Lord! Thou requirest unto this end the sacrifice of a human life, let this day be my last on earth, and this hour the last of my mortal pilgrimage."—*Catholic World*, May, 1872.

CHAPTER V.

A WONDERFUL MANIFESTATION OF THE REAL PRESENCE.

It was not enough for Protestants to deny the Real Presence of our dear Lord in the Blessed Sacrament; they committed even the most abominable outrages on His Sacred Person in this mystery of love. In France particularly, the Calvinists entered the Catholic Churches, overturned the altars, trampled the Blessed Sacrament under their feet, drank healths from the consecrated chalices, smeared their shoes with holy oil, defiled the church vestments with ordure, threw the books into the fire, and destroyed the statuary. They assaulted and massacred the Catholic clergy in the very discharge of their sacred functions, with cries of "kill the priests," "kill the monks." In France alone, the Calvinists destroyed 20,000 Catholic churches. They pillaged and demolished monasteries and hospitals. The monks at Chartres were all murdered with the exception of one, who concealed himself; but as soon as discovered, he was buried alive. In Dauphiny alone they murdered 255 priests, 112 monks and friars, and burnt 900 towns and villages.

Those were trying times for the Catholics in other countries as well as in France. Although the Bishops and priests did all in their power to strengthen their flocks in the faith, yet it required an extraordinary miracle to confirm the faith of many and confound the impiety of the heretics. This miracle was wrought by Jesus Christ in the Blessed Sacrament at Laon in France on the eighth day of February, 1566. It occurred in presence of more than 150,000 people; in presence of all the ecclesiastical and civil authorities of the city, of Protestants and Catholics alike. The account of this stupendous miracle I published last year. It is very interesting and instructive, and to it is added a plain treatise on spiritism. The title of the little volume is, "Triumph of the Blessed Sacrament, or History of Nicola Aubry." It is indeed a remarkable fact that, as the devil made use of Luther, an apostate monk, to abolish the Mass and deny the Real Presence, in like manner God made use of His arch-enemy, the devil, to prove the Real Presence. He forced him publicly to profess his firm belief in it, to confound the heretics for their disbelief, and acknowledge himself vanquished by our Lord in the Blessed Sacrament. For this purpose God allowed a certain Mme. Nicola Aubry, an innocent person, to become possessed by Beelzebub and twenty-nine other evil spirits. The possession took place on the eighth of November, 1565, and lasted until the eighth of February, 1566. Her parents took her to Father de Motta, a pious priest of Vervins, in order that he might expel the demon by the exorcisms of the Church. Father de Motta had tried several times to expel the evil spirit by applying the sacred relics of the holy Cross, but he could not always succeed; Satan would not depart. At last, inspired by the Holy Ghost, he resolved to expel the devil by means of the Sacrament of our Lord's Body and Blood. Whilst Nicola was lying in this state of unnatural lethargy, Father de Motta placed the Blessed Sacrament upon her lips, and instantly the infernal spell was broken; Nicola was restored to consciousness, and received Holy Communion with every mark of devotion. As soon as Nicola had received the Sacred Body of our Lord, her face became bright and beautiful as the face of an angel, and all who saw her were filled with joy and wonder, and they blessed God from their inmost hearts.

Nicola related that, during her trance, she saw herself surrounded by a crowd of horrid black men, who held glittering daggers in their hands, and threatened to kill her. She also beheld a number of wild grizzly monsters, who threatened to tear her to pieces. Flames of fire and brimstone shot forth from their eyes and nostrils, and almost suffocated her.

On the third of January, 1556, the Bishop arrived at Vervins, and began the exorcism in the church, in presence of an immense multitude.

"What is thy name?" asked the Bishop.

"Beelzebub, prince of the devils, next to Lucifer," answered the evil spirit.

"How many companions hast thou here at present?"

"There are nineteen of us now," answered Satan; "to-morrow there will be twenty. But this is not yet all, for I see that I must call all hell to my assistance."

"I command thee, in the name and by the power of God," said the Bishop, in a solemn voice, "to depart instantly with thy infernal companions!"

"Yes, we shall depart," replied the evil spirit, "but not *now*, and not *here*. My work is not yet done in this city."

"Where goest thou when expelled by the power of the Real Presence of our Lord in the Blessed Sacrament?" asked the Bishop.

"You want to know where I go, do you? Well! last night I paid you a visit," answered Satan; and then he related the very words the Bishop had said on hearing a noise in his room.

Satan was, at last, expelled again, by means of the Blessed Sacrament. On leaving, he paralyzed the left arm and the right foot of Nicola, and also made her left arm longer than her right; and no power on earth could cure this strange infirmity, until some weeks after, when the devil was at last completely and irrevocably expelled.

As the strange circumstances of Nicola's possession became known everywhere, several Calvinist preachers came with their followers, to "expose this popish cheat," as they said. On their entrance, the devil saluted them mockingly, called them by name, and told them that they had come in *obedience to him*. One of the preachers took his Protestant prayer-book, and began to read it with a very solemn face. The devil laughed at him, and, putting on a most comical face, he said: "Ho! ho! my good friend; do you intend to expel *me* with your prayers and hymns? Do you think that they will cause me any pain? Don't you know that they are mine? -*I* helped to compose them!"

"I will expel thee in the name of God," said the preacher, solemnly.

"You!" said the devil, mockingly. "You will *not* expel me either in the name of *God*, or in the name of the *devil*. Did you ever hear, then, of one devil driving out another?"

"I am not a devil," said the preacher, angrily, "I am a servant of Christ."

"A servant of Christ, indeed!" said Satan, with a sneer. "What! I tell you you are worse than *I* am. *I* believe, and *you* do not want to believe. Do you suppose that *you* can expel me from the body of this miserable wretch? Ha! go first and expel all the devils that are in your own heart!"

The preacher took his leave, somewhat discomfited. On going away, he said, turning up the whites of his eyes, "Oh Lord, I pray thee, assist this poor creature!"

"And I pray Lucifer," cried the spirit, "that he may never leave you, but may always keep your firmly in his power, as he does now. Go about your business now. You are *all mine*, and I am your master."

On the arrival of the priest, several of the Protestants went away—they had seen and heard more than they wanted. Others, however, remained, and great was their terror when they saw how the devil writhed and howled in agony, as soon as the Blessed Sacrament was brought near him. At last the evil spirit departed, leaving Nicola in a state of unnatural trance. While she was in this state, several of the preachers tried to open her eyes, but they found it impossible to do so. The priest then placed the Blessed Sacrament on Nicola's lips, and instantly she was restored to consciousness.

Rev. Father de Motta then turned to the astonished preachers, and said: "Go now, ye preachers of the new gospel; go and relate everywhere what you have seen and heard. Do not deny any longer that our Lord Jesus Christ is really and truly present in the Blessed Sacrament of the altar. Go now, and let not human respect hinder you from confessing the truth."

During the exorcisms of the following days, the devil was forced to confess that he was not to be expelled at Vervins, and that he had with him twenty-nine devils, among whom were three powerful demons: Cerberus, Astaroth, and Legio.

On another occasion, the devil was hotly pressed by the priest, to tell the hour of his final departure.

"At three o'clock in the afternoon," answered the three demons, Cerberus, Astaroth, and Legio.

"On what day?" asked the priest; but the demons would give no answer.

Beelzebub then began to howl wildly, and curse the hour when he first entered into the body of that wretched creature.

"Ah!" shrieked he, "if God would permit me, I would leave instantly; but I cannot. My task is not yet done."

"Dost thou, then, not know the hour of thy final departure?" asked the priest.

"Ah, yes! but if you promise that you will not take me to Liesse, I will leave instantly, and will not return until this day a year."

"God forbid that I should make thee any such promise," said the priest; "with the help of God, thou shalt leave this very instant;" and taking the Holy Eucharist in his hand, he compelled the evil spirits to depart.

22d to 24th of January, 1566.—The priests now resolved to take Nicola to the celebrated pilgrimage of our Lady at Liesse, especially since the devil seemed to fear the place so much. During the journey, the evil spirit opposed them in every possible way. At one time an accident happened; at another the horses stood still, and would not budge an inch. At other times the horses would rear and plunge in the most frantic manner. Sometimes the devil uttered the most frightful sounds—at times they were as loud as a clap of thunder. At last, by means of prayer and the exorcisms, and especially by the power of the Blessed Sacrament, all the obstacles of Satan were overcome, and the travelers arrived safely at Liesse.

Next day Father de Motta began the exorcism in the church of Our Lady at Liesse, in presence of an immense multitude.

"How many are you in the body of this poor creature?" asked the priest.

"There are thirty of us," answered the evil spirit.

The priest then sprinkled Nicola with holy water, and the devil spat upon it in contempt.

"As servant of the living God," cried the priest, "I command thee and thy associates to quit the body of this poor woman."

"No," answered Satan, in an impudent tone; "twenty-six of my companions will depart, but as for me, I will not go."

The priest then took the Blessed Sacrament in his hand, and showing it to the demon, he said: "I command thee, in the name of the living God, the great Emanuel Whom thou seest here present, and in Whom thou believest——"

"Ah, yes!" shrieked the demon; "*I believe in him.*" And the devil howled again as he made this confession, for it was wrung from him by the power of Almighty God.

"I command thee, then, in His name," said the priest, "to quit this body instantly."

At these words, and especially at the sight of the Blessed Sacrament, the devil suffered the most frightful torture. At one moment the body of Nicola was rolled up like a ball; then again she became fearfully swollen. At one time her face was unnaturally lengthened, then excessively widened, and sometimes it was as red as scarlet. Her eyes, at times protruded horribly, and then again sunk deeply into her skull. Her tongue hung down to her chin; it was sometimes black, sometimes red, and sometimes spotted, like a toad.

The priest still continued to urge and torture Satan. "Accursed spirit!" he cried, "I command thee in the name and by the Real Presence of our Lord Jesus Christ here in the Blessed Sacrament, to depart instantly from the body of this poor creature."

"Ah, yes!" cried Satan, howling wildly, "twenty-six of my companions shall leave this instant, for they are forced to do so."

The people in the church now began to pray with great fervor. Suddenly Nicola's limbs began to crack, as if every bone in her body were breaking, a pestilential vapor came forth from her mouth, and twenty-six devils departed from her, never more to return.

Nicola then fell into an unnatural swoon, from which she was roused only by the Blessed Sacrament. On recovering her senses, and receiving Holy Communion, Nicola's face shone like the face of an angel.

The priest still continued to urge the demon, and used every means to expel him. Satan grinned at him horribly, and shrieked at him in a rage. "Is it not enough for you to have expelled twenty-six of my companions? That is honor enough for the woman of this house!" By the "woman" Satan meant the Blessed Virgin Mary, who was especially honored in this place.

"I tell you," the devil shrieked, "that even if you remain here till midnight, even if you stay here a hundred years, I will not leave at your bidding."

"At whose bidding, then?" asked Father de Motta.

"I will not leave unless commanded by the Bishop of Laon," answered the demon, angrily.

That evening the priest gave orders that the church doors should be open next morning at five o'clock, so that the people could assemble early, and unite with him in prayer. During the night, the devil, who hates to see the people pray, stopped the clock in the church tower, as he afterwards confessed, so that the doors were not opened till an hour after the appointed time.

Nicola was now taken to Pierrepont, where one of the demons, named Legio, was expelled by means of the Blessed Sacrament. On leaving, a black smoke was seen issuing from Nicola's mouth, and the demon, in token of his departure, broke some tiles on the belfry.

Here the Calvinists, urged on by the evil spirit, tried to kill Nicola and the good priest who accompanied her; but a well-armed force came just in time, and dispersed these cowardly murderers.

Nicola was now brought to the town of Laon. On her arrival there the people locked their doors; and no one wished to receive her into his house, for all feared that the devil might reveal their most secret sins.

At last, after long and urgent entreaties, and especially after having placed a good sum of money in the hand of the inn-keeper, Nicola was permitted to stay over-night in an inn not far from the church.

Next morning Nicola was brought to the church. Scarcely had she quitted the house, when the devil again took possession of her.

The Bishop who was requested to exorcise Nicola, prepared himself for this terrible task by prayer and fasting, and other works of penance.

On the arrival of Nicola in the church, the exorcism began.

"How many are you in this body?" asked the Bishop.

"There are three of us," answered the evil spirit.

"What are your names?"

"Beelzebub, Cerberus, and Astaroth."

"What has become of the others?" asked the Bishop.

"They have been expelled," answered Satan.

"Who expelled them?"

"Ha!" cried the devil, gnashing his teeth, "it was *He*

whom you hold in your hand, there on the paten." The devil meant our dear Lord in the Blessed Sacrament.

"What were the names of those who were expelled?" asked the Bishop.

"What is that to you?" answered the devil, gruffly. "They were my dogs, my slaves; they have no name."

"Who is speaking now?" asked the Bishop.

"It is Beelzebub, the prince of devils."

"Let the other two speak also."

"They shall not," answered the proud spirit.

The Bishop then, in a solemn voice, commanded Cerberus and Astaroth to speak.

"You may talk till you crack your throat," answered Beelzebub, "I tell you they shall not speak in *my presence*. They are my servants, my slaves; I am their master. Did you ever see a slave speak in presence of his lord?"

"I will *force* them to speak," said the Bishop; "they must obey God."

"Very well! They will obey God; but I tell you they shall *not* speak. *I* am here for that. Go on, I will satisfy you."

"When wilt thou leave the body of this poor creature?" demanded the Bishop.

"Astaroth will leave next Sunday," answered the spirit.

"Thou shalt leave this very instant."

"No, I will not leave."

The Bishop then held the Blessed Sacrament near the face of Nicola. The demon writhed and howled in agony. "Ah, yes! I will go, I will go!" he shrieked, "but I shall return."

Suddenly Nicola became stiff and motionless as marble. The Bishop then touched her lips with the Blessed Sacrament, and in an instant she was fully restored to consciousness. She received Holy Communion, and her countenance now shone with a wondrous, supernatural beauty.

Next day Nicola was brought again to the church, and

the exorcism began as usual. The Bishop sprinkled Nicola with holy water.

"Faugh! you filthy papist" shrieked the devil in a rage, "away with your salt water!"

He then grinned horribly, and spat upon the holy water. The Bishop now began to read the gospel of St. John, and the devil mocked and mimicked him all the while, and repeated the very same words, sometimes before, sometimes after the Bishop,

The Bishop then took the Blessed Sacrament in his hand, held it near the face of Nicola, and said:

"I command thee in the name of the living God, and by the Real Presence of our Lord Jesus Christ here in the Sacrament of the altar, to depart instantly from the body of this creature of God, and never more to return."

"No! no!" shrieked the devil, "I will not go. My hour is not yet come."

"I command thee to depart. Go forth, impure, accursed spirit! Go forth!" and the Bishop held the Blessed Sacrament close to Nicola's face.

"Stop! stop!" shrieked Satan; "let me go! I will depart—but I shall return." And instantly Nicola fell into the most frightful convulsions. A black smoke was seen issuing from her mouth, and she fell again into a swoon.

During her stay in Laon, Nicola was carefully examined by Catholic and Protestant physicians. Her left arm, which had been paralyzed by the devil, was found entirely without feeling. The doctors cut into the arm with a sharp knife, they burnt it with fire, they drove pins and needles under the nails of the fingers, but Nicola felt no pain; her arm was utterly insensible. Once, while Nicola was lying in a state of unnatural lethargy, the doctors gave her bread soaked in wine (it was what the Protestants call their communion, or Lord's Supper), they rubbed her limbs briskly, they threw water in her face, they pierced her tongue till the blood flowed; they tried every possible means to arouse her, but in vain! Nicola remained cold and motionless as marble. At last the priest touched the lips of Nicola with the Blessed Sacrament, and instantly she was restored to consciousness, and began to praise God.

The miracle was so clear, so palpable, that one of the doctors, who was a bigoted Calvinist, immediately renounced his errors, and became a Catholic.

Several times, also, the Protestants touched Nicola's face with a host which was not consecrated, and which, consequently, was only bread, but Satan was not in the least tormented by this. He only ridiculed their efforts.

On the twenty-seventh of January, the Bishop, after having walked in solemn procession with the clergy and the faithful, began the exorcism in church, in presence of a vast multitude of Protestants and Catholics.

"I command thee in the name of the living God," said the Bishop solemnly, "answer truthfully to all that I shall ask thee."

"Speak on, I will answer;" replied the evil spirit.

"Who art thou that art now speaking?"

"It is myself."

"What is thy name?"

"I have told you before. My name is Beelzebub."

"Who are thy companions?"

"Astaroth and Cerberus."

"When wilt thou depart from the body of this creature of God?"

"Astaroth shall leave to-day. His hour is fixed, but I shall remain."

"What sign will he give of his departure?"

"He will break one of the window-panes, and take a piece of it with him."

"Whither will he go?"

"He will go to my brave Calvinist, Captain Dandelot, who would gladly put you all to death if he had the men at his command."

"Why do you keep possession of the body of this poor creature?"

"I do it to harden my Calvinists, or to convert them; and I swear by the Sacred Blood, that I shall yet drive them to the last extremity."

The names of Beelzebub, Astaroth, and Cerberus were now written on pieces of paper. The Bishop burned them in the flame of a blessed candle, and said: "Oh, wicked spirits! accursed of God! I here burn these names as a sign of the eternal torments to which you have been condemned; and you shall be tortured until you depart from this body." At this the demon shrieked and writhed in fearful agony. Three distinct voices were clearly heard; they resembled the bellowing of an ox, the howling of a dog, and the shrill squealing of swine.

The Bishop now holds the Blessed Sacrament close to the face of Nicola. Suddenly a wild, unearthly yell rings through the air—a black, heavy smoke issues from the mouth of Nicola. The demon Astaroth is expelled forever. At the same instant the crash of breaking glass is heard; a window-pane is broken and carried away. Nicola again falls into a deadly swoon, and is restored to consciousness only by the Blessed Sacrament.

During the exorcism which took place on the first of February the Bishop said:

"Oh, accursed spirit!" since neither prayer, nor the holy gospels, neither the exorcisms of the Church, nor the holy relics, can compel thee to depart, I will now show thee thy Lord and Master, and by His power I command thee."

"What do you mean?" shrieked Satan, gnashing his teeth. "Do you mean your white ——— ?"

(Here the devil used a very unbecoming expression for the Blessed Sacrament.)

"How darest thou call our Blessed Lord by such a vile name?"

"Ha! ha! I've taught my Calvinists to nickname Him thus."

"Why, then dost thou fear *Him* so much? Why dost thou fly in terror before His face?"

"Ha!" shrieked the devil, "it is that '*hoc*,' that '*hoc*,' that forces me to flee."

The devil here refers to the divine words of consecration by which the bread and wine are changed, in holy Mass, into the Body and Blood of our Lord Jesus Christ.

The devil kept on talking quite aloud during the holy Mass.

The moment of consecration came, and Satan was instantly struck dumb. Nicola was now seized with the most frightful convulsions. Fifteen strong men were holding her down; and so great was the strength of the demon, that they were all dragged with her aloft into the air. Nicola, her face turned away from the altar, remained suspended in space, over six feet above the platform, during the entire time of consecration. As soon as the consecration was over, she fell back heavily upon the platform.

During the exorcism which took place after mass, the Bishop held the Blessed Sacrament in his hand, and said: "O accursed spirit! arch-enemy of the ever Blessed God! I command thee, by the precious Blood of Jesus Christ here present, to depart from this poor woman! Depart accursed, into the everlasting flames of hell!"

At these words, and especially at the sight of the Blessed Sacrament, the demon was so fearfully tormented, and the appearance of Nicola was so hideous and revolting, that the people turned away their eyes in horror. At last a heavy sigh was heard, and a cloud of black smoke issued from the mouth of Nicola. Cerberus was expelled, and, in sign of his departure, he broke and carried away a pane of glass from one of the side-chapels.

Again Nicola fell into a death-like swoon, and again she was brought to consciousness only by means of the Blessed Sacrament.

During the exorcism which took place on the seventh day of February, the Bishop said to Satan: "What sign wilt thou give of thy departure?"

"I will cure Nicola's left arm, so that she can use it as well as ever. Is not this a splendid miracle? You will find another sign on the roof of the belfry."

"What hast thou gained by taking possession of this body? Many have been converted by witnessing the great power of the Blessed Sacrament. Depart, then! every one hates and despises thee."

"I know it," answered Satan. "Many have been converted; but there are also many who remain hardened in their sins."

"Tell me, then, why hast thou taken possession of this honest and virtuous Catholic woman?"

"I have done so by permission of God. I have taken possession of her on account of the sins of the people. I have done it to show my Calvinists that there are devils who can take possession of men whenever God permits it. I know they do not want to believe this; but I will show them that I am the devil. I have taken possession of this creature in order to convert them, or to harden them in their sins; and, by the Sacred Blood, I will *perform* my task."

This answer filled all who heard it with horror. "Yes," answered the Bishop, solemnly, "God desires to unite all men in the one holy faith. As there is but one God, so there can be but one true religion. A religion like that which the Protestants have invented, is but a hollow mockery. It must fall. The religion established by our Lord Jesus Christ is the only true one, which shall last forever; it shall increase. It is destined to unite all men within its sacred embrace, so that there shall be but one sheepfold and one Shepherd. This Divine Shepherd is our Lord Jesus Christ, the invisible Head of the holy Roman Catholic Church, whose visible Head is our holy Father the Pope, successor of St. Peter."

The devil was silent—he was put to shame before the entire multitude. He was expelled once more by means of the Blessed Sacrament.

In the afternoon of the same day the devil began to prate and make merry during the procession. "Ah! ha!" cried the devil, "you think that you can expel me in this way? You have not the proper attendance of a Bishop. Where are the Dean and the Archdean? Where are the Royal Judges? Where is the Chief Magistrate, who was frightened out of his wits that night, in the prison? Where is the Procurator of the King? Where are his Attorneys and Counsellors? Where is the Clerk of the Court?" (The devil mentioned each of these by name.) "I will not depart until all are assembled. Were I to depart now, what proof could you give to the king of all that has happened? Do you think that people will believe you so easily? No! no! There are many who would make objections. The testimony of these common country-people here will have but little weight. It is a torment to me that I must tell you what you have to do. I am forced to do it. Ha! cursed be the hour in which I first took possession of this vile wretch!"

"I find little pleasure in thy prating," answered the Bishop; "there are witnesses enough here. Those whom you have mentioned are not necessary. Depart, then! give glory to God. Depart—go to the flames of hell!"

"Yes, I shall depart, but not to-day I know full well that I must depart. My sentence is passed; I am compelled to leave; but, before I do so, you must fast a little more. You are not lean enough yet."

"I care not for thy jabbering," said the Bishop, "I shall expel thee by the power of God; by the precious Blood of our Lord Jesus Christ."

"Yes, I must yield to you," shrieked the demon wildly. "It tortures me that I must give you this honor. It is now twelve hundred years since a Bishop like you expelled the prince of devils."

"Thou art a liar!" said the Bishop, solemnly. "Every day the holy Roman Catholic Church triumphs over thee and thy hellish spirits."

"Thou liest thyself, my shell-pate!" answered Satan. "Poor, contemptible devils, nameless wretches, may have been expelled, but the prince of devils has not been expelled."

The Bishop now burned the name of Beelzebub, but Satan only laughed at him, and said: "Oh, my shell-pate, you are burning only paper and ink!"

At this every one was astonished, as the burning of the demon's name had hitherto always caused him the most frightful tortures.

"I see," said the Bishop, "that thou heedest neither the exorcisms nor the burning of thy name; I will, therefore, show thee thy Lord and Master."

"Whom do you mean?" shrieked the demon, in a fury "Do you mean your white——?"

Satan was at length expelled. On leaving, he cried out: "I depart, but I shall return again. My hour is not yet come."

The next day, as Nicola was being taken to the church, the demon instantly took possession of her. "Aha!" cried he, in a mocking tone, "I am not gone away yet." Then he ridiculed all that had been done the day previous. During the exorcism, the Bishop said: "Why dost thou not depart? The appointed day and hour have come."

"I will not go, because you are not fasting, because you have not been to confession, because you have not assembled witnesses enough."

The Bishop now took the Blessed Sacrament in his hand, and held it close to the face of the possessed woman.

"A thousand million devils take you, wretched shell-pate! Why do you torture me so horribly?"

At last, Satan was compelled to flee once more.

The next morning, after the procession was ended, the holy sacrifice of the Mass was offered up, as usual. As soon as the possessed woman was brought upon the platform, the devil looked around the church and said: "Ha! there are only papists here! The assembly is not yet full. Where is the magistrate Du Manche, who was in such mortal terror, that night, in the prison? Where is Bochet, the State's attorney? Where is the Archdean? I will not leave until all are present; for, by the Sacred Blood, I have good reasons for it."

During holy Mass, a German Protestant, named Stephen Voske, happened to be in the church. Hearing his name called by the demon, he went up to the platform to speak to him. Voske spoke in German, but the demon answered him in French.

"Ha! you want me to speak German with you; but I will not do it. Were I in your country, I would speak German better than you do. I can easily see that you were not brought up in Germany." (This was really the case.) "Here," said Satan "I speak only the language of the country, so that every one can understand me. You may speak German; I will answer you in my own language."

They continued thus to talk together for about half an hour, one speaking German, and the other French. When the time for the consecration approached, Satan said to Voske: "Stop, now! keep silence! They are going to show the white ——. Ha! it is my white ——. It is I who have nicknamed Him thus. I have taught all my servants and disciples to do the same."

Suddenly, Satan was struck dumb. The possessed woman was raised over six feet into the air, and then fell back heavily upon the platform. The same scene was repeated at the Elevation of the Chalice. The demon, wild with rage, shrieked: "Ha! Bishop, you shell-pate! if I had you now I would make you suffer for this. You torture me horribly."

(We must remark here, that the Bishop purposely prolonged the time of consecration, in order to cause Satan greater torment.)

As the Bishop, just before the Pater Noster, took the Saered Host once more in his hand, and raised it with the chalice, the possessed woman was again whisked into the air, carrying with her the keepers, fifteen in number, at least six feet above the platform: and, after a while, she fell heavily back on the ground.

At this sight, all present were filled with amazement and terror. The German Protestant fell on his knees: he burst into tears; he was converted.

"Ah!" cried he, "I now believe firmly that the devil really possesses this poor creature. I believe that it is really the Body and Blood of Jesus Christ which expels him. I believe firmly. I will no longer remain a Protestant."

After Mass, the exorcism began as usual. As soon as the Bishop appeared on the platform, Satan cried, in a mocking tone: "Ah, ah! my shell pate! you made a good confession this morning to the dean. I saw you, but I could not understand your words."

"Now, at last," said the Bishop, "thou must depart. Away with thee, evil spirit!"

"Yes," said Satan, "it is true that I must depart, but not yet. I will not go before the hour is come in which I first took possession of this wretched creature. Have patience, then; wait until three o'clock. Oh, accursed be that hour. Do not push on the clock. I know the hour well. My sentence is already passed."

"What sign wilt thou give of thy departure?" asked the Bishop.

"Never mind!" answered Satan, sullenly; "you shall have signs enough. I will heal the left arm of this creature. She has not been able to use it these three months, because I possessed it. And you, my shell-pate! you shall have *your* sign. I will strike such terror to your heart as you never felt before, and as you will not soon forget."

"Where wert thou last night?"

"I was in your palace," answered Satan, "I saw you right well. You got up last night to pray. It was about three o'clock. I know that your prayers have helped much to expel me."

Satan then turned to a gentleman present named Lancelot May, and publicly accused his brother Robert of some very grievous sins, which he named.

"Yes," cried Satan in a rage, "I swear by the Sacred Blood 'that what I say is true, even though he is your brother."

He then turned to a woman, who stood near by, and said: "He! Margaret, your husband Lancelot, lost two dollars last night. It was Nelly who won them."

At this, Lancelot, who was himself present, hung his head in shame, and all present were greatly surprised. Satan continued thus for some time to reveal, the sins of those around him. At last the Bishop took the Sacred Host in his hand, and said: "In the name of the Adorable Trinity, Father, Son, and Holy Ghost—in the name of the Sacred Body of Jesus Christ here present—I command thee, wicked spirit, to depart."

"What!" shrieked Satan, "you wish to expel me with your white —— ?"

"Accursed spirit!" said the Bishop indignantly, "who has taught thee to blaspheme God thus?"

"It was I who taught it to my Calvinists, who are my obedient servants," answered Satan.

"But it is the Sacred Body of thy Lord and Master; it is the Blessed Body of our Lord Jesus Christ. By His power thou shalt be expelled."

"Yes, yes, it is true!" shrieked the demon wildly; "it is true. It is the Body of God. I must confess it, for I am forced to do so. Ha! it tortures me that I must confess this; but I must. I speak the truth only when I am forced to do it. The truth is not from me. It comes from my Lord and Master. I have entered this body by the permission of God."

The Bishop now held the Blessed Sacrament close to the

face of the possessed woman. The demon writhed in fearful agony. He tried in every way to escape from the presence of our Lord in the Blessed Sacrament.

At length a black smoke was seen issuing from the mouth of Nicola. She fell into a swoon, and was restored again to consciousness only by means of the Blessed Sacrament.

8th of February.—During the procession, which took place in the afternoon of the same day, the devil said to the Bishop: "Oh Bishop, my shell-pate! you have taken no dinner. You are sick and weary." And then he began to sing—"Oh, he has eaten nothing! I knew that you had to fast before you could drive me out of the body of this worthless wretch."

After the procession Nicola was again placed on the platform, where she was held by fifteen strong men. The Bishop and clergy then offered up a solemn prayer in Latin, in which they called the devil a spirit accursed.

"Why do you use that word *accursed?*" asked the devil angrily.

"Because," answered the Bishop, "thou hast offended God so grievously, that thou canst never hope for pardon. Thou art lost to all love and hope; thou hast nought but eternal damnation to expect. Thy sentence is passed forever."

At these words Satan became silent, and turned away.

The Bishop now began the last solemn adjuration. During the exorcism, the devil said several times to the Bishop: "Ah, you have taken no dinner to-day! You are very weak." He then looked around, and said: "Ha, ha! are you here, Attorney-General Bochet? You were not here this morning!"

He then blew out the blessed candle which stood near the Bishop, and said, with a mocking laugh, "Ha, ha! how stupid you are to burn candles in the broad daylight!"

The Bishop read the gospels, prayers and exorcisms; he burned Beelzebub's name, showed him the relic of the holy cross, and solemnly commanded him to depart.

The devil answered impudently, that he did not feel like going yet.

"I shall not ask thee any longer," said the Bishop, "when thou intendest to leave; I will expel thee instantly by the power of the living God, and by the precious Body and Blood of Jesus Christ, His beloved Son, here present in the Sacrament of the Altar."

"Ha, yes!" shrieked the demon; "I confess that the Son of God is here really and truly present. He is my Lord and Master. It tortures me to confess it, but I am forced to do so." Then he repeated several times, with a wild, unearthly howl: "Yes, it is true. I must confess it. I am forced to leave, by the power of God's Body here present. I must—I must depart. It torments me that I must go so soon, and that I must confess this truth. But this truth is not from me; it comes from my Lord and Master, who has sent me hither, and who commands and compels me to confess the truth publicly. I shall go, but I shall not go empty-handed. By the Sacred Blood, I will have my booty. I shall take along with me the head of the little bailiff of Virvins. Perhaps I could also take with me some of my Calvinists—body and soul—for they belong to me. He! give me your head!" cried he, turning to the Bishop; "let me see whether I cannot carry it off?"

"No, never!" answered the Bishop; "thou shall depart, and thou shalt take nothing with thee. These men are baptized—thou canst not touch them."

"Yes," cried Satan, in a mocking tone, "they are baptized; but, after having renounced me in baptism, they gave themselves up to me again. Therefore they are mine—they are surely mine!"

"I forbid thee, in the name of the living God," said the Bishop, "to hurt either them or any one here present."

The Bishop then took the Blessed Sacrament in his hand, and, holding It on high, he said, with a solemn voice: "O thou wicked, unclean spirit, Beelzebub! thou arch-enemy of the eternal God! behold, here present, the precious Body and Blood of our Lord Jesus Christ, thy Lord and Master! I adjure thee, in the name and by the power of our Lord and Saviour Jesus Christ, true God and true man, Who is here present; I command thee to depart instantly and forever from this creature of God. Depart to the deepest depth of hell, there to be tormented forever. Go forth, unclean spirit, go forth—behold here thy Lord and Master!"

At these solemn words, and at the sight of our Sacramental Lord, the poor possessed woman writhed fearfully. Her limbs cracked as if every bone in her body were breaking. The fifteen strong men who held her, could scarcely keep her back. They staggered from side to side, they were covered with perspiration. Satan tried to escape from the presence of our Lord in the Blessed Sacrament. The mouth of Nicola was wide open, her tongue hung down below her chin, her face was shockingly swollen and distorted. Her color changed from yellow to green, and became even gray and blue, so that she no longer looked like a human being; it was rather the face of a hideous, incarnate demon. All present trembled with terror, especially when they heard the wild cry of the demon, which sounded like the loud roar of a wild bull.

They fell on their knees, and with tears in their eyes began to cry out: "Jesus, have mercy!"

The Bishop continued to urge Satan. At last the evil spirit departed, and Nicola fell back senseless into the arms of her keepers. She still, however, remained shockingly distorted. In this state she was shown to the judges, and to all the people present; she was rolled up like a ball. The Bishop now fell on his knees, in order to give her the Blessed Sacrament as usual. But see! suddenly the demon returns, wild with rage endeavors to seize the hand of the Bishop, and tries even to grasp the Blessed Sacrament Itself. The Bishop starts back—Nicola is carried into the air, and the Bishop rises from his knees, trembling with terror and pale as death.

The good Bishop takes courage again; he pursues the demon, holding the Blessed Sacrament in his hand. Satan endeavors to escape, and hurls the keepers to the ground.

The people call upon God for aid.

Satan departs once more with a noise which resembles a crash of thunder.

Suddenly he returns again in a fury, and casts a look of rage on some Calvinists present, who stood the whole time with covered heads.

"On your knees!" cried the people; "uncover your heads; kneel down in the presence of the precious Body and Blood of our Lord Jesus Christ."

Scarcely had these words been uttered, when a wild cry was heard, "to arms! to arms!" In an instant all was in confusion.

The Catholics thought that the Calvinists had come armed to church, in order to massacre them. The Calvinists, on the other hand, were filled with mortal terror. Soon this fear and confusion spread throughout the city. Every one was terrified, but no one could tell the real cause of such a sudden uproar.

The Bishop remained calmly at his post. Still holding the Blessed Sacrament in his hand, he turned towards the people and said in a loud voice, "My friends, do not be disturbed. Remain where you are. Here is the true Body of our Lord Jesus Christ; He will assist us; on your knees, and pray to God. I beg you, in the name of God, do not hurt one another."

Scarcely had the Bishop uttered these words, when all was instantly calm again. The people fell on their knees, and prayed to God for the possessed woman. The Bishop still pursued and urged Satan, holding the Blessed Sacrament in his hand, till at length the demon, overcome by the power of our Lord's Sacred Body, went forth amidst smoke, and lightning, and thunder.

Thus was the demon at length expelled forever, on Friday afternoon, at three o'clock, the same day and hour on which our Lord triumphed over hell by His ever-blessed death.

Nicola was now completely cured; she could move her left arm with the greatest ease. She now fell on her knees, and thanked God, and the good Bishop, for all he had done for her.

The people wept for joy, and sang hymns of praise and thanksgiving in honor of God, and of our dear Lord in the Blessed Sacrament.

On all sides were heard the exclamations: "Oh, what a great miracle! Oh, thank God that I witnessed it! Who is there now that could doubt of the Real Presence of our Lord Jesus Christ in the Sacrament of the Altar!"

Many a Protestant present also said: "I believe now in the Presence of our Lord in the Blessed Sacrament; I have seen it with my eyes! I will remain a Calvinist no longer. Accursed be those who have hitherto kept me in error! Oh, now I can understand what a good thing is the holy sacrifice of the Mass!"

A solemn Te Deum was intoned; the organ pealed forth, and the bells rung a merry chime.

The whole city was filled with joy.

CHAPTER VI.

THE WONDERFUL EFFECTS OF THE BLESSED SACRAMENT IN NICOLA AUBRY.

THE preceding chapter may lead the reader to think it strange that although Satan was repeatedly expelled by the Presence of our Divine Saviour in the Sacred Host, nevertheless, it appeared as if our Saviour was forced to yield to Satan, when he again took possession of Nicola's body. Why this struggle between our Lord and Satan, since our divine Saviour is his Lord and Master?

It is true that our Lord is the Master of Satan; and yet we read in the Gospel how He permitted the devil to touch Him and carry Him up to the pinnacle of the Temple and to the top of a high mountain. On these occasions it must be remarked that He suffered Himself to be touched by the devil, *only, when, and as long as* He gave him permission so to do. As soon as our Lord said to him: "Begone, Satan," he took to flight. In like manner did He permit Satan to take possession of Nicola's body, sometimes even for a considerable time, not only to sanctify this innocent woman, but also to confirm, by these repeated miracles, the Catholics in their faith in His Real Presence in the Holy Eucharist, and to convert or confound the Protestants, who denied that Real Presence and committed so many shocking outrages on His Sacred Person. For this reason also, did our Lord force Satan to make a public profession of his faith in the Real Presence, not once only but on several occasions, and in several places, in presence of thousands of Catholics and Protestants.

Moreover, it is to be remarked, that Satan had no power

over the soul of Nicola Aubry. He could not take away her own free will. She retained her own consciousness, her own intellectual and moral faculties unimpaired, and never confounded herself with the evil spirit. She always retained the power of internal protest and struggle. She always exercised this power most effectually, never yielding to any of the evil intentions of the devil. She derived this power from the Body of our Lord, which she received in Holy Communion.

During His life the body of Jesus Christ had a peculiar healing, life-giving power. A virtue went forth from His body to heal all those that came near Him, and to expel demons from the possessed. He touched the blind and they saw; He touched the deaf and they heard; He touched the dumb, and they spoke; He touched the sick, and they were healed; He touched the dead, and they were restored to life. Even before His passion and resurrection, before His body was glorified, Jesus made His body invisible, as we see in various parts of the Gospel.*

The Nazarenes once tried to cast Him down a hill.† The Jews wished to stone Him,‡ but in vain: He walked on the waves of the sea. On Mount Thabor Jesus showed His body to His disciples, as it would have always appeared, had He not chosen to hide His glory. And then His face shone as the sun, and His garments were whiter than snow. After His resurrection, His body became glorified and assumed the qualities of a spirit. He could pass through a wall without breaking it, as a sunbeam passes through glass. He passed through the tomb, though it was sealed; He entered the supper room, though the windows and doors were barred. He became visible and invisible at will. He appeared under different forms. To St. Magdalen, He appeared as a gardener; to the disciples going to Emmaus, He appeared as a stranger and traveler. Now it is this wonder-

---

* Luke iv., 30. † John viii., 59. ‡ John x., 39.

ful Body, this glorified Body, this life-giving, divine Body, this Body, possessing the qualities of a spirit, that Jesus Christ gives us when He says: "Eat My flesh, drink My blood."

By original sin—the sin of our first parents—man was injured in body and soul. After the fall, reason grew darkened, will weakened, the heart of man became more inclined to evil than to good. Now, as body and soul were both injured by sin, so there must be a medicine for both the body and soul; a heavenly medicine, which weakens our inclination to evil, enkindles in the heart the love of virtue, the love of God. This heavenly medicine for body and soul, is the sacred Body and Soul of Jesus Christ. It is His Flesh and Blood, united with His Soul and Divinity. By sin, our body has been doomed to death and corruption; but by eating the Flesh and Blood of Jesus Christ, the seed of immortality is implanted in it. Our flesh and blood mingling with the Flesh and Blood of Jesus Christ, are fitted for a glorious resurrection. Leaven or yeast, when mixed with dough, soon penetrates the entire mass and imparts new qualities to it. In like manner the glorified Body of Jesus Christ penetrates through our entire being, and endows it with new qualities, the qualities of glory and immortality. Our divine Saviour Himself assures us of this, for He says: "He that eateth My flesh and drinketh My blood, abideth in Me, and I in him. As the living Father hath sent Me, and I live by the Father: so he that eateth Me, the same also shall live by Me, and I will raise him up in the last day." *

There is an old proverb which tells us that "evil communications corrupt good manners." The converse of it is true. Why is it, that association with the great and good improves our manners and our morals? Intercourse or communion with a great and good man leaves us ever after different to what we were before. A virtue seems to have gone

---

* John vi., 55, 57.

forth from him and entered into our life. What is the explanation of this fact? How happens it that we are benefited by intercourse with the good, and injured by intercourse with the bad. How is it that one man is able to influence another, whether for good or for evil? What is the meaning of influence itself? Influence,—inflowing, flowing in—what is this but the fact that our life is the joint product of subject and object? Man lives and can live only by communion with that which is not himself. This must be said of every living dependent existence. Only God can live in, from, and by Himself alone, uninfluenced and unaffected by anything distinguishable from His own Being. But man is not God, is not being in himself, is not complete being, and must find out of himself both his being and its completeness. He lives not in and from himself alone, but does and must live in and by the life of another.

Cut off man from all communion with external nature and he dies, for he has no sustenance for his body, and must starve; cut him off from all communion with moral nature, and he dies—starves morally; cut him off from all moral communion, with a life above his own, and he stagnates and can make no progress. All this everybody knows and concedes. Then to elevate man, to give him a higher and nobler life, you must give him a higher and nobler object, a higher and nobler life with which to commune. To elevate his subjective life, you must elevate his objective life. From the object must flow into him a higher virtue—an elevating element.

To illustrate this point: What is the good of each being? It is that which makes the being better and more perfect. It is clear that inferior beings cannot make superior ones better and more perfect. Now the soul, being immortal, is superior to all earthly or perishable things. These, then, cannot make the soul better and more perfect, but rather worse than she is; for he who seeks what is worse than himself, makes himself worse than he was before. Therefore, the good—the life of the soul—can be only that which is better and more excellent than the soul herself is. Now God alone is this Good—He being Supreme Goodness Itself. He who possesses God, may be said to possess the goodness of all other things; for whatever goodness they possess they have from God. It follows, then, most clearly that the closer our union is with God, or the more intimate our relation to Him is in this life, the more contentment of mind, and the greater happiness of soul shall we enjoy.

Communion between God and man is possible, for like communes with like. Man has in his own nature a likeness to God. The human soul is a likeness of God, and hence there is nothing that hinders intercommunion between God and the soul of man. Though God, as the object, is independent of the soul, and does not live by communion with it, yet the soul lives only by communion with God: as, in all cases, the subject lives only by communion with the object, and not reciprocally the object by communion with the subject. By this communion the subject partakes of the object—the soul of man of the Divine nature.

The soul of man, then, to live, to be strong and to remain enlightened, must be, and remain, in communion with Almighty God. The more intimate its communion with God, the greater will be its light, strength and happiness. Now, God wishing to establish this intimate union between the soul and Himself, wishing to unite His divine nature to our human nature, took upon Himself human nature, and commands us to receive His humanity, that we may become partakers of His divinity. His human nature, His human Flesh and Blood are, then, the means which God has chosen from all eternity for the purpose of uniting us to Himself. By partaking of His human nature, by partaking of His sacred Flesh and Blood we become, as St. Peter says, partakers of the divine nature. We bear about God Himself in our bodies, as St. Paul forcibly expresses it.

This explains why Nicola Aubry, after receiving the Body and Blood of Jesus Christ, became as terrible to Satan as a furious lion is to man, and why her face became bright and beautiful as the face of an angel.

From the history of Nicola Aubry we learn, moreover, the implacable hatred and malice with which Satan studies to disturb our temporal happiness and to compass our eternal ruin. Yet it is certain that he can tempt and assail us only up to a certain degree; he can go only the length of his chain, that is, as far as God permits him. In the case before us, God permitted Satan to take possession of a body that was the temple of the Holy Ghost, and so frightful were the sufferings that he caused Nicola to undergo, that the people turned away their eyes in horror. God gave this permission to Satan from wise motives—from motives that proceeded from his kindness for men. Alas! what must be the power of Satan over those who live in mortal sin, who are his slaves, his obedient servants, who never receive Holy Communion, who even deny the Real Presence! In our days the number of these is immense, and there can be no doubt that the power and influence of Satan over them will increase in proportion as they approach heathenism and infidelity, and abandon the true religion. However, as long as they live in this world they experience the mercy of God in a certain degree, and Satan has no permission to exercise all his power and torment them as much as he desires. But let them leave this world in their state of unbelief and final impenitence, who shall be able to give us an adequate description of the sufferings that Satan will inflict upon them for millions and millions of years—nay, for all eternity! For then it is that God, from motives of justice, gives Satan unlimited power to torment his victims as he pleases. Then it is that God uses the demons as the cruel executioners of His divine justice, and none of the damned will experience the severity of this justice, and the unspeakable cruelty of Satan more keenly than unbelievers and the falsifiers of the word of God.

Let us be wise, let us receive Holy Communion as often as possible, but let us receive it worthily, in order to make sure of life everlasting. Were the Blessed Virgin to pay us a visit every day, and converse with us familiarly for the space of half an hour, what a favor it would be! And yet, it would be but a union of familiar intercourse with a creature—the holiest and highest of all pure creatures; but when Jesus Christ comes into us in communion, we are united to a Man-God—our Lord enters into the powers of our soul according as we are disposed to receive Him; He unites really His Flesh to our flesh, and His Spirit to our spirit, although we know not how this union is brought about. It is wholly interior, and infinitely more perfect than all the favors that angels and saints, and the Mother of God herself, can ever show us. Communion is truly the beatitude of our life. A single one, did we but bring to it, the necessary dispositions, would fill us with more delight and cause us greater transports of joy, than to see and converse with all the saints and angels together.

If we do not experience the effects of this admirable union, it is only from our want of disposition. "If after Communion," says St. Bonaventure, "you do not feel any effect of the spiritual food you have eaten, it is a sign that your soul is either sick or dead. You have put fire into your bosom, and you do not feel its heat; you have put honey into your mouth and you do not taste its sweetness."

Let us prepare ourselves for Holy Communion as well as we can, and then let us rest assured that our souls will be wonderfully changed and perfected. Our Lord will gradually remove all our weakness; He will encourage us and assist us to uproot our evil habits and passions; He will quench in us the fire of concupiscence in proportion to the disposition we bring to the holy table and finally He will lead us up to life everlasting. "He that eateth My flesh and drinketh My blood hath life everlasting." Admirable words, the meaning of which, we shall only perfectly understand when we see them verified in heaven.

Oh, what returns of gratitude and acknowledgment ought

we then to make to our Lord for having contrived this expedient to abide with us to the end of time! "Behold I am with you all days, even to the consummation of the world."* Should not our belief in His Real Presence in the Eucharist, enkindle in us the most ardent desires to visit and receive Him frequently, with the most profound humility, respect and veneration? Should not this our belief, excite us to testify our love and esteem for Him, with all the affections of our souls, and to invite Heaven and Earth to join with us in proclaiming the excess of His goodness and mercy? O amiable Jesus, it is in this mystery of the Blessed Sacrament, that Thy charity has exerted itself in such a wonderful manner as to seem to cast forth all its flames. Praise, honour and glory forever to Thy goodness and mercy! O grant, I beseech Thee, that I may duly correspond with the designs of Thy mercy, and partake of this banquet of Thy boundless love with such dispositions as are pleasing to Thee, and necessary to qualify me for receiving Thy grace in so superabundant a measure, as to change me entirely into Thee, that I may thus be able to say with Thy great Apostle: "I live, now not I, but Christ liveth in me."†

---

* Matt. 28.   † Gal. II. 20.

CHAPTER VII.

FURTHER WONDERFUL MANIFESTATIONS OF THE REAL PRESENCE.

WHAT has been said in the preceding chapters is certainly sufficient to establish the most solemn truth of the Real Presence. But our Lord Jesus Christ in the Blessed Sacrament has often been pleased to manifest His Real Presence in wonderful ways. Even when Jesus was loaded with infamy and tortured with pain, when He had almost lost the semblance of man, He knew how to prove to the world His divinity; it was then that He made all nature speak and testify to His innocence. The earth shrouded itself with the dark pall of mourning; the rocks burst asunder; the sun veiled its face and even the very dead arose from their graves to bear witness to the divinity of the dying Jesus. "Now the centurion and they that were with him watching, having seen the earth quake and other things that were done, were sore afraid, saying: 'Indeed this was the Son of God.'"[*] So when we look upon the Sacred Host, it is true, we see there, no mark of His Majesty, no token of His Sacred Presence, no vestige of His perfections, not a single ray of His Divinity. Yet, for all that, Jesus does not lack the power and means to manifest Himself in the Sacred Host, as the Lord of heaven and earth and the Redeemer of the world. Our dear Saviour has indeed been pleased on hundreds of occasions to manifest His Real Presence in the Blessed Sacrament in a most striking manner.

There exist a great number of hosts which are called miraculous, because of the wonderful facts connected with them. The history of that of Augsburg, in Germany, is

---

[*] Matt. xxvii. 54.

one of the most celebrated and most authentic. In 1194 a certain woman went to receive holy communion, in the Church of the Holy Cross in Augsburg. Immediately after receiving, she took the Sacred Host and put it between two slices of wax and thus kept it for five years. During all that time she suffered an agony of interior torments. To rid herself of her remorse of conscience she at length took the Blessed Sacrament to Father Berthold, a pious priest, the prior of the Convent of the Holy Cross, and declared to him her great crime and readiness to perform any kind of penance in expiation of it. The good priest consoled and encouraged the truly penitent woman to hope in the mercy of God. On taking the two pieces of wax apart, he beheld, instead of the species of bread, human flesh, and even the muscular fibres. When he tried to detach the wax from both sides of the Host, the better to contemplate the Blessed Sacrament, the Sacred Host split at once in two so as to remain, however, attached to the wax and united by the muscular fibres. Almost beside himself at this wonderful occurrence he was at a loss as to whether he should keep it secret or make it public. After mature reflection he concluded to consult several men of discretion on the subject. He was advised to put the wax with the Host in a sealed box and keep it until the Bishop of Augsburg should have given his decision on the matter.

On learning this miraculous event, Udalskalk, then Bishop of Augsburg, was greatly amazed. He went immediately with his clergy and a large number of the laity to the Church of the Holy Cross and in solemn procession, carried the Sacred Host with the wax to his Cathedral. After the wax had been taken off they all were surprised at seeing the Host become three times thicker than it was before. From this time to the feast of St. John the Baptist the Sacred Host used to increase in thickness, especially during Mass, to such an extent that the wax came off by itself without any human intervention.

Bishop Udalskalk, convinced of the truth of the miracle put the wax with the Blessed Sacrament, which kept the appearance of human flesh, in a crystal vase and carried it again in solemn procession to the Church of the Holy Cross, where it has been preserved with the greatest reverence to the present day. Every year processions numbering from twenty to thirty thousand men have come to this church to adore our Lord in this miraculous Host.

It would scarcely be expected that such an event should escape contradiction. In 1486 Leonard Stunz, a priest of the Cathedral, called the miracle in question. He ascended the pulpit several times and most vehemently inveighed against the devotion to the Blessed Sacrament, maintaining "that all that had been said about this Host was but a fiction and the story of an old devotee." The people felt highly indignant with him, whilst all unbelievers applauded what he had said. As soon as Frederick III, then Bishop of Augsburg, heard of the scandal, he ordered this priest to leave the city, withdrew the Sacred Host from public veneration, and kept it under lock and key in a wooden box until it had been examined anew. Just about this time Henry Justitutoris, the Papal Legate, came to Augsburg. The Bishop showed him the miraculous Host and related to him all that had happened. At the request of the Bishop, the Papal Legate examined the Sacred Host, after which he wrote a learned dissertation on the subject, showing that the Blessed Sacrament is still a Real Sacrament, containing the Body of Our Lord, even though the species of bread should disappear and instead human flesh and blood should become visible. This he wrote against Leonard Stunz, who had maintained that the Sacred Host should no longer be worshipped, since, instead of the appearance of bread, human flesh could be distinctly seen.

The Legate and Bishop, then referred the matter to the learned professors of the celebrated Universities of Jngolstadt and Erfurt, who unanimously declared that the Sacred

Host in the Church of the Holy Cross in Augsburg was the Blessed Sacrament, and should as such be venerated and adored. After this, the Bishop again examined the Sacred Host in presence of his clergy and other learned men. They distinctly saw human flesh as before, and as indeed it may be seen to the present day. The result of this examination and the declaration of both Universities were forthwith announced from the pulpit and the miraculous Host was again, to the great joy of the people, exposed on the altar for public veneration and adoration. From that time thousands of pilgrims flocked to the Church of the Holy Cross to worship Our Lord in the miraculous Host. The number of pious pilgrims, however, considerably increased in proportion as the extraordinary favors which Our Lord in the miraculous Host bestowed on the pious worshippers became more generally known. I will here relate three of those extraordinary favors for the edification of the pious reader.

In 1611, Mary Maximiliana, sister of William V., Duke of Bavaria, was taken sick with acute pain in her chest. The physicians had tried every remedy to procure her some relief, but in vain. One day the duke happened to speak to his sister of the great miracles wrought by Our Lord in the miraculous Host in the Church of the Holy Cross at Augsburg. On hearing the account of these wonders, Mary Maximiliana conceived great confidence in Our Lord in the Blessed Sacrament. She dismissed her physicians and caused herself to be carried from Munich to the Church of the Holy Cross in Augsburg, where she asked Our Lord in the miraculous Host to cure her. Her prayer was immediately granted. She rose up unaided by any one, perfectly cured. To show her gratitude to Our Lord, she had this miracle announced in all the Catholic Churches of Bavaria, and requested the clergy and the people to join her in giving thanks to Our Lord in the Blessed Sacrament for her miraculous cure.

In 1620 Bartholomew Holzhauser, a great servant of God,

was attacked by the pestilence which then raged in Augsburg. He had recourse to Our Lord in the miraculous Host and was delivered from the epidemic.

In 1747 a poor man in Augsburg who had been dumb from his very infancy, and was known by all in the city, prayed several times to Our Lord in the wonderful Host to obtain his speech but apparently without being heard. One day, however, he prayed with unusual confidence and with tears in his eyes to obtain the same favor. This time his request was granted. Full of joy he ran home to make known the miracle Our Lord had wrought in him.

After the Bishop had sufficiently convinced himself of the miraculous fact, he had a solemn Te Deum chanted, and all the bells of the churches rang out in thanksgiving.

The miraculous Host has often been examined since, and every new examination furnished new proofs of the Real Presence. All the Bishops of Augsburg, to the present day, have venerated and adored Our Lord therein, thus forming a chain of the most trustworthy witnesses of the great truth. But the faithful too have been most anxious to pay their homage to Our Lord in this miraculous Host. Up to the present time their devotion to Him has not diminished in spite of all the impious clamors of infidelity. And oh! how many prayers has not Our Lord there heard! How many extraordinary favors has He not bestowed upon the pious pilgrims who went thither, and had recourse to Him in their necessities whether temporal or spiritual.*

If we pray then to Jesus Christ in the Blessed Sacrament and obtain the favors we ask, it is a clear proof that Jesus is there present, for no favor can come forth from a piece of bread.

There are on record numberless favors granted by Jesus Christ to those who prayed to Him in the Blessed Sacrament. Cardinal de Noailles, Archbishop of Paris, relates in his pas-

---

* Ott's Eucharisticum.

toral of August 10th, 1725, the following cure of Mme. Anne de la Fosse, which took place on the feast of Corpus Christi in 1725. This lady had been suffering for twenty years from an incurable issue of blood. So weak had she become, that she was no longer able to walk even with the aid of crutches; nay, it very often happened that she fainted from sheer exhaustion. Many a time she was compelled to leave her bed on account of acute pains in her side, and when out of bed she had to be carried from one place to another. Sixty most trustworthy witnesses testified to the fact that Anne de la Fosse was in the pitiable condition mentioned at the approach of the feast of Corpus Christi. It happened that about this very time she felt strongly inspired by Almighty God to beseech our Lord Jesus Christ to cure her at the moment when the Blessed Sacrament would be carried by her house in the solemn procession of Corpus Christi. She was taken down and set before the door of her house, where she patiently waited and most fervently prayed until Our Lord was carried by. On being told, "Behold there is the Blessed Sacrament," she knelt down to adore, and, being too weak to remain in a kneeling posture, she threw herself on the ground and cried in a loud voice, "Lord, if Thou wilt, Thou canst cure me, for I believe that in the Blessed Sacrament there is the same Lord present who one day entered triumphantly into Jerusalem; forgive me my sins and I shall be cured." Then she tried to advance with the procession by dragging herself on her hands and knees, constantly crying aloud, "My Lord Jesus Christ, if Thou wilt, Thou canst cure me." Many of the people were perfectly astonished at her behavior, whilst others took her for a drunken or crazy woman. So the people insisted on her retiring and keeping silence; but she would not be intimidated or silenced, but continued crawling after Our Lord in the Blessed Sacrament saying, "Let me follow my Lord and my God." This great faith of hers could not go unrewarded. On a sudden she felt strength increasing in her limbs. She rose up, but fearing she might not be strong enough to walk to the church, she cried still louder than before, "Lord, let me enter Thy Temple and I shall be cured." She now requested her two companions to allow her to walk without their assistance, and, to the great astonishment of all present, she walked unsupported to the parish church, whither the Blessed Sacrament was being carried. As soon as she entered the church, she felt perfectly cured of the issue of blood, and so strong as to walk about with ease. After spending a considerable time in thanking, praising, and blessing our Lord Jesus Christ in the Holy Eucharist for the immense benefit He had bestowed upon her, she returned home accompanied by a great crowd of people. Many who had witnessed her intense suffering for years came now to behold the great miracle which Jesus Christ in the Blessed Sacrament had wrought upon her. To make sure that she was perfectly cured, they requested her to walk up and down in their presence, which she did with the greatest delight in order thus to give honor, and glory, and thanks to her Divine Benefactor in the Blessed Eucharist. Many non-Catholics even there were who praised God for this great miracle. One of them, who had often visited her when so very sick and who knew in what a pitiable condition she had been, took a solemn oath testifying that this cure was the wonderful effect of God's power, and that, according to his opinion, there could be no miracle more authentic than this.*

It will never be heard that God punished a man for turning into ridicule falsehood and error, idolatry and heresy, superstition and the like; on the contrary, God takes pleasure in those who confound heresy, idolatry, superstition and all kinds of falsehood and error. But when the truths and the mysteries of our holy religion are attacked, contra-

---

* Le Brun, "Explication des prieres et des ceremonies de la Messe," tom 3. For other examples see "Blessed Eucharist," p. 226, No. 22; p. 260–263, p. 213, No. 9.

dicted, or turned into ridicule, God in many instances, has shown the greatest displeasure by inflicting terrible punishments on those who mockingly spoke of the sacred mysteries of our religion, and who tried to make others also hold them in contempt and derision. Every truth is from God. Therefore, to contradict truth, to deny it, to turn it into ridicule, is to contradict God Himself, who uttered it—to mock the Lord of Heaven and earth. No wonder then, if we often hear of instances in which the wrath of the Lord fell upon such enemies of the true religion. In these punishments God gives us so many proofs to confirm that truth which is ridiculed and attacked. There are on record most frightful punishments with which the Lord has visited those who denied and insulted His Real Presence in the Blessed Sacrament.

I will relate here some of those lamentable occurrences, May they be a salutary warning to the miserable men who scoff and sneer at holy mysteries.

In the village of Edinghausen, situated not far from the town of Bielfield, in Rhenish Prussia, an impious blasphemer of religion took it into his head one day to turn the Holy Eucharist into derision. He sits down to table with some companions, not as infamous as he, although not much better. He takes some bread and wine and pronounced over it with mock solemnity the words of consecration: "This is my body! This is my blood!" After this sacrilegious parody he distributed them amongst his companions, saying to them with an ironical smile, "Take ye all!" When he had given some to all, and his turn came to take the bread and wine, he felt unwell, let his head fall on his chest and in a few seconds ceased to live. This took place on the 5th of January, 1807. The wretch was buried outside the cemetery, on the very feast of the Epiphany.*

---

* Schmid et Belet, Cat. Hist. II., 146. See other examples of Divine chastisements in "Blessed Eucharist," p. 209 ; then p. 212, No. 5 ; p. 213, No. 8; p. 214, No. 10 ; p. 218, No 12 ; p. 221, No. 15 ; p. 304, No. 2; and p. 182, 183.

History informs us how the Emperor Frederic II. persecuted the holy Church of God. He accepted the services of the Saracens, the sworn enemies of the Christian religion. By fire and sword they laid waste the environs of Spoleto in Italy. They showed their hatred against the Catholic religion, particularly by destroying churches and convents. Whilst they were besieging the city of Assisium, they tried to plunder and sack the convent of St. Damian, in which St. Clare lived, and was abbess at the time. The holy virgin had no one to defend herself and her convent against these enemies of God and religion. So in her firm confidence in Jesus Christ in the Blessed Sacrament, she had herself carried, sick as she was, to the gates of the convent. In her hands she held the Blessed Sacrament, the God of armies. As soon as the Saracens beheld in her hands the God of Infinite Majesty and Holiness, they were seized with terror, they trembled in every limb, their weapons fell from their hands, they turned their backs and fled. Had an army in battle array stood before them, those fierce barbarians would have fought to the last; they would either have conquered or left their bleeding corpses on the plain. But when the holy virgin, St. Clare, stood before them bearing in her hands the God of armies, that God, who rules the lightning and the thunder, they could not bear the sight of His awful Majesty and they fled in terror from the face of their Eternal Judge. St. Clare conquered, because Jesus, her divine Spouse, was with her; and as her enemies fled in terror, the heavens opened, she heard the sweet voice of her heavenly Bridegroom: "Do not fear, it is I, I will always watch over thee." Now would it not be ridiculous to say that a large army was panic-stricken and took to flight in great confusion at the sight of a piece of bread? It was not a piece of bread, but our Lord Himself Whom St. Clare held in her hands and Who at her prayer, and to reward her faith and confidence, struck terror into the enemies of His religion and made them raise the siege in spite of themselves.

We read in the Gospel that our dear Saviour one day performed most wonderful things. When the chief priests and scribes saw these wonders they were filled with indignation. What excited their rage most was that the children cried aloud in the Temple, saying: "Hosanna to the Son of David!" (that is, to Jesus Christ). And they said to Our Lord: "Hearest thou what these say?" And Jesus said to them: "Yea, have you never read; 'Out of the mouths of infants and of sucklings thou hast perfected praise.'"*
What happened then, happens still. Many non-Catholics are filled with indignation when we speak to them of the wonders that Jesus wrought—when we speak of the institution of the Mass, of the Real Presence of Our Lord in the Blessed Sacrament. But Jesus knows how to inspire even little children to proclaim His Real Presence and confound the unbeliever.

A Calvinist nobleman was once disputing about the Real Presence with the father of St. Jane Francis de Chantal; Frances was at that time only five years of age. Whilst the dispute was going on she advanced and said to the nobleman. "What, sir! do you not believe that Jesus Christ is really present in the Blessed Sacrament, and yet He has told us that *He is present*? You then make Him a liar. If you dared attack the honor of the King, my father would defend it at the risk of his life, and even at the cost of yours; what have you then to expect from God for calling His Son a liar? The Calvinist was greatly surprised at the child's zeal, and endeavored to appease his young adversary with presents, but full of love for her holy faith, she took his gifts and threw them into the fire, saying: "Thus shall all those burn in hell who do not believe the words of Jesus Christ!"

A visitor to Bologna may see the tombstone of a child called Imelda. The history of the child is written on the tombstone. She died at the age of *seven*, in the year 1393.

---

* Matt. xxi. 15. 16.

On Easter Sunday morning there were many children in the church, assembled to make their first communion. Little Imelda had begged hard to make her first communion, but the sisters justly thought that she was too young and too childish in her ways. They told her she must wait until she was older. So the child was obliged to stay far away from the altar, at the bottom of the church. She was alone in sadness and tears, because she could not receive Jesus Whom she loved. But there was One watching her who measures not the years, but the love of souls. Jesus could not bear that the child should be lonesome and sorrowful, because she wished to receive Him and could not. The bell sounded for the communicants to approach the altar. The altar rails were filled with a long line of happy children. The priest was standing on the highest step, holding the Blessed Sacrament in his hand, saying—" Behold the Lamb of God." At that moment a ray of dazzling light went forth from the Blessed Sacrament to the little Imelda, at the bottom of the church. Then the priest saw, with astonishment, that the Blessed Sacrament which he held in his hand the moment before, was no longer there! He had seen the ray of light, reaching to Imelda, and now above her he beheld what seemed a star of light. Imelda's eyes were also lifted up, looking at the bright star that glittered in her beautiful eyes. She knew it was the light of Jesus Himself who had come to His dear child. The priest left the altar, following the bright path. The people made way for him, hushed in deep and solemn silence. He reached Imelda, and to his wonder saw the sacred Host, suspended in the air over the head of the child. With trembling hand he took the Blessed Sacrament and gave it to Imelda, who thus received her Jesus. A short time after the little girl was seen to lean on one side, with pale face, as though she were ill. The sisters gathered around her and took her in their arms thinking she had fainted. On her face there was an angelic smile, the arms were crossed over the breast, as though holding fast to the treasure she had received. The joy of the little child in receiving Jesus had been too great to be able to part with Him again. The frail life went back to Him who sent it forth. The Master had need of her, and she went home.

Now to this miraculous occurrence apply the remarks which one day the saintly Curé of Ars made relative to a similar event. "Whilst catechising the people," said this holy priest, "two Protestant ministers came to me who did not believe in the Real Presence of Our Lord in the Blessed Eucharist. I said to them: 'Do you think a piece of bread could detach itself and of its own accord place itself on the tongue of a person who came near to receive it?' They replied 'no,' 'Well then,' said I, 'it is not bread.'" The holy priest then related the following fact: "There was a man who had doubts about the Real Presence. He said what do we know about it? It is not certain what consecration is, and what takes place at that time on the altar? But this man wished to believe and prayed to the Blessed Virgin to obtain faith for him. Listen attentively to this. I do not say this happened somewhere, but that it happened to myself. At the moment that this man came up to receive Holy Communion, the Sacred Host detached itself from my fingers, whilst I was yet some distance from the Communion rail, and placed itself on the tongue of the man." (Spirit of the Curé of Ars) St. Bonaventure and others received Holy Communion in the same miraculous manner.*

Do you believe our Lord would employ the ministry of an angel or a saint, instead of a priest, to take without the least necessity a small particle of bread to one of His servants? No, you reply. Well then it was not bread but His Body that at His command was taken to St. Stanislaus by St. Barbara, to blessed Gerard Majella by the Archangel St. Michael, and to other saints by the Blessed Virgin.†

---

* See Blessed Eucharist. p, 82. p. 211. No. 4.
† See Bl. Euch., p. 81.

Do you think that whilst Mass is being said the Angels would descend from heaven and surround the altar in the humblest attitude to adore and honor a piece of bread? You answer, no. Then it is not bread, but the King of Heaven under the appearance of bread whom the angels come to adore.*

Do you imagine that rays of brilliant light could naturally come forth from a little piece of bread, or that small particles of bread could raise themselves into the air and shine like stars, to the great astonishment of a multitude of people? Certainly not. But our Lord can do so under the appearance of bread and allow some rays of His Heavenly glory to escape through the outward species of bread.

In the monastery Philoxenes, situated in the Island of Cyprus, lived a poor man who wept incessantly day and night for several years. One day a celebrated religious, named John Mosch, having come with several others to visit this monastery, was greatly surprised at the sight of this singular monk. He was asked to cease weeping and tell the cause of so extraordinary a grief. "Father," one said to him, "why do you weep so? Do you not know that it is God alone who is without sin?" "Ah! Father, you never found in the whole world a sinner like unto me; no, there is no crime to equal that which I had the misfortune to commit, and for which I will never cease asking pardon of God. Hear me and judge for yourselves.

"While I was still in the world my wife and I had the misfortune to follow the heresy of the Severians. Returning home one day, I was surprised at my wife's absence; I inquired and sought for her for some time. At last I learned that she was gone to the house of a neighbor who was a Catholic, that she had been converted, and that they were to receive Holy Communion together that same morning. Full of rage at hearing this, I ran to the neighbor's house to pre-

---

* Bl. Euch., p. 308, No. 10 11; p. 295, 296, and p. 22, No. 13.

rent it; but it was too late, I arrived at the very moment when my wife was receiving Communion. Listening only to my impious rage, I threw myself upon her, seized her by the throat, and never let go my hold till she had thrown out the Sacred Host." Here the penitent monk stopped a moment overcome with grief. •At length he resumed, "The Holy Host fell into the mire, but to the great surprise of all who witnessed this sacrilegious scene, it appeared *all luminous and sending forth rays of brilliant light.* We prostrated to adore it. Two days after a devil appeared to me, as black as an Ethiopian, who said to me only these words, 'We are both condemned to the same torment.' I was seriously frightened at my crime, gave up my heresy, became a Catholic and shut myself up in this monastery, where, as you see, I have nothing better to do than weep over my crime. Oh! that I may obtain pardon from the mercy of God."*

Do you think a piece of bread could change itself into a beautiful living infant, or into the form of a living grown person? Certainly not. But Our Lord, under the appearance of bread, can so show Himself, and has frequently wrought such a miracle to prove His Real Presence.

Tillemand of Bredembach † relates a wonderful fact that happened to the famous Wittikind, duke of the Saxons, one of the most barbarous nations of Germany, in the eighth century. "Whilst Wittikind was still a pagan, and waging an obstinate war against Charlemagne, emperor of the Franks, he was curious to know what was passing in the camp of the Christian soldiers. For that purpose he disguised himself as a pilgrim. It was just at the time of the festival of Easter, when the whole Frankish army was engaged in receiving the Paschal Communion. He entered the camp without being recognized, admired the ceremonies of the Holy Sacrifice of the Mass, and assisted thereat with an

---

* John Mosch, Pré-Spirituel, Chapt. xxx. See other examples "Blessed Eucharist," p. 223, No. 23; p. 16 and 19.

† Lib. I. collat. c. 1 ex Hist. Eccl. Alb. Cranzii, L. 2, c. 9.

attention and a pious curiosity not to be expected from a barbarian and a pagan. What surprised him most was to see in the Host at consecration, and also in each Host the priest distributed to the soldiers at the time of communion, a child of wondrous beauty, all radiant with light. This child seemed to enter with extreme joy the mouths of some, while He struggled not to enter that of others. At the same time Wittikind experienced a great interior joy which he never felt before. He knew not what all this meant. After the divine service, he placed himself among the beggars and asked an alms of the emperor as he passed. At the same moment an officer recognizing the duke, whispered to the emperor: 'Your majesty, this pilgrim is the duke of the Saxons.' Whereupon the emperor, ordering the duke to go with him, said: 'Why is it that you come among us in the disguise of a pilgrim.' Wittikind humbly asked pardon and excused himself, saying, that he did not come as a spy, but from a desire of knowing something of the divine service of the Christians. 'What, then, did you see?' asked the emperor. 'Your majesty,' replied the duke, 'I saw such wonderful things as I never heard of, or witnessed before.' Then he related all he had seen and asked an explanation of the emperor. Charlemagne was perfectly amazed at the goodness of Our Lord who had appeared in the Host to this pagan in the form of the Divine Infant, and said to him: 'You have received from God a favor which He never granted to many of the saints.' He then instructed Wittikind in our holy religion and induced him to embrace it, as also did all his subjects, which happened in the year 804."

Do you believe that real blood could issue from a piece of bread as thin and small as a little Host? You answer, no. But it can happen by the permission of Christ hidden in the Host. Whilst the French were preparing for war with Aus-

---

* See other examples in "Bl. Euch.," p. 16–19; p. 24; p. 208, No. 1 p. 215, No. 11; p. 313, No. 15.

tria, there were seen during Mass several large drops of blood issuing from the consecrated Host in the parish church at Vrigne-aux-Bois near Sedan. This miracle was witnessed by many persons on the 7th of February, the 29th of April, the 8th and 15th of May, 1859. The last of these miraculous Hosts is still preserved in the new church of Vrigne-aux-Bois.*

There have been many holy persons who had a supernatural instinct by which they were sensible of the Presence of Jesus Christ in the Blessed Sacrament, even when it was hidden and at a distance from them. They could distinguish a consecrated Host from one that was unconsecrated.

Goerres in his celebrated work entitled "Christian Mysticism" notices this fact and thus prefaces the enumeration of the few cases which he cites:

"In reference to the holiest of all things—the Sacrament of the Eucharist, we find that those saints who have succeeded in raising themselves to the higher regions of spiritual life, were all endowed with the faculty of detecting the Presence of the Blessed Sacrament, even when it was hidden and at a considerable distance.

"Blessed Margaret of the Blessed Sacrament, a Carmelite nun in France, had an extraordinary devotion to and love of Jesus Christ in the Holy Eucharist even from her earliest childhood. Her sisters in religion had reason to believe that she could distinguish a consecrated host from an unconsecrated one. To find out for certain whether she enjoyed this extraordinary gift they gave her the following trial. Having locked the doors of the church, they lighted the candles on the altar, placed the remonstrance with an unconsecrated host in it, and then all passed and knelt in adoration to Jesus Christ as He is in Heaven. But Margaret, although she knew nothing of the sisters' intention, could not be de-

---

* Les Hosties sanglantes de Vrigne-aux-Bois. Trois lettres de M. l'Abbé Jules Morel. See Bl. Euch., p. 19, 21; p. 210, No. 8; p. 315 No 17; p. 314, No. 16.

ceived. She passed by the altar with the sisters, but did not kneel down, nay, she passed by hastily without making even the least sign of reverence, although she had always been in the habit of kneeling down and kissing the floor out of love and reverence for Jesus Christ in the tabernacle. On being asked by some of the sisters why she did not prostrate herself there to pray to Our Lord, she said: 'It is because Our Lord Jesus Christ is not there,' and she hastened to the Oratory where the Blessed Sacrament was kept.

"The sisters gave her another trial for the same purpose. They knew that Margaret found great relief from her sufferings whilst she was in the presence of the Blessed Sacrament, but they knew also that she could not tell whether she was in the church or elsewhere because she was blind, so they often took her before the Blessed Sacrament to procure her relief. Once, however, before taking her thither they carried her to various places, where the Blessed Eucharist was not kept, and then exhorted her to pray to Jesus Christ. But she answered in a plaintive tone: 'I do not find my Saviour here,' and addressing herself to Our Lord she said: 'My Lord, I do not find here *Thy Divine Truth*,' after which she besought her sisters to carry her into the Presence of the Blessed Sacrament." *

Our God is indeed a hidden God, as the Prophet Isaias calls Him; and nowhere is He more hidden than in the Blessed Eucharist. But He is only a hidden God in this mystery to those who love Him not. To those who truly love Him, He makes Himself strongly felt in their hearts. The appearances under which He conceals Himself are sufficiently transparent to the eyes of the faithful soul to make her thrill with joy in His presence, and to plunge her into the contemplation of His infinite love for man, like the Seraphim in the rays of His eternal splendor. Yes, in the mo-

---

* Her life by P. Poesl, C. S. S. R., see seven more instances in the "Blessed Sacrament," p. 22 to 24.

ment of holy Communion, the soul all inflamed with love for her Saviour, sees Him, feels Him and touches Him. "Such a soul touches Him," says St. Bernard, "with the fingers and with the embraces of love." She speaks to Him, listens to Him, answers Him and the Presence of the Lord in the heart causes something like the happiness of the elect. A certain convert to the faith used to say. "If I had not been convinced of the Real Presence of Jesus Christ in the Holy Eucharist by unanswerable proofs, as I have been, what I experience within me at the foot of the holy altars and more especially in holy Communion would soon dissipate all my doubts." More may be read on the wonderful effects of holy Communion in "The Blessed Eucharist," Chapt. viii.—Our Lord says in the Gospel, that we cannot gather grapes from thorns, and figs from thistles, that is to say, there must be a certain proportion between effect and its cause. Now as the effects of Holy Communion are most admirable and divine in the worthy recipient, divine, also, must be the cause which produces them. It is evident that a little piece of bread cannot be such a cause. Holy Communion, therefore, or the sacred Host we receive, is the Creator of Heaven and earth, Who alone is capable by means of holy Communion of manifesting Himself to the soul in so wonderful a manner.

"Yes," said a pious and learned missionary, "I have often been witness to the dispositions of numbers of Christians who approached the sacraments at the time of some festival or during a retreat. In giving them the holy Communion, in seeing their profound recollection, the piety, the heavenly joy depicted on their countenances, aware of the generous efforts of those souls to be reconciled to God, to free themselves from their passions, to give to others what charity or justice demanded of them, to live in peace and faithfully perform all their duties, knowing the delicacy of their consciences and their anxiety to prepare themselves worthily to receive this divine Sacrament.—'No, no!' said I to myself with eyes bathed in tears, 'none but a God could make such deep impressions on the soul, none but a God could thus absorb our minds and make us forget all creatures; none but a God could thus silence the most furious passions; none but a God could so change hearts, draw them to Him, and constitute their happiness here below!' I have often wished that our separated brethren, those who are enemies of the Eucharist, could be present at this spectacle of religion, they would soon be converted."

It may excite surprise to learn that even irrational animals can teach us lessons of faith in the Real Presence of Our Lord in the Blessed Sacrament. But such is really the case. There are several instances on record which prove that the Divine Author of nature has been pleased sometimes so to direct the instinct of brutes that, by their behavior, they might confound the pride and unbelief of heretics and infidels, or awaken the faith and devotion of lukewarm and indifferent Catholics. Holy Scripture tells us that one day God spoke to Balaam by means of his ass. "And the Lord opened the mouth of the ass, and she said: ' What have I done to thee?'"*

A similar, but more wonderful, instance is found in the life of St. Anthony of Padua. As Almighty God by the Prophet Isaias, purposed the docility of the ox and the ass for a rebuke to the stubbornness of the children of Israel, so, in this instance, He made use of a brute beast to reprove the folly and rashness and impiety of those who reject the mystery of the Real Presence.

In the time of St. Anthőny of Padua there lived at Tolosa, in Spain, a very obstinate heretic, Bovillus by name, who denied the Real resence of Jesus Christ in the Blessed Sacrament. Although compelled by St. Anthony to acknowledge in his heart the truth of the doctrine Bovillus persisted obstinately in his heresy. At last he professed his willingness to believe provided he should see a miracle wrought in proof of it. "What then do

---

* Numbers xxii, 125.

you desire?" asked St. Anthony, "I will keep my mule three days without food," said Bovillus, "afterwards I will bring him to you. On one side I will place food before the hungry animal, and on the other side you shall stand with the Blessed Sacrament. In case the mule leaves the food and goes to you, I will believe that Jesus Christ is truly and really present in the Blessed Sacrament." St. Anthony agreed to the proposal. On the day appointed a great concourse of people were assembled in the public square to see the issue. The Saint, after having said Mass, took the Blessed Sacrament and carried it with him to the square. Then when the hungry animal had been brought near and food put before him, St. Anthony holding in his hands the Blessed Sacrament, spoke thus: "In the name of my Creator, Whom I am not worthy to hold in my hands, I command thee to draw near and prostrate thyself before thy God, to give due honor to Him, that the heretics may learn from thee how they ought to worship their God in the Blessed Sacrament." And behold! no sooner had St. Anthony uttered these words than the mule left his food, went before the Blessed Sacrament, and bowed his head to the ground as if to adore It. At this sight Bovillus and his whole family together with many other heretics were converted and professed their faith in the Real Presence. Some time after he built a church in honor of St. Peter, and his grand children, inheritors of his zeal for God's glory, also built a church where they caused this miracle to be sculptured upon the wall of the archway, in order thus to show their gratitude to God for the gift of faith and to perpetuate the memory of His Goodness and Power for centuries to come.*

Maximilian I., Emperor of Germany, sometimes called the "Last Knight," for his chivalrous character, was in his youth remarkable for high courage and love of adventure, which at times led him to feats of rash daring.

---

* See other examples in "Blessed Eucharist," p. 224, No. 20 and 21.

Among the many lands over which he ruled, none was so dear to him as the mountainous Tyrol; partly from the simple and loving loyalty of the hardy race of shepherds and mountaineers who dwelt there, partly also because hunting among the Tyrolese Alps was one of his chief pleasures.

On Easter Monday, in the year 1493, the young emperor, who was staying in the neighborhood of Innspruck, rose before dawn for a day's chamois hunting. He took with him a few courtiers and some experienced hunters.

At sunrise they were already high up on the mountain pastures, which are the favorite haunts of the chamois; the valleys beneath them were still covered by a sea of white mist, while the golden rays of morning shone from an unclouded sky on the snowy peaks and ridges above them.

Maximilian fixed a longing gaze on the rocky summits, which stood out clear and sharp against the blue heavens. He felt the power of the fresh mountain air and the sublime scenery, and it filled him with the spirit of enterprise and daring.

"I wish," said he, "that I could gain to-day some spot where the foot of man has never trod before, and where no man should be able to follow; a spot amid the homes of the chamois and the eagle; where the busy hum of men should be lost to my ear, and all the crowded earth should lie beneath my feet; where even the thunder clouds should mutter far below me, while I stood in eternal sunshine! That would be a fit spot for the throne of an emperor!"

The courtiers replied that his majesty had but to wish and it would be fulfilled—to such a renowned hunter and intrepid mountaineer what could be impossible?

At this moment, one of the huntsmen gave notice that he had sighted some chamois; the whole party, guided by him, cautiously approached a rocky point, behind which the animals were grazing. On this point of rock stood a single chamois, its graceful head raised, as if to watch. Long before they were within shot range, they heard it utter the

peculiar piping cry by which the chamois gives notice of
danger to its fellows, and then off it bounded with flying
leaps toward the rocky solitude above. Maximilian on its
track, had soon distanced his attendants. To be a good
chamois hunter, a firm foot and a steady head are required,
for these beautiful little animals lead their pursuer into
their own peculiar domain, the rocky wastes just below the
regions of perpetual snow, and there they climb and spring
with wonderful agility, and if they cannot escape, it is said
that they will leap over a precipice and be dashed to pieces,
rather than fall into the power of man.

Maximilian had all the qualities necessary for this adventurous chase and was generally most successful in it. Now
he reached the brink of a chasm, which the chamois had
passed; black yawned the abyss at his feet, while beyond, the
rocks rose steep and forbidding, with but one little spot where
a man could find footing. One moment he paused, then with
a light spring gained the other side while a shout, half of
admiration, half of terror, burst from his astonished suite.

"That was a royal leap! Who follows?" cried Maximilian, with an exulting laugh. Then he sped onward,
intensely enjoying the excitement of the chase.

For a moment he lost the chamois from view, then it
appeared again, its form standing out against the sky, on
one of those rocky ridges that have been compared to the
backbone of a fish, but are perhaps more like the upper edge
of a steep gable roof. To gain this ridge it was needful to
climb an almost perpendicular precipice; but Maximilian,
nothing daunted, followed on, driving small iron holdfasts
into the rock in places where he could gain no footing, and
holding on by the hook, at the upper end of his iron-pointed
Alp-stick. At last, he seized a projecting piece of rock with
his hand, hoping to swing himself up by it, but the stone
did not bear his weight, it loosened and fell, and the emperor fell with it.

Breathless and stunned, it was some minutes before he

recovered consciousness after the fall. When he came to himself, he found that he had received no injury, except a few bruises, and his first thought was that he was most lucky to have escaped so well. Then he began to look about him. He had fallen into a sort of crevice, or hollow in the rocks; on one side they arose above him as a high wall which it was impossible to scale; on the other they were hardly higher than his head, so that on this side he had no difficulty in getting out of the hollow.

"Lucky again," thought Maximilian; but as he emerged from the crevice and rose to his feet, he remained motionless in awe-struck consternation. He stood on a narrow ledge, a space hardly wide enough for two men abreast, and beneath him, sheer down to a depth of many hundred feet sank a perpendicular wall of rock. He knew the place; it was called St. Martin's Wall, from the neighboring chapel of St. Martin; and the valley below it, which was now concealed from his view by white rolling vapors, was the Valley of Zierlein.

Above him rose the "wall," so straight and smooth, that it was utterly hopeless to think of scaling it. The only spot within sight, where a man could find footing, was the narrow shelf on which he stood. The ledge itself extended but a few feet on either side, and then ceased abruptly.

In vain Max gazed around for some way to escape.

No handsbreadth was there to which to cling; no hold for foot or hand of the most expert climber—beneath, a sea of cloud; above, a sea of air.

Suddenly he was startled by a whir and a rush of great wings in his face;—it was a mountain eagle which had swooped past him, and the wind of whose flight was so strong that it had nearly thrown him off his balance. He recollected that he had heard how these eagles try to drive any large prey, too heavy to be seized in their talons, to the edge of a precipice and so, by suddenly whirling round, they may dash it over the brink; and how they had tried this manœuvre more than once on hunters whom they found in critical and helpless positions. And then his wish of the morning occurred to him. How literally and exactly it had been fulfilled! And how little could the Emperor exult in his lofty and airy throne! He merely felt with a shudder his own exceeding littleness in the face of the great realities of Nature and Nature's God.

Beneath, in the valley of Zierlein, a shepherd was watching his flocks. As the sun rose higher and drew the mists off which clung around the foot of St. Martin's Wall, he noticed a dark speck moving on the face of the rock. He observed it narrowly.

"It is a man!" he cried; "what witchcraft has brought him there?"

And he ran to tell the wonder to the inhabitants of the valley. Soon a little crowd was collected and stood gazing up at St. Martin's Wall.

"God be with him!" was the compassionate exclamation of all. "He can never leave that spot alive—he must perish miserably of hunger!"

Just then a party of horsemen galloped along the valley, and rode up to the crowd, which was increasing every moment. It was the Emperor's suite, who, giving up all hope of following his perilous course, had gone back to where they had left their horses in the morning, had ridden around, hoping to meet their master on the other side of the mountain.

"Has the Emperor passed this way?" one of them called out. "He climbed up so far among the rocks that we lost sight of him."

The shepherd cast a terrified look at the wall, and, pointing upward, said:

"That must be he up yonder. God have mercy upon him!"

The Emperor's attendants gazed at the figure, and at each other in horror. One of them had a speaking-trumpet with him such as mountaineers sometimes use for shouting among the hills. He raised it to his mouth, and cried at the pitch of his voice:

"If it is the Emperor who stands there, we pray him to cast down a stone."

There was a breathless hush of suspense now among the crowd, and down came the stone, crashing into the roof of a cottage at the foot of the rock.

A loud cry of lamentation broke from the people and was echoed on every side among the mountains. For they loved their young Emperor for the winning charm of his manner, for his frank and kindly ways, and his especial fondness for their country.

The sound of the wail reached Max's ears, and looking down, he could see the crowd of people, appearing from the giddy height like an army of ants—a black patch on the bright green of the valley. The sound and sight raised his hopes; he had completely given up all thought of delivering himself by his own exertions, but he still thought help from others might be possible. And now that his situation was discovered, the people he knew would do whatever lay in the power of man for his deliverance. So he kept up his courage and waited patiently and hopefully. It was so hard to believe that he, standing there in the bright sunshine, full of youthful health and strength, was a dying man, and never would leave that spot alive.

Higher and higher rose the sun. It was midday now, and the reflected heat from the rocky wall was well nigh too great to bear. The stones beneath his feet became hot as a furnace, and the sunbeams smote fiercely on his head. Exhausted by hunger and thirst, by heat and weariness, he sank down on the scorching rock. The furious headache and dizziness which came over him made him think that he was about to become insensible. He longed for some certainty as to his fate before consciousness had forsaken him, and, following a sudden thought, he drew from his pocket a small parchment book, tore out a blank leaf and wrote on it with a pencil, then tied the parchment to a stone with some gold ribbon he happened to have with him, and let the stone fall down into the valley as he had done the first. What he had written was the question, "Whether any human help was possible?" He waited long and patiently for the answer; but no sound reached his ear but the hoarse cry of the eagle. A second and a third time he repeated the message, lest the first should not have been observed—still there was a silence, though the crowd in the valley had been increasing all day; and now a vast assembly—the inhabitants of Zierlein and all the district round—had gathered at the foot of the fatal throne which the emperor had desired for himself.

Terrible indeed—who can tell how terrible—were those hours of suspense to Max. Many deep and heart-searching thoughts visited him—thoughts of remorse for many sins, of self-reproach for the great responsibilities unfaithfully fulfilled.

The day wore on; the sun was fast sinking toward the west, and Max could no longer resist the conviction that there was no help possible, that all hope must be over for him. It seemed, as soon as he had faced this certainty, that a calm resignation, a high courage and resolve, took possession of his soul. If he was to die, he would die as became a king and a Christian—if this world were vanishing from him, he would lay firm hold of the next.

Again he tore a leaf from his book, and wrote on it. There was no more gold ribbon to bind it to the stone, so he took the chain of the Order of the Golden Fleece—what value had it for a dying man?—and from that high and airy grave he threw the stone down among the living.

It was found, like the others before it. None had answered these, because no one was to be found willing to be a messenger of death to the much-loved Emperor. The man who found the stone read the letter aloud to the assembled crowd, for the Emperor's messages were addressed to all Tyrol.

And this was the last message:

"Oh, Tyrol, my last warm thanks to thee for thy love which has so long been faithful to me.

"In my pride and boastfulness I tempted God, and my life is now the penalty. I know that no help is possible. God's will be done—His will is just and right.

"Yet, one thing, good friends, you can do for me, and I will be thankful to you even in death. Send a messenger to Zierlein immediately for the Holy Sacrament, for which my soul thirsts. And when the priest is standing by the river, let it be announced to me by a shot, and let another shot tell me when I am to receive the blessing. And when I pray, you unite your prayers with mine to the great Helper in time of need, that He may strengthen me to endure the pains of a lingering death.

"Farewell, my Tyrol, Max."

The reader's voice often faltered as he read this letter amid the cries and sobs of the multitude.

Off sped the messenger to Zierlein, and in all haste came the priest.

Max heard the shot, and, looking down, could see the white robe of the priest standing by the river, which looked like a little silver thread to him. He threw himself on his knees, in all penitence and submission, praying that he might be a spiritual partaker of Christ, though he could not receive in body the signs of salvation. Then the second shot rang on the air, and through the speaking-trumpet came the words of the blessing:

"May God's blessing be upon thee in thy great need— the blessing of the Father, the Son, and the Holy Ghost, Whom heaven and earth praise for ever."

The Emperor felt a deep peace filling his heart as the words of blessing were wafted to his ear.

The sun had by this time sunk behind the mountain range beyond the valley of Zierlein; but a rosy blush still lingered on the snowy summits, and the western sky glowed in crimson and gold. Beneath, in the deep purple shade of the valley, the people all knelt and the emperor could hear the faint murmur which told him that they were praying for him.

Touched by their sympathy, he continued kneeling in prayer for the welfare of his subjects.

It was quite dark now, and one by one the stars came forth on the deep blue sky, till at last all the heavenly host stood in glittering array. The sublime peace of those silent eternal fires stole into Max's heart, and drew his thoughts and desires heavenward to eternal Love and eternal Rest. So he knelt on, wrapped in prayer and in lofty and holy thoughts.

Suddenly a bright gleam flashed on his eyes, and a figure in a flicker, and a dazzle of light stood before him. No wonder that in his present mood his spirits raised above earthly things, this vision should seem to him more than human.

"Lord Emperor," it spoke, "follow me quickly—the way is far and the torch is burning out."

Hardly knowing whether he was still in the worlds of mortals or not, Max asked:

"Who art thou?"

"A messenger sent to save the Emperor"

Max rose; as he gazed it seemed to him that the vision assumed the form of a bright-haired, bare-footed peasant youth holding a torch in his hand.

"How didst thou find thy way to the cliff?" he asked.

"I know the mountains well, and every path in them."

"Has heaven sent thee to me?" asked Max, still feeling as if he were in dream-world.

"Truly it is God's will to deliver thee by my hand," was the simple answer.

The youth now turned and slid down into the hollow out of which Max had climbed that morning, then glided through a crevice in the rock behind, which the emperor had failed to detect. Stooping low, he with difficulty squeezed through the narrow chink, and saw the torch flickering below him, down a steep, rugged fissure which led into the heart of the rock. Leaping and sliding he followed on, and the torch moved rapidly before him, its red light gleaming on metallic ores, and glittering on rock crystals. Sometimes a low thundering sound was heard as of underground waterfalls, sometimes water dripping from the rocky roof made the torch hiss and sputter. Downward they went, miles and miles downward, till at last the ravine opened into a long, low, nearly flat-bottomed cavern, at the end of which the torch and bearer vanished. But at the place where he had disappeared there was a glimmer of pale light. Max groped his way to it, and drew a long breath as he found himself again in the open air, with the silent stars above him and the soft grass beneath his feet. He soon perceived that he was in the valley of Zierlein, and afar off he heard the confused noise of an assembled multitude. He followed the sound, but was forced to rest more than once from extreme weakness and weariness, before he reached the foot of St. Martin's Wall, and saw priest and people still kneeling in prayer for him. Deeply moved, he stepped into their midst and cried:

"Praise the Lord with me, my people. See he has delivered me."

The Emperor was never able to discover who had been the instrument of his wondrous rescue. A report soon spread among the people that an angel had saved him. When this rumor reached the emperor's ears, he said:

"Yes, truly, it was an angel, my guardian angel, who has many a time come to my help—he is called in German 'The People's Loyal Love.'"

Indeed, we may firmly believe that it was an angel of the Lord, that saved the Emperor's life. This great monarch had made a solemn profession of his faith in the Real Presence. He made it in the midst of the greatest danger, he made it at a moment which he and his people thought was his last; he made it in writing and threw it down to his faithful subjects. Ah! how much has he not edified the whole world by this lively faith of his in the Real Presence.

Such a faith could not go unrewarded. As our Lord one day marvelled at the faith of the centurion, and said to those that followed him: "Amen I say to you, I have not found so great faith in Israel," so must He have been exceedingly pleased with the great faith of Maximilian when He saw how the Emperor requested the priest through his people to carry the Blessed Sacrament as near to him as possible. Indeed, I believe that our Lord then said to His angels: "Do you see the great faith of this Emperor in My Real Presence? Let us do to him as he has believed. When visible among men on earth, I restored many sick people to health because they believed Me to be their Saviour, so let us also now save the Emperor's life for the sake of his faith in My Real Presence, a faith which is still greater than that of the Centurion." Then the Lord commanded one of his angels to conduct the Emperor safe back to his people, as He one day delivered His great servant Daniel from the lion's den, and St. Peter and Paul out of prison.

Such, then, are many of the wonderful manifestations of the Real Presence of our Lord Jesus Christ in the Blessed Sacrament. To this grand truth more than to any other do the words of the Gospel apply, "And the apostles went forth and preached everywhere, the Lord working withal, and confirming the word with signs that followed."* Not one of the truths preached by the Apostles has been confirmed by more striking miracles than that of the Real Presence. We can say in truth with St. John the Evangelist: "Many other signs also did Jesus (in confirmation of the Real Presence) in the sight of His disciples (and even of multitudes of people) which are not written in this book. But these are written that you may believe that Jesus Christ the Son of God (is present in the Holy Eucharist) and that believing you may have life in His name."†

Now after all that has been said, we may in truth apply to all unbelievers and heretics what the great Prophet Isaias

---

* Mark xvi., 20. † John xx., 30–31.

said of the Jews: "Hear, O ye heavens, and give ear, O earth, for the Lord hath spoken. I have brought up children and exalted them, but they have despised me. The ox knoweth his owner, and the ass his master's crib, but my people hath not known nor understood me."* The ox and the ass know their master and his voice and follow it, but the unbeliever, less docile than an irrational animal, turns his back upon Jesus Christ and disbelieves or misinterprets His sacred word. For " an understanding at once inexperienced and indocile," says St. Cyril of Alexandria, " utterly scoffs away in its disbelief and rejects as false whatever is beyond and exceeds its comprehension ; out of untutored ignorance it proceeds to the last degree of pride. For to be unwilling to yield to others and think no one above us, how can this be anything but the last degree of pride?" On looking into the nature of the matter before us, we shall find that the Jews, and with them all heretics, fell into this disorder, for they ought to have received without hesitation, the words of that divine Saviour whose power and irresistible authority over all things had already, on many occasions, excited their wonder, and they ought to have gladly inquired about what was hard to be understood, and begged to be instructed in those things which seemed to create in their minds a difficulty. "Further, that word *how* is uttered by the Jews without any sense in connection with God, as though they knew not that such a word is clearly full of nothing but blasphemy. For it is His to be able to do all things without an effort. But being carnal, as St. Paul says, they received not the things of the spirit of God ; but His mystery, though full of wisdom, seemed to them foolishness. We ought therefore to derive advantage from this and from the falls of others regulate our own conduct, to have uninquiring faith in the divine mysteries and not say *how* when anything is said, for it is a Jewish word, and is therefore the source of the greatest punishments. For to dishonor by our unbelief

---

* Chapt. I. 2, 3.

that God Who is the Creator of all things is to be guilty of a grievous crime.

"Since then there lie before us, for a viaticum of immortality, those gifts of the Lord which surpass all language, come all ye who feed daintily on things ineffable, ye sharers of the Heavenly invitation, and speedily clothed with the nuptial robe of sincere faith, let us hasten together to the mystic supper. Awful is what is said; awful what is done; the fattest calf is sacrificed, the Lamb of God that taketh away the sins of the world is slain! The Father is gladdened; the Son is willingly sacrificed, not to-day by God's enemies, but by Himself, that He may show that the saving passion was voluntary.

"The giver of great gifts is ready, the divine gifts lie open to view; the mystic table is fairly set forth; the life-giving chalice is mingled; the King of Glory sends His invitation. The Son of God receives us; the incarnate Word of God invites us; the hypostatic wisdom of God the Father, that built for itself a temple not made with hands, distributes its body as bread and bestows its life-giving blood as wine. Fearful mystery! Oh, ineffable dispensation! Oh, humility incomprehensible! Oh, goodness unsearchable! The Creator sets Himself before the work of His hands to be partaken of; the Self-existent gives Himself to mortals for food and drink. *Come eat my bread,'* is His invitation, *and drink the wine which I have mingled for you!'* I have prepared myself for food; I have mingled myself as drink for those that desire me. Eat me, who am life, and you shall live for this is my desire; eat life that never fails. For this did I come that you may have life, and may have it more abundantly.*

Oh my God! may I always be one of those little ones to whom Thou revealest Thy mysteries whilst Thou hidest them from the wise and prudent of the world!

---

* T. iv. Com. in Joann. in loco. l. iv. see also T. iv. Frag. lib. 7 and 8. and l. xi. and xii. and T. v. Par. ii- Hom. in Myst. loenam.

CHAPTER VIII.

THE SACRIFICE BEFORE THE COMING OF CHRIST.

If it is reasonable and natural for a man to make an offering as a token of esteem to those whom he loves and regards in this world, how much more reasonable and natural is it for him to make an offering to his best and dearest friend—to God his Creator.

It is, therefore, no matter for surprise to find that from the very beginning of the world, men were accustomed to make offerings to the Being to whom they felt bound to render supreme honor—the honor of adoration. Reason alone convinced man of the necessity and propriety of expressing by some external form his obligation of dependence on God. Especially was this the case after the fall. Our first parents, Adam and Eve, acknowledged their guilt before God with great sorrow and confusion. They knew that they deserved death, even hell itself. Their grief was so overwhelming that they were ready to sacrifice their lives at once in expiation of their sin and in reparation for the insult they had offered to Almighty God by their disobedience.

But God gave them to understand that any multitude of penances and good works together with the sacrifice of their lives would not suffice to cancel their deep debt. So He consoled them by the promise of a Redeemer who would live and die in perfect submission to His holy will in order to blot out their sin, who by His obedience would honor Him far more than He had been or could be dishonored by them or by their children.

This promise was a great consolation to our first parents, it gave them hope, and with hope the resolve to live up to God's holy will for the remainder of their life, with the idea of, by so doing, obtaining forgiveness and life everlasting through the merits of the Redeemer to come. Thus were our first parents disposed towards God. They heartily repented of their sins, and earnestly strove for the rest of their life to render that honor and homage to Almighty God which were due to Him as the Supreme Lord and Master of the Universe. They understood perfectly that they were bound in conscience to spend their life in serving God most faithfully, nay that God was worthy even to be honored by the sacrifice of their life, especially after they had offended Him so grievously. But at the same time they understood that it was not God's will that they should destroy their own life by way of rendering Him due honor and homage. They knew that God wished them and their descendants always to bear in mind that He was worthy of all homage and that they were under obligation to render it to Him, and that their salvation depended on their firm hope in the merits of the Redeemer to come.

Notwithstanding these good dispositions of our first parents, they had become much inclined to evil. Their will was considerably weakened in consequence of their sin; they were very apt to forget themselves, break their holy resolutions, even so far as to neglect their most sacred and essential duties towards their most benevolent and merciful Creator. God knew all this. And it cannot be doubted that, in order to strengthen our first parents in the good sentiments of their heart, He gave them a positive command to offer Him sacrifice, that is to say, such external acts of divine worship as would appropriately express the sentiments of their heart. He therefore instructed them to substitute for the sacrifice of their life the offering of other sensible objects; to destroy or otherwise change the same, in order to declare and acknowledge by this destruction or change of sensible things that He was the Supreme Lord of the Universe, the Sovereign Master of life and death; that were He to require it they would be willing even to sacrifice their own life in order thus to render Him an honor and homage of which He alone was worthy and well deserving.

God gave them also to understand that these sacrifices were to remind them of the Redeemer to come and of the sacrifice which he would make in expiation of their sin: that these sacrifices of theirs as figures of the sacrifice of their Redeemer to come would be pleasing to Him if made with the proper dispositions of the heart. Besides, it is most probable that it was not natural reason, but rather God Himself, Who dictated that particular species of oblation which has been in use amongst nations, *animal* sacrifice. For although the sense of guilt which has weighed upon all men ever since the fall of Adam would naturally have suggested to them the necessity of some expiatory offering whenever they were about to approach God, yet we cannot see why they should have chosen to sacrifice an animal for that purpose. On the contrary, the offering to God of the life of a harmless creature in expiation of the sins of men, considered apart from Divine Revelation would seem to be even absurd. It is, therefore, most probable that God Himself instituted animal sacrifice in the beginning of the world, to foreshadow the meritorious sacrifice of the Redeemer, and to give man a means of acknowledging his guilt and dependence on His Divine Majesty.

Domestic animals have been generally chosen for sacrifice for two reasons chiefly: first, because they stood in the nearest relation to man, and consequently were the most fitting substitutes to bear a penalty which he had incurred; and secondly, because by their gentleness and innocence they served to represent the meek and spotless Lamb of God.

It is thus by the teaching of God Almighty Himself, in the first instance, or by an impression made by Him on the hearts of men from the beginning that we can adequately explain and easily account for the fact that all nations have agreed not only upon the propriety of making oblations to the Being to whom they give supreme honor, but also even in the end for which and in the manner in which those oblations should be made. In all the sacrifices, sacred as well as profane, the sensible and visible thing offered was invariably destroyed or changed. Animals were slain, other sensible objects were burned or poured out, such as wine, oil, and the like. It never happened that the simple oblation of a thing went by the name of sacrifice in the strict theological sense. The character or essence of sacrifice was always held to consist in the destruction, or change of the thing offered, as without this destruction, or change, it seemed that man did not fittingly express his interior acknowledgment that God was the Supreme Lord of the Universe, the Sovereign Master of life and death, and, as such, worthy even of being honored by the sacrifice of man's life, were He to require it. Such acknowledgment alone could adequately express the principal object and meaning of sacrifice.

It is easy to understand then, how it never came to pass that sacrifices were offered to any one except God, they having always been considered the highest act of worship, an act which could not be rendered to any creature. If history informs us that in some instances sacrifices were offered to creatures, it informs us also that those very creatures were worshipped as gods, or deities, never as mere human beings.

To this prime intention which men had in offering sacrifice were added others. Sacrifices were also intended to obtain favors from God, to thank Him for particular graces received, or as propitiatory after having offended Him. Even from the beginning of the world sacrifices were offered to Almighty God for such intentions. Holy Scripture, the most ancient of all histories, tells us that Cain and Abel offered sacrifice to God soon after the fall of our first parents: Cain the fruits of the earth, and Abel the firstlings of his flock.*

As soon as Noah had quitted the ark after the deluge he erected an altar and offered " whole burnt offerings to God." †

---
* Gen. iv. 3.
† Gen. viii. 20.

The great patriarch Job offered up a holocaust every day for his children.*

Abraham sacrificed a ram in place of his son.

Melchisedech, King of Salem and priest of the Most High, offered up a sacrifice of bread and wine.†

Again Holy Scripture tells us that Jethro, the father-in-law of Moses, was priest of Madian ‡ and that Putiphar, the Egyptian father-in-law of Joseph, was priest of Heliopolis,§ and that Putiphar offered holocausts and sacrifices to God.‖

We find also in the book of Numbers that Balaam, a priest of Mesopotamia, offered up sacrifice to God. In fact, all the ancient Egyptians, the Greeks and Romans, even the American Indians had their sacrifices. Travel where we will over the wide world, open the pages of history, and look into the past, and we shall find that never yet was there a nation having a form of religion, that did not at the same time offer up some kind of sacrifice. Sacrifice, religion, and divine worship have ever been regarded as one and the same. In fact, sacrifice is so essential that there can be no religion without it. To imagine a religion without sacrifice is simply impossible. Sacrifice, therefore, was even under the Law of Nature, and among the patriarchs, from the beginning of the world, the essential form of religion. Such sacrifices, if offered with the proper dispositions of the heart, were agreeable to the Almighty, as we may gather from Holy Scripture telling us that, "the Lord had respect to the offerings of Abel." ¶ The precise manner in which God manifested His pleasure in the offerings of Abel is not known. It is believed by many grave authors that He sent fire from heaven to consume them, as he did on other occasions in after ages. From the very fact that God showed His pleasure in such sacrifices, we are naturally led to believe that He

---

* Job i. 5. † Gen. iv. 18.
‡ Exod. iii. 1. § Gen. xli. 45. ‖ Gen. xviii. 12.
¶ Gen. iv. 4.

Himself taught men, even from the beginning, to worship Him in this manner.*

However, this original revelation concerning sacrifice, traces of which are found among all nations, became, like many other revelations, very much corrupted in the course of time. Supposing that that which they loved and prized the most would be the most acceptable offering to God, at last men came to sacrifice their fellow-men, nay, even their own children. Of course, such sacrifices were in the highest degree hateful in the sight of God.

In order, therefore, to teach men how to worship Him properly, the Lord chose a particular people to whom He gave express and minute directions about the sacrifices that they were to offer.

This particular people was the Jewish nation. Out of this nation God chose a particular family—that of Aaron—who were to offer Him sacrifices. These sacrifices ordained by God were of various kinds. They were offerings of adoration, offerings of impetration, sin-offerings, and thanksgiving offerings. In some the victim was only partially, in others entirely, consumed by fire: these latter were called holocausts—whole-burnt offerings. It was God Himself who prescribed most minutely all the rites and ceremonies to be observed in that most solemn act of public worship. God Himself commanded that a lamb should be sacrificed every morning and every evening. On Saturday—the Sabbath—as also on all great festivals, more abundant sacrifices were offered. Sacrifice was not only the essential worship of the entire nation—of God's chosen people—it was also the essential worship of each individual. Whenever an Israelite committed a sin he was bound by the law of God to confess that sin and to offer sacrifice. The sinner led to the priest the animal destined for sacrifice. He then laid his hand upon the head of the victim, in order to acknowledge before God that this innocent animal was intended to bear his sins and to die in his place.

The animal was then slain by the priest, and its blood was poured round about the altar. This kind of sacrifice was thus offered up not only to atone for sin, but also to obtain favors from God, or to thank Him for favors received. As sacrifice was instituted by God Himself in the very beginning of the world for the most sacred ends, it was never to cease so long as human beings remained on earth. This continual, daily sacrifice, ordained by God Himself, was kept up until the coming of the Redeemer. As long as the temple remained, the fire on the altar was never suffered to go out, the blood of victims never ceased to flow, the smoke of sacrifices went up continually to God.

---

religion and the rite of sacrifice;" that is, Adam taught his sons the way in which it pleased God that men should worship Him. Abel observed those instructions, whilst Cain neglected them. Hence the difference between the two brothers. Cain's faith was not a living, practical faith, based on the divine tradition from Adam; it was but a sort of speculative faith. That he did in a certain way acknowledge God and His dominion as Creator, is clear, from the fact of his offering sacrifice. But there is nothing in his sacrifice to show that he looked upon himself as a sinner, as condemned to death, as having need of a victim that shall take his place before God and be immolated for him. What he offers is compatible with the state of an innocent man—the fruits of the earth, signs of gratitude, proofs that he looked on God as the Author of temporal goods. But there is nothing in Cain's sacrifice which relates to the Mediator, nothing gives one the idea of it, nothing helps towards the remembrance of it. He did not offer *the victim appointed by God*—a victim which was of such a nature as to shadow forth the true *Victim* for the sins of the world. "He sinned," says St. Clement, "in the choice of his offering." He was not a true worshiper in his heart. This is the reason why "the Lord had no respect to Cain and his offerings."

But Abel's faith, on the contrary, was lively and practical. He offered the prescribed *victim* in sacrifice—the first born of his flock and the fattest. He offered it in the prescribed manner, by the shedding of blood, and with the proper intention and disposition of heart, by worshiping God in trustful obedience to His directions, and in firm hope in His promises. There was in his sacrifice an outward character, typifying the sacrifice of Christ on the Cross. The shedding of blood was entirely a religious act; it was a "crying unto God," an appeal to God of the most solemn kind, pointing forward, by its expiatory character, to the great shedding of blood on the Cross, and pleading the great Atonement and anticipating its effects. Hence it is that St. Paul says, it was "by faith that Abel offered to God a sacrifice exceeding that of Cain, by which he obtained a testimony that he was just, God giving testimony to his gifts." Heb. xi. 4.

CHAPTER IX.

THE SACRIFICE OF THE NEW LAW.

AFTER our first parents had repented of their sin, God like a good father forgave them, and promised to send a Redeemer who should destroy sin and restore man to his lost inheritance. This Redeemer was to be the Blessed Son of God Himself. As has already been remarked, to keep before the mind of man the continual remembrance of his sinfulness,—in consequence of which he was deserving of death,—and especially to keep alive the remembrance of the promised Redeemer, God instituted bloody sacrifice. The sacrifice of corn and wine and the like, is a sacrifice which an innocent sinless creature might offer to his Creator, but a bloody sacrifice is the only befitting offering of a sinful creature to his offended God.

The victim which was slain and whose blood was poured out and body consumed, represented the sinner himself; and by this sacrifice the sinner publicly acknowledged that by his sins he deserved death, and that, were God to treat him with strict justice, he should even suffer eternally. Moreover, by this sacrifice man publicly and solemnly testified to his faith in the promises of God and his firm hope in the future Redeemer.

But the sacrifices of the Old Law were all institutions of a temporary nature; they were to last for a time, but to give way to a more perfect one that was to succeed them, as the imperfect light of the stars and the moon fades away and disappears before the full blaze of the sun. They were emblems, figures, and representations of that undefiled oblation, which Christians were to possess. From this indeed they derived all their merit, and to this, of course, they were destined to yield when it appeared. They were good in themselves, because appointed by God, and though imperfect, proportioned to the state of man at that time, and to the degree of knowledge which he then possessed. They served to prepare him for the better things which should be revealed in the new dispensation.

Our divine Saviour came on earth not to destroy the law of Sacrifice, but to fulfill it, to make it perfect; whatever was essential in the Old Law, in the Jewish religion, remained essential also in the New Law, the Christian religion. Sacrifice, then, which was the very essence of the Jewish religion, remained also the essence of the Christian religion. Our Blessed Saviour indeed substituted a more perfect victim for the victims offered up in the Old Law—for sheep, oxen, lambs and the like. Our reason tells us that all the blood of sheep and oxen, that ever was shed, could not of itself blot out the sins of free, intelligent man, "For it is impossible," says St. Paul, "that sin should be taken away with the blood of oxen and goats."* The blood of sinless animals could atone for sin only in as far as it was ordained by God, and represented the precious blood of the promised Redeemer.

As soon, then, as the Redeemer—the true victim—came and shed His precious blood for our sins, the types and images were set aside, because they were no longer pleasing to Almighty God, as St. Paul assures us in his epistle to the Hebrews: "Wherefore when he entered the world, thou wouldst not have sacrifice and oblation, but thou hast fitted a body to me. The sacrifice of propitiation for sins is no longer pleasing to thee; then said I: behold I come, according as it is written of me in the beginning of the book, that I may do thy will, O My God!"† God gave a body to His only Son that He might do the will of His Father, by offering Himself in sacrifice upon the cross for us; and immediately all the ancient sacrifices—the types and

---

* Heb. x. 4.
† Heb. x. 5.

figures of the sacrifice of the cross—ceased to be pleasing to God and disappeared.

Our Lord Jesus Christ did not abolish priesthood and sacrifice, but He substituted a more exalted priesthood and a more perfect sacrifice for those of the Old Law. The various prophets foretold in the clearest terms that the Jewish people would one day be rejected on account of their sins, and that the heathens would be chosen in their place. The prophets foretold also that the Jewish sacrifices would cease, and that a more pure and perfect victim would be offered instead. In the prophecy of Isaias, God says, " of those of My people that shall be saved,"—*i. e.* the Apostles— " I shall send some to the heathens, and I will take men from the heathens and make them priests and Levites." * God says again in the prophecy of Malachy, where He speaks of the Jews: " I have no pleasure in you, and I will not receive a gift from your hand. For from the rising to the setting of the sun My name is great among the heathens, and in every place there is a sacrifice, and there is offered to My name a clean oblation." †

This prophecy contains several very important facts. In the first place, it is declared that the Jewish sacrifices would be rejected. "I shall receive no gift from your hand" saith the Lord of Hosts. In the second place it is declared that another sacrifice would be substituted for the Jewish sacrifices. " In every place there is a sacrifice offered to My name." Again, it is declared that this new sacrifice is to be more perfect than the old, for God calls it " a clean oblation, a pure sacrifice," and finally it is declared that this pure sacrifice shall be offered up in every part of the world, " from the rising to the setting of the sun." Now on looking around we find every circumstance of this remarkable prophecy literally fulfilled. The Jewish sacrifices have ceased; the Jewish people are scattered all over the earth: they have no country, no nation, no

---

* Chap. 46.
† Malachy i. 10, 11.

priesthood, no altar, no sacrifice. The second part of the prophecy also is fulfilled. At the Last Supper, our Lord Jesus Christ, the promised Redeemer, instituted a new and pure and perfect sacrifice—that of His Sacred Body and Blood, which He substituted for the typical sacrifices of the Old Law. And now this adorable and perfect sacrifice of our Lord's Body and Blood is offered up all over the world, at every hour of the day and every part of the night, "from the rising to the setting of the sun."

There existed before the coming of the Redeemer two distinct kinds of sacrifice—the bloody, or the sacrifice of animals, and the unbloody, or the sacrifice of bread and wine, of the fruits of the earth. These two kinds of sacrifice were offered up even in the very beginning of the world, for Abel sacrificed a lamb and Cain offered to God the fruits of the earth. There were not only two distinct kinds of sacrifice but also two distinct classes of the priesthood. The one was the priesthood of Aaron, who offered the blood of animals; the other the priesthood of Melchisedech, who offered bread and wine.

In His own divine person our Blessed Saviour united both these classes of the priesthood. He offered up bread and wine at the Last Supper according to the rite of Melchisedech, and on the following day He offered up *Himself* in a bloody manner, as the victim of our sins, according to the rite of Aaron.

Thus did He also unite the two kinds of sacrifice of the Old Law in the one adorable sacrifice of His Body and Blood, which He offered up under the appearance of bread and wine.

On the eve of His passion, after our divine Saviour had washed His disciple's feet, He ordered a table to be prepared so as to resemble an altar, and to be covered with a rich and beautiful cloth. On this table they laid a plate and a cup like a chalice, to contain the wine requisite for the designs of the Lord, Who had prepared and foreseen everything by

His infinite wisdom. When seated at the table and surrounded by His Apostles, He asked first for unleavened bread, which He laid upon a plate, then for pure wine, which, mingled with a small quantity of water, He poured into the chalice. After praying for a long time, He took the bread into His hands, and offered a prayer internally to the Eternal Father, begging that, in virtue of the words He was about to pronounce, the Sacrament He was going to institute might be perpetuated in His church throughout all ages. With great majesty He raised His eyes towards heaven, that is towards the two divine persons, He pronounced over the bread and wine the words of consecration, by which they were changed into the Body and Blood, Soul and Divinity of our divine Redeemer.

The body of Jesus Christ was then in the host and His blood in the chalice. The consecration of the chalice being made immediately after that of the host, is a lively representation of the effusion of the blood of Jesus Christ upon the cross, and His death or the separation of His soul and body which followed this effusion of blood. Our Lord then deposited the holy Victim upon the table, placing it there in the state of a sacrifice, and offering it to His Father in a mystic and unbloody manner. To complete the sacrifice by a kind of mystic death,—the loss of His sacramental life—He partook of it Himself, and then commanded the Apostles to partake of it also, accompanying the precious treasure with an imperative injunction, which, at the same time that it commanded them to do as He had done, conferred upon them the sacerdotal dignity required for the due discharge of such an ordinance. They began to exercise this sacerdotal dignity at the moment they communicated each other at the command of our Lord. At the closing of this stupendous ceremony they chanted their thanksgiving in a holy canticle.* And thus was Mass, the sacrifice of the New

---

* Math. xxvi.

Law, that is, its essential parts,—consecration and communion,—instituted by our holy Redeemer.

In the Holocaust, which was the most perfect of all sacrifices, besides the victim being slain or immolated, it was also totally consumed upon the altar. Therefore it was necessary in this perfect sacrifice of the New Law, which includes every perfection of former sacrifices, that there should be a similar consummation, which is nowhere found but in the Communion. It is this act, therefore, which completes the sacrifice, makes it perfect in all its parts, and leaves nothing more to be desired. Hence, according to the best theologians of the church, the essence of this Eucharistic sacrifice which our divine Saviour thus offered to His Father consisted in producing by the words of consecration the holy victim —His sacred body under the two species—and in the oblation which He made of it to His Father, and the same words of consecration which produced the sacrifice served also to make the oblation thereof. But as the bloody sacrifice which Jesus Christ offered for us upon the cross to His Eternal Father was entirely accomplished at the same instant that our Saviour rendered up His spirit; so the Eucharistic sacrifice, which is a true representation of that of the cross and is in effect the same, is only consummated by communion, in which our Lord undergoes a kind of mystic death by losing His sacramental life. It was then our divine Saviour Himself who first offered up the sacrifice of the New Law—the sacrifice of His Body and Blood, which Catholics call the holy sacrifice of the mass. The first mass then that ever was celebrated on earth was offered up by our Lord Jesus Christ Himself at the Last Supper. Hence St. Gregory of Nyssa in the fourth century says: " By a method of sacrifice ineffable and invisible to men, He (Jesus Christ) offered Himself an oblation and a sacrifice for us, being at the same time both the priest and that Lamb of God that taketh away the sins of the world. When was this? When He made His own body eatable, and His blood drinkable to those who were with Him. He, therefore, who gave His body for food to His disciples, manifestly demonstrates that, under the appearance (figure) of the Lamb, the sacrifice was perfectly made. When, therefore, He gave His disciples His body to be eaten, and His blood to be drunk, that body was already sacrificed ineffably and invisibly according as was well pleasing to His power who had the economy of that mystery. Wherefore he will not err from the truth, who, from that time, dates the period from which the sacrifice was offered unto God by the great High Priest, who sacrificed ineffably and invisibly the Lamb of His own Self, for the common sinfulness. For it was evening when that sacred body was eaten." *

At that very time the Apostles were empowered and commanded to celebrate Mass. The words of Jesus were too distinct and explicit not to be intelligible. "Do this for a commemoration of me." Our Saviour meant to be thus understood. As I took bread and brake, and gave to you, saying, this is My body; and really and substantially made it, by My heavenly power, what I said it was, My body, which is given for you; and as I, having taken the chalice, giving thanks, gave to you, saying, this is My blood; and really and substantially made it what I then declared it was, My blood, which shall be shed for many; and thus offered to My heavenly Father, in a mystic and unbloody manner, that same victim, My own very body and blood, which is to be immolated on the cross in a visible and bloody manner; so do you take bread, and blessing it, make it My body; and taking wine, bless it, and make it My blood; and thus continually present to heaven in an unbloody manner, not a different, but the self-same sacrifice which shall be offered up in a bloody manner once upon the cross:—Do this for a commemoration of me, for as often as you shall eat this bread, and drink this chalice, you shall show the death of the Lord

---

* T. iii. In Christ. Resurrect. Orat. 1. p. 889

until He come. In obedience to Our Lord, the Apostles offered up the holy sacrifice of the Mass. We observe them most exact in exercising that marvellous prerogative, with which He had invested them, of doing what He Himself had done in their presence, a prerogative which He bestowed upon them when he said: "Do this for a commemoration of Me." This we can see clearly from the Acts of the Apostles,* where St. Luke informs us that as the Apostles were *ministering*, that is to say as they were *sacrificing to the Lord*, the Holy Ghost said to them: "Separate me Saul and Barnabas." The same sacrifice which the Evangelist distinguishes by the term "ministration," we Catholics, at the present day, call the "Mass." St. Matthew, the Apostle, as history informs us, was pierced with a lance, whilst celebrating the holy sacrifice of the Mass.

The tyrant Aegeas said to St. Andrew, the Apostle, "You may say those things to those who believe in you; but unless you obey me, so as to offer sacrifice to the all-powerful gods, I will command you to be beaten with rods, and fastened on that same cross which you praise." The Apostle answered, "To the Almighty God I offer up a living sacrifice, not incense-smoke, not flesh of bellowing bulls, not blood of goats; but I offer daily to God on the altar of the cross a spotless lamb, whose flesh after the believer has eaten, and drunk its blood, the lamb that was sacrificed remains entire and living." Aegeas said, "How can this be?" Holy Andrew answered. "If thou wishest to know how this can be, take upon thee the character of a disciple, that thou mayest learn that which thou inquirest after." Aegeas said, "I will seek the cause of this from thee by torments." Holy Andrew said, "I wonder that thou, a sensible man, shouldst have fallen into so great a folly, as to think that thou canst by torments make known to thyself the divine sacrifice. Thou hast heard the mystery of the sacrifice; if thou wilt believe

---

* xiii. 2.

that the Christ, the Son of God, He who was crucified by the Jews, is true God, I will discover to thee in what way the Lamb liveth which, after having been sacrificed and eaten, remains still entire and spotless in His kingdom." Aegeas said, "And how does a lamb remain in a kingdom, whereas it is slaughtered, and, as you say, is eaten by all the people?" Holy Andrew said, "If thou wilt believe with thy whole heart, thou mayest learn, but, if thou wilt not believe, thou wilt not be able to attain to the perfection of the truth." *

The Fathers of the Church, the successors of the Apostles, speak in the plainest terms of the Holy Sacrifice of the Mass. In consequence of the terror of the times, and the malice of the enemies of Christianity, the early Christians were obliged to meet in private to celebrate the divine mysteries of the Eucharist and the Sacrifice of the Mass. This privacy caused a report to be circulated that the Christians were child-murderers, cannibals, and partakers of human flesh. So St. Justin, who lived in the second century, defended his brethren in the faith, by describing their faith as well as the ceremonies which took place.

"On the day called 'Sunday,'" he writes, "there is an assembly in one place of all who live in the cities or country, and the Acts of the Apostles, or the writings of the prophets, are read as long as circumstances permit. Then when the reader has ceased, the one who presides delivers a discourse, in which he reminds and exhorts to the imitation of the good things. We then all rise together and pray. Our prayers being finished, we embrace one another with the kiss of peace. Then to him who presides over the brethren is presented bread and wine tempered with water; having received which, he gives glory to the Father of all things in the name of the Son and the Holy Ghost, and returns thanks in many prayers. These offices being duly performed, the

---

* Galland, t. I. p. 157.

whole assembly, in acclamation, answers, Amen. Then the ministers, whom we call deacons, distribute to each one present a portion of the blessed bread and wine. Some is also taken to the absent. This food we call Eucharist, of which they alone are allowed to partake who believe in the doctrines taught by us and have been regenerated by water for the remission of sin, and who live as Christ ordained. Nor do we take these gifts as common bread and common drink, but as Jesus Christ our Saviour, made man by the word of God, took flesh and blood for our salvation; in the same manner we have been taught that the food which has been blessed by the prayer of the words which He spoke, is changed into the flesh and blood of that Jesus incarnate, and it is thus that we are nourished by His flesh and blood. The Apostles in the commentaries written by them, which are called gospels, have declared that Jesus so commanded when, taking bread, having given thanks, He said: 'Do this in *commemoration of me; This is my body.*' In like manner taking the cup, and giving thanks, He said: 'This is my blood:' and that He distributed both to them only." *

St. Cyprian, in the third century, calls the Mass "an everlasting sacrifice." St. Augustine, in the fourth century, declares it to be, "A true and august sacrifice, and that it has supplanted all former sacrifices."† "Old things," he says, "have passed away, and new things have been made in Christ, in such a way that altar has yielded to altar, bread to bread, lamb to lamb, blood to blood."‡

St. Ambrose writes in his letter§ to the Emperor Theodosius as follows: "When other emperors gain a victory they order triumphal arches, or other trophies of their triumph to be prepared: but your highness prepares a victim unto God, desires oblation, and thanksgiving to be celebrated unto the Lord by his priests. Therefore though I am unworthy

---

* Apo. i. n. 65, 67. † De Civit. Dei, xx.
‡ Ep. xxxvi. ad Casulanum. § Ep. 61, n. 4, 5.

and unequal to so great an office, yet do I acquaint you with what I have done. I carried the letter of your friendliness with me to the altar; I placed it on the altar, I held it in my hand that your faith might speak by my voice, and the letter of Augustus might perform the function of a sacerdotal oblation."

"*Jesus Christ,*" says St. John Chrysostom, in the fifth century, "has ordained a sacred rite and changed the sacrifice, and instead of the slaughter of animals, has commanded Himself to be offered up." *

"What then? Do not we offer up daily? We offer indeed making a commemoration of His death, and this oblation is one, not many. How one and not many? Because it was offered once, as was that which was offered in the Holy of Holies. This is a type of that, and that of this. For we always offer up the same; not in sooth to-day one lamb, and another to-morrow, but always the same thing, so that the sacrifice is one. According to this reasoning, as He is offered up in many places, are there also many Christs? By no means, but one Christ everywhere; both here entire, and there entire,—one body. Wherefore as He that is offered up in many places is one body, not many bodies, so also is the sacrifice one. Our High Priest is He that offered up that sacrifice which cleanses us; that same sacrifice do we offer up now—that which was then offered—that sacrifice which cannot be consumed. This takes place for a commemoration of that which then took place. '*For this do ye in remembrance of me.*' Not a different sacrifice, as did the high priest of those Jewish days, but the same do we always celebrate, or rather we make a commemoration of a sacrifice."†

"The oblation which has place this day, and that which was celebrated yesterday, and that which takes place day after day, is like to, and the same as that which took place

---

* J. x. Hom. 24, in 1 Cor.
† J. xii. Hom. 17. in Ep. ad Heb. n. 3, p. 241.

on that Sabbath day, and in nothing was that more venerable than this, nor this less valuable than that, but one and the same, equally awful and saving." *

"Many divine pastors and teachers of the Church," writes St. Proclus, "who have succeeded the holy Apostles, have left in writing, and delivered to the Church, the exposition of the mystic liturgy. Of these the first and most celebrated are, Blessed Clement, the disciple and successor of the Prince of the Apostles—the Apostles themselves dictating to him. After Our Saviour was taken up into heaven, the Apostles, before being scattered over the whole world, being together in oneness of mind, passed whole days in prayer, and having found the mystic sacrifice of the Lord's body a great consolation, they sang Mass at very great length, for they considered this, and teaching, preferable to anything else. With very great gladness and joy were they instant in this divine sacrifice, ever bearing in mind the Lord's word, which says, '*This is my body, and do this in memory of me:*' and, 'He that eateth my flesh and drinketh my blood, abideth in me and I in him.' For this cause, too, with a contrite heart, they sang many prayers, earnestly imploring the divine aid: yea, they also accustomed those who had been recently baptized to the things of the dispensation of grace, teaching them to leave aside those which were before that dispensation of grace, as being but shadows of that grace. Through these prayers, therefore, they expected the coming of the Holy Ghost, that by His own divine presence He might make and render the bread that lay there for a sacrifice, and the wine mixed with water, that very same body and blood of our Lord Jesus Christ, which is no less done even to this day, and will be done even unto the consummation of the world." †

Thus, what the holy Church teaches on this sublime subject, is clear, viz.: "Because under the former Testa-

---

* J. i. Or. iii. Contus. Jud. n. 4, p. 745.
† Tract. De Tradit. Divinæ Missæ, p. 680, t. ix. Gallandii.

ment," as the Apostle St. Paul testifies, "on account of the weakness of the Levitical priesthood, there was no consummation or perfection, it was necessary—God the Father so ordaining it—that another priest, according to the order of Melchisedech, should arise—our Lord Jesus Christ—who might be able to consummate, and to lead to what is perfect all that were to be sanctified. Wherefore this our Lord and God, although He was about, *by means of His death*, to offer Himself once to God the Father on the altar of the cross, that on it He might operate an eternal redemption; yet because by death His priesthood was not to be extinct, He, at the last supper—the same night on which He was betrayed—that He might, as the nature of man requires, leave to His spouse the Church a visible sacrifice, by which the bloody sacrifice, once to be completed on the cross, might be represented, and its memory might continue to the end of the world, and its salutary virtue be applied to the remission of the sins which we daily commit, declaring himself constituted *a priest forever according to the order of Melchisedech*, He offered to His Father His body and blood, under the species of bread and wine; and under the symbol of these things, He delivered His body and blood to His Apostles, whom He then appointed the priests of the New Testament; and to them and to their successors in the priesthood He gave a command to offer by these words: 'Do this in commemoration of me.'* So the Catholic Church has always understood and taught. This is the clean oblation, which the Lord by Malachias foretold would be offered *in every place to His name, which would be great amongst the Gentiles.* This, in fine, is that oblation which was prefigured by the various typical sacrifices, during the period of nature and the law, in as much as it comprises whatever good things they signified, as being the consummation and perfection of them all."†

---

* Luke xxii. † Council Trid., Sess. 22, c. 1.

It is related in the life of St. John a Facundo, O. S. A., that he was unusually long in saying Mass, so that no one liked to serve it. The Father Prior told him that he should try not to be longer in saying Mass than the other fathers of the convent. The holy priest tried to obey, but finding obedience in this point so extremely difficult, he begged his prior to permit him to say Mass in the same manner as before. After hearing his reasons, the prior most willingly granted this permission. With Father John's leave, he told these reasons to the fathers of the convent. "Believe me," said the prior to them, "Father John's Mass lasts so long because God bestows on him the grace of seeing the mysteries of the holy sacrifice, which are so sublime that no human mind can understand them. Of these mysteries he told me things so wonderful that I was overwhelmed with holy awe and almost beside myself. Believe me, Jesus Christ shows Himself to this father in a most wonderful manner, converses with him most sweetly, and sends forth upon him from His sacred wounds a heavenly light and splendor so refreshing for both body and soul that he might live without any nourishment. Father John sees also the body of Christ in its heavenly glory and beauty shining like a most brilliant sun. Now, considering how great and how unspeakably sublime the graces and favors are which men derive from saying Mass, or from hearing it, I have firmly resolved never to omit saying or hearing Mass, and I will exhort others to do the same." *

Although we do not see with our eyes the stupendous wonders that take place in Mass, yet let us believe them most firmly, nay even more firmly than if we could see them with our eyes, in order that we may belong to the number of those of whom Our Lord has said, "Blessed are they that have not seen and have believed." †

---

* Henschen, in Act. Sanct., ad xii. diem Junii.
† St. John xx. 29.

CHAPTER X.

THE SACRIFICE OF THE NEW LAW—CONTINUED.

A MOST solid argument to prove the holy sacrifice of the Mass is taken from the use of altars in the Catholic Church. St. Paul expressly declares in his epistle to the Hebrews [*] that "We have an *altar* whereof they (the Jews) may not eat, who serve the tabernacle." Now an altar always implies a sacrifice, since it is used for no other purpose.

The use of altars for the purpose of religion, is coeval with the preservation of the human race by Noah; and from times of the remotest antiquity, the greatest respect has been ever exhibited for the place which had been more especially set apart for the worship of the Supreme Being as well as for the altar which was erected there.

That a particular ceremonial, accompanied by an especial form of prayer, has been invariably followed at their respective dedications, seems indubitable. Every one will immediately remember not only the solicitude with which Noah, on issuing from the ark, immediately hastened to erect an altar for sacrifice,[†] but also the injunctions delivered by Almighty God to Jacob that he should make to him an altar at Bethel.[‡] Moses, too, was thus commanded by the Lord: "Seven days shalt thou expiate the altar and sanctify it, and it shall be most holy," [§] and in the book of Numbers [∥] we find enumerated the many splendid presents which were offered by the princes of Israel on the occasion of the solemn consecration of the tabernacle, in the dedication and anointing of the altar. The excellence and holiness with which

---

[*] Chap. xiii. 10. [†] Gen. viii. 20. [‡] Gen. xxxv. 1.
[§] Exod. xxix. 37. [∥] Numb. vii. 84.

the altar of the New Testament is invested, are asserted by St. Paul, who admonishes the Hebrews* in the words above quoted, "We (Christians) have an altar whereof they have no power to eat who serve the tabernacle." To claim our religious respect for the temple of God, and to assure us of the hallowed nature of its altar, the same Apostle contrasts the table of the Lord, upon which the Eucharistic Sacrifice had been offered, with the table of devils, or the altars upon which meats had been presented in sacrifice to idols; † and after assuring the Corinthians that they could not be partakers of the table of the Lord and of the table of devils, he interrogates them in a manner which involves a severe reprimand on the slightest irreverence displayed towards either altar or temple. "What, have you not houses to eat and drink in? Or despise ye the Church of God?" ‡

On consulting the various monuments of antiquity, it will be found that throughout the Christian world, from the apostolic era up to the present moment, the same idea has prevailed, that the temples of the Christian faith were erected for no other purpose than to offer up therein the sacrifice of the Body and Blood of Jesus Christ, and that the table on which this offering was made became a true, a hallowed altar, while the spot on which it stood was regarded as a consecrated sanctuary, shut off from the footstep of even the holiest laymen—the Holy of Holies of the New Testament, sacred from the tread of any other than the priest of God and His ministers duly appointed.

To confirm his exhortations to the Philadelphians concerning their unity of faith, their harmony of preaching and their participation in the same Eucharist, the apostolic father St. Ignatius gives this reason: "The flesh of our Lord Jesus Christ is one, and His blood is one, which was poured out for us; one bread is broken for all, and one chalice is distributed to all: in every church there is but *one altar*, and

---

* Heb. xiii. 10. † 1 Cor. x. 19. ‡ 1 Cor. xi. 22.

one bishop, with the company of elders and deacons, my fellow-servants."

Tertullian, in his book on prayer, combats the scruples which began to disturb many who thought that on fasting-days it was better not to be present at the celebration of the Eucharistic Sacrifice, lest, by participating of the Body and Blood of Christ—for the custom of those times was that each one who assisted at Mass should also receive the Blessed Sacrament—they should thus violate the precept of fasting. He asks such persons, if the participation of the Eucharist, instead of superinducing a breach of duty towards God, will not rather draw the communicant closer to him? "Will not," he goes on to observe, "your fasting be more solemn if you stand before the altar of God? By receiving the body of the Lord, and reserving it, both duties will be fulfilled; the participation of the sacrifice, and the discharge of your obligation."

St. Optatus Milevitanus thus exclaims: "What is so sacrilegious as to break down, to erase, to remove God's altars upon which you yourselves have once sacrificed? What is the altar but the seat of the Body and Blood of Christ?" St. Ambrose, speaking of the martyrs SS. Gervasius and Protasius, whose relics he had recently translated to his new Church, exultingly exclaims: "Let those triumphant sufferers succeed to the place where Christ is the victim. But He who suffered for all men is upon the altar, they who have been redeemed by His passion are under the altar."

The eloquent Bishop of Constantinople observes that "the altar which we now use is admirable on account of the victim which is deposited upon it. . . This wonderful altar, by its nature, is indeed of stone, but it becomes holy after it has received the body of Christ." "Thou holdest," continues St. Chrysostom, "the altar in veneration, because it sustains Christ's body." "Who," inquires St. Augustine, "who amongst the faithful ever heard a priest, standing at the altar, though it was erected to the honor and worship of

God over the holy body of a martyr, say in the prayers: I offer sacrifice to thee, Peter, or to thee, Paul?"

That for the first three centuries the altar was more generally, though not always, of wood, is evident from a variety of testimonies. Tradition has handed down the altar in the form of a wooden table, upon which St. Peter, as it is said, was accustomed to offer up the Eucharistic sacrifice of the Mass, in the house of the patrician Pudens, at Rome, where it is still preserved with much respect in the Church of St. Prudentiana. From the earliest times, however, it is certain that it was customary to celebrate Mass in the Catacombs upon the tombs of the Apostles and martyrs, not only at Rome, but throughout the Church of Christ. The slab of marble which covered the sepulchre was made to serve as the altar-table, and the low-browed arched recess that spanned it, merely left sufficient space for the priest to perform the sacred Eucharistic mysteries. When the altar, as occasionally happened, was not the tomb of a martyr, it resembled a quadrangular table supported in the centre by a single column, or upheld at its extremities by two, or at its angles by four low columns. For almost fourteen centuries it has been a universal custom to have that part of the altar on which the Eucharist is consecrated, of stone or marble.

Judging from the piety of the primitive Christians, who never performed any action without hallowing it by prayer, or some religious ceremony, it is more than probable that from the apostolic times no altar was ever used for offering up the holy sacrifice of the Mass, without having been previously consecrated by a special solemn rite peculiar to that holy purpose, and it is no ill-founded presumption to suppose that the pastors of the Church, in the dedication of their temples and altars, copied the example of the saints of old, who were directed by heaven itself to consecrate the altar and to dedicate the temple erected to the Deity, by a particular and splendid ceremonial. We have the most authentic documents to prove the use of such a rite at the commencement of the fourth century. The ceremony of dedication, which must, in times of persecution, necessarily have been performed in privacy, began to be celebrated with much public magnificence during the tranquil reign of Constantine. It was then a gratifying spectacle, as the ecclesiastical historian, Eusebius, informs us, "to witness how the ceremony of consecration and dedication of the recently erected churches was solemnized in every city." After describing the dedication of the Church of Jerusalem, the same writer relates how it concluded by the mystical service or offering of the unbloody sacrifice to God. St. Gregory Nyssenus, who was born in 330, observes: "This holy altar at which we assist is constructed of stone, which by nature is common and nothing different from other flags of stone with which the walls of our houses are encrusted, and our pavements ornamented. But because it is consecrated and dedicated to the worship of God, and has received a benediction, it is a holy table, an immaculate altar, which is no longer to be touched by all, but by priests only, and even by them with veneration."

St. Ambrose has left us a prayer which he employed in the dedication of the churches and altars erected by him. "O Lord!" devoutly prayed the holy Bishop of Milan, "I now beseech Thee to look down as daily high-priest upon this Thy house; upon these altars which are this day dedicated; upon these spiritual stones, in each one of which a sensible temple is consecrated unto Thee; and in Thy divine mercy receive Thy servants' prayers that are poured out to Thee in this place. Let every sacrifice which is offered up in this temple, with an entire and pious sedulousness, be unto Thee as an odor of sanctification."

Not only did the Church bear in mind the divine command issued to Moses, of celebrating the dedication of the altar, but she also remembered that the holy table was more particularly consecrated to the purposes of religious worship, by being anointed with rich and precious unguents. In the book of Genesis we read that the patriarch Jacob, awaking out of his sleep, exclaimed concerning the spot on which he had been taking his repose: "How terrible is this place. This is no other but the house of God, and the gate of heaven. And Jacob arising in the morning, took the stone which he had laid under his head, and he set it up for a title, pouring oil upon the top of it." Moses was thus directed by Almighty God: "Thou shalt make the holy oil of unction, an ointment compounded after the art of the perfumer. And therewith thou shalt anoint the tabernacle of the testimony, and the ark of the testament. And the table with the vessels thereof, and the candlestick and furniture thereof, and the altars of incense. And thou shalt sanctify all, and they shall be most holy;"[*] a command which the Jewish lawgiver carefully complied with, as we find recorded in the book of Numbers: "In the day that Moses had finished the tabernacle, and set it up, and had anointed and sanctified it, with all its vessels, the altar likewise, and all the vessels thereof."[†] The Church conceived that the anointing of her altars was an emblematical ceremony which she could appropriately borrow from the Old Law.

Whenever an altar is consecrated, some small portion, at least, of the relics of saints is invariably enclosed in it. This universal and established usage has descended from a venerable antiquity. From the earliest periods of the Church it was usual to employ the tomb of a martyr for the purpose of the altar. Not only did this custom call to the remembrance of the faithful the brethren whose souls are described by St. John as reposing under the mystic altar of heaven, but it furnished them with an admonition of their duty of laying down their lives like the martyrs, if required, in the profession of the faith of Him who was crucified for their redemption.

Anciently, as now, the table of the altar was overspread

---

[*] Exodus xxx. 25.   [†] Numb. vii. 1.

with linen cloths. The linen cloths are directed to be blessed and consecrated, as they are to serve for enfolding the Body and Blood of Jesus Christ: "Deign, O Lord," says the prayer, "to sanctify, bless, and consecrate these linen cloths for the use of Thy altar, to cover and envelop the Body and Blood of Thy Son, our Lord Jesus Christ."

The altar may be likened, at the same time, to the sepulchre and to the throne of Jesus; so the linen cloths which cover it are considered to represent both the shroud that enveloped His blessed Body and the mantle of His glory.

That the ancient fathers of the Church, whether Greek or Latin, were unanimous in exhibiting much religious reverence towards the altar, and in requiring the faithful to regard it with similar respect, is evident from those unequivocal epithets indicative of honor and of sanctity, under which they designate it in their writings and discourses. The sacred, the divine table; the holy, the most holy altar; the altar of Christ; the table of the Lord, are the common appellations under which they mention it. Nor did this reverence consist in words alone; it was unceasingly manifested by other proofs of homage.

On entering a church, Latins, Greeks, and Orientals, have from time immemorial been accustomed to bow towards the altar. We still continue to show this token of our homage to the sacred table. That not only the threshold and door-posts of the Church were reverenced by the prostrations and embraces of the pious, but that similar honors were also paid to the altar, is evident from the testimony of ancient writers. St. Ambrose particularly mentions the joy which animated the soldiers as they entered his church at Milan, and crowded round the altar, kissing it devoutly as they published the news that the emperor had revoked his edict for surrendering the churches in that city to the Arians; and St. Athanasius bore witness to the devotion of many whom he beheld going to the altar, embracing it with tear mingled with joy.

On perusing the foregoing remarks, the most superficial observer cannot have failed to notice the similarity in the language employed and the uniformity of ideas exhibited by all antiquity with reference to the altar. It is a matter of fact that forces itself upon every one's attention, that from the apostolic era up to the present moment, the pastors of the Church have invariably spoken of the sacred table, however incidentally they may have happened to refer to it, as the altar of the living God, the holy, the sacred, the tremendous altar, upon which there is offered up a true, a real sacrifice: the victim of which sacrifice they have unanimously proclaimed to be the Son of God—Christ Jesus—whose same Body and whose same Blood, once immolated in a bloody manner on the Cross, are now daily, nay, hourly, sacrificed in an unbloody manner on our altars, and afterwards partaken of both by the sacrificing priest and the attendant people. Not only do we hear such a doctrine insisted on as a necessary and universally accredited article of faith, and that, too, in expressions free from the faintest shade of ambiguity, and by the teachers of the Christian religion dwelling in regions widely separated from each other, and flourishing at epochs with the lapse of centuries dividing them; not only do we witness the entire body of the faithful assenting to such a tenet, and echoing it back, but we everywhere behold the profound and well-defined impression with which this belief has stamped the entire Church of Christ, pastors as well as laymen. From the birth of Christianity this belief has not only extended its influence to the arrangement of every Liturgy, and the construction of the house of God, has determined the distribution of its parts and the style of its ornaments, but insinuated itself into the civil institutions of so many nations. If we take the trouble to peruse and collate the ancient Liturgies, we shall immediately discover that each of their respective authors had no other object in view, while arranging them, than to draw up a rite or ceremony for offering up sacrifice;

for in all these venerable documents of primitive belief, without one solitary exception, the correlative terms of victim, sacrifice, priest, and altar, are invariably found. If we search amongst the earliest monuments of Christianity, in every nation, whether those monuments consist of edifices dedicated to the worship of the Deity, still standing,* or whether they be descriptions of splendid temples now dwindled into dust, and known only by an enumeration of their beauties and magnificence recorded in the writings of the ancients; everywhere shall we behold an altar for sacrifice, occupying the principal and most conspicuous situation, and regarded by all as an object of peculiar respect, the immediate boundary of which was considered so hallowed on account of the sacrifice of Christ Jesus there, that to desecrate it was a heinous crime. At its threshold not only the demon-sisters, Hatred and Revenge and Persecution, but Justice herself, glowing with lawful indignation, would reverently pause, nor dare go forward and drag the object of her pursuit from the horns of that altar where he sought refuge. We shall see, too, that it was profound devotion towards the Victim offered there, that stimulated the piety

---

* So indissolubly associated in the minds of the inhabitants of England, Ireland, Germany, France, Holland, etc., were the ideas of altar and sacrifice, that, on the breaking out of the great heresy, at the commencement of the sixteenth century, the patrons of the new belief soon began to encounter the difficulty of eradicating the old doctrine of the Eucharistic sacrifice of the Mass, as long as the sacred table upon which it used to be offered was permitted to continue standing. Their innovating zeal was, therefore, immediately employed in overturning every altar which could be discovered, in cathedral, humble parish church, or private oratory, and such was the searching diligence with which they perpetrated the annihilation of the altars of the most High God, that but few of the many thousands which once stood in England can now be pointed out to satisfy the cravings of the antiquarian, the scholar, or the architect. How much the turbulence of the religious innovators in the sixteenth century resembled the outrages committed in the fourth by the Donatists and Arians, who burned and overturned the altars of the Catholics!

of the faithful to spread the richest carpets around it, to hang the most gorgeous veils on every side of it; to pile chalices of gold and precious stones upon it; to render it, in fine, as glorious as possible. Having ascertained the use of altars and the sense of the Church upon this article of doctrine through such a variety of testimonies, the sincere Christian will recognize the Mass to be a true and real sacrifice.*

---

* Dr. Rock's Sacra Hierurgia.

CHAPTER XL

MASS APPLIES TO US THE MERITS OF CHRIST.

THE love of our dear Saviour for His Heavenly Father and for men was so great that, had it been necessary, He would have been willing to remain on the Cross till the end of the world.

But since it was neither necessary nor becoming the sacred Person of our Lord to remain so long in so ignominious a condition, He instituted the holy Sacrifice, of the Mass, in order thus to be ever in a state of sacrifice, to renew His Passion, apply more effectually to our souls its all-sufficient merits, and to manifest His most wonderful love for us, His creatures.

The prophet David foretold that the Redeemer of the world was to be a priest forever, "according to the order of Melchisedech." Melchisedech was, as the holy Scripture assures us, a priest of the Most High. Our Lord Jesus Christ, therefore, must also be a priest. Melchisedech offered up bread and wine. Our Lord Jesus Christ did the same at the Last Supper. He then changed the bread and wine into His Body and Blood, and offered up His Body and Blood under the appearance of bread and wine, not "of" the order of Melchisedech, but "according to" the order of Melchisedech.

The Royal Prophet says that Jesus Christ is a priest forever. Therefore He must offer up sacrifice forever. For a priest means not merely one who prays, but one who offers sacrifice. The angels and saints pray for us in Heaven, but they are not called priests, because they do not offer sacrifice. Now, our Saviour offered Himself but once as a sacrifice on the Cross. But, as His priesthood lasts forever, He must offer sacrifice forever. The only sacrifice which our Saviour offers up forever, and which continues forever, is the Sacrifice of His Body and Blood in the Mass.

In the holy sacrifice of the Mass our Lord Jesus Christ is the true High Priest who really, though invisibly, offers the Sacrifice; the priests of the Catholic Church are only His visible agents, His ministers.

Sacrifice is the most perfect form of worship; it is the very essence of religion; therefore, it must be found in the religion which alone is true religion—the Christian.

Sacrifice was offered up every day in the Jewish religion; therefore, it must be offered up every day in the Christian religion also, since the latter is perfect.

The Christian religion, then, must have a daily and perpetual sacrifice; otherwise it would be inferior even in a great essential to the Jewish religion. But the Christian religion is *perfect;* it is a divine religion; it must, therefore, have a perfect sacrifice, a divine sacrifice, and one that must last forever.

On earth there is no perfect and divine sacrifice save that of the Divine Body and Blood of our Lord Jesus Christ, which is in reality offered up every day in the Holy Sacrifice of the Mass.

While our divine Saviour was hanging on the Cross on Good Friday, He performed every act of worship of which the human soul is capable. He prayed, He loved God, He praised Him, He gave thanks, He made acts of resignation, in a word, He offered to God perfect worship.

In the Holy Mass, the very same worship is offered to God. The Victim offered on Calvary was the living Body and Blood of our Lord Jesus Christ, and in the Holy Sacrifice of the Mass, the Victim is also the living Body and Blood of the same, our Lord Jesus.

The Priest that offered the Sacrifice on Calvary was our Lord Jesus Christ Himself: in the Holy Sacrifice of the Mass the same Priest offers the same Sacrifice.

On Calvary Jesus Christ was really and visibly present;

on the altar, during Holy Mass, Jesus, though invisible, is also truly present.

On the Cross our Saviour died a painful and bloody death; but in the Holy Mass He dies only in appearance, or, as it is called, a mystical death.

In the Holy Sacrifice of the Mass, the Body and Blood of our Lord Jesus Christ are not dead; no, it is the living Body, the living, warm heart's Blood—the living rational soul of Jesus, united to his Divinity, that we offer to God.

This is what renders the Mass a "reasonable service," as St. Paul expresses it, a spiritual Sacrifice; this is what gives it infinite value, and makes it the highest worship we can ever offer to God.

"In this divine Sacrifice of the Mass," says the Council of Trent, "the same Christ is contained and is immolated in an unbloody manner, Who on the altar of the Cross offered Himself once in a bloody manner. It is one and the same Victim, the same Christ offering Himself by the ministry of the priest, Who then offered Himself on the Cross; the manner alone of offering being different." *

The Sacrifice of the Mass, then, is the very same in all essentials as the Sacrifice of the Cross. It differs from it only in appearance.

It is true that by the bloody Sacrifice of Himself upon the Cross, our Blessed Redeemer fully atoned for all the sins of men, past, present, and to come.

It is true that the price He paid on the Cross for our salvation is of infinite value, and that nothing can be added to that value. It is true also, that only through His merits does the way of pardon lie open to us; and that all the graces we have or can have, are due to that precious bloodshedding. But the question is, how are these merits of our Saviour to be applied to our souls, so that we may profit by them? The mere fact of His death does not save all, other-

---

* Sess. xxii. c. 2.

wise all men would be saved, no matter who they are, or how they live, or how they die.

We believe that the merits of Jesus Christ must be imparted to us, so that they may be a healing and health-giving medicine to our souls. They must be applied to the soul so as really to cleanse and transform her into a true copy of Christ crucified.

To illustrate our point: In a city there is a large reservoir always filled with pure, fresh water, which is a great blessing to the inhabitants. The quantity of water is more than sufficient to supply the wants of every one. But for one who is in great need of water, what does it avail to know that an immense reservoir is there, if he cannot get at it? If a person wishes to get water, he must either go to the reservoir, or the water must be conveyed thence to him by some means.

It is just so with the graces of redemption, which our Blessed Saviour merited for us by His death. They form an infinite—an inexhaustible fountain open to all. But the pure water of this fountain must be applied to our souls, else we shall perish. And for this reason our Lord Jesus Christ not only *merited* these graces for us, but established also certain channels, whereby these graces are communicated to us, which channels are the Sacraments, and the Holy Sacrifice of the Mass.

The Scripture tells us that after God had created the world, He rested from His labors.* Nevertheless, our Divine Saviour assures us that He and His heavenly Father are "working continually." † And, indeed, if we look around us, we shall see that the work of creation is being constantly renewed. Year after year, the living breath of Spring brings a new face to the earth. The trees and plants and flowers bud and bloom again. Every shrub, every animal, every human being that is brought forth into the

---

* Gen. † St. John.

world is a new creation. The very work of *preservation* is an unbroken continuance of the divine creative act. The entire visible world is but an image of the invisible spiritual world. The work of Redemption is a second and more perfect creation. And just as God continually renews the work of creation, so also does He continually renew the divine work of the Redemption. This unbroken renewal of the work of the Redemption is wrought in the Sacraments, and especially in the Holy Sacrifice of the Mass.

It is not with our Redeemer as with some great man who lived and suffered eighteen hundred years ago, and of whom nothing remains but an historical remembrance. Jesus is ever living on the altars of His Church, and the Church is His living figure. It is through her ministers that He manifests Himself, and works through all ages; through them that He perpetually repeats and uninterruptedly continues His atoning and *redeeming* acts. In the announcement of His word He is the abiding Teacher: in Baptism He perpetually receives the children of men into His communion; in the tribunal of Penance He pardons the contrite sinner; in Confirmation He strengthens the growing youth with the power of His Spirit; in Matrimony He breathes into the bridegroom and the bride a higher conception of the nuptial relations. In Extreme Unction He consoles the dying; and in Holy Orders He institutes the organs whereby He works all this with an activity that never wearies, whereby, especially, He offers the commemorative unbloody Sacrifice of His Body and Blood, thus to apply to us more effectually the all-sufficient merits of the Cross. Christ on the Cross is, as it were, an object strange to us; there He is the universal Victim. But Christ in the Mass is our property, our Victim; He is there offered up for every individual amongst us; especially so, if we partake of the Sacrifice by receiving Holy Communion.

It is, therefore, evident that the Sacrifice of the Mass, by keeping the Oblation of Christ on the Cross, or rather His whole ministry and sufferings continually present, pre-supposes the same, and in its whole purport maintains the same. Far from obliterating, it stamps them all the more vividly on the minds of men; and instead of supplying the bloody Sacrifice of the Cross with heterogeneous elements, it brings that Sacrifice in its true integrity and original vitality to bear the most individual application and appropriation throughout all ages.

It is the same undivided Victim, the same High Priest, Who on Mount Calvary and on our altars offers Himself up an atoning Sacrifice for the sins of men. The consecrated Host at Mass is in Itself all that there is of most august in heaven and on earth, for it is our Blessed Redeemer Himself. All His divine perfections, His graces, merits, virtues, all that He is and all that He has, are mine when I receive Him in the Blessed Sacrament.

When I eat the living divine Victim, come down from heaven, Jesus is mine, *all* mine; His divinity as well as His humanity, His wisdom, power, mercy—all His adorable perfections are mine, since He offers them for my happiness. If we knew how to listen to Him every time He comes into our souls under the Holy Species, the words that He spake to the blind man on the way, would fall on our ears: "What wilt thou that I should do unto thee?" "When I became incarnate in the womb of Mary, and when I died upon the cross, it was for all men; but, at this moment, it is to thee that I give myself:" "what wilt thou that I should do unto thee?"

It is chiefly this mystery that establishes between Jesus and the soul which has been nourished by His Body that ineffable union of grace and life, compared by our Saviour to that which makes *one* His Father and Himself: "I and the Father are one; as I live by the Father, so he that eateth me, the same also shall live by Me;" life will flow from My Heart into his. Then can he say, in a manner, what I say to My Father: All that is Thine is mine.

After receiving our Lord in Communion, we can say with a just pride: Lord, I am no more unworthy of the regards of Thy majesty. O God, consider the face of Thy Christ: lovest Thou not to behold in me Him in Whom Thou art well-pleased? Does not justice please Thee? Behold, then, what justice, what sanctity burns in my soul united to the Soul of Jesus Christ! I complain no more, O Beauty ancient and always new, of not loving Thee as much as Thou shouldst be loved, since. at this moment, I love Thee with the Heart of Thy Son; I complain no longer of being destitute of merits, for now Thou beholdest me clothed with the merits of Jesus!

Far are we then from believing that anything is wanting to the Sacrifice of the Cross. We deem this sacrifice so fully sufficient and so perfect that, whatever is afterwards added, has been instituted to celebrate its memory and to apply its virtue.

We acknowledge that all the merits of the Redemption of mankind are derived from the death of the Son of God. When, therefore, in the celebration of the Divine Mysteries, we say, "We offer to Thee this Holy Victim," we do not mean by this oblation to make, or to present to God a *new* payment of the price of our salvation, but to offer to Him in our behalf the merits of Jesus Christ present, and that infinite price which He once paid for us upon the cross.

How unjustly and foolishly, then, do Protestants reproach us with obscuring the Sacrifice of the Cross by our daily Sacrifice of the Mass! Would it not be absurd to say that to desire baptism, and to place one's confidence in water, instead of in the blood of the Redeemer, would be a disparagement to the merits of Christ? Now, it is just as foolish to say that we, by our daily Sacrifice of the Mass obscure the glory of the Sacrifice of the Cross, and detract from its dignity; since we, by this very means only participate in it, and far from derogating from it, the Mass only brings it nearer to us, and renews and extends its effects in us in a wonderful manner.

Hence it is that our Lord once said to St. Mechtildis: "At the moment of consecration, I come down first in humility so deep that there is no one at Mass, no matter how vile and despicable he may be, towards whom I do not humbly incline and approach if he desires me to do so and prays for it; secondly, I come down with patience so great that I suffer even my worst enemies to be present, and grant them the full pardon of all their sins if they wish to be reconciled with Me; thirdly, I come with love so immense that no one of those present can be so hardened that I do not soften his heart and enkindle it with My love, if he wishes Me to do so; fourthly, I come with liberality so inconceivable, that none of those present can be so poor that I may not enrich him abundantly; fifthly, I come with food so sweet, that no one, however hungry he may be, may not be refreshed and fully satiated by Me; sixthly, I come with so great a light and splendor, that no heart, however blinded, may not be enlightened and purified by my presence; seventhly, I come with so great a sanctity, and treasures of grace so wonderful, that no one, however inert and indevout he may be, may not be roused from this state of sloth and indevotion."*

Our Divine Saviour, it is true, left all the splendors of Heaven. He became man in order that He, Who is life itself, might die to save us. He endured all the fury and barbarity of His enemies; He was torn, bleeding, abandoned by all on an infamous gibbet. Assuredly, this was too much, but it was not enough for His love to us. Hence it is that we behold Him in the Mass—this same God, again become a victim, giving Himself to us in perpetual sacrifice, in order thereby to apply forever to the souls of men the merits of His life and death. What can we say—what can we do while contemplating these prodigies, save to humble ourselves with the angels, in endless adoration, thanksgiving and love!

---

* Lib. iii. Rev. vi. 28.

CHAPTER XII.

MASS THE RENEWAL OF THE MYSTERIES OF THE LIFE OF CHRIST.

MEN are accustomed to erect monuments to commemorate extraordinary events, achievements, victories, and the like. The works of God, however, infinitely surpass those of men in greatness, power, and wisdom. What, then, more natural than to read in the Holy Scripture that God instituted the Sabbath day and solemn feasts to recall to the Jews the remembrance of His benefits; that for this same purpose He also had placed in the ark of the covenant the Tables of the Law and a vase of manna; that He left imprinted on the shore traces of the chariots of the Egyptians whom He had drowned in the Red Sea; that He commanded Joshua to take twelve stones from the bed of the Jordan over which he and his army had passed, in order that these things might be, as it were, monuments of what He had done for them. But what are all the wondrous works which God performed in favor of the Jews in comparison with the stupendous prodigies which the Son of God performed on earth for thirty-three years and a half! What more natural than that He should have left to His followers a perpetual memorial of all His prodigies?

Boleslaus, King of Poland, used to wear around his neck a golden medal with the features of his father stamped upon it. When about to undertake an important work he would take the medal in his hand, gaze at it with tearful eyes, and say: "O dearly beloved father, may I never do anything unworthy of thy royal name!" Thus, by means of a medal, did this king try to remember the blessings and example of his father. But our Lord Jesus Christ did not wish to be borne in memory by a medal or anything of such a nature. He wished to stay with us Himself in person, in order that His own Presence might constantly recall to our mind all that He had done for us. He instituted the holy Sacrifice of the Mass, not only to apply to our souls more effectually the all-sufficient merits of the sacrifice of the Cross, but to be a perpetual memorial of all that He has done and suffered for us and a sure pledge of His undying love for our souls.

It is now over eighteen hundred years since our Blessed Saviour died for us upon the cross. Our Lord knew well that men are apt to forget favors, especially those which are long past. What a contrast between "Hosanna to the Son of David: Blessed is He that cometh in the name of the Lord. Hosanna in the highest," and "Away with this man. Crucify Him!" What a contrast between spreading their garments in the way before Him and stripping Him of His garments, casting lots for them, and putting on Him the scarlet cloak of mockery! What a contrast between cutting branches of palm trees and strewing them where He passed, and platting a crown of thorns and putting it upon His head and a reed in His right hand, bending the knee before Him in mockery, and saying, "Hail, King of the Jews!" What a contrast between "King of Israel" and "We have no king but Cæsar!"

Our dear Saviour knew this fickleness and instability of the human mind and heart. So He instituted the holy sacrifice of the Mass, wherein the sacrifice of the cross is daily renewed, in order thus to remind us continually of His sufferings and death. "Do this," said He to the Apostles, "in remembrance of me." Just as if He had said; "I am about to accomplish the work of your Redemption; I then will return to my Father, Who is in heaven. Now I wish you never to forget Me and all that I have done for you. To make sure of this, I have instituted the sacrifice of the Mass as the only sacrifice of the New Testament, as the sacrifice in which are contained all the mysteries of My life and passion and death." St. Thomas of Aquin says: "In this sacrifice we have an abridgment of all His wonders, and a standing monument of all His prodigies."

And, indeed, in this marvel of the altar we find concentrated all the wonders displayed in the life of our Blessed Redeemer, all the sublime mysteries which He wrought for our salvation. In the Eucharistic sacrifice Jesus works prodigies like the sublimest mysteries and the most stupendous works of His Father and Himself.

To understand this better we must remember that our Divine Redeemer came into the world as a great High Priest to consecrate it by His Presence and to offer to His Eternal Father, in the great temple of the universe, a sacrifice worthy of the majesty of the Godhead. But as the whole earth could produce no victim worthy of God's sovereign majesty, He Himself became the Priest and the Victim by assuming human nature. His whole life on earth is one great act of sacrifice, one mighty action undertaken out of love for us. He commenced this great act of sacrifice interiorly at the first moment of His Incarnation, and exteriorly at His birth, appearing amongst us in human form to be immolated for the expiation of the sins of men, and the consequent reparation of His Father's glory, thus to consummate the great work of our Redemption. This mighty act of sacrifice consists, indeed, of various parts, yet of such a nature that no one is by itself, strictly speaking, the sacrifice. Every individual act of our Divine Redeemer forms but an integral part of His great work of the Redemption, and this work was to be only accomplished by the sacrifice of His life upon the cross. Hence, when on the point of dying, our Lord cried out in a loud voice, "It is consummated." He knew that He had accomplished all the prophecies and realized all the figures concerning Him from the beginning of the world: He knew that He had perfectly fulfilled all the designs of His Eternal Father in His regard; that He had achieved the Redemption of the human race by fully satisfying His Father's justice on the one hand, while on the other He had merited for men all necessary graces, "becoming to all that obey Him the cause of eternal salvation." *

He knew that He had secured those two great objects at the price of His own life. Not content with giving us all else, He concluded His career of suffering and love by the sacrifice even of Himself, and then indeed all was *consummated;* all that even He could do was accomplished.

As it was the will of the heavenly Father that His Son should assume human nature, be born, suffer and die to cancel our sins and satisfy the Divine Justice, so it was the will of God that the sacrifice of His Son should be constantly renewed to the end of the world. To accomplish this will of His heavenly Father Our Lord instituted the sacrifice of the Mass in such a manner that He is present there and offers Himself for us to His heavenly Father with all that He had done and suffered from the moment of His Incarnation to that of His death upon the cross.

The whole life of Our Holy Redeemer was but one great act of sacrifice. It took Him thirty-three years and a half to consummate it, whilst at Mass it takes but a few minutes to renew and consummate the whole of the great work of our Redemption.

Hence the Holy Mass is the solemn celebration of all the blessings imparted to mankind by God in Jesus Christ. In it the past becomes the present; all that Christ has merited for us, and whereby He has so merited it, is henceforth never separated from His Person; He is present as that which He absolutely is, and in the whole extent of His actions, as the Real Victim.

In holy Mass therefore is present our Saviour incarnate for us, born for us, dead for our salvation, risen for our justification, ascended to heaven as our eternal hope. Mass,

---

* Heb. v. 9.

then, is the renewal of His Incarnation, of His birth, of His hidden and public life, of His passion and death, of His glory; it is the living representation of the infinite love and compassion of God towards us, which He has revealed and still reveals daily in the delivering up of His only begotten Son. Mass is the worship most Christian, most pious, most sublime, most real; a worship wherein God is adored in spirit and in truth. The firm, unwavering faith that Christ before our eyes offers Himself up for us to His eternal Father cannot but produce most admirable effects, piercing into the inmost mind, heart, and will of man—far below the deepest roots of evil, so that sin in its germ should be plucked from the will, and the faithful soul be unable to refuse consecrating her whole life to God. When we see Him manifest His love, His benevolence, His devotedness to us, when we see Him even staying among us full of grace and truth, we cannot help rejoicing greatly in the excess of His condescending compassion, and expressing in hymns of praise and thanksgiving our pious emotions, so far as the divinely enraptured soul of man can express them. "But take from the Church," says Abbot Rupertus, "the daily sacrifice of our Saviour and see how well He then might say, 'of what utility is my Blood!' For were this sacrifice to cease, which now everywhere keeps alive His memory, all charity would grow cold, faith would be silent, hope would become languid, and into silence would lapse that great cry of His Blood for mercy."

We ought then to desire neither to see nor to admire anything on earth save the sacrifice of the holy Mass. Were God Himself capable of admiring anything He would admire nothing but this mystery and that of the Incarnation. Faith, supplying the defect of our senses, ought to make us remain as rapt with astonishment, as transported with love and joy at the sight of this divine mystery, as if what our Lord conceals—that splendor of beauty, majesty and glory, which are the delight of the beloved; those treasures, those riches, and those infinite perfections which are the admiration of the angels; that perfume of His glorious Body which regales all Paradise—were clearly manifested to us. To priests especially, this mystery, whose ministers they are, ought to be as much as possible the breath they inhale; they ought hardly to think of anything else. "Do this in commemoration of Me." Such is the last will of the Divine Victim. He asks but one thing, that having died for us; we should fondly cherish the memory of this ineffable benefit, particularly in approaching the altar. Jesus would Himself be our inheritance, our treasure, our patrimony, and for this purpose He leaves us His Body and Blood by His last testament. O testament of love! O inexhaustible treasure! O divine patrimony! O wonderful memorial of the prodigies of the Lord! be thou the principal object of all my thoughts and desires, the only treasure of my heart!

CHAPTER XIII.

MASS THE RENEWAL OF THE INCARNATION.

LET us picture to our minds that little house of Nazareth and the room in which Mary is praying, all alone, at the time of the Annunciation of the Incarnation of the Son of God. We gaze on her in silence: we think of her purity, her lowliness, of the graces which adorn her soul and make her a living temple of God. Suddenly there steals through the open casement a ray of soft light; it shines around this sweet Virgin, growing brighter and brighter the longer it shines. She raises her head and sees standing before her the beautiful form of one of God's angels. His silvery voice breaks the solemn stillness. He announces the glad tidings that she is to be the mother of God: " The Holy Ghost shall come upon thee, and the power of the Most High shall overshadow thee; and, therefore, the Holy which shall be born of thee shall be called the Son of God." The Blessed Virgin having thus learned that she was to become the Mother of the Son of God by the omnipotent power of the Holy Ghost, bowed to the divine decree and said: " Fiat mihi secundum verbum tuum "—" Be it done to me according to thy word." *

No sooner had she uttered those words than the Holy Ghost formed of her purest blood a perfectly organized body: the sacred soul of Jesus Christ was at the same moment created and united to that body, and the Divine Word Himself with both body and soul, in unity of person, so that God became man, and man was made God: " Et Verbum caro factus est "—" And the Word was made flesh."

---

* Luke, chap. i.

The Holy Church is struck with awe at the contemplation of this great mystery: "I considered Thy works and was afraid."* If God had created a thousand other worlds, a thousand times greater and more beautiful than the present, it is certain that this work would be infinitely less grand than the Incarnation of the Word: "He hath showed might in His arm." It required all the omnipotence and infinite wisdom of God to execute the great work of the Incarnation, in order to unite human nature to a Divine Person, and that a Divine Person should so humble Himself as to take upon Him human nature. Thus God became man and man became God: and hence the Divinity of the Word being united to the soul and body of Jesus Christ, all the actions of this Man-God became divine; His prayers were divine, His suffering divine, His infant cries divine, His tears divine, His steps divine, His members divine, His very blood divine, which became, as it were, a fountain of health to wash out all our sins, a sacrifice of infinite value to appease the justice of the Father, who was justly offended with men.

Thousands and millions, the patriarchs and prophets, for ages and ages had sighed and prayed and yearned for this great work of God. And now, while this awful mystery—this stupendous miracle is being accomplished, the whole world around sleeps in unconsciousness.

Surely such a scene would make a deep impression on those who witnessed it in reality. The heart would naturally incline to love and honor God for sending His dearly beloved Son to become man and suffer and die for man's Redemption.

Now turn for a moment to the Catholic altar. The holy Sacrifice of the Mass is being offered up. The bell has given the signal that the most solemn and awful moment of consecration is at hand. As yet there is only bread in the hand of the priest, and wine in the chalice before him. To wor-

---

* Resp. iii., Nocturn ii., in Fest.

ship these lifeless elements would be the grossest idolatry. But suddenly, amid the silence of the breathless multitude, the priest utters the divine life-giving words of consecration; and that which was bread and wine, is bread and wine no longer, but the true Body and Blood of our Lord Himself. It is that same Body that was born of the Blessed Virgin Mary, that died for us upon the cross, that was raised again to life, and that even now sits at the right hand of God the Father. In a hundred thousand Masses that may be said throughout the extent of the whole Church in the space of one hour, God works this miracle at the moment in which the priest finishes the words of consecration; so that in all these Masses the Blood and Body of our Saviour are present, and whether the consecration takes place in one spot or another, He is always the same.

Now in this mystery the power of the creation appears as much as in the mystery of the Incarnation. In the Incarnation the Son of God employed His omnipotence to make Himself man; but in the Mass the Son of God employs His omnipotence to change bread and wine into His Body and Blood. In the Incarnation the Son of God leaves, as it were, the bosom of His Father, descends from the height of His glory into the womb of a Virgin, and conceals His Divinity in taking human nature. But in the Mass He conceals His Divinity and Humanity under the forms of bread and wine, in order that we may eat Him. He is the same in a thousand hosts, as in one. Were a thousand millions to receive Him, all would receive Him whole and entire. He does what He pleases with His Body, putting it in this sacramental state and concealing it under the species, miraculously sustained by a continual miracle. In the Incarnation, God has received man into His bosom by uniting human nature to the Divine Word, and in the Mass He wishes man to receive Him into his heart. Man is united to God by the astounding miracle of the Incarnation. God and Man unite themselves to all of us by the prodigies wrought in the Mass; in the former, the communication and union is made with one individual nature—the sacred Humanity of Jesus Christ, personally united to the divine Word; but in the latter, a union is expected with all those who receive His Body and His Blood. He becomes the same thing with them, not indeed by a hypostatical and personal union, but outside of that, by the most intimate possible. "He who eats My flesh and drinks My blood abides in Me and I in him." What can be more admirable than this? The holy Catholic Church, contemplating the unutterable privilege of the Blessed Mother of God, cries out in admiration: "O blessed is the womb of the Virgin Mary, that bore the Son of the Eternal God." But we can say with even more justice: "O blessed, thrice blessed, are the hands of the priest into which the Eternal Son of God descends every day from heaven; blessed are those hands which bare, which handle, which sacrifice the ever-blessed Son of God!" The Son of God descended but once into the chaste womb of the Virgin Mary, but He descends every day into the hands of the priest.

"O venerable and sacred dignity of priests," exclaims St. Augustine, " in whose hands, as in the womb of the Virgin, the Son of God is incarnate every day. O stupendous mystery which God the Father and the Son and the Holy Ghost perform through the priest in so wonderful a manner."[*] "Should any one ask," says St. John Damescene, "how the bread is changed into the Body of Christ? I answer: the Holy Ghost overshadows the priest and operates through him that which He operated in the sacred womb of Mary."[†] "Indeed," says St. Bonaventure, "the miracle which God works in descending daily from heaven upon our altars, is just as great as was that which He wrought when He came down from heaven to assume our human nature."[‡] Hence Thomas à Kempis was right in saying, "As often as thou

---

[*] Sermo de dignitate Sacerdotum. [†] Lib. ii. c. 14.
[‡] Tom. vii. instit. Novit. p. 1 c. 11.

sayest or hearest Mass, it ought to seem to thee as great, new, and delightful, as if Christ that same day, first descending into the Virgin's womb, had been made man."* Five words of her humility brought the Eternal Word into her sacred womb. Five words of the power of the priest brings the same Eternal Word on our altar. If the consent which Mary gave was the conditional cause of the mystery of the Incarnation, the action of the priest speaking in the name and in the all-powerful virtue of Jesus Christ, is the efficient cause of Transubstantiation—of the change of the bread and wine into the Body and Blood of Christ—the New Incarnation, which is but an extension of the first. And what Mary did but once the priest does every day, while she gave to the Son of God a life of suffering, which ended by the torment on the cross, the priest renders Him present in his own hands, in a state immortal and impassible. "Ah! where are we?" exclaims St. John Chrysostom; "heaven has nothing, absolutely nothing more than earth; the earth has become a new heaven. Go up to the gates of heaven, or rather go up to the highest heaven; look attentively, and I will afterward show you on our altar that which struck you more than anything else in Paradise. For, as in palaces, it is not the gildings and tapestries we look at, but at the king seated on his throne, so I will not pause in heaven to point to you the angels, and the archangels, but the Lord who is the King of the angels, and the archangels, and you have Him upon the earth. It is indeed the same infinite God, the same all-powerful Creator of worlds, the same loving Redeemer, who only desires to be Emmanuel, or God with us, but a hidden God only, a God humbled through love, a Lamb full of divine meekness, a victim of propitiation for our sins."

How awful is that moment of consecration! On a sudden all is hushed, and men seem to fear to breathe. We

---

* Lib. iv. c. 2.

live for an instant in another world, among a crowd of blessed spirits silent and devout, speechless, allowing to escape from their hearts only the thought of prayer; copious tears flow down the cheeks at the thrilling sweetness of Jesus in the blessed hands of the priest. O Christ, how impressive, how blessed a moment is this! Truly, thy house of prayer is the earthly heaven in which Thou dwellest! The air of Paradise does fan Thy house, and angels minister all. These all are kneeling, with hands crossed upon their breasts, and eyes raised to the altar, as telling God,— I care for nought but Thee.

The Eternal Word keeps silence. There was the silence of Christ in the womb of His blessed Mother, the silence of Christ upon the Cross, and here is the silence of Christ in the Eucharist, as profound as that in the bosom of His Father. How awful is this silence of the Son of God in the blessed Sacrament. There under the sacramental elements, the Eternal Word dwells in silence till the end of the world. But He speaks to faithful souls in a manner that they know of, and the faithful worshippers see Him in the light of faith, and kneeling prostrate, praying in every posture of humble adoration, witness the tears, the smiting of the breast, the inimitable, the inconceivable expression of hearts impressed with a sense of the Real Presence.

The feasts of secular luxury last but for a short season. In our churches there is an eternal festivity, for nothing that passes away or that has a shadow of change is celebrated there. Eternal is the festivity of the Incarnation, in which we escape from our own mutability by beholding and receiving Him who is immutable.

Unlike all that belongs to the world, Mass is never altered by age from what it was found to be at first. It is like a treasury in which all the true joys of men are preserved. No one wearies of it as he grows old, but, on the contrary, the human heart loves and venerates it, if possible, each day more and more; for while it restores to the mind of man all the bloom and fragrance of the devotion of his early years, all that gave joy to his youth, it presents to it in prospect the fullness of joy and pleasure for evermore. At the altar the Catholic beholds and possesses whatever has rejoiced his soul in life; he sees the star whose radiance has guided him safely through all the gusts and tides of the world's mutability. There he hears I know not what sweet song in the ears of the heart, provided the world does not disturb it. This unearthly sound soothes the ear of him who considers the wonders of God in the redemption of the faithful, in the stupendous miracle of the Incarnation, renewed and extended in the holy sacrifice of the Mass.

Hail! sacred tabernacles, where Thou, O Lord, dost descend at the voice of a mortal! Hail mysterious altar, where faith comes to receive its immortal food. Oh! I love thy temple; it is an island of peace in the ocean of the world, a beacon of immortality! Thou art near to hear us. Is there a tongue equal to the ecstasy of the heart? Whatever my lips may articulate, this blood which circulates, this bosom which breathes in Thee, this heart which beats and expands, these bathed eyes, this silence,—all pray in me. So swell the waves at the rising of the King of day, so revolve the stars mute with reverence and love, and Thou comprehendest their silent hymn. Ah! Lord, in like manner comprehend me; hear what I pronounce not; silence is the highest voice of a heart that is overpowered with thy glory.

O happy Church! truly in Thee is a hidden God, an infinite treasure, a copious redemption, an everlasting safety. Human eye sees not, nor can any finite intelligence penetrate that ineffable mysterious presence of heaven's great Lord, the mighty foe to ill. "O Salutaris Hostia quæ coeli pandis ostium!" Wondrous things are related of Thee, to whom nothing is impossible, who canst in mercy or in judgment do all things in heaven and on earth! Let weak and frail man prepare himself then before he enters the church. Let him think of the majesty there veiled, and presume not of himself, but seek pardon with holy fear like the publican, that with Lazarus he may deserve in the country to come to find eternal rest. Let weak and frail man come here suppliantly to adore the Sacrament of Christ, not to discuss high things, or wish to penetrate difficulties, but to bow down to secret things in humble veneration, and to abandon God's mysteries to God. For truth deceives no man Almighty God can do all things.

CHAPTER XIV.

MASS THE RENEWAL OF CHRIST'S LIFE IN THE WOMB OF MARY.

PREVIOUS to the coming of our Redeemer, the whole unhappy race of mankind groaned in misery upon this earth; all were children of wrath, nor was there one who could appease a God righteously indignant at their sins. Man, being finite and nothing but a miserable creature, was unable by any punishment whatever to atone for the injury offered to an infinite majesty; there was need of another God to satisfy the Divine justice. But such a God did not exist. On the other hand, the person offended could not make satisfaction to Himself; so that ours was a desperate case.

But, "Be comforted, be comforted, My people," says the Lord through the prophet Isaias; "for her evil is come to an end:"* God Himself has found a way to save mankind. He has decreed that His only begotten Son is to be our Redeemer, for whose coming the Just of the Old Law sighed. This was He for whom Abraham desired, and the patriarchs and prophets longed to look upon. "Rain down, O heavens, and send us the Just one to appease the wrath of that God, Whom we ourselves cannot appease, because we are all sinners. Hasten and show us, O God of mercies, that greatest mercy which Thou hast already promised us, namely, our Saviour." Such were the longing aspirations and exclamations of the Saints. Nevertheless, for the space of 4000 years they had not the happy lot to see the Messias born.

---

* Is. xli. 1.

But at last came the happy time—"When God sent His Son that He might redeem them that were under the law." This happy time is called in Holy Scripture *"fulness of time,"* on account of the fullness of grace which the Son of God came to communicate to men by the redemption of the world.

No sooner, then, was the soul of Jesus Christ created, than it was united to His little Body in the womb of Mary; in the same instant it was also hypostatically united to the Divine Word, and so enlightened thereby with the light of glory, so overwhelmed with reverence, so inflamed with love, at the first view of the Divine Essence imparted to it at its creation, that it then offered itself to do and to suffer all that was necessary for the glory of the Godhead, and for the expiation of the sins of men. He knew that all the sacrifices of goats and bulls offered to God in times past, had not been able to satisfy for the sins of men; He knew that all these sacrifices were less than nothing before that great Being, Who could be worthily honored only by the homage of a God, and adequately worshipped only by the sacrifice of the life of God. Then it was, as St. Paul assures us, that our Blessed Redeemer exclaimed: "Father, sacrifice and oblation Thou wouldst not but a body Thou hast fitted to me —Then said I, Behold I come, to do Thy will."* "My Father," said Jesus, "all the victims hitherto offered to Thee have not sufficed, nor could they suffice to satisfy Thy Justice; but Thou hast given Me this passible body, in order that by shedding My blood I might appease Thee and save men: Behold, I come; here I am ready, I accept every thing, I submit Myself absolutely to Thy will."

The Eternal Father then intimated to His Son that He wished Him to die for the redemption of the world. At that same moment He presented to the view of His Son the entire tableau, so to say, of the sufferings He would have to

---

* Heb. x. 5.

endure, even unto death, in order to redeem mankind. He brought before Him the scourges, and Jesus presented to them His flesh; He brought before Him the thorns, and Jesus presented to them His head. He brought before Him the blows, and Jesus presented to them His cheeks; He brought before Him the nails, and Jesus presented to them His hands and His feet; He brought before Him the cross, and Jesus offered His life; He brought before Him all the labors, contempt, and poverty that were to be His portion through life, in Bethlehem, as well as in Egypt and Nazareth: all the sufferings and ignominy of His passion, all the weariness, the sadness, the agonies, and the abandonment in which He was to end His life upon Calvary, and Jesus embraced them all. Thus is it true that, even from His earliest infancy, our Blessed Redeemer every moment of His life suffered a continual martyrdom, which was as continual a sacrifice offered by Him for us to His Eternal Father.

No sacrifice was ever so acceptable to God as the one then made to Him by His dear Son, Who from His infancy even became a victim and a priest. If all men and angels together had offered their lives in oblation, it could not have been so dear to God as was this of Jesus Christ, because in this offering alone, the Eternal Father received infinite honor and infinite satisfaction.

Our Redeemer offered Himself voluntarily to His Father to satisfy for our sins. "He was offered, because it was His own will." * And His Father loaded Him with all crimes. "He has laid on Him the iniquity of us all." † And thus behold the Divine Word, innocent, most pure and holy, behold Him even from His infancy charged with all the blasphemies, the sacrileges, and the crimes of men, because He had bound Himself to satisfy the Divine Justice. So that Jesus charged Himself with as many evils as there have ever been, or ever shall be, mortal sins committed by all mankind.

Our Lord once showed to St. Catherine of Sienna the hideousness of one venial sin, and such was the dread and sorrow of the saint, that she fell senseless to the ground. What then must have been the sufferings of the Infant Jesus when, on His entrance into the world, He saw before Him the immense array of all the crimes of men for which He was to make atonement! Any one of our sins afflicted His soul more than crucifixion and death afflicted His body. He revealed to one of His servants that, from the commencement of His life, He suffered continually; and so much did He suffer for each of our sins, that if He had had as many lives as there are men, He would as many times have died of sorrow, had not God preserved His life that He might suffer more.* Hence St. Thomas Aquinas was right to say that "this sorrow which Jesus Christ felt at the knowledge of the injury done to His Father, and of the evil that sin would occasion to the souls that He loved, surpassed the sorrows of all the contrite sinners that ever existed; even of those who died of pure sorrow; because no sinner ever loved God and his own soul so much as Jesus loved His Father and our souls."

What a martyrdom must not the loving Heart of Jesus have constantly endured in looking upon all the sins of men! "He beheld every single fault." Even whilst He was in the womb of Mary every particular sin passed in review before Him, and each immeasurably afflicted Him.

But this is not all that Jesus Christ suffered in the womb of His Mother. Other infants, it is true, are in the same state; but they do not feel the miseries of it, because they do not know them. But Jesus knew them well, because from the first moment of His life He had the perfect use of reason. He had His senses, but He could not use them; He had His eyes, but He could not see; He had His tongue, but He could not speak; He had His hands, but He could

---

* Psalter B. Alani, p. 11, c. 12.

not stretch them out; He had His feet, but He could not walk; so that for nine months He had to remain in that state like a dead man shut up in a tomb. "I am become as a man without help, free among the dead." He was free, because He had of His own free will made Himself a prisoner of love in this prison; but love deprived Him of liberty, and bound Him there so fast in chains that He could not move. "Free among the dead!"

"Oh, great patience of our Saviour!" said St. Ambrose, while he considered the sufferings of Jesus in the womb of Mary. "Behold the state to which the Son of God reduces Himself for the love of men; He deprives Himself of His liberty and puts Himself in chains, to deliver us from the chains of hell. Oh, holy faith! If faith did not assure us of it, who would believe that a God of infinite majesty should abase Himself so far as to become a little infant, and shut Himself up in the womb of a Virgin, to suffer therein inconceivable pains for the sake of ungrateful man?"

Now let us turn to our altars. The Son of God annihilated Himself in the Incarnation, in the sacred womb of His Virgin Mother, but He has gone still farther in the holy sacrifice of the Mass. In the womb of His Mother He was a tiny, helpless infant. But on our altars He has surrendered even the appearance of a reasonable creature. There, too, He has eyes, but He cannot see; He has ears, but He cannot hear; He has a tongue, but He cannot speak; He has feet and hands, but cannot act, cannot move. He is living, and yet He is as if dead. The Eternal Word is mute, is divested of all the splendors of His divinity. He is enclosed in a little host, and even in each particle of the Host; He is imprisoned in the species of bread and wine, for these sacred species are only the covering which veils the Body of our Saviour; the womb, as it were, of His Virgin Mother.

There are three sorts of prisoners: criminals, debtors, and prisoners of war. Divine love has reduced the Incarnate Word to be a threefold prisoner in the sacred Host. He is, as it were, a criminal, although innocence itself, having become the victim of sinners that He may satisfy the justice of His Father, and restore them to grace. He is a prisoner for debt, having taken upon Him our sins, He was obliged to discharge their penalty, which He did from the first moment of His life, and continues to do in every Mass. He is a prisoner of war. Love has vanquished and reduced Him to this state. Love encloses His immensity in a point, His eternity in a moment, His immortality, His wisdom and omnipotence in the species of bread and wine. O wonderful prison! O devoted captive, who, to satisfy His beneficence, by a miracle of power and of love, whilst ascending into heaven, there to manifest His glory, remains at the same time on earth to dwell with and in us, by a Presence as real and true as it is secret and invisible.

Behold our Saviour twice the victim of charity, twice within a narrow prison, twice bound with the chains of love. And this narrow prison of His choice is multiplied in a thousand places at once.

Why does He choose to remain in this state of abasement and captivity? It is to offer to His Father for our sins all the acts of adoration, of love, and of prayer, which He made in the womb of His Mother, which served as His oratory for nine months: to present anew to the Divine Majesty, in our behalf, all the sufferings and pains which, during that time, He had endured to free us from hell. He is made a victim for our sins, in order that forgiveness through His merits might of right belong to us. There Jesus Christ is the "Prince of Peace," not of vengeance on poor sinners, but of mercy, constituting Himself the Mediator between God and sinners. If we cannot of ourselves make due atonement to the justice of God, at least the Eternal Father knows not how to disregard the cries and prayers and sufferings of the Divine Infant Saviour.

A knight, named Don Alfonso Albuquerque, made a sea-voyage once. A violent tempest arose, and his vessel was driven amongst the rocks. He had already given himself up for lost, when he saw near him a little babe crying bitterly. He took him in his arms, lifted him towards heaven, and said: "Though I myself am unworthy to be heard, give ear, at least, to the cries of this innocent child, and save us." Immediately the storm subsided, and they were saved. It is for sinners to do the like. We have offended Almighty God. Already has sentence of everlasting death been passed upon us. Divine Justice requires satisfaction, and rightly so. What have we to do? To despair? God forbid! Let us go to Mass and offer up to God this Infant, Who is His own Son, and let us address Him with confidence. O Lord, if we cannot of ourselves render Thee satisfaction for our offences against Thee, behold this Child on the altar. He is there to offer atonement for us, and to beseech Thy mercy in our behalf. Although we are undeserving of pardon, the sufferings and pains of this Thy guiltless Son have merited pardon for us, and He offers Thee His prayers to win it for us. Yes, says Jesus Christ to every one of us from the altar, after consecration, take Me, offer Me for thyself to the Eternal Father, and so shalt thou escape death and be in safety. Behold Me, descended from heaven, in all the amiability and with all the merits of My Infancy, behold Me, made your own on the altar.

If, then, we desire a cure for our wounded soul, He is our physician at Mass; if we are weak and infirm, and would be healed, behold, Jesus Christ heals us by His Blood; if we are troubled with the impure flames of worldly affections, behold the fountain to refresh us with His consolations. Do we fear the death of sin, He is our life. Do we wish for heaven, He is the way and the Good Shepherd. Let us then often be with Him at Mass in this world, and He will be with us forever in the next.

CHAPTER XV

MASS, THE RENEWAL OF THE BIRTH OF CHRIST.

PREVIOUS to the birth of our Lord, the Roman emperor had published an edict commanding all Roman subjects to go and be enrolled in their native country. So Joseph departed with his spouse Mary to have their names enrolled in Bethlehem. As soon as they arrived there, the time for Mary's delivery was at hand, and Joseph went about the town looking for a lodging. But being poor, they were driven away by every one, even from the inn where the other poor had been received. So they went away from the town in the night, and having found a cave, Mary entered. But Joseph said to her: "My spouse, how can you pass the night in this damp cold place? Do you not see that this is a stable for animals?" But Mary answered: "O my Joseph, it is nevertheless true that this cave is the royal palace in which the Son of God chooses to be born." And the hour of the birth being come, whilst Joseph was rapt in ecstasy, and the holy Virgin was kneeling in prayer, all at once she saw the cave illumined by a brilliant light, and casting her eyes upon the ground, beheld there the Son of God already born: a tender infant, weeping and trembling with cold; and thus she first adored Him as her God. Then she placed Him in her bosom, wrapped Him in the poor swaddling-clothes which she had with her, and finally laid Him on a little straw in the manger.

The birth of Jesus Christ caused a universal joy to the whole world. The angels came down from heaven and intoned the glad anthem, "Glory be to God in the highest; and on earth peace to men of good will." They communicated their joy to the good shepherds by announcing to them the advent of their long expected Redeemer. "Behold," said the angel to them, "I bring you good tidings of great joy that shall be to all people, for this day is born to you a Saviour, who is Christ the Lord, in the city of David." And the shepherds being filled with joy rose up in haste, saying one to another, "Let us go over to Bethlehem and see this word which has come to pass." Then the archangel St. Gabriel went to the just souls detained in Limbo to announce to them also the good tidings; and those souls rejoiced exceedingly because now heaven was soon to be opened to them by the Redeemer.

Entering that stable, and contemplating the Divine Infant wrapped in swaddling clothes and lying in a manger, we behold in Him, with the eye of faith, the God of Infinite Majesty, Whose throne is the highest heaven, Whose servants are the angels. Although stretched in an humble, comfortless crib, He dwells nevertheless in the bosom of the Father; although He utters no word, He is still the Word and Wisdom of God. He is clothed in poor and scanty raiment, yet is He the splendor of eternal light, whence all His creatures derive their brightness and their beauty. He subjects Himself to the sufferings of infancy, and is at the same time the joy and beatitude of angels. He requires the nourishment of ordinary babes, although on His liberal hand every creature in the universe depends for needful sustenance. He cannot move without being carried in some one's arms although He gives motion to the heavens.

Here we behold the sacrifice He offered to the offended God, interiorly, by sublime acts of adoration, love and acceptance of death: exteriorly, by His submission to corporal suffering, cold, poverty and privation of every description.

While St. Peter of Alcantara was one day meditating upon these prodigies of God's mercy, so inflamed was he with divine love that, in a state of ecstasy he was borne a considerable space through the air to the foot of the Blessed Sacrament. And the noble Paula, as she saw from afar the city that gave birth to the Saviour of the world, could not help exclaiming: "Hail! hail! Bethlehem; hail to thee so worthy of thy name (house of bread), since it was on thee that the True Bread from heaven deigned to descend for us." And in the ardent transports of her faith, her lips gave utterance to the most tender accents of admiration, gratitude, and love.

If the mere sight of the place where Jesus was born is capable of inflaming faithful souls with divine love; if the meditation on all that our Infant Saviour suffered in the stable of Bethlehem can make hearts overflow with a torrent of holy joy, what should be the delight of our souls at the consideration of the far more wondrous prodigies that take place in the holy Sacrifice of the Mass! There our Saviour is born every day in the hands of the priest, by the words of consecration. The Church is His birthplace, the altar is His crib. St. Bernard has well remarked that when the Church reads the martyrology for Christmas day, she uses the present instead of the past tense. At other times she mentions, for instance, the birth of St. John the Baptist, which took place at such a time, or the death of St. Peter, who suffered martyrdom on such a day, but the birth of our Lord and Saviour is proclaimed as taking place *now*. "Jesus Christus nascitur in Bethlehem. Juda." Jesus Christ *is* born in Bethlehem of Juda. Why this difference of phrase? Because He is every day really and truly born in the holy Sacrifice of the Mass.

Could we only see all the Catholics in the world, two hundred millions in number, assembled in one large church to hear Mass, and at the solemn moment of consecration, behold the prostrate multitude striking their breasts and adoring our Lord, while the priest elevates the Sacred Host and the blessed chalice, the sight would be a greater incentive to compel man to adore Him, in sacramental presence, than was offered to those who saw the Infant of Bethlehem and Jesus of Nazareth in the sorrows and the humiliation and passion of His humanity. "For when you see," says St. John Chrysostom, "the Lord slain and lying there, and the priest standing by the sacrifice, and praying over it, when you see all present reddened with that precious blood, do you still think that you are amongst men, and standing upon earth; will you not be at once translated to heaven, and casting forth from your soul every carnal thought, gaze around you on the things that are in heaven, with a naked soul and a pure mind? Oh, the marvel! Oh, the love of God towards man! He that sitteth on high with the Father, is held, at that hour, in the hands of all, and He gives Himself to those that desire to embrace and receive Him." At that solemn moment, the angels descend from heaven to tell us: "Behold we bring you good tidings of great joy, that shall be to all the people;" for this day—at this very moment of consecration—is born anew your Saviour.

Alph. Rodriguez, S. J., in his book, "Practice of Christian Perfection," * relates the following: "A holy man was one day at Mass, which was being said by a priest who was rather worldly. What was his surprise, at the moment of Communion, to see a charming child, surrounded by luminous rays, reposing on the paten in place of the species of bread! He was more astonished afterwards, for he saw that when the priest went to take Communion, the child turned away his head, struggling with his hands and feet, as if to prevent the priest from receiving him into his mouth. The same saint had several other times the same vision, which gave him much thought. One day this priest was conversing with him and confessed that as often as he received the body of our Lord at Mass he had great trouble in taking it, and knew not how that could come. The servant of God

---

* Eighth Treatise, chap. 18.

was very glad of this confidence; he took occasion to tell the priest what he had himself seen, and advised him to make a thorough examination of his conscience, a good confession, and change his life. Touched by this kind admonition, and the warning he had received, the priest applied himself to become more edifying. Some time after, the holy man who had warned him, when assisting again at Mass, perceived the same child between the hands of the priest, at the time of Holy Communion, but saw him enter now into his mouth and his heart joyfully and eagerly, which proved the sincerity of his conversion."

All this is in accordance with what other great saints have seen or said on this subject. "At the time of consecration," says St. John Chrysostom, "angels too stand by the priest, the whole order of heavenly powers cries aloud, and the space around the altar is filled in honor of Him Who liveth there. And this is indeed sufficiently made credible from the very things then celebrated. I once heard a person narrate that an old man—an admirable person and one accustomed to see revelations—told him that he had, on a certain occasion, such a vision as this vouchsafed him; and that, at this very time of the sacrifice, he saw of a sudden a multitude of angels—as far as was possible for him—clothed in shining robes, encompassing the altar, and bowing down, even as one may see soldiers standing in the presence of their king. And I believe it."

"That marvellous priest, St. John Chrysostom," relates St. Nilus of this saint, "that luminary of the great Church of Byzantium, yea rather of the whole world, being keen-sighted, often saw the house of the Lord not deprived or left for an hour even by the guardianship of angels, and this especially during the time of the divine and unbloody sacrifice, a circumstance which he, filled with awe and gladness, narrated privately to his spiritual friends. For, he says, 'when the priest begins to make the holy oblation, many of the blessed powers suddenly descend from heaven clothed in white robes, with their feet bare, with their eyes intent, but with their faces cast down; moving round the altar with reverence, and quietness, and silence, they stand around until the completion of the dread mystery; then scattering themselves through the venerable house of God, each of them here and there co-operating, aiding, and giving strength to the bishops and priests and to all the deacons present, who are administering the Body and the precious Blood.' These things do I write, that knowing the fearful nature of the divine liturgy, you be neither careless yourselves, heedless of the divine fear, nor suffer others to talk or whisper during the oblation." *

We read in the life of St. Oswald, bishop, that an angel used to assist him at Mass, and make all the necessary answers. Once on Easter Sunday, Pope Gregory I. celebrated Mass in the Church of St. Maria Maggiore, and when he said the words "Pax domini sit semper vobiscum," an angel of the Lord answered in a loud voice, "Et cum spiritu tuo." For this reason when the Pope celebrates Mass on that day, in that church, and says, "Pax domini sit semper vobiscum," no answer is made.†

No place on the earth is dearer to devout Christians than a church where the sacrifice of the Mass is daily celebrated. In the mere remembrance of the divine mysteries, they find an assistance in the great combat of life. "Alas! if I could go into a church," I hear one exclaim, "if I could be where our Lord is lifted up, and appears to the congregation in sacramental presence—then in that blessed moment, I should die of rapture!" In this mystic Jerusalem the prophecy is already in great measure fulfilled — "God wipes away all tears from the eyes of men, and there is no more death, nor any more grief, nor lamentation, nor sorrow, for the former things have passed away; and He Who sitteth upon the

---

* Lib. II., Epist. 294, p. 266.
† Life, by John the Deacon.

throne has accomplished His word and hath made all things new. The heart-rending sorrows of the poor, and the mighty woes of the rich, which the poor cannot conceive, are alike here forgotten." " O what grace has our Lord granted me," cried a poor recluse to one who was compassionating her condition: "I might be sick, and I am well; I might be living far away in pagan lands, and I am born here a Christian, in the neighborhood of beautiful churches and holy priests; I might be blind and deaf but I hear the peal of bells, and every morning my Saviour in Mass speaks to my heart in words of love in the Mass. I am dead, and I live only for grace, for the chants of the church, and for the holy Mass. Ah! my dear friend! when I enter the house of the Lord, every doubt, every earthly disquietude vanishes immediately. The smoke of the incense, the voice of the priest, which rises from the altar when I prostrate myself, awaken in my heart an impassioned fervor. The burning tapers remind me by their secret flame, of the secret of the world, and of creation, and a thrilling emotion spreads over my whole body when I think of the mysteries of which these are the signs. I meditate and I pray. The Creator and Saviour moves me with interior and ineffable words, which are heard at the bottom of my soul. I feel within me a love above all love—a happiness—a heavenly breath—and then the bell tingles and the mysteries of the Incarnation and birth of our Lord are renewed: a shuddering runs through my veins and through the marrow of my bones, for I feel that I am a Christian; that the Incarnate Saviour is near me, and that He looks upon me with love."

" Devout persons," says St. Bonaventure, " experience sometimes such a charm of sensible pleasure during Mass that they seem as if embalmed in the agreeable perfume which surrounds them, and melted in the sweetness of heavenly harmony. Perchance this is the grace of God to encourage the imperfect in their commencement of a holy life, or it is the fulness of spiritual perfection, which, by reason of the union of the soul with the body is communicated to the senses; or perhaps even it is a favor bestowed upon the body, that as it has been partaker of sorrow and mortification with the soul, it may now also share in its joy; for as the body labors with the soul, and both have their sufferings, there may be justice in imparting even to the body some consolation in the present as well as in the future life."

Numberless are the wretched men possessing lofty souls tortured by the feeling of isolation, and afflicted with unutterable anguish at the thought of remaining forever unknown. They thirst for society, for communion with congenial intellects. What society then can be found so amiable, so inspiring, so full of consolation, and of all remedies for human misery, as that of the angels and the faithful in the house of God, at the time of Mass? They wish to be entreated, and that their presence may be sought after, but what more noble invitation, or more worthy of all acceptance can they receive than that of our dear Saviour on the altar: "Come to Me all ye that labor and are heavy laden, and I will refresh you."*

Obey this loving invitation of our Lord, go to Mass, bow down and adore your Saviour, the heavenly King—the King of eternal glory, and according to your faith, will He have mercy on you. Are you tempted with unholy thoughts? You will be freed from them.

Are you a child of sorrow, wounded by the stern strokes of a calamitous life? You will be comforted.

Are you discouraged at the difficulties of your position—do you hunger and thirst after justice? You will be strengthened and refreshed. Mark and obey the prophetic invitation: "All ye that thirst, come to the waters, make haste, buy and eat." † Trust the experience of men who, long, like you, have trod the common ways of life, and who assure you that it will be so, that you will be filled with

---

* Mat. xi. 28. † Isai lv. 1.

blessings, filled with joy; that from the martyrdom of a deceitful world, you will come to this peace. Yes, it is so; we may well say it who have received the mercy of the Lord during the attendance at Mass, in the presence of assisting angels.

CHAPTER XVI.

MASS, THE RENEWAL OF THE LIFE OF CHRIST.

In the foregoing chapter I have expressed in a few words most sublime and consoling truths. I could wish I had it in my power to impress those truths upon the hearts of all men in indelible characters. Father Alvarez, S. J., tells us not to believe we have made much progress in the love of God so long as we have not constantly before our eyes the life and passion of our Lord Jesus Christ. Indeed it is our duty to form ourselves upon the divine model which our Heavenly Father has given us in His well beloved Son, Jesus Christ. We can therefore have no better intention in all our actions than to perform them, because our Divine Saviour has shown us the example, that is, to practise virtues because our Father has practised them. But to do this well, we must often consider them with great attention and make our mind dwell upon them with delight; for a child who loves his Father endeavors to acquire a conformity of dispositions and inclinations with his, to imitate Him in all His actions. Great indeed are the fruits, and wonderful are the effects produced in the soul by the frequent consideration of the mysteries of our Lord's life. This consideration is best calculated to produce in our hearts pious affections and fervent petitions for all the graces necessary for our salvation and sanctification, and to form resolutions to avoid some particular fault and to practise some particular acts of virtue; and this leads infallibly to the reformation of life. It is for this reason that in the opinion of the Fathers of the Church the mysteries of the passion and death of our Lord are the most useful subjects of meditation; for seldom, they say, does it happen that we do not profit by the consideration of the actions of our Lord. Now it is only natural that the fittest time for the consideration of the mysteries of our Lord's life is at the time of Mass, for then, as was shown in the preceding chapter, are these mysteries renewed in our presence in a most wonderful manner. Let us consider how it is done.

Let us enter once more in spirit into the humble dwelling of Nazareth. There we see our Lord leading, to all appearances, an ordinary existence as the son of a poor mechanic up to the mature age of thirty. The principal thing recorded of Him by the Evangelists for the long space of thirty years, is that He was subject to holy Mary and St. Joseph. So the Son of God, the Sovereign Lord of heaven and earth, obeys Mary and Joseph, who, though eminently holy, were immeasurably inferior as creatures to Him, their Creator and their God. He assists them in the lowliest offices, submitting to work in a poor carpenter's shop, and to help in the care of a very humble household; to saw wood, sweep the house, prepare the food, and the like. But with what promptitude and alacrity, with what perfection and exactitude, above all, with what interior resignation to the will of God did He discharge the lowest and meanest offices as willingly as He would have undertaken the most devoted and honorable functions? Thus, in the poor home of Nazareth, Jesus was a living victim, perpetually immolated to the glory, and consumed with the love of His Father. His exterior occupations never for a moment interrupting His interior dispositions of self-sacrifice. He offered to His Father a perpetual sacrifice of His Body and Soul, and in obedience to His Father's will passed thirty years in obscurity, employed in occupations which, to human reason, seem unworthy of His dignity as the world's Messiah. O wonder! O inestimable grace, to see a God serving as a boy, to behold a God sweeping the house! to see Him working and sweating to plane a piece of wood! to behold a God conversing visibly with men, to hear Him speak, to see Him work miracles, to behold resplendent in His countenance the features of divine Majesty, its benignity and sweetness; to receive Him under one's roof, to give Him food to eat, to talk familiarly with Him—this was a happiness which might have excited the jealousy of angels. How often have we not longed to see Jesus face to face in the innocent beauty of His childhood, as He appeared to the shepherds of Bethlehem! How often have we not wished to see Him in the bloom of boyhood, as He swept the cottage-floor and drew water for His Mother, or as He confounded the vain wisdom of the Doctors in the Temple! Who is there that has not wished to see Him in the vigor of manhood, as He walked on the Sea of Galilee, or ascended the mountain to teach the eager crowds that followed Him, thirsting for the word of life! Who would not wish to have seen our dear and compassionate Redeemer as He stood beside that tomb in Bethany and wept, while with the Almighty voice of a God He commanded the dead Lazarus to arise and come forth!

How often have we not yearned to look upon Him on that blessed farewell night when He instituted the sacrifice of the New Covenant, and left us His virgin flesh to be our food and His loving heart's blood to be our drink! How often have we not wished to stand beneath Him, whilst He hung on the cross for our sins, that we might gather every drop of His precious blood, and hear from His own lips those loving words: "Son, behold thy mother!" How great would be our joy could we have seen our Lord Jesus as He arose from the sealed tomb triumphant over death and hell, and, finally, could we have seen Him as He ascended to His throne of majesty in heaven! Truly, on that day, as the prophet had foretold, the moon did shine as the sun, and the sun shone with sevenfold brightness, like the brightness of seven days! "Blessed are the eyes," said our Saviour to His disciples, "that see the things which you see, and blessed are the ears that hear the things you hear, for amen, I say to you, many prophets, and just men, and kings, have desired to see the things that you see and have not seen them, and to hear the things that you hear, and have not heard them." *

If our Lord Himself then calls His disciples blessed for having seen and heard Him, it seems natural for us to wish for the same happiness and blessedness. But let us not deceive ourselves. It is true, our dear Saviour calls His disciples more happy than the just men of the Old Law, but He does not call them more blessed than those who were to live after Him under the New Law. On the contrary, of these He says: "Blessed are they who have not seen Me, but have most firmly believed in Me." Indeed, the Real Presence of our Lord in the holy Eucharist is far more advantageous to us than His sensible Presence was to the Jews. The Jews possessed Him only in one place. If He was at Jerusalem, He was not at Nazareth; and even if seen in the Temple at Jerusalem, He was not to be seen in any other part of the city. But as He is born anew, as He renews His whole life in the Mass, we possess Him everywhere at the same time in all our churches.

The Jews possessed Him only at certain times for a few days, for a few hours. The whole time He spent with them did not exceed thirty-four full years, while for thirty of those years he was unknown to almost all the world. In the Blessed Eucharist we possess Him every hour, day and night, and for how many centuries? Add to those that are past the centuries yet to come.

The Jews beheld our Lord only outwardly with their bodily eyes, and generally without advantage to themselves. But we behold with the eyes of the spirit His body, His blood, His soul, His divinity, and we never thus behold Him without the merit of acts of faith, adoration, and other virtues with which His Presence inspires us.

---

* Matt. xiii. 16, 17; Luke x. 24.

To the Jews our Lord did not show Himself except in a natural state, but we have Him on our altars in a state of pure grace, which it is as little possible to reckon up as it is to count the stars of heaven, the leaves on the trees, or the grains of sand on the sea-shore.

The Jews possessed our Lord only by means of the senses. But we possess Him in the Mass in a manner much more intimate, which is above sense! He comes into us, He unites His body and His soul to our body and our soul. But if our senses have no part in this possession, far from losing anything thereby it is exactly this that constitutes the merit of our faith.

Of all those who beheld our Lord, and who listened to Him while He conversed visibly with men, how many were there who joined themselves to Him? A very small number; there were not more than five hundred disciples when He ascended into heaven. Compare this little troop with the countless multitudes who adore Him in the Blessed Sacrament, and who, by faith in this mystery, instead of His corporal and sensible Presence, find His body and blood present under the species of bread and wine, and by concomitance, as theologians say, His soul and His divinity together with the treasures of all the possessions of grace and glory.

In the Holy Sacrifice of the Mass, in the mystery of the Eucharist, our Lord remembers His alliance, contracted with us by the Incarnation and Redemption. He renews the mystery of the Incarnation in every faithful soul by Holy Communion, for it is by Communion that He unites Himself, and restores to us that same nature which he vouchsafed to take of us; but with this advantage, that having taken it in its abasement and misery, He gives it back to us wonderfully elevated and united to God, in order to unite us also to Him, and to exalt us to the highest degree of greatness and glory to which it is possible for fallen man to rise. Who can say what our Lord operates by means of Communion in a pure soul? God only knows. The very soul in which these marvels are wrought is not conscious of them. A soul well disposed receives in a single Communion a fervor greater beyond comparison than all that flows from all the visions and revelations, which all the saints together have ever had.

By communion we are united immediately to the body and blood of Jesus Christ, and by means of His body and blood to His soul and His divinity. His body becomes blended with our body, His blood with our blood, His soul is joined to our soul; whence there results in us an accidental change, which makes us like unto our Lord, our body participating in the divine qualities of His body and our soul in the graces of His soul according as He is pleased to communicate Himself to us, and according to the disposition in which we receive Him. Thus, His imagination stays and regulates our imagination, His understanding enlightens our understanding, His will invigorates our will, His appetite moderates our appetite, and extinguishes therein the fire of concupiscence; His senses purify our senses. He roots up our evil disposltions, He destroys the seeds of sin; He mortifies our humors, and disposes everything in such a manner that the practice of virtue becomes easy to us.

This it is that was represented to a certain devout person, who, as Platus relates, once beheld in one of his communions the body of our Lord in the act of uniting Himself to him, His eyes, His arms, and each of His sacred members mingling with His own as one piece of melted wax mixes with another.

In the Mass the body of our Lord is the only sacrifice of the New Law. There He is our living victim before the eyes of His Father, appeasing His anger and satisfying His justice, communicating the life of grace and the seed of the life of glory to those who receive Him worthily. So that we ought to picture Him to ourselves upon our altars, as continually offering to God the sacrifice of His life and death for the very same ends for which He offered it on

Calvary, the sacrifice of the altar being the renewal of that of the cross. Is not this then an advantage that far exceeds the visible Presence of Jesus Christ among the Jews, a Presence from which, because of their evil dispositions, they derived so little fruits? Did the Jews, who beheld our Lord healing the sick and raising the dead, possess anything like this? The Apostles and disciples of our Lord themselves, before the institution of the Holy Sacrifice of the Mass, did not enjoy so great a privilege.

After all this, how does it happen that we are so little affected by this admirable Sacrifice of the holy Mass? How can we love anything on earth besides? How can we think more frequently of anything else? In the light of faith we behold the marvels it contains—the body and blood of Jesus Christ, the Majesty of a God, and the most astonishing excess of His love for men. And yet we have scarcely any other feelings at His Presence than those which the senses and the imagination give us! We are destitute of devotion; tepid and dull in regard to our Lord, so that at times He scarcely produces more effect by His Presence in the souls of a whole Christian congregation than on the walls of the Church in which He dwells. We suffer incalculable losses from failing to recognize the treasures we possess in holy Mass and in holy Communion; our stupidity in this respect is most deplorable. Generally speaking, we find ourselves after Mass and Communion as we were before, and after so many Masses and Communions we continue just the same, just as tepid, just as little mortified, just as imperfect as at the beginning; we attach our hearts to trifles, we place our happiness in them, we fill our mind with them. A wretched little attachment will deprive us of the marvellous effects which holy Communion and the celebration or devout hearing of Mass would operate in us were we well disposed.

This disposition consists chiefly in purity of heart, peace and tranquillity of soul, in noting and repressing the rebellion and resistance of our mind and will against grace, in discovering our illusions, our errors, our blindness, the depth of our malice, and in correcting all those disorders. When we have done this, we shall experience a hunger and thirst for holy Mass and Communion, we shall taste its sweetness, and it will produce in us from day to day a fresh increase of spiritual life.

In old days, it was a favorite devotion with Christians to visit the sacred spots in the Holy Land where our Lord lived and moved in the flesh, working out our salvation. Let ours be to abide with our Lord in the Mass. If pious Christians travelled so far, and faced so many dangers merely to see the country in which our Lord lived, in which He walked, and suffered death; if we regard it as a great favor to possess a little splinter of the wood of the cross; if the crib wherein He was laid, the river in which He was baptized, the garden where He prayed, the prætorium where He was judged, the pillar to which He was bound, the thorns with which He was crowned, the wood to which He was nailed, the rock in which He was buried, the mount where He ascended into heaven, are objects of such great veneration among Christians because of the relation they once bore with our Lord, with what ardor ought we not now to go to church, to hear Mass, to find there what is far more admirable—our Lord Himself in person.

Padbert, and also Paschasius relate that when St. Plegil said Mass, this holy priest used to see Jesus Christ in the consecrated Host, under the form of a beautiful child, stretching out his arms as if to embrace him. Let us go to Mass if possible every day of our lives; let us go to be embraced by the holy Infant Jesus—embraced in faith, hope and sweet charity. One day He will throw off His disguise and appear in His heavenly might and splendor. How happy will those then be who have endeavored often to assist at the Sacred Mysteries of Mass! They will not be confounded, but will "stand before Him with great constancy." They will "see His face" and rejoice for evermore.

CHAPTER XVII.

MASS, THE RENEWAL OF GOD'S WONDROUS WORKS.

From the beginning of the world, God has never ceased to perform miracles for the benefit of men, miracles so great that they will be the admiration of all nations to the end of time. But of all the wonders he has wrought two stand forth pre-eminent. So surprising does the prophet Isaias find them that he calls them the inventions of God: "Make known to the people," says he, "the inventions of God."* Indeed, it would seem that both in the one and the other, God has been careful, as it were, to study the manner in which He might best communicate and manifest Himself to us. The first of these wonders is the Incarnation, wherein the Word of the Father unites Itself to our nature, by a union so intimate that God and man become one and the same person. The secrets of this union will always remain incomprehensible to human reason, and known to God only; and so firm and indissoluble is it that, as St. Denis says, "what it has once joined, never has been, nor ever can be, separated." "Love," says this saint, "is a unitive virtue, which transforms the lover into the one beloved object, and of the two makes but one." Now, what no love in the world ever did, the love of God has done for man. It never happened in the world that of the lover and of the object beloved, love effectually made but one and the same thing. This was a marvel that seemed reserved for heaven, where the Father and the Son are indeed truly one. So great, however, was the love of God for man that God united Himself to him in such a manner as to make God and man one and

---

* xii. 4.

the same person; so that God is truly man and man truly God, and all that is truly proper to man, may be truly and properly said of God Himself. In a word, He whom men beheld speaking, walking, acting and suffering, was truly God, at the same time that He was truly clothed with human nature, and performing human actions. "Who ever heard of any such thing as this? And who ever saw any thing like unto it?"* A God to be wrapped in swaddling clothes! A God to weep! A God to become weary and feeble! A God to suffer! O Lord! did not the royal prophet say: "That Thou hast made the highest heaven Thy refuge, where no evil shall come to Thee; and no scourge shall approach Thy tabernacle"?† And yet the whips, nails, and thorns have overtaken Thee, and fastened Thee to the cross. What is farther from God than this? "It is an admirable work that proceeded from Him," says the prophet Isaias: ‡ a work which the Lord performed so as to lead up to one, in some manner, still greater, that should be the memorial of all His wonderful works.

This work is the institution of the Holy Sacrifice of the Mass—a work that exceeds the thoughts of man, and even those of the angels themselves, being to them a cause of perpetual admiration. Our Saviour would mark by the grandeur of His gift how far His love for "His own surpassed all the affection which had been manifested in the gifts which had preceded His great Presence. What was the tree of life to this? the manna to this? the waters of the rock in the desert to this? the brazen serpent to this? What are all the prophets and patriarchs, ever dreamt of, compared with this? There is no nation so blest as we that have our God so near us!" The Holy Sacrifice of the Mass is indeed an unfathomable abyss of the most astounding prodigies.

The first of these prodigies is that as soon as the priest

---

* Isaias, lxvi. 8.   † Ps. 90, 9, 10.
‡ xxviii. 21.

has pronounced the words of consecration over the host and the wine in the chalice, the Real Body and Blood of Our Lord Jesus Christ are present upon the altar. His Body is present under the appearance of bread, and His Blood under the appearance of wine.

The second miracle is that after the words of consecration there remains neither bread nor wine, though the contrary appears to our senses. When Jacob wished to obtain of his father Isaac the blessing which was designed for Esau, he covered his hands with the skin of a kid that he might the better resemble his brother. "It is indeed the voice of Jacob," said the holy old patriarch, "but they are the hands of Esau."* The same happens here—that which we touch with our hands, that which is exposed to our senses, appears to be bread and wine; but the voice and the word of faith assure us of the contrary, and faith must supply the defects of our weak senses.

Nor is there reason to be so much astonished at this; for is it not something far more wonderful that God should have made Himself man without ceasing to be God, than that bread, ceasing to be bread, should be changed into flesh? The same divine power whereby the Son of God became man, here changed bread and wine into His Body and Blood.

The third prodigy that happens in this change is not brought about as in natural things, wherein, when one thing is changed into another, there always remains something of the thing that is changed; for example, when earth is changed into gold or silver, or water into crystal, the matter or substance always remains the same; there is no change beyond one of form. Thus, for instance, you can make the form of a lion out of a piece of wax or clay, but the wax or clay remains. But here, after the consecration, there remains in the host nothing of the substance of bread, or in

---

* Gen. xxvii. 29.

the chalice, of the substance of wine, but all the substance of bread is changed into the Body of Jesus Christ, and all the substance of wine into His Blood. The Church properly calls this entire change—transubstantiation—*i. e.*, the changing of one substance into another.

There remains, therefore, in the Blessed Sacrament nothing of the substance of bread and wine; there remains only the color, smell, taste, and other accidents, and this is called the Sacramental species.

The fourth miracle that takes place in the Blessed Sacrament, is that the sacramental species or appearance remains without subject or substance. It is the property of such accidents to be inseparably attached to their substance. It is certain, for instance, that whiteness cannot subsist without being attached to some substance, and the same is to be said of taste and smell. But here, according to an order altogether above the order of nature, the accidents of bread and wine are miraculously sustained, without being united to anything, because nothing of the substance of bread and wine is any longer there to sustain them; and the Body and Blood of Jesus Christ, which take the place of bread and wine, cannot be the subject of these accidents, *i. e.*, of color, taste, smell, and the like. As the manna, which was the shadow and figure of this most wonderful sacrament, had the taste of all sorts of things, and yet was none of those things of which it had the taste, so this heavenly manna has the color, taste, and smell of bread and wine, yet is neither the one nor the other, so that by a continued miracle, God sustains these accidents by themselves.

The fifth prodigy is that not only the Body of Jesus Christ is under the appearance of bread and wine, but that Jesus Christ, true God and true man, is entire there, such as He is in heaven. So that the Blood of Jesus Christ, His sacred soul and His divinity, are conjointly with His body in the host under the species of bread; and His Body, His soul, and His divinity are also conjointly with His Blood in the chalice under the appearance of wine. But as divines observe, all these things are not in the Eucharist after the same manner. For some are there by virtue of the words of consecration, and others by way of concomitance. Those that are there by virtue of the words of consecration, are those which are expressed by the same words; hence there is only the Body of Jesus Christ in the host, and in the chalice only His Blood, because the words of consecration properly produce only what they signify, and they signify nothing else than: "This is my body, this is my blood."

The things that are in the Eucharist by way of concomitance, are those which are necessarily joined or united to that which is expressed by the words of consecration. For when divers things are necessarily joined together, it is necessary that where the one is, there the other should be also. Now at present the Body of Jesus Christ is not separated from His Blood, but is united with it as well as with His soul and divinity; therefore His Blood, His soul, and His divinity are also in the host with the Body. In like manner His Blood is not at present separated from His Body, but united with it and with His soul and His divinity; hence His body and soul and divinity are likewise in the chalice.

In order the better to understand this, divines say that, had St. Peter or any other of the Apostles consecrated during the three days that our Lord remained in the sepulchre, the soul of Jesus Christ would not have been in the host, because His soul was then in Limbo, and was not united with His Body; so that then there would have been in the host only the dead Body of our Lord, such as it was in the sepulchre, united, however, to the divinity from which it was inseparable.

In like manner, when Jesus Christ Himself had consecrated at His Last Supper, He was in the Eucharist true God and true man, but passible and mortal as He was at that time. Since His resurrection from the dead, however,

He is in the Blessed Sacrament, such as He is now in heaven —glorious, impassible, immortal.

The sixth prodigy wrought in the Blessed Sacrament is, that Jesus Christ is not only whole and entire in each host, whole and entire in the chalice, but He is also whole and entire in each particle of the host as He is whole and entire in the least species of wine. This is a truth which we read in the Gospel. For at the Last Supper Jesus Christ did not consecrate separately each piece of bread with which He communicated His Apostles; He only consecrated at once such a quantity of bread as was necessary to communicate all of them after it was divided. The Gospel, speaking of the consecration of the chalice, expressly takes notice that Jesus Christ gave it to His Apostles, saying to them: "Take and divide it amongst you,"* so that every Apostle receiving a portion of the consecrated bread and wine, received our Lord whole and entire under each species.

Finally, it is a great miracle that when the priest breaks the host or divides the chalice, it is not Christ Who is broken or divided. He always remaining as He does whole and entire in each part how little soever it may be; it is the species or appearance of bread and wine which is broken or divided.

This is what the Church teaches us in the hymn of the Blessed Sacrament, "He who receives the body of Christ does not bruise it, does not break it, does not divide it; he receives it whole and entire, he makes no division of it; he makes only a separation of the signs and accidents." "O illusion of the senses," exclaims St. Jerome; "the accidents with which Thou appearest to our senses to be clothed, are broken, but Thou, O Lord, remainest whole and entire. It seems to our senses that we chew Thee between our teeth, but we never do so to Thee. Thou remainest always whole and entire without any division, without any corruption, in

---

* Luke xxii. 17.

even the least particle."* Who can conceive the power manifested in the august sacrament in such a variety of ways! Thousands of places holding the sacred Body at the same time; God in one host the same as in a million; God in a million of hearts each moment, and two millions, and ten, and a hundred! God consoling and inspiring, and gently leading all these millions of hearts by various ways, all equally wonderful, and all at the same time. Whole and perfect under each morsel, as whole and perfect under a large mass, when once the mass has been divided; so that like the manna of which no more than a certain measure remained, no matter how much a person might have collected, the Christian has as much under the smallest particle as if the largest quantity were accumulated:—he has Christ the Lord. On thousands of altars, from the rising to the setting of the sun, and with perpetuity divine, day and night, all over the universe, offered up each instant and still in the glory of heaven! Hearing millions upon millions of prayers, and granting millions upon millions of petitions at the same time, of characters millions of times varying, through the length and breadth of the earth and of all time, and all for us! Doing what He pleases with His Body, putting it as He does in this sacramental state and concealing it under the species of bread and wine miraculously detached from their subject, but also at the same time sustained by a continued miracle!

Well may we exclaim here with the psalmist, "Who shall declare the power of the Lord?" † Who shall set forth all the wonders of His works? The Blessed Eucharist is truly the memorial of His wonderful works!

This power, this majesty, this all comprehending mystery, tells us in the midst of life's storms to "fear not!" in the midst of temptations, "I am here!" In the midst of doubts, difficulties, hesitations and depressions which surround His

---

* 4. Apud Euseb.   † Ps. cv. 2.

children, this memorial of power points to the altar saying, "I am with Thee all days even to the consummation of the world."

I will leave my children nothing to desire, Our dear Lord at the grand moment thought, I will leave all riches, all dignities, all felicity at their command. I will so accommodate the blessing to their capacity and their will, that their own desire shall regulate the number and the amount of the gifts. Neither shall they be limited in number, quality, or kind: they shall comprehend all things. They shall be all poured into the bosom of my beloved, for I will give gifts to men. And they shall have power of sending the wealth which I bestow to the remotest parts of the earth, to heaven and to purgatory. For them that wealth shall be sent all around the world, and pass even the confines of eternity. My children shall rule a royal priesthood, so that nothing shall draw them away from me, and we shall be one. And well we know how truly efficacious that same Presence has been. In dangers omniscient; in conflict omnipotent, it has been the real Emanuel through all the history of the world.

"All good shall come together with me to her." Our oneness and affection shall grow from never-ceasing communion. I will await her day and night. All I am, that she can desire or command, she may. For herself, for her friends, her cares, her needs,—for all she can employ me. She may offer me every day, she may command the repetition of my sacrifice on Calvary and make me the representative of her claims for anything that is not evil. She may offer up the blood, speaking better than that of Abel, and make the infinite ransom become ever repeated for her sins, and to attune her graces, until her soul becomes luminous with celestial light, and more powerful than embattled legions with the energy and arms of virtue. Nay, she may make that sacrifice her own for the far away, the erring, the unhappy, and the insecure. She may compass the whole world in her wishes, and have these wishes realized, and may even carry her power beyond the grave, and help the souls who are dear to her, and who suffer in the fire of Purgatory.

May Jesus in the Blessed Sacrament, all powerful and all wonderful, be praised for ever!

CHAPTER XVIII.

MASS, THE RENEWAL OF CHRIST'S PASSION.

AFTER our Saviour had fulfilled the office of teacher, He entered upon that of Priest and Victim; and as He had given us the treasure of His doctrine in pointing out the way of salvation, in like manner He wished to give us that of His blood to open the gate of heaven. St. Paulinus says: "He is Himself the Victim of His Priesthood, His life is the Victim of the world, and the Priest who immolates is His own love." Although Christ's love for us was the principal cause of the sacrifice of the Cross, yet the envy and hatred of His enemies and executioners had a share in it; but in the Mass *it is love alone that does all.*

In the Old Law it was God Himself who prescribed the sacred rites for the offering of sacrifices. It was very fatiguing to the priest to perform the whole of them. But how hard were the rites which the Heavenly Father prescribed for His Son when He was about to offer up His life in sacrifice for the atonement for our sins, and for the reparation of His honor and glory!

The simple narration of the frightful scenes of suffering through which our Saviour, the Lamb of God and the Victim of the Divine Vengeance, had to pass from the moment when He went forth with His Apostles to the Garden of Olives, until He expired upon the Cross, cannot fail to leave a most wholesome impression on the heart, and enable us the better to understand the value and dignity of the Mass, which is principally the commemoration of the Passion and Death of our dear Saviour. Let us accompany our Lord as He leaves His loving followers, and proceeds, unattended, to a solitary spot a little distance from them. There we behold Him voluntarily abandoning His sacred soul to the terrible impressions of excessive terror and oppressive sadness, and in His overwhelming anguish having recourse to prayer as His only refuge. We behold Him there prostrate on the earth, whence with profound respect and perfect resignation He sends up to heaven the piteous cry: "My Father, if it be possible, let this chalice pass from Me. Nevertheless, not as I will, but as Thou wilt."* It is thus that He expresses His voluntary acceptance of death. He had, no doubt, consented at the first moment of His Incarnation to die for us, but it pleased Him to ratify that consent in the solitude of the Garden of Olives, and to oblige the inferior part of His soul to concur in the great act of submission, notwithstanding all its natural repugnances. Representing to Himself His approaching death, with all its accompanying circumstances of horror, He permitted the inferior portion of His human nature to oppose the noble sacrifice, and to supplicate the Eternal Father, that the chalice might, if possible, pass away untasted; the superior part immediately manifesting its unshaken conformity to the divine decree by adding, "yet not My will, but Thine be done."

Amidst the conflict between the inferior portion, which shrunk from the dreadful death awaiting Him, and the superior part, which desired it for the reparation of God's glory and honor, an angel came from heaven to encourage the agonized Redeemer, representing to Him with profound respect the glory which would redound to His Father, and the blessings which would accrue to men from His all-saving sacrifice on the Cross. And then Jesus, passing once again in review each separate torment that awaited Him, accepted them all with most profound and reverential submission to the will of His Almighty Father, saying: "Yes, Father, I consent to be seized and bound as a malefactor, struck,

---

* Matt. xxvi. 89.

scourged, crowned with thorns, and crucified, since so it has seemed good in Thy sight." So ardent and so impetuous was the love which accompanied this act of acceptance that it reacted physically on His frame. The blood which terror had congealed around His heart, rushed through His veins, and forced its way through the pores of His sacred flesh, pouring itself out freely even before the barbarous executioners had bidden it to flow. Then, rising from His couch of agony, the generous Saviour of men entered bravely on the arena of His Passion by delivering Himself up of His own accord to the soldiers who had come to seize and bind Him.

The soldiers, who had witnessed or heard of Christ's miracles, thinking Him a magician, feared lest He should escape from their hands; therefore, they bound strongly His sides, arms, and neck with two long ropes and a heavy chain which had been used to open and close the prison-gate. At the end of this chain were manacles, wherewith they fastened His hands behind.

After binding Him thus cruelly, they set out from Mount Olivet with great noise and tumult, some dragging Him forward, others backward, so that He was cast violently to the ground. They vented their rage by inflicting blows on His face, head, and body. They tore His garments, plucked His beard, dragged Him by the hair, and forced the points of their sticks into His sides, struck Him on His shoulders, and dragged Him from one side of the street to the other. The Lord fell many times, striking His face against the ground with great pain, having His hands chained behind His back, His divine face becoming covered with wounds.

Thus they arrived in the city, uttering cries and execrations, as if they had arrested the chief of malefactors. The people rushed to the windows and doors with lights; they loaded our Blessed Lord with insults, injuries, and opprobrium, calling Him a false prophet, a deceiver, a wicked man, a robber, and a perverter of the people. They conducted Him to the tribunal of Annas. It was there that

Jesus received on His virginal face that cruel blow from the ungrateful barbarous hand of the servant whose ear He had miraculously restored in the garden of Gethsemane. So cruel was this blow that it broke all His teeth, and caused the blood to flow profusely from His eyes, nose, and mouth.

Sometime after midnight it was decided by the council that while they would retire to rest, Jesus should be thrown, bound as He was, into a dungeon, used for great robbers and murderers, so obscure that scarcely a ray of light could penetrate its darkness, and so loathsome as to be insupportable. Thither they dragged the Son of God by the cords and chains with which they had bound Him in the garden. There they chained Him in such a manner that He could neither lie nor sit. In going out they left one of their number on guard.

After the infuriated and intoxicated rabble had taken some refreshment, being excited by the devil, they hastened to the prison, where they unbound Jesus from the rock to which He was fastened, and placed Him in the middle of the apartment. They would fain have forced Him to speak and work some miracles; but the Incarnate Wisdom answered them not. They renewed their insults and outrages, and blindfolded Him with filthy rags. Striking Him violently on the neck and face, they cried out in derision: "Prophesy who it is that struck Thee."

At dawn of day, the priests and scribes assembled together, and the Divine Lamb was again led before them. It was a sight most worthy of compassion, to behold that innocent Victim with His face all bruised, disfigured, and defiled, without a merciful hand to wipe it, for His own were bound. Seeing Him in such a deplorable condition, even His enemies were startled. They again designedly asked Him whether He were the Son of God, and on His replying that He was, they cried out that He was worthy of death, and sent Him to Pilate, the Roman Proconsul—for whom all capital cases were reserved.

When the Jews arrived at the house of Pilate, he, although a Pagan, had regard to the ceremonial law, which forbade them to enter the prætorium; therefore he came out to interrogate the pretended criminal.

Finding that Jesus had been born in the jurisdiction of Herod, he sent Him to Herod. It is impossible to relate all that Jesus had to undergo from His enemies in this journey from Pilate to Herod, for they were continually excited by Lucifer to further outrages, in the hope that they might be able to learn if He were truly the Messiah. Herod had our Lord clothed in the robe of mockery, and then reconducted to Pilate. In this painful journey it happened many times that, by the pressure of the crowd, and the violence of those who dragged Him, Jesus was thrown upon the ground. His veins were opened by the fall and by the blows He received, for He could not rise because His hands were chained behind.

He was taken back to Pilate, who, seeing His innocence, and the envy and hatred of the Jews, tried to deliver Him. But finding that all his endeavors failed, he thought to have Him scourged, in the hope that the Jews might think such punishment sufficient, and allow Him to go free.

For the scourging they chose six young men remarkable for their strength and barbarous cruelty. They led Jesus into the court, where there was a pillar, and removed the handcuffs, chains, and cords. They tore off His garments, leaving Him almost entirely naked.

So tightly was He bound to the pillar, that the cords entered into the flesh, and His divine hands became much swollen. Afterwards they began to scourge Him, two at a time, with a cruelty of which mere human ferocity was not capable, but Lucifer had entered into the hearts of the executioners. The first two scourged the innocent Jesus with large twisted cords, exerting their utmost violence and greatest fury upon Him. The first blow that fell upon His delicate body inflicted large livid bruises, which swelled to a frightful extent, and seemed as if the blood was about to burst from them.

When these cruel men were exhausted from fatigue, they were succeeded by the second two, who, using heavy leather thongs, broke the flesh of the bruises inflicted by the first, so that the precious blood not only covered the body of Jesus, but also saturated the garments of the sacrilegious murderers, and fell upon the ground.

When exhausted, they were succeeded by a third party, who used as their instruments of torture the sinews of beasts, which were very hard and dry, resembling dried twigs. Their blows being repeated over the wounds inflicted by the first and second executioners, caused Jesus the most intense agony. But as His body was become one entire wound, they could no longer inflict new wounds; their blows therefore, falling on His sacred flesh, tore out pieces, which fell to the ground, and in many places left the bones exposed to sight. Not content with this, they satiated their cruelty by striking Him on the face, hands, and feet, and sparing no part of His body. So bruised, torn, and disfigured was the countenance of the Lord, as to be no longer recognizable.

But anxious to see Him die on the Cross, the Jews unbound Jesus from the pillar, and He sank to the ground bathed in His blood. They ordered Him to put on His garments, but one of the wicked wretches had hidden His seamless robe; therefore, while He remained there naked, they reviled and mocked Him. Some of them, going to Pilate, said, that as Jesus pretended to be the King of the Jews, it would be but just to crown Him with thorns. Having obtained His permission, they took Jesus, threw over His shoulders an old purple cloak, placed in His hand a reed for a sceptre, and violently pressed on His divine head the crown of thorns.

This crown was made of very long and sharp thorns, which, being pressed on, many penetrated the bones of the head, others came out at His ears and eyes.

After this ignominious and cruel ceremony, they adored as mock King Him, who, by nature and every title, was the King of kings, the Lord of lords. The soldiers set Him in their midst, and in presence of the priests and Pharisees loaded Him with injuries and blasphemies, while some, bending the knee before Him, cried out in mockery: "Hail, King of the Jews." Others struck Him violently on the face; others, taking the reed, struck Him on the head; others, again, defiled His countenance with spittle, while all conspired to load Him with injuries and blasphemies.

When sentence of death had been pronounced against Jesus of Nazareth, the soldiers drew Him aside, tore off the robe of mockery, and vested Him in His own tunic, that He might be the better known, and on His head they again pressed the thorny crown. The city was thronged with strangers who had come to celebrate the Pasch, and the streets leading to Pilate's house were filled, as all desired to know what was transpiring.

When Jesus was dragged into the midst of the crowd, a confused murmur arose amongst them, but nothing could be plainly heard save the insolent expressions of joy and blasphemy of the priests and Pharisees.

In presence of an immense crowd the executioners presented the Cross to Jesus, and laid it on His shoulders, all torn and covered with wounds, and that He might be able to carry it, they untied His hands, but did not remove the other bonds. They put a chain around His neck and bound His body with long cords; with one they dragged Him forward, with another backward. The Cross was of very heavy wood and fifteen feet in length.

The herald advanced first with sound of trumpet to publish the sentence; then followed the noisy and clamorous multitude, the executioners and soldiers uttering railleries, taunts, laughter, and cries of opprobrium; and thus in tumultuous disorder they traversed the streets of Jerusalem, from the palace of Pilate to Mount Calvary.

Our Lord continued His sorrowful way amid a thousand injuries. Many times He fell to the earth because they dragged Him this way and that, and because He was loaded with the heavy weight of the Cross. In those falls He received new and numerous wounds, which caused Him great pain, particularly those in His knees, and the load of the Cross made a deep wound on the shoulders. By dragging Him violently, they frequently struck His head against the Cross, and each blow forced the thorns deeper in, causing Him intenser suffering still.

The soldiers, seeing Jesus so weak and faint, and fearing that He would die on the way to Calvary, forced Simon of Cyrene to come to His aid; and at length the new Isaac arrived at the mount of sacrifice, spent with fatigue, faint from pain, and covered with blood.

All the sorrows of the Redeemer were renewed when His seamless robe, which clung to all His wounds, was violently torn from His body. They dragged it over His head, without removing the crown of thorns, and by this violence pulled it off with His garment, thus renewing all the wounds of His sacred head. Then they again fastened and pressed on the crown of thorns.

While the executioners were preparing to crucify Him, He prayed to the Eternal Father for the whole race of men, and for those about to crucify Him. They threw Him violently down upon the Cross, while He, raising His eyes to heaven, extended His arms and placed His right hand upon the hole. He offered Himself anew to the Eternal Father, and then they fastened His all-powerful hand with a large, pointed nail, which burst the veins and tore the sinews. The left hand could not reach the second hole on account of the contraction of the sinews, and also because they had purposely made the hole at too great a distance. Therefore they took the chain which had been fastened around His neck, and fastening it to the manacle of His wrist, stretched the arm and nailed it. The blood burst forth and flowed abundantly, causing incredible suffering to our Lord.

Attaching the chain to His feet they bound them together, one upon the other, and dragging them with great violence, nailed them with a third nail, larger and stronger than the other two. The Sacred Body was thus nailed on the Cross, but in such a state that all the bones might be counted, for they were entirely dislocated and dragged out of place. Those of the breast, shoulders, and limbs, were entirely disjointed by the cruel violence of the executioners.

After having nailed our Lord to the Cross, those monsters of cruelty began to fear that the nails would be loosened and the body fall to the ground; therefore they determined to prevent it. Raising the Cross, they turned it over in such a manner that our Saviour lay upon His face on the ground, and whilst He was in this position, they clinched the nails. At the sight of this new excess of barbarity the beholders shuddered, and many of the crowd, being excited, raised a tumult.

After the nails had been clinched, they raised the Cross, and let it fall into the hole in which it was to stand. Then those cruel wretches supported the body with their lances, making deep wounds under the arms, and thrusting the points into the flesh, whilst the others planted the Cross. At this painful sight the cries of the people were redoubled, and a still greater tumult was raised. The Jews blasphemed Him, the devout compassionated Him, and strangers were overwhelmed with astonishment. Many dared not look at Him for the horror that they felt. The sacred blood was gushing forth from the new wounds, and from those that were reopened.

The priests and Pharisees wagged their heads in mockery, and throwing dirt and stones at Him, cried out, "Thou who canst destroy the temple of God and in three days rebuild it, save Thyself." The thieves also insulted Him, saying, "If Thou art the Son of God, save Thyself and us."

Then the earth shook, the sun was eclipsed, the moon darkened, and the elements were thrown into disorder, the mountains burst asunder, the veil of the temple was rent, the graves opened and the dead arose. The executioners departed, groaning and contrite, because Jesus, in His agony, had, with excessive charity, offered the prayer, "Father, forgive them, for they know not what they do."

One of the thieves, called Dismas, hearing these words, was interiorly enlightened and filled with sorrow for his sins; he begged pardon of our Lord and received more than he asked, for our Saviour promised him, that on that very day he should be with Him in Paradise.

Jesus, being ready to give up His Spirit, reflects on all the labors, humiliations, opprobriums, and torments which Divine Justice had ordained Him to suffer in expiation of our crimes; and commencing from the moment of His entrance into the world until this in which He is going forth from it, He finds that the work of Redemption is consummated. He reflects on the work His Father had given Him. He considers all the actions of His life, with all the charges that had been committed to Him. He looks upon that of Mediator, Redeemer, Doctor, Legislator, Sovereign, Pontiff, Guide to eternity, and finds that all is consummated. He has preached the Gospel, and traced a model of every virtue. All is consummated.

He reflects on all the benefits He desired to confer on mankind in the course of His life, and finds He has spared nothing in his favor. "It is consummated." His blood, His strength, His merits are exhausted; He has not reserved a single moment of His life which He has not given us. Already a mortal paleness overspreads His countenance, His body grows cold, His eyes close, His lips fade; yet one sigh, and His soul goes forth and descends into Limbo. He languishes, He dies, He is dead! All is consummated!

CHAPTER XIX.

MASS, THE RENEWAL OF CHRIST'S PASSION—CONTINUED.

IN the preceding chapter, we have seen how the great sacrifice of atonement was accomplished. Let us now see how it is daily commemorated and renewed upon our altars, in the holy sacrifice of the Mass. Our divine Saviour wished that Mass should be, in a particular manner, the commemoration of His Passion and Death. His Passion and Death constituted the solemn crowning act of the great work of our Redemption. By this act was wrought our Redemption, and in it all the other acts of our Saviour's life were solemnly stamped by the seal of sacrifice. Our dear Lord, therefore, wished that this last act of His life should stand out forever before our minds in the most vivid manner. He wished the all-redeeming sacrifice of Mount Calvary to be offered daily until the end of the world, that its oblation should not be restricted to one particular period, nor to one particular place. He wished that in every land and clime, at every hour, from the rising of the sun to its going down, on every Catholic altar within the globe's circumference, His precious blood should mystically flow, His all-sufficient expiation should be renewed, and His all-pure holocaust should be consumed. This He Himself expressed most emphatically to be His will. After He had ordained His Apostles Priests of the New Law, and empowered and commanded them and their lawful successors in the ministry to consecrate and offer up the Blessed Eucharist for a perpetual commemoration of His Passion, and a grateful remembrance of His Death; He added these remarkable words," Do this in remembrance of Me;" that is, as St. Paul explains it, " to show forth the Death of

the Lord till His second coming at the end of the world." *
Such is the last will of our dear Saviour; He asks but one
thing, that having suffered and died for us, we should fondly cherish the memory of this ineffable benefit, especially by
the means of the holy Mass. It was for this purpose particularly that He made a separate consecration of the
chalice.

He might have instituted this holy sacrifice of the Mass,
by offering Himself under the appearance of bread alone,
saying, "This is My body and My blood," and the bread
would have been changed into His body and His blood. But
in this manner His Death would not have been so vividly
represented as it is by the separate consecration of the chalice
of wine into His blood, representing the separation of His
blood from His body, by which separation His Death was
caused. Thus does our Saviour perform in each Mass another
most astounding miracle, to place before our soul in a most
vivid manner His cruel Death upon the Cross, that we may
be reminded thereby of His love manifested in His sufferings and Death, and excited to love and serve Him with
more fervor, lest we be guilty of an ingratitude similar to
that of the Jews, "who forgot the God who had saved them." †
"The sacrifice of the Mass" therefore, says the Council of
Trent, "is the same as that which heretofore was offered
upon the Cross; it is the same victim, for He who offered
Himself then, is the same who daily offers Himself by the
hands of the priest; it is only the manner of offering which
is different." And the difference consists in this,—that the
sacrifice of the Cross was a bloody one; for then Jesus
Christ was passible and mortal; and what is now daily offered upon our altars is unbloody; because " Jesus Christ
being raised from death, can die no more, and death has
now no more power or dominion over Him." ‡ "Now the
Saviour of the world," says the Council, "having offered

Himself a sacrifice for us upon the Cross, was not content that this sacrifice should end there; but because He was a priest forever, He ordained that this sacrifice should forever continue in the Church as a most real and lively representation and renewal of His Passion and Death."

On the altar our Saviour Jesus Christ is really exhibited to His Eternal Father under the two separate species, without any visible sign of life, motion, or action, and under the figure and appearance of death, as if He were really dead, according to what was shown to St. John in the Apocalypse, when he said, "I saw a Lamb standing as it were slain," or under the appearance of being slain. It is true, Jesus, immortal and impassible as He is, can suffer and die no more; yet, as regards the effects to us, it is as if He really did bleed, agonize, and expire again each time He is immolated on the altar. His sufferings are not renewed in themselves; but in their fruits they are renewed for us, and applied to each soul separately and individually. What the sacrifice of Calvary did for the whole human race, one Mass can do for the one who assists at it with the requisite dispositions, who approaches the altar with humility, contrition, and sincere renunciation of sin. The blood which flowed on the Cross to ransom the world, will flow on the soul of such an one to wash away its defilements, to heal its wounds, to enhance its beauty, and strengthen its weakness; for "The sacrifice of the Mass," says St. John Chrysostom, "being but the application and repetition of the sacrifice of the Cross, is as efficacious as the sacrifice of Calvary for the good and salvation of men."* Hence the magnificent consequence drawn by this holy father of the Church: "A Mass is equivalent to the sacrifice of the Cross."† "Since, therefore," he continues, "we are about to behold Him who was nailed to the Cross, Him who as a lamb was slain and sac-

---

* In Cap. vi. Isaias.
† Apud Discip. Serm. 48.

rificed, let us approach with trembling, and much reverence and piety. Know you not how angels stood by the sepulchre which held not His body, stood by the empty tomb? Now we are going to stand, not at an empty tomb, but at the very table (altar) which holds that Lamb, and shall we approach tumultuously and disorderly? What dost thou, O man? When the priest stands before the altar with his hands stretched out toward heaven, invoking that Holy Spirit to come and to touch the things that lie to open view; when thou beholdest the Lamb slain and consummated, is that the time that thou introducest tumult, confusion, contention, and wrangling?

"Tell me why art thou hurried? for whose sake art thou in haste, beholding as thou dost the Lamb slain? For even if thou wert to gaze upon that sacrifice during the whole night, is that a thing of which to grow weary? Reflect what that is which lies before thee, and for what purpose it is lying there.

"He was slain for thee, and though thou beholdest Him slain, yet thou abandonest Him. Where the body is, there are also the eagles. But we approach not as eagles, but as dogs; such is our effrontery. Reflect what that is which is poured out. It is blood, that very blood which blotted out the handwriting of our sins; that blood which cleansed thy soul, which washed away its stain, which triumphed over principalities and powers." *

"None of those things, therefore, that take place in this sanctuary, is from man. Though it be man that stands at this sacred table, and offers up this tremendous sacrifice, yet is it God that operates through him. Wherefore attend not to his nature that is visible to thee, but rather fix thy mind on what is invisible."†

Were we only as enlightened in regard to the holy Mass

---

* Colos. ii. 15 ; T. ii. De Cœmeterio et de cruce, n. 3, p. 473.
† T. ii. Hom. i. de Sanct. Pentec. n. 4, p. 548.

as St. John Chrysostom and other saints; were our faith only as lively as theirs, assuredly, we should then see at a glance how Mass is, by excellence, the commemoration of the Passion and Death of our Lord; that to assist at it is to be on Mount Calvary with Mary, the blessed Mother of our Saviour, with St. John, and St. Mary Magdalen, witnessing the Passion and Death of Jesus Christ upon the Cross. It was for this very reason that the hearts of the saints, whilst at Mass, overflowed with sentiments of compassion for our Lord; of gratitude and love for His infinite charity, and of sorrow and contrition for their own sins.

In the life of St. William, Archbishop of Bourges, we are told that whilst celebrating Mass, this holy prelate was touched with deep, heartfelt sorrow for his sins—a sorrow that made him shed torrents of indescribably sweet tears. He used to say, "If I consider during the Mass that Jesus Christ offers Himself upon the altar as a victim to His Father, I feel as deeply penetrated with sorrow as if I saw Him with my own eyes hanging upon the Cross, and shedding His sacred blood for my sins."

St. Ignatius of Loyola was obliged to allow a day to intervene between his offering of the holy mysteries, which arose from the force of the impressions produced upon him each time he said Mass. From the extreme consolation which he experienced in the heavenly moment in which he possessed his God at Mass, he shed torrents of tears, a circumstance which drew the following remark one day from a man who witnessed it, and who assuredly knew but little of the gift of God: "That priest must be a great sinner; he does nothing but weep when he says Mass and receives Communion."

The life of St. Coleta, of the Order of St. Clare, was always holy and innocent from her very infancy. God bestowed upon her most extraordinary favors. Yet, when at Mass, she used to shed abundant tears over her sins. She often went to confession before Mass, in order to assist at the holy sacrifice with greater purity of conscience.

Some of the saints, when at Mass, imagined that they applied their mouths, as it were, to the precious wound of our Saviour's side, drank His blood, and participated in all the graces He had gained for us by the merits of His sufferings and Death. Others, at the time of Mass, represented to themselves our Saviour crucified, and planting His Cross in their hearts, as it was upon Mount Calvary, and casting themselves at the foot thereof, they gathered up with their lips all those drops of blood that fell from it. Now, these are not only holy thoughts, such as a meditation furnishes, but they are real truths taught by faith, for Mass is a real commemoration of the sufferings and death of our Lord, as is clearly signified by the words of our Saviour, "Take and drink ye all of this, for this is the chalice of My blood of the new and eternal Testament, which shall be shed for you, and for many, to the remission of sins."

Since it is Jesus Christ Himself who tells us that the Sacrifice of the Mass is the solemn commemoration of His Passion and Death, since the same truth is asserted by St. Paul the Apostle, and since this doctrine has been taught and firmly believed by the Catholic Church from the beginning, we need no particular miracles to confirm us in this belief. However, our dear Lord, in His goodness, has often been pleased to manifest Himself in the Mass as if in a state of suffering, bleeding and dying, in order to encourage the just in their resolution to serve Him faithfully, and the wicked in endeavoring to lead a better life.

Cæsarius of Heisterbach, who protests in his book that he has written nothing which he did not see himself, or hear he took it and kissed it, and experienced an unspeakable joy. After a little while, our Lord again assumed the form of the Host, and the priest finished Mass with unusual devotion. Soon after he fell dangerously ill. Before he died he revealed the wonderful vision to the superior of the convent, who related it to a certain parish priest, named Adolph of Deiseren. On hearing it, this priest was struck with great amazement and exclaimed with a deep sigh, "Why is it that God shows these wonderful things to His saints, who, without them, are perfect in faith? Why does He not show these things to me and other poor sinners, who are so easily inclined to doubt the truth of this sacrament?" One day Father Adolph took the sacred Host at Mass to divide it in two, when he beheld the Infant Jesus looking at him with a most gracious smile; but soon after the Divine Infant appeared in the state in which He was when hanging on the Cross, inclining His head as if about to die. At this touching sight Father Adolph commenced to shed bitter tears; he could hardly breathe, and almost fainted away. He beheld our Lord in a dying condition for a considerable time, and felt extremely perplexed, not knowing what to do. The people, too, were at a loss what to think of the priest, being so long in saying Mass and shedding so many tears. At last our dear Saviour assumed again the form of the Host, to enable him to finish Mass. After Mass he ascended the pulpit and related to those who were in the church the wonderful things he had seen on the altar. Now, when he tried to explain to them the dying condition in which he had seen our Lord, he felt so much overcome by the emotions of his heart that he could not utter a word; he did nothing but sob and weep. He left the pulpit and spent several days in shedding tears of repentance and in meditating upon the Passion and Death of our Lord. From that time he commenced to lead a retired and truly penitential life.*

---

* Lib. de illust. miraculis et historiis.

The holy Mass may also be called a commemoration of the Passion and Death of our Lord, because He constantly receives, in this august sacrament, insults similar to those which He had to undergo in the course of His Passion, and which He bears in the same manner in which He bore those that He suffered from Maundy Thursday until He expired on the Cross. Jesus, the Eternal Son of God, is mocked, not only by the most insolent of men—by the dregs of the people, in the house of Caiphas, and by the vile soldiery at the tribunal of Pilate; but also by Herod in his palace, by the scribes and priests upon Mount Calvary, in order that it might be believed that contempt was due Him, since the little and the great, the ignorant and the learned, the civil and the ecclesiastical powers united to insult His majesty, His sanctity, and His dignity. They blindfolded Him and gave Him blows, and yet He was silent; they beat Him with rods, and they tore out His hair, and He was silent; they spat in His face and insulted Him in a thousand other ways, and He was silent; He is treated as a mock-king and as a fool; He is chained like a ferocious beast, and cast into the mire like a vile slave; and He is silent. Oh, prodigy of humility and patience!

Similar insults have been offered to our dear Saviour in the holy Sacrifice of the Mass—in His sacrament of love, for more than eighteen hundred years, and will be offered to Him to the end of the world. He has been insulted by bad, unworthy priests, who have treated Him more shamefully than Judas did; He has been insulted by thousands of unworthy communicants, who have forced Him to enter their hearts, which were the abode of the devil; He has been insulted thousands of times by Jews and heretics, who have taken the sacred Hosts and thrown them into the foulest places or have treated them in the most shocking manner; and our dear Lord is silent and bears all these insults with the greatest patience. Although His sacred Body in its

Heart is not less sensitive to the injuries and ignominies it receives.

Among the miraculous Hosts preserved in different churches is that of St. Jean-en-Grève at Paris, the history of which is most authentic.

A poor woman, who had need of money, borrowed a small sum from a Jewish usurer, giving him in pledge all she had best in clothes and linen. The feast of Easter approaching, she entreated him to lend her, at least for that great day, what she had pawned him. "I will willingly do so," said he, "and I will even release you from the whole sum I lent you, if you promise to bring me the Host you will receive in Communion." The desire of having her clothes again, and not being obliged to repay the sum borrowed, proved a temptation which the unhappy woman could not resist. She promised to bring him the Host, and kept her promise. On the morrow she went to her parish church, and after receiving the sacred Host into her mouth, she hastened to take it out again, wrapped it in a handkerchief, and brought it to the wretched Jew to whom she had promised it. It was for the purpose of gratifying his hatred against our Lord that this man wanted to have a Host; he treated it with the greatest indignity, and Jesus Christ constantly showed him how sensible He was to the outrages offered Him. The Jew first put the Host upon the table, and struck it repeatedly with a penknife; blood immediately flowed from it in abundance, which caused the man's wife and children to shudder with horror. He nailed it to a wall and brutally struck it; then he pierced it with a lance, to renew, if possible, the frightful torments of our Lord's Passion. The Host shed blood anew, as though to prove to the execrable wretch that it was not merely material bread. He threw it into the fire, and it was seen flying here and there without receiving any injury. The infernal rage that animated the Jew led him to throw it into a pot

Host then appeared visibly under the form of Christ crucified. This sight so terrified the deicide that he went to hide himself in a dark corner of his house. But it was not long before his crime was discovered, and the discovery came about this wise:

One of his children, seeing people going to church, cried out simply: "Do not go to church any more to seek your God; don't you know my father killed him?" A woman hearing what the child said, entered the house under the pretext of asking for some fire, and she saw the Host, which was still under the form of Jesus on the Cross; but it soon resumed its former shape, and came to repose in the little vessel which the woman had in her hand. All amazed, she carried her treasure religiously to the church of St. Jean-en-Grève. Information was given to the magistrate. The Jew, nowise sorry for his fault, was condemned to be burned alive; but his wife, his children, and many other Jews were converted.

The house wherein our Lord showed that He is really in the Blessed Sacrament was changed into a church, and in course of time it was served by Carmelite monks. The religious who inhabited it were charged with repairing, by a perpetual adoration, the outrages offered to Jesus Christ in the sacrament of His love. This sad event took place in 1250.*

It is thus that the holy sacrifice of the Mass brings to our mind the Passion and Death of our Lord in the most impressive manner; it reminds us constantly of the cause of His unheard-of sufferings and cruel Death. We see, indeed, the sad effect of sin everywhere; but nowhere does it appear more fearfully than on Mount Calvary, and upon our altars during the holy sacrifice of Mass. Jesus suffered and died because we had sinned. To love sin, therefore, to continue to commit it, is to renew the Passion and Death of Jesus

---

* Lassausse, Exampl. du Cat. de l'Empire, 498.

Christ. As often as a mortal sin is committed, Jesus is crucified anew. The ever-blessed Son of God became man to take away the sins of the world. All the actions and all the sufferings of Jesus Christ were directed to this one end—to destroy sin. This was the object of all His thoughts, all His words, all His actions. This was the object of all His hardships, His labors, His life, and His death. Whosoever then commits a mortal sin, destroys, as far as in him lies, all the efforts and labors of Jesus Christ; he brings to naught the work of redemption. By his actions, if not by his words, he says clearly: Christ came on earth to destroy sin, and I, in spite of Christ, will cause sin to exist anew. Jesus in His Passion wished to honor His heavenly Father, and I, by my sins, will renew the Passion of Jesus Christ and dishonor God the Father.

By His death, Christ closed the gates of hell, but I, by my sins, will open them once more. Christ has opened heaven to me by His blood, but I, by my sins, will cause the gate of heaven to be closed against me.

Yes, whoever sins opposes Jesus Christ, and in his own person renders useless all His labors, His life, and His death. As often as we sin, we trample under foot the Son of God, we despise and dishonor the precious blood of Jesus Christ, we renew His bitter Passion and Death: we crucify Jesus anew. This is no mere figure of speech; it is the simple truth. In the first place, that for which Jesus was crucified is done—a mortal sin is committed. Our divine Saviour has taken upon Himself to atone for all our sins, and had His Death on Mount Calvary not been sufficient to atone for all the sins of the world, He would have to die anew each time that a mortal sin is committed. In the second place, as often as such a sin is committed, a crime is done which is more hateful and dishonorable to Jesus then were all the outrages of His Passion.

For, rather than be offended by a mortal sin, He would prefer to be scourged, to be crowned with thorns, to be mocked, and to be nailed to the Cross. By every mortal sin, then, Jesus is crucified anew in the heart of the sinner. Therein He feels again the scourges, the crown of thorns, the insults and the Cross. The Jews and the Jewish executioners were indeed cruel, hard-hearted, but yet they were not aware that He whom they crucified was the King of Glory, the ever-blessed Son of God; but the sinning Christian knows well that Jesus is the Son of God.

The executioners crucified Jesus but once; but we crucify Him as often as we sin. When the Jews saw that Jesus was dead, they were filled with remorse for their crime, and went away striking their breasts, and imploring God's mercy; but when we sin, we feel no sorrow, we sometimes glory in the wicked deed, and boast of it to others, as a noble exploit. The Jews and executioners of Jesus Christ indeed committed a heinous crime, for they were guilty of the murder of a God; but yet they accomplished thereby the loving designs of Providence, for Jesus was to die that the world might be saved; and amidst all the torments of His bitter Passion, He was consoled by the thought, that by His Death He honored His heavenly Father, closed the gates of hell, opened those of heaven, and saved those immortal souls which were so dear to His heart. But when we crucify Jesus by mortal sin, we open to ourselves the gates of hell, close the gates of heaven, pollute the precious blood of Jesus Christ, horrify the angels, and dishonor the Holy Trinity. So that mortal sin is a greater evil even than that of the Jews and the executioners of Jesus Christ. They were not Christians and friends of our dear Saviour, but His enemies; while we are Christians, friends, disciples of Christ.

Indeed, when an infidel sins, he deserves that a hell of torments should be created for him. On the day of judgment the unbelievers shall be judged by the voice of their conscience, by that law of nature which is inscribed in the heart of every human being; but Christians shall be judged by the very presence of Jesus Christ Himself. "Behold Me," He will say to them, "I am that God in whom you believed; I am that God whom you have outraged and crucified by your sins. Behold My hands and My feet, it is I."

Can there be any one who would have the madness to commit another mortal sin, knowing that Jesus became an object of horror to atone for these sins? Whenever we are tempted hereafter to commit sin, let us call to mind all that Jesus has done and suffered. Behold Him nailed to the Cross, see the streams of blood that flow from His hands and His feet and His blessed side. Behold His sacred head crowned with thorns. Gaze on His Godlike face, all livid with blows and defiled with spittle. Behold His virginal body, all mangled and bleeding. Look upon our good Lord loaded with contempt, while His blessed soul is weighed down with sadness. Consider all the sufferings that God has endured to atone for our sins, and then, if we have the heart, let us commit another mortal sin. When one has had the happiness of being baptized and well instructed in the Christian religion, he should, by right, never more offend Almighty God. There were saints, nay, even poor savages, who so lived. A pious missionary, whose name I have forgotten, was traversing the wildest regions of North America to win souls for Christ; he stopped at the principal villages, and often found there savages whom grace brought to him from a considerable distance. He instructed and baptized those whom he thought well disposed, and then went on his way to other places. A savage one day presented himself to him, whose fervor appeared to be something extraordinary; as soon as he was well instructed in the mysteries of our holy religion, the missionary administered baptism to him, and also gave him Holy Communion, which this good Indian received with the most lively transports of love and gratitude.

The missionary then went off on other apostolic excursions. A year after he returned to the place where dwelt this Indian convert. As soon as the latter was aware of the missionary's arrival, he ran to throw himself at his feet and bathed them with his tears; he knew not how to express the joy he felt in seeing again him who had begotten him to Jesus Christ. He soon entreated the Father to grant him once more the happiness he had made him enjoy the year before.

"Of what happiness do you speak?" asked the missionary. "Ah! my Father, do you not know? the happiness of receiving within me the Body of my God!" "Willingly, my child, but first you must go to confession. Have you examined your conscience well?" "Father, I examined it every day, as you charged me to do last year." "In that case, kneel down, and declare to me the faults you may have fallen into since your baptism?" "What faults, Father?" "Why, the grievous faults you feel you have wilfully committed against the commandments of God and the Church." "Grievous faults," answers the savage all amazed; "can any one offend God after they are baptized, and especially after having received Communion? Are there anywhere Christians capable of such ingratitude?" Saying these words he burst into tears, and the missionary, on his side, wept too, blessing God for having prepared for Himself even in the forests of America such worshippers, who may, indeed, be called worshippers in spirit and in truth.*

If we often consider that Mass is the solemn commemoration and renewal of the sufferings and Death of Jesus Christ upon the Cross, we shall, if possible, be present every day at this holy sacrifice, where the most precious blood of Jesus Christ falls upon the soul like a light dew, refreshing and reviving all that is drooping toward the earth. We shall see at Mass nothing but heaven; our virtue will take deep root; and the odor of a holy life will diffuse itself over our being like that of flowers in spring. All weak though we be, the corruption of sin shall not touch us, who have been pene-

---

* Dubussi Nouv. Mois de Marie, 135.

trated by the strength and the sweetness of the incorruptible Blood of Jesus Christ at Mass. "The statues of sovereigns have often served as asylums to men who flew for refuge to them; not because they were made of brass, but because they represented the persons of princes. In like manner, the blood of the lamb saved the Israelites, not because it was blood, but because it prefigured the blood of the Saviour, and announced His coming. Now, then, if the enemy perceives not the blood of the typical lamb on our doors, but the blood of the true Lamb shining on the souls of the faithful, he will depart farther from us. For if the angel of destruction passed by where he saw the figure, how much more terrified will not the enemy be at beholding the reality." *

---

* St. John Chrysostom.

CHAPTER XX.

MASS, THE RENEWAL OF CHRIST'S RESURRECTION.

Our divine Saviour remained in Limbo with the holy fathers from Friday night until Sunday morning, before dawn, when He came forth from the sepulchre accompanied by holy angels and the souls of the just whom He had redeemed. A great number of the angels kept guard over the holy sepulchre. Some gathered the drops of divine blood and the pieces of sacred flesh torn by the blows, as also everything which related to the integrity of the most holy Humanity. The souls of the holy fathers, on arriving, beheld at first this divine body covered with wounds and disfigured by the outrages and cruelty of the Jews; then the angels reverently replaced the sacred relics which they had gathered together, and at the same instant the most holy soul of the Redeemer reunited itself to the divine body and communicated to it life immortal and glorious.

In the time of His Passion, our divine Saviour had lost the four principal privileges that man may possess. His executioners deprived Him of His clothes, leaving Him in extreme poverty; they deprived Him of all honor by loading Him with the most outrageous contempt; they deprived Him of His health by inflicting upon Him most frightful torments; they deprived Him of His most precious life by inflicting on Him a most cruel death. But in arising from the tomb, He regained all these privileges, added to and multiplied beyond measure. He who before was poor and indigent became the Lord of the Universe. He who but three days before was a "worm of the earth, the opprobrium of men, the outcast of the people," is now crowned with glory and honor, and seated at the right hand of the Most High. He who was before " a man of sorrows and acquainted with infirmity, in whom there was no sound part, from the crown of His head to the sole of His foot," recovered His vigor, becoming victorious over hell and sin. He changes His weakness into power and strength, and the ignominy of His Passion into honor and glory. His body thenceforth shines resplendent for all eternity, endowed with the four qualities of glorified bodies. His countenance is more brilliant than the noon-day sun. He has overthrown in the Red Sea of His Blood " the horse and the rider," that is, the flesh, the world, and the demon.

O blessed day of the resurrection, that restores to us the divine Lamb—the Victim for our sins, whom love had immolated on the altar of the Cross! In His resurrection Jesus Christ restores to us with advantage the gift of the holy sacrifice of Mass. His resurrection is a re-establishment of this adorable mystery in its fullness and perfection. Previous to the Passion He gave His sacred body mortal and passible; after His resurrection He gives It immortal and impassible, such as He is now, seated in Heaven at the right hand of His Father. Not content with having employed His mortal life in laboring for our salvation, He would also in the excess of His charity employ therein His glorified life, and join eternity to time for the work of our sanctification. For this reason Mass is also the commemoration of the Resurrection of Jesus Christ.

When we considered Mass as the commemoration of the Passion and Death of our Lord, our attention was fixed on the real immolation of the Lamb; we looked upon the altar as a new Calvary, and our devotion was centred upon the divine Victim slain for our ransom. But when we come to consider Mass as the commemoration of the Resurrection of Jesus Christ, the divine Lamb presents Himself to us in another aspect; He is living, He is resplendent with glory, He is the Conqueror, although He still deigns to be immolated. Wherefore the priest commemorating the Resurrection of Jesus Christ, together with His Passion, on breaking the Host puts one part into the chalice, denoting thereby the reunion of the body and the blood of Christ on the day of His rising from the tomb. "Where, my brethren," says St. Augustine, "would the Saviour be known after His Resurrection, save in the breaking of bread? Be assured, we enjoy the same blessing; we break the sacramental bread and therein recognize our Lord; consequently, whoever is faithful, whoever bears not in vain the name of a Christian, let him be consoled in the breaking of bread. Jesus Christ, though seated at the right hand of the Father, is nevertheless present on the altar under the mystic species." For although the sacrifice of the Mass is in effect the same as that of the Cross, and Jesus Christ is on the altar in a state of mystic death; yet we commemorate therein the mystery of the Resurrection, because His sacred body is there also gloriously resuscitated. Hence it is that the Church in her chants of the Paschal time during Mass is untiring in her alleluias; she affectionately kisses her Saviour's wounds, which now dart forth rays of dazzling brightness. Her altar is the throne of the Risen God; she approaches it without fear, for the divine Conqueror of death, though so resplendent in His glory, is more loving and affable than ever. For this reason, during a considerable portion of the Paschal time, the Mass is celebrated in commemoration of the great mysteries which were accomplished at this season of the Liturgical year.

The Holy Mass, then, considered as the commemoration of the Resurrection of our Lord, reminds us in a special manner of a Victim, who is gloriously risen from the dead, and yet is still immolated in a real though unbloody manner; it brings to our minds a joyous banquet—the banquet of the Pasch, to which the Lamb of God invites us in order to give us to eat of His glorified body. Each church becomes a cenacle where Jesus celebrates the Pasch with His disciples. The holy table is no longer the feast of a chosen few; the guests come in in crowds, and the house is filled. Now is the great figure of the Old Law changed into a reality. "At this table of the great King, the new Pasch of the New Law puts an end to the ancient Passover. The new excludes the old, reality puts the shadow to flight; light expels night." We are the children of promise; we have not denied Christ, as did the Jews; but we acknowledged Him to be our King, whilst His faithless people were dragging Him to execution. He in return has invited us to His Pasch, and there makes Himself our Host and our food. At this table is likewise fulfilled the prophetic symbol of the ancient Paschal Lamb. For fifteen hundred years, it was the figurative lamb; the true Lamb has now reigned over eighteen hundred years, and this is the Lamb whom the holy Mass produces in all the efficacy of His sacrifice, and in all the magnificence of His glory. We should, therefore, be present at this great act of the Christian religion, especially in the Paschal time, with extreme joy of soul; for it is here that we have in all its reality the same Jesus who so gloriously rose again from the dead to die no more. We should unite with His holy Mother, Mary, with the Magdalen, and with His disciples in their sentiments of joy. They had the immense happiness of seeing and conversing with Him for forty days after His Resurrection. But our happiness is not less great. Jesus Christ has shown Himself in the Holy Eucharist oftener than He showed Himself to His Apostles and the pious women during those forty days. To them He appeared repeatedly to confirm their faith, and to prepare them for the persecutions that awaited them. With what charity did He not appear to St. Thomas the Apostle, who said he would not believe in the Resurrection of our Lord, unless he should see in our Saviour's hands the print of the nails, and put his finger into the place of the nails, and his hand into His side?

The incredulity of St. Thomas is inexcusable; he neither believed the prediction of his divine Master, nor the testimony of St. Peter, who had seen our Lord after His Resurrection. His presumption was extreme: for he preferred his own judgment to that of all the Apostles, whom he accused of simplicity. He is ungrateful to his Lord and Master for the graces he received, and the dignity to which he had been elevated. He has the temerity to prescribe laws to his Sovereign and his God; and were he not wanting in reverence and respect, the very thought of putting his hands in the sacred wounds of our Saviour would cause him to tremble with awe. Nevertheless, Jesus, with inconceivable meekness bears with the infidelity of His disciple, and prepares a sovereign remedy for his incredulity and the fortifying of our faith. In His unparalleled charity, our divine Saviour seeks out the faithless one. "He enters, the doors being shut." His custom is to knock at the door of the heart and await its opening. "I stand at the door and knock; if any man open to Me I will enter." But here He performs a miracle. "He enters, the doors being shut." To heal the incredulity of His disciples, He displays an act of that omnipotence which all creatures unresistingly obey. He shows him His wounds. "Put in thy finger hither, and see My hands, and bring hither thy hand and put it into My side." St. Thomas knew not that his Lord and his God was present when he said: "Except I shall see in His hands the print of the nails, and put my finger into the place of the nails, and put my hand into His side, I will not believe." Now he discovers that nothing can be concealed from the infinite wisdom of his Master, who, with a charity commensurate with that wisdom, sweetly invites the disciple to touch those sacred wounds, whence issues the light of faith to illuminate, as previously rushed the blood to redeem the human race. The charity of the Apostle is rekindled on touching the sacred wounds of his divine Master, who saved him from the dangers of the abyss into which he had fallen, by showing His hands and His side, the view of which raised him up, even to that admirable confession of the Divinity, "My Lord and my God."

Oh, what joy to this Apostle! With what ardent gratitude is his soul replenished in return for so singular a grace! Happy saint! how great the favor to put your hand into that heart of mercy, that side, the source of salvation, in which we are saved from the wrath of God, find healing for all our spiritual maladies, are engendered to grace, and elevated to eternal glory.

Alas! how many times has not our dear Lord in the Holy Eucharist treated men with the same charity and condescension. In this divine mystery He has appeared not only to infidels and heretics to convince them of His Presence and make them believe in it, but He has also frequently appeared to many of those of His priests who were faithless, like St. Thomas.

In the year 1263, during the Pontificate of Urban IV, occurred a very striking miracle at Volsia, a town near the city of Rome. A certain priest, having pronounced the words of consecration over the bread at Mass, had a temptation against faith, the devil suggesting to him to doubt how Jesus Christ could be present in the Host, when he could see nothing of Him. He consented to the temptation, but nevertheless continued saying Mass. At the elevation of the sacred Host, behold! he and all the people who were present, saw blood flowing abundantly from the Host down upon the altar. Some cried out: "O sacred Blood! what does this mean? O divine Blood! who is the cause of Thy being shed?" Others prayed: "O sacred Blood, come down upon our souls and purify them from the stains of sin." Others beat their breasts, and shed tears of repentance for their sins. When Mass was over the people all rushed to the sacristy in order to learn from the priest what had happened during his Mass. He showed them the corporal all stained with the sacred Blood, and when they beheld it they fell upon their knees imploring the divine mercy. The miracle became known all over the country, and many persons hastened to Volsia to see the miraculous corporal. Pope Urban IV. sent for the priest, who went to Rome, confessed his sin and showed the corporal. On beholding it, the Pope, the Cardinals, and all the clergy knelt down, adored the blood, and kissed the corporal. The Pope had a church built in Volsia in honor of the sacred blood, and ordered the corporal to be carried in solemn procession on the anniversary of the day on which the miracle occurred.*

Although we never witnessed such a touching spectacle, yet our sentiments when at Mass should be those of St. Thomas, after he had seen our Lord with his own eyes; we should exclaim with him, "My Lord and my God," I believe that Thou art here present, though hidden under the sacramental veil; I renounce my own judgment and the testimony of my own senses. Thou art my God and my Saviour; alas! what have I done? I have sinned against Thee, my Lord and my God. I am unworthy to approach Thee. O divine Lamb, that takest away the sins of the world, I conjure Thee by Thy sacred wounds, the only refuge of the sinner, to grant me mercy. My Lord and My God, grant that I may repeat these sweet words during my life, at the hour of my death, and in the unfading glory of eternity. My Lord and my God, dart forth from Thy sacred wounds a ray of light and love, to penetrate and transpierce my heart even to its inmost recesses. Enlighten my mind, inflame my will, that all the powers and affections of my soul may be consecrated with an eternal devotion to Thee, My Lord and my God.

---

* Platina's Life of Urban IV.

CHAPTER XXI.

MASS, THE RENEWAL OF CHRIST'S RESURRECTION—CONTINUED.

AFTER His Resurrection, our Lord appeared to His disciples not only to confirm them in their faith, but also in order to inspire them with an unbounded confidence in His goodness and divine protection. He still continues to do the same in the holy sacrifice of the Mass. The following examples are a powerful confirmation of this consoling truth.

In his Pastoral letter of June 22, 1823, The Right Rev. Dr. Doyle, of Kildare, Ireland, writes as follows: "We announce to you, dearest brethren, with great joy, a splendid miracle which the Almighty God has wrought even in our days, at the present time, and in the midst of ourselves. We announce it to you with a heart filled with gratitude to heaven, that you may unite with us in thanksgiving to 'the Father of mercies and the God of all consolation,' Who consoles us in every tribulation, and Who has even consoled us by restoring, miraculously, Miss Mary Lalor, to the perfect use of speech, of which for six years and five months she had been totally deprived!" Here the Right Rev. Bishop refers to the letter of the Very Rev. N. O'Connor, Rector of the Parish of Maryborough. This letter gives a detailed account of the miracle as it occurred. It reads as follows:

"MARYBOROUGH, June 11, 1823.

"MY LORD:—In compliance with your request I send you a statement of the facts relative to Miss Lalor, which I have heard from others and witnessed myself.

"I am now in the house where she was deprived of her speech. She is at present in the eighteenth year of her age; and as she is connected with most of the respectable Catholic families in this county, and has had frequent intercourse with them, her privation of speech during six years and five months is established beyond contradiction. Her hearing and understanding remained unimpaired, and she carried a tablet and pencil to write what she could not communicate by signs.

"Medical aid was tried by Dr. Ferris, of Athy, and Surgeon Smith, of Mountrath, but without effect. The latter gentleman (as a similar case never occurred in the course of his practice) resolved to have it submitted to the most eminent physicians in Dublin, eight of whom were consulted, and the result was, that no hopes could be entertained for her recovery. This decision was imparted by Dr. Smith to her father, apart from Mrs. and Miss Lalor, all which circumstances the Doctor recollected on the 14th instant, when he saw Miss Lalor and heard her case to be miraculous.

"You, my Lord, are already aware that, according to your directions, written to me on the 1st of June, I waited on Mr. Lalor and communicated to him and to his family all that you desired. They observed it with exactness; and on the morning of the 10th instant, Miss Lalor having confessed to me by signs, and disposed herself for receiving the Holy Communion, I read to her again from Your Lordship's letter the directions of the Prince De Hohenlohe, namely, that she should excite within her a sincere repentance, and a firm resolution of obeying God's commandments, a lively faith, and an unbounded confidence in His mercy, an entire conformity to His holy will, and a disinterested love of Him.

"I had previously requested the clergy of this district to offer up for Miss Lalor the holy sacrifice of Mass, at twelve minutes before eight o'clock in the morning of the 10th, keeping the matter a secret from most others, as you had recommended; however, as it transpired somewhat, a considerable number collected in the chapel, when my two co-adjutors, with myself, began Mass at the hour appointed. I offered the holy sacrifice in the name of the Church. I besought the Lord to overlook my own unworthiness and regard only Jesus Christ, the Great High Priest and Victim Who offers Himself in the Mass to His Eternal Father, for the living and the dead. I implored the Mother of God, all the angels and saints, and particularly Saint John Nepomucene. I administered the Sacrament to the young lady, at the usual time, when instantly she heard, as it were, a voice distinctly saying to her, '*Mary, you are well*'—when instantly she exclaimed, '*O Lord, am I!*' and, overwhelmed with devotion, fell prostrate on her face. She continued in this posture for a considerable time, whilst I hastened to conclude the Mass; but was interrupted in my thanksgiving immediately after by the mother of the child pressing her to speak.

"When at length she was satisfied in pouring out her heart to the Lord, she took her mother by the hand, and said to her, 'Dear mother,' upon which Mrs. Lalor called the clerk and sent for me, as I had retired to avoid the interruption, and on coming where the young lady was, I found her speaking in an agreeable, clear, and distinct voice, such as neither she nor her mother could recognize as her own.

"As she returned home in the afternoon, the doors and windows in the street through which she passed were crowded with persons gazing with wonder at this monument of the goodness and power of Almighty God.

"Thus, my Lord, in obedience to your commands, I have given you a simple statement of facts, without adding to or distorting what I have seen and heard, the truth of which their very notoriety places beyond all doubt, and which numberless witnesses as well as myself could attest by the most solemn appeal to heaven. I cannot forbear remarking to Your Lordship how our Lord confirms now the doctrine of His Church and His own Presence upon our altars, by the same miracles to which He referred the disciples of John, saying: 'Go, tell John the dumb speak,' etc.; as a proof that He was the Son of God who came to save the world.

"I remain, Your Lordship's dutiful and
affectionate servant in Christ,
"N. O'CONNOR."
"To the Right Rev. Dr. Doyle,
"Old Derrig, Carlow."

"Now here is exhibited a prodigy," continued the Right Rev. Bishop, "which is only different in kind, but not inferior in magnitude to the raising of the dead to life. He who at the gate of Naim put His hand to the bier, and raised the widow's son to life, and gave him to his mother, here spoke to the heart of a faithful servant, loosed the tongue which infirmity had paralyzed, and restored a happy daughter to the embraces of her parent. We ourselves have participated in their joy, on conversing as we have lately done with this favored child of heaven.

"Exult then, dearly beloved brethren, and rejoice that Almighty God has thus visited you His people, reanimating your faith, enlivening your hope, and exalting your charity, consoling your sorrows, relieving your distress, and healing your infirmities, preparing in your sight a table against all who afflict you, and urging, by these manifestations of His power and goodness, to rely upon His providence, 'Whereas He has care of you!'"

The Most Rev. Dr. Murray, in his Pastoral Letter, dated Dublin, August 15th, 1823, writes as follows:

"Beloved Brethren in Christ Jesus:—A delightful duty has devolved upon us; it is 'to reveal and to confess the works of God!'* With a heart at once struck with awe, and inflamed with gratitude to the 'God of all consolation,' we proclaim to you a new and wonderful manifestation of

---

* Job xii. 7.

His goodness which we have just had the happiness to witness. Mary Stuart, of the Convent of St. Joseph, Ranelagh, has through the extraordinary interposition of that Omnipotent Being, who 'killeth and maketh alive,'* been restored instantaneously to health, from a state of grievous and hopeless infirmity, for the relief of which all the resources of human skill had been expended in vain. The account of this wonderful cure reached us officially, on the 2d instant, in a letter from Mrs. Mary Catherine Meade, Prioress of St. Joseph's Convent, under date of the preceding evening. This communication stated in substance that one of the religious sisters of that community, by name Mary Stuart, had been afflicted with sickness for four years and about seven months; that during that period she had frequent attacks of paralysis, each of which seemed to threaten her with immediate dissolution; that the most powerful remedies had been applied, without producing any other than partial and temporary relief; that for several months past she had been confined to her bed, wholly deprived of the power of assisting herself, or of moving out of the position in which she was laid; that when moved by her attendants, how gently soever, she not only suffered much pain, but was also liable to considerable danger and to a temporary loss of speech; and that for the last five weeks she had entirely lost the power of articulation; that up to the morning of the 1st instant, she continued in this deplorable state, without any symptom of amendment, and apparently beyond the reach of human aid; that on a certain hour that morning, as had been settled by previous arrangement, she united her devotions (as did also her numerous friends) with the holy sacrifice of the Mass, which was to be offered by Alexander Prince Hohenlohe, in the hopes of obtaining immediately from God that relief which no human means could afford; that with this view, she received, though with much difficulty, the divine

---

* 1 Kings ii. 6.

Communion, at the Mass which was celebrated at the same hour in her chamber, for her recovery; that Mass being ended, she instantly felt a power of movement, a capability of speech; that she exclaimed 'Holy, holy, holy, Lord God of Hosts!' raised herself without assistance, to offer, on bended knees, the tribute of her gratitude to heaven; called for her attire, left that bed to which she had been for so many months as it were fastened, and walked to the convent chapel with a firm step, and there, in the presence of the community and congregation, joined her sisters in the solemn thanksgiving which was offered up to God, for this wonderful and manifest interposition of His goodness.

"What may be the views of God in the recent prodigies, which are now the admiration of Europe, and one of which has just occurred under our own eyes, it is not for us to determine. We may, however, safely conjecture, that this gracious God has some object beyond the mere addition of a few miserable years to the life of a favored individual. When our Blessed Redeemer raised His friend Lazarus from the grave, He did so to publish 'the glory of God.'* He did so to confirm the faith of His disciples. 'Lazarus,' says He, 'is dead, and I am glad for your sake that I was not there, that you may believe.'† Since, then, the same Blessed Redeemer now makes the unbloody sacrifice of His body and blood the visible means of calling back to life and health the victim that was ready to descend into the grave, is it unreasonable to suppose that He does so, in His mercy, for some general and exalted purpose? To awake, for instance, our slumbering piety, and animate the faithful throughout the Church to fly with more confidence, more reverence, more love, to those holy altars, on which the living Victim of salvation is working such wonders!"

In the year 1824, on the 25th of January, another miraculous cure was obtained during Mass in the case of Mary

---

* John xi. 40.   † John xi. 15.

Dorizon, which caused a great sensation in the diocese of Maux, in France, where it took place. Mary Dorizon, a poor woman, then forty-three years old, who was much respected for her virtues, was subject from the age of seventeen to a nervous disorder of a very extraordinary nature, and all the remedies administered to her proved unavailing. In the year mentioned, particularly, her disorder assumed an alarming character. She had daily convulsions, which rendered her person quite deformed; ulcers, swelling of the legs, and other maladies. It occurred to her friends to write to the Prince Hohenlohe on her behalf. The prince—as before—directed them to perform certain devotions, and on Sunday, the 25th of January, two Masses were offered up for her intentions. She fainted during both; but at the moment of the Elevation at the second, she recovered her senses, and exclaimed, "Thanks be to our dear Lord! give me my clothes." She rose without assistance and remained long enough on her knees to prepare herself for Holy Communion, which she received a little before nine o'clock. In short, her cure was so complete that the patient, incapable hitherto of moving a step, repaired alone to church, and assisted at High Mass, to the great astonishment of the spectators. Since that time she walks and works. Her person has become straight, her wounds have closed, and her diseases have disappeared.

On the 10th of February, in the year 1825, another miraculous cure was obtained in the case of Sister Elizabeth Beatrice Myers, of the Visitation Convent in Georgetown, D. C. According to the directions of Prince Hohenlohe the sisters began a novena on the 1st of February for this sister, for whom the skill of physicians gave them no hopes of relief. Thursday, the 10th inst., at three o'clock in the morning, corresponding to the time at which the prince must have said Mass in Germany, the spiritual father of the sisters carried the Blessed Sacrament to the sick sister, and after giving her the Holy Communion, and saying a short prayer, he retired. The Mother Superior and five other sisters were kneeling in the room joining in prayer with their sick sister who had received. Just as they thought of withdrawing to rest, leaving the success to God, Sister Beatrice called out "Mother!" The Mother Superior immediately went to her, and the sister, clasping her by the hand, said, "Mother, I think I am cured. Lord Jesus, may Thy name be glorified for ever!"—and made several other moving aspirations, inviting all to help her to thank God. Soon after she begged leave to go into the chapel, where, falling on her knees, she remained some moments in prayer, whilst the Mother Superior and other sisters who had followed her prostrated in thanksgiving and praise.*

St. Gregory the Great relates † that the holy Pope Agapetus, on his journey through Greece, cured a man who was lame and dumb, by saying Mass for him.

Now all these persons miraculously cured by our Lord in the Blessed Eucharist could truly say with the infirm man in the Gospel, "Sir, I have no man, when the water is troubled, to put me into the pond." ‡ For several years they had implored the aid of man without finding one to contribute to their relief. How little can we expect from creatures, and how long may we languish vainly awaiting their succor! What impotence, ignorance, and want of good-will, do we discover in them! In our greatest necessities they abandon us: Jesus alone remains constant. Let us, therefore, apply to ourselves and choose as our device these words of the paralytic: "I have no man!" That is, I desire not the favor or friendship of man. Jesus Christ alone in the holy Sacrifice of the Mass can satisfy my desires. He alone is necessary to my soul, that it may be enlightened with His knowledge: to my will, that it may be inflamed with His

---

* See a full report of the evidence in regard to all these facts, by Dr. England, Bishop of Charleston, in the third volume of his works, p. 893.   † Dial. l. 5, c. 8.   ‡ John v. 7.

love: to my faculties, that they may be governed by His justice: to my passions, that they may be subdued by His power: to my senses, that they may be purified and subjected to the spirit. "I have no man." That is, I desire no particular friendship prejudicial to fraternal charity. To the God-Man alone, present in the Holy Eucharist, I would attach myself, and be occupied only with Him Who is singularly great, good, and amiable. I wish not to live in the heart of any creature, I only desire a place in that of my Saviour in the Blessed Sacrament, Who is the universal friend given by the Father to men; Who has died for all, and makes Himself all to all in this great mystery; Who is the sovereign good of all. Therefore, one may appropriate to himself the words: my Jesus and my all! "I have no man!" I am satisfied to be unacquainted with creatures, provided that I be not ignorant of my Lord Jesus in the holy Sacrifice of the Mass, that I may love Him with my whole heart, may constantly have recourse to Him in all my temporal and spiritual wants, and thus be and remain His in time and eternity.

CHAPTER XXII.

MASS, THE RENEWAL OF THE VIRTUES OF CHRIST.

THE institution of the holy Sacrifice of the Mass may be regarded as the crowning act of mercy and love in the life of our dear Saviour. It perpetuated all the benefits which He brought into the world, particularly that of giving us the example of virtue. It may be said, that by the institution of the Mass our Lord fulfilled the prophecy that in the kingdom of grace all the children of the new covenant would be "taught of the Lord." Here He is Himself the present and ever-active teacher, and only those who open all the faculties of their souls to His voice, can know what a Master He is.

Instruction, reading, priesthood, and holy rite, were His servants and messengers of old; and they are so still. But not satisfied to see "those the Father has given Him" instructed by His representatives only, He wished to stay with them to the end of the world, and teach them in person. "They will respect My Son," said the Father, as of old. "I will be with them," said Jesus, in the Holy Eucharist to teach them lessons of sublime virtue—lessons of poverty, of humility, of obedience, the love of God and of their neighbor.

The poverty which surrounded the human life of our Lord lasted thirty-three years, but to convince mankind of the grandeur and holiness of this virtue, and to attract us freely to love it, as He did, Jesus Christ remains among us still in the state of poverty in the Holy Eucharist. It is voluntary poverty, chosen out of love—absolute poverty, depriving Himself of everything, even the appearance of existence. He does not so much as retain His liberty of action. It is a state of permanent poverty without interruption—generous poverty. He gives all that He has in giving Himself. His open heart, His pierced hands, can no longer hold back any grace. It is the same to Him whether He be in a city or in a village; He dwells as cheerfully in a ciborium of copper, as in one of silver or of gold. In heaven He has a royal retinue; but on earth, who keeps Him company? "I am a man," He says, "who sees his poverty."

We, too, see the poverty of Jesus; but oh! how slow are we to imitate it! Our affections are fixed on fine dwellings, good fare, soft garments, splendid retinue. We dislike to feel the want of anything, or to suffer the slightest inconvenience, just as though the Son of God had said, " Blessed are the rich, but not the poor; blessed are those that laugh, but not those that weep."

The example of our Lord's humility, in the holy Sacrifice of the Mass, is as conspicuous as His poverty. "Learn of Me, because I am meek and humble of heart," points to the altar as the great class-room wherein to learn. The God of heaven and earth so belittles Himself for man, under the appearance of bread, day and night a prisoner of love! while man, who has nothing, is so proud and so elate! The God of heaven reposes under the thatch, or is carried along the road by sinful men, while Christians, who say they adore Him, look only for marks of distinction. The God of heaven and earth remains silent in his lowliness, oftentimes the subject of mockery and outrage, oftentimes neglected and made to serve as a kind of witness against Himself, when hypocrisy kneels before Him to gain the name of devotion; yet men are dissatisfied at a correction, a small slight, a trivial injury, or a shade of misrepresentation. Oh! who can go thither and come away proud? Who can go thither and not come away humble? Who can go thither and not come away penitent? Who can go thither and not come away good?

Again, when our Lord lived upon earth He was "obedient

unto death, even to the death of the cross," * says St. Paul the Apostle. It was in obedience to His heavenly Father that the Son of God became man; it was in obedience that His blessed Mother conceived Him. He was born while obeying an earthly monarch; He lived under obedience to His parents, and died out of obedience to His heavenly Father and His unjust judges. Although he now reigns in heaven, yet is He ever ready to obey man. In the holy Sacrifice of the Mass, He becomes obedient unto the consummation of the world. He renders immediate, universal obedience to every priest who pronounces the words of consecration, a free and voluntary obedience, which exposes His adorable Person to the outrages of perverse men; an entire obedience, without reference to the virtue of the priest. During so many centuries, no interruption has ever occurred to this humble subordination, which, because of His love to us, is more dear to Him than His glory.

Jesus Christ has solemnly pledged Himself to continue this great subjection of Himself, to console our exile by filling up the void that separates earth from heaven, to which He ascended again after His resurrection. Out of love for us He prefers His obedience upon the altar to the exercise of His sovereign power.

Do we obey in this manner? Do we obey all our superiors without exception? Do we obey blindly, at all times, in all things, always showing that we are humble servants of the Lord, ready to follow the commands of our superiors?

We know that the glorified body of our Lord is no longer capable of suffering; yet the love of suffering, which ever consumed the heart of Jesus, is in no wise diminished. His divine Person is still sensible to every insult that is offered to Him. Oh! who can enumerate the outrages heaped upon Jesus in this Sacrament of love! How many affronts does He not daily receive from atheists, heretics, superstitious

---

* Phil. ii. 8.

persons, and particularly from bad Catholics! Think of the crimes, the sins of irreverence that are committed in His churches, in His own divine Presence. Think of all the bad and sacrilegious communions that are made! O Jesus! what admirable lessons of patience dost Thou not daily teach us in this divine sacrifice! But how little do we profit by them! We are so passionate, so impatient, so unwilling to suffer anything from God or man! We can bear nothing from our superiors, equals or inferiors. We are burdens to ourselves, yet wish that all should bear with us!

Most admirable also, is the example of mortification which our dear Lord sets us upon the altar. His whole life was a continual mortification. Although He is now forever happy in heaven, yet He has found a means to teach us by His own example, even to the end of the world, how to mortify our senses, our will, and our judgment. He mortifies His judgment by suffering Himself to be disposed of according to the good pleasure of His priests, to be carried withersoever they will, to be used for good or bad purposes, just as though He were utterly blind and helpless. He mortifies His will in bearing the numberless indignities that are offered to His holiness, to His majesty, and to His other divine perfections. He mortifies His senses by remaining present in the Sacred Host as if He were dead. He mortifies His tongue by preserving ever a profound silence; He mortifies His whole body by keeping it concealed under the lifeless appearances of bread and wine, by remaining days and nights upon our altars as in a prison of love. O my soul! addicted as thou art to sensual pleasures, what union can there be between thee and the mortified and crucified body of Jesus Christ! The holy sacrifice reminds thee of His Passion and thou holdest sufferings in horror; His life under the sacramental veil is entirely spiritual and thine is entirely sensual!

In the holy Sacrifice of the Mass, Jesus teaches us also how we ought to love God. If we love God truly, we will do His will in all things, we will keep His commandments, we will suffer much for Him and sacrifice ourselves to His honor. This is what Jesus teaches us on our altars. He sacrifices Himself daily, nay hourly, for the honor of His Father and for the good of men. He has thus found out a means of renewing His death in a mystical manner, at all times and in all places. All men should offer themselves to God, in order to acknowledge their dependence upon Him, to thank Him for His numberless benefits, to ask new blessings from Him, and to atone for their sins. Jesus Christ as the head of the human race has taken upon Himself this obligation, and daily offers Himself to pay homage to God for all men, to give thanks to God for all the graces they have received from Him, to make satisfaction to His justice, so often offended by their grievous crimes, and to obtain for them all the graces necessary for soul and body. O wretch that I am! A God takes upon Himself my sins: He lays down His life to deliver me from death, and He bears for love of me a thousand insults while I in return despise and offend Him, I only provoke His anger more and more; I am unwilling to suffer the least thing for Him, and thus I render His Passion and Death fruitless to me. What ingratitude! what hardness of heart! what cruelty and injustice!

One of the objects of the Incarnation was to reunite men in the bonds of charity which had been severed by sin. Jesus Christ made charity an express commandment; He calls it His only commandment; He declares that it is the true mark of His religion.

It was especially by His example that He taught us this divine virtue through the course of His whole life. There are two marks by which love is known. They are the fruits of true and solid love:—first, to *labor:* second, to suffer for the beloved object. Jesus labored for our souls as no one ever *did* or ever *will;* and He suffered as only a God-man can suffer in order to win our love. O, what a life was His, especially during the three years of His public ministry! The life of the most hard-working missionary that ever lived, is but a faint shadow of His unwearied labor. By dawn of day He is in the Temple. The gathering crowds find Him there, but they know not that He has had a journey already. He has been upon the Mount of Olives praying all alone among the peaceful trees. His whole day has been already mapped out. He has foreseen the souls to whom He is to do good, the afflicted whom He is to comfort, the people whom He is to meet in the hot streets and the public places, and the gracious words He is to speak to them all. And when He quits Jerusalem and goes up into Galilee, or passes through Samaria, there are wearisome journies on foot, over hill and dale, on the dusty highway, or in the savage wilderness. Whenever He comes to the habitations of men, on the village-green, or in the little hamlet hid among the mountains, He preaches. He has no time for rest, not a moment that He can call His own. Weary and hungry and footsore, He sits down beside a well. A woman comes from the neighboring town to draw water, and Jesus opens His parched lips and speaks to her of the delicious spring of living water, which He will give to all that ask for it.

This poor woman feels in her heart a great desire to drink of this water, and Jesus gives her to drink of the living fountain of grace, and she is converted. Again, He walks by the sea-shore, and the rude crowd press upon Him and almost thrust Him into the waves. At last, He is compelled to embark in one of the boats near Him, and the bark of St. Peter becomes His pulpit. One would think that night at least would bring Him rest; but no! He has no house of His own, He has no place whereon to lay His head. He is often tired—so tired that even in the daytime He throws Himself on the deck of a fishing-boat, and there, on that hard couch, falls asleep. His nights are often spent on the mountain side. There, kneeling on the cold ground, with the damp dews wetting His garments and steeping His hair, He prays for His poor erring creatures. Nicodemus comes to Him and finds Him up and watching, for He is ever foremost to meet those that seek Him. And even when He sleeps, His heart *watches* and *loves* and thinks of those immortal souls for whom He is to die.

It is thus that our Lord gave us the example of charity and zeal for the salvation of our fellow-men; and this example of charity, more than any other virtue, He continues to give us in a most striking manner in the holy Sacrifice of the Mass, which is but the perpetuation of that wonderful charity that culminated in the sacrifice of the Cross. It was to preserve that charity that He left us His Body and His Blood under the appearance of bread and wine, in order that partaking of one bread, we also may be one body and one soul. And the more to ensure the practice of charity among men, He has made our natural desire for happiness the motive for loving one another. He has commanded us to partake of His Body and Blood under pain of eternal damnation; and the indispensable condition to our receiving this heavenly food is charity. While other shepherds clothe themselves with the wool of their flocks, and feed on their flesh, Jesus Christ, the Good Shepherd, strips Himself in order to clothe us. He even gives us His flesh and blood for our food; and when a devout soul, transported at a favor so divine, asks how she may repay so great a benefit, He replies: "Do good to your fellow men, and I will hold you discharged of all your debts to me." Does it seem hard to you, He says, to love your neighbor? Consider, then, how much I have loved you. Does it seem hard to you to give and to forgive? Then think whether you are ever required to give anything so precious as the food which I give you. Think whether you have ever to suffer as many affronts as I have suffered for your sake in this sacrament of love! Is the disciple greater than his master, or the servant above his lord? Go, then, and do to others what I have done to you; "Whatsoever you do to them, I will count as done to Me." Be charitable to all with that constancy and perseverance with which I have stayed with you in spite of the deep ingratitude and numberless outrages that have been, and still continue to be, heaped upon my sacred Person in the mystery of Love. These are the silent lessons that our Saviour teaches us in the holy Eucharist. How sublime, how eloquent, how impressive are they to the faithful heart! O Jesus, Thou hast conquered. We give our hearts to Thee, that Thou mayest fill them with the spirit of humility, poverty, obedience, mortification, and self-sacrifice. O Thou, the Well-Beloved of the Father, who camest on earth and dwellest in our Tabernacles in order to impart to men Thy divine spirit of charity, take from us all selfishness and hardness of heart, and teach us how to love one another.

CHAPTER XXIII.

MASS, A SACRIFICE OF ADORATION AND INFINITE PRAISE.

THE God who created us—that God on whom we depend for every moment of our existence—is a God of infinite majesty and glory.

Look around upon the heavens and the earth, how sublime an idea do they convey of their Almighty Architect! What a stupendous mass is the ponderous globe upon which we stand; yet God poises it with one finger! How vast the abyss of its waters; yet He measures it, as the Scripture says, in the palm of His hand! How awful is the roar of the thunder; it is but the feeble echo of His voice! How terrific the glare of the lightning; it is only a faint scintillation of His brightness! All that we see around us, the vast luminaries that roll above us, the earth which we inhabit, with its endless diversity of animals and productions, with man, the lord and master of the whole, once were not. The Almighty spoke one word, and instantly we leaped into being, and we are! How the soul and all her faculties sink into insignificance before this idea of her Creator, God. How she longs to honor and glorify Him who is the centre of glory, towards whom tend all the works of the Creator. Yes, glory and honor essentially appertain to God. All that is in heaven, on earth, and under the earth, according to St. John, sing in concert the praises of one God, in three persons: and every creature which is in heaven, on earth, and under the earth, and such as are in the sea, and all that are in them; I heard all saying: "To Him that sitteth on the throne, and to the Lamb, benediction and honor, and glory, and power, forever and ever." *

---

* Apoc. v. 18.

The eternal occupation of the Blessed is to chant the sacred Canticle " Holy, Holy, Holy, the Lord God of hosts!"*

Their Alleluias, their hymns of gladness, are ascending before the throne of God forever and ever. In purgatory, in a special manner, is exemplified their profound esteem and homage to Almighty God, from the intense desire of the sufferers to enjoy Him.

Even hell itself glorifies the Lord, for the reprobate are constrained, in deploring their eternal loss of all the benefits of nature, grace and glory, to offer a reparation of honor to the power of the Father, the author of nature; to the wisdom of the Son, whose grace they have despised, and to the goodness of the Holy Ghost, whose saving inspirations they have criminally rejected.

Amongst all creatures, man is under special obligations to glorify and honor Almighty God. Man is the master-piece of the creation, a resplendent image of the three divine Persons. God has redeemed man preferably to the angels. In baptism he is consecrated to the Father, to the Son, and to the Holy Ghost by an inviolable character impressed on his soul. Man, therefore, is under the strictest obligation to honor God in the best manner possible! To comply with this obligation as far as in man lies, many holy kings, emperors, and lords had churches and monasteries erected where the name of the Lord might be honored and praised day and night.

Now, we cannot honor God better than by sacrifice; for sacrifice is that part of religious worship, whose special object is the honor of God. It is in this, particularly, that it differs from other religious and virtuous acts. It is true, we honor God by every act of devotion and virtue, by every good work that we do to please Him. Yet the honor which we render God by acts of devotion and good works, does not proceed from the nature of such acts and works, but

---

* Isaias, vi. 8.

rather from the intention with which we perform them. But the peculiar virtue of sacrifice consists in its having for the principal object the honor of God. In all other religious exercises, we strive for the most part to benefit ourselves rather than render honor to God. If we pray, it is to obtain the grace of God; if we repent of our sins and confess them, it is in order to become reconciled to God; if we go to receive communion, it is to unite ourselves more intimately with God: if we perform other good works, it is to increase our merits and receive a greater reward in heaven. But our chief intention in assisting at a sacrifice, in order to correspond to the end for which sacrifice was instituted, is, and must be, to render due homage to Almighty God. It is He alone who may be honored by sacrifice. Almost any other token of honor, respect, or reverence that is rendered to God, may also be, and often is exhibited to men, at least exteriorly. The title, "His Majesty," may be applied both to God and man. The title, "His Holiness," is applicable not only to the Lord of heaven and earth, but is also applied to His Vicar on earth—the Pope. We kneel down before God, and we light candles and lamps in His honor. The same may be done, and is often done, to honor bishops, kings, and emperors. We bow down profoundly before the Lord God, and the same is done before great lords of this world; nay, even before our equals, if necessary.

Holy Scripture tells us, that when Abraham wished to buy of the children of Heth a burying place for Sara, his deceased wife, "he rose up and bowed down to the people of the land, to wit, the children of Heth:"* In the same manner the patriarch Jacob honored his brother Esau, whose indignation he had incurred. When about to meet him, "he went forward, and bowed down with his face to the ground, seven times, until his brother came near.† When Abigail came to King David, "she bowed herself

---

* Genesis xxiii. 7.   † Ib. xxxiii. 8.

down with her face to the earth.* Men often bow down even more profoundly to their equals than to God.

Many of the tokens of deep respect and veneration, which it was customary to manifest only to the Divinity, have, in course of time, come to be manifested to such men as common opinion held in high esteem and veneration. But never did it happen that any nation offered sacrifice to a man. If instances to the contrary occur in history, it is because that man was believed to be a god. St. Paul, the Apostle, healed in Lystra a man who had been a cripple from his childhood. When the people saw this great miracle, they wished to offer sacrifice to him and Barnabas, his companion, because they took them for gods, who had come among them in human shape. "The people lifted up their voice, saying: The gods are come down to us in the likeness of men. And they called Barnabas, Jupiter; and Paul, Mercury." † But after the Apostles had persuaded them that they were no gods, but men like the rest, the people desisted. The honor rendered by sacrifice belongs, then, essentially and solely to God. This honor, as already has been seen, He demanded from the beginning of the world, but more strictly under the Mosaic Law. He prescribed that every day, morning and evening, the priest should offer a lamb for a continual burnt-offering, besides additional sacrifices on the Sabbath, the New-Moon, at the Feast of the Unleavened Bread, and at the Feast of the First-fruits. ‡

In the seventh month, for several days together, besides the daily sacrifice, there were to be extraordinary additional sacrifices, so that on the fifteenth day of the month the priest was to offer thirteen bullocks, two rams, and fourteen lambs; and in the seven days, from the fifteenth to the twenty-first, seventy bullocks, fifteen rams, and ninty-eight lambs.§

---

*1 Kings xxv. 41. † Acts xiv. 10. ‡ Numbers xxvi. 11.
§ Numbers xxix.

Every woman, after childbirth, was to bring a lamb for a burnt-offering, and a pigeon or a turtle-dove for a sin-offering, or two young pigeons for the two offerings.*

Anyone cured of leprosy was to bring a burnt-offering, and a sin-offering.†

In the case of "every burnt-offering, which any man shall offer," whether bullock, or sheep, or goat, or turtle-doves, the priests, Aaron's sons, were to sprinkle the blood upon the altar, and put fire upon the altar, and lay the wood in order on the fire, and lay the parts, the head and the fat, in order upon the wood, and the priest was thus to burn all on the altar, to be a burnt-sacrifice.‡

So in the case of a meat-offering, peace-offering, sin-offering, or trespass-offering, the priest had special duties assigned to him for the manner of making the offering.§

Now, if we Christians had to offer to God the same kind of sacrifices as the Jews offered to the Lord, if we had oxen, and sheep, and other animals slain and consumed by fire in sacrifice, it would be for us a holy religious act of divine worship to assist at such sacrifices—an act, by which we would greatly honor and please Almighty God, for we should make thereby a public profession of our faith in the supreme dominion of Almighty God over all creatures, who, as He made us out of nothing, could again destroy, or change us as He pleased. It would, at the same time, be a profession of our total subjection to Him, and our readiness to be treated by Him in whatever manner He pleased. Yet, however great might be the honor which we should thus render to God, it would fall far below the honor and homage due to Him. We usually honor men according to their rank and acquirements. We honor a man of learning, for instance, more than an ignorant rustic; a saint more than a sinner; a prince more than a peasant; a priest more than a layman. Now, God, being

---

* Levit. xii. † Ib. xiv. ‡ Ib. I.
§ Ib. ii., iii., iv. and v.

infinite in all His perfections, deserves an honor and reverence corresponding to His Greatness.

Only an infinite honor is adapted to an infinite Being; nothing limited is becoming a Being without limits. Where, then, in the whole range of created nature, shall we find a being that is capable of offering a homage such as this? Angels and men, principalities and powers, all creatures are before Him a despicable nothing, and homage, great as it may appear to us, can have nothing comparable to His Greatness. "Behold the nations are as a drop of water, and are counted as the smallest grain of the balance . . . . They are before Him as if they had no being at all, and are counted to Him as nothing and vanity." He alone, as Holy Scripture says, is "Blessed and Mighty, the King of kings and the Lord of lords; who alone has Immortality, and inhabiteth Light inaccessible; whom no man hath seen nor can see; to whom be honor and sacrifice everlasting."

How shall we be able to render to God the honor he deserves? Already we have seen that *sacrifice* is the mode by which we acknowledge the supreme sovereignty of God; but where shall we find a sacrifice pure and precious enough to oe offered to His Majesty? It is plain that we, finite creatures, have nothing of ourselves great enough to offer Him; even the sacrifice of our lives would be an inadequate homage. "What, then, shall we offer to the Lord that is worthy? Wherewith shall we kneel before the High God?"* How shall we acquit ourselves of our obligation to honor the Lord in a worthy manner, we who are under greater obligations to do so, than those who lived before Christ?

It is certain that, by all the sacrifices of the old Law, God could not be honored in a manner worthy of Him. The priests themselves, who offered the sacrifices, were all sinful or imperfect men; the victims offered were oxen, sheep, turtle-doves, and the like; the manner of offering consisted

---
* Micheas vi. 6.

in slaying those victims and consuming them by fire. What fitting proportion was there between such sacrifices and the supreme Majesty of God? None whatever. No wonder, then, to read in holy Scripture that on many occasions God expressed His displeasure at these sacrifices, and even rejected them. Any homage coming from a finite creature, necessarily partakes of the imperfection of its origin; it is essentially limited. Presented to the Almighty, it may serve in some sense to beautify and adorn the creature that presents it, but it cannot reflect any real glory on Him, who dwelleth in light inaccessible. Creatures may shine with a borrowed splendor; they may, like the stars of night, receive a foreign, an extraneous brightness; God, to be really and adequately glorified, can be glorified by no other than Himself. A God can be truly glorified only by a God.

This glorification has literally come to pass. Almighty God has given us a Man-God to supply our deficiency in adoring and honoring the Blessed Trinity, thus enabling us to discharge to the full a debt which would otherwise have remained eternally unpaid.

Jesus Christ came into this world to repair the fault of our first parents. He came to render infinitely more honor to His Father, than that of which the sins of all men had deprived Him. This honor He paid His Father by every action of His life, but particularly by his Passion and by His obedience unto the death of the Cross. Hence it was, that after Judas had left the Supper Room to betray our Lord, Jesus Christ said, "Now is the Son of man glorified, and God is glorified in him."* "Father, the hour is come, that thy Son may glorify thee."† The greater the dignity and rank of a person, the greater also is the honor which he pays to another. This honor is so much the more acceptable, the more it proceeds from the heart. No one can show his veneration and esteem for his sovereign, or his desire of seeing him honored better than by sacrificing his very life in honor

---
* John xiii. 31.   † Ib. xvii. 4.

and out of love for the potentate. As then the dignity of Jesus Christ is infinite, so was the honor which He paid to His Father by every act of His life, especially by His death upon the Cross; whilst the dishonor offered to His Father by all the sins of men that ever were or will be can never reach the infinite. He rendered this honor with an infinite love to His Father, and therefore it was most acceptable to Him—infinitely more pleasing than the dishonor caused by the sins of men could be displeasing. For this reason was it that the angels sang at the birth of our Lord: "Glory be to God in the highest, and on earth peace to men of good will."*

If we truly love and esteem a person, we rejoice exceedingly at seeing him honored as much as possible. Before the Incarnation of the Son of God, there was no one who loved the Lord of heaven and earth more than the angels. For this reason they had the greatest desire to see their God honored, praised, and worshipped as He deserved to be; and no one could rejoice more than they in beholding their Lord and King honored and glorified by the whole world. But knowing as they did, that God was worthy of infinite honor and glory, and knowing also that this infinite honor and glory could not be given to the Lord by any finite creature whatsoever, they rejoiced exceedingly in seeing the Son of God—a person of infinite dignity—become man, to give to His Father that infinite honor and glory which He had never before received. Hence it was that they sang most joyously at the birth of our divine Saviour: "Glory be to God in the highest, and on earth peace to men of good will," henceforth we are able for all eternity to give infinite honor and glory to our God through His Son Jesus Christ; now our joy has reached its height, and let all men of good will rejoice and be glad with us.

And indeed, though loud is the voice of nature in the

---

* Luke ii. 14.

praise of its author, harmonious the songs of thanksgiving which the Universe pours forth to its Creator, incessant the homage which the celestial choirs render to their eternal King,—all dwindles and totally disappears when compared with that honor, homage, and glory which Jesus Christ gave to His Father during His life on earth. This same infinite honor, praise, and glory Jesus Christ gives and offers still to His Father in every Mass, as He Himself declared one day to one of His servants who was burning with love for Him, and with an ardent desire to honor Him. "O," said this fervent soul, "would to God I had a thousand tongues, that I might praise the Lord always! O that I had hearts without number to love him! O that the whole world were mine, that I might see him loved and served by all men!" "My daughter," replied an inward voice, "thy zeal and love are extremely pleasing to Me; but know that I am more honored by a single Mass than by all the honor thou couldst ever conceive or desire."

The reason of this is plain. The victim, which is offered to God in the Mass, is our Lord Jesus Christ Himself, the well-beloved Son of His Father, equal to Him in all His divine perfections. Do we start at the expression? But daring as it may appear, it is literally true. We know it; we knew it before, only we did not sufficiently reflect upon it. To know how the mystery is to be comprehended, the highest angels are equally at a loss with ourselves. It is like all the other wonders of God, vast and incomprehensible; and all we have to do is, to bow down before it in silent adoration.

The holy Sacrifice of the Mass is, therefore, of infinite dignity and value. In it we offer to the Eternal Father all the honor which Jesus Christ gave Him during His whole life on earth, thereby atoning for our natural poverty. "Yes," says Father Paul Segneri in his "Homo-Christianus," *

---

* Diss. 12, p. 1.

"If, on the one hand, the blessed Mother of God, and all the saints and angels of heaven, were to prostrate themselves before God in the deepest humility and reverence; and on the other hand, the humblest priest on earth were to offer but one Mass, the offering of the priest would give more honor to God, than the united adorations of all the angels and saints." Hence it is that St. Ignatius, the martyr, calls the holy Sacrifice of the Mass " the glory of God ; " and the priest prays in Mass, when holding the sacred Host over the chalice, and slightly elevating both of them together: "Through Him, and with Him, and in Him, to God the Father Almighty, in the unity of the Holy Ghost, be all honor and glory."

Of this infinite honor and glory, the Lord is worthy in time and for all eternity. It is true, according to the prophecy of Daniel,[*] the public celebration of Mass will be discontinued during the reign of Anti-Christ for three years, six months and a half, or for the space of 1,290 days. Mass, however, will be said privately, for this holy sacrifice is never to fail for all eternity—Jesus Christ being a priest forever according to the order of Melchisedech;[†] and being also the victim at the same time, will offer to His Father for all eternity the same sacrifice which He one day offered upon the Cross for the honor of His Father and the salvation of mankind.

Blessed, therefore, thrice blessed the priest who gives this infinite honor and glory to Almighty God, by saying Mass every day of his life! To abstain from saying Mass occasionally, out of humility, is sometimes praiseworthy, for by such an act the Lord is also honored. But let it be remembered that this honor is finite, proceeding, as it does, from a finite and sinful creature; whereas the honor given to God in the Mass proceeds from a divine Person, and is infinite on that account. It is better, therefore, to say Mass every day than even out of humility to omit saying it.

---

[*] Dan. xii. 11.   [†] Ps. cix. 4.

A certain Cardinal of Rome was in the habit of saying Mass every day. But when his occupations became rather numerous and pressing, he easily omitted saying Mass in order to gain more time for the transactions of temporal affairs. No sooner had St. Cajetan of Naples, his bosom-friend, learned this, than he started without delay for Rome in spite of the extreme heat which endangered his life, in order to request the Cardinal to resume his former practice of saying Mass daily, and not deprive God any longer of so great an honor; the Blessed Virgin and all the saints, of excessive joy; sinners, of the grace of conversion and forgiveness; the just, of many actual graces; the souls in purgatory, of great relief in their pains; the Church of her greatest strength, and himself, of so powerful a means of salvation and sanctification.

One day Father John Avila, S. J., made a long journey. Having a great desire to say Mass, he continued his journey in spite of extreme fatigue, in order to reach a convent where he might offer up the holy sacrifice. But, at last, he felt so overcome with fatigue, that he gave up all hope of reaching the convent and saying Mass. Suddenly Jesus Christ appeared to him in the guise of a pilgrim, and, showing him all His wounds, said: "When I received these wounds I was certainly more fatigued than you are now." Having said this, our divine Saviour disappeared, leaving Father Avila full of courage to continue his journey, until he reached the convent to say Mass.

The lay reader may envy the priests their happiness of daily offering to God the Father, His well-beloved Son in the Sacrifice of the Mass. Indeed, if there is anything enviable, it is the happiness of priests. But it should be remembered that all can share in this happiness. Jesus Christ has not instituted Mass that it should be offered to His Father by Him alone. He has instituted it as a sacrifice which belongs to every one. In it He gives Himself not only to all the faithful in general, but also to every one in particular, in order that all present at Mass may offer Him to His heavenly Father. The holy Sacrifice of the Mass is, therefore, offered not only by the priest, but also by all those who assist at it with devotion, and are, as members of Christ, united with their Head. The only difference between the priest and the faithful is, that the priest has the power to change bread and wine into the Body and Blood of Jesus Christ by the words of consecration—a power which the faithful do not enjoy. But all who assist at Mass offer at the same time with the priest the Body and Blood, together with all the infinite merits of Jesus Christ to God the Father. It is for this reason that St. Peter, the Apostle, wrote to all Christians: "You are a chosen generation, a kingly priesthood, a holy nation, a purchased people: that you may declare His virtues who hath called you out of darkness into His marvellous light." *

Hence, as the priest in saying Mass offers the sacrifice for himself and others, even so, those who are present at it, may also offer it with him for themselves and others. When a city sends a present to a prince by its deputies, all the inhabitants have their share in the offering, though but one of them may speak on the occasion; in like manner, in the Sacrifice of the Mass, though none but the priest speaks and offers the sacrifice, yet all present fail not to have their share in it. It is true that with regard to the deputies of a city, each of them might speak, though but one be selected for the office. But in the Mass it is not so; because it belongs only to the priest, who is chosen by God for that purpose, to consecrate and celebrate. This, however, does not prevent those who assist at this adorable sacrifice, from offering it up with him. Nay, the very words of the priest show this when he says in the offertory: "Pray, my brethren, that *mine* and *your* sacrifice may be pleasing in the sight of God the Father omnipotent;" and in those other prayers of the

---

* 1 Peter ii. 9

Canon of the Mass, "for whom we offer this sacrifice, or for those who offer it unto Thee."

Again, we must take notice that the priest often says: "*Oremus*, let us pray," and not "*Oro*, I pray," because in reality all those who assist at Mass are invited and ought to pray with him, and because he prays in the name of them all. In order that this may be done with more fervor, the priest turns repeatedly towards the people and begs the assistance of the Holy Ghost in these words:—"*Dominus vobiscum*,—The Lord be with you," to which the people answer, "*Et cum spiritu tuo*,—and with thy spirit."

After the memento for the living, that is, for all those living persons to whom the priest may desire to apply in an especial manner the Mass, he prays: "Remember also all here present *who offer Thee this sacrifice* of praise for themselves and all theirs, for the redemption of their souls, for the hope of their salvation and safety, and who render their vows to Thee, the eternal, living and true God."

Again, immediately after the consecration, the priest prays: "Both *we*, Thy servants, and also *Thy holy people, do offer* to Thy most High Majesty, a pure Host, a holy Host, an immaculate Host, the holy Bread of Life Eternal and the Chalice of Perpetual Salvation." It is, then, a very consoling truth to know that all who assist at Mass with devotion, and are as members united with Jesus Christ their Head, do really offer at the same time with their Saviour and His priest, this most august sacrifice, and thus are, as St. Leo says, partakers of the priestly office. It follows then, that by assisting at Mass, Christians render to God the Father that same infinite honor which Jesus Christ, His only Son, gives Him in this holy sacrifice. In holy Mass we render this same infinite honor to every divine attribute.

We honor God as the Creator and Author of all things, by offering to Him the Incarnate Word, His well-beloved Son, the First-born and Head of all creatures; we honor God as our supreme Lord and sovereign Master, who as He made us out of nothing, can again destroy or change us as He pleases; this supreme dominion of Almighty God over all creatures, we acknowledge by offering to Him that same sacrifice in which the death of Jesus Christ, our supreme Head is represented and mystically renewed. In Mass we honor God as the principal and chief end of all our actions. Offering to Him as we do Jesus Christ, our supreme Head, we offer at the same time ourselves, whole and entire, as members which are united with their Head. It is thus that we declare our readiness to honor and worship God, to obey Him under all circumstances, and to love Him with our whole heart above all things in the same manner as Jesus, our Head, does on the altar.

In Mass we honor the mercy of God, by offering to the Eternal Father His Son, who saved us from eternal death by His bitter Passion and cruel Crucifixion.

In Mass we honor the wisdom of God, which invented this mystery—a mystery which neither any human nor any angelic understanding could ever have conceived.

We honor the power of God, which manifests itself in Mass more wonderfully than in all the other works of God.

We honor the liberality of God towards us, because by offering to Him a present of infinite value—the Body and Blood of His Son,—we make a worthy return for all the benefits He ever bestowed upon us. Lastly, in Mass we honor the justice of God, by offering to it a satisfaction more than sufficient for all our sins.

It is, then, at Mass that we, as members of Jesus Christ, render with and through Him, our Head, the same infinite honor to all the Divine attributes, which He Himself renders in this tremendous sacrifice. What a happiness for Catholics to be enabled to honor their God and Creator in a worthy manner! We must always bear in mind that at Mass we all honor God the Father by offering Him Jesus Christ, His well-beloved Son. With this thought always in our minds whenever we go to church, we cannot fail to acknowledge God's high dominion and our own absolute dependence upon Him; thus shall we worthily adore the sovereign Majesty of the Lord, and perfectly comply with our solemn obligations to offer to Him worthy and adequate homage.

There are numberless reasons for offering this honor and homage to God. Have we not dishonored Almighty God as many times as we have sinned? And have we not sinned many times every day since the time when we were first capable of sinning? How many insults have we offered to God by our lukewarmness: by the scandal given to our fellow men: by disobedience and want of submission to God's representatives! How often have we dishonored and insulted God in our neighbor by the hatred or contempt for his person! Have we not good reason to confess that by our whole life, by the greater part of our thoughts, words, and actions we have rather dishonored than honored Almighty God? Were one of our fellow-men to insult us, or cause us to lose our honor and good name, should we not require an adequate reparation? And will not God require the same at the hands of those who almost every day so grievously outrage Him in countless ways? How shall we pay off the enormous debt of years!

Let us thank Almighty God for having placed in our hands so easy a means of discharging all our debts to the Divine Justice in the holy Sacrifice of the Mass. Let us profit by it, not only on Sundays and holy days of obligation, but also on every other day, if at all possible. Then our love and veneration for this holy sacrifice will greatly increase, and in proportion as this love and veneration increase, so will our efforts to assist at Mass as often and with as much devotion and reverence as possible.

It is necessary to assist at Mass with all possible devotion and reverence, for, from what has been said, it follows that to assist at Mass with irreverence would be to offer a horrible outrage to God. Jesus Christ offers Himself upon the altar to His heavenly Father in our behalf, and thus renders Him an infinite honor. Now Catholics must go to Mass for no other purpose than to offer conjointly with Jesus Christ the same sacrifice and render to God the Father the same infinite honor. Would we like to hear Jesus Christ say to us when at Mass what He one day said to the envious and impious Pharisees, "I honor my Father, but you dishonor me?"* Whilst I am rendering infinite honor to my Father by offering myself to Him upon the altar, you dishonor and despise me and my heavenly Father by your immodest attire and unguarded eye, by your laughing and talking and irreverent behavior; when you hear the priest, who takes my place at the altar, say in a loud voice: "Lift up your hearts!" and the acolyth answers in the name of the people: "We have them with our Lord!" your heart is taken up with many worldly and unbecoming thoughts; you think of everything but me; at the very time that I humble myself before the Divine Majesty, nay, annihilate myself, as it were, you are standing there, casting around looks of pride and haughtiness and immodesty, just as though you had come to a theatre to display your vanity and gratify your curiosity, and to be seen and admired by every spectator; the very same holy sacrifice by which an infinite honor is rendered to my Father, you make use of to dishonor Him. Should we like to hear Jesus reproach us thus? Have we never given Him any reason to reproach us thus? God forbid that we should ever displease Him by want of faith, devotion, reverence, and recollection at Mass.

Cæsarius of Heisterbach relates that a pious priest named Andrew, together with many other devout Christians, made a pilgrimage to the Holy Land. The vessel in which they were to return was to set sail on Easter Sunday morning. So all embarked on that day except the holy priest, and

---

* John viii. 49

sailed off. This good priest preferred to let his fellow-pilgrims start than to omit saying Mass. Having finished his Mass, he went to the wharf to obtain, if possible, a small, fast-sailing bark to overtake the other pilgrims. Wonderful to relate, a beautiful youth suddenly appeared before him on horseback, and said: "You preferred not to start with the other pilgrims rather than lose Mass; get then on my horse with me and I will conduct you safely back to your own country." Andrew accepted the offer and soon fell asleep for a little while. When he awoke, the young man, who was an angel of the Lord, said to him: "Do you know where you are?" "Kind sir," replied the priest quite amazed, "I can hardly trust my eyes; it seems to me I am in my fatherland; this is the street in which I live; this is my house; these are the houses of my friends and neighbors; but how is it possible that I could come home by land in so short a time?" "Nevertheless it is so," said the angel; "your way has been shortened because you said Mass." Thus the good priest was taken home in a few minutes, whilst his companions remained exposed to all the storms and dangers of a sea-voyage for two months. It was thus that the Lord honored the holy priest, because He had been infinitely honored by him in the holy Sacrifice of the Mass.

In a similar way our Lord knows how to honor those even in this world, whose chief care it is to honor Him, especially by assisting at the holy Sacrifice of the Mass with all possible devotion and reverence. If He rewarded St. Peter of Alcantara with exceedingly great glory for all his corporal penances; if He made a pious student, after his death, shine with extraordinary heavenly splendor and brightness for having always prepared himself well for holy Communion, what will be the glory, splendor, and honor which the Lord will confer upon all who, during this life on earth, made it their chief duty to give infinite honor to the Almighty by hearing Mass as often as it was possible for them!

Let us, then, promise our Lord, that for the time to come

we will always assist at Mass, with all possible humility, devotion, and reverence in order to be able to say in truth with Jesus Christ, at the end of life: "Father, I have glorified thee on earth, I have finished the work which thou hast given me to do."[*]

---

[*] John xvii. 4.

CHAPTER XXIV.

MASS, A SACRIFICE OF PROPITIATION.

WHITHERSOEVER we may turn our eyes we behold the sad effects of sin, and the infinite hatred God bears to it. If we look up to heaven, we see that its brightest angels have been cast out for one single mortal sin. If we look into Paradise, we see how our first parents were banished from that abode of happiness for one single mortal sin. If we look upon the earth, we see it destroyed by water; cities consumed by fire from heaven, and all on account of mortal sin. If we look into the abyss of hell, we see lost souls there, we hear howling and gnashing of teeth for ever and ever, and all on account of mortal sin.

Were we to see a good and holy man, renowned for his wisdom and justice, a man who loved his children with the most tender affection, cast some of them into a fiery furnace, into a prison of frightful torments, and there suffer them to linger on in the midst of the most excruciating pains, with never a glance of pity, no relief, no deliverance for them, what should we think or say? How enormous must be the crime which could draw down such a punishment! This just, wise, and loving father is God. He loved the fallen angels with an unspeakable love, yet, for one mortal sin, He instantly cast them into hell, to burn, to be tortured for all eternity.

O how fearful an evil must mortal sin be, for an all-merciful God to punish it with such merciless rigor! The greatness of the punishment is the measure of the enormity of the crime. God is most just. The demons themselves confess that God has not punished them with all the rigor that their sin deserved. So great is the enormity of one mortal sin, that it has brought on the earth all the misery and woe that men have suffered since the beginning of the world and will suffer till the day of doom. So great is the malice of mortal sin that it kept heaven closed against us for a length of four thousand years, and it has opened wide the mouth of hell, which never ceases to swallow its countless victims. Yea, so great is the enormity of one mortal sin that God would see Himself obliged, as it were, to destroy man in the same instant he commits it, unless one interferes, and appeases His anger by offering a sufficient satisfaction to God's justice, and an adequate reparation to His honor.

We know that our first parents, Adam and Eve, transgressed their Maker's law, and in an evil hour undid the glorious work of their creation. Plunged in an instant into an abyss of miseries, they did not attempt to rise, and indeed had not left themselves the power. Their posterity, spread over the earth, adding sin to sin, insult to insult, carried with them their rebellion and their impieties. The iniquities of the father were multiplied in his children; one age improved on the vices of another; till at last almost the only intercourse between heaven and earth was the voice of crimes crying aloud for vengeance. And what was there to counteract the just demand? God stood not in need of these His worthless creatures; poor earth-born man had no connection with the eternal self-sufficient happiness of the Lord, Who in one moment might have crushed him without regret.

Hell, on the other hand, raised up its baleful voice, and demanded with seeming equity that he who had followed in guilt should follow also in punishment. The essential attribute of a God—impartial justice—seemed to second the terrible demand. And in this fearful moment, what was it that saved us? The unaccountable, incomprehensible love of God for the most wretched of His creatures. His impetuous love was too powerful for His justice, and, relenting into compassion, He pardoned us.

And in what manner? The Son of God Himself became

man to atone for our sins. Jesus was all innocent and holy, the only Son of God, loved by His Father with an infinite love, and yet, because He charged Himself with our sins, because He took upon Himself the semblance of a sinner, God punished Him with merciless rigor. On the night of His bitter Passion, our Blessed Redeemer knelt in the garden of Olives; His soul was sad unto death. His face was deadly pale; He trembled in every limb, and His heart's blood oozed out through every pore of His body. He struggled and prayed, He implored His heavenly Father to deliver Him from the shame and the torments that awaited Him. "Oh, My Father, if it be possible, take away this chalice from Me." But no, God's outraged justice must be satisfied. Jesus has taken upon Himself all our sins, He must also endure all our punishments. God treats His own beloved Son with justice, without mercy, in order that He might treat us with unbounded mercy. For our sakes God delivered up His beloved Son to the fury of His enemies, to all the malice of the demons, to the most infamous outrages, to the most atrocious punishments. For our sakes He made His only begotten Son to become an object of horror and malediction, for it is written in the Word of God: "Accursed is he who hangs on the cross."* And Jesus, the God of all glory, hung on the Cross, and died on the Cross in expiation of the sins of the world. The effusion of His blood is the price of our Redemption. It is thus that His Father pardoned us.

Pardoned us. Oh! look again upon the cross and behold the manner in which He has pardoned us! Who would have thought it? Had He but pardoned us, that alone would have been astonishing. Had He commissioned another to atone for our sins, it would still have been infinite mercy. But that He should think of this,—that He, the Omnipotent, the Eternal, the essential of all beings,

---

* Deut. xxi. 28.

should think of atoning for us Himself, that He should leave His celestial throne, invest Himself with our wretched clay, and hang for us upon the infamous gibbet of the Cross, —this surpasses all comprehension; it leaves us at once speechless and prostrate. Here we cannot understand; we can only be silent and adore.

But there is yet another circumstance wanting, to complete this stupendous wonder. For, was it necessary, if He must indulge His immense love, that He should descend to all this—that He should become as a worm, and no man, endure the very extremity of torment and ignominy? Faith teaches us, and reason itself seems sufficient to evince that, coming from a God, the slightest atonement would have been enough; that, in a being of His infinite dignity, the very first drop of His inestimable blood would have sufficed, nay, would have blotted out the sins of a thousand worlds ten times more wicked than our own. Yet for us alone He prodigally shed it all; He would observe no medium in His love, nor rest satisfied till He had selected and exhausted in His own person every refinement of suffering that the ingenuity of the most cruel of mankind could devise.

Behold, then, the grand wonder complete! Behold the grand act of atonement, the stupendous sacrifice of propitiation complete! Behold the justice of God fully satisfied and His honor more than abundantly repaired! Behold the unaccountable love and mercy of God to His guilty creature man, displayed on the Cross to an unthinking world!

But Jesus Christ was not content to offer Himself once a sacrifice for our sins upon the Cross; no, He wished to remain here below to be offered in sacrifice, not only once, but as often as we wish—even every day to the end of the world, in order that we might have in Him the most pleasing sacrifice that we could ever offer to His Father for our sins, and the most valuable present we could make to appease Him. For this reason it is that the Council of Trent declares that

Jesus Christ instituted the divine mystery of the Blessed Eucharist for two ends, namely, to be the food and life of our soul in the quality of a sacrament, and also in order that the Church might have a perpetual sacrifice to offer to God, in satisfaction for our offences. "In this divine sacrifice" (of the Mass) says the holy synod, "the same Christ is contained and is immolated in an unbloody manner, who on the altar of the Cross, offered Himself once in a bloody manner; hence it is that this sacrifice is truly propitiatory. If, with a sincere heart and a right faith, with fear and reverence, we come, contrite and penitent, unto God, we obtain mercy and find grace in seasonable aid.—For it is one and the same victim; the same Christ offering Himself in the Mass by the ministry of the priests, who on Mount Calvary offered Himself upon the Cross—the manner alone of offering being different. Wherefore, not merely is it rightfully offered, agreeably to the traditions of the Apostles, for the sins, pains, satisfactions, and the other necessities of the faithful who are living, but also for those who have died in Christ, and who are not as yet fully purified."*

"Now there are four things," says St. Augustine, "which are to be considered in a sacrifice: The person to whom it is offered; he who offers it; what is offered; and for whom it is offered. The infinite wisdom of God has here disposed things in such a manner that he who offers this sacrifice to reconcile us to God, is the same as He to whom it is offered; nay more, it is He Himself who is the victim, and He is so united to those for whom He offers it, that He is the same with them also. That true Mediator—whereas *in the form of God* He receives sacrifice together with the Father, with whom also He is one God, yet, *in the form of a servant*, He chose rather to be, than to receive sacrifice, lest, even on this account, any one might think that sacrifice was to be offered to any creature. For this cause also He is a priest, Himself

---

* Sess. 22. c. ii.

the offerer, Himself also the oblation," * Theodoret says the same of Jesus Christ, "He exercises the priesthood as man, but as God receives the things that are offered." † So that as upon the Cross He was both the priest and the victim, He is still upon our altars the victim and the priest, Who offers up Himself to His Eternal Father by the ministry of the priests. He who says Mass does but represent the person of Jesus Christ. It is in *His* name and as *His* minister that he offers this sacrifice. This is quite evident from the words of consecration; for the priest when consecrating, says not "*This is the body of Jesus Christ*," but he says, speaking in the person of Jesus Christ—"This is My Body;" from which words it is clear that Jesus Christ Himself is the High Priest who offers this sacrifice, using the priest as He does as a mere agent, to pronounce in *His name and place* the words of consecration over the bread and wine.

The royal Prophet and the Apostle St. Paul call Jesus Christ a "*priest forever according to the order of Melchisedech;*" and He is very justly called so, because every day in the Mass He offers to God that same sacrifice of propitiation which He once offered upon the Cross; and which He will never cease to offer to the end of the world. "Such a priest as this," says St. Paul ‡ "we should have, holy, innocent, undefiled, separated from sinners, and made higher than the heavens; who needeth not, as the other priests, to offer sacrifices first for his own sins and then for the sins of the people." We stood in need of a priest who was able to appease the wrath of God, not by the blood of victims, as ordained in the Old Law, but by His own blood, and His own Death and Passion.

From what has been said it is clear that this sacrifice is of so great price and value that it has not only sufficiently satisfied the Eternal Father for our sins and for those of the whole world—" He is the propitiation for our sins, and not

---

* T. vii. L. x. c. xx., col. 410.   † T. i. Interpret in Ps. clx,
‡ Heb. vii. 26.

only for ours, but for those of the whole world—,"* but it would be sufficient to satisfy for the sins of a million of worlds. It is not only a sufficient satisfaction, as theologians say, but it is a superabundant compensation; it is a payment that far exceeds the debt; it is a reparation of honor which pleases the Eternal Father far more than the sins of millions of worlds could displease Him. So that, as Jesus Christ is at the same time the sacrifice and the person who offers it, the sacrifice loses nothing of the value and merit when offered by the hands of a bad priest, and it ceases not to be always alike profitable to those for whom it is offered; just as an alms loses nothing of its merits if bestowed by the hands of a wicked man.

This sacrifice of propitiation is offered up daily, nay, hourly, all over the world. Ah! what would become of the world without it? To its efficacy, undoubtedly, must we attribute the less frequent occurrence, in later times, of those terrible punishments which God formerly inflicted on the wicked. The whole world was once destroyed by a deluge because of sin. Seventy thousand men fell victims to a pestilence sent by God to punish the vanity of King David. Fifty thousand Bethsamites were punished with death for the irreverent curiosity with which they gazed upon the Ark of the Covenant. Why are there so few instances of such punishments since the coming of Jesus Christ? Sin has lost none of its inherent wickedness; on the contrary, it has become much more malicious by reason of the more abundant graces of God. The Fathers of the Church tell us that without doubt it is, because in all countries and at all times Jesus Christ is offered up by the priests of the Catholic Church, and the hands of God are bound. Indeed, were it not for this sacrifice of propitiation, we should have been treated long ago as were Sodom and Gomorrha. Only for it, God would have punished us long before this, according as our sins have deserved.

---

* 1 John ii. 2.

"The Mass," says St. Odo, Abbot of Cluny, "is the act on which is based the salvation of the world."* "It is to the Mass," adds Timothy of Jerusalem, "that the entire world owes its preservation: without it, the sins of man would have annihilated it long ago." †

The property of this sacrifice, then, is to appease God; it is precisely this the Apostle expresses by the words: "He offered Himself to God for us to be a victim of an agreeable sweetness." ‡ For, as men are accustomed to forgive an injury in consideration of a service or gift, so God feels appeased and looks upon us with merciful eyes in consideration of the present of the sacrifice we offer to His divine majesty. Had we been at the foot of the Cross when our Saviour died, what consolation would we not have felt in our souls, and what hope of salvation should we not have conceived, had some drops of His most precious blood fallen upon us! A miserable wretch, whose life was spent in robbing, was filled with so much confidence at the side of our Lord, that, in an instant, from a robber he became a saint, and from the cross to which he was fastened he raised himself to the enjoyment of everlasting glory. The same Son of God Who then offered Himself for us upon the Cross, still daily offers Himself for us upon the altars, and the sacrifice offered in our churches is of as great a price and of as great virtue as that which was consummated upon Mount Calvary. Hence the Church is accustomed to say, "that the work of our Redemption is as often performed as we celebrate the commemoration of this Victim," § the fruits and graces of the bloody sacrifice of the Cross being applied to us by the unbloody sacrifice of the Mass. The voice of the blood of the Lamb of God prevails over the sins which cry to heaven for vengeance, and benedictions descend where punishments are due. How could it be otherwise? "Appeased by the

---

* Opusc. 2, c. 28.   † Orat. de Proph.   ‡ Eph. v. 2.
§ In orat. secret. Dom. 9, p. Pent.

Sacrifice of the Mass," says the Council of Trent, "God forgives even the most heinous crimes." *

However, we must not believe that the Sacrifice of the Mass is, properly speaking, the ordinary means which God makes use of to effect our justification. No, our sins are not directly and immediately remitted by Mass, as they are by baptism or the sacrament of penance; but this adorable sacrifice obtains the grace of repentance through which the sinner is disposed to go to confession, and by the reception of the sacrament of penance, in right and holy dispositions, to obtain the forgiveness of all his transgressions.

It would be a very wrong interpretation of the doctrine of the holy Council of Trent to pretend that, in order to recover sanctifying grace, when we had the misfortune of losing it by mortal sin, it is sufficient to assist at the holy Sacrifice of the Mass. The benefit we derive from our assistance at it, when we hear it with faith and the other necessary conditions, is the remission of venial sins, without the obligation of applying ourselves to the sacrament of penance, as well as several other spiritual graces. As for mortal sins, they can only be remitted by the sacrament of penance. Always remember that the sole effect with regard to such sins, of our assistance at Mass, is to appease the wrath of God, and to induce Him to grant us the requisite dispositions to receive the sacrament of penance worthily, which *alone* can effect our justification. And it is thus understood and explained that we say the Sacrifice of the Mass is propitiatory for the living.

"Unless you do penance," says our Lord in the Gospel, "you shall perish." Now, it is certain that no one will do true penance for his sins unless he is very sorry for them. But to have this sorrow requires a particular grace of God. Jesus Christ, speaking of the just, says: "As the branch cannot bear fruit of itself, unless it abide in the vine, so

---

* Sess. 23, c. iii.

neither can you, unless you abide in Me."[*] Now, if this be true of those who already enjoy the grace of God, it is especially true of sinners. The poor sinner, deprived of God's grace, is like a child that is helpless and abandoned. He is unable, of his own strength, to rise from the state of sin and recover the friendship of God. "If any one," says the Council of Trent, "asserts that without the preceding inspiration and grace of the Holy Ghost man can believe, hope, love, or repent in such a manner as he ought, let him be anathema." Consider well the word: "Repent in such a manner as he ought." Judas repented, for Holy Scripture says of him: "Then Judas, who betrayed Jesus, seeing that He was condemned, repenting himself, brought back the thirty pieces of silver to the chief priests and ancients, saying: I have sinned in betraying innocent blood."[†] But this was not such repentance as is required for justification; it proceeded only from natural motives, and consequently ended in despair. "And Judas," as Holy Scripture says, "went and hanged himself with a halter."

We may, indeed, fall into sin without any assistance; but rise from it we cannot, except by the special assistance of God. I can pluck out my eyes, but to set them in again properly is beyond my power. I can likewise lose the grace of God, but to recover it again without God's assistance, is more than I can do. St. Peter remained chained in prison until an angel came and said to him: "Arise," and the chains fell from his hands.[‡] Had St. Peter not been awakened by the angel, he would not have thought of rising; and had he thought of it, he would not have been able to free himself from his fetters. In like manner, the soul which has once been chained by sin will scarcely ever think seriously of being converted and returning to God. Should it even think of this, all its efforts will not suffice to break the chains of sin, and free it from the slavery of the devil, if God's grace does not come to its aid.

---

[*] John xiii. 4.   [†] Matt. xxii. 8.   [‡] Acts xii. 7.

One day St. Anselm met a boy playing with a bird. The poor bird tried to fly away, but it could not, as the boy held it by a thread which he had tied to its leg. The little bird tried to fly away again and again, but the boy always pulled it back, and laughed and leaped for joy, as he saw it flutter and fall upon the ground. St. Anselm stood gazing for a considerable time at this strange sport, and showed the greatest compassion for the poor little bird. Suddenly the thread broke, and the little bird flew away. The boy began to cry, but St. Anselm expressed the greatest joy. All present were astonished to see so great a prelate take such interest in this childish sport. But St. Anselm said: "Do you know what I thought of on seeing this boy amuse himself thus with the bird? Ah! it is thus, thought I, that the devil makes sport of sinners. He ties them at first, as it were, with a slender thread, and then sports with them as he pleases, drawing them from one sin into another." Some he ties by indifference to God and to their own salvation, others by too great love for the goods of this world; some, again, he ties by the sin of avarice, others by the sin of uncleanness, others by the sin of theft. Many a one of the unfortunate sinners, seeing his great misery, will cry out like St. Augustine: "How long, O Lord! Wilt Thou be angry forever? Remember not my past iniquities." And perceiving himself still held back by them, he cast forth miserable complaints, and reproached himself, saying: "How long? How long? To-morrow! To-morrow! Why not now? Why does not this hour put an end to my filthiness?" These complaints he uttered, and he wept with most bitter contrition of heart, not feeling courage enough to renounce his evil ways.

"Oh! would to God," cries many a sinner, "that I were freed from this accursed habit of drinking, of swearing, of sinning against the angelic virtue of holy purity! What am I to do?" Like the little bird, this poor sinner wishes to get free from his sinful habits, but in vain. The devil keeps him tied, and drags him back into his old sins. At last the unhappy wretch, seeing that he cannot get free, gives way to despair.

Many sinners become so hardened that they resemble incarnate demons;—even were hell open before them, they would still continue to sin. Others, again, are so unhappy that they do not see their misery, whilst some do not wish to see it, lest they should feel any stings of conscience, and conceive a desire of amendment. There are others who would indeed wish to amend, and even feel the good-will to do so, but they lack courage and energy.

Oh, unhappy state of sinners! Whence shall such men obtain light to understand their misery? Whence shall they receive the good-will, the courage, and energy to free themselves from their evil habits? From God alone: He can grant those graces. "The heart of man," says Holy Writ, "is in the hand of the Lord; He turns it whithersoever He wills." God can in one moment enlighten the sinner so that he understands the misery and danger of his state. The Lord can so move his will, that he makes a firm resolution to amend. He can in one moment inspire the heart of the sinner with so much confidence in His mercy, that he firmly hopes for the forgiveness of all his sins. Now it is this unspeakably great grace that the sinner surely obtains at Mass if he assists at it with proper devotion.

O! my sweet and most merciful Lord, Thou knowest the number of souls which Thou hast most wonderfully reclaimed from their evil ways by this sacrifice of propitiation! How many unnatural children, who had almost entirely renounced and forsaken Thee by the irregularity and the profligacy of their conduct, hast Thou not, by the influence of Thy grace, changed into sincere penitents, crying with bitter sorrow, "Father, I have sinned against heaven and before Thee, I am not now worthy to be called Thy son; make me as one of Thy hired servants."* How many crim-

---
* Luke xv. 19.

inals have returned from this new Mount Calvary striking their breasts and imploring mercy! How many lepers, after having earnestly solicited Thy assistance, have been inwardly urged to go and show themselves to the priests, and have been cured of their loathsome disorder!

St. Paul the hermit had received from God the gift of the penetration of hearts. By means of this gift he could discover the most secret thoughts of his fellow-men. On Sundays when the hermits went to hear Mass he often stayed at the entrance of the church, in order to tell those who in the state of mortal sin entered the house of God, to repent of, and do penance for, their evil deeds. One day he saw a man go to church whose face was quite disfigured, and who was followed by several evil spirits who kept him chained and pulled him to the right and to the left. His guardian angel followed at a distance, with great compassion for the unhappy man. At this lamentable sight, the holy hermit commenced to shed bitter tears; he struck his breast and greatly sympathized with the poor wretched sinner. But wonderful to relate, after Mass was over, he saw that great sinner come out with a bright countenance, and his guardian angel quite close by him. Full of joy, he exclaimed: "O most inconceivable, O most wonderful mercy of God! Behold, my brethren, I saw this man enter the church with a black face and surrounded by several evil spirits; and now, on coming out, I see him beautiful and bright like an angel." Then turning to that sinner, he said: "Give honor to God, and tell us in what state you entered the church." "I am a great sinner," said he; "I have spent many years in debauchery; but when I heard in the Epistle of the Mass, the words of the prophet Isaias, 'Wash yourselves, be clean, take away the evil of your devices from my eyes,' etc., 'if your sins be as scarlet, they shall be made white as snow.' I entered into myself and said to God: 'O my Lord, Thou Who camest into this world to save poor sinners, save me, the most wretched of sinners.' These were the sentiments of my heart during Mass. I firmly resolved never more to offend Almighty God. I besought the Lord to forgive me and to receive me once more in mercy. With these sentiments I left the church." Now, when the hermits heard this, they exclaimed: "Ah! how great is the mercy of God! He bestows the grace of conversion upon sinners in the holy sacrifice of Mass, and receives them again into His sacred embraces."*

What a consolation for us poor sinners to think that, as the sun in its course brings daylight to each successive spot on the earth, it ever finds some priest girding himself to go up to the altar; that thus the earth is belted from the rising of the sun unto the going down of the same, with a chain of Masses; that as the din of the world commences each day, the groan of the oppressed, the cry of the fearful and troubled, the boast of sin and pride, the wail of sorrow—the voice of Christ ascends at the same time to heaven supplicating for pardon and peace!

It is in this sacrifice of propitiation that the eagerness of God to save sinners is truly manifest. It is this eagerness for the salvation of sinners that makes Him come down from heaven in every Mass and say to them: "'Return, ye transgressors, to the heart.'† Sinners, enter once more into your own hearts; think on the benefits you have received from Me, on the love I have borne you, and offend Me no more. Turn ye to Me, and I will turn to you; I will receive you in My embraces.‡ My children, why will you destroy yourselves, and of your own free will condemn yourselves to everlasting death? Return to Me and you shall live.

"Have you forgotten that I am that Good Shepherd who goes about seeking the lost sheep, and on finding it makes a festival, saying: 'Rejoice with Me, because I have found

---

* Lives of the Fathers of the Desert. Lib. V. *in fine.*
† Isaias xlvi. 8. ‡ Ezech. xxi. 31.

My sheep that was lost?'* And He lays it upon his shoulders, and carefully keeps possession of it in His fond embraces for fear He should lose it again. Have you forgotten that I am that loving Father, Who, whenever a prodigal son that has left Him returns to His feet, does not thrust him away, but embraces him, kisses him, and as it were, faints away from the consolation and fondness which He feels in beholding his repentance? With what tenderness did I, the moment she repented, forgive Magdalen and change her into a saint! With what kindness did I forgive the paralytic, and at the same moment restore him to bodily health! And with what sweet gentleness, above all, did I treat the woman taken in adultery! The priests brought that sinner before Me, that I might condemn her; but I, turning towards her, said: 'Hath no man condemned thee? Neither will I condemn thee, I, who came to save sinners; Go in peace and sin no more.'†

"Remember it was out of compassion for sinners that I have been pleased to be bound in swaddling-clothes, that they might be released from the chains of hell; that I have become poor, in order that they might be made partakers of My riches; that I have made Myself weak to give them power over their enemies; that I have chosen to weep and shed My blood in order that by My tears and blood their sins might be washed away."

It is thus that the Lamb of God, the Saviour of the world, speaks at Mass to every poor sinner. And in very deed, all the sins ever committed are but a grain of sand beside a huge mountain when compared with the mercy of God. Hence it is that the Lord wishes every priest to tell poor sinners what He one day commanded the prophet Isaias to tell them for their encouragement: "Say to the fainthearted, Take courage, and fear not: behold, God himself will come and will save you."‡ Fear not, then, says the

---

* Luke xv. 6. † John viii. 10. ‡ Isaias xxxv. 4.

prophet; despair no more, O poor sinners! What fear can you have of not being pardoned when the Son of God Himself comes down from heaven in each Mass to save you? Has not He Himself made compensation to God by the sacrifice of His life for that just vengeance which our sins demanded? If you cannot by your own works appease an offended God, behold His Son upon our altars, Who can appease Him; this His very Son, with His tears, prayers, sufferings, and death, propitiates Him. You have no grounds for being any longer sad, on account of the sentence of death fulminated against you, now that Life Itself is upon our altars. If you are unable to render due satisfaction to the Divine Justice, look on Jesus during Mass, where He offers to His Father all the penances which He performed for thirty-three years in satisfaction for your sins. Hence, God, Who accepts on our behalf the torments and death of Jesus Christ, is obliged to pardon us in virtue of the compact made. He charged His beloved Son with all our iniquities, in order to release us from the punishment due to them.

Let us, then, not be afraid of Jesus Christ, but of our own obstinacy, if, after offending Him, we will not listen to His voice, inviting us to be reconciled. "Who is it that shall condemn?" says the Apostle; "Christ Jesus who died; Who also maketh intercession for us." [*] If we persist in our obstinacy, Jesus Christ will be constrained to condemn us; but if we repent of the evil we have done, what fear need we have of Jesus Christ? Who has to pronounce on us sentence? "Think," says St. Paul, "that the self-same Redeemer has to sentence thee who died for thee, and still descends from heaven every day, and dies mystically in each Mass, in order that He might not condemn thee; that self-same One Who, that He might pardon thee, has not spared Himself."

Go then, O sinner, go to Mass, give thanks to this your

---

[*] Rom. viii. 34.

Redeemer, Who there comes down from heaven to call you to Himself and to save you. If you are desirous of pardon, He is waiting there to pardon you. Go quickly, then, obtain your pardon, and forget not the excessive love which Jesus Christ has borne you.

Know, further, that should you love Him, your past sins will not stand in the way of your receiving from God those specially great and choice graces which He is wont to bestow on His most beloved souls: "All things work together unto good."* "Even sins," subjoins the Gloss. Yes, even the remembrance of the sins you have committed, contributes to your advantage, for the very fact that you bewail and detest them will make you more humble and more pleasing to God, and the reflection that God has welcomed you into the arms of His mercies, will be a powerful incentive for you to give yourself wholly and entirely to God. "There shall be joy in heaven upon one sinner that doeth penance, more than upon ninety-nine just." †

But what sinner is understood to give more joy to heaven than a whole multitude of just ones? That sinner, who, out of gratitude to the Divine Goodness, devotes himself wholly and fervently to the love of God, after the example of a St. Paul, a St. Mary Magdalen, a St. Mary of Egypt, a St. Augustine, a St. Margaret of Cortona. To this last saint in particular, who had formerly spent several years in sin, God revealed the place prepared for her in heaven, amongst the seraphim; and even during her life He showed her many singular favors, so much so, that beholding herself so favored she one day said to God: "O Lord, how is it that you lavish so many graces on me? Have you, then, forgotten the sins I have committed against you?" And God thus answered her: "And do you not know what I have before told you, that when a soul repents of her faults I no longer remember all the outrages she has been guilty of towards Me." This

---

* Rom. viii. 28. † Luke xv. 7.

same thing God had long ago announced by His prophet Ezechiel: "If the wicked do penance I will not remember all his iniquities." *

Our sins, then, do not prevent us from becoming saints. God readily offers us every assistance, especially at Mass, if we only desire and ask it. It remains for us to give ourselves entirely to God, and to devote to His love at least the remainder of our days in this life. If we fail, we fail of ourselves, and not through God. Let us never be so unhappy as to turn all the mercies and loving calls of God into subjects of remorse and despair upon our death-bed, at that last moment when no more time is left to do anything.

Let us acknowledge that if ever it be our misfortune to fall into hell, that place of eternal woe, the fault will be entirely our own. We shall not certainly have our God to blame. For what more could He have done to extricate us from it? It was indeed our destined and inevitable abode; but He has with His own blood effaced the terrible handwriting; and each time Mass is said, Jesus goes to Mount Calvary at the price of His blood, to keep down the ancient war between heaven and earth, to renew the treaty of solemn peace between God and man, and if, after this, we are eternally miserable, it is by our own free and deliberate choice. It is vain to allege that we have still a thousand enemies combining to drag us into the bottomless gulf. Have we not now an omnipotent arm stretched out at Mass to save us? It would be cruel to complain that unruly passions still clamor in our bosoms; can any of them speak so loud as an expiring God upon the altar? It would be injustice and insult to allege that we are surrounded by sin in every shape, and daily allured by its tempting baits: has it any persuasive power like the image of a crucified Saviour at Mass? No; if we can calmly look up at the Cross, and still embrace and continue in an evil which was so dearly expiated, we are hope-

---

* Ezech. xviii. 21.

less, we are beyond redemption, and must prepare without resource for that hell which he, for whom it was first created, had merited by such obdurate malignity.

Mass is the consolation for poor sinners! Why, then, do men go to it so seldom? Why do they hear it with such coldness? Do they not know that to do so is to offend Almighty God? Do we not wish to repair the injury done by our sins? Can we offer God a satisfaction more worthy than His well-beloved Son?

Have we not merited hell? What a consolation to be able to turn away the anger of God, and avoid the everlasting pains of hell at so small a price! Oh, happy souls who wash themselves often in the sacred laver of the blood of Jesus Christ at Mass! Unhappy souls! who prefer eternal death to a remedy so easy and efficacious! More miserable still are those who abuse and make subservient to their crimes the holy sacrifice which ought to put a stop to them.

Let us sing constantly with the prophet of the Lord this beautiful canticle of love and gratitude: "Bless the Lord, O my soul, and let all that is within me bless His holy name. Bless the Lord, O my soul, and never forget all that He has done for thee; Who forgiveth all thy iniquities; Who healeth all thy diseases; Who redeemeth thy life from destruction; Who crowneth thee with mercy and compassion; Who satisfieth thy desire with good things; thy youth shall be renewed like the eagle's."

CHAPTER XXV.

MASS, A SACRIFICE OF THANKSGIVING.

ABOUT three years ago a pious virgin, named Amelie Lautard of Marseilles, died in Rome. She was very sensitive to every outrage offered to God. There was, however, one, at which she seemed to be more pained than at all the rest. This was the ingratitude of men and their cruel neglect of our Saviour in His Eucharistic prison. During her solitary vigils before the altar, she conceived an ardent desire to make some reparation to the outraged love of Jesus Christ. The idea occurred to her of instituting a community whose mission should be to give thanks and console our divine Saviour for the ingratitude of the world by perpetual adoration before the Tabernacle, and at the same time of getting up a regular service of thanksgiving among the faithful at large, to have short prayers appointed and recommended by the Church to their constant use, for the sole and express purpose of thanking God for His countless mercies to us all, but more especially to those among us who never thank Him on their own account. In order to carry out these suggestions more effectively, she went to Rome to obtain the authorization and blessing of the Pope. She received the most affectionate welcome, for the Holy Father had been long acquainted with her by name and knew the apostolic manner of life she led. He approved of her design, encouraged her to carry it out, and gave his blessing to the work. She was in the habit of recommending to her friends the use of the *Gloria Patri* and the ejaculation *Deo Gratias*, as having been particularly commended to her devotion by the Holy Father himself.

An incident occurred to Amelie during her stay in Rome, which she often narrated as a proof of the extreme need we have of a service of thanksgiving. She went one morning to an audience at the house of a cardinal, and while waiting for her turn, she entered into a conversation with the superior of the Redemptorist Fathers in France. Always on the watch to gain an ally to the cause, she told him the motive of her journey to Rome, and begged that he would use his influence in his own wide sphere to forward its success amongst souls.

"Ah! madame!" exclaimed the Redemptorist, "it was a good thought to try and stir up men's hearts to a spirit of thanksgiving, for there is nothing more wanted in the world. The story of the nine lepers is going on just the same these eighteen hundred years. I have been forty years a priest, and during that time I have been asked to say Masses for every sort of intention, *but only once* have I been asked to say *a Mass of thanksgiving*."* Yes, truly the story of the nine lepers is being enacted now as in the old days when Jesus exclaimed sorrowfully, "Is there no one but this stranger found to return and give thanks?"

The duty of thanksgiving seems to be forgotten by most men, even by the good and pious. It would not be easy to exaggerate the common neglect of this duty. There is little enough of prayer; but there is still less of thanksgiving. For every million of *Paters* and *Aves*, which rise up from the earth to avert evils, or to ask graces, how many follow after in thanksgiving for the evils averted or the graces given?

Men are grateful to their fellow-men, grateful even to animals. But to be thankful towards God, their greatest benefactor, seems unaccountably to have fallen out of most men's practical religion altogether. If we have reason to pity God, if we may dare so to speak with St. Alphonsus, because men

---

* *Catholic World*, 1873.

sin against His loving Majesty, still more reason have we to do so when we see how scanty and how cold are the thanksgivings offered up to Him.

"This sin of ingratitude," says St. Bernard, "is an enemy of the soul that entertains it in every way, depriving it of the good it has acquired, and preventing the acquisition of more; it is a scorching wind that dries up the sources of piety, the streams of mercy, and the torrents of grace. I have an extreme hatred of ingratitude, because it is a murderer which directly attacks the soul's salvation, and in my opinion there is nothing in religious, and in persons who practise piety, so displeasing to God as ingratitude for His benefits. Why is it that often God does not grant what we ask of Him with the greatest earnestness? Is His power weakened? Are His riches exhausted? Has His affection for us waned? Alas, no! The true cause is that we do not thank God for His benefits. There are few who thank Him as they ought for His favors."

Indeed, there is nothing more odious even among men than ingratitude. "The ungrateful man," says St. Irenæus, "is a vessel of ignominy into which God pours the gall of His anger; while the grateful man is a vessel of election and honor, into which He continually pours the precious waters of His grace, making him a great instrument of His glory."

Now, to accomplish well our duty of gratitude towards Almighty God, we must consider attentively the excellence of His gifts and of the love with which He bestows them, and then make use of the means He has left us to thank Him in the most perfect manner. What are then the gifts which the love of God has bestowed upon us? To understand them in some measure, we must remember that the charity of God contains, in an eminent degree, three qualities, which, according to St. Ignatius, distinguish true from false love; for 1st, the love of God effects great things; 2d, it liberally communicates all it possesses to the beloved object; 3rd, it is always present to it in the most intimate manner.

In the first place, the love of God for us effects great things; He has drawn us from the abyss of nothingness in preference to so many other possible beings; He has formed us according to His own image; He has given us the three faculties of the soul; the entire use of the senses; He has granted us sound and perfect members; He has enriched us with happy natural qualities. Through love of us He preserves the universe; He multiplies animals for our use; He makes the trees grow, produces the plants, covers the meadows with grass, enriches the fields with harvests; He strengthens the earth under our feet, enlightens us by the sun, nourishes us by our food, refreshes us by water, warms us by fire, and cools us by air.

Add to these benefits of God the work of the Redemption of man when He became, not the deliverer of the angels, but of the human race; add the mission of the Holy Ghost to sanctify the world and to teach all truth; add our adoption as a child of God, as a brother of Jesus Christ, and heir of heaven by baptism; add moreover the benefit of a good education, our vocation to the true faith (perhaps, to the religious life), and say, Yes, " He who is mighty has done great things to me."

Secondly, God has bestowed great blessings upon us, and given Himself entirely to us when He gave the principal blessings which His almighty arm has created: namely, corporeal things for our use; the angels to guard us; grace to merit heaven; Jesus Christ for our master; His life for our example, His body for our ransom, His soul for our price; His sacred flesh for our food; His blood for our drink; in fine, when He lavished upon us all the riches of His love in the Eucharist, so that He Who knows everything knows of nothing better and has nothing greater to give. He has communicated the great and precious graces contained in His promises: viz., the assistance of His so-called *prevent-*

ing co-operating grace, the gift of faith, of hope, of habitual charity and sanctifying grace, that we might become partakers in the divine nature; for love gives itself liberally, with all its possessions, to the beloved object. Assuredly, if "God so loved the world as to give it His only Son," how could He refuse to give all things with Him? Yes, it is in this especially that the charity and benevolence of God has appeared.

Finally, God also shows His love for us in this, that He is always intimately present by His Essence, according to the doctrine of St. Paul the Apostle. "It is in Him," he says, "that we live, move, and exist," being more surrounded, filled, and penetrated with the Divinity than with the air we breathe.

He is present by His power, for He lives, He grows, He feels, He sees, He thinks, remembers, and speaks in us, by His concurrence in all these actions. He is present by His Providence, for He carries us in His bosom; He protects us as His children, removes evils both temporal and spiritual out of our path, provides us with food, and makes even temptation and all kinds of crosses and adversities profitable. In a word, God, to testify His benevolent love, is always intimately present in our body and soul, as in His temple; for He who loves, desires to be constantly united to the beloved object. There is no telling what He has done for men. "There are so many things,"* says St. John, "which Jesus did: which if they were written, every one, the world itself, I think, would not be able to contain the books that should be written." Yes, indeed, to lay open all God's blessings to the full, would be like a man trying to confine in a little vase the mighty currents of the wide ocean; for that were an easier work than to publish with human eloquence the innumerable gifts of God. Man, rightly considered, is a composition of God's benefits. This is why the royal prophet calls God his *mercy*. This means that David regarded

---

xxi. 25.

himself under every aspect as the work of the divine mercy.

Now, what enhances all the gifts and blessings of God in greatness and value, is the affection with which He bestows them. The love and affection with which He bestows His gifts is an eternal love, eternal with Himself, so ancient that we can never go back to its beginning; for God did not begin to love Himself before He began to love us, and intended to bestow His choicest graces upon us. He cast from all eternity those looks of mercy that drew us from our nothingness, in preference to so many others, who would have served Him much more faithfully than we.

Moreover, this love with which He bestows His favors is a gratuitous love, without any merit on our part, or advantage to Himself. St. John says, that the love of God for us appeared particularly in this, that we did not love Him first, thus meriting on His part a reciprocal love, but that He loved us first; that He loved us when we were His enemies, and by our nature, children of wrath. He bestows His benefits voluntarily, without having need of us, without any advantage to Himself. His eternal knowledge of the future could see in us only sin and nothingness, calculated to rouse His anger rather than gain His love; nevertheless this God, who has need of no one, who is happy in Himself, has enriched man with His benefits without any merit on his part, without any profit to Himself, even though He foresaw the many great faults that man would commit.

Finally, God has heaped upon us all His gifts and favors with an infinite love, with the same love, in its nature, with which He loves Himself, with which He loves Jesus Christ and His saints. Now, if we consider in all the gifts of the Lord the greatness and majesty of the Giver, and the infinite affection with which He gives them, we will come to understand that they are all unspeakably great, that there are no such things as small mercies. Hence it was that our Lord one day said to the Blessed Battista Varani, a Franciscan nun, "If you were never to sin again, and if you alone were to perform more penances than all the blessed in heaven have ever performed, and if you were to shed tears enough to fill all the seas, and suffer all the pains you are capable of suffering; all this could not be enough to thank Me for the very least blessing I have ever bestowed upon you." Another time, Battista said, God had given her to understand that the glorious Mother of God, and all men and angels, with their perfections, could not adequately thank the Divine Goodness for the creation of one of the least fieldflowers of the earth, which He has made for our use, in respect of the infinite gulf there is between His excellence and our vileness.

Hence, St. Gregory Nyssen was right in saying: "I think that if our whole life long we conversed with God without distraction, and did nothing but give thanks, we should really be just as far from adequately thanking our heavenly Benefactor, as if we had never thought of thanking Him at all. For time has three parts, the past, the present, and the future. If you look at the present, it is by God that you are now living; if the future, He is the hope of everything you expect; if the past, you would never have been if He had not created you. That you were born, was His blessing. And after you were born, your life and your death were equally His blessing. Whatever your future hopes may be, they hang also upon His blessing. You are only master of the present; and therefore, if you never once intermitted thanksgiving during your whole life, you would hardly do enough for the grace that is always present; and your imagination cannot conceive of any method possible by which you could do anything for the time past, or for the time to come." Since the benefits and blessings of God are unspeakably great, from their multitude, their magnitude, and their incomprehensibility, they are by no means to be concealed in silence or left without commemoration, though it be impossible to commemorate them adequately. They are to be confessed with the mouth, revered in the heart, and religiously worshipped, as far as the littleness of man can do so. For though we cannot explain them in words, we can make acknowledgment of them in the pious and enlarged affection of our hearts. Indeed, the immense mercy of our Eternal Creator condescends to approve not only that which man can do, but all He would desire to do; for the merits of the just are counted up by the Most High, not only in the doing of the work, but in the desire of the will.

Hence the spirit of thanksgiving has been in all ages the characteristic of the saints. Thanksgiving has always been their favorite prayer. They learned this spirit from our Lord Jesus Christ, who always thanked His Father in the beginning of His prayers, and when about to operate any miracle.

From the epistles of St. Paul we learn that this great Apostle constantly exhorted the Christians, "always to give thanks for all things, in the name of our Lord Jesus Christ, to God and the Father."

When the Archangel Raphael was about to make himself known to Tobias and his family, he said to them: "It is time that I return to Him that sent me: but bless God and publish all His wonderful works." Probably, as he parted from them, he showed them a glimpse of his angelic beauty, as they went immediately into an ecstasy of three hours, which filled them with a spirit of thanksgiving. "Then they, lying prostrate for three hours upon their face, blessed God, and rising up they told all His wonderful works."

The ancient Christians saluted each other with these words: "Thanks be to God." Those very words were always in the mouth and heart of the Blessed Virgin Mary. And in heaven, as St. John assures us, the blessed prostrate themselves before the throne of God to thank Him continually for all His benefits. St. Cyprian, on hearing the sentence of his death, said: "Thanks be to God," and gave twenty-five gold crowns to the man who was to cut off his head. St.

Lawrence thanked God on his gridiron. St. Boniface, in the midst of horrible torments, exclaimed: "Jesus Christ, Son of God, I thank Thee." St. Dulas, while he was being cruelly scourged, repeated: "I thank Thee, my Lord Jesus, for having deemed me worthy to suffer this for love of Thee." There is nothing more holy than a tongue which thanks God in adversity. To say but once "Thanks be to God" in adversity or illness, is better than to say it several thousand times in prosperity. Father Didacus Martinez, the Jesuit who was called the Apostle of Peru, because of his zeal for souls and his indefatigable labors in that province, used to say daily four hundred times and often six hundred times, "*Deo gratias*," "Thanks be to God," and he had some beads on purpose to be accurate. He tried to induce others to practise the same devotion, and declared that he knew there was no short prayer more acceptable to God, if only it be uttered with a devout intention.

These illustrious examples teach us how grateful we ought to be for the benefits of Almighty God. There are three degrees of the virtue of gratitude, says St. Thomas. The first engraves gratitude on the heart, causing a man to feel the good done him and acknowledge it; this is the lowest degree of gratitude, the very least that a benefit deserves. The second degree excites us to praise and magnify the benefit, and to thank the benefactor with words full of affection. The third and highest consists in adding to gratitude of the heart and mouth that of the hand, by giving something to our benefactor, and more than has been received; for, as the same Doctor remarks elsewhere, to fulfil all the duties of gratitude, we should give something *gratis*, that is, more than we have received, in as much as to give only the same, is to give nothing. How, then, shall we be able, as the word of God expressly declares, "to give to the Most High according to what He has given us?"* What can we

---

* Eccl. xxxv. 12.

do to repay God for all that He has done for us? Shall we search the depths of the sea, and offer to God its hidden treasures, its glittering pearls? Or shall we delve into the bosom of the earth, and offer to God its silver, and gold, and precious stones? Or shall we offer to God the birds of the air, the beasts of the field, the flowers and fruits of the earth? What shall we offer to God in thanksgiving for all His gifts?

Even had we offered to God all these gifts, we should still have done nothing; for the whole earth belongs to God with all its riches. The gold of the mountains, the pearls of the ocean are *His*. His are all the treasures of earth, and sea, and sky. Even were we to offer to Him our property, our honor, and our lives, we should still give to God only what He already possesses. What return, then, shall we make to God for all His favors? It is God Himself who, in His mercy, has given the devout soul a means of paying off this immense debt of gratitude. This means is the holy Mass. The Mass is an *Eucharistic* Sacrifice, that is to say, a sacrifice of thanksgiving. Jesus Christ has left us Himself to be offered in the Mass, by way of thanksgiving, to His heavenly Father. When the priest offers to God the sublimest act of homage possible, holding the body and blood of the Redeemer above the altar, suspended between heaven and earth, he presents the great thanksgiving as the source and object of all honor and glory, saying: "To Thee, O God, the Father Omnipotent, together with the Holy Ghost, through Christ, with Christ, and in Christ, is all honor and glory," [*] in which words the Church declares that she is incapable of offering up her thanks to God in any other way than by giving Him back who became the Victim for the world; as though she were to say: "Thou didst, O Lord, for Christ's sake look down, with graciousness and compassion, upon us as *Thy children;* so vouchsafe that we, with grateful hearts,

---

[*] Canon of Mass.

may revere Thee as *our Father* in Christ, Thy Son, here present. We possess nought else that we can offer Thee, save Christ; be graciously pleased to receive this our sacrifice of thanksgiving."

In order to understand, in some measure, the great return we make in the Mass to the Almighty for all the benefits bestowed upon us, we have but to consider the gift we offer to God in gratitude—the glorious privileges of the Sacred Humanity of Jesus Christ, and the excellence of our dear Saviour on account of His Divinity.

His body is the temple of God, because the plenitude of the divinity dwells in Him corporally, and not merely as in a cloud, of which Holy Scripture speaks when relating the manner in which, during the time of Solomon, the glory of the Lord appeared in the temple of Jerusalem. This body is the work, by excellence, of the Holy Ghost, for "the virtue of the Most High overshadowed Mary," and formed divinely this body of the pure blood of the Virgin, so that never, in all creation, has it produced any body of a delicacy, excellence, and perfection to be compared with that of the body of Jesus Christ. In His body are wrought miracles equally great and continual; in it are united infinite merits, because all the actions of Jesus Christ, without any exception, even those which are natural and necessary, are the actions of a Man-God, and are consequently of infinite value; so that, on account of the excellence and perfection of His Person, it is impossible that any actions more perfect or sublime could be found. This body is the sanctuary of sanctity itself, because Jesus Christ possesses a soul impeccable and endowed with intuitive wisdom. In fine, it is the worthy abode of the Divine Word. To form this body, the Father opened, with abundant liberality, the treasures of His power, the Son, those of His wisdom, and the Holy Ghost, those of His goodness; for if God displayed the power of His arm when He wrought astonishing miracles to glorify the "Ark of Alliance," and the Temple of Solomon, which he had caused to be built for His abode, and which were but feeble figures of the body of Jesus Christ, who would dare deny that the Most Blessed Trinity exhausted all the treasures of magnificence in ornamenting the sanctuary of the Divine Word?

The body of our Lord is gifted with incomparable beauty, consisting in the perfect proportion of all its parts, its brilliancy, and impassibility. These qualities it possesses in an eminent degree, because it is the head of the Church Triumphant, and the first-born among the dead. If, when He conversed on earth, there was seen in Him a divine majesty, tempered by a heavenly sweetness, so that many on beholding Him forgot the necessity of eating and drinking, to follow Him for several days; if, when He appeared on Mount Thabor, with so brilliant a beauty, the Apostles were ravished in ecstasy,—with what perfect graces does He not now shine in heaven, clothed in immortal glory! He must, indeed, be infinitely amiable and beautiful, whose face the angels vie with one another in contemplating; whom the Seraphim see eternally, without being satiated, and in whom our senses shall one day find their beatitude for all eternity; He, in fine, who was upon the earth the object of the complacency of His Father, as is said in St. Matthew: "This is My beloved Son, in whom I am well pleased."

But, if the beauty of the body of Jesus Christ is so great, what must not be the charms of His soul? To assert that these charms far surpass the beauty that all the saints and angels have received from nature and grace, is to express a truth as incontestable, as to say that the whole universe is greater than a grain of mustard-seed. The memory of Jesus Christ is the image of the invisible God, the living image of the divine perfections, which are ever present to Him, and which He contemplates incessantly. His understanding contains all the treasures of wisdom and knowledge. From the first instant of His creation, His understanding saw clearly, face to face, by intuitive vision, the whole divine essence; it comprehended the whole depth of the mystery of the Blessed Trinity; it knew in particular, and in all their immensity, the perfections of God; it clearly distinguished in God, as in the purest mirror, all things, past, present, and to come, even all possible things. The knowledge of all the angels together, is but darkness and ignorance, compared with the knowledge of Jesus Christ. His will is a continual practice of the most sublime truths, a lamp ever burning, of the most ardent love of God, and the perfect image of the divine will. His love, in fine, is embellished by the habit of all the virtues, ornamented with all the gifts of the Holy Ghost, in a perfect manner, as is becoming His dignity and glorious privileges. It is enriched with habitual grace, in so high a degree, that no created spirit, not even the angels, can comprehend its excellence. If the sanctifying grace with which the Blessed Virgin was filled, was so great, what must have been the measure of grace given to Jesus Christ? In a word, Jesus Christ is an immense ocean of prerogatives, of all virtues, of all perfections; the more we sound it, the deeper abysses of grace do we discover. Nothing, however, so much exalts the Sacred Humanity of Jesus Christ, as the privilege of being united by the Word to the Divinity. It is precisely in this that the eminent dignity of our dear Saviour consists—a dignity which the angels contemplate in an ecstasy of admiration—which Cherubim adore, and which all the affections and desires of the blessed never cease to glorify; for is there a prodigy equal to that of the human nature being so substantially united to the Word, as to make but one person? so that we may attribute to the human nature of Jesus Christ, that which belongs to the divine nature, and in like manner, may attribute to the divine nature that which belongs to the human nature. Consequently, in virtue of this hypostatic union, we may call God, weak, passible, mortal, dead; and say of the human nature, that it is immense, omnipotent, and omniscient. Who will not admire this truth, by which we believe that the Divinity fills and penetrates the Humanity of our Lord Jesus Christ, more than red-hot iron is penetrated by the fire; more than the air by light; more than the crystal by the rays of the sun? Hence it is that His amiability is so great, that, if heaven were opened one instant, all the demons in hell, instead of hating Him, as they do, would be compelled by a gentle violence to love Him with the most lively ardor. His beauty is so ravishing, that the lost souls would willingly suffer a thousand hells, could they contemplate it for for a single instant. His goodness has so many charms that, if the least effect of it could be experienced in hell, that horrible prison would more quickly than thought be changed into a paradise. Such is the excellence of His sanctity, that the displeasure caused Him by the least fault, far surpasses the joy afforded Him by the heroic action of all the saints. His wisdom is infinite, so that He forgets nothing that is past, He is ignorant of nothing present; and He sees the future as clearly as if all things were represented to Him in a mirror. His astonishing power equals His will. His age is eternity; His course immutability; His place, immensity, and His measure, infinity; He is so rich, that His wealth is inexhaustible; so provident, that He disposes everything without number, weight, or measure; so constant, that in Him there is no change, no shadow of vicissitude; so strong, that on three fingers He supports the world, weighs the mountains, places the hills in a balance; and so elevated is His power, that there is none like to Him; in a word, He is higher than heaven, deeper than hell, wider than the earth, vaster than the sea. Everthing is naked and open to His eyes. He holds in His hands the life and essence of every being. No one can resist His anger. Thousands and thousands of angels serve Him, and tens of thousands stand before Him.

From this feeble description of the present we offer to our Heavenly Father in the Mass for all the benefits He has ever bestowed upon us, may easily be understood what an immense return we make to God for all His blessings, and how fully we discharge by the Sacrifice of the Mass our duty of gratitude towards the Almighty.

Two pious souls were one day discoursing about the graces they had received from God. One of them complained of her inability to give due thanks to God for all she had received; the other smiled and said: "I give to God every day more than I ever received from Him." This answer naturally surprised the former, and she asked how this was possible. "Oh!" replied the latter, "I go to Mass every day, and offer up Jesus Christ to my heavenly Father for all the graces He has bestowed upon me; and Jesus Christ, the well-beloved Son of God, is certainly of greater worth than all the benefits which I ever received, or ever shall receive." Indeed, richer than if we had at our disposal all the elements and all the inhabitants of the heavenly Jerusalem, we have in the Sacrifice of the Mass, an offering which infinitely surpasses them all in dignity and power. On our altar the Eternal Son of God repeats in our name, as well as in His own, what He said in the days of His mortal existence: "O God, I give Thee thanks." What an abundant and inestimable resource in our extreme indigence! It is an inexhaustible source from which we are allowed to draw every day thanksgivings always acceptable to God. O Lord, we can never sufficiently acknowledge Thy infinite goodness in our regard. Our prayers, supplications, homage, and adoration are not worthy to be presented to Thee, but, in the Sacrifice of the Mass, it is not so much our interior acts of thanksgiving and adoration which we offer to Thee, as Thy divine Son Himself. These emotions of our heart are indeed excited, unfolded, sustained, and fostered by the presence and self-sacrifice of Thy Christ, our Saviour; but of themselves we deem them unworthy to be presented to Thee. Thy well-beloved Son, the victim in our worship, is the copious, inexhaustible source of our deepest devotion; it is to His personal Presence that we attach ourselves and unbosom all our affections. Thus, the expression of our gratitude and thanksgiving is no longer that of weak and imperfect beings, it is that of a God, equal therefore to Thy boundless and ineffable blessings.

Can we ever sufficiently bless God for having given us so easy a means of thanking Him worthily? From the moment that holy Simeon saw the promise accomplished, which the Holy Ghost had made him—that before his death he should see the Redeemer of the world—he burst forth into canticles of benediction; he received with ecstasy the holy Infant; he pressed Him in his arms, and, transported with joy and gratitude, cried out: "Now Thou dost dismiss Thy servant, O Lord, according to Thy word, in peace, because my eyes have seen Thy salvation."

The same sentiments of gratitude must animate our hearts; they should be apparent from the devotion and reverence with which we hear Mass, as well as from the eagerness with which we run to hear it, not only on days of obligation, but also on every other day, if possible.

There was a beautiful tradition amongst the Jews which Lancicius quotes from Philo. It was to this effect: When God had created the world, He asked the angels what they thought of this work of His hands. One of them replied that it was so vast and so perfect that only one thing was wanting to it, namely, that there should be created a clear, mighty, and harmonious voice, which should fill all the quarters of the world incessantly with its sweet sound, thus day and night to offer thanksgiving to its Maker for His incomparable blessings. They knew not how much more than this the holy Sacrifice of the Mass was one day to be. Happy he who faithfully discharges his duty of thanksgiving by hearing Mass every day, or, if lawfully prevented, offers up to God, as far as he can, all the Masses of the day, thus to thank the Lord for the innumerable graces He has received from Him. This spirit of gratitude is the key to the choicest gifts of the Almighty.

In one of the revelations of St. Catharine of Sienna, God

the Father tells her that thanksgiving makes the soul incessantly delight in Him, that it frees men from negligence and lukewarmness altogether, and makes them anxious to please Him more and more in all things. "Happy is he," says St. Bernard, "who at every grace he receives, returns in thought to Him in Whom is the fulness of all grace; for if we show ourselves grateful for what He has given us, we may make room for still further grace in ourselves. Speak to God in thanksgiving, and you will receive grace more abundantly."

St. Lawrence Justinian says: "Only let God see you are thankful for what He has given you, and He will bestow more and better gifts upon you." St. Mary Magdalen of Pazzi also received a revelation in which she was told that thanksgiving prepared the soul for the boundless liberality of the Eternal Word. Assuredly we shall experience this liberality of the Eternal Word in time and infinitely more in eternity by hearing Mass as often as possible, by offering to God in return for His favors multiplied, countless, immense, infinite as the Donor, His only Son, His beloved Son in Whom He is well pleased, Whose merits immeasurably surpass all our obligations; one word from Whose lips, one sigh from Whose heart is precious in His sight beyond millions of worlds, which, with their untold wealth, are but as dross before Him in comparison. "What shall I render to the Lord for all the things that He hath rendered to me? I will take the chalice of salvation and I will call upon the name of the Lord;"* and could my debt of gratitude be even greater than it is, my obligations heavier or more numerous, still would the return be more than sufficient, because infinite.

Surely these are very sweet and consoling reflections, which cannot fail to warm our hearts with the love of Jesus, and to inspire us with profound veneration for the great

---

* Ps. cxv. 12, 13.

sacrifice which has so justly been styled the golden key of Paradise. Let us endeavor by meditation and prayer to understand the value of the treasure we possess in the holy Mass, and far from requiring a recommendation to hear it as often as possible, the impulse of our own devotion will prompt us to do so. We will feel that no preparation could equal that involved in the loss of a Mass, and think little indeed of any sacrifice by which we can purchase the happiness of assisting at one.

CHAPTER XXVI.

MASS, A SACRIFICE OF IMPETRATION.

A TRAVELLER wishing to go to New York, will not arrive there by taking the train to New Orleans; he must take the cars that go to New York. It is just as certain that whoever wishes to go to heaven must follow the path that leads to heaven. If he takes another direction, he will certainly be excluded from the abode of the Blessed.

What, then, is the path that leads to heaven? There are but two; the one is the way of innocence, the other the way of penance. All who die after baptism, before they have committed any sin, all who have never lost their baptismal innocence, enter heaven by the first path: but for us who have lost that grace, who have soiled the pure robe of baptism, there is but one path left—the path of penance. Both ways are beset by three powerful enemies, the world, the flesh, and the devil, who are actively employed every instant of our life in laying snares for the destruction of the soul. This warfare will cease only with our earthly life, and must be carried on manfully to be crowned with life everlasting.

Even in this warfare the just are often in great danger of being overcome, on account of the weakness of human nature, and the malice and subtlety of their enemies.

St. Peter says, that "the devil goeth about like a roaring lion, seeking whom he may devour."* It was this arch-enemy who persuaded Adam and Eve to eat the forbidden fruit, who prevailed on Cain to slay his innocent brother Abel; who tempted Saul to pierce David with a lance. It

---

* 1 Peter, v. 8.

was he who stirred up the Jews to deny and crucify Jesus Christ our Lord; who induced Ananias and Sapphira to lie to the Holy Ghost; who urged Nero, Decius, Diocletian, Julian, and other heathen tyrants, to put the Christians to a most cruel death. He it was who inspired the authors of heresies, such as Arius, Martin Luther, and others, to reject the authority of the one, true, Catholic Church.

In like manner, the devil, at the present day, still tempts all men, especially the just, and endeavors to make them lose the grace of God. He tempts numberless souls to indifference towards God and their own salvation; he deceives many by representing to them in glowing colors the false, degrading pleasures of this world; he suggests to others the desire of joining certain bad secret societies; he tempts many even to conceal their sins in confession, and to receive Holy Communion unworthily; others, again, he urges to cheat their neighbor; he allures some to blind their reason by excess in drinking; some he tempts to despair; in a word, the devil leaves nothing untried which may cause the just to fall into sin. He finds the weak point of every man, and knows that this weak point is for many—very many—a strong inclination to the vice of impurity. The wicked spirit knows how to excite in them this degrading passion to such a degree, that they forget their good resolutions, nay, even make little account of the eternal truths, and lose all fear of hell and the Divine Judgment. It is the universal opinion of all theologians that there are more souls condemned to hell on account of this sin alone, than on account of any other which men commit.

But the just must not only wage war against their archenemy, the devil, they must also fight manfully against the seductive examples of the world. Were all those who have lost their baptismal innocence to tell us how they came to lose it, they would al answer: "It was by this corrupt companion, by this false friend, by this wicked relative. Had I never seen this person, I would still be innocent." One unsound apple is sufficient to infect all the others near it. In like manner, one corrupt person can ruin all those with whom he associates. Indeed, the bad example of one wicked man can do more harm to a community, than all the devils in hell united. Small indeed is the number of those who manfully resist bad example.

There is still another truth to be considered here. St. Paul the Apostle says: "All that live godly in Christ Jesus shall suffer persecution."* All those who endeavor to serve our Lord Jesus Christ faithfully, and to persevere in His service, will have to suffer, in some way or other, from their fellow-men. Sometimes it will be from jealous and envious neighbors; sometimes from bad comrades, whose company they have given up; again, they are blamed, rashly judged, and condemned; and what is the most painful of all, God, to try their patience and charity, often permits them to suffer most from those very persons from whom they should naturally expect sympathy and consolation. Very small, indeed, is the number of those who, under such severe trials, remain faithful to God. The greater part, even of the just, cannot bear detraction and calumny. To suffer a temporal loss seems almost insupportable; to forgive an injury or an insult is more than they can do; they try to avoid those who have offended them; they complain bitterly of, and sometimes even curse them.

The just must fight not only against the devil and the world, but also against their own corrupt nature. Had they not this enemy to contend with, the devil and the world would not so easily overcome them. Corrupt nature plays the traitor, and very often gains the victory, even when the other enemies have failed. This dangerous foe is always near, within their very hearts; and his influence is the more fatal because the greater number of the just themselves do not seem to be fully aware of his existence; hence it is that they are so

---

* 2 Tim. iii. 12.

little on their guard against his wiles, and fall a prey to his evil suggestions.

Ever since the fall of our first parents, we are all naturally inclined to evil. Before Adam had committed sin, he was naturally inclined to good; he knew nothing of indifference in the service of God, nothing of anger, hatred, cursing, impurity, vain ambition, and the like; but no sooner had he committed sin, than God permitted his inclination to good to be changed into an inclination to evil. Man of his own free will forfeited the kingdom of heaven; he exchanged heaven for hell, God for the devil, good for evil, the state of grace for the state of sin. It was, then, but just and right that he should not only acknowledge his guilt, repent sincerely of his great crime, but that he should also, as long as he lived, fight against his evil inclinations, and, by this lifelong warfare, declare himself sincerely for God.

Baptism, indeed, cancels original sin in our soul, but it does not destroy our natural inclination to evil, which we have inherited from our first parents. The great Apostle St. Paul bears witness to this when he says: "I do not that good which I will, but the evil which I hate, that I do." *
That is to say, I do not wish to do evil; I even try to avoid it; but I experience within myself a continual inclination to evil; I endeavor to do good, but I feel within myself a great reluctance thereto, and I must do violence to myself in order to act aright. Every one has from his childhood experienced this evil inclination. We naturally feel more inclined to anger than to meekness, to disobedience than to submission; we are more prone to hatred than to love; more inclined to gratify the evil desires of our heart than to practise the holy virtue of purity; we prefer our own ease to visiting Jesus Christ in the Blessed Sacrament, or receiving Him in the Holy Communion. We are naturally indifferent towards God and His holy religion; we lack fervor in His divine service; we often feel more inclined to join a

---
* Rom. vii. 15.

forbidden society than to enter a pious confraternity; we often find more pleasure in reading a bad or useless book than one that is good and edifying; we are more apt to listen to uncharitable and unbecoming conversation, than to the word of God; we feel naturally more inclined to vain glory, pride, and levity, than to humility, self-control, and the spirit of mortification.

When we consider seriously the continual war we have to wage against these three powerful enemies; when we consider our extreme weakness, and the sad fact that the greater part of mankind do not overcome even one of their enemies, we see clearly how terribly true are the words of our Lord: "Wide is the gate and broad is the way that leadeth to destruction, and many there are who go in thereat. How narrow is the gate and strait is the way that leadeth to life, and few there are that find it."* Ah! who shall find this strait way? Who will be able to conquer these three enemies of our salvation? Whence shall we obtain strength and courage to struggle bravely against them until death? Truly must we exclaim with King Josaphat: "As for us, we have not strength enough to be able to resist this multitude, which cometh violently upon us. But as we know not what to do, we can only turn our eyes to Thee, our God." By our own efforts alone we shall never be able to overcome even one of our enemies.

It is only by the constant efficacious grace and assistance of God that we can overcome them to the end of our life. But how are we to obtain this assistance? By prayer. But vile, abject, worthless, and undeserving as we are, by what right shall we venture to implore the numberless favors of which we stand in need in the order both of nature and grace? Certainly, by no right of our own, for in truth, we have not the very least. But happily for us, our dear Saviour came, and by His tears, His labors, and sufferings, by His blood and death upon the Cross, but especially by His

---

* Matt. vii. 13, 14.

prayers, He obtained for us from His Heavenly Father, the right to every grace and gift of the Lord. This right He obtained by His prayers particularly; for the Heavenly Father had decreed not to grant any grace to man, not even to His Divine Son, except through prayer, which is the channel through which all graces flow. Wishing to be glorified by His Father, Jesus had to pray for this favor: "And lifting up His eyes to heaven, He said : Father, the hour is come, glorify thy Son."* Jesus merited the empire of the whole universe; notwithstanding which He obtained it only by praying for it. "Ask, my Son," says the Heavenly Father, "all the nations of the earth, and I will give them to Thee for Thy inheritance."

Our dear Saviour, knowing this decree of His Father concerning the necessity of prayer to obtain the divine grace, was therefore not satisfied with preaching, laboring, fasting, nor even with the sacrifice of His blood and life for the salvation of mankind. To all this He added most fervent prayer. Prayer was His chief occupation from the moment of His Incarnation until that of His death. Thirty years of His life were consecrated to this holy exercise, and three years and a half only to the instruction of the people, and even of this short period of three years He spent the greater part in prayer. How often did He not say to His disciples: "Withdraw a little from the multitude." And for what purpose? That they might be more at liberty to pray. Moreover, do we not read in the Gospel that after having spent the day in instructing the people, He would retire to a lonely mountain, there to spend the whole night in prayer? "And it came to pass that He went out into a mountain to pray, and He passed the whole night in the prayer of God." † This was the custom of our Saviour, as we may gather from the fact that Judas, the traitor, did not go with the soldiers to seek Him in the city of Jerusalem, but went straightway

---

* John xi. 1. † Luke vi. 12.

to the Mount of Olives, because he knew that Jesus was accustomed to go thither to spend the night in prayer. We may say that prayer was His life, and His life a continual prayer. He had no sooner become man than He prayed, and He died with prayer on His lips. He perfectly accomplished that which He inculcates to His disciples, that we must always pray, to overcome our enemies and to sanctify our lives.

And for whom did He pray? He prayed for all men in general; but He prayed especially for those who would believe in Him, and follow Him faithfully. "I pray for them (His disciples); I pray not for the world, but for them whom Thou hast given me: that they may be one, as We also are one. I do not ask that thou take them away out of the world, but that Thou preserve them from evil. Sanctify them in truth. And not for them only do I pray, but for those also who through their word shall believe in Me: that they all may be one, as Thou, Father, in Me and I in Thee, that they also may be one in US; that the world may believe that Thou hast sent Me. Father, I will that where I am, they also whom Thou hast given Me, may be with Me; that they may see my glory which Thou hast given Me."* It is thus that Jesus prays to His Eternal Father for all His elect; it is He Who loves them with a love of preference, a love full of tenderness and strength, and in dying He recommends them with a particular affection.

What does He demand for them? The same riches, pleasures, and glory that He has chosen for Himself. His glory is to be the Son of God: He desires that His Father should cherish them as His brethren. He is the Holy of Holies: He would have them to be holy as He is holy. He is from eternity in the bosom of God; He will have them to dwell there, tasting with Him the delights of beatitude for eternity. He is one with the Father in essence and in love: He

---

* John xvii.

desires that they should be one with Him, and one among themselves.

O what a powerful advocate with the Heavenly Father had mankind in the Person of Jesus Christ during His life on earth for thirty-three years and a half! If the Lord of heaven and earth spared the Jewish nation for the sake of Moses' prayer; if He declared Himself ready one day to spare the city of Jerusalem for the sake of a just man's prayer, should one be found therein, assuredly from the moment that Jesus Christ commenced to pray for the human race, His Father felt reconciled with men and ready to grant them all graces. But alas! this divine, this all-powerful Advocate has left the world and ascended into heaven! Who will now pray for us and with us, to make our prayers acceptable in the sight of God, and obtain for us all we need for body and soul? Jesus knew that men could not advance in this world without His powerful intercession, without His continual prayer. He knew that the prayers of men were not powerful enough to obtain salvation unless they were supported by, and united to His. So, in the excess of His love He chose to stay with us by means of the holy Mass, to be in this holy sacrifice our perpetual Advocate with His Father. In Mass He renews all the prayers which He addressed to His Father in our behalf for the space of thirty-three years and a half, and offers them to Him to obtain for us the abundance of spiritual and temporal blessings. It is for this reason that Mass is also called a *sacrifice of impetration.*

Let us imagine that we are assisting at Mass, and that the solemn words of the Preface are uttered: "Holy, holy, holy, Lord God of Hosts, heaven and earth are full of thy glory. Blessed is He that cometh in the name of the Lord." The worshippers are warned that the Lord of glory is about to appear before them upon the altar. They rouse their best feelings to receive Him. And now the Redeemer comes from His throne at the right hand of God. He comes from among the Cherubim and Seraphim, from among the angels and archangels who have taken up our adoring cry of welcome, Blessed is He that cometh in the name of the Lord! This loving cry reaches the gate of Heaven; it is re-echoed on the mercy-seat. The Eternal Word replies: "*Ecce venio*, Lo, I come!" And the ancients fall down and cast their crowns at His feet as He passes, and the thousands of thousands of angels around the throne strike their golden harps and sing: "Worthy is the Lamb that was slain to receive power, and divinity, and wisdom, and honor, and glory, and benediction, for ever and ever." And *now* "the Lamb that was slain from the foundation of the world"—the Lamb of God—our Lord Jesus Christ, comes down from Heaven to offer Himself up again for each one present. The awful words of consecration are pronounced, and Jesus Christ, the King of glory, is really and truly present upon the altar as a Victim of impetration.

In the Old Law, the High Priest entered once a year into the Holy of Holies. His sacred place was separated from the rest of the temple by a veil; and while the High Priest prayed unseen behind the veil, the people prayed in silence without. Thus, too, it is in the holy Sacrifice of the Mass. The priest raises the Sacred Host on high; we see the white appearance of bread; that is the white veil which hides from our gaze the God of all holiness. Behind that veil our Lord Jesus Christ intercedes with His Eternal Father in our behalf. It is a most solemn moment. Let no sound be heard to break its awful stillness. Even the priest dares not raise his voice; he prays in silence. The Lord is present. He prays for us. "Let the whole earth be silent before Him." It is a moment rich in untold blessings. Would that Christians might understand better the great power of Mass to obtain all kinds of graces and blessings! Assuredly they would not so easily stay away, especially on days of obligation, nor would they assist at it with such lukewarmness.

In order to understand well how powerful a means Mass is of obtaining from God every blessing possible, one need only consider the qualities which accompany the prayer of Jesus at Mass. Holy Scripture tells us that prayer to be pleasing to the Almighty must be humble. "The prayer of the humble and the meek hath always pleased Thee."* Jesus Christ assures us in the Gospel that the Publican who prayed with so much humility went down justified to his house.† "To the humble God giveth grace; their prayer shall pierce the clouds," says Holy Writ. As God is severe and inexorable to the proud, so is He bountiful and liberal to the humble. "Know, my daughter," said Jesus Christ to St. Catherine of Sienna, "that whosoever shall humbly persevere in asking graces of Me, shall obtain all virtues." "Never did I," says St. Teresa, "receive more favors from God, than when I humbled myself before His divine Majesty." "Yes," says St. Alphonsus, "should a soul have committed ever so many sins, yet the Lord will not reject her if she knows how to humble herself." "An humble heart, O Lord, Thou wilt not despise." ‡

Holy Scripture § tells us that Achab was one of the most impious kings that ever lived. God sent to him the prophet Elias to tell him that in punishment for his enormous crimes the Lord would cut off his posterity, and that their bodies would be eaten up by the dogs in the streets and by the birds of the air. Now when Achab heard these words, he rent his garments, and put haircloth upon his flesh, and fasted and slept in sackcloth and walked with head cast down. When the Lord saw how the king humbled himself He again sent the prophet Elias to Achab, to tell him that as he had humbled himself before the Lord, the evils with which his house had been threatened would not be inflicted in his days, but in the days of his son.

If this impious king obtained forgiveness, if he was not punished by the Lord as he had deserved, because he humbled himself before God, what will not the humiliations

---

* Judith ix. 16.   † Luke xviii. 10.   ‡ Ps. l. 19.   § 8 Kings xxi.

of Jesus Christ at Mass be able to obtain for wretched sinners! When our dear Saviour is lying upon our altars as our Victim; when He offers to His Father in heaven all the humiliation He went through during His lifetime on earth, together with those He has been submitting to in the Blessed Sacrament—oh! then does the Heavenly Father say to His angels as He said to Elias: "Do you see how my well-beloved Son humbles Himself before Me for the salvation of men? Do you see the excess of humility with which He prays to Me for all men? With that same humility with which He prayed to Me in the Garden of Gethsemane and when hanging on the Cross?" "Ah, yes," the angels answer, "when we behold our King and Master lying in the crib, or prostrate on His face, we are almost beside ourselves at the sight of the infinite humility with which He prays." It is then that the Heavenly Father cannot help saying: "Because my well-beloved Son prays to Me with such unspeakable humility for sinners as well as for the just, I cannot refuse His prayers, I feel constrained to grant all He asks for them." It is for this reason that the Church prays that "our vices may be cured by the sacred mysteries, and that we may receive everlasting remedies; that her solemnities may both confer upon us the remedies of the present life, and grant us the rewards of eternity."

History records many memorable examples to show us the fulfilment of such prayers. Listen to the great poet who sung the recovery of Jerusalem, telling the story of his own conversion. "A time there was," says Tasso, "when I, darkening as I did my mind with clouds of sensuality, could only recognize Thee, O Lord, as a certain reason of the Universe; for I doubted whether Thou hadst created the world or endowed man with an immortal soul, and I doubted of many things which flowed from that source; for how could I firmly believe in the Sacraments, or in the authority of the Pontiff, or in hell, or purgatory, or in the Incarnation of Thy Son, if I doubted of the immortality of the soul? Willingly I would have kept down my understanding, of itself curious and wandering, and believed whatever the holy Roman Catholic Church believes and teaches; but this I desired, O Lord, not so much through love of Thy infinite goodness, as through a certain servile fear which I had of the torments of hell; for often there used to sound horribly to my imagination the angelic trumpet of the great day of rewards and punishments, and I saw Thee sitting upon the clouds, and heard Thee utter words full of terror,—Depart, ye cursed, into everlasting fire. And this thought was so strong in me, that sometimes I used to communicate it to some friend or acquaintance of mine, and in consequence of this fear I used to go to confession, and to communion, in the times and manner prescribed by Thy Roman Church; and if at any time I thought I had not mentioned any sin through negligence or shame, though it was ever so little and vile, I repeated my confession, and often made a general confession of all my errors. Yet Thou knowest that I always desired, though perhaps with a fervor more mundane than spiritual, that the seat of Thy faith and pontificate in Rome might be preserved for ever. And Thou knowest that the name of Lutheran or heretic was abhorred and detested by me, as a pestiferous thing, and that my doubts were merely an interior affliction, until Thou didst begin to warm and to rejoice my heart with the flames of Thy love: and then by degrees, *by means of frequenting oftener the sacred mysteries* of the Mass, and praying every day, my faith grew stronger from day to day, and I became sensible from experience that it is Thy gift, and I learned to see my past folly in having presumed to imagine that I could discover by my intelligence the secret things of Thy essence, and estimate by the measure of human reason Thy goodness, Thy justice, Thy omnipotence." *

---

* Torquato Tasso. Discorso sopra vari accidenti della sua vita, scritto a Scipion Gonzaga.

This affecting passage clearly shows the wonderful effect produced by the prayer of Jesus in souls, whilst assisting at the celebration of the sacred mysteries. Nor is there matter for wonder at this; for the Mass contains a spectacle that gives delight to angels; it is here that they behold the elevation of the innocent Lamb of God, praying to His Father with such deep humility as to obtain all.

Father Columbiere used to say: "When I pray, or fast, or give alms, or do penance for any sins, I do so with a certain diffidence, not knowing whether or not the intention is pure enough to make them pleasing in the sight of God. But when I say Mass, or assist at the holy Sacrifice, I am, O my God, full of confidence and courage; I dare challenge all the saints of heaven to offer something more pleasing to Thee than Mass; neither terrified by the number nor by the grievousness of my sins, I most confidently ask Thy pardon, not doubting in the least but Thou wilt grant it more abundantly than I could ask it; how great soever the desires of my heart may be, I do not hesitate in the least to pray Thee to gratify them all."

A prayer which is also infallibly heard by the Almighty is that which is accompanied with forgiveness of injuries, and great charity for our enemies.

To pray for those who wish us evil, is an extremely difficult act, and one full of the most heroic charity. It is an act free from self-love and self-interest, which is not only counselled but even commanded by the Lord.* The insults, calumnies, and persecutions of our enemies, relate directly to our own person; wherefore, if we forgive, nay, even beg of God also to forgive them, we give up our claim to our right and honor, thus raising ourselves to the great dignity of true children of God, nay, even to an unspeakably sublime resemblance to His divinity, according to what Jesus Christ says: "if you pray for those who hate you, calumniate, and

---

* Matt. v. 44.

persecute you, you will be children of your Father who is in heaven, who maketh His sun to rise upon the good and bad, and raineth upon the just and the unjust." * For there is nothing more peculiar to God than to have mercy and to spare; to do good to all His enemies, convert them into His friends and His children, and thus make them heirs of everlasting glory.

By imitating God's goodness in a point most averse to our nature, we give Him the greatest glory,—and do such violence to His tender and meek heart as to cause it not only to forgive the sin of our enemies, but even to constrain it to grant all our prayers; because He wishes to be far more indulgent, far more merciful, and far more liberal than it is possible for us ever to be. Holy Scripture and the lives of the saints furnish us with very striking examples in proof of this great and most consoling truth.

The greatest persecutor of St. Stephen was St. Paul the Apostle, previous to his conversion; for, according to St. Augustine, he threw stones at him by the hands of all those whose clothes he was guarding. What made him, from being a persecutor of the Church, become her greatest Apostle and Doctor? It was the prayer of St. Stephen: "for, had he not prayed," says St. Augustine, "the Church would not have gained this Apostle." St. Mary Oigni, whilst in a rapture, saw how our Lord made to St. Stephen a present of the soul of St. Paul before his death, on account of the prayer which the former had offered for the latter; she saw how St. Stephen received the soul of this Apostle, the moment of his death, and how he presented it to our Lord, saying: "Here, O Lord, I have the immense and most precious gift which Thou gavest me, now I return it to Thee with great usury." †

Most touching is what Father Avila relates of St. Elizabeth of Hungary. One day this saint prayed to God to give great

---

* Matt. v. 45. † Her Life, by Cardinal Vitriaco, Lib. 2, chap. xi.

graces to all those who had in any way injured her; nay, even to give the greatest graces to those who had injured her the most. After this prayer our Lord Jesus Christ said to her: "My dear daughter, never in your life did you make a prayer more pleasing to Me than the one which you have just said for your enemies; on account of this prayer I forgive not only all your sins, but even all temporal punishments due to them." Let us be sure that the greater injuries we forgive for God's sake, the greater graces we shall receive in answer to our prayer.

Now, no saint ever forgave more and greater injuries than our divine Saviour did; no saint ever forgave his enemies with so much charity and generosity, ever prayed for his persecutors with so much fervor as our Lord did. Who can think of Jesus hanging on the Cross and hear Him pray, nay, even cry to His Father for the forgiveness of His enemies, without feeling moved to tears at such an excess of divine charity! "Father, forgive them, for they know not what they do."* Let us rest assured that Jesus Christ said this prayer not only when hanging on the Cross, but every moment of His life. He had come down from heaven to be our Saviour, therefore it was His greatest desire that His Father should forgive us, and not forgive us only, but grant us every grace and blessing. To force His Father, as it were, to do so, He prayed constantly to Him with infinite charity for all of us who were His enemies. How could the Heavenly Father refuse to listen to such a prayer? It was by its effect that the good thief was converted, and that the centurion who led the soldiers to crucify our Lord, repented, and on leaving Mount Calvary, struck his breast, saying: "Indeed this man was the Son of God."† The powerful effects of that prayer will be known only on the day of judgment.

Let us remember that at Mass Jesus still prays for us with

---

* Luke xxiii. 34. † Mark xv. 35.

the same intensity of fervor and charity, with the same unspeakable desire to help and assist us in all our necessities. What He is most desirous to obtain for us is a complete forgiveness of our sins, that is to say, not only the forgiveness of eternal punishment, but also the full remission of all temporal punishments which often remain due to the divine Justice after the remission of the eternal punishment.

A criminal is often recommended to mercy because of his remorse and good conduct while in prison, and the extreme punishment of death, which he deserves, is commuted into one lighter. The same thing takes place in the government of God. Adam obtained pardon from God, and the hope of pardon for all his posterity, and yet a part of his punishment remained, the necessity of laboring for his bread, the miseries of this life, sickness, and death.

God pardoned the sin of the Israelite nation at the prayer of Moses, and did not destroy them, but left a penalty behind. Their children were allowed to enter the promised land of Canaan, but they themselves were kept back to spend their lives and die in the desert. When the prophet Nathan reproved King David for his two-fold sin of murder and adultery, David repented, confessing his guilt, and the prophet declared: "The Lord also hath taken away thy sin, nevertheless, since thou hast made the enemies of the Lord to blaspheme on account of this thing, the child which is born to thee shall surely die."*

Among the temporal punishments due to sin, after the remission of its guilt, the saints count the withholding of many of God's graces. From eternity God prepared for us all abundant graces to work out our salvation. Some of these graces were necessary to lead us to a high degree of perfection and to make us saints; others were so necessary for our salvation, that without them we should not be saved. In punishment of sin, even after its guilt has been remitted,

---

* II. Kings xii. 13.

God sometimes withholds these graces; and, therefore, our past sins, after they have been forgiven, may be the cause of our damnation, by preventing God from bestowing upon us certain graces without which we shall be certainly lost. Hence it is that the Holy Ghost tells us "not to be without fear about sin forgiven." * In order, then, to secure not only the pardon of all our past sins, but also the graces which may be withheld in punishment of them, and particularly the graces without which we should be lost, we must pray fervently and frequently for the complete and entire remission of all our sins, and of all the penalties due to them. By frequent and fervent petitions for these favors, every one, even the most abandoned sinner, however enormous his crimes may have been, can easily and infallibly avert the chastisement of sin, which consists in the withholding of God's graces; and may thus infallibly prevent the danger of his past sins being the cause of his damnation, after their guilt had been remitted.

Now, be it borne in mind that nowhere shall we obtain sooner the full remission of these temporal punishments than during the celebration of the holy Sacrifice of the Mass; for it is there that our divine Saviour Himself offers up His prayer for this very great favor. For this reason it is that St. Ephrem, who lived in the fourth century, prays: "Since Thou wast immolated a Victim for us, free us from *all defilement* by cutting off *all our sins;* for Thou hast been constituted our High Priest that, by the shedding of Thy blood, Thou mightest cleanse us from *all defilement* . . . . . An eternal Redemption having been obtained, Thou dost daily renew Thy sacrifice upon the altar, and dost present Thy saving chalice to our lips to be partaken of; to so great a benefit and gift grant such efficacy that, being freed in virtue of it *from every sin*, we may cling to Thee with the utmost love of which we are capable." †

---

* Eccl. v. 5. † Tom. III. Syr-Paraen 74, p. 555.

Oh, how advantageous it is to hear holy Mass! As St. Gertrude offered the adorable Host to the Eternal Father at the moment of the Elevation, in satisfaction for all her sins and in reparation for all her negligences, she beheld her soul presented before the Divine Majesty with the same sentiments of joy in which Jesus Christ, who is the splendor and living image of the glory of His Father, and the Lamb of God without spot, offered Himself on the altar to God His Father for the salvation of the whole world; because the Eternal Father considered her as purified from all sin by the merit of the spotless Humanity of Jesus Christ, and enriched and adorned with all the virtues which, through the same holy Humanity, adorn the glorious Divinity of His Son.

As the Saint returned thanks to God for these graces with all her power, and took pleasure in considering the extraordinary favors which He had communicated to her, it was revealed to her that whenever any one assists at Mass with devotion, occupied with God, who offers Himself in this Sacrament for the whole world, he is truly regarded by the Eternal Father with the tenderness merited by the sacred Host, which is offered to Him, and becomes like to one who, coming out of a dark place into the midst of sunlight, finds himself suddenly surrounded by brightness. Then the Saint made this inquiry of God: "Is not he who falls into sin deprived of this good, even as one who goes from light into darkness loses the favor of beholding the light?" The Lord replied: "No; for, although the sinner hides My divine light from him, still My goodness will not fail to leave him some ray to guide him to eternal life; and this light will increase whenever he hears Mass with devotion or approaches the Sacraments."

Let us, then, imitate the saints in their great desire to render to God a full satisfaction for their sins, and to obtain, as soon as possible, a complete remission of all their temporal punishments, in order to be sure that God, in punishment for their sins, would not withhold from them those efficacious graces which were necessary for them to overcome great temptations and withstand great trials, as well as to save them from being cast into the terrible flames of purgatory after their death. In order to accomplish these two objects, the saints were very careful to hear Mass as frequently as possible.

We are debtors to the Divine Justice, and we have a choice between two modes of payment. We may make satisfaction here below, of our own accord, and set about obtaining a full remission of all our indebtedness to God by assisting at Mass, or we may wait till God shall take satisfaction of us hereafter in purgatory. To prefer the latter, would be unpardonable cruelty towards ourselves and a great want of love for God, as such a mode would only be forcing God to punish us, and deprive us of the happiness of heaven for a long time. Such a want of love for God would render us unworthy to receive in purgatory the benefit of the prayers and good works which our friends on earth might offer up for us. Let us beware of falling into the hands of the Divine Justice, for it is a thing terrible beyond conception. Let us rather avail ourselves of His exceedingly great mercy while in this valley of tears. Let us wash our souls white in the blood of the Lamb during Mass. How great is the power of that cleansing blood! how little the labor that applies it!

St. Margaret of Cortona, reflecting on her many grievous sins, and wishing to atone for them all as far as possible, went to her confessor to ask him what was the best way for her to make satisfaction to God for all her sins. He told her to hear as many Masses as she could. From that time forward she was very careful not to miss a single opportunity of hearing Mass.

CHAPTER XXVII.

MASS, A SACRIFICE OF IMPETRATION—CONTINUED.

Holy Scripture tells us that a prayer accompanied with tears is most powerful with God. It is for this reason that the Fathers of the Church are profuse in bestowing praises upon humble tears of the soul. The Holy Scriptures and the lives of the saints abound in examples, to prove their power with God. "Oh, how great is the power which the tears of sinners exercise with God!" exclaims St. Peter Chrysologus. "They water heaven, wash the earth clean, deliver from hell, and prevail upon God to recall the sentence of damnation pronounced upon every mortal sin." "Yes," says Anselmus Laudunensis, commenting on the words of the Book of Tobias,—" Continuing in prayer, with tears he besought God,"—"prayer appeases God, but, if tears are added, He feels overcome, and unable any longer to resist. The former is for Him an odoriferous balm, the latter a sweet tyranny."

Hence Julianus exclaims, with truth: "O humble tears, how great is your power, how great is your reign! You need not fear the Tribunal of the Eternal Judge; you silence all your accusers, and no one dares prevent you from approaching the Lord; should you alone enter, you will not come out empty. Moreover, you conquer the unconquerable, you bind the Omnipotent, you open heaven, you chase away all the devils." "Indeed," says Peter Cellensis, "the infernal spirits find the flames of hell more supportable than our tears." Cornelius à Lapide says: "One tear of the sinner, produced by the sorrow of his heart, is capable of making God forgive and forget many, even the most atrocious crimes." For this reason St. Leo the Pope says of the tears of St. Peter, "O happy tears of thine, O holy Apostle St. Peter, which were for thee a holy baptism to cancel thy sin of denying the Lord." St. Magdalen asks of our Lord the forgiveness of her numerous and great sins; but in what manner? "She began to wash His sacred feet with her tears;" those tears moved His compassionate heart, and made Him say, "Many sins are forgiven her, because she hath loved much."

Why was it that the holy patriarch Jacob, when wrestling with the Angel of the Lord, received his blessing? It was because he asked it with tears in his eyes: "He wept, and made supplication to him." In the Fourth Book of Kings, we read as follows: "In these days Ezechias was sick unto death, and Isaias the Prophet came to him and said: Thus saith the Lord God; give charge concerning thy house, for thou shalt die and not live. And he turned his face to the wall, and prayed to the Lord, saying: I beseech Thee, O Lord, remember how I have walked before Thee in truth, and with a perfect heart, and have done that which is pleasing before Thee. And Ezechias wept with much weeping." What did he obtain by his tears? Holy Writ says: "And before Isaias was gone out of the middle of the court, the word of the Lord came to him, saying: Go back and tell Ezechias; thus saith the Lord: I have heard thy prayer and I have seen thy tears; and behold, I have healed thee; on the third day thou shalt go up to the Temple of the Lord. And I will add to thy days fifteen years."

Now, if the tears of a wretched sinner are so powerful with God, if the tears of a just and holy man are still more so, what power must not the tears of Jesus Christ have with His Father? Our dear Saviour shed torrents of tears in the course of His life. He wept in the crib at Bethlehem; He shed bitter tears over the obstinacy of the Jews; He wept at the grave of Lazarus; He was so compassionate that He wept out of love for His friends, and out of sympathy for the afflicted, but He wept far more bitterly over the sins of men.

St. Paul the Apostle assures us that He used to pray to His Father with tears in His eyes. "Who in the days of His flesh, *with a strong cry and tears*, offering up prayers and supplications was heard for His reverence." * And it is Jesus Himself Who assures us that His Father always hears His prayer. "Father," He said at the grave of Lazarus, "Father, I thank Thee that Thou hast heard me. And I know that Thou hearest me *always*." †

How was it possible for the heavenly Father to resist the prayers and tears of His well-beloved Son? With what confidence, then, ought we not to assist at the Mass, knowing as we do that the same Jesus who prayed and wept so much for us on earth, continues to do the same at this holy sacrifice? If our eyes are dry, if we cannot pray with tears, we should not feel discouraged; we have the tears and prayers of our dear Saviour to offer to our heavenly Father—prayers and tears far more precious, far more powerful than the prayers and tears of all the saints united. What grace and blessing is there that these prayers and tears will not obtain for us? In his comment on Zacharias, Cornelius à Lapide relates, that St. Dunstan, after the death of King Edwin, at whose hands he had received much ill-treatment, saw, whilst praying, several black men running off with the soul of the king in their hands. Forgetting all the injuries and ill-treatment which he had received from Edwin, he took pity on him in his miserable condition, shedding torrents of tears before the face of the Lord for the deliverance of the king's soul, and he did not cease weeping and praying until the Lord heard him. Soon after he saw the same black men again, but their hands were empty, and the soul of the king was no longer in their possession. They then commenced to curse and swear, and uttered the most abominable imprecations against the servant of God, to which St. Dunstan paid no attention, but thanked God for the extraordinarily great mercy shown to the king.

---
* Heb. v. 7. † John xi. 41, 42.

If the prayers and tears of this saint could obtain the deliverance of the king's soul from the hands of the devil, from what evils shall we not be delivered by the prayers and tears of Jesus at Mass, if we assist at it in the proper spirit! It would take whole volumes to relate all the favors that have been granted by means of the holy Sacrifice of the Mass. St. Bernard obtained a great number of them; his life contains several which took place, as we may say, before the whole city of Milan. One day, at the moment when he was going to celebrate Mass, there was brought to the church of St. Ambrose a lady of distinction who had been sorely afflicted for several years. She had lost at once sight, hearing, and speech; her tongue even had lengthened so that it protruded from her mouth in a monstrous manner. St. Bernard exhorted all the people present to unite their prayers with his, and began to celebrate the divine mysteries, making the sign of the cross over the poor infirm woman every time he made it over the Host or chalice. Having finished the Lord's Prayer, he took the Body of Jesus Christ, placed it on the paten, which he laid on the woman's head, and prayed our Lord to cure her. After that he turned to the altar to finish the holy Sacrifice. When he had made the division of the Host and distributed Communion to the people, the infirm lady, who was placed near the altar, felt herself suddenly cured; her tongue resumed its natural state, and she recovered at the same time sight, hearing, and speech. Quite transported with joy, she came to throw herself at the feet of St. Bernard, and returned a thousand thanks to the Lord. A cry of admiration arose from every part of the church; the bells rang out joyously, the people ran in crowds to see the person so miraculously cured, and the whole city magnified the power of God, so wonderfully manifested in that miraculous cure.[*]

St. Gregory relates that on certain days the fetters used to

---

[*] Abbé Favre, *Le Ciel Ouvert.*

fall from the hands of a Christian captive who had been taken prisoner by the barbarians, and after his deliverance he found out that on those days his relatives had Mass offered up for him.

When, in the year 871, the Danes invaded England, King Ethelred went with a small army to meet them. But trusting more in the protection and assistance of God than in the valor of his army, he went first to hear Mass. While assisting at the holy Sacrifice, messengers came to tell him that the Danes were quite near, and that he must prepare immediately for battle; but he answered that he would not go until he had received Holy Communion. So he stayed in church until Mass was ended, and then went forth with a lion's courage to attack his enemies. The Lord of armies was with him and fought for him, and thus, after a short conflict, the pious king succeeded in putting the enemies of his kingdom to a shameful flight.* Let us then rest assured that, as a mother cannot help consoling her weeping child, neither will the heavenly Father refuse to hear any of the petitions of His weeping Son at Mass.

The great power of Mass as a sacrifice of impetration appears also from the fact that a prayer united with good works is most powerful with the Almighty. "Prayer is good, with fasting and alms," said the angel of the Lord to Tobias;† and by the prophet Isaias the Lord says: "Deal thy bread to the hungry, and bring the needy and the harborless into thy house; when thou shalt see one naked, cover him, and despise not thy own flesh." ‡ "Seek judgment, relieve the oppressed, judge for the fatherless, defend the widow." § "Then shalt thou call, and the Lord shall hear; thou shalt cry, and He shall say: Here I am." ‖

And again it is said: "Blessed are the merciful, for they shall obtain mercy;" ¶ especially when they pray, for who-

---

* Baronius.   † Tob. xii. 8.   ‡ Isaias lviii. 8.
§ Isaias i.   ‖ Isaias lviii.   ¶ Matt. v.

soever is good and liberal to the brethren of Jesus Christ on earth, to him Jesus Christ must be good and liberal also; for He is, and He desires to be, and to exhibit Himself infinitely better than any one possibly could be.

In the life of the Bishop St. Julian, we read that he distributed among the poor and needy everything he possessed. Hence the Church says of him that, being inflamed with a great paternal charity for his fellow-men, he obtained from God many wonderful things. When the people were once suffering very much from a want of corn, he began to pray to God with tears in his eyes; at once several wagons of corn arrived, and no sooner were they unloaded than the men who brought the corn disappeared. Another time, when the epidemic spread rapidly throughout the diocese of this holy bishop, God caused it suddenly to cease, on account of the prayer of His servant. The Lord also heard his prayer for many who suffered from incurable diseases.

If the prayer of the saints is so powerful with God because their justice—"their good works go with them before the face of the Lord," * what shall be said of the power of the intercession of Jesus Christ with His Father? The least act which He performed was of greater merit and dignity and gave greater pleasure and honor to His Father than the good works of all the saints together with those of the Blessed Mother of God herself. All the good works of Jesus Christ are of an infinite value and dignity, and when He prays to His Father for us at Mass, it is not mere prayers that He offers in our behalf, but, in addition, all He has done for thirty-three years and a half to please Him. He offers to Him His blood, His very life itself, in sacrifice, and thus lays before His Father the greatest gift possible—a gift far more precious than all He can ask for us—as great in power and dignity as is the Father Himself. This is the precise reason why Mass is so powerful a sacrifice of impetra-

---

* Isaias lviii. 8.

tion, why it can obtain for us every favor possible. "Ask of Me," says the Father to His Son when lying upon the altar, "ask of Me and I will give Thee the Gentiles for Thy inheritance."* Every word that our dear Saviour spoke, every act of obedience that He performed, every step that He took, every breath that He drew, every pulsation of His sacred Heart, every drop of blood that He shed, every pain that He suffered, all are so many eloquent tongues with God the Father to defend our cause and obtain for us His choicest gifts and blessings.

Our divine Saviour has assured us "that whatever is asked of His Father in His name is granted." † If then the *name* of Jesus is so powerful, so efficacious, and of so great authority with the Father that, for the sake of His name alone He grants the most wonderful things, shall we hesitate to believe that Almighty God, for the sake of His well-beloved Son, interceding in His own Person for us at Mass, will grant us all we can desire, all we stand in need of, nay, far more and far greater gifts than we would dare to ask?

In a city of the West I made, about three years ago, the acquaintance of a Catholic lady whose husband was a Protestant. Wishing to obtain for her husband the grace of conversion to the Roman Catholic faith, she made an offering to Almighty God of what was most dear to her in this world—her only child. "My most merciful God," said she, "if Thou wilt vouchsafe to give the grace of conversion to my husband, I am willing to lose my darling child by death." God heard the prayer of this good lady, for her child died soon after. Now, when the child was lying dead in bed, she called her husband and said to him: "Where do you think the child is now?" "I have no doubt he is in heaven," was his answer. "Do you not wish," said she, "to be, one day, with him in heaven?" "Indeed I do," replied he. "Well, then," said his wife, "embrace the religion

---
* Ps. ii. 8. † John xvi. 23.

in which our darling child was baptized and died." At this moment God enlightened the mind of that man to know the truth of the Roman Catholic religion, and, at the same time, strengthened his will to embrace it.

Now, if the offering which this pious mother made of her child was so pleasing in the sight of God that He could not help granting her petition, the offering which Jesus Christ makes of Himself at Mass to His Father, is, no doubt, infinitely more pleasing to Him, and must, of course, obtain for us all he asks in our behalf. It is, therefore, not in vain that the priest prays during Mass that through this sacrifice "we may be filled with every heavenly blessing and grace."

Let us always remember, then, that in the holy Sacrifice of the Mass the Son of God not only worships His Father for us, but that He also prays for us, asks pardon and every kind of blessing for us.

Bollandus relates of St. Coleta that, one day, when she was hearing the Mass of her confessor, she suddenly exclaimed at the elevation: "My God! O Jesus! O ye angels and saints! O ye men and sinners, behold the great marvels!" After the Mass her confessor asked her why she had wept so bitterly and uttered such pitiable cries. "Had your Reverence," said she, "heard and seen the things which I heard and saw, perhaps you would have wept and cried out more than I did." "What was it that you saw?" asked her confessor again. "Although that which I heard and saw," she replied, "is so sublime and so divine that no man can ever find words to express it in a becoming manner, yet I will endeavor to describe it to your Reverence as well as my feeble language will permit. When your Reverence raised the sacred Host, I saw our Lord Jesus Christ as if hanging on the Cross, shedding His Blood, and praying to his heavenly Father in most lamentable accents: 'Behold, O My Father, in what condition I was once hanging on the Cross and suffering for the Redemption of mankind. Behold My wounds, My sufferings, My death: I have suffered all this in order that poor sinners might not be lost. But now Thou wilt send them to hell for their sins. What good, then, will result from My sufferings and cruel death! Those damned souls, instead of thanking Me for My Passion, will only curse Me for it; but should they be saved, they would bless Me for all eternity. I beseech Thee, My Father, to spare poor sinners, and forgive them for My sake; and for the sake of My Passion preserve them from being damned forever.'"

What a consolation to know that we have so powerful an advocate with the Almighty in heaven. Let us no longer say that we are poor, that we are weak, that we have nothing to offer to God. In the holy Mass we have an offering worthy of God—a prayer to present to Him, which is all-perfect—all-powerful, the prayer of His only begotten Son, in whom He is well pleased.

But our divine Saviour worships God for us, and prays for us in the Mass, not in order to exempt us from worshipping, but in order to *help* us to worship God *properly* and to pray to Him in a perfect manner.

On the night before His death Our Blessed Redeemer went with His Apostles to the Garden of Gethsemane. When they had come to the garden He said to them: "Remain ye here while I go yonder and pray." He went from them about a stone's throw and began to pray with great fervor. Then His agony came on, and His soul was sad unto death. His whole body was covered with a bloody sweat, and the blood which oozed through every pore fell down in drops to the ground. He was praying to His Eternal Father for the sins of His brethren: He prayed for all those souls whom He had created and for whom He was to die. The Apostles were sad and weary, worn out with watching; and instead of praying with our dear Lord they fell asleep. Then Jesus arose and went to them again and again. In a mournful voice He upbraided them for their weakness, their drowsiness; He exhorted them to watch and pray; desiring that they should unite their prayers with His.

It is thus that our Lord acts during the holy Sacrifice of the Mass; He withdraws a short distance from us in order to make intercession for us. He prays for us on the altar, and wishes us to kneel around Him in church, there to unite with His our feeble prayers. What we ask for in broken accents, He puts into glowing words, and as our prayers pass through His Sacred Heart, as they ascend to heaven from His divine lips, they are transformed, they become most acceptable in the sight of God, all-powerful, all-divine. Throw copper into molten gold and it appears at once to be all gold. Unite your prayers with those of Jesus at Mass and they go up to His Father as the prayers of His well-beloved Son.

St. Porphyrius, Bishop of Gaza, went once to Constantinople to ask a favor of the Emperor Arcadius. On his way he met the servants of the emperor carrying with them his infant son Theodosius. The holy Bishop immediately drew near and placed his petition in the hands of the young prince. The emperor, agreeably surprised at this singular artifice of the prelate, readily granted what he asked, through love for the little bearer.*

Let us adopt a similar means to obtain favors from God. In the Mass Jesus Christ, the Son of God, is ever ready to carry up our desires to the throne of His Father. Let us, therefore, in all confidence, charge Him with our petitions, and rest assured that, for His sake, they will be granted. Let our lips move in silence after consecration. Let us pray to Jesus according to the wants of our hearts, pouring out before Him our joys and sorrows, our hopes and fears.

Catholics do not go to church to hear a man pour forth an extempore prayer; they are not obliged to follow any man through the various moods of his thoughts and feelings. They are not obliged to join in any set form of prayer; for such a prayer, no matter how beautiful, must necessarily

---

* Schmid's Histor. Catech.

fail to express the different wants and feelings of the various members of the congregation. They go to church to take part in the most holy Sacrifice of the Mass—not to join in the prayers of a *man*, but in the prayers of our Lord Jesus Christ Himself, Who is really present on our altars. They are not bound by any set form of prayer; they can pour out their souls before God according to the various wants and desires of their hearts. There is around the altar the most complete liberty, the greatest variety, combined with the most perfect unity.

Let then the little children, let the young and innocent go to Mass; let them unite their joyous hearts with the heart of the Infant Jesus, Who is born again spiritually every day upon our altars. Let also the old and the weary go; let them pour out their sorrows before the face of God, and Jesus, "Who hath borne our sorrows," will comfort and console them.

And let those who are weak and sorely tempted go to Mass: Jesus will encourage and strengthen them by His heavenly grace. Let those who have sinned go to Mass; and weep, and mingle their tears with the tears which Jesus shed for them and for us all on the hard wood of the Cross.

Let those who are poor and sick and heart-broken go to Mass, and lay their wants before the compassionate heart of Jesus; He Who "filleth the hungry with good things" will not suffer them to go away empty-handed.

Let the rich and prosperous also go to Mass, and give thanks to God Who has blessed them with the good things of this world. Let all go: laying their fears, their joys, hopes, wishes, and tears—all at the feet of Jesus, and He will hear and sympathize with us. He will offer up our prayers and our tears in union with His own divine supplication. Our prayers, united with the prayers of Jesus, will ascend before the throne of heaven louder than the music of angelic choirs, sweeter than the sublime hymn of the virgins, more powerful than the intercession of all the saints.

And if ever there is a time when prayers are heard, it is during the holy Sacrifice of Mass. For this reason is it that in the office of consecrating a church, the Bishop prays that "here may be heard by God the prayers of all invoking Him, that the blessed and holy Trinity, which purifieth all things, and adorneth all things; that the blessed and holy hand of God, which sanctifieth all things, blesseth all things, and enricheth all things, might purify and bless and consecrate, by a perpetual out-flowing of His sanctification, that house; that here priests might ever offer to Him the sacrifice of praise, and here the faithful people pay their vows; that here the burden of sinners might be loosed, and the falls of the faithful repaired; that here the sick might be healed, the lepers cleansed, the blind enlightened, the demons expelled, and all invocations granted through our Lord Jesus Christ."

Oh, what a gift is the Holy Mass! How completely is the distance bridged over that separated the Creator and the creature! The time of the Mass is the time of grace; it is then that the earth has disappeared from view, and heaven is opened. The place on which we kneel is holy ground, we are in the presence of God, surrounded by myriads of angels.

Mass was the comfort of the Christians in the Catacombs. It was the glory of St. Basil, and St. Ambrose, and St. Augustine. So it is also our glory, our stay and support in this nineteenth century of unbelief and impiety. "Yes, strip our altars, leave us only the corn and the vine, and a rock for our altar, and we will worship with posture as lowly and hearts as loving as in the grandest Cathedral. Let persecution rise; let us be driven from our churches; we will say Mass in the woods and caverns, as the early Christians did. We know that God is everywhere, we know that Nature is His Temple, wherein pure hearts can find Him and adore Him; but we know that it is in the Holy Mass alone that He offers Himself to His Father as 'the Lamb that was slain.' How can we forego that sweet and solemn action? How can we deprive ourselves of that heavenly consolation? It is in Mass that man's heart has found a home and resting-place in this vale of tears. To us the altar is the vestibule of heaven."

Such be our thoughts about the Holy Mass. Go to Mass and go to pray. When the Lord drew near to Elias on the Mount, the prophet wrapped his face in his mantle; so when we come to Mass let us wrap our souls in a holy recollection of spirit. Remember what is going on. Now pray; now praise; now ask forgiveness; now rest before God in quiet love. So will the Mass be a marvellous comfort and refreshment to the Christian.

CHAPTER XXVIII.

MASS, THE HOPE OF THE DYING.

There are many now-a-days who view death merely as the dissolution of organs, the decomposition of a worn-out machine, as an extinction of the powers of life; in other words, they examine it simply with the eye of an infidel physician. It is not strange at all that these people should be insensible to the high moral grandeur which so often distinguishes the closing scene of mortal life, or that they should be surprised and offended at the importance which religion ascribes to this last act in the combat of her children. But far is it from the humble followers of a crucified Saviour to profess a scorn for death, which He Himself condescended to endure. Death is disarmed, it is true; it is vanquished; yet its aspect still bespeaks its origin, and the eye naturally turns from it in mourning. "Perhaps you do not know," says St. Leonard, "what sort of a grace it is to die a happy death. It is such a grace, that the greatest saints never thought it was their due for anything they had done for God. Even if God had denied a happy death to His own Mother, He would have done her no wrong, for it is a grace so great that no one can merit it. Though all angels and men should unite their power to give us a just knowledge of the importance of a good or bad death, it would be impossible for them to do so, because they themselves cannot adequately comprehend the good or evils resulting from a good or bad death."

Death is the end of all our works, of our earthly pilgrimage, the harbor where we cast anchor, or are wrecked for ever. On death depends eternity; eternal happiness or eternal misery is its necessary result. If we die well, we shall be saved eternally, if we die ill, we shall be eternally lost. We can die but once. Hence the infinite importance of this final act of our life. Yes, the day of death is the master-day—the day that judges all the others. It is for this reason, that this crisis naturally impresses every one with a feeling of awe. The pinched and pallid features, the cold and clammy skin, the heaving, laborious, rattling respiration, and the irresistible force of that disease which no earthly remedies can overcome, speak of something appalling, and suggest the idea of an Almighty power manifesting displeasure and inflicting punishment.

What especially increases the sufferings of the dying is their remorse for sin committed, their dread of the approaching judgment, and the uncertainty of eternal salvation. At that moment especially, the devil puts forth all his power to gain the soul that is passing into eternity, knowing that the time is short in which he may win her, and that if he lose her then, he has lost her forever. For this reason it is that the devil, who has always tempted her in life, will not be satisfied to tempt her alone in death, but calls companions to his aid. When any one is at the point of death, his house is filled with demons, who unite to accomplish his ruin. It is related of St. Andrew Avellino that, at the time of his death, several hundred devils came to tempt him, and we read that, at the time of his agony, he had so fierce a struggle with hell, as to cause all his good brethren in religion who were present to tremble.

Now, the path which we are pursuing leads us necessarily within view of death; this angel of destruction gains upon us more and more every day, and he comes upon many too often unawares. Happy are those who are always prepared to follow his summons. He has two keys in his hands; with the one he opens heaven for the good, and with the other he opens the gates of hell for the bad. The greatest gain, therefore, in this life is to prepare ourselves every day for a happy death.

Chief among the means which our Lord has left us for this end, is that of assisting, as often as possible, at the mystical renewal of His Death—the holy Sacrifice of the Mass. "Offer up the sacrifice of justice," says holy David, "and then trust in the Lord."* This sacrifice of justice is the holy Mass; by this sacrifice, as we have seen, the Lord is appeased, His justice is fully satisfied, and our sins and the punishments due to them are cancelled. We read in holy Scripture that a certain man, named Michas, said to a young Levite: "Stay with me, and be unto me a father and a priest, and I will give thee every year ten pieces of silver, and a double suit of apparel, and thy victuals." The Levite was content, and abode with Michas, and was unto him as one of his sons. Michas was overjoyed, and said: "Now I know God will do me good, since I have a priest of the race of the Levites." † If Michas was not afraid of the Lord and His punishments, if he felt quite confident that God would bless him because the priest of the Lord staid with him in his house, and prayed and offered sacrifice for him, how much greater must be the joy and confidence of a Christian in the hour of death, when he remembers that he assisted so many times at the holy Sacrifice of the Mass, where not only the priest of God, but the Priest of priests—Jesus Christ Himself—prayed, and offered Himself in sacrifice to His heavenly Father to obtain for him the grace of a happy death.

Saint Boniface, Archbishop of Mayence, relates the following: "A deceased Brother in a certain convent of my diocese had been raised to life again; he came to me and said: When I was conducted before the tribunal of God, every sin of mine came along with me in the shape of a most hideous person, and said to me, 'I am that vain honor and glory which made you consider yourself superior to others;' another said, 'I am that want of charity which you have shown

---

* Ps. lv.   † Judges xvii.

to your neighbor in thoughts, words, and actions;' another again said, 'I am that lie which you told on such and such an occasion.' It was thus that all my sins, one after the other, came and presented themselves to me, accusing me, and clamoring against me most frightfully before the Eternal Judge. Many devils, too, came at the same time, and bore witness that I had committed these sins at such a time and in such a place. Then there came also before me the few good works which I had performed during my life, and they said to me, one after the other, 'I am that obedience which you have rendered to your superior for the love of God;' another said, 'I am that mortification, that work of penance, by which you have chastised your body;' 'I am,' said another, 'that prayer and meditation which you have so often performed.' It was thus that all my good works, one after the other, came and presented themselves before me, consoling and defending me before the Eternal Judge, and many of the angels of the Lord, too, came and bore witness to my good works, and exalted them exceedingly."

What happened to this pious brother may also happen to us at the hour of death. At that moment our sins may rise up before us in hideous forms to terrify and throw us into despair. But then our good works, especially all the Masses we have heard with devotion, will also present themselves in the form of beautiful virgins, to inspire us with the greatest confidence in the mercy of God. They will say: we are the many holy masses you have heard with so much fervor; we will accompany you to the Tribunal of the Eternal Judge; there we will defend you and plead your cause; we will say to the Lord of heaven and earth: "It is true, this soul has often dishonored Thee by her many sins, but it is also true that she has infinitely more honored Thee by one Mass than Thou hast been dishonored by all her sins; it is true that by her sins she has contracted before Thee an enormous debt, but it is also true that one Mass alone, which she heard with devotion, was more than sufficient to cancel a thousand times more sins than she has committed. It is true that she has shown herself very ungrateful for the numberless graces thou hast bestowed upon her; but it is also true that by one Mass alone she returned to Thee far more than Thou hast ever bestowed upon her." Thus will each Mass become a most powerful advocate in our favor. What then will not the hundreds of Masses we have heard be able to obtain for us! The cry raised against us by our sins, and the accusations of the devil, will be hushed in a moment by the cry of the many Masses, that is, of the Blood of the Lamb of God which fell so abundantly upon us in each holy Mass. What consolation, what joy, what confidence will be ours at the hour of death, when we see ourselves surrounded by so many Masses as by so many faithful friends and most powerful advocates, pleading for our admission into paradise. Blessed, therefore, are those who persevere in their love and devotion for Mass until death. By a peculiar supernatural strength, which they derive from this holy sacrifice, they will also in a most wonderful manner either be preserved from all attacks of the devil, or rendered strong against the same in a manner most fearful to Satan.

We read in holy Scripture that the angel of destruction passed by all the houses of the Israelites without doing them any harm, because he found them sprinkled with the blood of the lamb. We have seen how at Mass the blood of the Lamb of God—of Jesus Christ—is shed in a mystical manner; that whenever we assist at Mass with devotion, our souls are sprinkled with this sacred Blood, and experience its powerful effects, especially the protection it affords them in all spiritual and temporal afflictions. When the devil comes to these souls at the hour of death, he loses all courage to win them, because he sees them sprinkled with the sacred Blood of the Lamb of God, at sight of which he trembles and flies away in rage, perceiving that no room is left for his temptation.

Eneas Silvius, who afterwards became Pope Pius II., tells us that in a certain city of Germany, called Svezia, there lived a gentleman of high social position, who, after losing nearly all his wealth, retired to a country-house for the sake of economizing. Spending his time in great seclusion, he soon became a prey to the most profound melancholy, so much so, indeed, that he was in a state bordering on desperation. While in this deplorable condition the devil often suggested to him that he ought to put an end to his life; "for," said the tempter, "there is nothing for the barren tree but the woodman's axe." In this conflict of mental agony and temptation, the gentleman had recourse to a holy confessor, who gave him the following good advice: "Let no day pass without assisting at the holy Mass, and make your mind easy." Pleased with the advice, the gentleman lost no time in carrying it out, and in order to prevent the possibility of ever losing Mass, he engaged a chaplain, who daily offered the adorable Sacrifice, at which he assisted with the most edifying devotion. But it happened that one day his chaplain went at an early hour to a neighboring village to assist a young priest, who was about to celebrate his first mass. The devout nobleman, fearing that he would that day be deprived of the Sacrifice, hastened to the same village in order to be present at it. On the way he met a peasant who told him that he might as well turn back, because the last Mass was ended. Much disturbed in mind, he began even to shed tears. "Alas, what shall I do?" he kept repeating, "What shall I make of myself to-day? Perhaps it may be the last of my life." The peasant was astonished to see him so much agitated, and being himself a man careless of his soul, he exclaimed, "Pray, do not weep, my lord, do not weep; for my part, if it is a thing that can be done, I don't mind at all selling you my share in the Mass I heard this morning. Give me that good cloak of yours, and for aught I care, my Mass is yours this moment." The nobleman, thinking he would take the chance of possibly getting something by it, at least for his good intention's sake, handed over the cloak and pursued his path towards the church. There he offered a short prayer, and on his return had hardly reached the place where the bargain had been struck, when he saw the miserable man who had conceived the profane design of selling his Mass, hanging by the neck from an oak-tree, and already dead, like another Judas. In fact, the temptation to self-destruction had passed into the unhappy peasant, who had voluntarily deprived himself of the aid which he might have had from the Sacrifice, and designedly left himself powerless to resist the malignant suggestion of the devil. Then the worthy nobleman began to perceive how effectual was the remedy which his confessor had advised, and he was from that moment confirmed in his holy determination—daily to assist at the divine mysteries, in order to be preserved from the temptation of the devil, and make a happy end. What Pope St. Gregory says is true: "The holy Sacrifice of the Mass preserves the soul from everlasting destruction."*

The Archangel Raphael said to Tobias: "Alms delivereth from death, purgeth away sins, and maketh to find mercy and life everlasting." † What the archangel said of alms, applies most assuredly, far more directly, to the holy Sacrifice of the Mass; for it delivers the soul from a bad death, cleanses her from sins, and makes her find mercy and life everlasting. "As many Masses as a good Christian has heard with devotion," said our Lord to St. Mechtildis, "so many of my angels do I send him in the hour of his death to console, and protect, and to accompany him to heaven." ‡ Although this revelation be not an article of faith, yet it is very authentic and agrees with what we read in the writings of St. John Chrysostom: "A certain person," says he, "told me—not having heard it from some other person, but himself found worthy to be an eye and ear witness of the fact—

---

* Lib. iv. Dial. c. 58.   † Tob. xii. 9.   ‡ Lib. iii. Revel. c. 19.

that persons about to depart this life, if they be found to have partaken of the mysteries (of the holy Mass) with a pure conscience, have, at the moment of breathing their last, angels as guards to conduct them away hence, for the sake of what they have received." *

A certain holy Bishop of Breslau, named Nanker, entertained a most tender devotion for the holy Sacrifice of the Mass. He used to say Mass daily, and heard as many Masses besides as he possibly could. When at the point of death, a most sweet, heavenly melody was heard, and a voice from above said: "The soul of Bishop Nanker has already left the body, and is now being carried by the angels into heaven. This grace and honor have been bestowed upon him on account of his great love and devotion for the holy Sacrifice of the Mass." † No wonder, then, that we read in the lives of holy bishops, priests, and Christians, how diligent they were in offering up daily the holy Sacrifice, and hearing Mass as often as possible. They found ample time to do so by quitting vain amusements, useless conversations, and frivolous pleasures.

Baronius relates of St. Theodore Studita that he begged God in his last illness to give him sufficient strength to say Mass once more before he died. His prayer was heard. So, to the great astonishment of all his friends, he rose up from his bed and said Mass with the utmost fervor and devotion, shedding at the same time a torrent of tears. This devotion of the saint made a deep impression upon all who saw him, so much so that they could not help shedding tears themselves. Immediately after Mass, St. Theodore returned to bed, feeling perfectly prepared to die, for he could say with holy Simeon: "Now Thou dost dismiss thy servant, O Lord, according to Thy word, in peace, because my eyes have seen Thy salvation." He soon after died a holy death.‡

Baronius relates also that St. Tarasius, patriarch of Con-

---

* T. i., L. vi. de Sacerd. n. 4, p. 518.   † Reinaldus ad ann. 1241.
‡ Ad ann. 826, Num. 44.

stantinople, said Mass as long as his strength did not fail altogether. When it was nigh exhausted, towards the end of his life, he would lean on and bend over the altar, in order to be enabled to finish Mass. By this great fervor and devotion for saying Mass, he obtained from God the grace to breathe his last with unspeakable happiness and consolation.* In all ages there have been many holy priests who knew no better preparation for death than that of saying Mass daily with great devotion.

Dom Basile in his last illness, though suffering from a severe cold, used to rise and say Mass a little after four o'clock. So also, Don Isidore continued to hear Mass every morning until he died. Hence, hospitals and convents are so constructed that the patients, who are in bed, can each see the altar in the chapel and hear Mass, and thus prepare for a happy death.

Good Christians try to imitate holy priests in their devotion and love for the holy Sacrifice of the Mass; they hear it as often as possible with the utmost fervor. Many even when grievously sick, try to obtain the privilege of having Mass said in their room, or, at least, to have it offered up for a happy death. Theodoret relates the following of an old man: "Though ninety years of age, his garments were of hair-cloth, and his food bread and a little salt. And having desired for a long time to see the spiritual and mystic Sacrifice (of the Mass) offered up, he begged that the oblation of the divine gift might take place there. And I (Theodoret) gladly yielded to him; and having ordered the sacred vessels to be brought, for they were at no great distance, and using the hands of the deacons instead of an altar, I offered up the mystic, divine, and saving Sacrifice. But the old man was filled with all spiritual joy and fancied that he beheld the very heavens, and declared that he had never experienced so great a gladness."†

---

* Ad ann. 806, Num. 1.   † T. iii. Hist. Relig. c. xx. p. 1288.

Such is the joy which the Lord keeps in readiness for the hour of death of those who know how to value, in the course of their life, the gift of the holy Mass, this inexhaustible treasure of grace.

But in what does this joy which good Christians experience consist? In this: that they bear the pains of their last illness with great patience; that they experience an unlimited confidence in the mercy of God and in the merits of Jesus Christ; that they have no fear of death, but greet it joyfully as their best friend, opening for them the gates of heaven; in a word, this joy consists in a perfect and most admirable resignation to the holy will of God, who calls them to a better life. To die in this manner is to die with a merit similar to that of a martyr; for "martyrdom," says St. Thomas Aquinas, "does not consist in suffering much for the faith; it consists rather in the conformity of the martyr's will to the will of God in the trials under which he dies." If, then, God makes use of sickness or any other cause to take away my life, and if I conform my will to His, declaring myself perfectly resigned to the manner of my death, my will, being in conformity with that same will of God to which the martyr conforms in the hour of death, must earn a merit similar to that of the martyr. As man cannot make a greater sacrifice to God than that of his life, the will being perfectly resigned to make this sacrifice in the manner God requires and manifests by sickness or any other cause, it follows that such an act of the will is an act of perfect charity for God, which cancels all sins and punishments due to them. To die in this way, is, of course, a very great grace, and yet we may rest assured that it is particularly this grace which the Lord grants in the hour of death to those who are careful not to miss Mass. If we pray for this grace in each Mass we hear, our prayer will undoubtedly be heard, so much so that we shall exclaim: "I never thought it was so sweet to die." There are, indeed, some things whose price we know not till we come to die. To have fought the good fight against the devil—to have said no to those who tempted us to sin—to have been patient when we were poor, or sorrowful, or in pain—to have been kind and merciful to many a poor creature—but especially to have often assisted at the holy Sacrifice of the Mass,—these are things the value of which we scarcely realize when death is far off. Their true value will appear only when it will no longer be of any advantage to us. We easily suffer ourselves to be prevented from hearing Mass by our friends and acquaintances, by our occupations, and by our sloth. Often it is a burden to us to go and assist at the Sacrifice, and when there we hardly know what to do. A day will come when a single quarter of an hour spent in hearing Mass will appear of more worth to us than all the riches of the world. Let us ever remember that we are advancing rapidly towards eternity, that the time of Mass is the best to prepare for it, and that eternity will not be too long for our regrets at the loss of one single Mass.

CHAPTER XXIX.

MASS, PROPITIATORY FOR THE DEAD.

A SHORT time ago, a fervent young priest of this country had the following conversation with a holy Bishop, on his way to Rome. The Bishop said to him: "You make mementoes, now and then, for friends of yours that are dead, do you not?" The young priest answered: "Certainly, I do so very often." The Bishop rejoined: "So did I when I was a young priest. But one time I was grievously ill. I was given up as about to die. I received Extreme Unction, and the Viaticum. It was then that my whole past life, with all its failings, and all its sins, came before me with startling vividness. I saw *how much* I had to atone for; and I reflected on how few Masses would be said for me, and how few prayers! Ever since my recovery I have most fervently offered the Holy Sacrifice for the repose of the pious and patient souls in purgatory; and I am always glad when I can, as my own offering, make the 'intention' of my Masses, for the relief of their pains." *

Indeed, no one is more deserving of Christian charity and sympathy, than the poor souls in purgatory. They are *really poor souls*. No one is sooner forgotten than they.

How soon their friends persuade themselves that the souls departed are in perfect peace. How little they do for their relief when their bodies are buried. There is a lavish expense for the funeral. A hundred dollars are spent where the means of the family hardly justify the half of it. Where there is more wealth, sometimes five hundred or a thousand

---

* *Freeman's Journal*, Nov. 1869.

and even more dollars are expended on the poor dead body. But what is done for the *poor living soul?* Perhaps it is suffering the most frightful tortures in purgatory, whilst the lifeless body is laid out in state and borne pompously to the grave-yard. It is right and fitting to show all due respect even to the body of a deceased friend, for that body was once the dwelling-place of his soul. But, after all, what joy has the departed, and perhaps suffering soul, in the fine music of the choir, even though the choir be composed of the best singers in the country? What consolation does it feel in the superb coffin, in the splendid funeral? What pleasure in the costly marble monument, in all the honors that are so freely lavished on the body! All this may satisfy, or at least seem to satisfy, the living, but it is of no avail whatever to the dead.

Poor, unhappy souls! how the diminution of true Catholic faith is visited upon them. Those that loved them in life might help them, and do not, for want of knowledge, or of faith!

Poor, unhappy souls! your friends go to their business, to their eating and drinking, with the foolish assurance that the case cannot be hard on one they knew to be so good! Oh! how much and how long this *false charity* of your friends causes you to suffer!

The venerable Sister Catherine Paluzzi offered up for a long time and with the utmost fervor, prayers and pious works for the soul of her deceased father. At last she thought she had good reason to believe that he was already enjoying the bliss of Paradise. But how great was her consternation and grief, when our Lord, in company with St. Catherine, her patroness, led her one day in spirit to purgatory. There she beheld her father in an abyss of torments, imploring her assistance. At the sight of the pitiful state his soul was in, she melted into tears, cast herself down at the feet of her heavenly spouse, and begged Him, through His precious Blood, to free her father from his excruciating sufferings. She also begged St. Catherine to intercede for him, and then turning to our Lord, said: "Charge me, O Lord, with my father's indebtedness to Thy justice. In expiation of it, I am ready to take upon myself all the afflictions Thou art pleased to impose upon me." Our Lord graciously accepted this act of heroic charity, and released at once her father's soul from purgatory. But heavy, indeed, were the crosses which she, from that time forth, had to suffer.

This pious sister seemed to have good reason to believe that her father's soul was in Paradise. Yet she was mistaken. Alas! how many are there who resemble her in this. How many are there whose hope as to the condition of their deceased friends is far vainer and more false than that of this sister, because they pray less for the souls of their departed friends than she did for her father.

"No defiled thing," says St. John, "shall enter the heavenly city of Jerusalem." How easy was it for the departed soul to defile itself in this life, where it was surrounded by all kinds of snares and dangers.

St. Severinus, Archbishop of Cologne, was a prelate of such great sanctity, that God wrought many remarkable miracles through him. One day after his death, he was seen by a Canon of the Cathedral to suffer the most excruciating pains. Upon being asked why he suffered so much, he who, on account of his holiness of life, ought to be reigning gloriously in heaven replied: "I suffer this torment, merely for having recited the canonical hours hurriedly and with wilful distraction." *

It is related in the life of St. Mary Magdalene de Pazzi, that one day she saw the soul of one of her deceased sisters kneeling in adoration before the Blessed Sacrament in the Church, all wrapped up in a mantle of fire, and suffering great pains in expiation of her neglecting to go to Holy

---

* St. Peter Dom. Epist. 14. Edit. Desid. c. vii.

Communion, on a day when she had her confessor's permission to communicate.

If St. Severinus, so holy a prelate of the Church, if a holy nun who spent her life in the convent, had to suffer most excruciating pains in purgatory in expiation of small faults, what reason have we to imagine so readily that the souls of our departed friends are already enjoying the beatific vision of God—who perhaps were never very much in earnest about leading a holy life—who perhaps made light of venial faults—who perhaps often spoke uncharitably of their neighbors—who perhaps neglected so many Holy Communions and other means of grace and sanctification—who in their youth may have committed hundreds of secret mortal sins of the most heinous kinds, and may never have conceived any other than imperfect sorrow or attrition on account of them—who perhaps spent their whole lives in the state of mortal sin, and were converted only on their deathbed?

Ah! how much combustible matter—how many imperfections, venial sins, and temporal punishments due to mortal and venial sins, may they not have taken with them to be burned out in the flames of purgatory?

The Venerable Bede relates that it was revealed to Drithelm, a great servant of God, that the souls of those who spend their whole lives in the state of mortal sin and are converted only on their death-bed, are doomed to suffer the pains of purgatory to the day of the last judgment.*

In the life and revelations of St. Gertrude, we read that those who have committed many grievous sins, and who die without having done due penance, are not assisted by the ordinary suffrages of the Church until they are partly purified by divine justice in purgatory.

After St. Vincent Ferrer had learned of the death of his sister Frances, he at once began to offer up many fervent

---

* Hist. Anglic. lv. c. 13.

prayers and works of penance for the repose of her soul. He also said thirty Masses for her, at the last of which it was revealed to him, that, had it not been for his prayers and good works, the soul of his sister would have suffered in purgatory to the end of the world.*

From these examples we may draw our own conclusions as to the state of our deceased friends and relatives. The judgments of God are very different from the judgments of men. "My thoughts are not your thoughts," says the Lord, "nor your ways my ways. For as the heavens are exalted above the earth, so are my ways exalted above your ways, and my thoughts above your thoughts." †

We know that souls of great perfection have been deprived of the beatific vision of God, for having committed little faults. This we learn from many apparitions of the souls of the faithful departed, who have been saved and who praised the mercy of God, declaring at the same time that the judgments of the Lord are strict and terrible beyond description, and that mortals could never reflect too deeply upon this truth. The true reason of this great rigor of the judgments of God is found in His infinite sanctity, justice, and love.

God's sanctity requires an adequate expiatory punishment, because everything that is not good and perfect, is essentially opposed to His divine nature; hence He cannot admit into heaven, to the contemplation of His divine Essence, a soul that is still spotted with the least stain of sin.

God's justice requires no less severity than His sanctity, because every sin is an offense and outrage against His divine Majesty; for which reason he cannot help defending His divine right and absolute dominion over all creatures by requiring full satisfaction from every soul that has offended against this divine Majesty.

Neither can God's infinite love be less severe, because He wishes to see the souls of His elect pure, beautiful, perfect

---

* Marches. Diar. Dom. 5 Apr.   † Isaias lv. 8.

in every way; for which reason He purifies them from every stain, as gold is refined in a furnace, until they become His true image and likeness, according to which He created the first man in sanctity and righteousness. He takes no pleasure in seeing these souls suffer, but, wishing to render them capable and worthy of being united to Him as to their supreme happiness, He makes them pass through a state of the most frightful sufferings, a state of the greatest poverty imaginable—the privation of the beatific vision of God.

No sooner has the soul departed this life, than it beholds God, and from this sight it receives at once so deep and vivid a knowledge of God and all His infinite perfections, that thenceforth it is utterly incapable of being occupied with anything else than the divine beauty and goodness; it feels so violently drawn towards God, the supreme Lord of all things visible and invisible, that it finds it altogether impossible to wish, to seek, and to love anything but God. It experiences at once an insatiable hunger and thirst after God; it pants for its Supreme Good with a most ardent desire. "God! God! I must be with God!" is its constant cry. But at the very moment when the soul is endeavoring to unite itself to God, it is repulsed by Him and sent to purgatory to cleanse itself from the sins not cancelled in this life. In this banishment from the sight of God, the soul finds the bitterness of its torments. As it is the height of happiness to see a God infinitely amiable, so it is the greatest of all pains to be rejected from His presence. It is true, during this life, the soul experiences but a feeble desire to see God, and, as it does not know the greatness of this heavenly benefit, it does not comprehend how great a pain and misfortune it is to be deprived of it. But once the soul has quitted the body, it conceives so high an esteem for the possession of the Supreme Good, it burns with so ardent a desire to obtain it, it tends with so much force to enjoy it, that the greatest of all its torments in purgatory is to be repulsed, if only for an instant, from the presence of its Creator. In a word, the soul suffers more from the privation of the beatific vision of God, than from all the other torments of purgatory. For such is the infinite beauty of God, that to have seen Him for a single instant, and in that same moment to be rejected from His presence, is to experience at once the torment of hell. In heaven, love for God is the happiness of the elect; but in purgatory, it is the source of the most excruciating pains. It is principally for this reason, that the souls in purgatory are called "poor souls," they being, as they are, in the most dreadful state of poverty—that of the privation of the beatific vision of God.

After Anthony Corso, a Capuchin Brother, a man of great piety and perfection, had departed this life, he appeared to one of his brethren in religion, asking him to recommend him to the charitable prayers of the community, in order that he might receive relief in his pains; "for I do not know," said he, "how I can bear any longer the pain of being deprived of the sight of my God. I shall be the most unhappy of creatures as long as I must live in this state. Would to God all men could understand well what it is to be without God, in order that they might firmly resolve to suffer anything during their life on earth rather than expose themselves to the danger of being damned and deprived forever of the sight of God." *

The souls in purgatory are poor souls, because they suffer the greatest pain of the senses, which is that of *fire*. Who can be in a poorer and more pitiful condition than those who are buried in fire? Yet such is the condition of these souls. They are buried under waves of fire. The smallest spark of this purgatorial fire causes them to suffer more intense pains than all the fires of this world. In this fire they suffer more than all the pains of distempers and the most violent diseases—more than all the most cruel torments undergone by malefactors, or invented by barbarous tyrants; more than

---

* Annal. PP. Capuc. ad 1548.

all the tortures of the martyrs summed up together. Could these poor souls leave the fire of purgatory for the most frightful earthly fire, they would, as it were, take it for a pleasure-garden; they would find a fifty years' stay in the hottest earthly fire more endurable than an hour's stay in the fire of purgatory. Our terrestrial fire was not created by God to torment men, but rather to benefit them; but the fire in purgatory was created by God for no other purpose than to be an instrument of His justice, and for this reason it is possessed of a burning quality so intense and penetrating that it is impossible for us to conceive even the faintest idea of it.

A religious of the Order of St. Dominic, when about to depart this life, most earnestly begged a priest to say Mass for the repose of his soul immediately after his death. The good religious had scarcely expired when the priest went to say Mass for him with great fervor and devotion. Hardly had he taken off the sacred vestments after Mass, than the soul of his deceased friend appeared, rebuking him severely for the hardness of his heart in leaving him in the torments of purgatory for thirty years. Quite astonished, the good priest exclaimed: "What, thirty years! an hour ago you were still alive!" "Learn then from this," said the deceased, "how excruciating are the pains of the fire of purgatory, since one hour's stay therein appears as long as thirty years." *

Another reason why these holy prisoners and debtors to the divine justice are really poor, is, because they are not able to assist themselves in the least. A sick man, afflicted in all his limbs, and a beggar, in the most painful and destitute condition, has still a tongue left to ask relief. At least they can implore Heaven—it is never deaf to their prayer. But the souls in purgatory are so poor that they cannot even do this. The cases in which some of them

---

* Da Fusian, Tom. iv.

were permitted to appear to their friends and ask assistance, are but exceptions. To whom should they have recourse? Perhaps to the mercy of God! Alas! they send forth their sighs plaintively: "As the hart panteth after the fountains of water, so my soul panteth after Thee, O God. When shall I come and appear before the face of God? My tears have been my bread day and night, whilst it is said to me daily: Where is thy God."* "Lord, where are Thy ancient mercies." † "I cry to Thee, and Thou hearest me not; I stand up, and Thou dost not regard me. Thou art changed to be cruel toward me." ‡ But the Lord does not regard their tears, nor heed their moans and cries, but answers them, that his justice must be satisfied to the last farthing.

Are they to endeavor to acquire new merits, and thereby purify themselves more and more? Alas! they know that their time for meriting is passed away, that their earthly pilgrimage is over, and that upon them is come that fatal *night in which no one can work*." § They know that by all their sufferings they can gain no new merit, no higher glory and happiness in heaven; they know that it is through their own fault they are condemned to this state of suffering; they see clearly how many admonitions, exhortations, inspirations, and divine lights they have rejected; how many prayers, opportunities of receiving the sacraments, and profiting by the means of grace within their reach they have neglected through mere caprice, carelessness, and indolence. They see their ingratitude towards God, and the deep wounds they have made in the Sacred Heart of Jesus; and their extreme grief and sorrow for all this is a worm never ceasing to gnaw at them; a heart-rending pain, a killing torment—that of knowing that they have placed themselves wilfully and wantonly in this state of the most cruel banishment. "O cruel comforts! O accursed case!" they cry out, "it is on your account that we are de-

---

* Ps. xli. 1.   † Ps. lxxxviii. 50.   ‡ Job xxx. 20, 21.   § John ix. 4.

prived of the enjoyment of God, our only happiness for all eternity!"

Shall they console themselves by the thought that their sufferings will soon be over? They are ignorant of their duration unless it be revealed to them by God. Hence they sigh day and night, hence they weep constantly and cry unceasingly: "Wo unto us, that our sojourn is prolonged!"

Shall these poor, helpless souls seek relief from their fellow-sufferers, all utterly incapable of procuring mutual relief? Lamenting, sobbing, and sighing, shedding torrents of tears, and crying aloud, they stretch out their hands for one to help, console, and relieve them. We are the only ones who have it in our power to assist them in their sufferings.

After the Emperor Henry had besieged a certain city for a considerable time, and found the inhabitants still unwilling to surrender, he notified them that he would give orders to his soldiers to take the city by assault, and massacre all its inhabitants, even the little children. Alarmed at this proclamation, and seeing no hope left of saving themselves except by moving the emperor to compassion, the inhabitants of the city had recourse to the following expedient: They collected all the little children from six to ten years of age, and after arraying them in procession, made them march before the emperor and throw themselves on their knees, striking their breasts and crying aloud in pitiful accents: "Have pity on us, O emperor: O emperor, have pity on us." This heartrending scene affected the emperor so much that he himself could not help weeping. He pardoned the inhabitants of the city, and raised the siege immediately.

Could we only open the dungeons of purgatory and see the immense procession of poor suffering souls coming forth and crying aloud in the most lamentable and heart-rending voice: Father, mother, have pity on me, your child! Brother, have pity on me, your brother! Sister, have pity on me, your sister! Husband, have pity on me, your wife! Wife, have pity on me, your husband! Friend, have pity on me, your friend!—how would this spectacle affect us? Would not their pains alone plead more pathetically than any human tongue? Would not our eyes stream with tears, and our hearts be moved with compassion at beholding innumerable holy and illustrious servants of God, suffering more than any human being can conceive! But, unable to let us witness their tears and hear their moans, they borrow a voice from the Church, their mother, and her priests, who, to express their moans and inconceivable distress, and to excite our compassion and charity, cry to us in the words of Job: "Have pity upon me, have pity upon me, at least you, my friends, for the hand of the Lord hath smitten me."*

Just and holy souls, illustrious servants of the Lord, noble sons of the heavenly Father, heirs of His celestial glory, chosen vessels of election, enriched with precious gifts and ornaments of divine grace, laden with the merits of so many good works, confirmed in grace, and no longer in a condition to offend God, dear spouses of Christ, but victims to the divine justice, shall we be so dead to compassion, so steeled to feelings of humanity as to refuse you our sympathy? Shall we be as deaf and unmerciful to you as the just God who punishes you. "*Quare me persequimini, sicut Deus?*" O what a cruelty! A sick man weeps on his bed, and his friend consoles him; a baby cries in his cradle, and his mother at once caresses him;. a beggar knocks at the door for an alms and receives it; a malefactor laments in his prison, and comfort is given him; even a dog that whines at the door is taken in; but these poor, helpless souls cry day and night from the depths of the fire in purgatory: "Have pity on me, have pity on me, at least you, my friends, because the hand of the Lord hath smitten me," and there is no one to listen!

---

* Job xix. 21.

It seems as though we heard these poor souls exclaim: Priest of the Lord, speak no longer of our sufferings and pitiable condition. Let your description of it be ever so touching, it will not afford us the least relief. When a man has fallen into the fire, instead of considering his pains, you try at once to draw him out or quench the fire with water. This is true charity. Let Christians do the same for us. Let them give us their feet by going to hear Mass for us; their hands, by frequently offering the honoraries for the "intention" of the Masses of a priest in our behalf; their lips, by praying for us at Mass; their tongue, by begging others to do the same; their memory, by constantly bearing us in mind at the holy Sacrifice; their body, by offering up for us to the Almighty all its labors, fatigues, and penances, in union with the merits of Jesus Christ at Mass.

Indeed, it seems to be a kind of folly to reflect long upon the pains of the souls in purgatory by way of inducing ourselves to assist them. To know that they are tormented by fire ought to be enough to bring us to their relief at once, especially as we can do so with so little inconvenience to ourselves.

We read in the Acts of the Apostles that the faithful prayed unceasingly for St. Peter when he was imprisoned, and that an angel came and broke his chains and released him. We, too, should be good angels to the poor souls in purgatory, and free them from their painful captivity.

But the most efficacious of all means to release them is undoubtedly the Holy Sacrifice of the Mass. This is the common doctrine of the Fathers. St. Jerome says, that by every Mass, not one only, but several souls are delivered from purgatory, and he is of opinion that the soul for which the priest says Mass suffers no pain at all while the holy Sacrifice lasts.*

St. Augustine writes: "The funereal pomp, the crowded

---

* Apud Bern. de Busto, Serm. 8, de Missa.

funeral, the sumptuous attention to the burial, the construction of costly monuments, are some sort of solace to the living, not aids to the dead. Whereas it is not to be doubted that the dead are aided by alms, prayers of the holy Church, and *by the salutary sacrifice.*" * And in another place: " Nor is it to be denied that the souls of the departed are relieved by the piety of their living friends when the Sacrifice of the Mediator is offered for them." † " Not in vain," says St. John Chrysostom, " were these things ordained by the Apostles that a memorial of the departed be made at the awful mysteries. They knew great gain and great aid accrues to them. For when all the people stand stretching out their hands—a priestly assemblage—and the awful Sacrifice lies to open view, how shall we not propitiate God for those departed when we call upon Him." ‡ " It is for this reason," continued this great saint, " that there is no time fitter to treat or converse with Almighty God than that of the divine Sacrifice; that the angels profit by this time as the most favorable to beg graces for men and the souls in purgatory; that at the moment in which the Sacrifice of Mass is offered, these heavenly messengers presently fly to open the prisons of purgatory, and to execute all that God has been pleased to grant by the prayers of the faithful and the merits of His Son."

The Fathers of the Council of Trent declare that, by the Sacrifice of the Mass, the souls in purgatory are most efficaciously relieved. It is for this reason that the Sacrifice is offered up not only for the living, but also for the dead; that is to say, God is implored for the sake of Christ's oblation to grant to all those who have departed this life in the Lord, the full remission of their indebtedness to His divine justice.

To consider merely himself, is an impossibility to the Christian; how much less is it impossible for him, in so

---

* T. v. Serm. 172, n. 2, 3, col. 1196.
† T. vi. De Octo Dulcit. Quaest. n. 4, col. 222.
‡ T. xi Hom. iii. in Ep. ad Philip.

sacred a solemnity, to think only of himself, and omit his supplication that the merits of Christ, which outweigh the sins of the whole world, may likewise be appropriated by the souls in purgatory.

In the time of St. Bernard, a monk of Clairvaux appeared after his death to his brethren in religion to thank them for having delivered him from purgatory. On being asked what had most contributed to free him from his torments, he led the inquirer to the church where a priest was saying Mass. "Look," said he; "this is the means by which my deliverance has been effected; this is the power of God's mercy; this is the salutary Sacrifice which takes away the sins of the world." Indeed, so great is the efficacy of this Sacrifice to obtain relief for the souls in purgatory, that the application of all the good.works which have been performed from the beginning of the world would not afford so much assistance to one of these souls as is imparted by a single Mass. The blessed Henry Suso made an agreement with one of his brethren in religion, that as soon as either of them died, the survivor should say two Masses every week for one year for the repose of his soul. It came to pass that the religious with whom Henry had made this contract died first. Henry prayed every day for his deliverance from purgatory, but forgot to say the Masses which he had promised, whereupon the deceased religious appeared to him with a sad countenance, and sharply rebuked him for his unfaithfulness to his engagement. Henry excused himself by saying that he had often prayed for him with great fervor, and had even offered up for him many penitential works. "Oh, brother!" exclaimed the soul, "blood, blood is necessary to give me some relief and refreshment in my excruciating torments. Your penitential works, severe as they are, cannot deliver me. Nothing can do this but the blood of Jesus Christ, which is offered up in the sacrifice of the Mass. Masses, Masses, these are what I need." We read of St. Gregory the Great, that he had Mass said for thirty days in succession for a deceased monk named Justin, who, according to a revelation, was detained in purgatory for having kept some money without permission. On the last day Justin appeared to his brother, telling him that he now was released from purgatory, after enduring intense torments.*

St. Bernard tells us that the renowned Irish Bishop, St. Malachy, had a sister who led a rather worldly life. After some time she fell sick and died. St. Malachy prayed for her every day during the holy Sacrifice of the Mass. This he continued to do for a long time. At last, supposing that she was in heaven, he ceased praying for her. One night, however, he had a strange dream or vision. It seemed to him that he saw his sister standing outside the graveyard. She looked pale and sad. She told him that she was famished with hunger, as she had tasted no food for thirty days. St. Malachy understood at once that the food of which she spoke was the holy Sacrifice of the Mass, as he had not offered it up for her during the previous thirty days. Next morning he began to pray for his sister. After some time he saw her once more. She was now standing at the entrance of the church, but unable to enter. He continued to pray for her, and he saw her again; she was now in the church, but at some distance from the altar. He prayed with redoubled fervor, and, at last, as he was standing at the altar, he beheld the soul of his sister quite near him. Her countenance was now beaming with heavenly joy, and she was surrounded by a multitude of blessed spirits. She thanked him for his prayers, after which she entered into the unutterable joys of heaven.

St. Teresa gives an account of a merchant who lived at Valladolid, in Spain. His life was not what that of a good Christian should be. However, he had some devotion to the Blessed Virgin. St. Teresa came to the town where the

---

* L. 4, Dial. c. 55.

merchant was living. She wanted to find a house for her nuns. The merchant heard that she was seeking a house; so he went to her, and offered to give her one that belonged to him. He said he would give the house *in honor of the Blessed Virgin Mary*. St. Teresa thanked him and accepted his offer. Two months after this the gentleman suddenly fell very ill. He was not able to speak or make a confession; although he showed, by signs, that he wished to beg pardon of our Lord for his sins. Soon after he died. "After his death," St. Teresa says, "I saw our Lord. He told me that this gentleman had been very near losing his soul; but He had mercy on him when he was dying on account of the service he did to His Blessed Mother, by giving the house in her honor." "I was glad," the saint adds, "that his soul was saved. For I was very much afraid it would have been lost on account of his bad life." Our Lord told St. Teresa to get the house finished as soon as possible, because that soul was suffering great torments in purgatory. It would not come out of purgatory till the convent was finished and *the first Mass said there*. When the first Mass was said the saint went to the rails of the altar to receive Holy Communion. At the moment of kneeling she saw the gentleman standing by the side of the priest. His face was shining with light and joy; his hands were joined together. He thanked her very much for getting his soul out of the fire of purgatory. She then saw him ascend to heaven.

"My children," said the Curé d'Ars one day, "you remember the story I have told you of that holy priest who was praying for his friend; God had, it appears, made known to him that he was in purgatory; it came into his mind that he could do nothing better than to offer the holy Sacrifice of Mass for his soul. When he came to the moment of consecration, he took the sacred Host in his hands, and said: 'Oh, holy and eternal Father, let us make an exchange. Thou hast the soul of my friend who is in purgatory, and I have the body of Thy Son who is in my hands. Well, do

Thou deliver my friend, and I offer Thee Thy Son, with all the merits of His death and passion.' In fact, at the moment of the Elevation, he saw the soul of his friend rising to heaven, all radiant with glory."

Let us do the same after consecration if we wish to obtain from God speedy relief for the souls in purgatory; let us offer up to Him His well-beloved Son with all the merits of His death and passion. He will not be able to refuse our prayer. Indeed, if He heard the prayers of the Jews when they asked Him anything in the name of His servants Abraham, Isaac, and Jacob, He will certainly hear a Christian who, during the celebration of the holy Sacrifice of the Mass, asks relief for the souls in purgatory in the name and through the merits of His Son.

We read in the Book of Esther that Aman, a very proud and wicked man, procured a decree of the king to destroy the whole nation of the Jews. When Queen Esther learned this, she felt quite inconsolable. She sought for an opportunity to prevail upon the king to repeal the decree and to spare her nation. To find this favorable opportunity she invited the king to dinner. Whilst at table, the king observed that the queen was in deep mourning. "What is thy petition, Esther," asked the king, "that it may be granted thee? and what wilt thou have done? although thou ask the half of my kingdom, thou shalt have it." Then she answered: "If I have found favor in thy sight, O king, and if it please thee, give me my people for which I request." She then related to the king how Aman, by intrigues, had obtained a decree of the king to destroy the whole nation of the Jews, and she requested him to repeal this decree. Her request was granted immediately.

Now, as Queen Esther was right in believing that the best opportunity to obtain the king's pardon for the Jews would be afforded her at the royal banquet, we, too, should feel convinced that one of the best opportunities of obtaining the Lord's pardon for the souls in purgatory is offered when assisting at Mass, at His sacred banquet, while receiving Him worthily in Holy Communion as a guest into our hearts. At that happy moment Jesus Christ unites Himself most intimately with the soul, and caresses her in the most endearing manner, saying to her: "Dear spouse of Mine, why is it that thou art cast down? Rejoice and be glad. I, thy God and sweet Saviour have deigned to come and dwell in thy heart; My grace has rendered thee most beautiful. Oh, rejoice exceedingly." And the soul should answer confidently: "O Jesus, my God and my all! how can I rejoice and be glad when I know that there are so many of my departed fellow-Christians who, at this very moment, suffer such bitter pains in purgatory? No, my dear Saviour, I shall experience no consolation if Thou dost not give me my people—these suffering souls, for whom I beg relief and offer up the merit of my Communion."

Is it possible to think that the sweet Heart of Jesus, so full of compassion, will not be touched and overcome by such an humble and tender prayer and offering? No heart can be sooner moved to compassion, and overcome by prayer and works of charity, than that of Jesus. St. Gertrude never felt happier than on those days on which she had heard Mass and offered up Holy Communion for the relief of the souls in purgatory. Once she asked our Saviour why it was that she felt so happy on those days. "It is," He replied, "because it would not be right for Me to refuse the *fervent* prayers which you, on these days of My visits, pour out to Me for the relief of My suffering spouses in purgatory." "It is not right for Me," says Jesus Christ, "to refuse the prayers which you, on Mass and Communion days, address to Me in behalf of My captive spouses." How consoling, then, and, at the same time, how encouraging must it be to hear Mass often, to receive Holy Communion thereat, and offer up the merit of these holy acts for the release of the poor suffering spouses of Christ. Then do they say to us what Joseph said to the chief butler of King Pharaoh: "Remember me when it shall be well with thee, and mention me to Pharaoh, that he may bring me out of this place." *

It is during Mass and after Communion that all is well with us, and that we must remember these poor souls. If it is a pleasure to give a crumb to a poor little dog that is near when at table, surely we can remember these poor sufferers that press around us when at Mass, and cry at the sacred banquet to share in the merit of our Mass and Holy Communion. Let some fervent prayers for their relief be part of our worship and thanksgiving. If we condemn the rich Dives in the Gospel, who feasted splendidly every day, for not giving, at least, the crumbs that fell from his table to poor Lazarus, who was sitting at his door, covered all over with ulcers, must not these poor souls, afflicted in so many ways, complain of us, if we withhold our charity from them; while we are feasting splendidly; that is, when the Lord of heaven and earth is present upon the altar, has become the guest of our heart, is so desirous to hear our prayers, but especially those which we address to Him for the release of the souls in purgatory? Were we always to remember these great sufferers after Communion, the Lord would much sooner shower down upon them the torrents of eternal delights; He would much sooner disclose to them the light of His glory, and admit them into the company of His angels and saints.

Let us call to mind again the words of our Lord to St. Gertrude: "Because it would not be right for Me to refuse the *fervent* prayers you offer up to Me for the souls in purgatory."

Our prayers, then, for these souls must be fervent, as otherwise they will not benefit them very much. This was one day expressly declared by our Lord to St. Gertrude when asking Him: "How many souls were delivered from purgatory by her and her sisters' prayers?" "The number," replied our

---
* Gen. xl. 14.

Lord, "is proportionate to the *zeal and fervor* of those who pray for them. Although the souls of the departed are much benefited by these vigils and other prayers, nevertheless a few words said with *affection* and *devotion* are of far more value to them." And this may be easily explained by a familiar comparison: it is much easier to wash away the stains of mud or dirt from the hands by rubbing them quickly in a little warm water than by pouring a quantity of cold water on them without using any friction; so a single word said with fervor and devotion for the souls of the departed is of far greater efficacy than many vigils and prayers coldly offered and negligently performed.

Dinocrates, the brother of St. Perpetua, died at the age of seven years. One day, when St. Perpetua was in prison for the sake of faith, she had the following vision: "I saw Dinocrates," she says, "coming out of a dark place, where there were many others, exceedingly hot and thirsty; his face was dirty, his complexion pale, with the ulcer in his face of which he died, and it was for him that I prayed. There seemed a great distance between him and me, so that it was impossible for us to come to each other. Near him stood a vessel full of water, whose brim was higher than the stature of an infant. He attempted to drink, but though he had water, he could not reach it. This mightly grieved me and I awoke. By this I knew my brother was in pain, but I trusted I could by prayer relieve him; so I began to pray for him, beseeching God with tears, day and night, that He would grant me my request, as I continued to do till we removed to the camp-prison. The day we were in the stocks I had this vision: I saw the place, which I had beheld dark before, now luminous; and Dinocrates, with his body very clean and well clad, refreshing himself, and instead of his wound, a scar only. I awaked, and I knew he was relieved from his pains." *

---

* Butler's Lives of the Saints.

After St. Ludgardis had offered up many fervent prayers for the repose of the soul of her deceased friend, Simeon, abbot of the monastery of Souiac, our Lord appeared to her, saying: "Be consoled, My daughter; on account of thy prayers I will soon release this soul from purgatory." "Oh, Jesus, Lord and Master of my heart," she rejoined, "I cannot feel consoled so long as I know that the soul of my friend is suffering so much in the purgatorial fire! Oh! I cannot help shedding most bitter tears until Thou hast released this soul from her sufferings." Touched and overcome by this tender prayer, our Lord released the soul of Simeon, who appeared to Ludgardis, all radiant with heavenly glory, and thanked her for the many fervent prayers which she had offered up for his delivery. He also told the saint that had it not been for her *fervent* prayers, he would have been obliged to stay in purgatory for eleven years.[*] "It is, therefore, a holy and wholesome thought," says Holy Writ, "to pray for the dead, that they may be loosed from their sins."[†]

---

[*] Life 1, I. c. 4. [†] II. Macchabees xii. 46.

CHAPTER XXX.

MASS, THE JOY OF THE BLESSED VIRGIN.

THE Blessed Virgin is that blessed tabernacle in whom the Son of God was conceived, made man, and dwelt for nine months. Her Son is the divine Victim that we offer at Mass to the Eternal Father: to her, after God, we are indebted most for this divine Victim; for unless Mary had consented to become His Mother, Jesus would not have been born. Divine grace no doubt disposed her to acquiescence, but the act was not the less one of her own free unfettered will, an act which it was in her power to have refused, and by refusing to have thwarted the divine plans. Omnipotence might have arranged it otherwise; but as certainly as man has been redeemed by the Incarnation and Passion of Jesus, so surely did God make the whole depend, in the first instance, on the assent and co-operation of Mary. When He created the visible universe He said "*Fiat*"—Let it be: and it was. When He wished to redeem the world, it was by a *Fiat;* but the word was uttered by the lips of Mary; "*Fiat mihi secundum verbum tuum.*" But why did God not act as before, without any intermediate agent,—why did He make the execution of His plans of mercy depend on the will and the word of a feeble woman? No one can say, because He has not revealed the reason. We only know that so it is, and it is for us to accept the truth that after God we are most indebted to the Blessed Virgin for the coming of the holy Redeemer.

As by her word He became incarnate, so was He supported by her from day to day, as infants are by their mothers. He was nourished by her substance, watched and tended by her love, and closely associated with her at every step of His advancing years.

"After the days of Mary's purification," according to the law of Moses, "were accomplished," says the Gospel, "they carried the divine Infant to Jerusalem to present Him to the Lord." Here is a new and important instance of the agency of Mary. It was no empty ceremony, that offering and redemption of the infant Redeemer. "He was offered," says the prophet Isaias, "because it was His own will." * It was the first installment of the sacrifice which from eternity He had designed to make; when, in the language of the Psalmist, He said, "Behold, I come: in the head of the book it is written of Me, that I should do Thy will. O my God, I have desired it; and Thy law is in the midst of my heart." † It was the symbolical and preparatory offering which was consummated on Calvary, and is perpetuated on our altars for a lasting memorial of His Death, Resurrection, and Ascension.

That offering was made by the hands of Mary. He lay in the hands of His Blessed Mother passive, and seemingly helpless, with no visible sign of His greatness, as He lies to-day in the hands of His priest. The Omnipotent had taken upon Himself our infirmity, had adopted our weakness; He could not walk, or stand, or speak. Mary must therefore sustain Him, and express for Him the interior longing desire of His Eternal love to offer Himself to His Father for man, which had as yet found in Him no voice to make itself known or to carry out its intentions. Beneath the form of an infant, there lay concealed a divine energy. That child was the very Word that created the world; but the conditions of our humanity, within which His infinite love had circumscribed Him, imposed silence upon Him, reduced His power to feebleness and inaction. Mary was chosen among all the generations of mankind to stand forth in the

---

* Is. liii. 7. † Ps. xxxix. 7-9.

plenitude of grace and power, to supply the means of action to the infant God, to become for the time being the voice of the Eternal Word.

She advanced along the aisles of the solemn temple, attended by Simeon and Anna and Joseph, to the place where the priest was waiting to receive her. She raised the child in her arms, and with an overflowing heart surrendered Him to the representative of His heavenly Father on earth. The first and long-desired act of His sacrifice was accomplished. He was not hers any longer, but God's—the victim of charity, ready to be immolated. The Eternal Priest according to the order of Melchisedech had ascended the mountain of sacrifice, and in this oblation of Himself, Mary was made the great agent and minister of His will. Thus "they presented Him to the Lord" for the salvation of mankind.

But the time had not yet come for the closing and bloody act of His sacrifice, when the Lord would lay upon Him the iniquity of us all; when the life of the victim was to be taken in expiation. His oblation of Himself, though essentially one and the same, must be prolonged and reiterated through a course of years: "He must first suffer many things and be rejected by His nation." * His Mother must therefore receive Him again, to foster and mature His natural powers, to watch the growing signs of His intelligence, His advance in wisdom and age, and in grace with God and man. † He was, therefore, ransomed for the small sum of money prescribed by the ceremonial law, and restored to Mary until the time of His Passion and cruel Death upon Mount Calvary. There, at the foot of the Cross, she stood to behold the eyes she had been the first to see opening to the light, closing in death; to hear His last cry as she had soothed His first; to offer to the Eternal Father all His prayers, labors, sufferings, life, and death for the Redemption of mankind, as she had done over and over again during the course

---

* Luke xvii. 25. † Luke ii. 52.

of His life, but especially when offering Him in the Temple. As the Son of God became man only at the consent of Mary, so He died only after His Mother had given her consent to His death.

As then, after God, it is to the Blessed Virgin that we are indebted for our holy Redeemer, so is it to her that we owe the holy Sacrifice of the Mass, because it is her divine Son who offers Himself to His Father in the Mass for our sins. Moreover, the Blessed Virgin alone had a true knowledge and just appreciation of the cruel sufferings and death of a God made Man for our Redemption. By reason, therefore, of the depth of her profound wisdom, she penetrated into all the mysteries of the sacrifice of our Redemption, which was to be accomplished by the ignorance of those who were to be redeemed. She worthily and truly appreciated the majesty of Him who suffered, because, as next to her divine Son, she possessed the gift of knowledge in the highest degree, so she most fully comprehended the dignity of Jesus Christ, in whom were united both the human and divine natures, with the perfections of each. Therefore, she alone among all pure creatures could fully estimate the value of the great sacrifice that He made for us of His life, and all the advantages that were to be derived from it to the end of the world. She understood that it was the will of her Son that the fruits of the sacrifice of the Cross should be applied to the souls of men by means of the holy Mass.

As then after Jesus Christ, no one ever suffered more for the salvation of mankind than did His Blessed Mother, so no one ever more ardently desired to see the fruits of His life and death applied to those who were redeemed than she. For this reason we piously believe that it was at her request the Apostles said the first Mass soon after having received the Holy Ghost. We read in the "Mystical City of God," by Mary of Jesus of Agreda, as follows: "After the descent of the Holy Ghost, the Apostles preached assiduously the word of God and confirmed their doctrine by miracles.

The number of believers continued to increase, and seven days after Whit-Sunday they were already five thousand. On the following day the catechumens assembled in the supper-room, and St. Peter begged the divine Mother to instruct the new converts more perfectly by her fervent words. The Mother of humility said to them with great modesty; 'My children, the Redeemer of the world, my Son and true God, because of the love He has for men has offered to the Eternal Father the sacrifice of His divine body and blood, in consecrating and concealing Himself under the species of bread, under which He has willed to remain present in the holy Church, in order that His children might have a sacrifice to offer to the Eternal Father, and might also possess the food of eternal life, and a most assured pledge of that which they hope for in heaven.

"'Thus, by means of this sacrifice, which contains all the mysteries of the life and death of the Son, we can appease the Eternal Father, and in Him and by Him the Church will render the actions of thanksgiving and praise, which are due to Him as God and sovereign Benefactor.

"'To you, O priests, to you alone belongs the right to offer it. It is my desire, if it be agreeable to you, that you commence to offer this unbloody sacrifice, in order to testify our gratitude for the ineffable benefit of Redemption which Jesus Christ has operated for us, and for the descent of the Holy Ghost upon His Church. The faithful in receiving it will begin to relish this bread of eternal life and its divine effects. Among those who have been baptized, they who are capable of it and well-disposed, may be admitted to receive it, but baptism is the first and necessary condition.'

"All the Apostles and disciples agreed to the desire of the Mother of wisdom, and returned her thanks; they determined that after the baptism of the catechumens, St. Peter, as head of the Church, should celebrate the first Mass. St. Peter consented.

"Whilst the Apostles went forth to preach, and the disciples to instruct the catechumens and prepare them for baptism, the divine Mother, accompanied by the holy angels and the Marys, went to prepare and adorn the hall in which her divine Son had celebrated the Last Supper; she swept it herself and arranged it for the celebration of the holy Mass. She begged the good master of the house to give her the same ornaments that had been used on the Thursday at the Last Supper, which he did immediately on account of the veneration he entertained for the holy Virgin. She also prepared the unleavened bread and the wine needed for the consecration, with the little plate and chalice used by the Redeemer.

"On the morning of the following day, the Octave of Pentecost, all the faithful and catechumens, with the Apostles and disciples, assembled together in the hall; St. Peter made a discourse to show the excellence of baptism, its divine effects and the obligations its reception entails on the receiver; he also announced the truth of the blessed Sacrament of the Altar. After this the Apostles baptized with their own hands more than five thousand persons; they rendered thanks to God and prepared themselves with the rest of the faithful to receive Holy Communion. They prostrated themselves upon the earth, adoring the infinite goodness of God and confessing their unworthiness to receive so great a gift. Then they recited the canticles and psalms which the Lord had said.

"St. Peter took in his hands the bread already prepared, and raising his eyes to heaven with great devotion and profound recollection, pronounced over it the divine words of the consecration of the sacred Body of Jesus Christ. The supper-room was at that moment filled with ravishing splendor and an infinite multitude of angels, and in the sight of all the assistants this divine light was especially directed towards the great Queen. St. Peter immediately consecrated the wine in the chalice, and with the sacred Body and precious Blood, he performed the same ceremonies as the Saviour; that is to say, he elevated them that they might be adored by all.

"After this he communicated himself, then the other Apostles. When the divine Mother received holy Communion from the hands of St. Peter, she was surrounded by the heavenly spirits, who were there present, with ineffable respect. Before reaching the altar, the great Queen performed three acts of humility; she prostrated upon the earth to the edification of the faithful, who were moved to tears. Then being entirely recollected and ravished in the Lord, she returned to the place where she had been kneeling.

"After the Communion of the Queen of angels, the other faithful communicated, but of the five thousand who had been baptized, only one thousand received Holy Communion, because the others were not sufficiently disposed and prepared. The manner in which the holy Sacrament was on that day administered was as follows: St. Peter communicated the Apostles, the holy Virgin, and all those who had received the Holy Ghost, under the *two* species of bread and wine. The faithful who had been baptized, afterwards received only under the species of bread. This difference was not made because the converts were less worthy of receiving one species than another, but because the Apostles knew that by receiving only under one species they received Jesus whole and entire in the Blessed Sacrament, and again because there was no precept to communicate under both.

"After the Communion, St. Peter finished the holy mysteries by prayers and acts of thanksgiving. Whereupon they spent some time in meditation. The great Queen returned thanks in the name of all, in which the Divine Majesty took His complacency. He heard and accepted the prayers of His beloved Mother for all the children of the Church, both present and future."

Thus did the Blessed Virgin on this occasion manifest her great desire to see offered up the holy Sacrifice of the Mass. She has still the same desire as she then had.

St. Bonnet, Bishop of Clermont, a great servant of Mary, betook himself one night alone to a church in order to give himself with more leisure and devotion to prayer. At the moment in which his affections were most enkindled, he heard a sweet and ravishing melody, and soon the whole church was filled with light. He then saw the Blessed Virgin enter, accompanied by a great number of angels and saints, who walked in procession, chanting the praises of Our Lord and of His holy Mother. Arrived at the altar, some of them asked who should celebrate Mass. Mary replied that her well-beloved servant Bonnet, bishop of the place, would celebrate. On hearing these words, the holy prelate was seized with fear, and so deeply penetrated with the sentiment of his unworthiness, that he sought to hide himself, and on retiring fell against a stone, which miraculously softened and received the impression of his body. His humility, however, but rendered him more worthy of the honor which he fled; he was constrained to obey. Being conducted to the altar some saints met him, and he celebrated Mass in the midst of this glorious assemblage, assisted and served by the saints. After Mass, Mary gave him a very white alb of a material so fine and delicate that the like was never before seen on earth. It was afterwards shown as a very precious relic.

Why is it that the Mother of God is so desirous of, and delights so much in seeing the holy Sacrifice of the Mass offered? It is because she desires so much to see God the Father honored and worshipped in a manner worthy of His infinite greatness; because she wishes to see men reconciled with Him; because she wishes to obtain for us all the graces necessary for our salvation and sanctification; because she wishes that fitting thanks should be offered to Him for all the blessings and favors He has in an especial manner bestowed upon her and the saints and the whole human race. She understands that it is by the unbloody Sacrifice of the Mass that all these objects are accomplished. It is for this very reason that all the angels and saints of Heaven also rejoice exceedingly whenever the holy Mass is being said. The Blessed Virgin knows that for the sake of the sacrifice of her Son upon the Cross, she was honored with the unspeakable privilege of being preserved from original sin; that to this sacrifice she is indebted for all the other graces and favors which are now hers in heaven, and that the time of Mass, during which the sacrifice of the Cross is renewed, is for her the time most favorable for obtaining every kind of blessing for men, but especially for her servants. Let us rest assured that we can never honor and praise her better, nor give her greater joy, than by having the holy Sacrifice of the Mass offered up in her honor.

Cæsar of Heisterbach relates the following: Some time ago two good priests passed through the country of the Albigensian heretics in France. On seeing a church quite desolate on the road-side, one said to the other, "It is Saturday; let us enter this church and say Mass in honor of our Lady;" for they carried with them everything necessary for the sacrifice. Before Mass was over, some heretics came and said to them: "Why have you said Mass in spite of our strict orders to the contrary?" The priest who said Mass replied boldly, as did the Apostles before the Jewish Council: "We must be more obedient to God than to man; for this reason I have said Mass in honor of God and the Blessed Virgin in spite of your unjust orders." Enraged at this answer, they dragged the pious priest out of the church, beat him, and tore out his tongue. It was with great difficulty that his companion led him to Cluny, where he commended him to the care of the monks. The servant of God suffered this most cruel pain very patiently. On the night of the Epiphany the sick priest made signs to be carried to the church. The charitable monks took him there and placed him before the altar. There he prayed with great fervor to the Mother of mercy, and this good Mother heard the fervent prayers of her servant. The Blessed Virgin appeared to him with his tongue in her hand, saying: "Because of the honor which you have rendered to God and to me by saying Mass, I herewith restore your tongue, requesting you at the same time to continue to say Mass." He thanked the Mother of God for this great blessing, and returning to the people showed them his tongue and confounded the enemies of the Mass. This miraculous cure inflamed the good priest with still greater love for the Blessed Virgin, and out of love for her he staid in the convent and became a monk.

The time of Mass is the most favorable moment for asking the Blessed Virgin to exercise her maternal power, and obtain for us every blessing, both temporal and spiritual. To understand this, we must remember that as before death every father of a family makes his will, so did Jesus Christ make His will on the Cross in concert with the Eternal Father. It remained sealed and hidden with regard to men, but was revealed to the Divine Mother as the co-operatrix in the Redemption. Our dear Saviour declared her heiress and testamentary executrix of His divine will, and all was remitted into her hands, as the Eternal Father had remitted all into those of His Son. Thus our great Queen was charged with the distribution of the treasures which belonged to her Son by virtue of His divinity, or had been acquired by His infinite merits. She was declared the depositary of the riches of her Son, our Redeemer, that all graces, favors, and helps might be given us by the holy Virgin, and that she might distribute them through her merciful and liberal hands.

If we remember this last will of our dear Saviour, if we think of the moment in which the Blessed Virgin was declared the depositary of her Son's wishes and the distributor of all His graces; if we remember that this privilege was bestowed upon her whilst her Son was consummating the great sacrifice of atonement upon Mount Calvary, then it will be clear that she executes her Son's wishes most cheerfully, and distributes to us His blessings and graces more abundantly at the very time when the great Sacrifice of the Cross is renewed, that is, during the time of the holy Mass, for then is she at full liberty to distribute to every one as many favors as he is capable of receiving.

One day St. Dominic was saying Mass in London, England, in presence of the king and queen and three hundred other persons. As he was making the memento for the living, he suddenly became enraptured, remaining motionless for the space of a whole hour. All present were greatly astonished, and knew not what to think or to make of it. The king ordered the server to pull the priest's robe, that he might go on with the Mass. But on attempting to do so, the server became so terribly frightened that he was unable to comply with the order. After an hour's time St. Dominic was able to continue the Mass, when, wonderful to relate, at the elevation of the Sacred Host, all who were present saw, instead of the Host in the hands of the priest, the holy Infant Jesus, at whose sight they experienced great interior joy. At the same time they beheld the Mother of God in heavenly splendor, and surrounded by twelve stars; and they saw her take the hand of her Divine Infant to bless with it all those who were present at Mass. At this blessing many experienced an ineffable joy, and shed tears of tenderness. At the elevation of the chalice every one saw above it a cross on which Our Lord Jesus Christ was hanging in a most pitiable condition, and shedding all His Sacred Blood; they also saw how the Blessed Virgin sprinkled, as it were, the sacred Blood over the people, upon which every one received a clear knowledge of his sins and a deep sorrow for the same. Mass being ended, St. Dominic ascended the pulpit and addressed the people in the following manner: "'Sing ye to the Lord a new canticle, because He hath done wonderful things.'*

---

* Ps. xcvii.

You have all seen with your own eyes, and experienced in your own hearts the wonderful things which Jesus Christ has done in the Most Blessed Sacrament. You have seen with your own eyes, and it has been given you to understand, how Jesus Christ, the Saviour of the world, and the Son of Mary, has been pleased to be born anew, and to be again crucified for you. In this divine and tremendous mystery of the holy Mass, you have witnessed things most holy, most sublime, most consoling, and most touching. It is not one or a few of you who have seen these wonders, but all here assembled, to the number of three hundred, have witnessed them. Now, if there be but one little spark of divine love in your hearts, sentiments of gratitude and hymns of praise in honor of the divine goodness ought incessantly to ascend to God from your hearts." *

This may help us to understand the all-powerful means which the Blessed Virgin has at *her* command, more than all the angels and saints united, a means which she makes use of every minute of the day, to obtain for us in abundance whatever temporal and spiritual blessings we stand in need of in this valley of tears.

She knows and understands the full extent of the great promise of her Son: "Amen, amen, I say to you, if you ask the Father anything in My name, He will give it to you." †
This promise is made to all men, to the Jews as well as to the Gentiles, to Catholics as well as to heretics, to the just as well as to sinners.

Were all men to profit by this promise, were all to pray to the heavenly Father to save them from everlasting perdition for the sake of His son, their Redeemer, all would be saved. But now the greater part of men do not mind this promise, they neglect prayer, and thus are lost. Not so the Blessed Virgin. She profits by this promise, she uses it in our favor, but especially at Mass, when her Son is lying upon the altar

---

* Ex. lib. intit. B. Alamos rediv. par. 3. cap. 22.   † John xvi. 23.

as a Sacrifice of impetration. It is then, more than at any other time, that she presents to the heavenly Father His and her Son, and obtains through Him all she asks. Let us then be careful to hear Mass in her honor as often as possible, resting assured that in life and death she will be to us the most tender of mothers, to lead us safely through all the dangers and troubles of this life to the everlasting contemplation of the glory of her divine Son in heaven.

CHAPTER XXXI.

REVERENCE AND DEVOTION AT MASS.

GOD is everywhere. Nevertheless He is said to be particularly in heaven, because He there displays His Presence by His glory and gifts. In like manner, He honors the Church with His special Presence, because He is there in a particular manner ready to receive our public homages, listen to our prayers, and bestow on us His choicest graces.

"How wonderful were the privileges which He restricted, how magnificent the promises which He made to the Jewish temple!"* With what religious awe did His servants honor it! There was then but one temple of the true God in the world: and that temple no infidel was ever suffered to enter farther than the outer inclosure, or Court of the Gentiles.

The Jews, that is to say, the faithful, had an inner Court allotted to them, where they beheld the offering of the sacrifices, and performed their devotions at a distance from the holy place; but they were never permitted to go any farther, nor even to enter this Court until they had been purified from all legal uncleannesses by the ablutions and other rites prescribed by the law. It is recorded by the Rabbins † that it was not lawful for any one to spit on any part of the mountain where the temple stood, ever to go through it to another place, or ever to gaze about in it; but entering with trembling and gravity, they went to the place where they performed their prayer. The Levites, though devoted to the divine service, were not admitted beyond the part allotted for the bloody sacrifices. None but the priests could enter the sanc-

---

* 2 Paral. vii. 2, 14–16.   † Lamy, in Appartu Biblico.

tuary or Holy Place, and of these but one a week, chosen by lot, could approach the golden altar to offer the daily sacrifice of frankincense. As for the Holy of Holies, or innermost sanctuary, which God sanctified by His more immediate Presence, where the ark, the tables of the law, and the rod of Aaron were kept;—this no one could ever enter on any account, except the High Priest alone, and even he only once a year, on the solemn feast of expiation, carrying the blood of victims sacrificed. Nor was he to do this without having been prepared by solemn purifications and expiations: and the smoke of perfumes was to cover the ark and the propitiatory or oracle, called the seat of God, before the blood was offered.

Whoever dared profane the temple was visited with terrible punishments by the Lord.

It is related in Holy Scripture that Heliodorus was sent by King Seleucus to take away the treasures which were deposited in the temple of the Lord in Jerusalem. When Heliodorus entered the holy place, " Almighty God gave a great evidence of His presence, so that all who had presumed to obey Heliodorus, falling down by the power of God, were struck with fainting and dread. For there appeared to them a horse with a terrible rider upon him (an angel of the Lord), adorned with a rich covering, and he ran fiercely and struck Heliodorus with his forefeet, and he that sat upon him seemed to have the armor of gold.

" Moreover, there appeared two other young men beautiful and strong, bright and glorious, and in comely apparel (two angels), who stood by him, on either side, and scourged him without ceasing with many stripes. And Heliodorus suddenly fell to the ground, and they took him up covered with great darkness, and having put him into a litter they carried him out. So he that came with many servants and all his guard into the aforesaid treasury, was carried out, no one being able to help him, the manifest power of God being known. And he, indeed, by the power of God lay speechless, and without all hope of recovery. But the Jews praised the Lord because He had glorified His place; and the temple, that a little before was full of fear and trouble, when the Almighty Lord appeared, was filled with joy and gladness.

"Then some of the friends of Heliodorus forthwith begged of Onias that he would call upon the Most High to grant him his life, who was ready to give up the ghost. So the High Priest Onias, considering that the king might perhaps suspect that some mischief had been done to Heliodorus by the Jews, offered a sacrifice of health for the recovery of the man. And when the High Priest was praying, the same young men in the same clothing stood by Heliodorus, and said to him: Give thanks to Onias the priest, because for his sake the Lord hath granted thee life. And thou, having been scourged by God, declare unto all men the great works and the power of God. And having spoken thus, they appeared no more.

"So Heliodorus, after he had offered a sacrifice to God, and made great vows to him who had granted him life, and given thanks to Onias, taking his troops with him, returned to the king. And he testified to all men the great works of God, which he had seen with his own eyes.

"And when the king asked Heliodorus who might be a fit man to be sent yet once more to Jerusalem, he said, If thou hast any enemy or traitor to thy kingdom, send him thither, and thou shalt receive him again scourged, if so be he escape: *for there is undoubtedly in that place a certain power of God. For he who hath his dwelling in the heavens, is the visitor and protector of that place, and he striketh and destroyeth them that come to do evil to it.*" *

Pompey's boldness and presumption in viewing the temple of the Lord all over when he had conquered the country, in the opinion of the Jewish historians, caused the misfortunes with which he was afterwards overwhelmed. It

---

* 2 Macchabees iii.

was thus, by frightful punishments and other wonderful signs, that Almighty God inspired the Jews and the Gentiles with reverence and awe for his holy place.

Yet, the temple of Solomon and the Holy of Holies were only types of our sacred tabernacles, in which is offered not the blood of sheep and goats, but the adorable blood of the immaculate Lamb of God. "Verily, the Lord is in this place, and I knew it not."* When the Jewish temple was consecrated, to inspire the people with awe for the holy house, God filled it with a cloud; nor could the priests stand and minister, by reason of the cloud: for the glory of the Lord had filled the house of God. This miracle was repeated when the holocausts were first offered in it. The like wonder had often happened when Moses and Aaron entered the tabernacle. When God came to give the law, Moses himself was affrighted and trembled, and the people stood terrified afar off. Yet all these things were but shadows to our tremendous mysteries, in which we are sprinkled with the precious blood of our Redeemer, and associated to the company of angels.

When our dear Saviour was crucified on Mount Calvary, the sun was darkened, the rocks were rent, and the whole earth quaked. Why did our Lord permit these awful disturbances in nature? In order to impose silence on His enemies, whilst He was offering His life in sacrifice for the expiation of their crimes; and that the Jews, terrified by these prodigies, might leave Him in a repose suited to the sanctity and importance of the action. For the same reason He also remains three hours in silence, recollection, and prayer. Many indeed were at that time deeply impressed with sentiments of faith, reverence, and repentance. The Roman centurion, seeing the things that were done, was greatly afraid, struck his breast, and said: "Indeed this was the Son of God." The Mass, being the mystical

---

* Gen. xxviii. 16.

renewal of the sufferings and death of our Lord, will always excite emotions of faith, reverence, and love in those who assist at it with sincere hearts.

The Catholic has within himself the rule of deportment during the time of Holy Mass—his faith in the Real Presence. He needs nothing else to teach him what is proper or improper during Mass. Yet, although our faith is sufficient to teach us how to behave during Mass, it is possible to remain irreverent, indevout, and cold at so sacred a mystery. In the very temple of God, our Lord found those that sold oxen, sheep, and doves, and the changers of money sitting. The devil understands well how important it is for Christians to assist at Mass with reverence and devotion. Hence he makes every effort to distract them while they are present at the holy sacrifice. It has often been remarked that infidels and idolaters never behave disrespectfully at the sacrifices which they offer to their false gods. Now, this is not strange, for, as Picus Mirandola justly remarks, there is no reason why the devil should tempt them to irreverence, since it is he himself who is honored by their superstitious ceremonies, but knowing how highly God is honored by the great Sacrifice of the Christians, he does all in his power to keep the faithful from church, or, at least, to make them irreverent and indevout while they are there. Once, when the Israelites were fighting against the Philistines and were on the point of being defeated, they had the Ark of the Covenant brought to the camp. As soon as it came they all raised a great shout, so that the earth rang again. The Philistines heard the shout, and were struck with terror on learning that the God who had done such wonderful things against the Egyptians was come into the camp of their enemies. "Woe, woe to us!" they cried, "who shall deliver us from the hands of these high gods?" However, driven to desperation by the greatness of their danger, they exhorted one another to fight manfully. "Let us take courage," they cried, "let us behave like men, O Philistines, lest we become the servants of the Hebrews, as they have served us; let us take courage and fight bravely."[*] In like manner, when the signal is given for beginning Mass, the great adversary of mankind is seized with rage and terror. "Woe, woe!" he cries, "what shall we do? This is that Sacrifice which every day snatches so many souls from our grasp; this is the weapon with which Anthony and Francis, and so many others, have defeated us, and weakened our power. What shall we do?" Then, urged on by the rage he feels at his own impotence, he employs all his cunning to destroy, at least, some part of the good fruits of the Mass: he prevents the sinner from escaping his power by placing before him some dangerous object on which his eyes or imagination may rest; he deprives the devout Christian of the strength and consolation which he would have received during Mass by filling his mind with vain thoughts and worldly cares, so that he cannot attend to what is going on. It is thus that notwithstanding the Presence of our Lord Jesus Christ on our altars, and the infinite value of the Sacrifice, so many precious graces are lost during Mass.

The author of the "Magnum Speculum" relates the following example. Three maidens made a pilgrimage to a certain church. The priest who said Mass was wrapt in ecstasy; he saw how an angel descended with a crown of red roses, and placed it on one of them; he also saw how another angel descended with a crown of white roses, and placed it on the second; while, at the same time, a demon enveloped the third with a fur tippet, and danced before her. After Mass the priest asked them what had been their thoughts during Mass. The first said she had meditated on the crowning of our Lord with thorns; the second, that she had thought of the boyhood and innocence of our Lord; and the third avowed that she had been thinking how slow the priest was in saying Mass, and that she wished it over, that she might buy a new tippet, and hasten to a dance.

---

[*] 1 Kings iv. 5–10.

In a book, named Dormiscuro, it is told, as a well-founded story, that a woman, for a long time suffering deep poverty, wandered about in a sort of despair through solitary places, and that there, in some way or other, an evil spirit intimated to her that if she had conducted herself in church as some did, entertaining those near with idle whisperings and useless and impertinent talk, he would have befriended her and made her better off. The miserable woman accepted the bargain thus suggested, applied herself to the devilish work, and succeeded marvellously; for whoever happened to be placed beside her found it impossible to attend devoutly to Mass, so constant were her observations and questions, and so many the little methods of interruption which she applied. But no long time passed before she felt the avenging hand of God. One morning there came on a violent thunder-storm, and a thunderbolt fell among the crowd, which slew her alone, reducing her to ashes.

Learn then at another's cost and avoid those who, with idle talk and with so much irreverence in church, make themselves truly the servants of Satan; spurn them, if you do not yourself wish to incur the wrath of God.

"The Lord sometimes vehemently impelled me," says Marina de Escobar, "to reprove the faults which others committed against the divine Majesty, and if I ever omitted it through the consideration of my being a poor woman, I felt obliged to return through a mighty scruple. It happened once that being in a church, a certain noble lady entered, who wishing to sit in a place occupied by a poor woman, ordered her angrily to yield it up, beginning at the same time to rebuke her maids for not driving her away instantly; for she was choleric by nature and had an inveterate habit. Then the Lord said to me, 'Rise up and accost that lady, and tell her that she remembers not the nothing from which she is made, and admonish her to be humble.' I heard the divine voice, and I was troubled, as I did not like to perform this unpleasant duty, which was so very contrary to my inclination, and unsuitable to my vile condition; but so absolute was the injunction that I could not help obeying it. Therefore I rose up, and approaching the lady said to her with as loving and sweet a tone as I could find the words with which the Lord inspired me, and she received them with great humility, embracing and returning me immense thanks for having showed her such charity, and beseeching me to commend her to God, and also her son, who was sick. Thus I was consoled, seeing how souls could be inflamed with divine love through such a miserable instrument."

Since the devil has never ceased to tempt the Christians to irreverence and indevotion at Mass, and since there are so many in whom the love of the world soon deadens the appreciation of the most holy mysteries of our religion, the Church has always found it necessary to exhort Christians to behave with great reverence in the house of God. "Reverence My sanctuary, I am the Lord." * "For My house shall be called the house of prayer." † And as exhorting by example is much more impressive than that by precept, word, or writing, a few striking instances may serve to impress deeply upon the mind the duty of reverence during the time of holy Mass.

"And I saw an angel come, who stood before the altar, having a golden censer: and there was given to him much incense, that he should offer up the prayers of all the saints upon the golden altar. And the smoke of the incense of the prayers of the saints ascended up before God, from the hand of the angel." ‡ From this and other similar passages of holy Scripture, the Fathers of the Church infer that God has deputed a particular angel to assist the priest at the altar, whilst celebrating the holy Sacrifice of Mass, to offer to the Almighty the august Sacrifice and the prayers of the priest. Nor is there reason for surprise at this, for holy Scripture tells us that angels assisted even at the sacrifices of the Old

---

* Levit. xxvi.   † Matt. xxi. 13.   ‡ Apocal. viii. 3, 4.

Law, which were but the shadows of the Sacrifice of the Mass.

We read in the Gospel of St. Luke,* that when the priest Zachary was offering incense to the Almighty in the temple of Jerusalem, the archangel Gabriel appeared to him and said: "Fear not, Zachary, for thy prayer is heard, and thy wife Elizabeth shall bear thee a son, and thou shalt call his name John." In the book of Judges † we read that an angel appeared to Manue, and promised him a son, and assisted at his sacrifice. "And when the flame of the altar went up towards heaven, the angel of the Lord ascended also in the flame." We read in the same book ‡ that when Gedeon was offering sacrifice to God, an angel of the Lord was present. "And the angel put forth the tip of the rod which he held in his hand, and touched the unleavened loaves; and there arose a fire from the rock and consumed the flesh and the unleavened loaves."

When Abraham was about to sacrifice his son at the command of the Lord, an angel was present, who prevented Abraham from killing his son Isaac, and supplied him with a ram to be offered to the Lord instead of his son.§ If God then sent His angels to be present at those sacrifices which but prefigured the Sacrifice of the Mass, we may rest assured that He sends them to assist the priest at the altar to celebrate Mass with reverence and devotion, and also the people to hear Mass with proper sentiments of respect and awe. It is related in the book, "Spiritual Meadow," that the Abbot Leontius went one Sunday to church to celebrate Mass. When he came to the altar, he saw an angel standing close by it, who said to him: "Since this altar has been consecrated, I have been commanded to stay here all the time."

One day, whilst St. John Chrysostom was celebrating the holy mysteries, soldiers were sent by the Empress Eudoxia to take him prisoner. Now, when they came to the church,

---

* Chap. I. † Chap. xiii. 20. ‡ Chap. iv. 21. § Gen. xii. 11.

they saw an angel standing at the entrance, brandishing his sword to prevent the soldiers from entering, so that they were obliged to go home without having accomplished anything.*

Something similar is related by Ado,† where he tells us that when the Saxons were about to enter sacrilegiously into a church which had been consecrated by St. Boniface, they found two young men of exquisite beauty and heavenly brightness standing at the entrance. They were angels of the Lord, who prevented them from entering the church, and put them to a shameful flight. Now this angel may be either the guardian angel of the priest, of the altar, or of the church, who assists the priest at the altar, in order that he may be enabled to celebrate the sacred mysteries with greater devotion and reverence. It is for this reason that the priest, after consecration, prays in every Mass in a posture of profound humility: "We humbly beseech Thee, Almighty God, that Thou wouldst command these to be carried by the hands of *Thy holy angel* to Thy sublime altar before the sight of Thy sublime Majesty." Besides this guardian angel of the altar or the church, there are also many other angels present at the holy Sacrifice of the Mass. St. Euthemius, when saying Mass, used to see many angels assisting at the sacred Mysteries in reverential awe. St. Guduvalus, Archbishop, often saw how the angels descended from heaven during Mass, chanting hymns of praise with unspeakably great reverence; but he himself would be standing at the altar like a majestic column of fiery flame whilst he was celebrating the holy sacrifice. St. Basil and St. Chrysostom ‡ testify to having seen at the time of the Mass many hosts of the angels in human form, clothed with white garments, and standing round the altar as soldiers stand before their king. But what was their attitude and deportment? Their heads

---

* Life of St. John Chrysostom.   † In Chron. ætat. 6, anno 774.
‡ De Sacerd. lib. 6, c. 4.

were bowed, their faces covered, their hands crossed, and the whole body so profoundly inclined as to express the deepest sense of their own unworthiness to appear before the Divine Majesty.

Father Balthazar Alvarez, S. J., whilst saying Mass, used to see an angel of the Lord who assisted him in the offering of the holy Sacrifice, and made known to him the particular wants of those for whom he offered up the Mass.* St. John Damascene tells us † that St. Gregory I. used to see the angel of the Lord whilst he was celebrating the sacred mysteries. In the Liturgy of the Mass of St. James the Apostle, we read: "When the moment of consecration is arriving, every one should be silent and trembling with reverential awe; he should forget everything earthly, remembering that the King of kings and the Lord of lords is coming down upon the altar as a victim to be offered to God the Father, and as food to be given to the faithful. He is preceded by the angelic choirs in full splendor, with their faces veiled, singing hymns of praise with great joy." Of these hymns of praise St. Bridget writes thus: "One day, whilst a priest was celebrating Mass, I saw, at the moment of consecration, how all the powers of heaven were set in motion; I heard at the same time a heavenly music most harmonious, most sweet. Numberless angels came down, the chant of whom no human understanding can conceive, nor the tongue of man can describe. They surrounded and looked upon the priest, bowing towards him in reverential awe."‡

Who can wonder at this behavior of the angels during Mass, and at the great preparations which the celestial spirits make when it is being celebrated, in order that the most august mystery may be performed with the greatest pomp and dignity possible? But wretched men as we are, we see for want of a lively faith but little of the supernatural

---

* His Life, by Louis de Ponte.
† Orat. de iis qui cum fide dormierunt.   ‡ Lib. 8, c. 5, 6.

that is going on during Mass. Were Our Lord to show us what He deigned to show St. Bridget and so many other saints, how we would prostrate ourselves to the earth, dazzled, overwhelmed, crushed down by the overpowering splendor of heaven's glory! Not seeing these wonders with our eyes, we come not to appreciate them, and to assist at Mass with levity and indevotion. But why not exercise our faith, and dissipate by its clear light the obscurity of the senses? "Faith is the evidence of things that appear not," * and if we appeal to its aid, it will reveal to us the existence of the wonders concealed from our corporal vision. Believing, on its unerring testimony, that the God of the altar is the God of heaven and earth, the Judge of men—while that thought holds dominion it will be impossible to forget for a moment the respect due to His Majesty; to permit the mind to wander, to whisper, or smile, or look about to recognize acquaintances, or assume any other than a reverential attitude. In a well-instructed Christian such practices would be quite inexcusable and extremely disedifying, therefore we must never allow ourselves to be drawn into them by example. The temple of the Lord is holy; it is "a terrible place, the home of God and the gate of heaven."† Let us take the angels, its invisible guardians, for our models, and contemplating them as they hide their faces with their wings in presence of the God of power and majesty, bow down our souls in profound and humble adoration with them, and for the time, at least, forget all else, to think only of Him Whom, with the eyes of faith, we behold present on the altar. When we think how the angels, those pure spirits, shrink before the Infinite Holiness of God, can we allow vain, worldly, and even sinful thoughts to insinuate themselves into our minds in His Presence? The angels tremble before His Greatness, and shall we dare to talk and laugh before It? The angels, those princes of heaven, are all humility and modesty, and shall we, the dust of the earth,

---
* Heb. xi. 1.   † Gen. xxvlii. 17.

and miserable sinners, be all impertinence and pride? The angels veil their faces before His splendor, and shall we not do even so much as cast down our eyes, but stare rudely and gaze around to see every one who comes in or goes out? The angels, full of awe, fold their hands upon their breasts, and shall we allow ourselves every freedom of attitude and movement? The slightest noise is sufficient to disturb and cause us to forget the Presence and Majesty of the Lord. Shall the reproach which Jesus Christ made to St. Peter when he said, "O ye of little faith," become applicable to us? When approaching these sacred mysteries, let us put off from our hearts the shoes of all earthly thoughts and affections, for the *ground on which we stand is holy*: let us cover our faces with the veil of a deep reverential awe, put upon our senses the guard of profound recollection, tremble with the Seraphim in the Presence of the Lord, and, like the Jews upon entering the temple, bow toward the Mercy-seat of God, saying with the Publican in the Gospel, "Be merciful to me a sinner."

But to assist at Mass with reverence is not enough; we must also assist with devotion, to derive from it the blessings of Our Lord's Passion. The Mass in itself is indeed always of the same value, whether those who assist at it be devout or indevout; but the fruit we derive from it is greater or less according to our dispositions. When Our Lord offered His life on the Cross as a sacrifice for the sins of the world, those who were present received the fruits of that sacrifice in very different proportions. Some received no grace at all, but went away as hardened as they had come, while others received great and special favors. The good thief obtained an entire remission of all his sins, and the punishment due to them. St. Mary Magdalen received a large increase of sanctifying grace. So it is at Mass. The Council of Trent says that God gives the grace of contrition and forgiveness of sin to those who assist at this Sacrifice with a sincere heart, with faith and reverence.

These graces are given more or less in proportion to the devotion and purity of intention of those who assist at Mass. In one of the prayers which the priest recites in the canon of the Mass he says: "Be mindful, O Lord, of all here present whose *faith* and *piety* are known to Thee." It follows from this that one person may gain more graces from a single Mass, than another would gain from twenty or thirty. When we go to the well to draw water, we can only take as much as our vessel will hold; if it be large, we can draw a great quantity; if it be small, we can draw but little. Now, the Mass is an inexhaustible fountain of blessings; it is, to use the language of the Scripture, the Saviour's fountain, from which the precious graces He has merited for us gush forth upon our souls, and the vessel in which we receive these graces is our faith and devotion. If our faith be lively, and our devotion ardent, the blessings of heaven will fill our hearts; if our hearts be filled with the thoughts of this world, we shall receive but a small share of those blessings. All this was once shown in a vision to Nicholas de la Flue, a holy hermit of Switzerland, who was greatly enlightened by God in spiritual matters. While this good man was present at Mass one day, he saw a large tree full of the most beautiful flowers. He soon noticed that the flowers began to fall down upon those who were present. But some of them, as soon as they fell, withered and became dry, while others retained their freshness and fragrance. After Mass he related this vision to his brother, and requested him to explain its meaning. The brother replied that he, too, had seen the vision, and he explained it as follows:

"The tree," said he "is the holy Mass; the withering of many of the flowers signifies that many of the graces which Our Lord distributes in the Mass are lost because Christians are not recollected and devout while they assist at this Sacrifice, or because they afterwards allow worldly thoughts to stifle all the good inspirations which they have received; the flowers which retained their odor and beauty signify the permanent fruits which those Christians derive from the Mass who assist at it with reverence and devotion." Such Christians, when about to enter the church to hear Mass, say with St. Francis: "Now, ye worldly affairs and thoughts of business, leave me and remain outside, while I go into the sanctuary of the Most High to speak to the great Lord of heaven and earth;" and when Mass is over they leave the church with such sentiments of humility and piety as if coming from the awful scene of the death of Jesus Christ on Mount Calvary; they go forth to their duties with the same resolution with which they would have gone had they stood with Mary and St. John beneath our Saviour's Cross, namely, to merit heaven by fulfilling the obligations of their state of life, and by bearing with patience all sufferings, trials, and hardships, and injuries, for the love of Jesus Christ, who loved them to such an excess, and whom, they feel, they will never be able to thank sufficiently, nor repay His ever-burning love.*

Fornerus, Bishop of Bamberg, relates of the great Duke Simon Montfort: "This famous Duke was accustomed to hear Mass daily with great devotion; and at the elevation of the sacred Host, he used to say with Simeon: 'Now Thou dost dismiss Thy servant, O Lord, according to Thy word, in peace, because my eyes have seen Thy salvation.'† His regular attendance at Mass was known to the Albigenses, his bitterest enemies, against whom he had been waging war for twenty years. The Albigenses, being driven to despair, determined to make a sudden attack upon the Duke's army in the morning whilst he was at Mass. They executed their design, and really surprised his soldiers. Officers came to him whilst he was hearing Mass, announcing the great danger in which the whole army was, and begging him to come to their assistance. The Duke answered: 'Let me serve the Lord now, and men after-

---

* Dr. Herbst, Vol. II., p. 409.   † Luke ii. 29.

wards.' No sooner were those officers gone, than others arrived, making the same most earnest request. The Duke replied: 'I shall not leave this place until I have seen and adored my God and Saviour Jesus Christ.' Meanwhile he recommended his whole army to Our Lord, beseeching Him by the most august Sacrifice of the Mass to assist his people. At the elevation of the sacred Host he poured out his heart in humble prayer to his Saviour, offering up to the Heavenly Father the Body and Blood of His well-beloved Son, and making at the same time an oblation of his own life in honor of the Blessed Trinity. At the elevation of the chalice he prayed: 'Now Thou dost dismiss Thy servant, O Lord, according to Thy word, in peace, because my eyes have seen Thy salvation.' Then, feeling inspired with great courage and confidence in the Lord, he said to his officers: 'Now let us go, and if God pleases die for Him who has deigned to die for us on the Cross.' His whole army consisted of but sixteen thousand men. With this little force he attacked in the name of the Blessed Trinity the grand army of the Albigenses commanded by the Count of Toulouse, who was supported by the army of Peter, king of Arragon, his brother-in-law. Now, of this grand army, Simon Montfort, the Christian hero, killed twenty thousand men on the spot, and the rest of his enemies he put to a shameful flight. Every one said and believed that Montfort had gained this glorious victory more by his fervent and devout prayers at Mass than by the strength of his army."*

How many and how great would be the victories which we should gain over the devil, the world, and the flesh, were we always to hear Mass with as much faith, fervor, and devotion as did this pious Duke! How great would be our humility to bear contempt and contradictions with a tranquil heart! how great our patience to carry the crosses and trials of this life until death! how great our charity for our

---

* Miser. conc. 78.

neighbor! how great the light of our understanding in religious matters and the devotion of our hearts to relish the same, if we profited by the gift of God in the holy Mass! What the holy patriarch Jacob said after his wrestling with the angel of the Lord, we too might say, but with more truth: "I have seen God face to face, and my soul has been saved." "For as often as one hears Mass," said Our Lord Jesus Christ to St. Gertrude, "and looks with devotion upon Me in the sacred Host, or has at least the desire to do so, so many times he increases his merits and glory in heaven, and so many particular blessings and favors and delights shall he receive."* How consoling are those words of Our Lord! Let us beware of depriving ourselves of the great blessings of our dear Saviour by inexcusable irreverence and indevotion at Mass.

It is related of St. Basil, that he would not finish Mass unless he had been favored by a heavenly vision. One day, however, this favor was denied him on account of a lascivious look of his assistant. The saint then sent him away, whereupon the vision returned, and he finished the holy Sacrifice.

If God withheld from a great saint certain favors at Mass on account of the sin of another, how many blessings will He refuse to bestow upon us on account of our own wilful faults which we commit during the celebration of the Sacred Mysteries!

Blessed Veronica of Binasco relates of herself the following: "One day, whilst at Mass, I cast a glance of curiosity at one of my sisters in religion. Immediately after, my guardian angel gave me such a severe reprimand for this fault as made me almost die from fright. Ah! how severe was not the look he cast at me, and how sharp the words he spoke to me! 'Why did you give such unbecoming liberty to your eyes?' said he; 'why did you cast that look of curiosity at

---

* Lib. 4. Revel. c. 25.

your sister? Indeed this is not a little fault!' Then he gave me in the name of Jesus Christ a penance for my sin, over which I shed bitter tears for three days. Since that time I hardly ever again dared to make the least motion at Mass for fear of being punished by the Divine Majesty." *

Let us be persuaded that the amount of graces and favors to be derived from the adorable Sacrifice of the Mass depends upon the dispositions of our heart. The Mass is an infinite treasure. Our share, however, rests upon the extent of our claim in the sight of God. When the cathedral of Salzburg was being built, St. Vigilius presented a purse to his workmen, and allowed each man to take what he could. By a supernatural restraint, however, no one could take more than was justly earned. In like manner our dear Lord presents to us in Mass the fulness of the treasure of His blessings, but we can take only the amount which our faith, fervor, reverence, and devotion of the heart will have earned.

---

* Bollandus in Vita ejusdem 13. Jan. Lib. 3. c. 9.

CHAPTER XXXII.

WHY CATHOLICS MUST HEAR MASS.

We have already seen that sacrifice is as old as the world. False or true sacrifices always existed, and have ever been employed for the same purposes. Mankind adopted some victim which was destroyed as a recognition of the supreme dominion of God over all His creatures, or, as the case might be, to expiate sin, propitiate the divine Majesty, or to thank Him for favors received. This is so universal and so uniform, even among nations that could not have known one another, that only the original teaching of God Almighty Himself, or an impression by Him in the hearts of men from the beginning, can adequately explain its universality.

The reason why religion requires a sacrifice is this:—to express our duty of offering to the divine Majesty a fitting worship, to thank Him for the innumerable benefits He has conferred on us, in a manner worthy of the giver and the magnitude of His gifts, to expiate the sins we have committed against God, and to secure for ourselves and others all the blessings needed for soul and body.

Now, the holy Sacrifice of the Mass is the only suitable means of accomplishing all this. For the excellence of the Christian sacrifice consists in the Victim offered being a living, reasonable Divine Victim, even the incarnate Son of God Himself, Who by His life and death offered to His Father the four-fold offering of adoration, impetration, propitiation, and thanksgiving, and Who still, in every Mass, continually, with heart and soul offers this four-fold offering anew. For this, then, the Mass is given, and for this we are required to assist at it, that we may, in a perfect and fitting manner recognize God's sovereignty and our dependence on Him. When we assist at Mass the meaning of our action, if put into words, would be something of this kind: "I acknowledge Thee, O my God, for my Sovereign Lord and the Supreme Disposer of my life and death: and because I am not able worthily to express Thy greatness, I beg of Thee to accept as if it were my own, all the submission with which Thy Son honored Thee on the Cross and now honors Thee in this Holy Sacrifice. I intend, moreover, by this divine Victim to propitiate Thee for my sins, to lay my wants open to Thee, through the pleading tongue of Jesus; and to thank Thee as becomes me and as is worthy of Thee, for all the blessings Thou hast bestowed upon me and upon the whole world."

The spectacle is beautiful, indeed awful, in its sublimity. "Have I not said, you are gods!" comes up before one's mind when we think of it. All nature seems to turn to us at that moment: each of us is its representative. Intelligent and unintelligent, in heaven above, on earth, and under the earth, they all turn towards the priest, who gives expression to their feelings and their dependence, who represents their desires at the throne of eternity. The saints and angels look down with Holy Mary at their head, because we bring them increased glory and honor; the souls in purgatory look up to where we kneel, because we are about to make the Blood of the Lamb plead for the eternal union to which their holy souls are tending; the wants and woes and sorrows, the crimes and penitence of the universe turn to us, because everything, outside hell, is interested in the adorable Sacrifice, which it is given us to offer up. At Mass we are enabled to place in the Sacred Heart of the divine Lamb all our thoughts, words, and actions, that they may be purified and sanctified. In this Sacred Heart of the divine Victim at Mass we find a supplement for our deficiencies, and a substitute for our incapabilities. In the Mass we can offer to the eternal Father, to atone for the coldness and distraction of our prayers, the petitions which this compassionate heart of Jesus poured forth in the silence of night on the lonely mountains of Judea, its supplications in the garden of agony, its piteous appeals for mercy for men on the Cross. At Mass we can offer the burning zeal and love of the Heart of Jesus to supply for our insensibility to the divine attractions, our indifference to heavenly things, our fatal self-love, which blinds the understanding and enslaves the affections: at Mass we can clothe ourselves in the virtues of Jesus Christ, and hide our miseries under the mantle of His perfections.

If we go often to Mass, this holy Sacrifice will correct our faults without bitterness; will heal our wounds without pain; will purify our heart without violence; will sanctify our soul without alarm, and almost without a struggle; it will detach us from ourselves without the convulsion of death; it will withdraw us from creatures and unite us to God without agony. It is the remedy which Jesus Christ has left us in all its sweetness. The poor and the rich, the mechanic and the merchant, the married and the unmarried, the sick and the strong, all can easily participate in this adorable Sacrifice without leaving the world, without injuring their health, or abandoning their family, or employments. The holy Sacrifice of the Mass, then, is the most beautiful, the most sublime, the most powerful, the most acceptable, and withal the easiest worship that we can ever offer to God. This is the reason why Holy Church commands her children under pain of mortal sin to hear Mass, at least every Sunday and holy-day of obligation; why she forbids us to come too late to Mass; why we always find good Catholics so eager to assist at the divine Sacrifice. This explains also the great difference between Catholics and Protestants while on their way to their several churches.

One may see Protestants taking their time, loitering on the way as if they were going to a lecture-room, which, in fact, is really the case; while, on the contrary, good Catholics are hastening on to church with a certain eagerness, as having some very important duty to perform.

Why this strict obligation of hearing Mass? Why this eagerness in going to assist at it? Can we not worship God just as well at home? No! For, although God, by His immensity, is present everywhere—yea, even in hell—nevertheless He is present on our altars *in a most special manner*. He is present there as God and man, as our Redeemer, our Intercessor, our High Priest, Who offers His own innocent Heart's Blood as the atonement for our sins.

What a consolation to know that as the sun in its course brings the light of day to each successive spot on earth, it ever finds a priest girding himself for the altar, preparing to celebrate holy Mass. Thus, from the rising to the setting of the sun, the pure oblation is offered up to God. Each day, as the busy din of the world begins, as the groan of the down-trodden and the wail of the heart-broken, the tear of the helpless victim and the insolent boast of pride, rise up before the throne of God, there also ascends before that throne from our altars the sweet voice of Jesus supplicating for pardon and for peace.

But, say some: "There is no need of going to Mass; we can pray just as well at home."

Now, do we really pray to God at home? But, whether we do or not, the question is *not* can we pray well at home, but whether God requires us to hear Mass on Sundays and holy-days of obligation. God *does require* this. God speaks to all Christians through His Church, and the Church of God commands us to hear Mass on Sundays and holy-days under pain of mortal sin, that is, she commands you under pain of eternal damnation to be present, with attention and devotion, at the three principal parts of the Mass: that is, at the Offertory, Consecration, and Communion. Should you, through your own fault, miss one of these parts, you would not comply with your obligation of hearing Mass. In this case you are bound to hear another Mass, if possible, under pain of eternal damnation. It is true that we are distinct individuals, with distinct individual duties, but it is also true that we are a religious body. This society, this Church of which we are members, has certain duties to fulfil towards God, one of which is public worship; and the public worship of this Christian society is precisely the holy Sacrifice of the Mass. To stay away from this act of public worship is to neglect a most sacred duty; it is, in a certain sense, to renounce all our share in the merits of Jesus Christ. For our sake the heavenly Father sends His well-beloved Son upon the altar; for our salvation, the Holy Ghost changes bread and wine into the Body and Blood of Jesus Christ; for our sake the Son of God comes down from heaven, and conceals Himself under the species of bread and wine, humbling Himself so much as to be whole and entire in the smallest particle of the Host. For our sake He renews the Mystery of His Incarnation, is born anew in a mystical manner, offers up to His heavenly Father all the prayers and devotions which He performed during His life on earth, renews His Passion and Death to make us partakers of its merits, cancelling our sins and negligences, and remitting many temporal punishments due to the same. And we reject these graces and blessings, despise this offering every time that we carelessly stay away from the holy Mass.

Now, can we think that God will allow this carelessness of ours to go unpunished? Listen to the following example: St. Anthony, Archbishop of Florence, relates that two young men went hunting on Sunday. The sky was cloudless, not a leaf was stirring. Presently they heard the low rumbling of distant thunder. A dark smoke like a vapor began to spread over the face of the heavens. Flashes of lightning succeeded one another rapidly, and the voice of the thunder was heard in one continuous roar. In a few moments the sky grew black as sackcloth. Soon the vivid flashes of lightning lit up the heavens with a lurid preternatural glare. At times the whole universe appeared to be on fire; the peals of thunder followed one another with astounding rapidity. Many trees were struck by the lightning within view of the hunters, and presently one of the largest was shivered to splinters directly in their path. Suddenly they heard above them in the air a wild unearthly yell. "Strike! strike!" cried the voice, and instantly a flash of lightning killed one of them —the one that had not heard Mass. The other young man was panic-stricken at this, especially as he heard at the same time, a voice saying: "Strike him too." A little after he felt encouraged by another voice, which said, "I cannot strike him, because he heard Mass this morning."*

We know that we can do nothing better for our parents, friends, for the poor and distressed, for our benefactors, for the dying, for the conversion of sinners, for the just, for the souls in purgatory, than to hear and offer up for them the holy Sacrifice of the Mass; and that we cannot give greater glory and joy to the blessed Trinity, to the Blessed Virgin, and to all the saints, than by assisting at Mass with devotion. But whenever we stay away from Mass through neglect, especially on Sundays and holy-days of obligation, we thereby give to understand that we do not care to give glory to God and His saints, as little as we care to obtain the graces of God for ourselves and others by so powerful a means as that of the Mass. And do we imagine that this contempt of ours for God's glory and His blessings will go unpunished? We cannot complain that the Almighty should treat us with similar neglect, if He bestows His choicest gifts upon others and passes us by unnoticed. We made the choice and we must abide the issue.

Three merchants of Gubbio went to a fair held in the town of Cisterno, and having disposed of their goods, two of them began to speak of returning home, and arranged to start the next day at dawn, so as to arrive by evening in their own

---

* Ant. ii. p. Theolog. ix. c. 10.

neighborhood. But the third would not consent to start at that time, protesting that the next day being Sunday he would never think of commencing a journey without first having heard holy Mass. His companions refused to wait for him, and set out by themselves. But when they arrived at the river Corfuone, which had risen to a great height in consequence of the rain that fell during the night, the bridge gave way and they were drowned. The third, who had waited to hear Mass, found his two companions dead on the bank of the river, and gratefully acknowledged the grace which he had received on account of having heard Mass.*

We may rest assured that whenever we miss Mass through carelessness, we expose ourselves to the greatest dangers of soul and body; for it is then that the devil obtains from God great power over both; which power is refused him in regard to those who comply with their duty of hearing Mass with devotion on all days of obligation. It is an unquestionable truth that devout attendance at Mass has protected many souls from vices into which they would otherwise have fallen; it has saved many a one from sudden death and calamities which God has permitted to fall on others; it has conferred a blessing on many a family—given peace and unanimity, where discord would otherwise have reigned; and made parents happy in the conduct of children, whose hearts would otherwise have been broken by their disobedient and disorderly behavior.

It is related of Drahomira, the mother of St. Wenceslaus, a very impious Duchess of Bohemia, how she one day went in a carriage to Saes in order to take a solemn oath on her father's grave, to extirpate all the Christians in her dominions. Passing a chapel in which Mass was being said, the driver, on hearing the bell ring for the Elevation of the Host, stopped the carriage and knelt down on the bare

---
* Lohner.

ground to adore our Lord Jesus Christ on the altar. At this the impious Duchess flew into a violent passion, cursing the driver and the Blessed Sacrament. In punishment for her horrible blasphemies, the earth opened and swallowed her and her whole escort. They cried for help, but in vain. In a moment they were gone forever. The driver was glad indeed for having stopped the carriage to adore our Lord in the Blessed Sacrament; his faith and devotion saving him from destruction.*

Mass alone of itself is an inexhaustible treasure of graces. Yet how little is this most august Sacrifice valued by most men! If it were said, "At such a place and at such an hour a dead person will be raised to life," men would run to witness the miracle. But is not the consecration which changes bread and wine into the Body and Blood of Christ, a much greater miracle than the raising of a dead person to life? If Christians only knew the value of the holy Sacrifice of the Mass, or rather, if they had more faith, assuredly they would not absent themselves from it on the most trivial pretexts. There are indeed grievous reasons which dispense with the obligation of hearing Mass, for instance, when a person is confined to bed by sickness, when he is in prison, or when he is blind and has no one to conduct him to church, or when he cannot go to Mass without exposing himself to the danger of some grievous temporal or spiritual evil. Hence, the persons on guard in cities, or in armies, or entrusted with the care of herds of cattle, or of houses, or of infants, or of the sick, are exempt from the obligation of hearing Mass, *when they have no person to take their place.* A grievous inconvenience is also an excusing cause. Hence, the sick who are convalescent and unable to go to church without great pain or danger of relapse, are excused from the obligation of hearing Mass. Servants, also, are excused who cannot leave the house without grievous

---

* Hagec in chronic. Bohemic. ad ann. 9. 30.

inconvenience to their master, or to themselves. A considerable distance from the church is also an excusing cause. A less distance excuses from sin when it is raining or snowing, or when a person is infirm, and the road to the church very bad. But there are numbers for whom a little rain, a damp mist, the slight inconvenience of heat, a little moisture under foot, rise up as a sufficient excuse. They will be judged by St. Elizabeth, who, as Rutebeuf tells us, repaired early in the morning to Mass so poorly and humbly, through the mire of the road, without horse or carriage, holding her lighted taper in her hand.

These lukewarm Christians will be judged by that Christian young lady who, when on her way to Mass, was perceived by the guard of the Emperor Diocletian; he was struck with her modesty, and going rudely up to her he said: "Stop! whither are you going?" The young lady was frightened; she feared that he would insult her. She made on her forehead the sign of the Cross, in order to obtain the divine protection. The soldier, deeming himself affronted by her silence, seized her violently and said: "Speak! who are you? whither are you going?" She courageously replied: "I am a servant of Jesus Christ, and am going to the assembly of the Lord." "You shall not go," said the soldier; "you must sacrifice to the gods; to-day we worship the sun; you must worship him with us." He then attempted to pull off the veil which covered her face. This she endeavored to prevent, and said: "Wretch, Jesus Christ will punish you!" At these words the soldier became furious, and plunged his sword into the heart of the Christian virgin. She fell, bathed in her blood, but her holy soul flew up to heaven, there to receive an unfading crown of glory.[*]

There are also many who find an excuse in the fact that their friends and acquaintances, as well as occupations, make large demands upon their time. But these will be judged

---

[*] Fleury.

by Sir Thomas More, who never omitted hearing Mass, notwithstanding his numerous friends and occupations. One day, whilst he was assisting at Mass, the King's messenger came and told him that his majesty required his immediate presence, in order to transact with him business of the greatest importance. The Chancellor said to him: "Yet a little patience. I have to present my homages of respect to a sovereign of greater power and authority; and I think it necessary to remain at the audience of heaven until it shall be over." He considered it a high honor to serve Mass. "I deem it," he used to say, "a high honor to have it in my power to render this slight service to the greatest of sovereigns."

There are others who say: "Father, I oversleep myself." Shame on such! Let them break off useless conversations and go to bed in due time; not turning night into day and day into night, and they will awake easily enough, as they do when there is question of some temporal gain. But when the question is one of obtaining the blessings of the Mass, graces and blessings which have cost our dear Saviour His most precious Blood, they are too lazy to get up in time. Certainly they will be judged by that good and faithful Christian who, as Gillois relates, lived in Roibon, a town of the diocese of Grenoble. He was a peasant whose great devotion at Mass edified every one who saw him. Although living three miles from the church, he never failed to be one of the first worshippers in the morning. In the latter years of his life he was subject to severe pains in his legs, which prevented his walking so far in the winter season, but as soon as the spring came on, he used to rise about one o'clock in the morning, and supporting himself by means of crutches, he would reach the church after a painful and laborious walk of four hours.

But some may say, "It is more necessary for us to labor than to hear Mass; because, without work, we cannot even earn a subsistence for ourselves and family." On the contrary, it is even more necessary to hear Mass than to labor, because it is a most powerful means of keeping oneself in the state of grace, and obtaining the blessings of God. This does not mean that men are to neglect their work, but they can easily break off for half an hour, and devote that short time to God. Those who do so will soon find that their business will not suffer, as God's blessing will be upon it. Men who neglect to hear Mass, either from temporal interest or from sloth, inflict upon themselves a loss for which there is no compensation; they lose a hundred-fold more than the work of a whole day could bring in.

In the life of St. John the Almoner is an instructive narrative of two artisans who pursued the same trade; one was burdened with a family: wife, children, grandchildren; the other was alone with his wife. The first brought up his family in great comfort, and all his transactions turned out wonderfully. Thus he went on till he found himself putting by every year a good round sum, to serve in time for marriage portions for his daughters. The other, who was without children, at one time got very little employment, was half famished, and in short, a ruined man. One day he said confidentially to his neighbor: "How is it with you? On your home rains down every blessing of God, while I, poor wretch, cannot hold up my head, and all sorts of calamities fall on my house." "I will tell you," said his neighbor; "to-morrow morning I will be with you and point out the place from which I draw so much." Next morning he took him to church to hear Mass, and then led him back to his work-shop; and so for two or three days, till at last the poor man said: "If nothing else is wanted than to go to church to hear Mass, I know the way well enough, without putting you to inconvenience." "Just so," said the other; "hear holy Mass, my friend, with devotion every day, and you will see a change in the face of your fortune." And, in fact, so it was. Beginning to hear holy Mass every morning, he was soon well provided with work, shortly after paid his debts, and put his house once more in a prosperous condition.

Some again say: "Father, I am in a place where I have too much work to do; after I have finished it is too late for Mass; and were I to leave my work unfinished and go to Mass, the family I live with would be much displeased with me, and might discharge me."

Now, there is good reason for believing that this difficulty is not so great as is imagined by those who raise it. If the family they live with are Catholics, they know that it is their duty to see that all Catholics get to Mass in due time; if they are Protestants or Jews, they will be glad to see those in their employ anxious to comply with their religious duties, knowing that if their employees are faithful to God, they will also be faithful to them; and this is the reason why they like to have Catholic workmen and servants. Should, however, the demand to go to Mass be refused, other places are open, and sensible employers will scarcely object at the risk of parting with a conscientious Catholic workman or servant. In order to avoid all difficulties, it is best to tell the family into whose service one is about to enter, that he or she only enters on condition that full liberty be given to comply with religious duties on Sundays and holy-days of obligation. Should they not agree to this, one should not go to them so long as there are prospects of finding another situation. However, it may be taken for granted that generally speaking, a good Catholic laborer or servant who is very anxious to hear Mass on Sundays and all holy-days of obligation, easily finds a good situation, for this is a blessing which Jesus Christ grants to those who never miss Mass through neglect. It may be also taken for granted that those who really value and rightly appreciate the blessings of Mass, will know how to arrange their work so as not to allow it to interfere with their regular attendance at Mass. Show a little more anxiety to serve the Lord, to keep the soul in the state of grace, and to advance in holiness of life, and all imaginary difficulties in this matter of staying away from church will soon disappear. Be just as careful and desirous to obtain the blessing of God as to avoid a little temporal loss, and you will soon be a better Catholic.

St. Isidore was hired by a wealthy farmer to cultivate his farm. He would, however, never commence his work in the morning before he had heard Mass. He was accused to his master by some of his fellow-laborers, of staying too long in church, and on that account of being always late at work. His master, in order to examine for himself the truth of the accusation, went out early in the morning to see whether or not Isidore came in due time to the farm; but how great was his astonishment when he beheld two angels, dressed in white, ploughing with two yoke of oxen, and St. Isidore in their midst. From that time forward Isidore was held in great veneration by his master as well as by all those who heard of the wonderful occurrence.

Why is it that Mass is said, especially on Sundays and holy-days of obligation, at different hours, from break of day till noon? Precisely for the convenience of the early traveller, laborer, the domestic, the student, the charitable matron, the pious father of a family, the children; to remove as far as possible every pretext for missing Mass. Indeed, there were, and there still are many Catholics who heard Mass under greater difficulties and inconveniences than those who are so ready with excuses. They will judge and condemn on the day of the last judgment all who neglect this most important duty of their religion.

After the miserable Henry VIII., King of England, had consummated the schism and heresy of the Anglican Church, there were enacted several penal laws against those who had the courage to practise the Catholic religion; a heavy fine even was imposed on those who assisted at Mass. It happened one day that a fervent Catholic, who enjoyed a large fortune, was condemned to pay five hundred gold pieces, because he had dared to fulfil publicly that duty of religion.

The gentleman was very happy in that he was judged worthy to endure this persecution. He sought out the finest pieces of Portuguese gold that were to be had, because they bore the impress of the Cross, and went himself to present the entire sum in the court of law. As he counted out the new coins before the Protestant official, the latter asked him in a jeering tone, what was the reason of his selecting such beautiful pieces to pay the fine. To this ironical question the Catholic gentleman merely replied: "I would think it wrong to pay with common and ordinary money the favor I received in being enabled to adore my Lord and Saviour in the holy Sacrament of the Altar. Know, sir, that between the Cross you see stamped on this coin and the holy Sacrifice of the Altar, there exist numerous points of analogy; both are, in fact, monuments of our Saviour's infinite love, and no Catholic may ignore them." And so saying he went on quietly counting out the five hundred gold pieces which were the price of assisting at the holy Sacrifice.*

But, granting that our facilities for hearing Mass may not always be so great as our wish, yet if we understand and value the gift of God to us in the Mass, we will not only think it well worth some additional trouble in the purchase, but feel that the sacrifice of a life would be too well repaid by the high honor and unsurpassed happiness of assisting even once at the most adorable Sacrifice. There is no Christian incapable of feeling the pleasure that is produced by the knowledge of what is contained in the holy Sacrifice of the Mass. All that is necessary for that is to esteem the blessings of grace, to desire your salvation, to sigh after heaven, and to remember that the august Sacrifice is the source of all temporal and spiritual riches, and the most efficacious means of satisfying all holy desires.

Unless so circumstanced that to hear Mass even daily is a moral impossibility, or a decided infringement on the duties

---

* Schmidt's Histor. Catech.

of your state in life, maintain inviolably the good habit of hearing Mass every day. Go gladly to the altar of God, there to draw down the multiplied graces of which it is the copious source, thence to extract the spiritual treasures of which it is the inexhaustible mine; thence to procure a balm for all miseries and a remedy for all wants. Think seriously of all that we have in the wonderful and adorable Sacrifice, thus to enliven faith, to reanimate confidence, to inflame devotion, and powerfully to confirm the determination to be ever the fervent, devoted, loving adorer of Jesus, the divine Victim of the Altar. If circumstances render it really impossible to hear Mass daily, endeavor at least, as far as in you lies, to indemnify yourself for the very great privation. Desire with all the ardor of your soul that you could enjoy so great a happiness.

It is well for those who can do so in the course of the morning to retire to their room nearly at the time which they know to be the hour when the holy Sacrifice of the Mass is being offered in the church, and, after having implored the grace of God, to perform with recollection and fervor the duty of religion, to kneel down before the Crucifix, and with all the sentiments of devotion possible to unite heart and soul to the Heart of Jesus in the holy Mass, and then read or say the same prayers which they would have said had they been actually present in the church, never forgetting to make the spiritual Communion, which may be made in any place, and at any hour of the day or night. The good Catholic, then, will always feel himself impelled to hear Mass, unless a very urgent reason prevents him from so doing.

In the South of Ireland, County Cork, there are two islands with only one church. When the sea is too stormy the inhabitants of one island assemble upon the beach at the appointed hour and turn to the church. There they kneel in the sand, arise at the Gospel, bless themselves at the Consecration, and thus unite themselves in spirit with the holy

Sacrifice from which they are separated by the wind and waves.

St. Louis, King of France, used to hear two Masses every day; sometimes even three or four. Some of his courtiers murmured at this, but the king gave them a sharp reprimand, saying, "If I were to ask you to play, or to go hunting with me, three or four times a day, you would find no time too long, and now you feel weary of staying in the church during one or two Masses for the honor of our Lord and Saviour."*

Henry III. of England used to assist each day at three High Masses, besides several Low Masses. One day St. Louis conversed with him on this devotion and observed that it was not always necessary to assist at so many Masses, but that as many sermons as possible should be heard. King Henry replied, "I prefer seeing my friend often to hearing any one speak of him, however excellent may be his discourse."

When St. Anselm, Archbishop of Canterbury, was no longer able on account of his old age to say Mass, he had himself carried to the church every day to hear it.†

Blessed Armella was a poor, but holy servant girl. We read in her life that whenever she was prevented from going to church, she used to kneel down in the place where she had to work, with her face turned towards Jesus in the Blessed Sacrament, and thus performed her devotion. She used to do this particularly at the time when she knew the Holy Mass was being celebrated, or that the Blessed Sacrament was exposed on the altar.

Would that we had some of this spirit of the saints still left among us! Has devotion forsaken the greater part of Christians altogether, that they leave Jesus at present such a stranger upon our altars? Are their necessities less numerous or less urgent than were those of old? No, but it is true that their weaknesses are greater and they are less

---

* Reinaldus in Annal. 1270, No. 19. † His Life, by Eadmer.

sensible of them. They take less pains to acquire strength. If there were a day on which they were not exposed to sin; a time in which they were not surrounded by enemies; if they had no virtues to acquire, no homage to pay, they might be excused from hearing Mass. But if, on the other hand, they are pressed by all these motives, let them not be so thankless to the Almighty, so thoughtless of themselves, as to neglect the only means they have of performing all these duties. Let us endeavor to imitate the saints in their zeal in hearing Mass. Early in the morning, when angels are descending from heaven to take their stand around the altar of the Most High, let us too set out to assist at Mass, and emulate their devotion during the performance of this stupendous mystery.

Let us not think the time is lost which is spent in hearing Mass; it will prove most profitable to us in this life and in the next. See how many sins are expiated by it! how many punishments averted! how many graces drawn upon ourselves and others! how many merits stored up for heaven! Let us be diligent in hearing Mass, and we shall surely find in it all that we need, our happiness here below and our happiness hereafter. Amid all the vicissitudes of life, at the altar we shall find true peace and support. At one time it will be Mount Calvary for us, where we may weep tears of sympathy for our Saviour, and of grief for our sins and for those of others; at another time it will be Mount Thabor, where heavenly joy will be poured into our sorrowing heart, and tears will be wiped away from our eyes. Again, that same altar will be a crib of Bethlehem, where we may gather strength to bear contempt, poverty, pain, and desolation. Yes, at the altar we shall find that Mount of Beatitude, where we may learn the vanity of all earthly things, and the way to true and lasting pleasure. In fine, it will be to us Golgotha, where we may learn to die to ourselves and to live to Him who died for us! All this and more we find in the Mass, if we cherish a tender devotion to it: let us persevere in this devotion, and we will soon taste the sweets of those inspired ejaculations: "How lovely are Thy Tabernacles, O Lord of Hosts! Thou hast prepared a table before me against those that trouble me. Better is one day in thy courts above thousands! Blessed are they that dwell in thy house, O Lord: they will praise Thee forever and ever: They will drink hereafter at the torrent of delight, which, flowing from the Heart of Jesus as its source, inundates from end to end the everlasting kingdom of God's glory."

CHAPTER XXXIII.

HOW TO HEAR MASS.

WHEN we go to church to hear Mass, we must remember that, though it is only the priest who speaks in the holy Sacrifice and offers it up to God, yet all who assist at Mass also offer it up in union with the priest. Our Lord has instituted Mass in such a manner as to serve for all and each of us as a sacrifice worthy of being offered to the Divinity, and as a Victim most agreeable to Him, so that Mass is a common good to all and to each in particular. Every Christian has a claim to this Divine Host, and can offer it in his own name and for his own good, as if it belonged to him alone, and also as a gift common to all and peculiar to each.

In order to gather the wonderful fruits of the Mass, we must assist at it in the right spirit and with proper dispositions. Every grand and solemn action in human life is preceded by a suitable preparation. As there is nothing more sublime in heaven and on earth than the celebration of the Holy Mass, it is our duty to prepare ourselves worthily for performing or assisting at the sacred mysteries. On this preparation depend in great measure the blessings and favors of this august Sacrifice.

There are many who live quite close to the church, and they are, generally speaking, the very persons to be regularly late at Mass, seeming to be afraid of being a minute too soon in church. Others are in the habit of standing outside the church until the organ commences to play, and then noisily rush in so as to disturb the priest at the altar and the devout worshippers in their prayers. As all these come to Mass without preparation, they assist at it, of course, without devotion. Many of them remain behind in the church. They have eyes, and see not; ears, and hear not what is going on at the altar. They have hearts, and feel not, lips, and pray not. They have neither prayer-book nor rosaries in their hands. They are there like marble statues. Like these, they neither hear nor draw the least profit from Mass. They do not comply with the command of the Church, prescribing *to hear Mass with devotion.* How sad it is to see Catholics manifest less devotion and recollection at the tremendous Sacrifice of the Mass than heathens manifest at their idolatrous worship!

There are others whose preparation for Mass is still worse. It frequently happens that the nearest neighbors of a Catholic church are generally the proprietors of drinking saloons. It was not the Holy Ghost, but the devil, the enemy of God and of prayer, that inspired these men to establish the offices of Satan as close to the church as possible, so as to make it convenient for lukewarm Catholics to enter first these little chapels of the devil, and pay their homage to the god of their belly before entering the house of the Lord. What is still worse than all this is, that the near neighborhood of these houses causes lukewarm Catholics sometimes to leave the church during the time of the sermon, in order to spend it in these chapels of the devil. They are afraid of listening for half an hour to the word of God, which might make them become better Christians; they prefer to listen to the word of the devil, to the obscene language which prevails in these establishments. Some of these lukewarm Catholics remain there during the whole time of High Mass, and leave but too often in a state of intoxication; while others leave when they think that the sermon is over. It is hardly necessary to say that to this class of Catholics the words of the Gospel apply: "This people honoreth me with their lips, but their heart is far from me."* They leave the church as

---

* Mark vii. 6.

little touched and benefited by the sacred mysteries as the stones in the wall. But woe to the men who thus draw Catholics from the worship of God! Can there be a greater blindness, a greater cruelty to one's self and to our fellow-men, than that of making a living by offending Almighty God, and ruining many souls redeemed at the infinite price of the most precious Blood of Jesus Christ?

How, then, must we prepare for hearing Mass? We must remember that Mass is not only a commemoration and representation of the Passion of Jesus Christ, and of the Sacrifice which He Himself offered upon the Cross to His Eternal Father for our sins, but that it is also really the same Sacrifice which was then offered, of the same virtue, efficacy, and value.

On the way to the church we may imagine that we form part of the crowd who accompanied our divine Saviour in His last journey to death. We may think over some of the circumstances of that sorrowful journey, or represent to ourselves the closing scene on Calvary. Before Mass begins, we should acknowledge our unworthiness to assist at the most holy and august Sacrifice, as well as our incapability of doing so with suitable dispositions, and beseech our Lord to inspire us with the thoughts and sentiments which should occupy our mind and heart on so solemn an occasion.

After this preparation it would be well to unite the intention at the beginning of Mass with that of the priest, and endeavor to follow and imitate him in all he does, remembering that, at the time of the Sacrifice, we are not only in the church to hear Mass, but also to offer with the priest the most adorable Sacrifice of the Body and Blood of Jesus Christ. This may be briefly done thus: "O my God! I offer to Thee this Sacrifice for the same ends for which Thou didst institute it, and for which Thy priest is now celebrating it; I beseech Thee to grant that the souls of the living as well as the souls in purgatory may share in its fruits."

After this, the time of Mass may be spent in such prayers

as devotion may suggest. According to St. Leonard of Port Maurice, it is a very good plan to divide the whole Mass into four parts, corresponding with the four principal objects for which Mass is offered; that is to say: To consider the Mass from the beginning to the Gospel as a sacrifice of propitiation; from the Gospel to the Elevation, as a sacrifice of impetration; from the Elevation to the Communion, as a sacrifice of adoration; and from the Communion to the end, as a sacrifice of thanksgiving.

In the first place, we may consider the holiness of God and the enormity of sin, and, bewailing our offences, offer the Immaculate Lamb to the Father, and ask in the name of Jesus a more complete forgiveness of our sins, and of the temporal punishments due to them, and a more profound spirit of penance.

In the second part we may offer this sacrifice to obtain special graces from God for ourselves and others, for the welfare of Christendom, for the propagation of the Catholic faith, for the extirpation of heresy, for peace among Christian rulers, for grace to fight against our besetting sin, and in remembrance also of the poor souls in purgatory.

In the third part we may consider our own nothingness and God's greatness; then offer up to Him the homage of His well-beloved Son, and in union with the same sublime homage of Jesus Christ our own acts of adoration to the Heavenly Father. We may rejoice in His glory, and desire that all men render Him due honor.

In the fourth part we may consider what God is in Himself and what He is in His Saints, and offering to Him the thanksgiving which Jesus Christ makes in the Mass, add an affectionate oblation of ourselves and of all we have in return for the great mercies He has shown us. Here an especial acknowledgment of the graces which the Lord has bestowed on the Blessed Virgin Mary, our Mother, and on all the angels and saints of heaven, may be made.

These intentions are just and appropriate at the beginning

of Mass, and afterwards the Book of Devotions may be used, or the Rosary of the Blessed Virgin may be said. If the Rosary, it would be well to say the Hail Mary in the usual manner as far as the word Jesus, adding in the first decade, "Whom I offer to God as a sacrifice of propitiation for my sins," and then continue the Hail Mary as usual; in the second decade, add after Jesus, "Whom I offer to God as a sacrifice of impetration;" in the third and fourth decade, "Whom I offer to God as a sacrifice of adoration;" and in the fifth decade, "Whom I offer to God as a sacrifice of thanksgiving." By these means the time of Mass will never seem irksome, and great fruit will be derived from the most holy Sacrifice.

The best method, however, of hearing Mass is to recall the sufferings of our Lord's Passion, and to consider with what an excess of love He devoted Himself for us to the death of the Cross; one of the chief ends for which He instituted the holy Sacrifice of His Body and Blood, being that we might have His Passion ever present to our minds. "As often," says the Apostle, "as you shall eat this bread and drink this chalice you shall show the death of the Lord until He come."* The reason why this method of hearing Mass is the best of all is because it is best calculated to produce in us the spirit of sacrifice, which is the spirit of Christianity, the spirit of Christ Himself. It is necessary that when we offer the Sacrifice of the Mass, we should offer ourselves also to God in sacrifice; and since we celebrate the mysteries of the Passion of our Saviour, we ought to imitate what we celebrate Jesus Christ will be truly a Victim for us if we become a victim with Him. In this sense St. Peter calls all Christians a *holy priesthood.* What is more royal, more sacerdotal, than to subject the mind to God and the body to the Spirit? Many offer to God their prayers, alms, fasts, and mortifications; but few offer *themselves,* and make an obla-

---

* 1 Cor. xi. 26.

tion of their *hearts*. They always secretly reserve to themselves the disposal of their own will. This division is displeasing to God; it is not the sacrifice of Abel, but of Cain, who offered to God the fruits of the earth, but reserved to himself his heart and will, as St. Augustine says.

We should remember, therefore, that as we are associated with the priest of Christ in offering the adorable Victim to God, so should we be associated with the divine Victim, in the spirit of self-sacrifice; we should offer ourselves with Him; we should lay on the altar the oblation of our soul and body, our memory, will, and understanding; our thoughts, words, actions, and intentions of the day; our life, death, and whole being, that all may be sanctified by union with Him Who is immolated for the love of us. We should offer all generously to God, with self-renunciation, that the mystic death of Jesus in His temple may produce in our souls a similar death—the death of our evil inclinations to worldly pleasures and allurements, but above all, the death of our self-will, in order thus to become a fit holocaust in the sight of God, of which He may dispose according to His good pleasure, for His greater glory and for that of our own soul and the souls of our fellow-men.

The holy Mass is a worship of sacrifice, and a worship of sacrifice implies a life of sacrifice. This is most beautifully illustrated in the lives of the martyrs and of all the saints. One who reads the Acts of the Martyrs cannot help seeing this.

The evil spirit seems, indeed, to have left nothing untried to overcome the grace of God that upheld the martyrs, the faithful witnesses and champions *of the faith;* and the divine Wisdom appears to have allowed every excess of cruelty to have been put to the test and found futile against His followers, in order more deeply to humble for ever His enemies, to exalt and glorify His own adorable name, and heighten the splendor of the triumphs of the Church, His spouse.

Some martyrs, like Metrius, a venerable old man of Alexandria, had splinters of reeds thrust into their eyes.

Some, like the aged and venerable matron, Apollonia in Egypt, had their teeth knocked out of their jaws.

Some had their tongues as well as their teeth pulled out, as was done to Andronicus in the persecution of Diocletian.

Some were cut open, filled with grain and thrown out to be devoured by swine, as in Phenicia.

Some, like the holy man Serapion, were thrown headlong from the tops of their houses upon the pavement.

Some, like Quinta, were dragged by the heels over a pavement of sharp pebbles.

Some, like Marcellus, were buried up to the waist, and left there to perish after many days of suffering.

Sometimes the holy martyr's body was broiled on every side, as if prepared for the crowd to devour it.

Sometimes the martyrs were burnt "according to law," that is, condemned to die by slow fire, according to the rules laid down in the imperial edict: First, a slight flame was applied to the soles of their feet, until the callous sole shrank so as to fall off; then torches, with little flame, or smoking, were moved along every member of the body until no spot was left unharmed: meanwhile, prolonging the torture, the face was sprinkled with cold water, and the lips moistened frequently, lest the drought of the parched throat should bring forth too soon the last breath. When the surface of the whole body and limbs had gone through an entire day's cooking and the fire reached the entrails, the martyr died.

Many were put into large marble mortars, and actually pounded to death with a pestle.

Others were cut into pieces and their chopped limbs thrown before their companions to terrify them.

But the grace of the Divine Redeemer made men and women triumph even over the arts and ingenuity and most cruel outrages of paganism.

In those days of persecution, the truth of the words of our

Lord, "Unless you eat My flesh and drink My blood, you shall not have life in you: but he who eats my flesh and drinks my blood shall have life everlasting," was most evident. The Bishops and priests and the Christians knew and perfectly understood it; hence they not only celebrated the sacred mysteries in some chamber of the Catacombs, or in the well-concealed hall of some mansion in Rome, or elsewhere, but they also partook of them to become strong with the strength of God. They could not be prevailed upon to stay away, *being fully persuaded* that they could not fight the battle of the Lord and gain the final victory by the sacrifice of their lives, unless they were fortified and encouraged by the celebration of the holy Mass and receiving holy Communion.

During the reign of the Emperor Galerius, thirty men and seventeen women were arrested in the city of Aluta, in Africa, for having heard Mass contrary to the orders of the emperor. While on their way to Carthage they never ceased singing hymns of praise in honor of God. Having arrived at Carthage, where they were to be tried before the emperor, an officer of the guard said: "Behold, O emperor, these impious Christians, whom we have arrested at Aluta for having heard Mass contrary to the orders of your Majesty." The emperor at once had one of them stripped of his clothes, placed on the rack, and his flesh torn to pieces. Meanwhile, one of the Christians, Telica by name, cried out in a loud voice: "Why, O tyrant, do you put but one of us to the rack, since we are all Christians, and we all heard Mass at the same time." At once the judge treated this one just as cruelly as the other, saying: "Who was the author of your meetings?" "Saturninus, the priest," replied the Christians, "and we all together; but you, O impious wretch, act most unjustly towards us; for we are neither murderers nor robbers, nor have we done any harm." The judge said: "You should have obeyed our orders and stayed away from your false worship." Telica replied: "I obey the orders of the true God, for which I am ready to die." Then by the emperor's orders Telica was taken off the rack and thrown into prison.

After this, the brother of St. Victoria came forth, accusing Datiorus for having taken his sister Victoria to Mass. But the saint replied, "Not by the permission of man, but of my own accord, I went to hear Mass. I am a Christian, and as such, I am bound to obey the laws of Christ." Her brother replied, "You are crazy, and talk like a crazy woman." She said, "I am not crazy, but I am a Christian." The emperor asked her, "Do you wish to return home with your brother?" She answered, "No, I will not; I take those for my brothers and sisters who are Christians like me, and suffer for Jesus Christ." The emperor said, "Save your life, and follow your brother." She answered, "I will not leave my brothers and sisters, for I confess to you that I heard Mass with them, and received Holy Communion." The judge then tried every means to make her apostatize, for she was very beautiful, and the daughter of one of the noblest families of the city. When her parents wanted to force her to marry, she jumped out of the window and had her hair cut off. Then the judge addressed the priest, Saturninus, saying, "Did you, contrary to our orders, call these Christians to a meeting?" The priest replied, "I called them, in obedience to the law of God, to meet for His service." The emperor then asked, "Why did you do this?" Saturninus replied, "Because we are forbidden to stay away from Mass." "Are you, then, the author of this meeting?" asked the emperor. "I am," said the priest, "and I myself said the Mass." Upon this the priest was taken and put to the rack, and his flesh torn by sharp iron points, so much so that his entrails could be seen; finally he was thrown into prison.

After this, St. Emericus was tried. "Who are you?" he was asked. "I am the author of this meeting," he replied, "for the Mass was celebrated in my house." "Why did you," said the emperor, "permit them, contrary to my orders, to enter your house?" "Because they are my brothers," said Emericus, "and we *cannot do without Mass.*" Then his flesh was also mangled, after which he was also led into prison to the other martyrs.

The judge then said to the other Christians: "You have seen how your companions have been treated; I hope you will have pity on yourselves, and save your lives." "We are all Christians," they cried out with one voice, "and we will keep the law of Christ, being ready to shed our blood for it." Then the iniquitous judge said to one of them, named Felix, "I do not ask you if you are a Christian, but I ask you if you were present at this meeting and heard Mass?" "What a foolish question this," replied Felix, "just as if Christians could do without Mass; incarnate devil, I tell you that we were very devout at the meeting and prayed fervently during the holy Sacrifice." At these words, the tyrant felt so much enraged that he knocked the holy martyr down, and beat him until he expired. The remainder of the Christians were also thrown into prison, where they died from starvation.*

From the answers of these Christians we may see in what esteem they held the holy Sacrifice of the Mass, of what importance it was to them. "We cannot do without it," they say. It was at this holy Sacrifice that they obtained that wonderful spirit of sacrifice which taught them to give their lives for the love of Jesus Christ, Who offered Himself daily for them upon the altar. We have another most beautiful illustration of this truth in the life of Saint Lawrence, the martyr and deacon.

St. Lawrence was one of the seven deacons of the city of Rome in the third century of the Christian era. As deacon, it was his office to serve the Mass of St. Xistus, who was at that time Pope. When the persecution broke out under the Emperor Valerius, St. Xistus was seized and carried off to martyrdom. As he was on his way, St. Lawrence followed

---

* Baronius.

him weeping and saying: "Father, where are you going without your son? Whither are you going, O holy priest, without your deacon? You were never wont to offer sacrifice (to celebrate Mass) without me, your minister; wherein have I displeased you? Have you found me wanting in my duty? Try me now, and see whether you have made choice of an unfit minister for dispensing the Blood of the Lord." And St. Xistus replied: "I do not leave you, my son; but a greater trial and a more glorious victory are reserved for you who are stout and in the vigor of youth. We are spared on account of our weakness and old age. You shall follow me in three days."

And, in fact, three days after St. Lawrence was burnt to death, his faith rendering him joyful, even mirthful, in his sufferings.

In the words of St. Lawrence we see the sentiments with which he was accustomed to assist at Mass. As he knelt at the foot of the altar at which the Pope was celebrating, clothed in the beautiful dress of a deacon, his soul was filled with the thoughts of God's greatness and goodness, and together with the offering of the heavenly Victim, he used to offer his fervent desire to do something to honor the Divine Majesty; the color sometimes mounting high in his youthful cheek as he thought how joyfully he would yield his own heart's blood as a sacrifice if the occasion should present itself. Martyrdom to him was but a natural completion of Mass. It was the realization of his habitual worship.

In the early history of the city of St. Augustine in Florida, it is related that a priest who was attacked by a party of Indians, asked permission to say Mass before he died. This was granted him, and the savages waited quietly till the Mass was ended. Then the priest knelt on the altar steps and received the death-blow from his murderers. With what sentiments must that priest have said Mass! with what devotion! with what reverence! with what self-oblation! So I suppose St. Lawrence, St. Xistus, and the Christians of the olden time were accustomed always to assist at Mass with the greatest desire to honor God, in the most complete spirit of self-sacrifice.

This spirit of self-sacrifice was not required in bishops, priests, and Christians in those days of cruel persecution only; the same spirit has always been required in the true followers of Christ. Without this spirit, parents will do but little good to their children, and children to their parents; without this spirit of self-sacrifice, pastors of souls will be but hirelings to their respective flocks, and Christians will be Christians only in name, but not in deed. To celebrate Mass and to assist at it daily without any increase of the spirit of sacrifice is to be ignorant altogether of one of the principal fruits to be derived from it, or to remain a faithless and lukewarm Christian. Indeed the numberless enormous sins of so many Christians proceed from no other source than from the want of the spirit of sacrifice. The miser does not want to sacrifice his passion for money; the revengeful his passion of avenging himself on his neighbor; the slothful finds it too difficult to overcome his laziness in order to comply with his Christian duties; the lustful finds it too hard to sacrifice his sensual and brutal pleasures. Thus, wherever the spirit of sacrifice is wanting, there can be no faithful compliance with the commandments of God and the Church; there can be no faithful correspondence to the divine inspirations; there we find nothing but egotism or selfishness. It is, therefore, of the greatest importance for pastors of souls to celebrate Mass in this spirit of sacrifice, and it is also not less important to teach the faithful to assist at Mass in this same spirit—as otherwise they are wanting in what is most essential to a true follower of Christ. This great truth cannot be illustrated better, nor impressed more forcibly on the mind of the pious reader than by relating what our Lord one day said to St. Catherine of Sienna.

We read in the life of this saint that from her very childhood she experienced a great desire to become a perfect holocaust to the Lord. The older she grew the better she understood that this was the duty of every good Christian, and that she could not please the Lord perfectly unless she became His without the least reserve. So she most fervently begged God to teach her the shortest way to become His own, and lead the life of a holy Christian. Our Lord heard her prayer and said to her: "Know then, that the salvation of My servants and their perfection consists in this only, that they do My will, and that they endeavor with their whole strength to do it always; that they obey, glorify, and look to Me alone at all times. The more carefully they do this, the more they advance in perfection; for then it is that they adhere and unite themselves more closely to Me, who am Supreme Perfection Itself.

"In order that you may understand this sublime truth, expressed in a few words, consider My Christ, in whom I am well pleased. He annihilated Himself, taking the form of a servant, being made in the likeness of man, in order that by His example and word, He might lead you back to the way of truth, from which you had gone astray so very far, walking in the greatest darkness of the intellect. He was obedient unto death, teaching you by His persevering obedience how your salvation depends altogether on your firm resolution to do nothing but My will alone. He who carefully reflects and meditates upon His life and doctrine, will soon come to understand that the summit of perfection consists in nothing else than in the uninterrupted, persevering, and constant accomplishment of My will. This He has declared repeatedly. 'Not every one who says to Me, Lord, Lord, shall enter into the kingdom of heaven, but he who obeys the will of My Father who is in heaven, shall enter into the kingdom of heaven.' He means to say that no one, whosoever he may be, and whatsoever exterior good works he may perform for My name's sake, shall be admitted to the glory of life everlasting, if he has not performed all according to My will.

"He has said again: 'I have come down from heaven not

to do My own will, but the will of Him who sent Me. And: 'Not My will, but Thine be done.' Now, if, in imitation of your Saviour, you will do My will, in which alone your salvation consists, you must necessarily renounce your own will in every thing; you must make it die, as it were, having no longer any regard for it. The more you die to yourself, the more you endeavor to empty yourself of what is your own, the more will I fill you with what is My own. But no one will arrive at this perfection unless he constantly renounces his self-will. He who neglects this, neglects also this sublime perfection; but he who practises it, does My will in a perfect manner, and I am well pleased in him. I am always near such a one; for nothing gives Me greater pleasure than to be with you and to co-operate with you. My delight is to be with the children of men, and to change you, by My grace, into Myself, so that you may become one with Me, by partaking of My perfections, of My peace, and of My joy. But this I will not do unless you so wish; for I will never violate the privileges of your free-will.

"Now, in order that you may be inflamed with a vehement desire of submitting your will most closely to Mine, you have but to consider My ardent desire of being with you. This you will understand the better, the more deeply you reflect how I have willed that My only-begotten Son should assume flesh, that My Divinity, stripping itself, as it were, of its majesty, should be united to your humanity, in order that, by this inconceivable love of Mine, you might be induced, drawn, nay, sweetly forced, to unite your will in the same manner with Mine, and to remain thus always united with Me.

"Moreover, consider how I have willed that this My Beloved Son should give Himself up to so horrible and cruel a death as that of the Cross; that by His sufferings He should cancel your sins, which had separated you so far from Me.

"Finally, consider how I have prepared for you a precious banquet in the most august Sacrament of His own Flesh and Blood, in order that, receiving Him you might be transformed into Me; for as bread and wine which you take become one with the substance of your body, so you too by receiving Him become spiritually changed and transformed into Myself, because He is one with Me.

"It is certain that your perfect welfare depends on your perfect renunciation of self; for I will fill you with My grace in proportion as you empty yourself of your will. This participation in My will effects your perfection by My grace, without which you would be totally destitute of all virtue and dignity. Now, in order to obtain this grace, you must, in profound humility and in deep knowledge of your own misery and poverty, ardently desire and strenuously endeavor to obey Me only, and do nothing but My will. In order to be enabled to effect this, you must, by means of your memory and intellect, build for yourself a cell out of My will. You must keep this cell entirely close, remaining shut up within it, so that whithersoever you go, you may not go out of it; and whithersoever you look, you may not look out of it. Regulate all your affections according to My will. Think, speak, and do nothing but what is pleasing to Me, and what you know to be in accordance with My will. Then the Holy Ghost will teach you everything you have to do.

"There is yet another means by which you may attain to a perfect renunciation of your will, viz.: if there are servants of Mine who will teach and guide you to do My will, submit yourself to them, by giving up into their hands your own self and all that is yours, always obeying and following their advice. You hear Me, if you listen to My wise and faithful servants.

"Moreover, I wish that you should often meditate, with an unyielding faith and an elevated mind, upon Me, your most glorious God, who created you, in order to make you capable of partaking of My own happiness; of the happiness of the Most High and All-Powerful Being; who does for you everything that I please; whose will no one can resist; without whose will nothing can happen to you, as I spoke by the Prophet Amos. Meditate upon Me, your God, whose wisdom and knowledge are infinite; who see and penetrate everything at a glance; who cannot be deceived nor disturbed by any error; who govern you, and at the same time heaven and earth; because I am God, the All-Wise Being.

"And in order that you may understand something of the effects of this My wisdom, you must know that, from the evil of guilt and punishment I can draw a good which surpasses by far the extent of the evil itself. Furthermore, I wish that you should meditate upon Me, your God, as being most perfect in love and in kindness; whence I cannot will anything but what is good, salutary, and profitable to you and to others; for no evil can go out from Me. I hate nothing, and, as I have created man through love, so do I continue to love him with infinite love.

"To these truths you must always cling with steadfast faith. From a constant meditation upon the same it must be clear to you how, under My wise Providence, afflictions, temptations, hardships, sickness, and other adversities, are permitted to befall you for no other reason than for your own good, in order that by them you may be induced to amend what is bad in you, and to commence to walk in the road of virtue, which leads you to Me, your Supreme Good.

"If this light of faith shines on you, you will also understand that I, your God, know better how to promote your welfare, and wish more for it, than you yourself; and that you, without My grace, would be ignorant of it, unable to promote it, nay, even not able to will it.

"This being true, you must endeavor with your whole strength to submit your will to Mine, then peace will always reign in your heart, for I will be with you; because My habitation is in peace. There will be no scandal of sin for you, that is to say, no occasion of sin; for great is the peace of those who love My Name; they shall not fall, because they love nothing but My law, that is to say, My will; My law is that rule according to which all things are directed. Their union with Me is so close, and their delight in doing My will so great, that, happen whatever may, nothing but sin is able to disturb or disquiet them. Their souls being totally purified, they see without deception that from Me, the Ruler of the Universe, Who govern all things with wonderful wisdom, charity, and order, nothing but good can proceed, and that, consequently, I can take care of both their temporal and spiritual welfare far better and with more salutary effect than they themselves.

" Persevering in the consideration that all things which happen and which they may endure, proceed from Me and not from their neighbor, they feel animated with unconquerable patience, baffling every attack, so that they suffer everything, not only with a tranquil mind, but also with a cheerful heart, because in all things, whether exterior or interior, they taste the sweetness of My unspeakable love.

" And this is to give true honor to My goodness, namely, to believe and consider with a thankful and cheerful heart, in all difficulties and adversities, that I order all things sweetly, that everything proceeds from the profound source of My love, and that nothing but your own will and self-love hinder and destroy the fruit of this consideration and the union of your will with Mine. Were you to do away with them, there would be no longer any hell for you, either in the world to come, with its perpetual torments of both soul and body, or in this world, by continual disquietudes of mind and the ever-recurring anxieties of exterior and interior troubles.

" Well, if you wish to live, endeavor to die to this life, drowning yourself in the unchangeable life of perpetual glory, and doing away with your own self-will. ' Blessed are the dead that die in the Lord,' and, ' Blessed are the poor in spirit.' These see Me in mutual love in their earthly pilgrimage, and will see Me in heaven in everlasting bliss and glory."

These are the lessons which our Lord gave to St. Catherine of Sienna, and which He still gives to us at Mass. If we assist at it in the proper spirit, like St. Catherine, we shall experience in our soul a great desire to become a holocaust to the Lord, in order to be altogether His as He is altogether ours in the Sacrifice of the Mass. It is at this holy Sacrifice that He inspires such a desire, and the manner of resolutely carrying it out. What is the source of the Catholic charity that is so productive of wonders, and so superior to worldly philanthropy and to Protestant generosity? Ask it of all those Sisters of Charity of different denominations in the Catholic Church—those angels here on earth, who have consecrated themselves and their fortunes to the alleviation of human infirmities, to the instruction of the little ones, especially of the poor orphans; ask it of the Catholic missionary buried in the midst of trackless deserts and barbarous nations, and all will answer by pointing to the altar, to the holy Sacrifice of the Mass. Yes, indeed; this august Sacrifice is the true source of the wonderful charity of the Catholic Church. Wherever the belief in, or the participation of this great mystery of the Mass ceases, there charity dies out and gives place to egotism or philanthropy. Except amongst Catholics who often hear Mass, there is no such thing as heroic consecration of one's self to the aid of suffering man; no missionary, no true Sisters of Charity.

The Protestant, the philanthropist, may bestow greater or less donations of money, but never will he give himself; his religion does not go so far. "I could wish to be like you," said a young Protestant lady to some nuns whose assiduous attention to the sick excited her admiration, "but I feel full well that our religion does not go so far."

But the devout worshipper at Mass says to himself: My Lord and my God, Who suffered and died for my salvation, comes down in person upon the altar to renew for me His

Passion and Death: in exchange for His heart He asks for mine; for His life my life; what can I refuse Him? But as He wants nothing for Himself, He yields His rights to the poor, to the sick, to the unfortunate, to the ignorant, and to the little orphans; they are His brethren; for them He asks me to give my heart and my life. To repay His love I have but this means alone; but He is content with it. And then a low, sweet voice is heard in the depths of the soul, a heavenly joy diffuses itself over it, an overpowering impression seizes it, and the Catholic, carried off, as it were, by a sweet force, makes an offering of himself. And here, if God wills, is a new missionary, a martyr, a Sister of Charity, a servant of the poor, a whole life of devotedness and self-sacrifice.

Does the fire that consumed the holocaust begin to smoulder? If so, the Catholic knows how to rekindle it at the perpetual Sacrifice of the Mass; he returns to the altar where the burning fire of the love of God is kept up. As the blood returns from the extremities of the body to the heart whence it first set out, to start afresh, heated and purified, in order to carry to the members heat and life, in like manner does the adorable Sacrifice of the Mass, the focus of heat and spiritual life, operate in the moral body of the Catholic Church. Yes, it is even here, to this Eucharistic Sacrifice, that our best Christians of to-day come to receive the riches of their souls and the treasures of their love. Here it is that the good soldier learns how to die in defence of his country, good parents to sacrifice themselves for the temporal and spiritual welfare of their children. Here it is that good children learn their filial obedience, respect and love to their parents, and good servants their submission to their masters in all lawful matters. Here all good Christians not only receive the power, but put themselves under the obligation of offering to God continual sacrifices—the sacrifice of their passions, their perverse inclinations and evil propensities, by self-denial and mortification; the sacrifice of their own will, by submission to the dispensations of Providence; the sacrifice of their pride by humility; of their resentment by charity; of their anger by meekness. "By such sacrifices," we may add, in the words of St. Paul, "God's favor is obtained." *

In the life of St. Casimir, son of Casimir, King of Poland, we are told that this king spent more of his time in the church than in his own palace. His devotion and love to Jesus Christ in the most Blessed Sacrament were astonishingly great and ardent. He used to rise about midnight and go barefooted quite alone to the church to adore our Lord in the Blessed Sacrament. On leaving he used to kiss the door and threshold for love of Jesus Christ, Who dwelt in it in His mystery of love. Early in the morning he went back to the church to assist at all the Masses which were celebrated. During the holy Sacrifice he was so deeply absorbed in prayer that he seemed to be beside himself, and often forgot to take his meals. One of the great divine favors which he obtained at Mass was a wonderful spirit of self-sacrifice—a grace which sweetly compelled him to consecrate his virginity to Almighty God, and brought down upon him many other choice graces. He died in the odor of sanctity at the age of twenty-three, and God glorified His great servant by many miracles which He wrought at his intercession.

Let us, then, celebrate or assist at Mass, daily, if possible, in the spirit of sacrifice, and this spirit will make our prayers all-powerful; it will prevail upon the Lord to grant all our petitions. "If thou hear the voice of the Lord thy God," † or, as Isaias says, "If thou turn away thy foot from doing thy own will," ‡ in order to follow Mine, as it is expressed in My commandments, in the doctrine of My Son, and thy Redeemer, and in thy rules, if thou art a religious; in the precepts of those who keep My place with thee on earth, and

---

* Heb. xiii. 16.   † Deut. xxx. 10.   ‡ Chap. lviii. 13.

in My inspirations, I also will listen to thy voice when thou prayest to Me. Hence, Cornelius à Lapide says: "If you wish that God should do your will when praying, you must first do what He wishes and commands you. If you wish that He should turn to you, you must go to meet Him; if you desire that He should delight in you, you must delight in Him." "Delight in the Lord," says the Psalmist, "and He will give thee the requests of thy heart." *

Now who can be said in truth to go and meet the Lord at Mass and delight in Him? He alone who with a cheerful heart does the Lord's will. "His petitions" as the royal prophet says, "shall be granted." Our Lord said one day to St. Gertrude, when she was praying for one of her sisters in religion, who wished that God should grant her prayer for divine consolations: "It is she herself who puts obstacles to the consolations of My grace, by attachment to her own will and judgment. As one who closes his nostrils cannot enjoy the fragrance of fresh flowers, so the sweet consolations of My grace cannot be experienced by him who is attached to his own will and judgment."

The response to our petitions at Mass depends, then, on our faithful fulfilment of the will of God. "You ought to know, brethren, that God will comply with our wishes in prayer only in proportion as we try to comply with His commandments." † We must not be astonished, therefore, if we see or hear how the saints obtained everything from God. "He who honoreth his father, . . . in the day of his prayer he shall be heard." ‡ Those who honor their Heavenly Father perfectly, by an exact compliance with His Divine will, He honors by doing their will.

St. Francis of Assisium would often stop on his journey suddenly, as soon as he perceived within himself an interior inspiration of God, and giving it all his attention, he would

---

* Psalm xxxvi. 4.   † St. Aug. vol. x., Serm. 61.   ‡ Eccles. iii. 6.

say: "Speak, O Lord, for Thy servant heareth!" He would stop as long as the inspiration lasted, listening to it in all humility, and promptly executing whatever our Lord would inspire him to do. For this reason did he become so great and powerful with God. One day as he was praying in these words, "Lord, have compassion on poor sinners," Jesus Christ appeared to him, saying: "Francis, thy will is one with Mine; I am therefore ready to grant all thy prayers."

Thus, Cornelius à Lapide exclaims: "Oh, how powerful should we be with God, were we always ready to lend a ready ear and an obedient heart to His voice!" Like St. Dominic, we would experience that there is nothing that could not be obtained by prayer. Indeed, so good is our Lord to those who do His will perfectly, that He not only grants their prayers, but even anticipates them. Tauler relates of a pious virgin, whose spiritual director he was, that many people used to come and recommend their affairs to her prayers. She always promised to pray for them, but often forgot to do so. Nevertheless, the wishes of those who had recommended themselves to her were fulfilled. These persons then came and thanked her, feeling persuaded that through her prayers God had helped them. The pious virgin blushed, and confessed that although she had intended to pray for them, she had forgotten to do so. Wishing to know the reason why our Lord blessed all those who recommended themselves to her prayers, she said to Him: "Why, O Lord, is it that Thou dost bless all those who recommend themselves to my prayers, even though I do forget to pray for them?" Our Lord answered her: "My daughter, from that very day on which you gave up your will, in order always to do Mine, I gave up Mine to do yours, wherefore I even comply with the pious intentions which you forget to carry out."* Thus is verified what the Lord promised by

---

* Serm. I. De Circumcis

the prophet Isaias:* "And it shall come to pass that before they call I will hear."

Would that all Christians would understand what has been said in this chapter, and practise faithfully the lesson inculcated! How happy would they make themselves, and thousands of their fellow-men!

---

* Chap. lxv. 24.

CHAPTER XXXIV.

HOW TO HEAR SEVERAL MASSES AT ONCE.

SOME persons are under the impression that it is impossible to reap more advantage from many Masses heard at once, than from a single Mass. This is a mistake. That two or more Masses may be heard at the same time, when they are obligatory, or in accordance with a vow, or enjoined as a penance, is not true. But a person may profit as much by assisting at several Masses simultaneously, as if he assisted at each singly.

In a previous chapter, we saw the obligation every priest is under, of praying and of sacrificing the unbloody Victim in behalf of the faithful present. Take the case, then, of one priest at the altar: he is in duty bound to pray for every individual in the church. Increase the number of priests celebrating at the same moment to two, three, five, or any number possible, the whole body unite in recommending each individual to God, and thus, their combined mementoes are certainly more powerful than that of a single priest.

It has also been remarked elsewhere that the angels are very busy in bearing up to heaven the petitions of all the faithful present at the august mysteries. Accordingly, the greater the number of Masses offered up at the same moment and in the same church the more numerous the holy angels hovering about the altars, and bearing the requests made on their airy wings to the throne of the Most High.

The spotless Lamb Himself offers His atoning Blood, not only for the welfare of His Church at large, but in a most special manner for those assisting at the divine Sacrifice then and there. Their wants, their necessities, their pe-

titions, are the peculiar objects of His solicitude in every
Mass. For Christ, having died for all, laid down His life for
every one in particular; according to the words of St. Paul
—" Christ, having loved me, laid down His life for me."*
In like manner, every Mass, which is the unbloody renewal
of that great Sacrifice on Calvary, may be said to be offered for
each one in particular, since Christ interposes His mediation
and pours out mystically His Blood for every individual
present. This happens at every Mass. Supposing, then, more
Masses than one going on at the same time in our presence,
the prayers of Christ multiply in our behalf in proportion,
whilst innumerable blessings, graces, and spiritual treasures
of every kind are showered down upon us.

It is hardly necessary to add that one must be in a state of
grace in order to be enriched with so many gifts and treasures. It is well, then, to endeavor to assist at as many Masses
as possible, and never to make light of the multitude of blessings, both spiritual and temporal, which roll in one united
stream from as many altars as the unspotted Lamb is immolated on simultaneously. In order to hear several Masses at
the same time, something more is required than a mere recommendation in all that are being, or are about to be, said.
He who so desires must contribute to each Sacrifice by means
of prayer; must adore Jesus Christ really present; must offer
Him up as a sacrifice of propitiation, and have the hearty
desire of hearing all the Masses. If a priest approaches the
altar, he must say to himself: I purpose to hear this Mass
too, and I offer it up to God in advance. He must renew the
intention as often as another priest begins the divine mysteries. If upon entering the church, he perceives a priest just
at the Introit, he must not forget to make the proper intention. Up to the moment of Consecration, he may occupy
himself with reciting prayers from his book, telling his beads,
or, if he belong to some confraternity, saying the prayers

---

* Gal. ii.

appointed for its members will be very suitable. At the moment of the Consecration, it is well to close the book and make an act of lively faith in the Real Presence: to prostrate one's self in spirit before the Lord, as the priest elevates the Sacred Host. Arouse your faith anew, at the Consecration of the Chalice, uniting in all the fervor of your soul with the breathless host of angels who surround the spotless Lamb. Excite acts of love, adoration, and thanksgiving, till you see another priest about to consecrate. Bow down again in respectful awe during the Elevation, repeating at the same time the prayer of adoration. Thus do briefly at each succeeding Mass; and then signal advantages will accrue from each Mass, to say nothing of the abundant merits thus laid up in heaven.

But it may be objected; "Suppose I am to recite the prayer for the Elevation at every Mass, I should have no leisure for the other prayers, not even for my daily devotions." Let the objector weigh well the moral contained in the following parable, which bears directly on this point: A vine-dresser went forth into his vineyard to till the soil. He had struck but a few blows, when he hit upon a treasure. Overjoyed at his good fortune, he hastened home, carefully stowed away the sparkling gems and glittering coins, and returned to his work. To his unbounded delight another heap of wealth met his gaze after a short time. He quickly secured the prize, laid it up safely with the first, and betook himself again to his task in high glee. It was not long before he struck upon a third treasure. He hastened to gather up the precious diamonds, hurried home, and related his good fortune to his wife. "Say rather," rejoined his wife, "that a great misfortune has befallen us. Because, if you spend your time in carrying home treasures, our vineyard must remain untilled this year, and we shall have no grapes." "Would," exclaimed her husband, "that I could find such heaps of gold all day long: depend upon it, I would not put a hoe into our vineyard. For one of these treasures is worth ten abundant harvests."

Apply the parable to your case, devout soul, and rest assured that the advantages to be derived from all other prayers combined cannot be compared with the golden fruit which one reaps from the renewed act of adoration and the repeated recital of the proper prayer at the Consecration. If on entering the church, the Priest is at the *Pater Noster*, *Agnus Dei*, or even on the point of receiving, the usual prayer of Consecration, if said at once, will draw down a considerable share of merit as a reward.

When two priests consecrate at the same moment, pronounce the prayer but once, adoring your Lord on both altars at the same time. Nor is it necessary to see the priest; the signal given with the little bell is quite sufficient to direct the thoughts to the altar. More is not required. And even suppose one not hearing the signal should miss the precious moment—still no loss would be incurred, provided one had the intention at the beginning to hear all the Masses likely to be celebrated at the same hour. If, on leaving the church, you perceive a priest about to consecrate, tarry a moment to assist at the Elevation of the Body and Blood of Jesus Christ.

It is related in the life of St. Elizabeth, Queen of Portugal, that she was extremely charitable to the poor. She had ordered her almoner never to refuse charity to any one, but, over and above, she also gave continual alms by her own hands or those of her domestics. She usually employed for that purpose a young page named Pedro, in whom she had discovered great piety. Another page, whether through envy of him or to ingratiate himself with King Denis, husband of St. Elizabeth, accused Pedro of having a secret understanding with the queen. Although the king did not absolutely give credence to this story, still, as he was already somewhat displeased with his wife, a suspicion entered his mind, and he resolved to get rid of the page. The means adopted for that purpose were rather extraordinary. Passing one day by a kiln where men were

20

baking lime, he sent for the people whose business it was to keep up the fire, and told them that, on the following morning, he would send a page to ask them *if they had executed his orders*, and that they must not fail, as soon as he uttered those words, to throw him immediately into the fire. Thereupon he returned to his palace, sent for the suspected page, and ordered him to go next morning early to deliver the message in question. But God, who always takes care of His own, ordained it so that as he passed by a church on his way to the limekiln, he heard the bell which announced the Elevation of the Host at Mass. Piety having induced him to enter the church, he heard the rest of that Mass, and two others that were said in succession. Meanwhile King Denis, impatient to know if he had been obeyed, chanced to meet in his ante-chamber the wicked page who had accused the queen, and commanded him to go in haste and ask the men at the limekiln if they had done as he ordered. The page went thither without a moment's delay, and delivered his message; but no sooner did they hear what he said, than, taking him for the one of whom the king had spoken, they seized him and threw him into the fire. The other, who by this time had finished his devotions, went on his errand, and being informed that the king's orders had been obeyed, returned to Denis with the answer. Imagine the king's amazement when he saw that things had turned out so differently from what he expected. He asked Pedro where he had stopped so long. The page answered unsuspectingly: "Prince, as I passed by a church, on my way to the place where your majesty had sent me, I heard the bell for the Elevation and was induced to go in; I remained till the end of the Mass. But just as it was finishing another was commenced, and then a third before the other was finished, and I heard them all, because my father, in giving me his last blessing before he died, told me, above all things, to hear to the end of every Mass I saw commenced." Then the king, entering into himself, easily understood that it was owing to the three Masses that his faithful servant had escaped his doom. He adored the divine Providence, and banished from his mind all the injurious suspicions he had conceived against his wife, whom he venerated ever after as a saint.*

Not a few eminent theologians maintain that to recommend one's self at the moment all Masses begin is to share largely in their merits. Others, on the contrary, without blaming these recommendations or stripping them of merit in the sight of God, deny openly that any one can participate in this way in the merits of such Masses as are celebrated elsewhere, because he does not contribute anything towards the Sacrifice. For, they say, allowing the contrary opinion to prevail, it would be no longer necessary to go to Mass on ordinary days, the mere intention to hear Mass sufficing. Nevertheless, it must be granted that, when assisting at one Mass, if a person feels a fervent desire and makes an earnest intention to hear all the Masses going on at that hour elsewhere, he is surely entitled to a share in their merit. For we do what lies in our power and would gladly do more if we could. We would fain, were it possible, multiply ourselves, in order to be present everywhere in body where we can only assist in spirit. God is content with our good will, when the execution of our praiseworthy desires is out of the question. Our Lord said as much to St. Gertrude.†

What consolation does this thought afford! In one hour not less than fifty thousand Masses are offered up throughout Christendom, and we have free access to their overflowing merits. This practice should be especially dear to religious who have no leisure to assist at many Masses. Seculars, too, who are prevented by domestic duties from being present at more than one, should profit by their short hour and multiply it diligently. It cannot be denied, further, that the practice of many pious Christians, who are deprived of the holy Sacrifice entirely, either by distance of place,

---

* Life of St. Elizabeth of Portugal. † Life, iv. c. 15.

sickness, or other impediments—the laudable custom of going through the prayers of Mass with zeal is beyond doubt very meritorious, their merit will not be much less than that which they would acquire were they really present. God exacts nothing unreasonable of us, but He expects us to show ourselves in earnest, and then He is ready to supply our shortcomings. If such be the case, if I can hear all the Masses celebrated throughout the world during the half hour I am in church, why not make the intention to assist at all the Masses to be said that day, or even during the rest of my life, asks some one. This opinion is not condemned, neither does it appear extravagant; still it cannot be more than probable, and as such it may be maintained. For my part, I affirm that one has no claim to the merits of any Mass other than that he really assists at, or offers up. But a man cannot be supposed to assist at all the Masses which will be offered up during the day, or even during his lifetime. He may, indeed, desire to hear every Mass even till the day of judgment, still such a desire is necessarily vague, and affords little or no room for its fulfilment. The case is far different if we confine ourselves to the Masses said during the time we are present at the holy Sacrifice. For then our prayers are not limited to the particular Mass at which we assist, but are extended so as to embrace, as it were, all the Masses going on at the same moment. We place ourselves at the foot of every altar and unite our glowing intentions with those of every priest. By our intention we invoke grace from on high for the minister of Christ that he may offer worthily; we pay Christ supreme homage on every altar, imploring blessings for ourselves and for our neighbors. Hence arises our claim to a share in all these merits; we have done our best, we have contributed our mite. God requires no more.

In conclusion may be added the beautiful sentiments of P. Marianus Schott.[*] "You ought to rejoice," he says,

---

[*] Vide "Fundamentum Perfectionis," Tract. 2. cap. 6. 12.

"when a priest promises to remember you in his Mass; indeed you should frequently ask this favor yourself, for thus you share largely in the merit of their Masses and unlock for yourself the treasury of Christ. As I said before, when you would heartily wish to hear Mass and find it impossible, remember that God is satisfied with the sincere desire of your heart. And, what is more, suppose you would like to assist at Mass some morning at Jerusalem or Loretto, recollect that you are enabled to do so any time by assisting in thought at the Mass celebrated there. It is even likely that you will derive more profit in this way, than another who is really present but distracted. Certainly they who are present usually receive the largest share of spiritual gifts, still his merit is double who assists in spirit only because holy obedience so disposed."

Were I to rejoice in all the sins that are being committed at the time I hear Mass, or even during the day; nay, were I to desire to share in them actually, I would, no doubt, become accessory to them all, and God would without fail punish me accordingly. But God, by reason of His infinite goodness, is far more inclined to reward me for good intentions and hear my holy desires than He is to punish me for wicked ones. If I have the sincere intention and real desire to share in all the Masses that are going on at the time I am hearing Mass, nay, that are being said during the whole day, or to share particularly in those Masses which are being said in certain sanctuaries of our Lord or the Blessed Virgin, why should God not let me share in them to a certain degree, and thus reward me for my good desires and intentions? It is therefore a very laudable practice for all pious Christians to make, in the morning, the good intention of sharing in all the Masses of the day.

CHAPTER XXXV.

THE DIGNITY AND SANCTITY OF THE MASS.

FROM the title—the Dignity and Sanctity of the Mass—the reader must not expect an adequate description of the infinite excellence of this holy Sacrifice. If the subject were the sacrifices of the Old Law, it would not be so difficult to place before the mind a high idea of their excellence. Merely to call to mind the great pleasure which God took in the sacrifices of animals—a pleasure which He so wonderfully manifested in sending fire from heaven to consume the victims, and in rendering His Presence visible by a bright cloud which filled the entire temple of Jerusalem with the glory of heaven and by its dazzling brilliancy obliged the people to prostrate themselves with their faces to the earth—might suffice. But the Lord, Who instituted those sacrifices, and manifested great pleasure in them for a certain number of years, abolished them also, as we have seen, and in their stead instituted the holy Sacrifice of the Mass, which they only foreshadowed—a sacrifice of such great dignity and sanctity, that it is not within the range of mortal mind to comprehend and describe its infinite excellence.

The holy Sacrifice of the Mass is one of those works greater than which the omnipotence of God cannot produce. St. Thomas Aquinas asks whether God could make works still greater than those already created, and he answers, yes. He can, except three—*the Incarnation of the Son of God, the maternity of the Blessed Virgin Mary, and the everlasting beatitude of the saints in heaven.* In other words, God can create numberless worlds, all different one from another in beauty, but He cannot make anything greater than the Incarnation of Christ, the maternity of the Blessed Virgin, and the happiness of the Blessed in heaven. But why can He not? Because God Himself is concerned in, and most intimately united to each of these works, and is their object. "*Hæc tria Deum involvunt et. pro objecto habent,*" says St. Thomas.

Now, as there is nothing greater than God, so there cannot be a work greater than any of these, with which His Divinity is so intimately united. As there can be no greater happiness than the beatific vision and enjoyment and possession of God in heaven, where the soul is as it were transformed into God, and most inseparably united to His nature, and as there can be no mother made more perfect than the Mother of God, so also there can be no man more perfect than Christ, because He is the Man-God. These three works are, in a certain sense, of infinite dignity on account of being so intimately united to God, the infinite Good.

But in the holy Sacrifice of the Mass it is the Son of God incarnate, Jesus Christ Himself, Who is at once our High Priest and Victim. And thus, in order to form an adequate idea of the dignity and sanctity of the Mass, it would be necessary for us to be able to form an adequate idea of the Victim that is there offered, of the sanctity of the High Priest who offers it, to measure the depth and the height of the mysteries of our Lord's Life, Passion, and Death, which are here represented, continued, and renewed. But this is simply an impossibility. In order to compass the idea of the dignity and sanctity of Jesus Christ, our High Priest and Victim at Mass, it would be necessary to comprehend the greatness of His Godhead. But what mind of man or angel can conceive the greatness of the Divinity of Jesus Christ, which is indeed infinite? To say that His Godhead is greater than the heavens, than all kings, all saints, all angels, is to fall infinitely below it. Jesus Christ, as God, is greatness itself, and the sum of our conception of greatness is but the smallest atom of the greatness of His Godhead. David, contemplating the divine greatness, and, seeing that he could not and never would be able to comprehend it, could only exclaim "O Lord, who is like unto Thee!"* O Lord, what greatness shall ever be found like to thine? And how in truth could David understand it, since his understanding was finite and the greatness of Jesus is infinite? "Great is the Lord, and of His greatness there is no end." † To form some idea of God's greatness, let us remember that although this world of ours is only one of a vast system of planets, yet it is twenty-seven thousand miles in circumference, and it would take two years and a half to traverse it completely at the rate of thirty miles a day.

The sun being nearly three millions of miles in circumference, could not be traversed at the same rate of speed in less than two hundred and seventy-four years; yet this sun, so immeasurably greater than our universe, is supposed to be immeasurably less than certain of the fixed stars. Let us reflect again that the sun is distant from us at least ninety-five millions of miles. It is impossible to conceive in the mind so vast a space. Yet there are planets twenty times farther removed from us than the sun, and even their distance is nothing, humanly speaking, in comparison with that of the fixed stars. The light of some of those stars, according to the opinion of astronomers, has not yet reached us, although it has been travelling towards us at the rate of twelve millions of miles a minute since the creation of the world. And each of those stars is the centre of a planetary system vastly greater than our own.

Now, what are those millions of worlds that bewilder calculation or even conception when compared to God, their wonderful Maker! "Do I not fill heaven and earth, saith the Lord." ‡ Thus, all of us, according to our mode of understanding, are nothing but so many miserable atoms existing in this immense ocean of the essence of the Godhead. "In Him we live, move, and be." §

All men, all the monarchs of the earth, and even all the

---

* Ps. xxxiv. 10. † Ps. cxliv. 3. ‡ Jerem. xxiii. 24. § Acts xvii. 28.

saints and angels of heaven, confronted with the infinite greatness of Jesus Christ, are like or even smaller than a grain of sand in comparison with the earth. "Behold," says the prophet Isaias, "the Gentiles are as a drop of a bucket, and are counted as the smallest grain of a balance; behold, the islands are as little dust. All nations are before Him as if they had no being at all." *

It is an utter impossibility for any human or angelic understanding to conceive an adequate idea of the Mass. All we can say is that its dignity and sanctity are infinite. Indeed, in this sacrifice there is nothing to be seen but the Infinite; the Priest is God, and the Victim is God. For this reason, "All the good works together" as the saintly Curé of Ars says, "are not of equal value with the Sacrifice of the Mass, because they are the works of men, and the holy Mass is the work of God. Martyrdom is nothing in comparison; it is the sacrifice that man makes of his life to God; but the holy Mass is the sacrifice that God makes of His Body and Blood for man." So sublime is this sacrifice that in order to establish it, our Lord Jesus Christ had to die. To redeem the world it was not necessary that He should die. A single drop of His sacred Blood, a single tear, a single prayer of His would have sufficed for that purpose; but to leave to His holy religion a fitting sacrifice, a victim pure, undefiled, worthy of God, He had to die, as in the whole Universe not any victim nor High Priest could be found of equal worth with Himself.

Hence the inestimable dignity and sanctity of this Sacrifice are such that it can only be offered to God; for though it is customary to say Mass in honor of the saints, yet it is not to the saints that this sacrifice is offered. The priest says not, I offer to you, St. Peter, or I offer to you, St. Paul; but, I offer to Thee, O Lord, rendering thanks to God for those crowns and victories which the saints have obtained by the assistance of His grace, and begging their protection, that

---

* Isaias xl. 15, 17.

those whose memory we celebrate on earth may vouchsafe to intercede for us in heaven.

Awful, indeed, are the mysteries of the altar. "Fearful and most awful," exclaims St. John Chrysostom when speaking on the dignity and sanctity of the Mass, "were the things that were *before* the times of grace; but if one inquire into those that are *under* the times of grace, he will find those fearful and awful things under the Old Law trifling indeed. Imagine with me Elias before thine eyes, and a countless crowd surrounding him, and the sacrifice lying on the stones and the prophet alone in prayer, whilst all the rest are in profound silence; then of a sudden the flame of fire cast down from heaven upon the sacred victim. These things are admirable and wonderful.

"Then pass thence to the things now consummated on our altars, and thou wilt not only see things wonderful, but that surpass all wonder." For "when the moment of consecration is arriving," says St. James the Apostle in his Liturgy of the Mass, "every one should be silent, and trembling with reverential awe; he should forget everything earthly, remembering that the King of kings and the Lord of lords is coming down upon the altar as a Victim to be offered to God the Father and as food to be given to the faithful; He is preceded by the angelic choirs, in full splendor, with their faces veiled, singing hymns of praise with great joy." "Then it is," says St. John Chrysostom, "that a fountain is opened which sends forth spiritual rivers—a fountain round which the angels take their stand, looking into the beauty of its streams, since they more clearly see into the power and sanctity of the things that lie to open view, and their inaccessible splendors."

This mysterious fountain is the paradise of the true Christian; it is his life, his happiness, his rapture; the centre of his religion, the heart of devotion, and the soul of piety. From this mysterious fountain gush forth upon the entire Church torrents of benediction, life, and abundance.

It is this fountain to which the martyrs came to inflame their charity, the doctors to draw thence science and light, and the anchorites their life of contemplation and love. It is to this fountain that the king comes from his throne, the beggar from his hovel, the professor from his study, the simple peasant from his labor, the merchant from his store, the mechanic from his work-shop, the soldier from the tented field, and the mariner from the billowy sea: all, all draw from this ever-flowing fountain of spiritual riches in proportion to the measure of their faith, confidence, fervor, and devotion. To this fountain of healing water the poor walk free and favored as in presence of nature; they can approach it as near as kings, and can enjoy equally with the pomp and glory of nobility, the splendor and loveliness of the altar of God; here ends the land of malediction. No more of its restrictions, of its conventional barriers, of its miscalled social forms; here the ceremonies of the secular court would be a profanation. No one marshals you, no one heeds you; here you may kneel and weep in secret, or lie prostrate before the Good Shepherd and the Lamb of God in the Blessed Sacrament; here each sun that rises will find you more consoled, with healthier looks, less pale; here the workings of an uneasy conscience are sanctified, or rather, here it is that you find time and opportunity for reconciliation with God.

Here the poor sinner is assisted to enter upon the way of salvation; here he is supplied with that living water, of which those who drink shall never more feel thirst; here God is your Father; the angels and saints your friends; here you find what is most sublime in nature, most beautiful in the whole universe. Here you can feed yourself, solitary and unobserved by any eyes save those of your angel guardian who watches over you; here, before the Sacramental Presence, you behold your one, ancient, and ever-constant friend—the friend of your childhood, the friend of your youth, your friend for eternity. Oh! how mysterious and solemn a thing is it thus to be as a disembodied spirit, as it were, in the presence of the Lord of Lords, thirsting after justice and the streams of a happier world!

Since the opening of this fountain—the institution of the Mass—Paradise blooms again, the heavens wax purple, the angels shine in white, and men are exhilarated. This sublime and profound mystery which scandalizes the obstinate unbelievers, and arouses the pride of Protestants, is nevertheless that which renews the face of the earth, satisfies the justice of God, redeems man unto salvation, opens heaven, sanctifies the world, and disarms hell. It is this mystery which has engendered a more holy religion, a more spiritual worship, and a purer virtue, because it is more interior; from it springs the most efficacious Sacrament, more abundant graces, more sublime ceremonies, more perfect laws; it is that which is substituted for the more ancient alliance founded upon servile fear, the tender adoption of men as children of God. This mystery is the striking manifestation of all the truths, and the censure of all errors; all vices find their condemnation therein, all virtues their principle, all merits their recompense; it is, in short, the foundation of faith, the support of hope, and the most powerful motive for the love of God.

From this mystery proceeds the instruction of the ignorant, the science of doctors, the efficacy of preaching, the courage of martyrs. It restores those who are overcome with fatigue; it gives strength to the weak, purifies those who are defiled, enriches the poor, grants liberty to captives, health to the sick, and life to the dead. It is a powerful defence for those assailed by temptation; it gives consolation to the afflicted, and hope to those who hoped no longer. It is in this mystery that sinners obtain pardon, the cowardly encouragement, and the indifferent fervor. Through this mystery the saints attain perfection, the just perseverance, and the elect their crown.

This mystery of the Mass is truly called the Pasch, or *transitus*, that is, the passage. What is this transit? Whence and whither is this passage? Who is it that passes? Whence and whither does He pass? Christ our Lord passed from this world to the Father, from death to life, from shame to glory, from servitude to a kingdom, from insults to honor, from the floods of the world to the port of heaven, from being between two thieves to the throne of His Father.

We, too, have passed; for Christ is our Pasch, our passage—Christ is immolated. Whither then have we passed? From what distance? From twofold perdition to twofold salvation of body and of soul, from the devil to God, from an enemy to our Father, from a tyrant who is neither God nor man, to our king who is both God and man. We have passed from darkness to light, from weariness to rest, from lamentations to canticles of joy, from nakedness to clothing, from poverty to opulence, from guilt to grace, from pain to glory. The holy Mass is the Sun of Christianity, and the summary of all that is grand and magnificent and most prodigious, both in the triumphant and in the militant church of God. The angels almost envy us this divine Sacrifice. Protestants and infidels may say with a sneer that it is the pomp and glitter of our ceremonies and altars that draw the faithful to the church. Not so. Our fickle nature cannot be charmed long by such transitory things. Our altars indeed we adorn, we decorate our churches, we embellish the priestly vestments, we display the gorgeous ceremonies of the church, but not to attract the people. Simply because our Lord Jesus Christ is present there—our Saviour and our God, surrounded by countless myriads of angels. This is the grand source of the magnificence of our architecture, the gorgeousness of our vestments, the diversity of our ornaments, the sound of our organs, the religious harmony of our voices, and the grandeur and order of all our ceremonies, both in the consecration and dedication of our churches and in the solemn celebration of the Mass.

This is the reason why we adorn ourselves with our gayest attire, why we rifle the gardens of their sweetest and choicest flowers to decorate our altars, and scatter them in lavish profusion before the feet of our sacramental King. This is the reason why our sacred altars glitter and sparkle with cheerful lights, while clouds of sweet-smelling incense float up and around the sacred Victim. This is also the very reason why we read in the Apostolic Constitutions: "Let some of the deacons walk about in the church, and watch the men and the women, that no noise be made, that no one nod, or whisper, or slumber; and let the deacons stand at the doors of the men, and the sub-deacons at the doors of the women, that no one go out, nor a door be opened, although it be for one of the faithful, *at the time of the oblation*." *

This, again, is the reason why the primitive Christians never entered the churches without washing their hands and putting on their cleanest apparel; why kings, on entering the same, took off their crowns; why in some countries it was even the custom to bare the feet at the threshold; and why the very doors of many churches, as at the four Basilicas of Rome, are literally worn down with the kisses of the faithful.

Again, it is precisely on account of the infinite Dignity of Jesus Christ, Our High Priest, and the unspeakable Sanctity of the Lamb of God, Our Victim at Mass, that the Fathers of the Church denounce so severely all those students who become priests from worldly motives; that they so unmercifully condemn the hasty and inconsiderate ordination of priests, asking, "Who is he that thus fashions, as if it were an ephemeral thing of clay, Truth's guardian, him that shall take his stand with angels, that shall give glory with archangels, and that shall send up the sacrifice to the altar on high, that shall share in the priestly office together with Christ, and, to say something greater still, shall be a God and the maker of a God."

The Church, during eleven centuries, excluded from this

---

* Lib. viii. c. 12.

holy state every one who had committed even one mortal sin after baptism; and if any one, after having received Holy Orders, fell into a mortal sin, he was deposed forever from his sacred office, for the simple reason that he who is not holy should not touch what is holy.

This severe discipline of the Church, it is true, has been greatly mitigated; but it has always been required that he who in his past life had become guilty of grievous sins, and desired to receive Holy Orders, should first lead a pure life for some time previous to his ordination. It would certainly be a mortal sin to receive any of the Holy Orders while still addicted to a sinful habit. "If I consider your vocation," says St. Bernard, "I am seized with horror, especially if I see that no true penance has preceded your ordination."

And should a priest know himself to be in a state of utter unworthiness to say Mass, the Church obliges him, under pain of mortal sin, to go to confession previous to the celebration of the holy Sacrifice, for "Thou dost not dare," says St. John Chrysostom, "to touch with unwashed hands the sacred Sacrifice, however great the necessity that urges thee; approach not, therefore, with an unwashed soul."

"He who is to act as priest," says the same Father of the Church, "must needs be as pure as though he stood in heaven itself, in the midst of those heavenly powers."

No wonder that many saints would never consent to receive Holy Orders. To escape Ordination, St. Ephrem feigned derangement of mind; St. Mark cut off his thumb, St. Ammonis his ears and nose, and when the people still insisted upon his being ordained priest, he threatened to cut out even his tongue.

St. Francis of Assisium once beheld, in a vision, a crystal vase filled with most limpid water. God revealed to him that the soul of a priest must be as pure as this crystal vase. This vision made such a deep impression upon him, that he could never afterwards be prevailed upon to accept the dignity of the priesthood.

The Abbot Theodore had received the Order of Deacon. One day he beheld a fiery column, and heard, at the same time, a voice saying: "If thy heart be as fiery as this column, thou mayest exercise the functions of thy sacred Order." He would never afterwards consent to exercise the sacred functions of his office. Every one, even the most wicked man, feels naturally that the candidate for the priesthood should be holy; the least fault in him is considered unpardonable.

No wonder, then, if we read in the lives of holy priests that they were so careful to prepare themselves in the best manner possible for the celebration of the tremendous Sacrifice of the Mass, and on that account were often visited with most extraordinary favors during the oblation of the sacred mysteries. St. Leonard of Port Maurice said Mass every day. He prepared himself for this tremendous Sacrifice by confessing twice in the day. He never approached the altar without being girt with hair-cloth, and having first offered thirty-three times to the Eternal Father the most sacred Blood of Jesus Christ, praying Him to grant, by virtue of His Sacrifice, that his heart might be always pure and clean, free from every stain of sin. In going to the altar, he pictured to his mind the awful scene of Calvary, and saw with the eye of faith the Holy Trinity, surrounded by angels and saints, ready to receive the sacrifice he was about to offer. His deportment was that of a man raised above the world, recollected and absorbed in contemplating his God. If sometimes he was told that he was a long time in celebrating Mass, he used to reply: "Do you not know that my greatest consolation is to celebrate the Holy Sacrifice, and my great sorrow is to see some priests celebrate it with so much haste. If all had a lively faith, they would be unwilling to leave the altar." In fact, so strong was his faith, that he found his greatest delight in offering the Divine Son to the Eternal Father, especially in the consecration, when he appeared quite inflamed with love and joy, and during the whole time of Mass he seemed in an ecstasy.*

The great and famous Archbishop of Cologne, St. Herbert, was touched with such devotion in saying Mass, that his face, which bore habitually marks of the virtues with which his holy soul was adorned, became then so luminous and resplendent, that he seemed an angel rather than a man.

What were the transports and sentiments of St. Lawrence Justinian? His body became, as it were, immovable, and had only sufficient motion to serve his soul, which was totally taken up with this most sublime action; his face shone with angelic modesty, his eyes distilled tears, and his mind was transported by the force of his ravishments.

John of Alvernia, whilst one day saying Mass, was so wrapt in a divine and ineffable sense of God, that he was hardly able to proceed. After he had pronounced the words of consecration, he became, as it were, unconscious of himself, being wholly lost in the divinity of the mysteries which he was performing.

The Abbot Euthymius used to tell in private conversation that often, while saying Mass, he saw troops of angels who stood around.

We read of St. Thomas Aquinas that, in saying Mass, he seemed to be in raptures, often quite dissolved in tears, and melting with love in contemplation of the immense charity of Jesus Christ.

Severus relates that while St. Martin was saying Mass, a fiery globe used to appear above his head.

St. Euthenius used to see a great fire and light coming down from heaven, and enveloping him and his assistant to the end of the holy Sacrifice.† In the same manner the Holy Ghost came upon St. Anastasius, and surrounded him in the form of a fiery flame whilst celebrating the sacred Mysteries.‡

---

* His Life. † His Life, by H. Cyrillus. ‡ His Life, by St. Basil.

"Yes, the priest stands at the altar," exclaims St. John Chrysostom, when considering these sublime mysteries: "the priest stands there and makes a long supplication, not in order that fire from heaven may consume the things that lie to open view, but that grace, lighting on the Sacrifice, may thereby inflame the souls of all, and show them brighter than silver purified in the fire. Art thou ignorant that the soul of man could never bear this fire of the Sacrifice, but that all would be utterly consumed, were not the aid of the grace of God abundant? For if one would but consider how great a thing it is for a mortal, and one still clothed with flesh and blood, to be enabled to be nigh to that blessed and immortal nature, he would then see how great an honor the grace of the Spirit has vouchsafed to priests. For through them both these things are done, as also others, nowise inferior to them, which concern both our dignity and our salvation." *

Can we wonder if the holy Sacrifice of the Mass has ever been, and still is, the delight and the glory of truly Christian souls, of hearts devoted to Jesus Christ! Indeed, this holy Sacrifice ought to be the incessant study of every Christian, but especially of every Roman Catholic priest. Happy shall we be if, in applying our minds to it, we also fix our hearts upon it. "Where thy treasure is, there is thy heart also." †

---

* T. L. L. iii. de Sacerd. n. 4, 5.   † Matt. vi. 21.

CHAPTER XXXVI.

SATAN'S HATRED FOR THE MASS.

BEFORE the coming of our Redeemer, mankind was groaning under the tyranny of the devil. He was lord, and even caused himself to be worshipped as God, with incense and with sacrifices, not only of animals, but even of children and human lives. And what return did he make them? He tortured their bodies with the most barbarous cruelty, he blinded their minds, and by a path of pain and misery led them down to torment everlasting. It was to overthrow this tyrant, and release mankind from its wretched thraldom that the Son of God came; that the unfortunate creatures, freed from the darkness of death, rescued from the bondage of their eternal enemy, and enlightened to know the true way of salvation, might serve their real and lawful Master, who loved them as a Father, and from slaves of Satan wished to make them His own beloved children. The prophet Isaias had long ago foretold that our Redeemer should destroy the empire which Satan held over mankind: "And the sceptre of their oppressor Thou hast overcome."[*] Why does the prophet call Satan oppressor? It is because this heartless master exacts from the poor sinners who become his slaves, heavy tribute in the shape of passions, hatreds, disorderly affections, by means of which, while he scourges, he binds them in a still faster servitude.

Our Saviour came to release us from the slavery of this deadly foe; but in what manner did he effect this release? By offering His sufferings and death in satisfaction to the

---

[*] Isaias, ix. 4.

divine justice for the punishment due to our sins; by the sacrifice of His life upon the Cross He overthrew the empire of Satan over mankind.

The holy Evangelists tell us that after Jesus left Jerusalem on the eve of His Passion to go to the Mount of Olives, He crossed the torrent of Cedron. The Cedron flows at the eastern extremity of a valley which separates Jerusalem from the Mount of Olives. In this valley was a thick forest, which the superstition of the degenerate Jews, according to St. Jerome, had consecrated to Moloch. To such an excess of stupid impiety and barbarous folly had this nation come, that fathers went there in crowds to sacrifice their little children to an infamous idol, and burn them alive in its honor; and lest they should be moved by the cries of those innocent victims, they were careful to drown their voices in the noise of drums and other instruments. The ashes of the horrible sacrifice they cast into the waters of the torrent, which for this reason was called *Cedron*, signifying *black* and *obscure*, because of the remains of the blackened corpses which were thrown into its waters.

This place, then, was the most corrupt in the whole world; the very seat, as it were, of the empire of Lucifer on earth, where he received, even from the people of God, and within sight of the Temple of the Lord, divine honor and worship, in which atrocity was added to sacrilege.

All these circumstances explain why our Lord was desirous of commencing His Passion near the torrent in this same valley; why He chose by preference so infamous a place, solemnly to devote Himself to death. Our Saviour wished to attack the devil in the very centre of his sacrilegious empire; and, therefore, crossing Cedron, and repairing to the opposite shore, the Redeemer goes forward to face Lucifer, in order to humiliate, confound, and disarm him; to overthrow his power by His agony and sufferings, as a generous and magnanimous warrior who descends the first into the arena to meet his enemy, confident of conquering and triumphing over him. During the whole course of the life of Jesus Christ, our sovereign Lord, divine Providence never permitted the demons to recognize Him to be God and the Redeemer of the world. Lucifer remained in his blindness to the last; for although, from the splendor of His miracles, he sometimes suspected that Jesus might be God, yet again, seeing Him so poor and humble he could not believe it.

"At the moment when our Lord received His beloved Cross," said the Blessed Virgin to blessed Mary of Jesus d'Agreda, "Lucifer and his demons lost all strength; they were vanquished and enchained, and the end of their chains placed in the hands of His Mother, that by the virtue of her divine Son she might hold him and his legions in subjection. They tried to precipitate themselves into the abyss, but were constrained by the great Queen to witness the end of those mysteries and to remain around the Cross.

"When Jesus Christ began to speak upon the Cross, He willed that the demons should hear Him, and understand the sense of His words and the profound mysteries expressed in them. Hearing Him pray to His Eternal Father for His executioners, they clearly understood that He was the Messiah, and were filled with rage at His infinite charity. When He promised Paradise to the good thief, they understood the virtue of His redemption, and Lucifer being unable to endure that sight, humbled his pride so far as to supplicate our great Queen to allow him and his legions to precipitate themselves into the infernal abyss, but he was refused in order to add to his greater torment. When Jesus, in recommending His Mother to St. John, called her 'woman,' they clearly understood that she was that great woman who had been shown to them after their creation, and that it was she who was to crush the head of Lucifer, as had been foretold him in the terrestrial paradise.

"At the fourth word, which testified the desolation of Jesus, they learned His incomprehensible charity, which led Him to complain to the Eternal Father, not because He was suffering, but because He wished to undergo even more agony, to save mankind. But at the words 'I thirst,' they were filled with rage, because they saw that He complained not of bodily thirst, but that ardent desire which He felt in His soul for man's salvation.

"At the sixth mysterious word, 'All is consummated,' they received a clear knowledge of the mystery of Redemption, which was already accomplished to their eternal shame and confusion. The reign of Jesus was established and the empire of Satan overthrown.

"When Jesus pronounced the words, 'Father, into Thy hands I commend my spirit,' and bowing His head, expired, the ground opened, and the demon, with all his companions, was in a terrific manner swallowed in the bottomless pit of hell, more quickly than a flash of lightning passes through the air. He fell, disarmed and vanquished, and his head was crushed beneath the feet of Jesus and His Mother."

Each Mass is the same sacrifice as that which Jesus Christ offered to His heavenly Father on Mount Calvary for the overthrow of Satan's power over mankind. Hence, each Mass shakes the very foundations of the devil's empire in this world; it causes him to tremble and take flight, giving him unspeakably great pain.

When St. Bridget was assisting at Mass one day, she saw at the moment of consecration how all the powers of heaven were set in motion; she saw how numbers of angels came down, and the devils commenced to tremble and take to flight in the greatest confusion and terror.[*]

St. Augustine relates the following: "We have amongst us a Tribune, Hesperius, who has a farm called Zubedi, in the district of Fussalæ. Having learned that his house there, besides the tormenting of his cattle and servants, was suffering under the noxious violence of malignant spirits, he requested of our priests in my absence, that some one of them

---

[*] Lib. viii. c. 56.

should proceed thither, at whose prayers these spirits might give way. One went thither; he offered up there the Sacrifice of the body of Christ, praying to the best of his power that the annoyance might cease. At once by the mercy of God, it ceased."*

Presbyter of Africa relates this story as having fallen under his own observation: "An Arabian girl was, in consequence of a sin against purity, given over to the evil spirit, and was unable, for a considerable time, to partake even of ordinary food. She was admitted into a nunnery. Having remained for a fortnight without food, a priest going thither with me to offer as usual the morning sacrifice there, the superior of the nunnery led the girl to the altar. There, by the noise of her weeping, she moved all who were present to tears and sighs. The people implored the Lord to remove from her so great an evil. A certain deacon suggested that the priest should apply the saving chalice to her throat. No sooner was this done than the devil, by the command of our Saviour, left the place he had besieged, and the girl cried out with praise of the Redeemer. Then followed universal joy; another Mass was said for the girl, in thanksgiving for the favor she had received.†"

No wonder, then, that Satan has always borne an implacable hatred to the Mass as to the most powerful weapon against all his evil machinations. It is for this reason that ever since the institution of the holy Sacrifice he has repeatedly tried to destroy this impregnable fortress of the Catholic Church by undermining the faith in the Real Presence, being fully persuaded that a complete success in this point is the only means for him of opening the way to the introduction of idolatry. It took Satan more than fifteen hundred years to gain any great victory over the faith in the Real Presence among European nations. Meanwhile his en-

---

* T. vii. Lib. xxii. c. viii. Col. 1063.
† De Promiss. et Praedic. Dei. T. I. c. vi. p. 193.

deavor to re-establish his fallen empire was untiring. Not being able to reconstruct it on the same basis of idolatry—the worship of himself—he has, at all times, endeavored to indemnify himself by the introduction of new sects and heresies, such as the erroneous and infernal doctrines of Arius, Pelagius, Luther, Henry VIII., and other wicked heresiarchs. In this undertaking he has succeeded admirably among many nations who had renounced idolatry and embraced the only true doctrine of the Catholic Church, but afterwards listening to perverse men—the agents of Satan, in the reconstruction of his empire on earth—apostatized and fell into heresy or false doctrines—a finer and more subtle species of idolatry, according to what holy Scripture says: "It is like the sin of witchcraft to rebel, and like the crime of idolatry to refuse to obey"* the voice of the Lord speaking through His representatives, St. Peter and all his lawful successors—upon whom Jesus Christ built His Church, and of whom He has said: "He who heareth you heareth me, and he who despiseth you despiseth me," and, therefore, such a one shall be damned.

The great and long hoped-for day arrived for Satan at last; the hour had struck in which he found two men according to his heart—men who listened most attentively to all his crafty suggestions, and carried out most faithfully all his malicious designs. These men were Martin Luther, an apostate priest of the Catholic Church in Germany, and Henry VIII., King of England. By those two agents and their associates Satan succeeded in depriving their numerous followers of the faith in the Real Presence in the holy Sacrifice of the Mass. It is, however, a well-known fact that Luther, even after his apostasy from the Church, adhered for some time to his faith in the Real Presence of our Lord in the Blessed Sacrament. He condemned all who denied the Real Presence. He says: "That no one among the Fathers, nu-

---

* I Kings, xv. 23.

merous as they are, should have spoken of the Eucharist as these men do, is truly astonishing. Not one of them speaks thus: '*There is only bread and wine;*' or, '*the body and blood of Christ are not present.*' And when we reflect how often the Fathers of the Church treat of this subject and repeat it, it ceases to be credible—it is not possible, that not even once such words as these should not have dropt from some of them. Surely it was of moment that men should not be drawn into error—still they all speak with such precision, evincing that they entertained no doubt of the presence of the body and blood. Had not this been their conviction, can it be imagined that, among so many, the negative opinion should not have been uttered on a single occasion? But our sacramentarians, on the other hand, can proclaim only the negative or contrary opinion. These men, then, to say all in one word, have drawn their notions neither from the Scriptures nor the Fathers."* But as an evil spirit came upon King Saul, because he had left the Lord and assumed the office of the priest of the Most High, in like manner one of the worst of evil spirits came upon Luther, because he left Jesus Christ by turning his back upon the Vicar of Christ and His Church. This evil spirit caused him to change his language speedily as to the Real Presence.

Previous to his apostasy, Henry VIII., King of England, had entered the lists with Luther in defence of the Sacrifice of the Mass. But now the apostate monk replied: " To establish this sacrifice Henry has recourse at last to the words of the Fathers. Heaven well knows that I care not if a thousand Austins, a thousand Cyprians, or a thousand other such were against me."† Such is the impious language of Luther. No longer caring for the Chief of Pastors, for the centre of Christian faith and unity, the learned Doctor and founder of Protestantism carried his ravings so far as to

---

* Defensio verborum Cœnæ, T. vii., p. 391. Edit. Wittembergae, 1557.
† Contra Regem. Angliæ. T. II. p. 334.

pretend to have been taught by the devil, to boast of it, to found new doctrines on so powerful an authority, and to leave us in his works the evidence of his interview with Satan. Certainly it is impossible to carry fanaticism farther than to boast of having had such a master. Luther tells us himself that he had many colloquies with the devil. I. M. V. Audin informs us, in his Life of Luther, how one night at the Wartburg the devil appeared to this apostate monk, and shook a bag of nuts which had been presented to him. Luther, growing impatient, roared out: "Begone!" but the devil was not to be dislodged so easily. He changed himself into a fly, and by his buzzing annoyed the acute hearing of the monk, who at length took his inkstand and threw it at the wings of the insect. Now, whenever visitors came to the Wartburg, the keeper of the chateau would point out to them the place at which Luther threw his inkstand, saying: "See, this is the stain of the ink which time has not been able to efface." But worthy of attention above all, is the vision in which, as he relates in the most serious manner, Satan by his arguments compelled him to proscribe private Masses. He gives us a lively description of this adventure. He wakes suddenly in the middle of the night; Satan appears to him. Luther is seized with horror; he sweats; he trembles; his heart beats in a fearful manner Nevertheless the discussion begins: "Listen to me, learned doctor," says he. "During fifteen years you have daily celebrated private Masses. What if all those Masses have been a horrible idolatry? What if the body and blood of Jesus Christ be not present there, and that yourself adored, and made others adore, bread and wine? What if your ordination and consecration were as invalid as that of the Turkish and Samaritan priests is false and their worship impious? How, then, could you consecrate at Mass, or really celebrate it, since you had not the power of consecrating, which, according to your own doctrine, is an essential defect? What a priesthood is that! What a consecration!

What a Mass! What sort of a priest are you? And you make your Mass a propitiatory sacrifice before God? O abomination, which surpasses all other abominations!

"I maintain, then, that you have not consecrated at Mass, and that you have offered and made others adore simple bread and wine. In your Mass is wanting a person who has the power to consecrate. You stand there by yourself as an ignorant and faithless monk. If, then, you are not capable of consecrating, and ought not to attempt it, what do you do while saying Mass and consecrating, but blaspheme and tempt God? You are not a real priest, nor do you really consecrate the body of Jesus Christ. And you, who are an impious and incredulous man, are no more capable of receiving the sacrament than the bell is capable of receiving baptism. Show me where it is written that an impious and incredulous man can ascend the altar of Jesus Christ, consecrate, and make the sacrament? If no one can administer any of your sacraments to himself, why do you wish to reserve this sacrament for yourself alone?"

The devil having said these and many other things to shake Luther's faith in the holy Sacrifice of the Mass, said finally: "You are not ordained, you have only offered bread and wine, like the Pagans. What an unheard of abomination!"*

Luther acknowledges, at the close of this conference, that he was unable to answer the arguments of Satan. The devil, like a good disputant, pressed him so hard with his arguments, that he left him without reply. Luther is conquered, which fact ought not to astonish us, since he tells us that the logic of the devil was accompanied with a voice so alarming that the blood froze in his veins. "I understood," says he, "how it often happens that people die *at the break of day;* it is because the devil is able to kill or suffocate men, and without going so far as that, when he disputes with

---

* Audin's Life of Luther, chaps. xix. and xx.

them, he places them in such embarrassment that he can thus occasion their death. I have often experienced this myself."

Immediately after, he wrote to Melancthon, his fellow-laborer in the vineyard of the devil, "I will not again celebrate private Masses forever."* It was the devil who introduced idolatry, or devil-worship, into the world; he it is who tries to keep it up and promote it everywhere to the best of his power. In the discussion which he held with Luther, he tried to persuade the learned doctor, as he mockingly calls him, not to say Mass any longer, in order that he who said it, and others who assisted at it, should not continue to commit the abominable crime of idolatry. But Luther was perfectly blinded, or else he would have answered: "If to say Mass and to assist at it is to commit the sin of idolatry, why is it then that you persuade me to abolish Mass? Why is it that you wish me to abolish your own worship? to destroy your own empire on earth? You are certainly no such fool; you only wish to deceive me; you know too well that Mass is that mighty Sacrifice by which your strength has been crushed; it is this great power which prevents you from spreading your kingdom as you please, from exercising that power which you held over mankind previous to the coming of Christ. This is the very reason why you wish me to be your agent in abolishing Mass, the interpreter and executor of your will and evil designs! Begone, Satan! for you are a great deceiver and a liar."

Had Luther but known his catechism well he could have easily refuted all the objections of the devil, and proved to him that he was a deceiver and a liar. But the great "Reformer" was too mild with his adversary, too obedient a disciple to his master; so he never again said a private mass.

No wonder if from henceforward Satan succeeded with

---

* Letter to Melancthon, August 1, 1521.

all who followed Luther's fundamental principle of "private judgment" in religious matters, which private judgment ended in their renouncing all belief in the Real Presence. Thus, for instance, Zuinglius, the founder of Protestantism in Switzerland, tells us that while he was in great perplexity and deep meditation how to explode the doctrine of the Real Presence of Jesus Christ in the Eucharist, he was furnished with an argument for that purpose by a nocturnal monitor, "whether black or white he did not remember."*

Every one knows that the first duty of man is to adore God. No sooner was man created than this necessary homage became due. All know likewise that the perfect way of expressing this homage is by sacrifice: the mode of adoration revealed by the Almighty Himself to man. We find it prevalent wherever man exists. No nation, however barbarous, no religion, however false or idolatrous, but has had its sacrifices. From the foundation of the world, no age or nation ever pretended to adore God without a sacrifice, until Luther, Calvin, Zuinglius, Henry VIII., King of England, and other heresiarchs with their followers came up as the first sectarians among Christians to deprive the Almighty of this right of worship.

On the day when Luther and men of the same stamp denied the Real Presence of Jesus Christ in the Mass, and succeeded by means of the civil authority to abolish this holy Sacrifice, they deprived all their followers of the greatest gifts and consolations that God, in His infinite power, wisdom, and love, had bestowed upon the world. The hearts of their fellow-men they left utterly void; they flung back Christianity, as far as their tenets obtained, two thousand years into the realms of Judaism; they stripped the Christian altar bare, and left it poorer than the altar in the temple of Jerusalem, for man had no longer the comfort nor the help of a visible Sacrifice.

---

* Lib. de subsidio Euchar.

The domain of Protestantism presents indeed in its bleak and dreary waste a sad proof of what the absence of the life-giving Lamb of God really is.

Until Protestantism appeared to cast a blight on worship, who ever heard of a religion, Christian or Pagan, whose very essence did not consist in an external sacrifice? In this respect the Reformation has *protested* against the unanimous voice of mankind, and therefore the Protestant service is as contracted in its nature as it is meagre in its details, as it is cold and unimpressive in its general effect. In the Protestant service almost everything is for the ear, and scarcely anything for the eye and the heart. Protestants, those in Germany even, lately began to understand and to deplore this desecration and desolation of God's holy sanctuary. Isidore, Count Von Loeben, considering the splendid old Catholic worship, exclaimed: "Admirable ceremonial, replete with harmony! It is the diamond that glitters on the crown of faith!" * Elsewhere he says: "The Catholic Church, with its ever-open door, with its undying lamps, its joyful and mournful strains, its hosannas or its lamentations, its hymns, its Masses, its festivals and reminiscences, resembles a mother who ever holds forth her arms to receive the prodigal child. It is a fountain of sweet water, around which are assembled multitudes to imbibe vigor, health, and life." †

Leibnitz ‡ breaks forth into this exclamation: "How beautiful is the music of the Catholic Church! How it addresses both mind and sense! Those melodious notes and voices, those canticles which breathe so pure a spirituality, those clouds of incense, those chimes which a disdainful philosophy condescends to despise; all these please God. Architects and sculptors, you have acted wisely and ennobled your art, by raising churches to the Divinity! Enter their portals, and your soul expands with the presence of

---

* In his Lotos Blätter, 1817. † Ibid, p. 1. ‡ Syst. Theol., p. 205.

God; you involuntarily exclaim: 'Truly this is the house of God, and the gate of heaven!'" It is related of Frederick II., King of Prussia, that after having assisted at a solemn High Mass celebrated in the Church of Breslau by Cardinal Tringendorf, he remarked: "The Calvinists treat God as an inferior, the Lutherans treat Him as an equal; but the Catholics treat Him as God." Yes indeed, it is only the Catholic Church that is the home for our dear Saviour. His Presence fills her halls to overflowing with joy and gladness. Her propitiatory altars are the anchors of hope for the sinner; her sanctuaries the ante-chambers of heaven. Take away the Blessed Sacrament, and you take away her Saviour. Give her the Blessed Sacrament and you give her a glory, an honor, a triumph the greatest possible this side of Paradise. Her altars are the altars of joy, because they are the altars of the Saving Victim for the sins of the world, for which reason the robed priest begins the tremendous Sacrifice with the antiphon; "I will go unto the altar of God, to God who rejoiceth my youth."

> "O Salutaris Hostia!
> Bella premunt hostilia,
> Da robur, fer auxilium!"
>
> "Oh Saving Host! Our foes press nigh;
> Thy strength bestow, Thine aid supply!"

Who can fail to be impressed by the grandeur, the solemnity, and the noble dignity of the Catholic ceremonial? Who has not felt a sentiment of reverence and of awe creep over him, when at the most solemn part of the service the peal of the organ ceases, the voice of music is hushed, and, while clouds of incense are ascending, the priests, the ministers, and the people, fall prostrate in silent prayer before the altar in which the Lamb is present "as it were slain!" Who has not felt a thrill of rapturous emotion, when, after this solemn moment has passed, the music again peals forth, mingling joyous with solemn notes, and pouring out a stream of delicious melody over the soul! Who has not been struck with the pathetic simplicity, the unction and the massive grandeur of the Gregorian chant, especially in the Preface and the Pater Noster! And who has failed to mark the reverential awe with which Catholics are wont to assist at the service, as well as the general respect they pay to the Church of God!

Is it not an evident demonstration of the Real Divine Presence which presides over the celebration of the Mass, to mark the universality of that intense devotion, reverence, and respect of Catholics during the divine Sacrifice? "In our time," writes a convert to our faith, "after such a successive diminution of truth, affecting both the spiritual and temporal hierarchy of society, nothing can be more monotonous than an assembly of Protestants. There are the rich, cuirassed in egotism, initiated in no other rites but those of Bacchus, bred up with the same feeling of disdain for every outward manifestation of piety and fervor: there are the poor, parked in from all observation or contact with the rich, thoroughly subdued and moulded into one form of servile respect. But in our churches, during the celebration of the divine mysteries, it is a very different picture. What do we find here amidst the pious throng? We find the simple peasant come from his woods, the shepherd from the mountains, the young and thoughtful clerk, the solemn religious man, the devout student, whom nothing but the divine service could tear from his books, the holy recluse, who may be looked for elsewhere in vain, the laboring youth, with joy and triumph in their looks, the innocent child with its baptismal robe unsullied, the penitent sinner who has atoned, or who is atoning, for having stained the purity of his soul.

"At times, indeed, may be discovered some awful figure, who seems moved and yet unable to call on Heaven for mercy—one like those we read about in legendary tales, from whose eye no tear can fall, and at whose heart there seems to lie an icy coldness, unrelieved, though ever so many voices join to raise the solemn hymn, and hearts are thrilled, and eyes are filled with tears, by that full harmony.

"There we find the female sex, gifted with great faith and ardent devotion, who turn their steps, or at least their hearts, to the Catholic altar, whether in joy or sorrow, in sickness or in health, like the innocent child, who always runs thither for help where he trusts most—here the poor pilgrim wearied with fatigue, kneels down on the altar-steps to thank Him who has watched over him during a long and perilous journey; here a distracted mother comes into the temple to pray for the recovery of her son, whom the physicians have given over; all persons dissimilar in habits, in disposition of mind, in the cultivation and direction of their intelligence, and yet who have one centre and bond of union—Jesus Christ in the Eucharistic Sacrifice."

Thus there is a common sacrifice, but there are particular wants; and therefore, while the priest chants aloud at the altar, the internal desires of innumerable hearts are sent up to Heaven. And here it is that fine arts have been lavish of their tribute to religion and to God, speaking with silent eloquence of Christ, of His Mother, of His Apostles, and of His Saints. Let us cast one more contemplative look upon the wondrous and tender scene. What an assembly is present! This is the blessed vision of peace. Here the race of men seems amiable. Here we feel how near we are to God, who thus showers down His mercy upon us in His temple.

"Yes, sweet is the air of temples to those who have endured the thirst of the Babylonian exile, to those who have wandered sufficiently long in the land of malediction, as to discover how tasteless are its fruits, and how void of perfume its most gorgeous flowers. At the first step on entering this garden of God, it is as if one emerged from a withering atmosphere to feel the healthful and delicious breeze of mountains. What a glow of charity suddenly transports the heart and revives the fancy, though joy and hope had before seemed dead. No distrustful, or malignant, or inquisitive looks cause you to feel yourself a stranger, for it seems to be here, as it is in Paradise, where the blessed hail each new arrival, crying, 'Lo, one arrived to multiply our loves!'" *

"Ah! how blind, therefore, were our reformers," exclaims Fessler, † when openly censuring the intemperate vandalism of the reformers in destroying the most beautiful portions of Catholic worship. "Nay," exclaims the famous Novalis, "Luther knew nothing of the spirit of Christianity." "What is more natural for man," says Father Burke, O. P., "than that he should seek His God! God has stamped this desire upon Catholics and non-Catholics alike. No matter how keen the pleasure of the world; no matter how joyous the cup of life may be; no matter how bright the promise of youth; how serene the mature pleasures of the man of old age—there is in the heart of the non-Catholic, as well as of Catholics, one secret chamber which God alone can enter and fill. Hence it is that he who had tasted all pleasures—St. Augustine—exclaimed: 'Thou hast made me, O God, for Thyself, and my heart was uneasy within me until it found its rest in Thee.'

"What says another one of the greatest men of our age, a man upon whom God had showered every human gift, the poet Byron? He sought to feed his soul upon every pleasure of sense, and when he was thirty years of age he sat down to write, and this is what he wrote:

> 'My days are in the yellow leaf;
> The fruit, the flower of life are gone;
> The worm, the canker, and the grief,
> Are mine alone.'

"And why? Because God was not there."

One day, a certain Irishman, who, at the time of great famine in Ireland, had turned Protestant for the sake of

---
* Dante. † Theresia 2, p. 101.

food and raiment, came to Father Thomas Burke, O. P., and put himself into his hands, truly repentant, and sincerely sorrowful for what he had done. The good Father, who had the pleasure to receive him back into the Church, asked that man a question; and the answer made is interesting. He said to him, "Tell me this: you were two years amongst them?" "I was, your reverence, God bless you." "Now what sort of feeling had you—what impression did the Protestant religion make upon you?" "Well, your reverence, I felt like as if it were not natural-like. I went in of a Christmas morning; there was a sermon. I went in on Easter Sunday; and there was a sermon; and there was no difference at all between one day and another; and I felt even if it were a true religion, as if it were not natural, as if it would not *help* a man." There was a man who had his natural cravings—who had his natural feelings, and he could find nothing harmonious with those cravings and feelings the moment he left the Catholic church.

Indeed, the Protestant service in itself is neither inviting nor impressive; it has nothing in it to stir up the fountains of feeling; to call forth the music and poetry of the soul; to convey salutary instruction, or to awaken lively interest; it possesses no single trait of grandeur or sublimity; it has certainly not one element of poetry or pathos. Generally cold and lifeless, it becomes warm only by a violent effort, and then it runs into the opposite extreme of intemperate excitement and sentimentalism; nay, it is no exaggeration to say that religiousness among the greater part of Protestants in our day and country seems to have well nigh become extinct. They seem to have lost all spiritual conceptions, and no longer to possess any spiritual aspiration. Lacking as they do the light, the warmth, and the life-giving power of the sun of the Catholic church—the holy Mass—they seem to have become or to be near becoming what our world would be if there were no sun in the heavens. Having boldly denied and lost faith in the Real Presence of Jesus Christ in the Blessed Sacrament, they gradually began to deny with the same boldness almost all the Gospel truths. Why should the one who cares not for Jesus Christ upon the altar, be expected to care for Jesus Christ in heaven, and for all that He has taught us? For this reason is it that Protestants are so completely absorbed in temporal interests, in the things that fall under their senses, that their whole life is only materialism put in action. Lucre is the sole object on which their eyes are constantly fixed. A burning thirst to realize some profit, great or small, absorbs all their faculties—the whole energy of their being. They never pursue anything with ardor but riches and enjoyments. God—the soul—a future life,—they believe in none of them, or rather, they never think about them at all. If they ever take up a moral or a religious book, or go to a meeting-house, it is only by way of amusement—to pass the time away. It is a less serious occupation than smoking a pipe, or drinking a cup of tea. If you speak to them about the foundations of faith, of the principles of Christianity, of the importance of salvation, the certainty of a life beyond the grave—all these truths which so powerfully impress a mind susceptible of religious feeling,—they listen with a certain pleasure, for it amuses them, and piques their curiosity. In their opinion all this is "true, fine, grand." They deplore the blindness of men who attach themselves to the perishable goods of this world; perhaps they will even give utterance to some fine sentences on the happiness of knowing the true God, of serving Him, and of meriting by this means the reward of eternal life. They simply never think of religion at all; they like very well to talk about it, but it is as of a thing not made for them—a thing with which personally they have nothing to do. This indifference they carry so far—religious sensibility is so entirely withered or dead within them—that they care not a straw whether a doctrine is true or false, good or bad. Religion is to them simply a fashion, which those may follow who have a taste for it. By-and-bye, all in good time, they say—one should never be precipitate; it is not good to be too enthusiastic; no doubt the Catholic religion is beautiful and sublime; its doctrine explains with method and clearness all that is necessary for man to know. Whoever has any sense will see that, and will adopt it in his heart in all sincerity; but after all, one must not think too much of these things, and increase the cares of life. Now, just consider we have a body, how many cares it demands. It must be clothed, fed, and sheltered from the injuries of the weather; its infirmities are great, and its maladies are numerous. It is agreed on all hands that health is our most precious good. This body that we see, that we touch, must be taken care of every day, and every moment of the day. Is not this enough without troubling ourselves about a soul that we never see? The life of man is short and full of misery; it is made up of a succession of important concerns that follow one another without interruption. Our hearts and our minds are scarcely sufficient for the solicitudes of the present life—is it wise then to torment oneself about the future? Is it not far better to live in blessed ignorance?

Ask them what would you think of a traveller, who, on finding himself at a dilapidated inn, open to all the winds and deficient in the most absolute necessaries, should spend all his time in trying how he could make himself most comfortable in it, without ever thinking of preparing himself for his departure, and his return into the bosom of his family? Would this traveller be acting in a wise and reasonable manner? "No:" they will reply; "one must not travel in that way; but man, nevertheless, must confine himself within proper limits. How can he provide for two lives at the same time? I take care of this life, and the care of the other I leave to God." If a traveller ought not regularly to take up his abode at an inn, neither ought he to travel on two roads at the same time. When one wishes to cross a river, it will not do to have two boats, and set a foot in each; such a proceeding would involve the risk of a tumble into the water, and drowning oneself. Such is the deep abyss of religious indifferentism into which so many Protestants of our day have fallen; and from which they naturally fall into one deeper still—infidelity.

It is a well-known fact that, before the Reformation, infidels were scarcely known in the Christian world. Since that event they have come forth in swarms. It is from the writings of Herbert, Hobbes, Bloum, Shaftesbury, Bolingbroke, and Boyle, that Voltaire and his party drew the objections and errors which they have brought so generally into fashion in the world. According to Diderot and d'Alembert, the first step that the untractable Catholic takes is to adopt the Protestant principle of private judgment. He establishes himself judge of his religion, leaves it and joins the reform. Dissatisfied with the incoherent doctrines he there discovers, he passes over to the Socinians, whose inconsequences soon drive him into Deism. Still pursued by unexpected difficulties, he finds refuge in universal doubt; but still haunted by uneasiness, he at length resolves to take the last step, and proceeds to terminate the long chain of his errors in infidelity. Let us not forget that the first link of this chain is attached to the fundamental maxim of private judgment. It is, therefore, historically correct that the same principle that created Protestantism three centuries ago, has never ceased since that time to spin it out into a thousand different sects, and has concluded by covering Europe and America with that multitude of free-thinkers and infidels who place these countries on the verge of ruin. And what is easier, from this state of irreligion and infidelity, than the passage to idolatry?

This assertion may seem incredible to some at this day, and may be esteemed an absurdity; but idolatry is expressly mentioned in the Apocalypse as existing in the time of Antichrist. And, indeed, our surprise will much abate, if we take into consideration the temper and disposition of the present times. When men divest themselves as they seem to do at present, of all fear of the Supreme Being, of all respect of their Creator and Lord; when they surrender themselves to the gratification of sensuality; when they give full freedom to the human passions and direct their whole study to the pursuits of a corrupt world, with a total forgetfulness of a future state ; when they give children a godless education, and have no longer any religion to teach them, may we not say that the transition to idolatry is easy ? When all the steps leading up to a certain point are taken, what wonder if we arrive at that point? Such was the gradual degeneracy of mankind in the early ages of the world that brought on the abominable practices of idol-worship.

Of course it will be said that we have the happiness of living in the most enlightened of all ages; our knowledge is more perfect, our ideas more developed and refined, the human faculties more improved and better cultivated than they ever were before ; in fine, that the present race of mankind may be reckoned a society of philosophers, when compared to the generations that have gone before. How is it possible then that such stupidity can seize upon the human mind as to sink it into idolatry?

This kind of reasoning is more specious than solid. For, allowing the present times to surpass the past in refinement and knowledge, it must be said that they are proportionately more vicious. Refinement of reason has contributed, as every one knows, to refine upon the means of gratifying the human passions.

Besides, however enlightened the mind may be supposed to be, if the heart is corrupt the excesses into which a man will run are evidenced by daily experience.

If the philosopher is not governed by the power of religion, his conduct will be absurd and even despicable to the most ignorant individual of the lowest rank.

A Socrates, a Cicero, a Seneca, are said to have been acquainted with the knowledge of one supreme God, but they had not courage to profess His worship, and in their public conduct basely sacrificed to stocks and stones with the vulgar. When men have banished from their heart the sense of religion, and despise the rights of justice (and is this not the case with numbers?) will many of them scruple to offer incense to a statue, if by so doing they serve their ambition, their interest, or whatever may be their favorite passion? Where is the cause for surprise then, if infidelity and irreligion be succceded by idolatry? That pride alone, when inflamed with a constant flow of prosperity, may raise a man to the extravagant presumption of claiming for himself divine honors, we see in the example of Alexander, the celebrated Macedonian conqueror, and of several emperors of Babylon and ancient Rome. From suggestions of that same principle of pride, it will happen. that Antichrist, elevated by a continued course of victories and conquests, will set himself up for a God. And as at that time the propagation of infidelity, irreligion, and immorality will have become universal—this defection from faith, disregard for its teachers, licentiousness in opinions, depravity in morals, will so far deaden all influence of religion and cause such degencracy in mankind that many will be base enough even to espouse idolatry—to yield to the absurd impiety of worshipping Antichrist as their Lord and God; some out of fear for what they may lose, others to gain what they covet.

Let it be remembered that Satan will succeed in introducing idol-worship universally through Antichrist, because the great power in his way will then have been removed—the holy Sacrifice of the Mass will not be offered for three years and a half. Then will it become evident that, as our dear Saviour had St. John the Baptist as His forerunner, to prepare the hearts of men by penance for His reception, so Antichrist had Luther, Calvin, Henry VIII., and men of the same stamp as his forerunners to abolish Mass, and thus prepare the hearts of their followers by pride, arrogance, want of submission to Christ's Vicar, irreligion, infidelity, and immorality, to follow and worship him—the son of perdition—

as their sovereign Lord and God. During that dreadful time, the sun shall rise only to show that the altar has been torn down, the priest banished, the lights put out; it will be a time of calamity, of darkness and sorrow for the faithful worshippers of Jesus Christ in the Blessed Sacrament. When there shall be no Mass any more, when sacrifice and libation are cut off from the House of God, when Jesus Christ shall not be allowed to be worshipped on our altars in the Eucharistic Sacrifice, then the tie between earth and heaven shall have been broken; then will the heavens over our head be brass and the earth under foot iron; then the power and blessings of the Mass will be better known and understood than ever before.

The description in the Apocalypse of the time of Antichrist paints it in colors leaving no room for doubt that it will be the most turbulent, the most calamitous, and the most persecuting of all periods. How alarming and how terrible those extraordinary and unnatural signs in the sun, moon, and stars, the earthquakes, the enormous swelling and roaring of the sea, the bloody wars and battles. Our Saviour in the Gospel and St. John in the Apocalypse give us to understand the impression these calamities will make on mankind, by saying that "men will sink away for fear, and call upon the mountains to fall upon them and cover them." How dreadful will be the destruction made by the army of Antichrist! How cruel and bloody his persecution, lasting for three years and a half! What degree of fortitude will therefore be requisite to support those that are faithful on so trying an occasion.

Who are those that will remain firm in their faith in those days of unheard-of tribulation? Who will not be conquered, but will fight the good battle of the Lord? They will be those especially who, in the course of their life, assisted regularly at Mass with fervor and devotion. We have seen how the early Christians prepared themselves for their severe trials, by assisting at, and partaking of, the sacred mysteries. They knew that it was only from the Lamb of God, sacrificed on the altar, that they could receive that heroic courage which was requisite to sacrifice all, even their own lives, for the sake of Him who sacrificed Himself upon their altars. In like manner Catholics who will live in the days of Antichrist and have heard Mass regularly, will be endowed with a strength supernatural to baffle all the efforts of the son of perdition and his infernal agents to make them apostatize and to pass over to his army.

It might be well for parents and pastors to begin to inculcate this lesson upon those who are committed to their care; for if we consider the general decay of religion which now prevails, if we see how little the practice of morality is attended to, how little even religion is thought of, we cannot help thinking that mankind has already made gigantic progress towards that apostasy, as St. Paul calls it, or towards that general defection from the faith and that degeneracy of morals which will take place before Antichrist, the great minister of Satan, appears. How swift indeed must be the decline of true faith, while free-thinking, religious indifferentism, infidelity, and godless education of the young grow at such a pace? While every one seems to accept as a fixed principle to believe nothing more than his reason comprehends or what coincides with his own private humor. What practice of morality can be expected from people who are immersed in worldly pleasures, or in pursuits of private interests, in the gratification of their shameful passion of lust; who never spend a thought about eternity, or scarce ever address their God and Creator in a short prayer? Is not this the general course of life of the present generation of mankind? Certainly, then, due care should be taken to prevent as many of the rising race as possible from being infected with this pestiferous corruption, and to prepare them to be enrolled in the list of the few elect of the approaching time. When a tide of irreligion and infidelity has broken in, and is seen to swell in volume day by day, what wonder if the period approach when God will bring all to the test, and try them as metal in the fiery furnace in order to discriminate between the good and the bad, and to separate the sound from the unsound grain? The few that will remain firm and staunch under all temptations and persecutions, will shine with great lustre in those days, when the bulk of mankind suffer themselves to be so far seduced as to go over to Antichrist, adore him as a god, and renounce their Creator, their religion, and their own conviction. Notwithstanding the great power of Antichrist, and his faculty of performing surprising wonders, the small body of the faithful will bear away the palm of victory by their constancy in maintaining the cause of God at the expense of their lives, and by their fortitude in not yielding to promises, threats, or torments. And thus the fruit of their perseverance will be to see their victory completed and the cause of religion fully vindicated by the just judgments of God upon the impious, when He will annihilate before their eyes that satanic man, Antichrist, with his associates, extirpate idolatry from the earth, and restore peace to the Church, so that it shall shine with greater lustre than in all preceding ages.

CHAPTER XXXVII.

WHY MASS IS CELEBRATED IN LATIN.

THE celebration of Mass and the administration of the sacraments in the Latin tongue form for some Protestants a subject of surprise, for others of complaint; as if there were something unnatural or wrong in the practice. Among Catholics it never excites either surprise or complaint; they never think themselves in the slightest degree aggrieved by it. If strangers to the Catholic religion think otherwise, their complaints proceed from ignorance.

When a Protestant goes to church he generally seems to consider the principal acts of religion to consist in *reading, praying,* or *preaching;* nay, he seems to attach most importance to the last office. He seems to look upon his clergyman merely as a *teacher* of morality, as one whose chief business is to read prayers in an audible tone for the people, so that all may join in. His character lacks that *sacredness* which arises from the sublime duty of offering sacrifice; preaching and praying are the two great acts of his ministry, the former of which any clever man without the help of ordination, may perform as well as he; and for the latter any good reader is equally capable. For a religion like this, which acknowledges nothing more sublime in its ministry, a foreign language, or an *unknown tongue,* as it is commonly called, would certainly not be very appropriate in public service; hence proceeds the error of judgment so common to Protestants when they conclude it is equally unfit for Catholic worship.

How different are such ideas from ours and from the truth! We venerate in our priests a character of a much higher order, and an office infinitely more exalted. We look upon them as the representatives and vicegerents of Jesus Christ, our great High Priest; as having power, by virtue of their ordination, to consecrate and offer sacrifice, and to administer sacraments; thus divinely commissioned, to become, as St. Paul expresses it in admirable terms, "the ministers of Christ, and dispensers of the mysteries of God."

The Catholic looks upon his priest as a *minister of Christ*, whereas the Protestant considers his preacher more as a *minister of the people*. When the Catholic priest stands at the altar, he stands there as a mediator between God and the people; he has an office to perform in which they have nothing to do *with* him, or for him, as *assistants* or *coadjutors;* in a word, he has a sacrifice to offer, which is an act that passes between God and himself alone, to complete which, or to render it more acceptable, no assistance of the people is *necessary*. He offers it indeed *for* the people, and in *company with them*, but not that they have any part in *offering* it in the strict sense of the word. For the character of a priest is essentially distinct and separate from that of a layman, and nothing marks this distinction so absolutely as the power of offering sacrifice, which is his exclusive right.

Taking, then, this view of the subject, can it *in itself* be a matter of any consequence at all what is the language in which the Almighty is addressed at the time? Cannot He who is the Author of all, equally understand any language? And if the priest understands the language in which he is addressing the Almighty what more is required? The words by which sacrifice is offered are addressed to God, not to the people, nor by the people, and if he who addresses them and he to whom they are addressed understand them, every useful object is attained, and nothing more can be wanting. This is the case in the Mass, and for this reason all the essential parts of the Mass—the Offertory, the Consecration, and the Communion—are performed in *secret* or in *silence*.

It is true that both prayers and instructions accompany

the essential parts of a sacrifice, and these are spoken aloud so that all may hear them; but the fruits and blessings of the Mass are not the consequence of these prayers, nor produced by them, but by the essential act of the sacrifice alone. In like manner the administration of the sacraments is properly performed in Latin, for though these also are *sometimes* accompanied by prayer and instruction, or ceremonies, which, when properly understood, may affect the minds and excite the devotion of the people, yet the effect is not produced by any of these means, but by the actions rightly performed and the words properly pronounced by the priest, as ordained by Jesus Christ. In both these instances of sacrifice and sacraments, the priest is performing the highest offices ever given to man to perform—offices totally and incommunicably peculiar to himself, to which an unchangeable and a dead language is expressly and justly assigned. If the Mass or the sacraments were nothing but a common prayer, read for the people, then perhaps the common language of each country would be the most proper to use; but then, also, would religion lose its chief character of Divinity, and the priesthood be stripped of the only character which distinguishes its members from the laity. We do not, therefore, blame the Protestants for using the common language of the people in their public prayers, for as they have neither sacrifice nor priest, they were only consistent in laying aside the language when they rejected the sacrifice and the priesthood. But on the other hand let them not object to us; for as we have still retained the sacrifice and the priesthood, there is no reason for rejecting the use of a language which is most convenient for our purpose.

Thus the complaints so common among Protestants about the use of the Latin language in the Mass are purely founded on a want of knowledge of our religion. Let them inform themselves upon this subject, and all difficulties will disappear at once. To Catholics it is a great consolation to reflect that, in this as in every other respect, the Church always adapts her discipline to the necessities of her flock, or to the dignity and order of her public service.

It has been said that the use of any language *in itself* was immaterial, but in its consequences, or in view of the commands of the Church, it is by no means immaterial. The Church has wisely ordered the Latin tongue only to be used in the Mass and in the administration of the sacraments, for several reasons.

I. Latin was the language used by St. Peter when he first said Mass at Rome. It was the language in which that Prince of the Apostles drew up the Liturgy which, together with the knowledge of the Gospel, he or his successors the Popes imparted to the different peoples of Italy, France, Belgium, Spain, Portugal, England, Ireland, and Scotland, Germany, Hungary, Poland.

II. From the time of the Apostles down, Latin has invariably been used at the altar through the western parts of Christendom, though their inhabitants very frequently did not understand the language. The Catholic Church, through an aversion to innovations, carefully continues to celebrate her Liturgy in that same tongue which apostolic men and saints have used for a similar purpose during more than eighteen centuries.

III. Unchangeable dogmas require an unchangeable language. The Catholic Church cannot change, because it is the Church of God, Who is unchangeable; consequently the language of the Church must also be unchangeable.

IV. Mass is said in Latin because a universal Church requires a universal language. The Catholic Church is the same in every clime, in every nation, and consequently its language must be always and everywhere the same, to secure uniformity in her service.

V. Variety of languages is a punishment, a consequence of sin; it was inflicted by God that the human race might be dispersed over the face of the earth. The holy Church, the immaculate Spouse of Jesus Christ, has been established for the express purpose of destroying sin and uniting all mankind; consequently she must everywhere speak the same language.

VI. It is a fact well known that the meaning of words is changed in the course of time by every-day usage. Words which once had a good meaning are now used in a vulgar or ludicrous sense. The Church, enlightened by the Holy Ghost, has chosen a language which is not liable to such changes. The sermons and instructions, and in short everything that is addressed directly to the people, are all in the language of the country; even the prayers of the Mass are translated in almost every Catholic prayer-book, so that there can be no disadvantage to the Catholic worshipper in the fact that Mass is celebrated in the Latin tongue; especially as the pastors of the Church are very careful to comply with the injunctions of the Council of Trent, to instruct their flocks on the nature of that great Sacrifice, and to explain to them in what manner they should accompany the officiating priest with prayers and devotions best adapted to every portion of the Mass. In the second place, faithful Catholics know well that the holy Sacrifice of the Mass is the self-same sacrifice that Jesus Christ offered to His Father on the Cross, because both the priest and the Victim are the same; their faith in the Real Presence is abundantly sufficient to enkindle devotion in their hearts, and to excite in their souls appropriate acts of adoration, thanksgiving, and repentance, though they may not understand the prayers which the priest is uttering. For this reason it is that the faithful, pressed by different wants, go to the adorable mysteries of the Mass, never thinking of the language in which they are celebrated. Some, moved by the force of calamities, hasten thither to lay their sorrows at the feet of Jesus. Others go to ask some grace and special mercy, knowing that the heavenly Father can refuse nothing to His Son. Many feel constrained to fly thither to proclaim their gratitude, and to pour forth the love of a thankful heart, knowing that there is nothing so worthy of being offered to God as the sacred Body and Blood of the eternal Victim. More press forward to give glory to God and to honor His saints, for in the celebration of these mysteries of love alone we can pay worthy homage to His adorable majesty, while we bear witness to our reverence for those who served them.

Lastly, men hasten to Mass on the wings of charity and compassion, for it is there that they can hope to obtain salvation for the living and rest for the dead. Thus to the thirsty pilgrims through the rocks of the desert do the fountains of water appear. Thus do the generation of those who seek justice receive benediction from the Lord and mercy from God their Saviour.

Pity for those who know not this heavenly sacrifice! What a misfortune to see one driven from this Eden, and yet to do nothing to obtain the favor of readmittance! How unhappy too are those Catholics who, though knowing it, by their unpardonable indifference deprive themselves of this exhaustless mine of inestimable riches!

CHAPTER XXXVIII.

THE HONORARY OF MASS.

In preceding chapters we have seen that the holy Sacrifice of the Mass is the most august, the most efficacious form of prayer, the most sublime act of worship that can be offered to God, and that the best time for prayer is during Mass. For this reason it has been always customary among Catholics to request the priest to offer up the holy sacrifice for some special intention, in order to obtain from God certain graces and favors.

Some offer a Mass to obtain from God the grace to overcome a certain vice, or to acquire a certain virtue. Others request the priest to offer up the holy Sacrifice for a son, or a brother, or a father, who is engaged in a dangerous expedition, or intent on gaining some laudable object.

Many request the priest to offer the Mass in thanksgiving for certain favors received; others again for a sick person, in order to obtain either a speedy recovery or the grace of a happy death. Others request him to offer up the Mass for the conversion of a neighbor, or a dear friend, or a relative.

Some years ago the Redemptorist Fathers gave a Mission at St. Stephen's Church, in New York. A young man of the parish, after attending a few sermons, resolved not to go any more, as he did not wish to go to confession. When his mother saw how careless he was to profit by the time of grace, she went to one of the Fathers giving the Mission to request him to offer up the holy Sacrifice of the Mass for the conversion of her son. The following night the young man fell dangerously ill; he suffered the most excruciating pains. Not wishing to die in the state of mortal sin, he begged his mother and sister to assist him in examining his conscience and preparing for a good confession. Whereupon the mother returned to the missionary, and with tears of joy related to him her son's remarkable conversion. He was truly contrite, made a good confession, suffered still for a few weeks, and after having confessed and received communion, recovered. He was exceedingly grateful for the mercy which the Lord had shown him, acknowledging that, had it not been for his sickness, he would not have gone to confession.

Not long ago the Redemptorists gave a Mission at Genevieve, near St. Louis. In order to escape attending the services, a young man left for St. Louis under pretext of transacting business in that city. His mother went to one of the Fathers asking him to offer up the holy Sacrifice of the Mass for her son. From that very moment the young man had no rest in St. Louis; he returned without delay to Genevieve, attended the Mission, and went to confession and communion.

Others ask the priest to offer up the Mass for the repose of the soul of a deceased friend or relative. And here it may be well to call attention to a custom sanctioned by the Church. It is customary to give an "honorary" to the priest on the occasion of a christening, or a marriage, or a funeral. It is also customary to give an *"honorary"* to the priest whenever he is requested to say Mass for a particular intention, whether for the living or for the dead. Custom has established that this honorary should amount to the sum required for the decent maintenance of a priest for *one* day. Now, whatever is given to the priest on the reception of the sacraments, or on the celebration of the Mass, is not given as *payment*. No one, therefore, should say to the priest, "How much does a Mass cost?" Mass is of infinite value. To buy or sell the holy things of God would be a grievous sin—the sin of simony. The sum is not given as *pay;* it is merely an offering given in obedience to the express command of the Church to support our pastors. It is also given to the priest as a slight return for the time and labor he has sacrificed.

The custom of giving an offering to the priest with the request to offer up the Mass, is one of the most ancient in the Church. We find it even in the Old Law. The Jews were obliged by the Law of God to bring offerings, part of which were consumed in sacrifice and part given to the priests. The Holy Scripture tells us that Judas Maccabæus sent a very large sum of money to the priests with the request that sacrifices might be offered up for those who died in battle. The early Christians were accustomed to bring offerings during the holy Sacrifice of the Mass, and one part of the Mass is on this account still called the *Offertory*. The fourth Council of Lateran says that "though the sacraments are given *freely*, nevertheless the faithful should be exhorted to give the customary offerings."

St. Epiphanjus, who lived about three hundred years after the death of our Lord, tells us that a certain Jewish Rabbi, who became a convert to the Church, gave, after his baptism, a large sum of money to the bishop who baptized him, with the request to offer up the holy Sacrifice for him. We find numerous examples of this kind in history. It is related, in the life of St. John the Almsgiver, who was patriarch of Alexandria in Egypt in the beginning of the seventh century, that a certain man brought him a large sum of money, with the request to offer up a Mass for his son, who had set out on a dangerous voyage.

St. Paul says "that he that ministers at the altar should live by the altar." This is certainly just and reasonable, for the priest cannot support himself by working at a trade or by entering into business. The Church forbids it, and the faithful would be scandalized. He must devote all his time —his whole life—to spiritual things, to the care of souls. In this country especially, where a young man living in the world has so many opportunities of growing rich, no one but a madman would ever become a priest for the purpose of making money; and indeed no one would anywhere become a priest except from the highest and holiest motive.

A person engaged in a lawsuit will willingly pay a lawyer or advocate to take his case in hand to obtain justice. A sick man sends for a physician and pays him liberally for his visits and advice. The priest is the spiritual advocate; he pleads men's cases with God, and obtains mercy and pardon. The priest is the physician of the soul; he devotes his energy, his faculties of mind and body; he sacrifices his health, his time, for the welfare of Christians. It is then most reasonable that they should make some return for his services.

CHAPTER XXXIX.

THE USE OF CEREMONIES.

THE word *Ceremony* is derived from the ancient word "*cerus*," which means *holy*. "Men cannot be collected in any name of religion," says St. Augustine, "unless the bond of certain signs, as if of visible sacraments, should unite them together;"* from which Duns Scotus infers that even under the law of nature there must have been ceremonies divinely instituted;† for though they are nothing in themselves they are yet acts of religion exteriorly manifested, by which the mind is excited to veneration of holy things, and elevated to heavenly objects; and by them piety is nourished, charity enkindled, faith increased, the worship of God is adorned, and religion maintained. The simple are thus instructed, and the true faithful kept distinct from false Christians. Christ Himself hardly ever performed a miracle without using some ceremony, as when He made damp clay, and stretched out His hand to touch, and wrote upon the ground. The body should pay its homage as well as the soul. External homage is the natural and necessary appendix to internal worship; for we are so constituted by nature that all the sentiments of our soul show themselves in the exterior, and become painted in the demeanor of the whole body; insomuch that it is scarcely possible to love God sincerely with all the heart, and not break forth in His praise, and manifest the interior sense of divine charity by external signs.

Why do men love ceremony in religion? Because they wish to enjoy life in all the faculties and divisions of their

---

* Contr. Faustum, Lib. xix., c. xi.   † In Lib. iv., Leut. Dist. l. 9. 7.

nature. To live is to be happy; and the highest life is that which is spiritual and divine. Therefore we desire that in this life all our perceptions should participate in, and consequently that our senses, as well as our reason, should be excited by, a divine object. Even the disposition of body in relation to things external, resulting from a habit of devotion, instead of being a scandal to a profound thinker, may only remind him of what Malebranche says, " that everything which passes mechanically within us is worthy of the wisdom of our Maker." Besides, man being constituted of a body and a soul, it is just that the body, with its various capabilities, which are so many gifts of God, should come forward on the side of religion, especially as it is the nature of man to need external assistance to enable him to rise to the meditation of divine things.

Internal piety, therefore, requires to be excited and nourished by ceremonies, or certain sensible signs.

Moreover, every man ought to be religious and pious, not only so as to be conscious within himself that he worships God, but also to the extent of promoting the piety and instruction of his fellow-men, especially of those who are entrusted to his care; and this cannot be done, unless we profess by some external sign the intimate sense of religion with which we are animated.

In the ceremonial and discipline of the Church there is no part without its use. That which might seem the most trifling has its proper object, and serves in some way or other to promote habits of humility, order, patience, recollection, and religion, so as to build up the Catholic character. Hence the Fathers of the Council of Trent pronounce an anathema against all who should say that the received and approved rites of the Catholic Church may be despised or omitted "*ad libitum*," by the priests, or that they may be changed by any pastor of the churches.* A most important

---

* Sess. vii., Can. 13.

and incalculably beneficial sentence, which saves Catholic piety from being at the mercy of weak, ignorant, though perhaps well-meaning men, who, in proportion to their weakness and ignorance, are generally vain of being reformers or modifiers of ancient things.

These approved ceremonies of the Church are called by Hugo de St. Victor Sacraments of Devotion. He divides them into three classes—the first consisting in things, such as the aspersion of water, the reception of ashes, the blessing of palms and tapers; the second in actions, as the sign of the cross, the insufflations, the extension of hands, genuflexions; and the third in words, as the invocation of the Blessed Trinity, and that of *Deus in adjutorium*, for words themselves are sometimes sacraments.* There would be no end to following theologians in remarking all the uses of these external rites in imprinting the mysteries of our faith on the understanding. They show that, from the exorcisms and insufflations used in baptism, it was easier to understand than the unlearned would have found it from the Scriptures, that children are born under the yoke of the demon and infected with original sin; that, in like manner, the ashes strewed on the heads of men at the beginning of Lent teach them in a most forcible manner the vanity of all earthly things, and that in Holy Week the solemn ceremonies of the Church recall to and imprint on their minds a knowledge of the mysteries of human redemption. Certain it is that the Catholic ceremonies, besides answering these ends, conduce in all ages to the defence of the faith against innovators.

The Church, however, has not only ordained her ceremonies with a view to aid the understanding of the unlearned, but she also presents these rites to the affection and understanding of the instructed people. Can one suppose that no permanent moral change would be wrought in the mind by the mere act of slowly and deliberately tracing the sign of

---

* Erudit. Theol. de Sacram. Lib. ii. pars ix. 1.

the Cross on the forehead, on the lips, and on the heart, when the Gospel is announced in the divine mysteries? Can we suppose that the man accustomed to this practice is as likely to blush at the Cross in society, and to show vile submission to worldly respect, as another who knows of no such practice?

At the end of each lesson in the choral office the reader turns to the altar, saying, "*Tu autem, Domine, miserere nobis;*" because, as holy writers say, even that act of reading cannot be performed without some fault, since, if he read well, the mind is tempted with elation, and if ill, confusion follows; therefore he who reads stands always in need of the mercy of God, lest a work in itself good should be either corrupted by pride or rendered ineffectual by false shame. Can it be thought that to one instructed in this meaning the mere ceremony does not incline him to humility, and warn him to beware how he hears as well as reads the divine word?

The solemnity of the ritual itself has been known to produce permanent conversion. "Brother Theodoric, our monk," says Cæsar of Heisterbach, "as he often told me, when a youth in the world, came merely to visit a certain novice who was his relation, without any idea of being converted. It happened that a certain monk was buried on the same day, and when the community, having said the antiphon *Clementissime Domine,* proceeded then round the grave with great humility, imploring pardon, saying, '*Domine miserere super peccatore,*' he was so struck and excited that he who before had resisted all the exhortations of the Abbot Gerrard now sought with many prayers to be received to conversion. Such a little matter sufficed to accomplish so great a work."*

After King Clovis had been converted to the faith, and initiated by the holy Bishop Remigius in the truth necessary to be known, this prince went to the church to receive the holy sacrament of baptism. The road between the royal

---

* L. c. 21.

palace and the church was superbly adorned, shaded by hangings suspended from above; the walls of the houses were draped with costly silks; the church in which the king was to be baptized was decked out in all its splendor, and in it a sumptuous baptistery was erected, while the air was laden with delicious perfumes. The solemn procession was headed by the whole body of the clergy, one of them bearing the Book of the Holy Gospels. It was preceded by the Cross and a great number of lighted torches, and all implored in melodious tones the help of God and His saints, in the usual prayers of the Church. The king followed, being led on by the hand of the saintly bishop. The queen came next, and in her train an innumerable crowd. Now when the king saw the long line of sacred ministers, when he heard their hallowed chants, and witnessed the devout splendor and magnificence of the function, he was inwardly moved, and filled with such joy and consolation that, turning round to the prelate, he asked whether perhaps this were the kingdom of God which had been promised to him should he embrace the faith? "No, sire," replied St. Remigius, "this is not the kingdom of God I promised you, but the way that leads thereto."* From this we may learn the powerful influence which the sacred ceremonies connected with God's worship can exert over our minds, since they availed to soften the heart of the fierce conqueror, accustomed to live amid regal splendor, and to make him think that he was in heaven, when only on the path to the heavenly kingdom.

"Were I to enter the Catholic Church now," says a Protestant writer of the last century, "it would be apt to put me in mind of what St. John tells us he saw once in a vision: 'Another angel came and stood at the altar, having a golden censer; and there was given unto him much incense, that he should offer it with the prayers of the saints upon the golden altar which was before the throne of God.

---

* In Vita S. Remig. Apud Surium, 13, Jan.

And the smoke of the incense with the prayers of the saints ascended up before God out of the angel's hand.' These lighted altars made me naturally think of what the good old Simeon said of Christ, 'A light to enlighten the Gentiles, and the glory of thy people Israel.'"

Similar are the sentiments expressed by the celebrated Lavater, on finding himself in a Catholic Church. "He does not know thee, O Jesus Christ, who dishonors even Thy shadow; I honor all things, where I find the intention of honoring Thee. I will love them for Thy sake. I will love them provided I find the least thing which makes me remember Thee. What then do I behold here? What do I hear in this place? Does nothing under these majestic vaults speak to me of Thee? This cross, the golden image, is it not made for Thy honor? The censer which waves round the priest, the *gloria* sung in choirs, the peaceful light of the perpetual lamp, these lighted tapers—all is done for Thee! Why is the Host elevated if it be not to honor Thee, O Jesus Christ, who art dead for love of us, because it is no more bread, it is Thy Body; the believing Church bends the knee. It is in Thy honor alone that these children, early instructed, make the sign of the Cross, that their tongues sing Thy praise, and that they strike their breasts thrice with their little hands. It is for love of Thee, O Jesus Christ, that one kisses the spot which bears Thy adorable Blood; for Thee the child who serves sounds the little bell, and for Thee he does all that he does. The riches collected from distant countries, the magnificence of chasubles—all that has relation to Thee. Why are the walls and the high altar of marble clothed with verdant tapestry on the day of the Blessed Sacrament? For whom do they make a road of flowers? For whom are these banners embroidered? When the *Ave Maria* sounds, is it not all for Thee? Matins, vespers, prime, and none, are they not consecrated to Thee? These bells within a thousand towers, do they not bear Thy image, cast in the very mould? Is it not for Thee that they send forth their solemn tone? Is it not under Thy protection, O Jesus Christ, that every man places himself who loves solitude, chastity, and poverty? Without Thee the orders of St. Benedict and of St. Bernard would not have been founded. The cloister, the tonsure, the breviary, and the chaplet render testimony of Thee. O delightful rapture, O Jesus Christ, for Thy disciple to trace the marks of Thy finger where the eyes of the world see them not! O joy ineffable, for souls devoted to Thee to behold in caves and in rocks, in every crucifix placed upon the hills and on the highways, Thy seal and that of Thy love! Who will not rejoice in the honors of which Thou art the object and the soul? Who will not shed tears in hearing the words, 'Jesus Christ be praised?' O the hypocrite who knows that name and answers not with joy, 'Amen;' who says not with an intense transport, 'Jesus be blessed for eternity! for eternity!'" *

It is thus that many of those who have distinguished themselves by their hostility to the "*religion of our fathers,*" have admitted that that religion and its rites were venerable. Many of those who have been foremost in vilifying its principles, or in misrepresenting its tenets, have, in the midst of their bigoted bitterness, been compelled to acknowledge that its ceremonies were splendid and impressive. One may often see revilers of this stamp bowing during the celebration of the Mass, and owning that in the forms before them there was something indescribably awful—something in the objects around them that proclaimed the Presence of the Deity— something that was calculated to awaken the inattentive, animate the lukewarm, and shed even over the spirit of the irreligious a feeling of sacred reverence, leading to penitence and to piety. Such have been the admissions of those who had not "faith in them"—the confessions of men who merely gazed upon externals, and looked not beyond the

---

* Empfindungen eines Protestanten in einer Katholischen Kirche.

surface. They knew not that the ceremonies which they witnessed were so many high and holy symbols, portraying to the eyes of the faithful the progress, the precepts, the struggles, and the sufferings of Him who was offered for the transgressions of mankind. They knew not that *these* constituted the parts, and the aggregate of a sacrifice, enjoined from the beginning as a sacrifice, that to the true children of Christianity is at once a sign of remembrance, and an instrument of propitiation.

It is the Catholic, and he only, who beholds these sacred forms in their true light, who joins rightly in those ceremonies, and derives a spiritual advantage from their daily celebration. How necessary is it then that we be thoroughly acquainted with their meaning, with their general tendency, and with each and all of the wonderful incidents which they represent? All, at least all those who are capable of reading, should endeavor to acquire this most interesting and most salutary information. For if the various ceremonies of the Mass are well understood, they will greatly incite and foster reverence and the spirit of devotion at the holy Sacrifice; they will inflame the hearts of the faithful with greater love for this inexhaustible treasure of grace, and make them hear Mass in the proper spirit and to the greatest advantage of their souls. Culpable ignorance, then, on this point, amounts to a crime. Reverence and love for our dear Saviour will avoid the reproach of this crime. Reverence and love, too, are our best instructors at Mass, because where they are, not a single movement of the Liturgy can ever be lost, and not a single one will pass without imparting instruction. The Liturgy is the manner which Jesus adopts for the purpose of renewing the great Expiation; every variation and every shadow of variation has a significance quite its own.

Reverence and love will take pains, therefore, to examine and understand them in every detail, that not a movement, a word, a whisper, of our dear Lord be lost upon us during the whole time of the holy Sacrifice. From this we learn that we should look well to the explanations which teach with authority the mystic meanings attached to the various parts and movements of the Mass; and that they ought to become as much a part of our minds as the meanings which spring up when we hear a sentence spoken or see it written down, or when we look at a picture of some scene which we know well.

We shall not have placed ourselves in a condition perfectly to gather the riches of grace spread at the foot of our unbloody Calvary, unless we have accomplished this small task. Deep reverence and true love will leave nothing undone to learn the lesson well. Again, let us repeat, each movement of the Mass ought to awaken thoughts, like spoken language, in the soul of the "child of benediction."

Wherever there are love and reverence, we may feel assured, not only of a perfect acquaintance with the symbolism of the holy rites and the holy vestments, but of that profound attention and devotion which the august Sacrifice should demand and inspire.

The heart and mind will be united with every proceeding about the altar, will be ever warm and watchful, so that nothing shall be presented to God without the companionship of the rational affection and worship of the adorer. Attending at Mass, we shall ever know what we do, and ever do it as we know; and thus nothing will be lost to us of the mighty favors there to be obtained. Our minds will become the form of that wonderful work of God for man, and we shall assist every day with a renewed and increased feeling of gratitude and awe, because every day is an increased wonder in the increasing number of countless miracles performed before our eyes, for our salvation and the salvation of fallen man generally.

The acquaintance with the meanings of the various movements and proceedings of Mass, will make it easy for us to follow the various stages of the Passion in a spirit of love, reverence, gratitude, and sorrow, which is, no doubt, the best way to hear Mass. At every stage our hearts will overflow with affectionate recognition of the love of Jesus, and at every stage we can whisper a prayer for the special objects of our desire on the occasion. Nothing so concentrates the powers of the soul as always to have some special objects to be obtained by the holy Sacrifice. We know it is infinite in value, and therefore impetrates more than a million of worlds could ever need; and we know, moreover, that as the harvest-time is given to the reaper's sickle, the abundance is given here to be gathered by the sickle of devotion. The Passion and Death of Jesus have placed and continue to place, the luxuriant growth at our command; we need only the energy of grace and the sickle of holy prayer, to depart filled with the good things of God's husbandry. We are poor, only because we will not be rich; weak, only because we will not be strong; hungry and thirsty, because we seek fountains which God has not made to flow, and forget where the rod of His wisdom and power has left us "the rock which is Christ."

CHAPTER XL.

THE USE OF SACRED VESTMENTS.

In all public functions of his office, the priest has certain appointed robes or vestments to wear, particularly when he offers the holy Sacrifice of the Mass.

The use of special dresses for public functionaries is congenial to the very nature of man, and is adopted alike by the most savage and civilized nations. God Himself condescended to deliver to Moses minute instructions concerning the vestments which each Priest or Levite in the Old Law should wear. In the Christian dispensation, the Church has done the same.

The ordinary garment of the priest, which he ought at all times to wear, is the cassock, over which he puts others when performing his public duties. The cassock is common to all orders of the clergy, varying only in color, according to the dignity of the wearer. Priests wear black; prelates and bishops, purple; cardinals, scarlet; and the Pope, white.

Before robing himself in the sacerdotal vestments, the priest, clad in his cassock, washes the tips of his fingers. It has been the invariable custom of all times and of all nations, for the ministers of the altar to wash their hands previous to offering sacrifice. The Old Law expressly commanded this observance.[*]

Though respect for the decorum of religion alone would inspire such a practice, still the Church attaches a spiritual signification to it, and studies by the symbol of exterior ablu-

---

[*] Exod. xxx. 18–20

tion to convey to her ministers instructions to cleanse the heart by an interior purity, which she teaches them to solicit in a prayer particularly adapted to the purpose: "Grant," exclaims the priest, while washing his fingers—"to my hands, O Lord, a virtue that shall cleanse away every stain, so that I may be able to serve Thee without impurity of body and soul."

The priest first puts on the *Amice,* a small piece of white linen, which being drawn over the head, is suffered to rest on the shoulders. The meaning of this is sufficiently explained by the prayer he recites at the time: "Put, O Lord, on my head the *helmet* of salvation, to repel all the assaults of the devil."

The *Alb* comes next, a white garment that covers the priest all over, and represents the purity and innocence which ought to accompany him at the altar, also expressed by the prayer: "Cleanse, O Lord, my heart, that being made *white* by the Blood of the Lamb, I may possess eternal joys." The alb is fastened by a *cord,* to remind us of the necessity of girding our loins with the virtue of purity, as is expressed in the prayer which is said at the time, in imitation of what our Saviour said, as recorded in Luke xiv. 35. Then the *Maniple* is placed on the left arm. Its ancient service is by no means forgotten in the ornaments which decorate it: for the prayer which accompanies the action is a pious and consoling admonition to the priest, that he should bear the evils of this life, and endure the toils and anxious labors of his ministry with the anticipation of a certain and eternal recompense. It is on this account that the Church directs her ministers to recite the following prayer as they assume this vestment: "O Lord, may I be found worthy to bear the maniple of sorrow and affliction, that I may reap with joy the reward of my labors."

The priest next puts the *Stole* on his neck, and crossing it on his breast, fastens it by the girdle. The stole is the emblem of authority, is worn by the bishop hanging straight down in front; by the priest, crossed on the breast; and by the deacon, upon one shoulder only, like a soldier's cross-belt. The sub-deacon does not wear it at all. These are all signs of the different degrees of authority attached to the different degrees of Holy Orders. The prayer used while putting it on expresses a desire that we may be clothed with the stole of immortality, which had been lost by the transgression of our first parents.

The *Chasuble* is the outer vestment worn by the priest, generally richly ornamented and embroidered, with a large cross in front or on the back, to signify that the priest should also bear his cross in imitation of Christ; while putting it on he prays that he may so bear the sweet yoke of Christ as to merit his grace. These are the vestments which the priest wears when he proceeds to the altar to say Mass.

At solemn High Mass, the outer vestment of the deacon and sub-deacon is the *Dalmatic*. During this solemn function also, the sub-deacon, for a portion of the ceremony, has his arms and shoulders muffled with a species of scarf of an oblong shape, which is usually composed of the same material as the vestments, and is called a *veil*.

In primitive times, the number of those who partook of the Blessed Sacrament every Sunday, together with the priest at the holy Sacrifice, was very great, and consequently, the *paten* or sacred disk, from which the Sacramental species used to be distributed, was so large in its dimensions, that convenience required it to be moved from the altar as soon as the oblation had been made, and not brought back until the period arrived for giving the communion to the people.

Instead of depositing the paten upon either of those tables which stand near the altar, or carrying it to the sacristy, the Roman ritual considered it more decorous and appropriate to consign it to the sub-deacon, who, by holding it in an elevated position, might thus announce to the assembly that the period for receiving the Blessed Sacrament would very soon approach, and silently admonish them to pray with greater fervor.

The custom of enveloping the sub-deacon with a veil during the time he holds the paten was suggested to the Church by the ancient law, which prohibited the Levites from touching the consecrated vessels, or bearing them about uncovered. "Take," said the Lord to Moses, "the sons of Caath from the midst of the Levites. And when Aaron and his sons have wrapped up the sanctuary, and the vessels thereof, then shall the sons of Caath enter in, to carry the things wrapped up, and they shall not touch the vessels of the sanctuary, lest they die."* To exhibit an equal reverence towards those instruments dedicated to the service of her altars and used in the sacrifice of the new and better covenant, the Church directs the sub-deacon, officiating at solemn High Mass, to hold the paten enfolded in a veil, and prescribes to each inferior member employed about the sanctuary, as well as to every layman, not to touch any of her vessels. Moreover, she directs that the officiating priest who gives benediction to the people with the Blessed Sacrament, should also have his hands, out of reverence to It, enveloped with the veil which he wears on the occasion, in such a manner that they do not touch the monstrance or vessel in which it is enclosed.

The *Cope* resembles in its shape a flowing and ample cloak. It is open in the front, and fastens on the breast by clasps. To the part which corresponds with the shoulders of the wearer is attached a piece of the same material, in form like the segment of a circle, resembling a hood, which is usually adorned with lace and fringe.

The prototype of our cope is found among the garments of the ancient Romans; like the chasuble, it was a mantle deriving its origin from the *pœnula*, which it perfectly re-

---

* Num. iv. 2–15.

sembled, with this variation: that while the *pænula* encircled the entire person, the cope was open in the front, and adapted to defend its wearer from the severities of the season, the variations of the weather, and from rain, by the addition of a cowl or hood. Necessity, not splendor, introduced this robe amongst the sacred vestments, and the Latin *Pluviale*, or rain-cloak, the term by which it still continues to be designated, will immediately suggest its primitive use to every learned reader. Its appropriateness as a sacerdotal garment may be referred to that epoch when the Popes were accustomed to assemble the people during the penitential seasons of the year at some particular church, which had been previously appointed for that purpose, and thence proceed with them in solemn procession and on foot to some one or other of the more celebrated basilican churches of Rome, to hold what was called a station. To protect the person of the Pontiff from the rain that might overtake the procession on its way, the *pluviale*, or cope, was on such occasions assumed by him at the commencement of the ceremony. It has been employed at the altar ever since, and is worn by bishops and priests on different occasions, but particularly at vespers.

The *Surplice* is that white linen garment which is worn, not by the priest only, but is permitted to be assumed by the lowest minister who officiates at the celebration of divine service. It represents the robe of innocence, purity, and righteousness, that our divine Redeemer purchased for the human race by the price of His glorious atonement, and with which He arrays the soul of the regenerated or repentant sinner, and effaces man's iniquities, figured by the skins of animals; since it was in garments formed from such materials that fallen Adam, after being chased from Paradise, was covered.

The surplice is very appropriately assigned to the Acolytes, or youths, who answer and attend upon the priest at Mass;

for "Samuel ministered before the face of the Lord, being a child, girded with a linen ephod." *

In her vestments the Church employs five different colors. On the feasts of our Lord, of the Blessed Virgin Mary, of the angels, and of those amongst the saints who were not martyrs, she makes use of white, not only to signify the stainless purity of the Lamb and of His Virgin Mother, but to figure that "Great multitude, which no man could number, of all nations, and tribes, and peoples, and tongues, standing before the throne, and in sight of the Lamb, clothed with white robes." † On the feasts of Pentecost, of the Invention and Exaltation of the Cross, of the Apostles and Martyrs, she uses red, to typify those fiery tongues that rested on the heads of the Apostles, when the Holy Ghost descended visibly among them; and in reference to the effusion of blood by Christ and his faithful followers. On the most of the Sundays the vestments are green. Purple is the color assigned for the penitential times of Advent and of Lent, for the Ember days, and for the several vigils throughout the year; whilst black is reserved for the office of Good Friday and for Masses of the dead.

When the priest proceeds to the altar, he is the representative of Christ. To make this representation still more complete, each particular vestment reminds us of something which our dear Saviour bore at the time of His Passion. The *Amice* reminds us of the handkerchief with which our Lord was blindfolded. The *Alb* is literally the *white* garment with which Herod clothed Him in mockery. In the *Girdle* we see the cord by which our Saviour was bound to the pillar when He was scourged. The *Maniple*, by its weight on the arm, represents the weight of our sins which our Saviour bore; and the *Stole*, being put like a yoke on the shoulders, calls to our remembrance the obedience and humility to which He submitted for the expiation of those

---

* 1 Kings ii. 18. † Apoc. vii. 9.

sins. The *Chasuble*, with the Cross on the back, very aptly expresses the purple garment and the carriage of His Cross.

Thus adorned, the priest approaches the altar, as our dear Saviour ascended Mount Calvary, to offer the very same sacrifice, but in an unbloody manner.

CHAPTER XLI.

LOW MASS.

THE unbloody Sacrifice of the New Law has been known under a variety of names at the several periods of the Christian era. For more than fourteen hundred years, however, it has been called almost exclusively by the title Mass. The Latin word *Missa*, is a contraction of *Missio*, which signifies a dismissal or permission to depart as soon as the sacrifice is completed. Such abbreviations are not unusual with profane as well as ecclesiastical writers.

The naming the holy Eucharistic Sacrifice by the term Mass or dismissal, arose originally from a ceremony which in the earliest ages of the Church was observed on two several occasions, and still continues to be practised once during its celebration.

Immediately after the reading of the Gospel, and the delivery of the sermon by the Bishop, the Deacon turned to the assembly, and in an elevated tone of voice admonished the different persons who composed it, that the initiated only might remain, and consequently the unbaptized and unbelieving were required to depart.

The formula employed on this occasion was to the following effect: "The Catechumens are dismissed, the faithful shall remain." Hence it was, that the portion of the Divine service which preceded the Creed and Offertory was denominated the "Mass of the Catechumens," since those who were distinguished by such an appellation were dismissed from the church, and not permitted to assist at the Sacrifice which was then beginning.

As soon as the Eucharistic Sacrifice was terminated, the

Deacon proclaimed to the faithful assembled that they might withdraw. This he announced by a form of speech which to the present day remains in use—*Ite Missa est:* "Go, leave is given to depart;" hence arose, in the earliest ages amongst our venerable predecessors in the faith, a custom of denominating the second part of the divine service "the Mass of the faithful." From this we gather that the whole of the Liturgy or public service was by the ancients comprehended under two general divisions, to each of which they assigned a different appellation. The first was termed the Mass of the Catechumens—"*Missa Catechumenorum;*" the second, the Mass of the faithful—"*Missa Fidelium.*" In order to express these two portions of the Liturgy in the language of the present time, we should denominate the first, ante-communion service; the other, the communion service. When the discipline of the secret fell into disuse, and public penance was abolished, an exclusion from the sacred mysteries, and consequently the distinction between the Mass of the catechumens and the Mass of the faithful, ceased to be observed; and the entire form of prayer employed in offering up the Eucharistic Sacrifice, was denominated by the exclusive term Mass, as at present.*

There are two forms which the Church employs for offering up the Eucharistic Sacrifice; one called *High Mass*, the other *Low Mass*. Both are the same in essence, and differ in the ceremonies only, which are more numerous and solemn in the celebration of High than in that of Low Mass. By Solemn High Mass is signified the Mass at which a Deacon and Sub-deacon minister.

When the priest goes to say Mass, he first clothes himself in the sacred garments of his office. They have each of

---

* The Catechumens were such as had abandoned the Synagogue, or passed over from Gentilism to become Christians, and, as their names imply, were under a course of catechetical instruction, previous to their being admitted to the sacrament of Baptism.

them particular significations, and are emblems of particular virtues; but altogether they serve to hide the littleness of man, and to make him forget himself while clothed in the robes of a superior character, and to gain the respect of the people, who no longer, on that occasion, regard what he is, as a man, but lose sight of the individual, who is lost in the character of Jesus Christ, which he represents. For, let a priest be either edifying or not, amiable or otherwise in his private character, that should all be forgotten at the moment of saying Mass—he is then a priest of the Most High, even if an unworthy one, a representative of Jesus Christ, Who has said to his minister: "He that despises you, despises Me;" for it is to God, not to the minister, that is referred all the honor paid the man.

The entry of the priest into the sacristy to put on the sacred vestments, represents the descent of the Son of God into the sacred womb of the Blessed Virgin Mary, where He clothed Himself with our human nature in order thus to become a perpetual Victim upon our altars.

The priest, thus vested, leaves the sacristy and goes to the altar to celebrate Mass. This reminds us of Jesus Christ leaving the sacristy of His Mother's womb on Christmas Day to make His Introit or entrance into the world.

The priest, coming down from the altar to commence Mass at the foot of the altar, represents Jesus Christ going to Mount Olivet to commence His Passion.

When the priest begins Mass, he says with the server some prayers at the foot of the altar, during which he bows very profoundly. This signifies Our Lord entering upon His Passion in the Garden of Gethsemani, where He sweat blood and prayed prostrate on the ground. These prayers of the priest are a kind of preparation for Mass. He begins by saying: "*In nomine Patris, et Filii, et Spiritus Sancti*— In the name of the Father, and of the Son, and of the Holy Ghost." It is as much as to say: "I act now by the authority of God the Father, whose priest I am; and in the name of the Son, in Whose place I am priest; and of God the Holy Ghost, by Whom I am priest;" or, "I offer this Sacrifice in the name of the Father, to Whom I offer it; and of the Son, Whom I offer; and of the Holy Ghost, by Whom I offer it."

Then he says the forty-second psalm, expressive of humble trust in God, which is followed by the *Confiteor* and the ordinary prayers accompanying it. The reciting of the *Confiteor* signifies that Our Lord has vouchsafed to charge Himself with our sins, and to atone for them, and that He would appear a sinner and be considered as such, in order that we might become just and holy.

While reciting the *Confiteor*, the priest, with his hands joined, lowly bows his head, to express his confusion for his sinfulness, and to imitate the humble "Publican who would not so much as lift up his eyes towards heaven." *

At the words "through my fault," he strikes his breast. This manner of expressing grief for sin is both ancient and scriptural. The Publican mentioned in the Gospel struck his breast, saying: "O God, be merciful to me a sinner;" and at the Crucifixion the multitude that saw the things that were done, returned striking their breasts.† The striking of the breast is meant to signify, not only that we are indignant with this bosom of ours, which has so often rebelled against Heaven; but our desire that it may be bruised and softened by compunction, and that the stony heart may be exchanged for one of flesh.‡ In the Old as well as in the New Law, the confession of sins has invariably preceded sacrifice. Under the Mosaic dispensation, before the High Priest offered the emissary goat, he was directed "to confess all the iniquities of the children of Israel, and all their offences and sins."§ The priest finishes the prayers at the foot of the altar, by saying, "*Dominus vobiscum.*"

These words "*Dominus vobiscum* — The Lord be with

---

* Luke xviii. 13.   † Luke xxiii. 48.   ‡ Ezechiel xi. 19.   § Levit. xvi. 21.

you"—are found in several passages of the Old Testament. Booz said to the reapers: The Lord be with you. And they answered him: The Lord bless thee.* Such, too, was the salutation of the Angel Gabriel to the Blessed Virgin Mary.† The response—"And with thy spirit"—is furnished by the words of St. Paul to Timothy: The Lord Jesus Christ be with thy spirit.‡ All this the priest says with his head partially inclined to the altar, as though still preserving the character of a penitent. At length he stands erect and says, "Let us pray," after which he ascends the steps of the altar, saying in a low voice a short prayer to be delivered from all his sins, and to obtain grace to enter the Holy of Holies with right dispositions. He then prays, by the merits of those saints whose relics are here deposited in the altar, and of all the saints, that God would be pleased to pardon all his sins, and at the same time kisses the altar out of respect and affection towards that spot on which Jesus Christ is daily immolated; for we may well exclaim with St. Optatus Milevitanus, who lived about the year 308, "What is the altar but the seat of the Body and Blood of Christ?"

The priest is directed to kiss that part of the altar whereon is placed the stone under which it is usual to deposit the relics of some saint or martyr. Thus there is furnished another testimouial of reverence to our Divine Redeemer, through the respect which is exhibited towards the earthly remains of those who have borne witness to His precepts by their virtues, or sealed the profession of His doctrines with their blood. In the earliest ages of the Church the holy Sacrifice of the Mass used to be offered on the tombs of the martyrs; whence arose the custom of enclosing a portion of their relics in the altar-stone. It is but becoming that beneath our earthly altars should repose the relics of the saints, since St. John remarks of them, in his vision of the heavenly sacrifice, "I saw under the altar the souls of them

---

* Ruth ii. 4.   † Luke i. 28.   ‡ 2 Tim. iv. 22.

that were slain for the word of God, and for the testimony which they held." *

This part reminds us also of the seizure of Our Lord by the Jewish multitude, into whose hands He was betrayed by the perfidious kiss and cruel treachery of Judas.

And now begins what may be called the preliminary part of the Mass, which answers to the time when Our Lord was interrogated about His doctrine before the tribunals of Caiphas and Pilate; it lasts till the end of the Creed.

After saying the short prayer, on first coming to the middle of the altar, the priest goes to the book at his right hand, and making the sign of the Cross, reads the Introit, or Entrance upon Mass, that is, some short verses from Holy Scripture. The reciting of the Introit by the priest, or the singing thereof by the choir, at High Mass, represents the ancient patriarchs who expected the coming of the Messiah, and who begged God to send Him in these words: "Send, O Lord, the Lamb, the Governor of the earth." † The priest and the choir also repeat the Introit to mark the holy impatience the just of the Old Law were in, and the frequent prayers they made to God to send the Redeemer.

After reading the Introit, the priest returns to the middle of the altar to recite the *"Kyrie eleison*—Lord, have mercy on us," which represents the miserable state that men were in before the coming of the Redeemer.

"*Kyrie eleison*" are two Greek words, which signify " Lord, have mercy." Such a petition is most appropriately recited at the commencement of the tremendous mysteries. Then it is that we should supplicate the mercies of Heaven in cries like those of the blind man of Jericho; ‡ with the perseverance of the Canaanean mother; § and as humbly as the ten lepers. ‖ "*Kyrie eleison*" is repeated three times in honor of God the Father; "*Christe eleison*" three times in

---

* Apoc. vi. 9. † Isaias lxiv. 1.
‡ Matt. ix. 27. § Matt. xv. 22. ‖ Luke xvii. 13.

honor of God the Son; and "*Kyrie eleison*" three times in honor of God the Holy Ghost. Our dear Saviour said the *Kyrie* when lying in the crib, and on other occasions, when He prayed with tears for our salvation. Immediately after the *Kyrie* follows the "*Gloria in excelsis.*"

This has been denominated the "Angelic Hymn," because it commences with the words chanted by angelic voices in the midnight air at the birth of our Divine Redeemer, which was announced to the shepherds by an angel zoned in light, with whom "there was a multitude of the heavenly army, praising God, and saying, Glory be to God in the Highest, and on earth peace to men of good will." * This Canticle, as the Fathers of the fourth Council of Toledo, held in the year 633, observed, consists of the strain sung by the multitude of the heavenly army, and of pious aspirations composed by the pastors of the Church.

In commencing this hymn, so beautiful for its devout sentiments, and venerable for its antiquity, the priest stretches out and elevates his hands, and turns his eyes towards heaven. A pious sensibility naturally suggests such gestures. They exhibit in a feeling manner those profound inward emotions, and that religious elevation of the soul experienced by the fervent Christian, and testify that whilst his lips are resounding with those angel notes of praise— Glory be to God on High—they echo but the accents of a heart that sighs to embrace and retain the joys of Heaven for all eternity. Glory to the Divine Wisdom, which by this wonderful sacrifice has devised a daily means of satisfying His justice, and at the same time of delivering man from the death he had deserved; Glory to the Divine Power, destroying, by so signal a Victim, the powers of hell; Glory to the Divine Love, which induced God to become a little Child, poor and lowly, to live a hard life, and to die a cruel death, and become the food of men in the Blessed Eucharist,

---

* Luke ii. 13, 14.

in order to show them the love He bears them, and to gain their love in return.

The inclinations of the head at the name of God manifest our worship of God made man for our redemption. At the conclusion the priest makes the sign of the Cross, according to the custom of the ancient Christians, who sanctified all their principal actions by calling to their minds the sacrifice of Christ's atonement by this holy symbol. The "*Gloria in excelsis*" being a canticle of gladness, is omitted at Masses said in black for the dead, and also during the penitential seasons of Lent and Advent, unless the Mass be of some saint.

After the "*Gloria*" the priest bows down before the altar, because he who wishes to communicate a benediction unto others must first of all, by his humility, incline Heaven to bestow the blessing he desires to impart. He kisses the altar, because it is the throne of Jesus; he turns round towards the congregation, because he speaks a holy greeting in the words "*Dominus vobiscum;*" and he holds his arms extended, to signify, by such a natural expression of sincere and warm affection, that he is acting in the name of Jesus, the loving Father of His people, who was hanging on the Cross with outstretched arms, in token of His readiness to receive all sinners who are truly penitent in His arms, and press them to His Heart in remembrance of His undying love for them. After the priest has said "*Dominus vobiscum*," the server, in the name of the people, answers, "*Et cum spiritu tuo*," a salutation and response which occur very often during Mass. The Church intends, by this frequent interchange of holy affections between the priest and the people, to excite devotion, and teach us how we should desire above all things to remain always in the peace of God. Then the priest goes to the book to recite, with extended arms, the "Collects," or prayers of the day, saying, "*Oremus*—Let us pray," thus inviting the people to join him in those prayers.

Nothing can be more impressive than this scriptural and very ancient custom of extending the arms during the time of prayer. It was thus that Moses prayed upon the mountain while the children of Israel were contending on the plain with the Amalekites.* The Psalmist makes frequent mention of it. "Hear, O Lord," he cries, "the voice of my supplications when I lift my hands to Thy holy Temple."† "Lift up your hands to the holy place." "I stretched forth my hands to Thee." St. Paul refers to this ceremony when he says, "I will that men pray . . . lifting up pure hands." ‡ That such was the method of praying observed by the primitive Christians is evident, both from the testimony of the earliest writers of the Church and from those monuments of Christian antiquity which are extant. Tertullian, in his book on prayer, and Prudentius, in his hymn on the Martyrdom of St. Fructuosus, particularly mention it. In the fresco-paintings with which the Christians of the first ages adorned the chambers of their catacombs at Rome, are still visible many figures with outstretched hands, in the act of praying. Anciently this gesture was common both to the clergy and laity during the time of prayer; but now, with the exception of some places where the people still employ it in the churches, it is observed by the priest only.

Amongst ancient ecclesiastical authors the word "Collect" signifies a meeting of the faithful, for the purposes of prayer. In the early times of Christianity it was usual for the people to assemble in a particular church on fast days, but especially during the season of public calamity, in order afterwards to proceed in regular procession to another church, previously determined upon, for the celebration of what was called, in the language of the period, a Station.

When the clergy and the people had assembled at the place appointed, the Bishop, or the priest who was to officiate, recited over the assembled multitude a short prayer, which, from the circumstance, was denominated the Collect, or the gathering prayer.

---

* Exod. xvii. 11.   † Psalm xxvii. 2.   ‡ 1 Tim. ii. 8.

As the Mass is the principal service of the Church, for the celebration of which the faithful are collected, we see the propriety of denominating, by the term Collect, that prayer which the priest sends up to God in behalf of those amongst His servants who have come together to adore Him. In fact, the ancient mode of saying the Collect furnishes another warrant for the propriety of such a title. Before the celebrant began the prayer itself, he exhorted, as he does now, the people to offer their petitions to Heaven, by saying, "Let us pray." The deacon then proclaimed aloud, "Let us kneel down," and after a pause, which was employed by all present in silent supplication, he cried out a second time, "Stand up again," whereupon the priest, rising from his knees, prayed aloud.

In conclusion it may be observed that as it is the office of the priest to stand between the altar of God and the people, to collect the vows and the petitions of those around him, and offer them up all together to the throne of grace and mercy, the formula employed for such a purport has been very properly, from this circumstance alone, denominated Collect, from the collection which the pastor makes of the prayers of his flock, and from his afterwards compressing into one common summary the requests of each single individual. Jesus Christ said the Collects when He spent the nights in prayer for our salvation.

By making a reverence before the Crucifix, by bowing his head as he says "*Oremus*," or pronounces the sacred name of Jesus, and by kissing the text of the Gospel, the priest intends to honor and worship not an image, nor a book, nor a sound, but Jesus Christ Himself in heaven, Who is represented and called to his remembrance by these several sensible signs and figures. To these symbols of Jesus he exhibits no more honor than the Jewish priesthood by express command of God manifested towards the Ark of the Testament and to the Temple. The Catholic neither worships, nor prays to, nor reposes any trust in images, as did the heathens in their idols; nor does he believe any power or virtue to reside in them. He is expressly taught by his Church that "images have neither life nor sense to help us."

The Acolyte in the name of the people answers "Amen" at the end of the Collect, Post Communion, and other prayers, thus ratifying what the priest has been saying, according to the custom of the Jews and primitive Christians. Amen is a Hebrew word employed to confirm what has been announced; and according to the tenor of the discourse to which it is appended, signifies either "that is true," or "may it be so," or "I agree to that." It is in reality a form of speech indicative of an assertion, a desire, or a consent. First: When the Amen is uttered after a declaration of the truths of Faith, as, for instance, the creed, it is a simple assertion, and signifies "that is true." Second: The Amen indicates a wish when it follows a prayer in which the priest expresses a desire for some blessing or a spiritual good; for example, the conversion of nations, health of soul and body, and rest to the spirits of departed brethren. Third: When the priest recites a prayer which pledges us to the performance of anything, the Amen repeated after it declares our determination to comply with the engagement. After the Collect follows the Epistle.

The Jews commenced the public service of their Sabbath by reading Moses and the Prophets.* The first Christians followed their example, and during divine worship on the Sundays, read passages from the Old or New Testament. But as these extracts were more generally made from the letters of St. Paul, the Doctor of the Gentiles, this scriptural lecture received the appellation of the "Epistle." The Epistle of each Sunday is taken from the letters of St. Paul, or of the other Apostles, and not without a spiritual meaning; for in causing the writings of God's envoys to be recited previous to the lecture of the Gospel, the Church appears to imitate the example of Jesus Christ, Who deputed some among His disciples to go before Him into those quarters which He was about to honor with a visit. It is thought that the present distribution of Epistles and Gospels throughout the year, was arranged by St. Jerome at the desire of Pope Damascus, about the year 376. When the Epistle is ended, the server, or the choir, answers: "*Deo gratias*—Thanks be to God," that is to say, for the good instruction contained in the Epistle.

After the Epistle, in order to unite prayer with instruction, the whole, or part of some of the Psalms is recited; and this anthem is called the Gradual, from an ancient custom which once prevailed of chanting it on the *Gradus*, that is, steps of the *Ambo*, or pulpit, in which the Epistle used to be recited. These versicles, composing the Gradual, used to be chanted sometimes by one chorister alone, without any pause or interruption; sometimes alternately and by many voices, which responded one to another. When the chanting was performed by one voice, and without interruption, it was distinguished by the appellation of Tract, from the Latin *Tractim*, "without ceasing." When it was sung by several of the choir, or by the whole congregation, who took up some of the strophes, it was called the Anthem, sung in versicle and response. Hence the origin of the generic term Gradual, and of the specific ones, Tract and Response.

As there is something plaintive and melancholy in solemn, long-drawn strains of a single voice, the Tract is chanted in penitential seasons, or during the time the Church is occupied in commemorating the Passion of our Divine Redeemer. But during the period that the Church is busied in solemnizing the joyful mysteries of our religion at Easter, and on those Sundays when she more particularly commemorates the resurrection of her Spouse, and on other festivals, the swell and harmony of many voices blended together, and the bursts of alternate choirs singing Alleluia, are admirably adapted to exhibit her joy; hence the versicle begins and ends with that word of jubilation. Alleluia is a Hebrew term, which signifies "Praise the Lord," but as it expresses a transport of joy which cannot be adequately rendered by any term in Greek or Latin, it has been retained in its original form. Tobias, wishing to signify the joy which is to distinguish the flourishing periods of the Church of Christ or of the New Jerusalem, proclaims that Alleluia shall be sung in all its streets;* and St. John assures us that the inhabitants of heaven hymn their praises in Alleluias.†

There are certain rhythms which, on particular festivals, are chanted after the Gradual, and on this account are called Sequences. They are called, also, Proses, because, though written in a species of verse, they are not fettered by any of the recognized laws of metre. The introduction of these hymns into the Liturgy is thought to have originated in the devotion of Blessed Notkems, Abbot of the Monastery of the Irish St. Gall, in the diocese of Constance, towards the close of the ninth century. Of the many Sequences, or Proses, which have been composed, four only are inserted in the Roman Missal. The first of them is the "*Victimae Paschali*," sung at Easter, and which, according to Durandus, is the production of Robert, King of the Franks, in the eleventh century; the second is the "*Veni, Sancte Spiritus*," for Pentecost, and is considered to have been written in the eleventh century also, by Blessed Hermannus Contractus; the third is the "*Lauda Sion*," for the feast of *Corpus Christi*, and is ascribed to St. Thomas Aquinas; the fourth is the justly celebrated "*Dies irae*," which, according to some, issued from the pious pen of Cardinal Latino Orsini, a Dominican Friar, who lived in the thirteenth century; according to others it is the production of Thomas de Celano, a Minorite, who lived A. D. 1360. The beautiful and celebrated hymn,

---

* Tob. xlii. 22.   † Apoc. xix.

"*Stabat Mater dolorosa*," is attributed to Pope Innocent III. by Pagi, in the life which he wrote of that Pontiff.

The server next carries the Missal to the other side of the altar for the reading of the Gospel, at the left, to signify how Our Lord was led about from one iniquitous judge to another. The carrying of the book from the right to the left signifies that when the Jews had rejected the Gospel it passed over to the Gentiles, who received it with joy.

Whilst the book is being removed to the other side of the altar, all the people rise up, to indicate, by the posture of standing, their eagerness to hear and readiness to follow the call of Our Divine Saviour, and obey the precepts of His Gospel.

The priest also, as he passes from one side of the altar to the other, bows down in the middle, and reflecting how unworthy he is to utter with his own mouth the inspired words of Christ, begs that the Almighty would purify his heart and lips, as he once did those of the Prophet Isaias, with a burning coal, and enable him worthily to announce the sacred Scriptures to the people. When he begins the Gospel he makes the sign of the Cross on the book to signify that the Gospel he is about to read is the book of Jesus Christ crucified, and that Our Lord died for the truth of His doctrine; then he makes the sign of the Cross on his forehead, on his lips, and on his heart, and the people do the same. This action is very significant, and should never be omitted. By signing the forehead with the sign of the Cross we declare that we entirely submit our minds to the teaching of faith; by signing the lips we testify our readiness to profess our faith before men; and by signing the heart we remind ourselves of the duty of carefully preserving a great affection for the word of God in our hearts. Again, we impress the sign of the Cross upon the forehead, not only in reference to that mystic law, which, on the day of judgment, will be the characteristic of divine election, to distinguish the favorites of Heaven from the objects of its vengeance, but to manifest a desire that the wisdom of the Cross may beam upon and illuminate the darkness of our minds, and make us understand the words of God which are about to be spoken to us. It is imprinted on the mouth, in order to bring to our remembrance that saying of the Royal Prophet: "Let a watch, O Lord, be before my mouth, and a door round about my lips;" and to instruct us to keep such a guard upon our tongue that it may never utter anything irreverent towards God, or uncharitable towards our neighbor. It is signed upon the bosom in order to banish from the heart every disorderly affection, every dangerous inclination, and every sentiment of pride or vanity, that ill become the followers of Jesus, "Who humbled Himself, becoming obedient unto death, even the death of the Cross." The priest and people here, and at the last Gospel, sign first their foreheads with this emblem of Christianity, to manifest, as St. Augustine observes, so far are they from blushing at the Cross, that they do not conceal this instrument of redemption, but carry it upon their brows, and with St. Paul, glory in the Cross;* then their mouths: "For with the heart we believe unto justice; but with the mouth confession is made unto salvation;" † and, finally, upon their bosoms, by way of admonition that the precepts of Christ should be imprinted in indelible characters upon the heart of every true believer in the Cross. At the end of the Gospel the priest kisses the book. This is done both out of reverence for the word of God and to signify that everything which emanates from such a hallowed source is sweet and venerable. When kissing the sacred text the priest says, "By the evangelical words may our sins be blotted out."

This is in accordance with what we read of the great multitude of people who came to hear the words of Jesus, and to be healed of their diseases. The server says, in the name of the people, "*Laus tibi, Christe*—Praise be to Thee,

O Christ," to testify our reverence, and to express our joy in the Gospel and affection towards Jesus, inspired by His divine words. At solemn High Mass, after the Gospel, the priest is incensed. This tribute of respect is offered to him because he is the principal sacrificing minister, who should "manifest the odor of his knowledge in every place," according to the language of St. Paul.* The Gospel is followed by the Creed.

The Creed is an abridgment of the Christian doctrine, and is usually denominated the Symbol of Faith.

The word symbol means a sign to distinguish things one from another. To the primitive Christians the Symbol, or Creed, was what the watchword is now to an army in the field—a signal by which a friend may be immediately known from a foe. As the Creed was the medium through which the true believer was recognized amid heretics and Gentiles, it became customary to say, *"Da signum," "Da Symbolum"*—give the sign, repeat the Symbol, Creed.

The Creed is said every Sunday during the year and on all those feasts, the objects of which are in a manner comprehended in it: such as the different festivals instituted in honor of Christ and His Apostles, of the Blessed Virgin Mary, and of the Doctors of the Church, by whose arduous labors and writings the doctrine included in this symbol of Christianity has been disseminated through the world. When the priest commences the Creed he raises his hands towards heaven to signify that whenever we address ourselves to the Divinity we ought to elevate our hearts towards Heaven. The exterior lifting up of the hands is a figure of the interior elevation of the mind to God.

While reciting the Creed the priest inclines his head as he pronounces the name of God. He exhibits by this action his profound respect for the ineffable perfections of the Deity. At the words *"Et incarnatus est,"* "and He—the Son of God—was made man," all kneel down to venerate the mysteries of the Incarnation, and to adore God made man,

---
* 2 Cor. ii. 14.

"who being in the form of God thought it not robbery to be equal with God; but debased Himself, taking the form of a servant, being made in the likeness of a man, for which cause God also hath exalted Him and hath given Him a name which is above all names: that in the name of Jesus every knee should bow, of those that are in Heaven, on earth, or under the earth." *

By kneeling down in adoring gratitude to the Son of God for having become man for us and rising up again, we endeavor to express that our hopes of a joyful resurrection and of the happiness of eternal life are founded solely on the merits of Jesus crucified.

---

* Philipp. ii. 6, 7, 9, 10.

CHAPTER XLII.

LOW MASS—CONTINUED.

WE now come to that part of the Mass, which, in importance, is above all that has been so far explained. In former times, as soon as the Creed was finished, all who had not been baptized, or were under a course of penance, or had not been admitted to Communion, were ordered to leave the church; for the remaining part of the Mass was considered too holy to allow any such persons to be present. The Church has changed her discipline, and she allows even the greatest sinners to remain during the whole of the sacred rites. She does this out of compassion, hoping that the sight of her august mysteries may convert those hardened sinners who withstand everything else.

Before uncovering the chalice, the priest recites the Offertory or an anthem prior to the Oblation. In some places, the Offertory is chanted by the choir immediately after the *Dominus vobiscum.* It owes its name to a practice anciently observed in the church by the faithful, who, at this part of the Mass, presented at the altar their offerings of bread and wine, to be consecrated at the holy Sacrifice. Having recited the Offertory, the priest uncovers the chalice, removes it from the centre of the altar, and there unfolds the *Corporal.*

The *Corporal* is a square piece of linen, so-called because it touches the Body of our Lord. It has been known by this appellation for more than ten centuries. In the Ambrosian rite, which received its present arrangement from St. Ambrose, the *Corporal* is likened to the linen cloths in which the Body of our Saviour was shrouded in the sepulchre. Germanus, Patriarch of Constantinople (A.D.

1222), says: "It signifies the linen cloth in which was wrapped the Body of Christ when it was taken down from the Cross, and deposited in the monument." At a much earlier period (A.D. 412), an eminent saint of the Greek Church attached the same meaning to the *Corporal;* St. Isidore, who spent the greater part of his life at Pelusium, on the Nile, and was at first the disciple, afterwards the bosom friend and strenuous vindicator of St. John Chrysostom, observes, in one of his epistles, when speaking of the *Corporal,* "that this piece of linen cloth which is spread under the divine gifts, serves the same purpose as the one employed by Joseph of Arimathea. For, as that holy man enveloped with a winding-sheet and deposited in the sepulchre the Body of the Lord, through which the universal race of mortals participated in the resurrection; in the same manner, we who sacrifice bread of proposition on the linen cloth (Corporal), without doubt, find the Body of Christ." This spiritual signification, which has been attributed from all antiquity to the piece of linen called the *Corporal,* as well as the very term itself by which it is denominated in the Greek and Latin churches, though an indirect, is a very convincing argument in favor of the belief of the real and corporeal presence of Jesus Christ in the Blessed Sacrament, which has been professed at every age and by every nation of the Christian world.

The priest then takes the unconsecrated bread, which we call the *Host* (from the Latin *Hostia,* or Victim), placed upon the paten or gilt plate, and lifting it up to heaven, with his eyes raised, offers it to Almighty God, saying this most beautiful prayer: "Receive, O Holy Father and Eternal God, this unspotted Host, which I, thy unworthy servant, offer to Thee, my true and living God, for my innumerable sins, offences, and negligences, as well as for all here present —as also for all faithful Christians, both living and dead, that it may avail both me and them unto life everlasting. Amen."

The matter, as it is called, of the Sacrifice is composed of wheaten bread and wine of the grape. The Church, in imitation of our divine Redeemer,* employs unleavened bread in the celebration of the Blessed Eucharist. Though merely bread, nevertheless, the Host is by anticipation called an *unspotted* Host, or Victim, as it is about to be converted by Almighty God into the Body of Jesus Christ, the One, the only Victim without stain or imperfection.

The priest pours the wine which is to be consecrated into a chalice, and at the same time mixes with it a small quantity of water. This is done according to the tradition of the Church which teaches us that water was mingled with the wine in the Eucharistic cup, by our divine Saviour Himself. The mixing of the water with the wine represents the blood and water which flowed from our Saviour's side when He was pierced with the lance upon the Cross.

The Chalice is offered up to the true and living God in the same manner as the bread had been before. On this occasion, when about to bless the offerings, the priest bows down his head in a spirit of humility, then lifts up his hands and eyes to heaven in imitation of Christ, Who thus invoked the omnipotent power of His Heavenly Father, makes the sign of the Cross upon them, and says: "Come, Thou Sanctifier, and bless this sacrifice which is prepared for Thy holy name."

The sign of the Cross is frequently made during the celebration of the Mass, and in blessing anything dedicated to the service of Almighty God, to indicate that all our hopes of obtaining the blessings prayed for, are founded solely on the merits of Christ's passion, which He endured on the Cross.

Having made the oblation of the Host and the Chalice, the priest retires to one side of the altar, and there washes his fingers. In the meanwhile he recites the twenty-fifth

---

* Matt. xxvi. 17; Mark xiv. 12.

Psalm, beginning at the sixth verse, with the words: "I will wash my hands among the innocent and encompass the altar of the Lord." To wash the hands is very often used in Scripture as an emblem of innocence. It is with great propriety, therefore, that the Church has adopted into her service a ceremony so expressive of the innocence and purity with which we ought to approach to the Sacrifice of the Mass. St. Cyril of Jerusalem, who lived in the middle of the fourth century, makes the following observation concerning this ablution of the hands: "You have seen," he says, "the deacon furnish water to the sacrificing priest, and presbyters standing about the altar to wash their hands. Did he give it to cleanse away any stain of dirt that soiled their bodies? By no means. For we do not enter into the church with soiled hands; but that washing of hands is a symbol, and indicates that you ought to be pure from every sin and prevarication." At the end of the psalm the priest adds: "Glory be to the Father," etc. · As this is a hymn of joy, it is properly omitted in the service for the dead, and at the time when the pains and sufferings of Christ are commemorated.

This prayer being finished, the priest returns to the middle of the altar, and bowing down his head, continues to pray a short time in silence. This silent prayer is addressed to the Holy Trinity, that the Almighty would vouchsafe to accept the offering the priest has just made in memory of Our Blessed Saviour's Passion and His glorious Resurrection, through the intercession of the Blessed Virgin and all the saints, that it may be available to their honor as well as to our salvation, and that they may intercede for us in heaven, whose memory we celebrate on earth.

Having thus begged the powerful intercession of the saints, he kisses the altar, turns towards the people, and solicits their prayers, saying: "*Orate Fratres*—Brethren, pray." This is the last time that he turns towards the people till the Sacrifice is accomplished, and the Communion received. The reason of this is because he now enters upon the solemn part of the Mass, which includes both the Consecration and Communion, and therefore requires his utmost attention; an attention that must not henceforward be distracted by turning away from the object. It will be observed, also, that during the exposition of the Blessed Sacrament upon the altar, as at Benediction, the priest never turns his back upon it, lest by such a posture he should seem to forget Him, or to be thought to offer even an unintentional irreverence to Him, upon Whom all our senses and powers of body and soul ought to be concentrated. When, therefore, the priest turns to the people for the last time, at the *Orate Fratres*, he may be considered as having taken his leave, and entered, as the High Priest did of old, into the Holy of Holies. Let the faithful consider him as oppressed by the knowledge of his unworthiness, seeking the assistance of their prayers to support him in the sacred functions he is about to perform. Hitherto he has prayed as one of themselves, standing in the midst of them, speaking aloud, that they may join with him. With them and for them he has made the confession of his sins—given praise to God at the *Gloria*—read the Epistle and Gospel for their instruction—joined in one common profession of faith at the Creed, but now he separates himself from the people. Like Moses, he leaves them at the bottom of the mount, while he ascends to the top to converse with God alone. Called to the performance of a ministry so much exalted above human nature, yet feeling that he still carries about him all the infirmities of humanity, what can he do otherwise than turn with eyes downcast, and in a low and suppliant voice say, " *Orate Fratres*," "Pray, brethren, that my sacrifice, which is also yours, may be acceptable to God the Father Almighty." This is a most interesting part of the Mass. How many does the priest see among the faithful by whom he is surrounded, whose greater innocence, whose greater purity, whose greater fervor of prayer might ascend up to Almighty God, might supply his defects, and make his sacrifice acceptable. If, therefore, Christians have compassion for the defects from which no human nature was ever exempt, if they have charity, if they have brotherly love, they will at that time unite and pray most fervently for him who is their brother, their priest, and their minister; who is there occupied in a ministry that regards themselves as much as it does him. Yes, they will pray and answer his addresses cordially in these words of the response: "May the Lord receive this sacrifice from thy hands, for the praise and honor of His own name, for our benefit and that of the whole Church." When the priest and the people are thus united in mutual prayer for each other, well may they expect that Our Saviour will fulfill His promise, and be in the midst of them, to grant their petitions.

What follows is called the *Secret*: it is one or more prayers corresponding always to the *Collect*; they are the same in number, and always have reference to the same subject, that is, to commemorate the same solemnity, or to beg the intercession of the saint mentioned in the Collect. These are always said by the priest in an undertone, audible to himself, but not heard by the people, for which reason they are called Secret.

When St. John Chrysostom speaks of the moment in which the tremendous Sacrifice of the Mass is consummated, he says: "So great is then the abstraction of the pious mind from all sublunary things, that it seems as if one were caught up into Paradise and saw the things that are in heaven itself." It is possible that when he wrote those words he may have had in his mind that part of the service which comes next in order; for now the priest calls upon the people to banish all earthly thoughts, and to think of God alone, saying in an audible tone: "*Sursum corda*—Lift up your hearts;" at the same time he elevates his hands, to impress more deeply upon the people by such an outward sign the necessity of lifting up their hearts to the Almighty;

and the people, in obedience to the call, answer by mouth of the server, "*Habemus ad Dominum*—We have lifted them up to the Lord."

Once more he appeals to them, saying, in view of the countless mercies of God, "*Gratias agamus Domino Deo nostro*—Let us give thanks to the Lord our God." Whilst pronouncing these words, he joins his hands and bows his head, to express as significantly as possible, by this corporal homage, that it is the worship of the spirit which God insists upon. The people answer: "*Dignum et justum est*—It is meet and just." Whereupon, taking up the words which they have just uttered, he proceeds: "It is very meet and just, right and salutary, that we should always, and in all places, give thanks to Thee, O holy Lord, Father Almighty, Eternal God, through Christ our Lord." This part of the service is called the *Preface*, from its being the introduction to the prayers of the Canon of the Mass. It is an invitation to elevate our hearts to God, and to offer Him our thanksgivings for the stupendous work which He is about to accomplish through the ministry of His priest by the words of consecration. In this instance the Church purposes to imitate her Founder, Jesus Christ, Who returned thanks to His Eternal Father before He called back to life Lazarus from the tomb in which he had been four days buried; when He multiplied the loaves,* and converted bread and wine into His own Body and Blood.†

Different Prefaces have been used on different holy-days from the most ancient times. The purport of this variety was, that in each particular Preface might be designated some amongst the chief characteristics of that especial mystery for which thanks were rendered to God by the Church on that annual festival. The Preface ends with a petition that our praises be accepted before the altar of the Most High, in union with the adoration of the angels, who rest not day or night, saying, "Holy, Holy, Holy, Lord God of Hosts!"

---

* John vi. 11.　　† I Cor. ii. 24.

At these words the bell is rung to give notice of the approaching Consecration.* Here all should kneel down and keep as quiet as possible, avoiding even coughing or moving unnecessarily, for now the *Canon*, or most solemn part of the Mass begins, and the *Consecration*, or the second and most essential part of the Mass, follows.

The parts of the Mass thus far explained, have varied, been lengthened or shortened, in fine, have been changed at different times and places. Though most holy prayers and exercises, yet they form no essential part of the Sacrifice, being only immediate preparations for it. We cannot say the same of the part now coming, for it is the very *Action* of the Sacrifice, as this prayer is sometimes called. At other times it is called the *Canon*, which word means a *Rule*, because this prayer has been laid down as the Rule or Canon which is to be rigidly followed by the priest who offers up the Holy Sacrifice. The minutest variation from it can never be tolerated. The prayers of the Canon are always said in complete silence by the priest, because, being about to offer the adorable Sacrifice, he turns his thoughts to the Almighty alone, forgets all other objects, and neither turns to the people, nor invites them any more to unite with him in fervor. He has retired, as it were, into the inner sanctuary, to converse with God alone, where he continues in silent worship until the *Pater noster*. Nor is it necessary that the people should hear every prayer he now says. It is sufficient for them to know that he is performing the most sublime part of his office—offering sacrifice—without their being acquainted with the exact terms in which he offers it. If any one can enter into the meaning of these prayers, and repeat them with the priest, it will be a great help to devotion. For those who cannot do this, an attention to the following short instructions may be useful.

After the recital of the "Holy, Holy," etc., the priest lifts up his hands to heaven, and by that posture expresses whither the heart ought to be raised; then joining them, and bowing down his head in humble supplication, he begins this prayer: "We humbly beseech Thee, therefore, O most merciful Father, that, through Our Lord Jesus Christ, Thy Son, Thou wouldst accept and bless these gifts, these presents, these holy and unspotted sacrifices which we offer to Thee." Whilst reciting this prayer, he kisses the altar as a sign of reverence and affection towards the spot which, in a few seconds, is to serve as the Throne whereon will repose the Body and Blood of Jesus, verily and indeed present, but veiled under the appearances of bread and wine. He also makes the sign of the Cross over the Host and Chalice as he repeats the words: "Bless these gifts, these presents, these unspotted sacrifices," because we neither demand nor do we hope to obtain the benediction of Heaven, except through the merits of Jesus, Who paid our ransom on the Cross.

These gifts and these presents are by anticipation called unspotted sacrifices, because they are shortly to become the Body and Blood of Christ, the Lamb of God, the only Victim without spot or stain. We then pray that the merits of the Sacrifice may be applied to the holy Catholic Church, which we beg God to direct, govern, and unite throughout the whole world; to our chief Pastor, the Pope; to the Bishop of our diocese; to our temporal rulers; to all orthodox believers and professors of the Catholic and Apostolic faith. It is our duty to pray for the spiritual welfare of the Church, of which St. Paul says: "Christ loved it, and delivered Himself up for it, that He might present it to Himself a glorious Church, not having spot, or wrinkle, or any such thing; but that it should be holy and without blemish." *

As the God of Truth cannot violate His promises, the Church has ever been, is, and ever will be holy. In praying for the Unity of the Church it is but just that we should, in the first place, remember its visible head and centre upon

---

* Ephes. v. 25.

earth, the Pope, or Bishop of Rome; since as long ago as the year 177, St. Irenæus, in noticing the successors of the Bishops who had been appointed by the Apostles, says: "As it would be tedious to enumerate the whole list of succession, I shall confine myself to that of Rome, the greatest, most ancient, and most illustrious Church founded by the glorious Apostles Peter and Paul; receiving from them her doctrine, which was announced to all men, and which, through the succession of her Bishops, has come down to us. For, to this Church, on account of its superior Headship, every other must have recourse; that is, the faithful of all countries in whose Church has been preserved the doctrine delivered by the Apostles." One of the bonds which connect us with the Chair of Peter, the centre of Unity, is prayer for its actual occupant.

We also pray for our temporal rulers, because not only do Catholics honor the king,* because, as St. Paul observes, "he is God's minister to thee for good; but if thou do that which is evil fear, for he beareth not the sword in vain," but however widely they may differ from him in religious belief, and though he even be a persecutor of the Church, they nevertheless pray for him. In this they not only obey the voice of the Apostle, who desires that supplications, prayers, and intercessions be made for kings; † but they imitate the faithful of the Old Testament, since we learn that the Jews who were captives in Babylon accompanied the collection of money which they sent to Jerusalem to Joakim the priest, for the service of the altar, with this particular request: "Pray for the life of Nabuchodonosor, the King of Babylon, and for the life of Baltassar, that their days may be upon the earth as the days of heaven." ‡ Moreover, they follow the example of the primitive Christians, who, as Tertullian informs us in his first Apology, prayed for the Emperors, though they were Pagans; and, as we gather

---

* I Peter ii. 17.   † I Tim. ii. 1, 2.   ‡ Baruch i. 7.

from the letters of St. Dionysius of Alexandria, continued to offer up fervent prayers for the health of the Emperor Gallus, notwithstanding that he was persecuting them.

To this general prayer for the whole Church, we immediately add the particular prayer for our friends, called the *Memento of the living*, because at present we name only our living friends, another part of the Mass being appointed for the remembrance of the dead. On this occasion, the Church has adopted the prayer of the good thief upon the cross: "Remember me when Thou comest to Thy Kingdom." So we pray: "Remember, O Lord, Thy servants, men and women, whose faith is best known to Thee; for whom we offer this sacrifice, or who offer it themselves to Thee, the true and living God, for present safety and the future salvation of their souls," etc.

Our prayer for all the members of the Church living on earth being ended, we naturally lift up our minds to those members of the same Church, who, having completed the time of their probation, are now enjoying their reward in heaven. Thus having done what we can by our own prayers for the welfare of the whole Church on earth, we are anxious to secure their prayers also for the same purpose, as the Apostles' Creed teaches us to believe in the Communion of Saints. We therefore say: "Communicating with, and venerating the memory of the glorious and ever Blessed Virgin Mary, Mother of God; of the twelve Apostles, of the martyrs, and all the saints, by whose merits and prayers grant we may be armed with the help of Thy protection, through the same Jesus Christ our Lord."

The Lord announced to King Ezechias by the mouth of the Prophet Isaias, that He would protect and save Jerusalem against the Assyrians for His own sake and for the sake of David, His servant. The Israelites frequently entreated the Almighty to hear their prayers for the sake of Abraham, Isaac, and Jacob. The Church, in like manner, refers to the memory of the Blessed Virgin Mary, the

Mother of our Lord, and of the saints of the New Law, to render God more propitious to her supplications for their sakes. In the above prayer to the twelve Apostles are united the names of twelve from amongst the most illustrious martyrs who watered the foundation of the Church with their blood. Linus, Cletus, and Clement were fellow-laborers with St. Peter in the preaching of the Gospel at Rome, and all three severally became his successors in the Pontifical Chair. Xystus and Cornelius were two other Popes; the former was martyred in the reign of Trajan, the latter in the year 252. Cyprian was the celebrated martyr and Bishop of Carthage. Lawrence was Deacon to Pope Xystus II. Chrysogonus was an illustrious Roman, martyred at Aquileia, under Diocletian. John and Paul were brothers, who, rather than worship marble gods and idols, underwent a cruel death by order of Julian the Apostate. Cosmas and Damian were physicians, who, for the love of God and of their neighbor, exercised their profession gratis.

The priest then, holding his hands extended over the Host and the Chalice, continues this devout prayer: "We beseech Thee, therefore, O Lord, that having been pacified, Thou wouldst accept this Oblation of our service, and dispose our days in Thy peace, and command us to be delivered from eternal damnation, and numbered among the flock of Thy elect."

Thus far the priest has recited the Canon with his hands lifted up to heaven; he now joins and spreads them over the bread and wine. This ceremony is borrowed from the Old Law. The Almighty commanded Aaron to put his hand upon the head of the Victim he was going to offer, and it should be acceptable. By this ceremony was expressed the act of devoting or consecrating the animal as a victim—praying that God would transfer the iniquities from His people to the head of that victim, and accept its immolation in place of that death which they had merited for their sins. In the same manner we confidently ask the Almighty Father to look down upon His only Son, Who is about to appear on the altar in the state of an expiring Victim, and for His sake, and for His sufferings, transfer our sins from us. In this prayer, which we call the Oblation, we are making an *oblation* of ourselves and *of our service*, because one of our principal duties towards God is to offer sacrifice to Him. We solicit three great favors, which, indeed, include every other that the heart of man can desire:

First. That He would dispose our days in His peace; that He would let us pass our days in love and harmony with one another, and above all, give us that interior peace of mind which arises from a good conscience, which He alone can give.

Secondly. That He would deliver us from eternal damnation, and, as a prelude, that He would preserve us from mortal sin, which alone can expose us to damnation.

Finally, That He would number us among the flock of His elect. This would form the completion of all our happiness, the object which we strive to obtain by all our prayers and exertions in the service of God.

We then continue this prayer, as connected with the one just explained: "Which Oblation, we beseech Thee, O Lord, vouchsafe to bless, approve, ratify, and accept, that it may be made for us the Body and Blood of Thy Beloved Son, Our Lord Jesus Christ."

This is the last prayer the priest says before the Consecration, and the nearer he approaches to that moment, the more interesting his words become. This last prayer deserves that every word should be well considered.

We pray first that this oblation may be blessed, that is, that it may be raised from the mere elements of bread and wine, and by the Divine benediction be changed into a more noble substance, which is capable of conferring a blessing upon us: that it may be *approved*, not rejected, as all the sacrifices of old were, and that he who offers it, as well as those for whom it is offered, may be also approved; that it may be *ratified*, that is, accomplished, and made a pure and spotless offering; that we also being approved, may be placed among the number of the elect; that it may be *reasonable*, that is, as St. Austin explains, differing from all the sacrifices of beasts, which are irrational creatures; that it may be acceptable—acceptable it must be when it becomes the Body and Blood of His well-beloved Son by the words of Consecration.

In the act of consecrating, the priest performs the same action which Jesus Christ performed at the Last Supper. He takes the Host into his hands, and lifting up his eyes to heaven, repeats the words which our Lord made use of; and by the Divine power of those words of Consecration, the bread is changed into the true Body of Our Saviour. After this he pronounces the words of Consecration over the Chalice. The moment after the priest has pronounced the words of Consecration, he kneels down to adore his Divine Redeemer, Whom he at that moment holds in his hands concealed under the humble appearance of bread and wine. He then elevates, that is, lifts up first the sacred Host, and afterwards the Chalice, in both hands, that the people also may see and adore. At each Consecration the server tinkles a little bell, to give notice to such as may be at too great a distance to see, as well as to rouse the attention of such as may be indolent or inattentive. In the meantime the people also kneel down on both knees, bow their heads, strike their breasts, and either occupy their silent thoughts in most fervent acts of adoration, or those who are less able to form their own prayers, recite out of their prayer-books those acts of adoration which have been composed for their assistance.

The Elevation and Adoration of the consecrated Host and Chalice have been in use from the beginning of the Church, as may be seen from the Liturgy of St. James, St. Basil, and St. Chrysostom.

To the eleventh century, however, the Elevation did not

take place until about the end of the Canon. Towards the year 1047, Berengarius began to broach his errors concerning the Holy Eucharist. Not only were the heterodox opinions of this innovator immediately anathematized by several councils, but the Church unanimously adopted a ceremonial at the celebration of Mass—the *Elevation*—which should at the same time furnish a most significant condemnation of the new doctrine of Berengarius, and be an unequivocal and practical profession of faith concerning the Real Presence of Jesus Christ in the Blessed Sacrament, in which bread and wine are changed into the Body and Blood of our Saviour, uplifted by the priest, and adored by the people at the Elevation. In the Greek and Eastern Churches the ceremony of the Elevation, which has always been observed by them, does not take place until just before the Communion.

As to the adoration of the Eucharist, it is attested by all antiquity. St. Cyril of Jerusalem, a Father of the Greek Church, thus addresses the recently baptized, who were about to make their First Communion: "After having thus communicated of the Body of Christ, approach to the Chalice of the Blood, not stretching out your hands, but bowing down in the attitude of homage and adoration, and saying, Amen." St. Ambrose, who died in the year 397, says: "The very Flesh of Jesus Christ, which to this day we adore in our Sacred Mysteries." St. Augustine remarks that "This Flesh Christ took from the flesh of Mary, and because He here walked in this Flesh, even this same Flesh He gave us to eat, for our salvation; but no one eateth this Flesh without having first adored it, and not only do we not sin by adoring, but we sin even by not adoring it."

"'The Wise Men," says St. John Chrysostom, "came a long journey to adore the Saviour with fear and trembling. Let us, who are citizens of heaven, imitate their example. For seeing only the stable and manger, without having seen any of those great things which we have witnessed, they still came and adored with the greatest reverence. You see that same Body, not in a manger, but upon the altar; not carried in His Mother's arms, but elevated in the priest's hands. Let us, therefore, be roused, and tremble, and bring with us more devotion to the altar than those eastern kings did to the manger, where they adored their new-born Saviour."

CHAPTER XLIII.

LOW MASS—CONCLUDED.

ALL the prayers which precede the Elevation are preparations for the Sacrifice; all that follow must be explained as applications of the virtues of the Sacrifice to our wants. In every sacrifice there must be an offering. We have already had in the Mass an Offertory, in which we presented to the Almighty the simple elements of bread and wine to receive His blessing. That blessing having now been received, by the Consecration, we have an offering worthy of Himself, which we present to the Divine Majesty in these words: "Wherefore, we, Thy servants and Thy holy people, being mindful of the Blessed Passion as well as of the Resurrection from the dead, and the glorious Ascension into heaven of our Lord Jesus Christ, offer to Thy most excellent Majesty of Thy own gifts conferred upon us, a pure Host, a holy Host, an unspotted Host, the holy Bread of eternal life, and the chalice of everlasting salvation." This prayer is in exact conformity with our Saviour's command, when He bade us to do this in commemoration of Him. We are, therefore, mindful of His Passion, Resurrection, and Ascension into heaven. Having our hearts filled with the gratitude which comes from the memory of those three great mysteries, we style ourselves the servants of Almighty God, and a holy people. By the former title of servants, we are reminded of our humble and dependent state; by the latter title of a *holy people*, we call to mind our dignity by which Jesus Christ has chosen us for Himself, to become a royal priesthood, and a sanctified flock. By both we learn that the priest and people form but one body, and are united in heart and mind for one great object, namely, to offer to the divine Majesty a *pure,* holy, and *spotless Victim.* In the spirit of humility, we acknowledge at the same time, that even what we do offer are His own gifts conferred upon us.

Having nothing of our own worthy His acceptance, it was necessary that He should provide for us even the sacrifice we offer to Himself. It is with propriety called the *Bread of eternal life and the Cup of everlasting salvation,* because our Saviour has promised that he who eats His Flesh and drinks His Blood shall live for ever. In repeating these words, the priest makes frequent signs of the Cross over the Host and the Chalice, not, of course, to bless them as before the Consecration, because they are already consecrated, and so far from wanting a blessing they are capable of conferring a blessing upon everything else; but the object of the frequent signs of the Cross over the Host and Chalice after the Consecration is this: the Church avails herself of every occasion to impress upon the minds of the priest and of the people this truth, that the Sacrifice of the altar is the very same as that which was offered on the Cross. She is solicitous that the priest, especially after the Consecration, should behold with an eye of faith Jesus Christ immolated on the Cross, as St. Paul observes to the Galatians, "before whose eyes Jesus Christ hath been set forth crucified among you."* To produce this effect, she has ordained in her Liturgy that all these words which designate the Body or the Blood of Jesus Christ, should be accompanied by the sign of the Cross, in order to signify that the consecrated Host and contents of the Chalice are the same Body which was crucified, and the same Blood which was shed upon the Cross.

Continuing the above prayer, the priest proceeds: "Upon which we beseech Thee, omnipotent God, to look down with a propitious and serene countenance, and accept them as

Thou wert pleased to accept the offerings of Thy righteous servant Abel, the sacrifice of our father Abraham, and that which Thy High Priest Melchisedec offered to Thee, a holy sacrifice and a spotless victim." These most beautiful and impressive words require no explanation. It is only necessary to observe, that when we beseech the Almighty to look down upon our offerings with a propitious countenance, the prayer is referred entirely to ourselves—that He would look down upon us with a mild countenance. The *Victim Itself*, we know, He always beholds with complacency, but our offering may not be so acceptable. To remove this obstacle is the object of this prayer; and we beg that He would extend that kindness to us which He formerly did to His servants in the Old Law, and accept from our hands a more noble gift than ever they had to offer. We call theirs, indeed, a holy sacrifice and a spotless victim; and so they were, if they be considered figures of the Victim of the Mass, that alone contains the plenitude of sanctity within Himself. The mention of the three Patriarchs is also introduced with the greatest propriety, to remind us of the dispositions which rendered their offerings acceptable.

Abel offered the first-fruits of his flock; he is called the Just, on account of his upright intentions; he is called the Child, for his simplicity and innocence. Abraham was the Father of the faithful, and will ever be celebrated for his great faith, when, in obedience to the command of God he prepared to slay his only son, and still hoped against all hope that he should be the father of a great nation. Melchisedec is the holy priest of the Most High, and is always considered as the most direct representative of Christ, because he blessed and offered bread and wine, whence Jesus Christ did not disdain to have His priesthood called "according to the Order of Melchisedec." In calling to mind, then, these great characters at so sacred a time, the Church wishes us to cherish their virtues, and strive to adopt into our lives some share of their excellence.

The prayer which follows hardly needs any explanation; it is, however, one of the most beautiful prayers that are made after Consecration. The attitude of the priest is also changed when he comes to this part. Hitherto he has recited the prayers of the Canon in an erect posture, generally with his hands lifted up to heaven. But at this prayer he joins his hands before his breast, and bows down his head as low as the altar will admit. In this posture of prostrate humility he recites the prayer, till, towards the conclusion, kissing the altar, he resumes his former upright posture. These august ceremonies alone might seem to show the great importance of this prayer, the words of which correspond to the ceremonies, and are: "We most humbly beseech Thee, Almighty God, command these things to be carried by the hand of the angel (there are always many angels present at Mass) to Thy Altar on high, into the presence of Thy divine Majesty; that as many as partaking of this altar, shall receive the most sacred Body and Blood of thy Son, may be filled with all heavenly grace and blessings." After this prayer follows what is called the *Memento of the dead*. From the very beginning of the Church it has been customary to pray for the dead, that is, for those who died in union and society with Jesus Christ and His Church. As for those who died out of the Church, there is no law to exclude our charity towards them. We may pray for them *privately*, especially if they led a good life, and there be ground to hope that their error was not wilful. Besides, we do not know what grace the Lord may have granted them in their last moments; as He enlightened the good thief in his last moment to know and profess Him as his God and Redeemer, in His exceedingly great mercy, may He enlighten many of those who die out of the Church, to know and embrace the Catholic faith in desire, and be very sorry for their error and all their sins; and thus they die in the Church before God. Not knowing what passes between God and these souls in their last moments, charity will induce us to hope for the best in their regard and pray for them, at least *conditionally*. The Church, however, forbids their names to be mentioned in the public Mass, to show her detestation of the guilt of heresy and disobedience.

At the memento of the dead the priest joins his hands before his breast, and in the meantime mentions any names of persons for whom he particularly wishes to pray or offer up the Mass. Then he extends his hands to pray for all that are detained in Purgatory, that the Lord may grant them " a place of refreshment, light, and peace." This is done, in order, as St. Augustine remarks, " that such religious duty, whenever it becomes neglected by parents, children, relatives, or friends, may be supplied by our common mother, the Church."

Having finished our prayer for the dead, who, though sinners, are yet eternally secured in the grace of God, which they can never lose, we again turn our thoughts upon ourselves, who are sinners of a very different kind, not knowing whether we possess the favor of God, and if we do, uncertain whether we shall persevere to the end in that favor. At this part the priest elevates his voice a little, that he may be better heard in this humble acknowledgment, and striking his breast in imitation of the publican in the Gospel, says: "To us sinners also, Thy servants, trusting in the multitude of Thy mercies, vouchsafe to grant some part and fellowship with Thy holy apostles and martyrs, and with all Thy saints, into whose company we beseech Thee to admit us; not in consideration of our merit, but of Thy own gratuitous mercy, through Jesus Christ, Our Lord, by whom O Lord, Thou dost always create, sanctify, and quicken, bless and grant to us all those good things. By Him, and with Him, and in Him, to Thee, O God, the Father Almighty, in the unity of the Holy Ghost, be all honor and glory, for ever and ever, Amen." In saying the last words of this prayer, the priest holds the sacred Host in his right hand over the Chalice, which he takes in his left hand, then elevates a little both the Host and the Chalice.

Up to the eleventh century the Body and Blood of Christ were here held up to receive the adoration of the people. But, as has been already observed, about the year 1047 a more solemn elevation was adopted by the Church, to furnish a public and daily profession of its ancient faith concerning the Real Presence, in contradiction to the impious novelties of Berengarius. This, in consequence, is denominated the minor or second elevation, in contradistinction to the first, which preceded it, and takes place immediately after the Conseoration.

The above prayer finishes the Canon, and the priest now for the first time breaks the silence he has observed since the Preface, by saying: "*Oremus*—Let us pray." The reader may perhaps have observed that the priest begins every other part of the Mass with this invitation to the people to join him in prayer, but neither in the beginning nor in any other part of the Canon does he make use of it. The reason is, because at that time, as has already been said, he is supposed to have entered into the Holy of Holies, and to be engaged in earnest prayer *alone*, separated, as it were, for a time from the people. This is in memory of those awful hours during which Jesus Christ hung on the Cross, and bore in silence the scoffs and blasphemies of the Jewish multitude, and silently prayed for all His enemies to His Heavenly Father. But at the *Pater noster*, which now follows in order, the priest raises his voice and recites aloud the seven petitions of the Our "Father"; this is to remind the faithful of the last seven words which our Saviour spoke in a loud voice when hanging on the Cross. As the Mass contains every perfect form of adoration, the Lord's Prayer was sure to be introduced into some part of it. It is inserted here as the first prayer towards a preparation for Communion, to which we are now approaching. The priest dwells particularly on the last petition: "Deliver us from evil," and immediately continues it in silence in these words: "Deliver us, O Lord, from all evils past, present, and to come, and through the intercession of the Blessed Virgin and all Thy saints, mercifully grant us peace in our days, that, assisted by the help of Thy mercy, we may be free from all sin and secure from all trouble, through Jesus Christ our Lord."

At these words he makes on himself the sign of the Cross with the paten, which he afterwards kisses as the instrument of peace, and the disk on which is about to be deposited the Blessed Eucharist—the peace of Christians. He employs it in making the sign of the Cross, because it was by the Cross that Christ became "our peace . . . and hath reconciled us to God in one body by the Cross, killing the enmities in himself, and coming, he preached peace." *

At the conclusion of the above prayer, the priest kneels down to adore the Blessed Sacrament; then taking the Sacred Host and holding it over the Chalice, he divides it into two parts. In this ceremony he imitates our dear Saviour, who broke the bread after He had consecrated it, before giving it to His Apostles. During this ceremony he says: "May the peace of our Lord be with you," to which the people by the server answer: "And with Thy spirit." Whilst saying these words he makes the sign of the Cross three times over the Chalice with a small part of the Host which he has broken off from one division of the Host; and this being done, he puts it into the consecrated wine, saying: "May this mixture and consecration of the Body and Blood of Christ be effectual to eternal life to us who receive it." This union of the two species signifies that though presented under two forms, they are but one and the same substance, each containing equally the Body and Blood of Christ.

Now follows what is called the "*Agnus Dei*," "Behold the Lamb of God." This was the exclamation of St. John the Baptist when he pointed out our Saviour to the un-

---

* Ephes. ii. 14.

believing Jews. The Church, acknowledging the fitness of this title, has adopted it into her service, and we repeat three times, "O Lamb of God, who takest away the sins of the world, have mercy on us!" On the third petition, instead of the last words we say, "Grant us Thy peace." By this threefold repetition of the same prayer, the Church teaches us how ardently we should desire, and how fervently and constantly we should pray for the peace of the Lord, that is, for a complete forgiveness of all our sins, and all punishments still due to them. We also strike our breasts three times, in testimony of our sorrow, except in Masses for the dead, when this action is omitted, and instead of "Have mercy on us," we say, after each invocation, "Grant them rest." This is reasonable; for as we are not then praying for ourselves, we have no occasion to strike our breasts.

The priest then continues the same request for peace in another prayer. But as we cannot enjoy the peace of God unless we live also in peace with our fellow-men, and as this twofold peace is the best preparation for holy Communion, the custom arose in the Church that the Christians of former times saluted one another with a holy kiss of peace. This custom was especially adopted at the celebration of the Mass. The priest, after the recital of the prayer for peace, gave the salutation of peace to the deacon, and the deacon went on to proclaim solemnly that they should salute one another with a holy kiss, and so the clergy saluted the bishop, and laymen their fellow-laymen. This custom is still kept up partly at solemn High Mass, when the priest, after the above prayer for peace, gives the salutation of peace to the deacon, saying, "Peace be with you," the deacon answering, "And with thy spirit." The deacon then in the same manner salutes the sub-deacon. When the people witness this pious ceremony, they also should in their hearts forgive all injuries, not entertaining any antipathies or unchristian enmities, especially if they are about to receive holy Communion. As the priest is about to receive holy Communion, he recites, after the prayer for peace, two others, by which he disposes himself still more particularly for the worthy reception of the Body and Blood of our Lord.

These prayers being ended, he kneels down in the act of adoration, and taking the sacred Host into his hands, says: "I will take the heavenly Bread, and call upon the name of the Lord." It is here called the *heavenly* Bread in allusion to the manna of the Israelites, which was a figure of this sacrament. Being then about to receive so great a blessing, and to perform so sacred an action as receiving the Body of our Saviour, what can we do better than call upon the name of the Lord? Yes, call upon His name for help, succor, and assistance to enable us to perform it well. As humility is one of the most necessary conditions for making a worthy Communion, whilst he still holds the sacred Host in one hand, looking upon it with affection mingled with dread, he strikes his breast with the other hand, and says: "O Lord, I am not worthy that Thou shouldst enter under my roof, say but the word and my soul shall be healed." This prayer is repeated three times, and at each repetition the little bell is tinkled to excite the attention of all to this important part of the Mass, which exceeds every other part except the Consecration.

It may be well to remark here that the ringing of this bell serves also as a signal for such of the laity as receive Communion to approach the sacred table. For if, as soon as these words are finished, they rise from their places in the church, and proceed to the communion-rail, they will have time to arrange and place themselves in decent order, and recollect themselves a moment before the priest comes to communicate them.

The Communion is given in the following manner: The acolyte, kneeling on the epistle side of the altar, repeats the *Confiteor*, as a public declaration of sorrow for sin on the part of those who are about to receive the Blessed Eucharist.

The priest then turns to the people and says: "May Almighty God be merciful unto you, and forgiving you your sins, bring you to life everlasting." "Amen." "May the Almighty and merciful Lord grant you pardon, absolution, and remission of your sins." "Amen." Having adored on his knees, he then takes the sacred Host into his hands, and turning about, says: "Behold the Lamb of God, behold Him Who taketh away the sins of the world. Lord, I am not worthy that Thou shouldst enter under my roof; say but the word and my soul shall be healed." This last sentence he repeats thrice, which is as oftentimes recited along with the priest by the communicants, who, at each repetition, strike their breasts in attestation of their sorrow for having ever sinned, and of their unworthiness to receive the Body and Blood of their Redeemer. The priest then descends to the rails, bearing within a kind of vase, called the *Ciborium*, or upon the Paten, the Blessed Eucharist. Holding the communion-cloth spread over their hands, with their eyes reverently closed, the head modestly raised, the mouth conveniently opened, and the tip of the tongue resting upon the lip, the communicants successively receive the Body of Christ, which is administered in the following manner: the priest holding one of the consecrated particles in his right hand, makes with it the sign of the Cross, and afterwards imparts it to the communicant with these words, "The Body of our Lord Jesus Christ preserve thy soul unto life eternal." The communicants, on receiving the Sacrament, bend down and adore in silent but most fervent worship. They then retire from the rails, not with a hasty, but decorous step, with downcast eyes, and a becoming gravity.

Before receiving the Body and Blood of our Lord, the priest makes with each the sign of the Cross over himself, to express in a lively manner that the sacred Body and Blood which he is about to receive, are the same as were sacrificed for us upon the Cross.

The priest who celebrates Mass receives under both kinds,

because he must consume the sacrifice offered up under two species. At the Last Supper, when Christ commissioned His Apostles to do as He had done, He said to them: "Drink ye all of this." No one, however, was present but the Apostles, all of whom were then ordained sacrificing priests. The priest or bishop, nay, even the Pope himself, who partakes of the Blessed Eucharist without saying Mass, receives the Communion like any layman, under one kind only.

As soon, then, as the priest has taken the sacred Blood, all the essential parts of the Mass are finished—the object of our prayer is attained—the Victim has disappeared from our altar—the Sacrifice is accomplished. The wine and water which are subsequently taken into the chalice, are merely for the purpose of consuming completely any remains of the sacramental species, and are therefore called purifications.

The prayers which are said after the Communion are very short and few. The priest having finished his Communion, retires to the epistle side of the altar, and reads from the missal one single verse called *Communion*, which varies with each Sunday and festival, and is generally, though not always, a versicle extracted from the psalms. It is called communion, because in ancient times it used to be chanted by the choir, while the priest was distributing the Blessed Eucharist to the people.

The whole of this part of the Mass is considered as an act of thanksgiving due to the Almighty after the offering of the Sacrifice. The priest, therefore, again salutes the people with "*Dominus vobiscum*," as if he were to say, You have now gone through the different parts of the Mass with me, you have communicated either in reality or in spirit of the Victim which I have been offering, I therefore wish that the Lord may always remain in you, and take up His abode in your souls, by a permanent residence, according to His promise: "He that eateth My flesh and drinks My blood, abideth in Me, and I in him." The prayers called the *Post Communion* are then said, which in number and subject are the same as in the Collects. There is only this difference, that in these latter prayers, whatever be the subject of them, there is always mention made of the Blessed Sacrament which has been received. The following is an example, and will serve to show the nature of these prayers, which differ every day: "Help us, O Lord our God, and forever protect those whom Thou hast refreshed with Thy sacred mysteries, through Jesus Christ, our Lord."

These prayers being finished, the priest again salutes the people, and says, "*Ite, missa est*,—Go, the Mass is finished;" to which answer is made, "Thanks be to God." This, again, is the true spirit of gratitude, for eternal and infinite thanks are due to the Almighty every time He confers upon us the happiness of having been present at so wholesome a sacrifice. Thanks be to God for having left us this Victim—thanks be to God for having given us the opportunity of assisting at the immolation, of which blessings so many other Christians, far better than ourselves, are almost perpetually deprived.

The priest now turns to the altar, and mindful of how great an action he has presumed to perform, bows down his head, and says in a spirit of humility this last prayer of the Mass, which is extremely suitable to the occasion: "May the obedience of my service be pleasing to Thee, O blessed Trinity, and may the Sacrifice which I, though unworthy, have offered in the sight of Thy divine Majesty, be acceptable to Thee, and through Thy mercy, be a propitiation for me, and for all those for whom I have offered it, through Jesus Christ, our Lord."

Though these words require no explanation, it is well to call attention to the very first words, "the obedience of my service." It is as much as if the priest had said—The service I have been performing is so great, that I never should have presumed to do it, had it not been in obedience to the commands of my Saviour, who has chosen such an unworthy creature as myself to offer so great a service to him. May

His goodness supersede my unworthiness, and grant a blessing to me and to all for whom the Sacrifice has been offered.

The only ceremony that now remains to be explained is the blessing with which the people are dismissed and the Mass concluded. The blessing of a man venerable for his age, of a parent, of a priest, or of any one remarkable for sanctity, has from the beginning of the world been asked and received with gratitude by the religious part of mankind. And with great reason; for who is there so devoid of religious sentiment as not to be desirous of the prayers and good wishes of a virtuous man? Even the blessing of a bad man is much more desirable than his curse. No child in a well-regulated family ever retires to rest without a father's blessing. No parent would choose to leave this world without conferring his blessing in his dying words upon all his offspring. These are the dictates of human nature, and are valued and respected alike by the good and by the bad. In conformity with these principles we find that Abraham, returning in triumph over his enemies, was glad to receive the blessing of the high-priest Melchisedec. The manner in which Jacob blessed the children of Joseph, his son, is affecting and edifying. Joseph, taking his two children, placed them before his aged father, and bowed down with his face to the ground. Jacob, stretching forth his hands, put his right hand upon Ephraim's head, and his left upon Manasses', and blessed these two sons of Joseph, saying: "The God in whose sight my fathers walked, the God who hath fed me from my youth until this day, the angel who delivereth me from all evils, bless these boys, and let my name be called upon them." In like manner Aaron, the high-priest of the Jews, when he had finished the sacrifice, stretched forth his hands and blessed the children of Israel. In the Old Law the priests were commanded to bless the people, as we see in Numbers vi. 23: "Thus shall you bless the children of Israel, and you shall say to them:

The Lord bless thee and keep thee, the Lord show His face to thee and have mercy on thee, and give thee peace. And they shall invoke my name upon the children of Israel, and I will bless them." We also read in the Gospel that our dear Saviour gave His blessing to His Apostles when He was about to leave them and ascend into heaven. "And lifting up His hands, He blessed them, and whilst He blessed them He was carried up to heaven."* A ceremony so conformable to nature, so much practised in the Old Law, and even by Jesus Christ Himself, has with reason been adopted in the Christian ritual. At no time could it be exercised with so much dignity and propriety as at the conclusion of the august sacrifice of the New Law.

It should be remembered that when a priest is ordained, one of the powers he receives is to bless both persons and things. Nor is it to be supposed that the blessing of the priest may be undervalued by reason of his personal character. If priests had nothing to confer upon the faithful in their blessings but what comes from themselves, there might be no reason for setting so high a value upon them. In this as in all other public functions, priests are but the channels through which the blessings flow. Without arrogating any merit to themselves where none is due, they are bound to acknowledge themselves to be the representatives of Christ. In His name, by His authority, and from His resources do they confer His blessing upon His people. Therefore His people value it as coming from Him. When the end of the Sacrifice has come, then let the faithful kneel down and bow the head to receive the proffered blessing in a spirit of humility. The priest, in the meantime, lifting up his hands to heaven, joins them, then turning to the people, makes the sign of the Cross over them, and pronounces, "May the Almighty God, Father, Son, and Holy Ghost bless you. Amen." Then he usually recites the Gos-

---

* Luke xxiv. 50, 51

pel of St. John. But in some of the Masses the Church has appointed another Gospel to be said in its stead. The Gospel of St. John may be considered in some respects as a short summary of our faith, pointing out the source of grace in this life—Jesus Christ, our divine Redeemer, Who, by His grace and merits, is to conduct us to the future glory in the next. Towards the end of the Gospel, when the words are said: "And the Word (the Son of God) was made flesh," all kneel down with the priest to adore Him Who condescended to become man, and conceal His glory under the vile form of a slave for our sakes. Rising up again immediately, the priest finishes the Gospel, and the people reply by the server, "Thanks be to God," for this, the mystery of the Incarnation, the source of all our blessings.

CHAPTER XLIV.

SOLEMN HIGH MASS—LIGHTS AND INCENSE.

It is in the nature of man to dedicate all his powers, faculties, and possessions, to any object to which he is vehemently attached. Religion, which acts more powerfully than anything else on the human heart, prompts us to manifest our love to God by every means in our power. The internal affections of the soul are first engaged, and soon discover themselves by external actions. The warm feelings of the soul summon everything within their reach, to aid them in proclaiming the praises of our great Creator. This has been the effect produced on religious men in every age and in every country. Hence all the resources of art have been called in to adorn the temple and the worship of God, from the time when David and Solomon first set the example, down to the present day.

We love to demonstrate our joy in the occurrences of this world by illuminations; our festivity by joyful airs of music; our sorrow by mourning; our honor and respect by processions, and so of the rest. Shall these natural affections of the soul then have no corresponding external expressions in the single instance when they are directed to God? Oh, no! It is natural to make use of them, and never are they better employed than in the service of religion. The ignorant and the profane may scoff, but the wise and the educated will allow the justice of the following observations, which come from the pen of a Protestant: "Every person who has attended the celebration of High Mass at any considerable ecclesiastical establishment, *must have felt* how much the splendor and magnificence of the Roman Catholic worship tends to exalt the spirit of devotion, and inspire the soul with rapture and enthusiasm. Not only the impressive melody of the vocal and instrumental music, and the imposing solemnity of the ceremonies, but the pomp and brilliancy of the sacerdotal garments, and the rich and costly decorations of the altar, raise the character of religion, and give it an air of dignity and majesty unknown to any of the reformed Churches." *

These are the dictates of an unprejudiced mind. In conformity with these first principles of our nature, the Catholic Church has exhausted the resources of the arts, of architecture, sculpture, painting, music, and the rest, to adorn her temples and enhance the beauty of her divine worship. She has instituted most becoming and sublime ceremonies, besides those already mentioned in the explanation of Low Mass, for more solemn occasions and high festivals.

On great solemnities or solemn occasions, when a Bishop or a priest celebrates solemn High Mass, he is accompanied by a deacon and a sub-deacon. Besides these, several acolytes are in attendance to perform their respective duties; some to carry the incense, some the candles, the cruets of wine and water, and whatever is necessary for the celebration. These numerous attendants, in imitation of the ancient Levites who served the altar, add much to the solemnity of this awful Sacrifice, and furnish an excellent representation of that eternal worship which is continually paid in heaven to God, as described in the Apocalypse: "And I heard the voice of many angels sound about the throne, saying with a loud voice, the Lamb that was slain is worthy to receive power, and riches, and wisdom, and strength, and honor, and glory, and benediction."

When the Mass is about to begin, they proceed from the vestry in procession to the altar, and each takes the place assigned to him, according to the office he has to fulfil.

---

* Pain Knight on Taste, 863, 2d edition.

It is the part of the priest or Bishop only, in all Masses, to offer sacrifice; the rest, therefore, are only solemn ministers to assist and attend on the priest. The deacon approaches nearest to the priest, and it is his duty and privilege to sing the Gospel in a solemn manner. Taking the Missal, he lays it upon the altar, whilst he kneels down and prays that the Almighty would cleanse his heart and enable him to announce His heavenly truths worthily. Having obtained the priest's blessing, he gives the book to the sub-deacon, who holds it whilst he sings the Gospel. When the Gospel is finished, the book is conveyed to the priest, who kisses it in token of the respect and affection he bears in his heart towards the holy truths therein contained.

After the Gospel, it is the duty of the deacon to prepare for the Sacrifice; to offer the priest the bread and wine, to cover and uncover the Chalice, and to perform every other little office which regards the Sacrifice. The sub-deacon comes after and performs the next most important offices. It is his privilege to read aloud or sing the Epistle; he also receives the cruets from the acolytes, supplies the wine to the deacon, and pours the water into the Chalice. After the Offertory, his presence being no longer necessary at the altar, he takes the paten, and covering it with the end of the veil which he wears, retires to the bottom of the steps, where he remains till the *Pater noster*, except occasionally going up to join the priest in prayer, as at the *Sanctus*. The rest of the ministers supply the other requisites of public worship, such as the incense, the tapers, the book.

After the Communion the sub-deacon wipes the Chalice, arranges the corporal and paten, and conveys them covered with a veil from the altar to the Credence Table at the side. Soon after the deacon, turning to the people, and singing aloud the "*Ite Missa est*," announces that the Sacrifice is over, and that they may depart. After the blessing and last Gospel, all who assisted at the altar depart in procession as they came, and return to the vestry for the purpose of unvesting and spending some time in acts of thanksgiving and prayer.

At Solemn High Mass a great number of lights are burning on the altar; whilst the Gospel is being sung, two servers hold lighted tapers, one on each side of the sub-deacon, and, during the Elevation, all the assistants kneel down in profound adoration, and either themselves hold burning tapers, or others are introduced bearing lighted torches. In order to understand the reason why the Church uses lights at Mass, we must remember that in the Holy Sacrifice of the Mass, the Christian has the most abundant cause imaginable for joy. The altar then becomes the throne of God made man, and angels and cherubim surround it in prostrate adoration. The Church, in her primitive days, to manifest her lively faith and joyfulness, produced this emblem of lights. She still continues to retain their use. While these wax-tapers, therefore, proclaim our exultation for the actual presence of our Blessed Redeemer, they testify the light and glory of the Gospel diffused throughout the earth by that Orient from on high, Christ Jesus. St. Jerome, as we have already seen, observed in his answer to Vigilantius: "Whenever the Gospel is to be read, lights are produced; not certainly, to banish darkness, but to demonstrate a sign of joy, hence these evangelical virgins always have their lamps burning;"[*] and to the Apostle it is said: "Let your loins be girded, and candles in your hands;"[†] and of St. John the Baptist it was remarked: "He was a lamp burning and shining,"[‡] that under the type of corporal light, that light may be manifested of which we read in the Psalmist, "Thy Word, O Lord, is a lamp to my feet, and a light to my paths."[§]

The twofold mystic signification which the Church attaches to the paschal candle is also no less appropriate than beautiful and edifying. The paschal candle is regarded as

---

[*] Matt. xxv.   [†] Luke xii.   [‡] John v.   [§] Ps. cxix.

an emblem of Christ. While it remains unlighted, it is figurative of His death and repose in the tomb; when lighted, it represents the splendor and the glory of his resurrection. Before it is blessed, the officiating deacon inserts the five grains of incense, to signify that the sacred Body of our divine Redeemer was bound in linen cloths with spices, and thus consigned to the grave by Joseph of Arimathea and Nicodemus.* The five incisions made to receive the grains of incense, which are so arranged as to form the figure of the Cross, represent the five wounds that were inflicted on the body of Christ at His crucifixion.

Though it be usually reserved to priests only to pronounce benediction over anything, an exception is made in the present instance, as it is the deacon, not the celebrant, who blesses the candle. This, however, is not destitute of a mystic meaning, for it signifies that the Body of Christ was deposited in a sepulchre that had been prepared with a mixture of myrrh and aloes, "as was the manner of the Jews to bring," † not by His Apostles, but by the disciples.

The paschal candle is thought by some to have a second meaning. Before being lighted, it is considered to be a figure of the column of cloud which moved before the Israelites by day; lighted, it is thought to represent the column of fire that burned by night, to point out the land of promise. This figurative meaning, though at present forcible and appropriate, was still more obvious in the early ages of the Church, when it was usual for the baptismal font to be blessed and public baptism to be administered on Easter eve to a crowd of catechumens; when the paschal candle, which had been recently blessed, was carried before them in the solemn procession which they made towards the waters of regeneration. It was then the catechumens were happily assimilated to the Israelites. Like them, these new believers had escaped an Egyptian bondage, and were about to pass through the

---

* John xix. 38–40.   † John xix.

Red Sea, in the waters of baptism, in order to arrive at the real promised land, a state of grace, which was indicated by that heavenly column, shining on them day and night—the Gospel-light of Christ. The column which is generally employed in the churches in Italy, but especially in those of Rome, to support the paschal candle, has a reference to the second meaning of this ceremony.

In the service peculiar to Holy Saturday or Easter eve, the attention will be arrested by the lighting of the triple candle, the branches of which all arise from one stem, affixed to the top of what is called the reed. This three-branched candle is intended to indicate a Trinity of persons in one God; or the light and glory of the triune God beaming forth upon mankind through the person of our Redeemer Jesus.

The Purification, a festival common to the Latin and Greek churches, is rendered peculiar by the blessing of wax-tapers, which are carried burning by those who form the procession that takes place afterwards. The symbolical meaning attributed to this ceremony is, that the faithful should, with the holy Simeon, recognize in the infant Jesus the salvation which the Lord had prepared before the face of all people—"A light to lighten the Gentiles, and the glory of the people of Israel,"* and be admonished by the burning tapers which they are carrying in their hands, that their faith must be fed and augmented by the exercise of good works, through which they are to become a light to shine before men. †

From what has been said we gather, that from the earliest periods of the Church the use of lights prevailed; that they were employed to shed splendor and impart a dignity to the ceremonies of religion, as well as to create a solemnity of thought, and inspire reverence in the minds of the assistants.

Though on some, but not on all occasions, the employment of lights was indispensable, either from convenience or ne-

---

* Luke ii. 31, 32.   † Matt. v. 16.

cessity, still they had invariably attached to them a spiritual, a mystic signification. Lamps and glowing tapers, from their number and their brilliancy, were regarded as lively emblems of joy and exultation. Hence, to express these emotions, it was a custom of the Church to use lights at the celebration of the Holy Eucharist, at the public services, at the administration of baptism, and at the funeral obsequies of her spiritual children. But she particularly delighted to suspend them around the tombs of the martyrs and confessors, upon their festivals; or, to speak more accurately, upon the annual celebration of their nativity to the bliss of Heaven, in order to exhibit a becoming honor to those amongst her sainted but departed children, and to stimulate her living sons and daughters to earn the glory and the happiness by emulating the virtues and the heroism of their holy brethren.

Moreover, at Solemn High Mass incense is used at the beginning, at the Gospel, at the Offertory, and at the Elevation. Indeed, of the several rites which the Catholic Church employs for the celebration of her Liturgy, and in performing the other functions of divine worship, the burning of incense is not the least conspicuous.

Moses received particular injunctions from God to employ incense in the service of the Tabernacle: "Thou shalt make an altar to burn incense of setim-wood, and thou shalt overlay it with the purest gold, and thou shalt make to it a crown of gold round about; and Aaron shall burn sweet-smelling incense upon it in the morning."[*] "Take unto thee spices, stacte, and onycha, galbanum of sweet-savor, and the clearest frankincense, all shall be of equal weight, and thou shalt make incense compounded by the work of the perfumer, well tempered together, and pure, and most worthy of sanctification. And when thou hast beaten all into very small powder, thou shalt set of it before the tabernacle of

---

[*] Ex. xxx. 1, 3, 7.

the testimony, in the place where I will appear to thee. Most holy shall this incense be unto you. You shall not make such a composition for your own uses, because it is holy to the Lord." Directing how the high-priest was to enter into the Sanctuary, the Lord commanded that, "taking the censer which he had filled with the burning coals of the altar, and taking up with his hand the compounded perfume for incense, he should go in within the veil into the holy place, that when the perfumes were put upon the fire, the cloud and vapor thereof might cover the oracle." * Among the vessels which Solomon provided for the service of the house of the Lord, are particularly enumerated the censers, which he caused to be made of the most pure gold.†

The primitive Christians imitated the example of the Jews, and adopted the use of incense at the celebration of the Liturgy. In the third of the Apostolical Canons, we find it enacted, that, amongst the very few things which might be offered at the altar whilst the Eucharistic sacrifice was celebrating, were oil for the lights and incense. The testimony of St. Ambrose concerning the use of incense at the altar is lucid. "Oh!" exclaims the illustrious Bishop, "Oh, that with us while incensing the altar, and offering up sacrifice, an angel would assist, nay, would render himself visible!"

If we come to inquire, we shall find that it would be difficult to select anything which could be a more appropriate symbol of prayer than the use of incense.

First. The burning of incense at the altar indicates that the place is holy and consecrated to the worship of Almighty God, in whose service every creature ought to be employed, and if necessary, consumed, to exhibit a proper homage and to proclaim His glory.

Second. A venerable antiquity informs us that the incense burnt around the altar, whence as from a fountain of delicious

---

* Lev. xvi. 12, 13.   † 3 Kings vii. 50.

fragrance it emanates and perfumes the temple of God, has ever been regarded as a type of that good odor of Jesus Christ which should exhale from the soul of every true disciple.

Third. Incense has invariably been considered as beautifully figurative of the sincere Christian's prayers. In fact, it would be impossible to select any symbol better calculated to signify to us what our prayers should be. The incense cannot ascend on high, unless it first be enkindled; so our prayers, which are, in reality, the desires of the heart, cannot mount before the throne of heaven, unless that heart be glowing with the fire of God's holy love. Nothing arises from the incense but what is of a grateful odor; we should, therefore, ask of God that He would prepare our hearts in a manner that such petitions might be breathed from them as have a holy fragrance. We should exclaim with the Psalmist—" Let my prayer, O Lord, be directed as incense in Thy sight." The whole of the incense is consumed, and every particle of it ascends in odorous vapors; so, also, all our aspirations should tend upwards to our God; nor ought any of them to hover on the earth.

Fourth. This spiritual perfume, to which all the ancient liturgies refer, is not only symbolical of our petitions, but especially typifies the prayers of the saints, which are so often described in Holy Scripture to be an odor of sweetness before heaven. "The four-and-twenty ancients," says the sacred writer, "fell down before the Lamb, having every one of them harps, and golden vials full of odors, which are the prayers of the saints." *

It was from this religious custom of employing incense in the ancient temple, that the royal prophet drew that beautiful simile of his, when he petitioned that his prayers might ascend before the Lord like incense. It was while " all the multitude was praying without, at the hour of incense, that there appeared to Zachary an angel of the Lord, standing on

---

* Apoc v 8.

the right side of the altar of incense." That the oriental nations attached a meaning, not only of personal reverence, but also of religious homage, to an offering of incense, is seen in the instance of the Magi, who, having fallen down to adore the new-born Jesus, and to recognize His divinity, presented Him with gold, and myrrh, and frankincense.*

The ceremony then of burning incense at the Gospel should figure to us, that as a grateful perfume exhales from the glowing thurible, so a sweet odor is diffused throughout the soul by the Gospel of Jesus Christ, whose bosom glowed with love for man. The incense, which is burnt in honor of Jesus Christ, at the Elevation, is a symbol of what our prayers should be, and of the oblation which we ought to make of ourselves to heaven.

If the angels, who always see His face, fall down to adore Him, what can we do sufficiently to express our astonishment and gratitude when He comes to visit us upon our altars? If the wise men of the East, recognizing their God in the helplessness of an infant, offered Him their choicest treasures (none of which he required), in acknowledgment of His divine presence, and as tokens of their interior sentiments, what can we ever do sufficiently to testify our respect for His condescending to be present upon our altars, in the state of a sacrifice—an immolated Victim?

The incense with which the bread and wine are perfumed, is meant to indicate that the assistants unite their vows and prayers with those of the celebrant who offers this oblation. The priest encircles the altar with the fuming thurible, to signify, that as the altar is the throne of Jesus Christ, an odor of sweetness is diffused around it. The ministers of the sanctuary are incensed: first, to admonish them to raise their hearts, and to make their prayers ascend like grateful incense in the sight of God; secondly, to put them in mind that they are those members of the Church who should con-

---

* Matt. ii. 11.

tinually strive to be able to say with truth;—" We are the good odor of Christ unto God in them that are saved," * and of whom it may be truly observed by men,—" God always manifesteth the odor of His knowledge by them in every place."

---

* 2 Cor. ii. 15.

CHAPTER XLV.

MUSIC AT HIGH MASS.

In all ages men have been convinced that music was a thing divine, and belonging to the worship of God. Strabo says that music is the work of God (descended from heaven). The early Fathers agree in saying that nothing is better adapted to the human soul than music.

"The science of music," says St. Augustine, "is probably the science of moving well the mind. To sing and to chant psalms is the business of the lover of God." "Nothing," says St. John Chrysostom, "so exalts the mind, and gives it as it were wings, so delivers it from the earth, and loosens it from the bonds of the body, so inspires it with the love of wisdom, and fills it with such disdain for the things of this life, as the melody of verses and the sweetness of holy songs."

Music throws the soul into an enthusiastic rapture, so much so, that no art harmonizes so marvellously with the sentiments and idea of infinity, and the relations of God and man. Music rouses a longing desire which charms and even seizes upon the soul with a magical power.

St. Albertus, a monk, while he was a secular in the world, being present at a certain play with its music, respecting the life and conversion of St. Theobald, was suddenly, by divine grace, so filled with compunction, that he began from that hour to lead a life of great sanctity.[*]

St. Ansbertus, a monk and Bishop of Rouen, while as yet a layman, and living in the court of the king, hearing some instruments of music, said within himself: "O glorious

---

[*] Surius, 7 Apr.

Creator, what will it be to hear that song of the angels who love Thee, which is to sound forever in the celestial courts! How sweet and admirable will be that chorus of saints, when Thou ordainest that the sounds of a mortal voice, and the skill of human instruments,, should be able to excite the minds of the hearers to praise Thee devoutly, their God and their Creator!"

St. Dunstan, while a youth, withdrew from the world to devote himself to music and to the meditation of celestial harmony.*

Osbert, in his life of St. Dunstan, relates that the holy archbishop had recalled many from the turbulent affairs of the world by means of his musical science.

Brother Pacific, one of the first disciples of St. Francis, had been celebrated, while in the world, for his musical science, and the holy father employed him to instruct the other brethren in singing the hymn of the sun, which he had composed in honor of God; for he wished that they should always sing it after their sermons, and that they should tell the people that they were God's musicians, and that they wished no other payment for their music, but to behold them doing penance for their sins.

Grievous enmity existed between the Bishop and the Governor of Assisium. St. Francis deputed two of his friars to present themselves before the Governor, and invite him on his part to repair, with as many persons as he could collect, to the Bishop's house, whither he had deputed two others to apprise the Bishop. When all were assembled, the friars said: " Lords and brethren, beloved in Jesus Christ,—Father Francis being prevented by sickness from coming here in person, has sent us here to sing a canticle which he has composed, and he implores you to listen to it devoutly." Then they commenced this song, to which St. Francis had added a strophe appropriate to the occasion. The Governor heard

---

* Osbert, Monachus Cantuar. in ejus Vita.

them with hands joined and eyes raised to heaven, weeping. When they had finished, he professed his desire to be reconciled with the Bishop, who, on his part, only lamented that he had not been the first to show an example of humility. Then they embraced and kissed each other, mutually demanding forgiveness, and filling the beholders with wonder and joy.*

"Music," says Cassiodorus, "dispels sorrow, soothes anger, softens cruelty, excites to activity, sanctifies the quiet of vigils, recalls men from shameful love to chastity, by the sweetest rapture expels the disease of the mind, and soothes, through the medium of the corporeal senses, the incorporeal soul." †

The celebrated Italian musician, Alexandro Stradella, had the misfortune to give offense to an entire Roman family. The haughty nobles determined to have revenge. They hired a band of assassins to waylay the musician on his return from a church and murder him.

On the appointed evening they came to the church. Alexandro, little dreaming of any danger, entered the choir, and began to play and sing a most sweet and touching melody. He had just composed the piece, and he was now playing it for the first time. "*Pieta, Signore, di me dolente;* Have mercy on me, O Lord, have mercy on me, look on me in my sadness; condemn me not in justice, but pardon me in mercy." These were the words he sang. And as the touching melody rose and swelled, filling the whole church with its melancholy strains, and then sank and died away like the sad wailing of a broken heart, there was not one there who could repress his tears. Even the hardened assassins, those men of blood who, without a shudder, could murder the innocent virgin and the helpless babe, even they were moved, and the tears glistened in their dark eyes. They sheathed their poniards, and they vowed a vow that they would never strike at the heart of him who could sing so sweetly.

---

* Les Chroniques des Freres Mineurs.   † Lib. ii. Var. Ep. 40.

Music has power to raise the drooping spirits, and to soothe the troubled soul. The Holy Scriptures tell us that when King Saul saw that God had abandoned him on account of his sins, a deep melancholy settled on him, and his soul was harassed by an evil spirit; and when those fits of sadness came on him, his face looked dark and scowling, like one in despair. Messengers were sent all over the land to find a good musician who would play for the king and charm away his grief. They found the youthful David, who was renowned for his skill in playing on the harp.

Now, whenever the evil spirit came upon Saul, David stood before him, and sang and touched his harp with such marvellous sweetness that the evil spirit was forced to flee away, and hope and joy revived again in the bosom of the unhappy king.

No wonder, then, if the Church has employed music to enhance the sublimity and grandeur of her divine worship, and to raise the minds of the faithful to God, and fix them as it were upon their future home in heaven. But it is not every kind of music that produces upon the soul such wondrous and wholesome effects. It is only true ecclesiastical music that has such sweet, enrapturing power. The character of this music is described by St. Bernard, in a letter to the Abbot Aerremacens: "The style of church music," he says, "is full of gravity, being neither lascivious nor rustic; sweet without being frivolous, soothing to the ear, but so also as to move the heart. It should appease sadness and mitigate anger; it should fecundate rather than diminish the sense of the words."

There was never any affectation or levity in true ecclesiastical music. The Church was so impressed with a sense of the importance of it, as being the only kind adapted to Catholic worship, that all music composed by heretics was prohibited from being used in the Church, by a synod in the year 1567. In fact, Catholic music is the sister of Catholic manners. It is the expression of faith, hope, and charity;

it is the voice of penance, of simplicity and love. However rich, however ravishing, this was its essential character. What musicians were those who composed the sublime Masses that raised souls to heaven, wherein the music consisted entirely in a simple phrase of the chant in an artless and even popular air, but which, directed by an all-powerful harmony to suit the different parts of the Mass, could express so many various passions. At the "*Kyrie*" those of submission and piety; at the "*Gloria in excelsis*," those of admiration and adoration; at the "*Passus*," suffering; at the "*Resurrexit*," joy; at the "*Agnus Dei*," gratitude and peace. The plain chant in Holy Week irresistibly affects the soul with a sadness unutterable. The "*Stabat Mater*" places the Blessed Virgin before our eyes, as if with the pencil of Raphael; the "*Miserere*" moves the soul to its centre; the funeral office is terrific with the voice of death, sublime like the angel's announcement of Resurrection; and one turns pale with fear and admiration at the "*Dies irae*" which is sung at the dead man's bier. The style of music for singing the Preface and the '*Pater noster*,' and for chanting the psalms at Vespers, and at other parts of the divine service, has about it a simple grandeur, and is so exquisitely touching that, independent of those claims to our respect which it possesses by its venerable antiquity, it has been regarded with enthusiasm, through its own intrinsic merits, by some amongst the most celebrated composers and writers on music.

But these were the inspirations of men in the thirteenth and fourteenth centuries; a Dufai de Chimai, a Binchois de Paris, an Ockeghen of Bavaria, a Leteiutwier of Nivelle, a Josquin of Cambray, and such like.

The moderns have cultivated more and more the luxury of harmonic accompaniments and instrumental concord, but only to promote the fantastic interest of a confused entertainment. The best judges sigh after the simple elevation of the ancient style, and recognise their chief masters in the first composers of the old simple harmonies of the Church.

Under the inspiration of faith, art was a great and holy thing. It was the reflection of God. It was the invisible world, the soul-world. Palestrina and Mozart composed figured music equal in solemnity and feeling to the noblest tones of the Gregorian Chant.

Under the influence of Catholicity, music sent forth sounds such as the ear of man had never before heard. Truly, no tongue can be adequate to give an idea of the impression produced by the plain song of the choir. While the Gregorian Chant rises, you seem to hear the whole Catholic Church behind you responding. It exhales a perfume of Christianity, an odor of penitence and of compunction which overcome you. No one cries—How admirable! but by degrees the return of those monotonous melodies penetrates one, and as it were impregnates the soul, and if to these be added personal recollections a little sad, one feels oneself weep without ever dreaming of judging, or of appreciating, or of learning the airs which we hear.

In regard to art, we may pronounce without hesitation that men who never in their hands bear the olive branch, having lost the faculty of prayer, the thrilling emotion in presence of the Father and Creator of the world, who, in short, experience nothing but ordinary sensations when they hear the chants of the Church, must be degraded beings, insensible to the magnificence of nature, deaf to the nightingale or to the murmur of the woods, dead to music, and susceptible of no enthusiasm but for objects disgusting and absurd.

Such, then, was the ecclesiastical music during the Middle Ages, till the commencement of its decline, which, according to the natural order of things, was contemporaneous with the decline of faith and the introduction of the new opinions; for a change of manners necessarily superinduced a change in the style of music. In the fifteenth century a profane theatrical music began to be introduced into churches, which was censured by Pope Benedict XIV. in his encyclical letter in the year of the Jubilee, and in his works, in which he called upon all bishops to correct this abuse. It arrived at such a height that the Fathers of the Council of Trent deliberated whether they ought not to abolish all music in the churches except the Gregorian. Satan seemed to have again crept into the paradise of man on earth, the house of God. The chants were left to profane artists, who substituted a hypophrygian style, consisting of fanciful digressions and exaggerated bombastic flourishes, for the ancient simplicity, the dignity of the priesthood, and the reverence of God. Anthems were sacrificed to exhibit the fantastic powers of vain men, who knew nothing of devotion. False character, false expression, and frivolity, under the title of brilliant execution, became the prevailing vices of music. This kind of music, full of insolent grandeur, noisy, tedious, and abounding in insipid repetitions, adulatory and suited to unstable minds, indicated clearly enough the influence of the new spirit which had superseded the reign of faith and Catholic devotion. Such music is an abomination in the holy place; it is a mockery of what is most holy, and an insult to Catholic faith and worship. What should we say if at the funeral of a dearly beloved friend or relative the hired musicians would play some giddy or voluptuous waltz? How great would have been our indignation had we been present on Mount Calvary while our Blessed Lord hung bleeding and dying on the Cross, to hear the music of some lascivious dance at that awful moment when the sun hid its light, when the rocks burst asunder, when even the very dead rose from their graves to take part in the universal sorrow of nature at the death of the Creator! But we still celebrate the death of our dearest and best friend, our Lord and Saviour Jesus Christ; what propriety is there then for lascivious music at such a solemn moment? In the holy Mass is renewed the awful scene of Calvary. What room can there be then for senseless, sensual music at this holy and tremendous sacrifice? Unfortunately, many of our so-called Catholic choirs remind one of the motley crew that were present at the crucifixion of our Blessed Saviour. At that awful moment there might be seen sneering Jews, and cold and indifferent heathens; there were present proud, self-conceited men, and vain, lascivious women, whose presence only served to increase the sufferings of the dying Saviour.

But how sweet, how devotional, on the contrary, is the harmony of youthful and aged voices, joining in saintly chorus. By such homage of praise we join the heavenly spirits in their uninterrupted songs of adoration, love, and praise, and it is such music and singing that even the holy angels join in to help us to honor and praise our Lord and Saviour.

In a procession at Valencia, in which Blessed Nicholas Fattori was carrying the Blessed Sacrament, there came all at once a flock of birds, forming a crown just above our Lord in the Blessed Sacrament, singing most melodiously, and steadily accompanying the procession, their warbling notes harmonizing beautifully with the ecclesiastical chant. The great servant of God, being afterwards asked what he thought of those birds, answered with a smile, that they were angels who had come from heaven to join the procession, to honor and sing with them the praises of their Divine Lord and King.

It is by such music that we express the spiritual joy of our hearts in this heavenly mystery, and excite both ourselves and others to holy jubilation and devotion.

St. Augustine tells us that soon after his conversion to God, he was moved by the sacred singing at the church to shed abundance of sweet tears.

But such holy joy, such interior devotion cannot be produced by opera music, and by hired opera singers. They do not and they cannot represent the angelic choirs. Those sudden bursts of deafening noise, those tempests of sound, mechanically sent forth in impetuous streams, are not in accordance with the still, peaceful voice of heaven; but are well calculated to draw the hearts of the devout worshippers from the altar and make them violate the precept of the Church prescribing to hear Mass with devotion. They are calculated to make many go to church as to a theatre, and behave there, in presence of the Divine Majesty, as in a place of amusement. Instead of being honored by such music and singing, the Lord feels deeply offended. It is only the devil who is delighted and honored thereby. Let such soft and effeminate music be forever shunned with abhorrence and banished from every Catholic Church, as the corruption of the heart and the poison of virtue.

CHAPTER XLVI.

THE USE OF HOLY WATER BEFORE HIGH MASS.

The ordinance of Almighty God, promulgated by the lips of Moses, concerning the water of aspersion and the mode of sprinkling it, are minutely noticed in Chapter xix. of the Book of Numbers. In the Book of Exodus we read that the Lord issued the following directions to Moses: "Thou shalt make a brazen laver, with its foot, to wash in, and thou shalt set it between the tabernacle of the testimony and the altar. And the water being put into it, Aaron and his sons shall wash their hands and feet in it when they are going into the tabernacle of the testimony, and when they are to come to the altar, to offer on it incense to the Lord." *

That it was a practice with the Jews, not confined to the members of the priesthood merely, but observed amongst the people, for each individual to wash his hands before he presumed to pray, is a well-attested fact. The Church adopted this, as well as several other Jewish ceremonies, which she engrafted on her ritual; and St. Paul apparently borrows from such ablutions the metaphor he employs while thus admonishing his disciple Timothy: "I will that men pray in every place, lifting up pure hands." † That in the early ages the faithful used to wash their hands at the threshold of the church before entering, is expressly mentioned by a number of writers.

The introduction of blessed or holy water must be referred to the times of the Apostles. That it was the custom in the

---

* Exod. xxx. 18-20.   † 1 Tim. ii. 8.

very earliest ages of the Church, not only to deposit vessels of water at the entrance of those places where the Christians assembled for the celebration of divine worship, but also to have vases containing water mingled with salt, both of which had been set apart from common use, and blessed by the prayers and invocations of the priest, is certain. Special mention of it is made in the Constitutions of the Apostles; and the Pontiff Alexander, the first of that name, but the sixth in succession from St. Peter, whose chair he mounted in the year 109, issued a decree by which the use of holy water was permitted to the faithful in their houses.

The holy water is blessed in the following manner: Having signed himself with the sign of the Cross, the priest commences the benediction of the salt and water before him in these words: "I exorcise thee, O creature of salt, by the living God, by the true God, by the holy God; by that God Who, by the prophet Eliseus, commanded thee to be cast into the water to cure its barrenness; that thou mayst by this exorcism be made beneficial to the faithful, and become to all of those who make use of thee, healthful both to soul and body; and that in what place soever thou shalt be sprinkled, all illusions, and wickedness, and crafty wiles of Satan may be chased away, and depart from that place; and every unclean spirit commanded in His name, Who is to come to judge the living and the dead, and the world by fire. Amen.

"Let us pray.

"O Almighty and everlasting God, we most humbly implore Thy infinite mercy, that Thou wouldst vouchsafe by Thy power to bless and to sanctify this Thy creature of salt, which Thou hast given for the use of mankind; that it may be to all who take it for the health of mind and body, and that whatever shall be sprinkled with it may be freed from all uncleanness and from all assaults of wicked spirits, through our Lord Jesus Christ."

After this the priest proceeds to the blessing of the water:
"I exorcise thee, O creature of water, in the name of God the Father Almighty, and in the name of Jesus Christ His Son our Lord, and in the virtue of the Holy Ghost, that Thou mayst, by this exorcism, have power to chase away all the power of the enemy; that thou mayst be enabled to cast him out and put him to flight with all his apostate angels, by the virtue of the same Jesus Christ our Lord, Who is to come to judge the living and the dead, and the world by fire. Amen.

"Let us pray.

"O God, Who for the benefit of mankind hast made use of the element of water in the greatest Sacraments, mercifully hear our prayers and impart the virtue of Thy blessing to this element, prepared by many kinds of purifications, that this Thy creature, made use of in Thy mysteries, may receive the effect of Thy divine grace for the chasing away devils and curing diseases, and that whatsoever shall be sprinkled with this water in the houses or places of the faithful, may be free from all uncleanness, and delivered from evil; let no pestilential spirit reside there, no infectious air; let all the snares of the hidden enemy fly away, and may whatever envies the safety or repose of the inhabitants of that place, be put to flight by the sprinkling of this water, that the welfare which we seek by the invocation of Thy holy name may be defended from all assaults, through our Lord Jesus Christ."

Then the priest mingles the salt with the water, saying:
"May this salt and water be mixed together in the name of the Father, and of the Son, and of the Holy Ghost. Amen." "The Lord be with you." "And with thy spirit."

"Let us pray.

"O God, the author of invincible power, King of an empire that cannot be overcome, and for ever magnificently triumphant, who restrainest the forces of the adversary, who defeatest the fury of the roaring enemy, who mightily conquerest his malicious wiles; we pray and beseech Thee, O Lord, with dread and humility, to regard with a favorable countenance this creature of salt and water, to enlighten it with Thy bounty, and to sanctify it with the dew of Thy fatherly goodness; that wheresoever it shall be sprinkled all infestation of the unclean spirit may depart, and all fear of the venomous serpent may be chased away, through the invocation of Thy holy name; and that the presence of the Holy Ghost may be everywhere with us, who seek Thy mercy, through our Lord Jesus Christ."

It is the never-ceasing solicitude of the Church to render her children holy and undefiled, and to preserve them from everything which may contaminate or injure them. In laboring to achieve this object, she connects her prayers and aspirations with all those exterior signs and ceremonies which are most likely to express her benevolent desires. The property of water is to cleanse, and it is the type of purity, while salt is used as a preservative against corruption, and is an emblem of wisdom. Water and salt commingled, blessed, and sprinkled on the people, form a very appropriate symbol to exhibit the desire felt by the Church for our purification and preservation from everything contagious.

When the men of Jericho complained to Eliseus that the waters were bad and the ground barren, the prophet said to them: "Bring me a new vessel, and put salt into it. And when they had brought it, he went out to the spring of the waters and cast the salt into it, and said: Thus saith the Lord, I have healed these waters, and there shall be no more in them death or barrenness." * The Church, in imitation of the prophet, invokes the divine power on the salt, that it may have an efficacy from God to preserve her members from everything that can be noxious to them.

---

* 4 Kings ii. 19–21.

The priest exorcises the salt and the water. Exorcise is a Greek term, which signifies "to conjure—to speak imperatively." The Church is well aware that man, by his corruption, had perverted to the service of the demon those things which were intended for the service of God, and she hears St. Paul proclaim that "the creature was made subject to vanity, not willingly."* But she knows that everything "is sanctified by the word of God and prayer." †

Hence it is that she exorcises and blesses many creatures. She exorcises salt and water by commanding them, on the part of God and through the merits of the Cross of Jesus Christ, not only to be innocuous to man, but to become serviceable to him while laboring in the work of salvation.

This, in reality, is the object of all her exorcisms pronounced over inanimate creatures, and it should not be forgotten that it is a pious custom with her to bless everything which is assigned for holy purposes.

It is usual to sprinkle the altar and the people on Sundays, immediately before commencing the celebration of High Mass. As holy or blessed water was instituted for the express design of insinuating to Christians that they were to keep a cautious guard against the attacks of Satan, and to preserve themselves as much as possible immaculate from the contagion of sinfulness, the purpose of this aspersion is to warn the faithful to purify themselves before they presume to assist at the holy Sacrifice, that clean oblation predicted by the Prophet Malachias.‡ The words recited by the priest and chanted by the choir during the ceremony are quite appropriate: "Thou shalt sprinkle me, O Lord, with hyssop, and I shall be cleansed; Thou shalt wash me, and I shall be made whiter than snow." §

The same pious motives have induced the Church to place vases containing blessed, or as it is denominated, holy water,

---

* Romans viii. 20.   † 1 Tim. iv. 5.   ‡ Mal. i. 11.   § Ps. l. 9.

at the entrance of her temples. Into these the faithful immerge the tips of their right hand fingers, and afterwards make the sign of the Cross, as they repeat the following invocation to the holy and undivided Trinity: "In the name of the Father, and of the Son, and of the Holy Ghost." In this manner it is that the Church endeavors to address her children at the very threshold of the tabernacle, and to exhort them to understand, by the water which she holds out to them, that they must bring a purity and cleanness of heart to the sanctuary, and thus comply with the exhortations of St. Paul, "lift up pure hands" to the throne of Him whose Cross they have just figured on their foreheads, through the merits of Whose death and suffering they can alone expect to receive the pardon of their sins, and obtain eternal happiness.

Thus is a satisfactory reason given for every ceremony made use of in our public worship. They are all, no doubt, calculated to inspire us with reverence for the sacred mysteries. They are outward signs of the interior dispositions with which we ought to be animated, and are means of exciting such dispositions within us. Let us look upon them with eyes of faith; let us practise or behold them with sentiments of humility and reverence. Let us never forget that they are but means and helps of acquiring the true dispositions of devotion. For, as the psalmist justly observes of the soul, "All beauty is from within." Not external pomp of worship, but the interior virtues of the soul—faith, hope, love, devotion, compunction, adoration, gratitude, praise—these are the beauties which should adorn every Christian soul. Let it be our constant endeavor to acquire these virtues by every act of religion, and thus render ourselves pleasing to our Creator. This is the only object of our existence, the only thing that will profit us for eternity when everything else has passed away. May the Almighty grant us this happiness.

CHAPTER XLVII.

HOW AND WHY CATHOLICS BUILD CHURCHES.

WE have seen, so far, that the holy Sacrifice of the Mass is the most abundant source of peace and blessings; that it is the fountain of the Saviour, from which the priest must derive the sanctity that ought to adorn his character, and the people the spirit of religion that is equally necessary for them. We have seen that in this holy Sacrifice every state of life finds the means of obtaining the peculiar virtues necessary for it; the merchant, honesty; the laborer, diligence; the parent, watchfulness over those children for whose souls he will have to answer; the child, respect and obedience to those whom God has placed over it; the young, purity, modesty and sobriety.

No wonder if the holy Catholic Church has always endeavored to make this mysterious fountain flow everywhere. Her churches are built at short distances from one another, in which the divine mysteries are celebrated, in order that the merchant, the tradesman, the laborer, and the servant, may be able to assist at them every morning without interruption to their duties, as also to give facility to infirm persons who cannot go far from their houses; while in the country churches are multiplied to afford a similar assistance to persons engaged in agriculture.

But there is still another reason why the Church loves to multiply her temples, chapels, and oratories, and place them amidst the woods and the mountains; it is to make men love the Author in the Blessed Sacrament, while they admire the works of nature. How richly adorned England was in this respect, is recorded by Strype, Leland, Dugdale, and other historians, who speak of the destruction which attended the first establishment of heresy. In Ireland there are only ruins left which appear thickly scattered over the country. In Spain there are more than seventy thousand churches; there were no fewer than a thousand raised in the reign of King Don Jaime I., of Aragon, alone.

A French writer tells us that there were in France 30,000 churches, 1,500 abbeys, 18,500 chapels.

In Rome there are as many churches as days in the year, ancient piety having left there as many stations as the sun has in the sky, each of them being, as Gerbet says, "the monumental expression of some mystery of faith, or of some great example of virtue drawn from the lives of saints; so that, if we could embrace them in view all at once, we should have before our eyes the plan of the whole religion."

The Church knows too well the propensity of wretched mortals to be occupied incessantly with creatures, and to depart from Him Who made them. Hence she seeks, by the erection of churches and chapels, to make the whole life of man a continual hymn or act of praise to God.

The cock on the summit of the steeple calls to our mind the vigilance, eloquence, and prudence of the preacher, who excites himself with his own wings of zeal for the salvation of souls before he calls others. It turns against the wind to show that he argues against the evil customs of the world, and applies himself to resist the wolves. It is seated on an iron rod, which denotes the straightforward and just doctrine of the preacher; and this rod is placed upon a cross, surmounting a globe, to represent the triumph of the faith over the world.

The bell sounding in the lofty tower reminds us in the morning, at noon, and in the evening toward sunset, of the Incarnation of the Son of God, and we say the *Angelus*. On Sundays it reminds us of our duty to assist at Mass and other devotions; at the Elevation of the Host, it reminds those without the Church, of Jesus Christ offering Himself upon the altar for their sins; at the death of a person it tells the people to pray for the repose of his soul. Moreover, at the sound of the bell, the demons tremble and take to flight, and the angels come to protect us from temporal and spiritual harm; for in the office of the Consecration of a bell, the Bishop prays, that as the voice of Christ appeased the troubled sea, God would be pleased to endue that sound with such virtue, that it may intimidate the enemy and encourage the faithful; and that, as the Holy Ghost formerly descended upon David when he struck the chords of the harp, and the thunder of the air repelled adversaries when Samuel offered up the lamb, in like manner, at the sound of that vase (bell) passing through the clouds, flights of angels may surround the assembly of the Church, and save the minds and bodies of the believers with an everlasting protection. Well might we conclude that the arch-heretics had read this prayer with trembling, when with such a determined will they refused permission to the Catholics under their subjection to make use of bells. Indeed, for their zeal in removing them from the churches which they seized, one may not otherwise account. "When I was a child," says Sir Thomas Spelman, " I heard much talk of the pulling down of bells in every part of my country of Norfolk, then fresh in my memory. And the sum of the speech usually was, that in sending them over sea, some were drowned in one haven, some in another, as at Lynn, Wells, or Yarmouth.

"Sir Hugh Paulett-pulled down the bells of the churches of Jersey, and sending them to St. Malo's, in Britain, fourteen of them were drowned at the entrance of that harbor. Whereupon it is a by-word at this day in those parts, when any strong east wind bloweth there, to say 'The bells of Jersey now ring.'"

Such are the reasons why the Catholic Church, in all ages and countries, has been so indefatigable in constructing and preserving numerous churches. The recollections of every traveller who has visited a Catholic country will bear testimony to the wisdom of this discipline, and even history itself has been obliged in many instances to record its effects. During the dreadful storm which so dismayed the English army under King Edward after leaving Rheims, it is said that the troops and the king himself looked upon it as a mark of God's wrath, and that at the same moment the king, turning towards the church of Chartres, whose lofty tower rose in the distance, made a vow to consent to peace.

The Archduke Leopold used always to salute the patrons of the different churches that he passed. Thus the whole face of a country is like a book which recalls a thousand holy images to inspire devout meditation, and to confirm salutary thoughts.

But in order to succeed still better to draw men to their Creator, to inspire them with devout meditation and salutary thoughts, to remind them of their heavenly country, the Church has always exhorted her children to spare neither labor nor cost in the erection and decoration of churches. St. Gregory Nyssen is astonished at the superb temple of the martyr Theodore, which, with its gold arches and azure tablets, impels the mind to the contemplation of eternal beauty. In his description of this church he says: "When you enter this temple you are filled with delight. On viewing the magnificence of everything around you, you behold with wonder the vastness of the structure, and the elaborate finish of every one of its splendid decorations; here the skilful carver has brought out life-like animals from the block of precious wood; there the marble incrustations are so beautifully polished as to reflect your image like a mirror of burnished silver. Before you glows a picture of the richest coloring and in the highest style of excellence, portraying deeds of heroism, from which you apprehend, as vividly as you would from a plainly-told narrative, the struggles and toils of the holy martyr. How calm and undaunted Theodore there stands in the midst of his tortures and his enemies! How grim and fierce the forms and the looks of the tyrants that frown on him, or rush forward to drive him through flames and fire into the blazing furnace that is to consummate his triumph! Sweetly represented in His human form, you see Christ appear above the scene of conflict, as an umpire to witness and quickly reward his glorious victory." *

The loftiness and lavish richness of this great church, and the continual ebb and flow of the immense crowds that visited it, formed altogether a proud spectacle of religion, that the devout mind might well call royal and superb, if not truly sublime, as it seemed to Prudentius.

The blessed Patiens, Bishop of Lyons in the third century, built in that city a most splendid church of marble and gold; there were precious stones and variegated marbles to adorn it.† In the fourth century the Church of St. Eulalia, at Merida, in Spain, was ornamented with magnificent columns, beautiful marbles, and lofty towers.

Before the tenth century the church of St. Martin at Tours was encrusted with red, green, and white marble, and even the exterior was adorned with gold and beautiful stones. Old men, in the time of St. Odo, who had seen it, used to say that when the building was seen against the sun, it resembled a mountain of gold. Indeed, the palaces of Genoa and of Venice, without their superb churches, would not compensate for their scorched and formal hills, and unhealthy marshes.

The monotonous plain of Milan would be no delightful recollection without the thought of its Cathedral.

The low sandy banks of the Arno would not arrest pilgrims at Pisa if there were not the soil of Calvary in the Campo Santo, the Cathedral, and the Baptistery.

Who would be attached to Sienna if it were not for its

---

* Greg. Niss. Serm. de St. Theod.
† Sidon. Apol. Seg. II. Epist. 10.

Cathedral and its Gothic towers? And what pilgrim from the North would be attracted to Ancona by the scenery of that level shore of the Adriatic, if it were not for the hope of arriving at the house of our Blessed Lady?

Anastasius shows us Rome and her churches, laden with the spoils of the converted world. Fancy, if you can, the appearance of a tabernacle made of solid silver, in the construction and ornamenting of which two thousand and twenty-five pounds of the metal have been used. In front of the tabernacle sat the Saviour, nearly as large as life, and around Him stood the twelve Apostles, each five feet in height, all wearing crowns; the chair, the twelve Apostles, and the Saviour, were all of solid silver. Four angels of the same size, also of solid silver, stood at the four corners, resplendent with gems. Upon four waving branches, wrought of pure gold, stood twenty-scones for candles, each composed of fifteen pounds of silver, chased into the form of a dolphin. Around the church there was a profusion of similar riches; seven altars, enriched with massive silver ornaments, and crowded with one hundred and sixty silver candlesticks, each containing from twenty to thirty pounds of pure silver. There was also the gold sanctuary lamp of twenty pounds of the precious metals, and a gold censer weighing twenty pounds, which was brilliant with forty-two precious stones. The baptistery, with its large porphyry font in the centre, and its lamb and other ornaments shone with a like profusion of silver, and gold, and gems.

Such was the Lateran before the barbarians.

Among the most superb churches built between the tenth and eleventh centuries, are the cathedrals of Winchester, Canterbury, and York; the churches of Westminster and Bristol in England; that of Sainte Croix, at Orleans; the cathedrals of Chartres, Paris, Rheims, and Amiens, in France; in Germany, the church of Halberstadt, the Elizabeth Kirche at Marburg, and the cathedrals of Vienna and Cologne; in Italy, the cathedrals of Pisa, Sienna, Milan, the

Carthusian church at Pavia, and the church of St. Petronio at Bologna.

Look at those majestic monuments of architecture. Behold the tranquil grandeur of a gothic cathedral—a vast symphony, as it were, of stone, colossal work of a man and of a people, one, and yet complex—a kind of human creation, powerful and fruitful, seeming to have attained the double character of divine creation, variety, and eternity. Behold within it those myriads of statues which people all the intercolumnization of the nave and choir, images on their knees, on foot, on horseback; men, women, children, bishops, kings, warriors, in stone, in marble, in gold, in silver, in brass and wax.

Such magnificent churches cannot fail to make a most wholesome impression on the mind of the beholder, and especially to remind him of the holy Catholic Church, which is constructed in heaven of living stones. This house of the Lord is firmly built, the corner-stone of its foundation being Christ, upon which, and not beside it, is the foundation of the Apostles and Prophets, while the upper stones are Jews and Gentiles from the four parts of the world, coming unto Christ. All the stones are polished and square; that is, holy, pure, and firm, disposed by the hand of the great Architect, so as to remain forever. Of these some are borne and do not bear, answering to the simple members of the Church; others are borne and do bear, answering to those of the middle class; and others only bear and are not borne, excepting by the foundation, which is Christ; for, in this edifice, by how much anyone excels more eminently, by so much the more does he humbly sustain others; but one charity cements all together in one body.

All who see such superb churches naturally ask themselves the question: How were these marvellous edifices raised? That the erection of these magnificent churches cannot be attributed to any ordinary cause, will appear most evident on a reference to the history of their construction.

The history of their construction exposes three sources which supplied the means required: consisting in the substitution and performance of such works instead of other works of penance, zeal, and charity; in the devotion of the multitude, and in the munificence of kings and religious Orders and particular families. All these, it is obvious, must be referred to the faith of the people, which will be found fully adequate to explain the phenomenon.

To witness those causes in operation, we have only to open the first ecclesiastical chronicle which presents itself.

About the twelfth century, the Western nations, in their desire to wrest the sepulchre of Christ from the hands of the infidels, originated the wars which we call the Crusades. Peter the Hermit led the first. Godfrey de Bouillon conquered Jerusalem, and was proclaimed King of the Holy City. By degrees, all the kings, princes, and Christian lords of Europe enrolled themselves under the standard of the Cross, from Frederick II., Emperor of Germany, to St. Louis, King of France. For the space of two centuries they nobly combatted the Saracens.

The kingdom of France had been frequently invaded, pillaged, devastated, and burned by Moors, who made hostile irruptions from Africa and Spain. The northern provinces had been desolated by incursions of the Normans, who ravaged the country with fire and sword. Magnificent abbeys and cathedrals, reared by the pious munificence of the Merovingian and Carlovingian kings, had been attacked by bands of marauders, plundered, and, in most instances, set on fire and destroyed. A vast number of villages were sacked, the ramparts of strongholds levelled, wooden bridges cast burning into the streams, and their stone arches demolished. The Hungarians at divers times invaded Bavaria, Burgundy, and Italy. They swept through those countries in a blood and fire, burning, consuming, reducing to dust the harvests and forests, leaving in their passage signs of horror and desolation. Germany, on the other side of the Rhine, was laid waste by the Prussians; Bohemia and Moravia by the Tartars and Sclavonic tribes; the shores of the Baltic by the Swedes and Thuringians; Flanders by the Frisons. But England, enriched by its Saxon kings with abbeys, cathedrals, and hospitals, was the greatest sufferer, from the havoc made by the Danes. These barbarians strewed the soil with ruins, and made the country a desert.

During the eleventh and twelfth centuries the Mussulmans and Northern tribes had flung back into barbarism the nations of Europe. Churches, monasteries, fortified cities, were devastated. The inhabitants resumed the manners of forest savages. Every city, castle, and territory was insulated like islands in the sea, as all intercommunication was cut off. Roads, bridges, barks, means of transportation, richly-endowed hospitals, monasteries whose doors were ever open to the wayfarer, had disappeared. The eye beheld, on every side, thickets, swamps, pools, fallow and waste lands, so that in many places neither man nor horse could pierce a way. God had pity on society. He raised up high-minded men, endowed with eminent wisdom and sanctity. They established, according to the rules of St. Benedict, new monastic congregations, which gradually softened the manners and dispelled the ignorance of the people. France was gloriously resplendent with the lustre of the monks of Citeaux, Cluny, and Chartreuse, under the government of St. Bernard, St. Odo, and St. Bruno. Germany was blessed with the Order of Premonstratensians, founded by St. Norbert, Archbishop of Magdeburg. England, with the monasteries of St. Alban, St. Dunstan, St. Columbanus, restored by Lanfranc and Anselm, Archbishops of Canterbury. Italy ranked among her benefactors St. John Gualbert and St. Romuald, founders of Vallambrosa and Camaldoli, who, with heroic courage, combated the abuses of the epoch. In fine, at the close of the twelfth century the two great luminaries of the world appeared, St. Francis of Assisium and St. Dominic. Their Orders dissipated the darkness of barbarism which had settled on Christendom. At this period the orders of chivalry, especially of the Knights Hospitallers and the Knights Templars, were formed to civilize and rule the boorish and rugged nations. They introduced the polished and elegant manners of the East, and contributed powerfully to the progress of European refinement.' The Church, whose maternal heart is ever full of tenderness and solicitude for her children, studied to provide for their wants in the West, as she had striven by the Crusades to promote their interests in the Levant. In those ages of faith, the desire of Christians to draw holy indulgences from her treasury, prompted them to undertake journeys to Palestine. The Church availed herself of this popular movement, and gave it a more advantageous direction. It was deemed inadvisable to exhaust the fountains of European wisdom and strength in behalf of Eastern nations, to bereave France, Burgundy, England, and the Germanic Empire of their defenders, guardians, and counsellors. Hence the same spiritual favors were dispensed to Catholics who devoted themselves to the service of the Church and the exercise of works of charity.

Among such works was reckoned the rebuilding of hospitals, monasteries, and temples to the Almighty. The indulgence granted to the Crusaders was extended to all contributors who, by money or labor, founded or restored edifices of public utility. Thus many of the counts and barons, disabled by age or infirmity from joining the Crusaders, desired to share their merits; thus many high-born ladies, rich and powerful castellans, were animated with the same spirit, and generously promoted the accomplishment of those noble projects.

To this principle, France, England, Germany, Italy, and the entire West, after the year 1000, owed those majestic monuments which are the objects of our admiration; monuments which modern times, notwithstanding the progress of arts and sciences, have been unable to surpass or even approach in their poor imitations. It was a beautiful spectacle to see these margraves, landgraves, counts, barons, lords of castles, presenting themselves to the bishops and abbots, and zealously co-operating with them in the restoration of the abbeys, priories, and churches of their dioceses; not only offering their treasures, but lending their horses, mules, wagons, for the good work, allowing them the use of their lands, quarries, and forests.

But the Church knows the value of organization, by rule, order, and harmony. She is the head which directs the members to a common end. The bishops and abbots divided these zealous Catholics into orders and classes, appointed managers under the leadership of a chief, who was to control the entire body. This is the origin in France, and afterwards in England and Germany, of the religious guilds of Masons. The members consecrated themselves to the erection of churches, monasteries, priories, chantries, collegiate churches, pastoral residences, hospitals for the sick, inns for travelers, asylums for lepers, bridges for streams and rivers.

The head of these confraternities was styled *Grand-Master of the Masons;* the subordinate chiefs, *Masters;* the ordinary workmen, *Masons;* the others, *Apprentices* or the initiated. Around the church were built temporary huts or shelters for the workmen. These were called *lodges.*

The members of these communities saluted one another by the Christian name of *brethren.* To gain admission and the indulgence attached to the guilds, it was necessary to go to confession and communion, swear obedience to the Grand Master, and execute the work allotted by the director of the lodge, but, above all, to forgive one's enemies and be reconciled with them. This last condition was essential in those warlike times, when villages and communes were engaged in continual conflicts with their neighbors, under the influence of those barbarous manners which perpetuated feuds, hatreds, and bloody retaliations. According to the most reliable histories we can trace the history of these confraternities to Chartres, at the beginning of the twelfth century, when the cathedral of that city was constructed. From Chartres they spread into Normandy and the rest of France. Thence they passed into England, Scotland, and particularly Flanders and Germany. It was a spectacle worthy of those heroic ages of faith which had succeeded the dismal period of barbarism to see noble and puissant barons approach the bishop with humble and reverential air, and ask his blessing, then offer their aid to the grand master, who admitted them as associates, and sent them to the masters to discharge assigned functions. It was an admirable spectacle to behold haughty marchionesses, and the daughters of landgraves, barons, counts, and even kings, earnestly soliciting the lowly and laborious condition of female masons, and congratulating themselves on their enrolment as sodalists.

When it was announced that a cathedral or monastic church was to be erected, masons and apprentices, in numerous bands, preceded by priests carrying the cross, were seen converging to the appointed place from the neighboring dwellings. They presented themselves to the masters, and repaired to their respective lodges to wait for orders. And now they began operations. They built the walls, dressed the stone, hewed the timber, formed the arch-frames, laid the floors, and raised the parapets. One slaked the lime and made the mortar, another sifted the gravel, one brought brush-wood and fagots for the furnaces, and another kneaded the clay or moulded tiles and bricks. Noble matrons and young ladies of wealth and station carried stone and wood upon their shoulders; they bore vessels of lime and sand; they drew water at the moats and rivers, and sometimes they were so numerous as to form an unbroken chain, and pass the water from the stream to the scene of labor.

The workmen, in the midst of these toils, maintained silence and recollection, demonstrative of the faith and religion which animated their souls. They chaunted at their work sacred hymns and canticles, in honor of Mary, the

Virgin Mother of God. They fasted on the eves of the great solemnities, and the priests urged them to offer to God their pains, fatigues, and all discomforts, under a burning sun, cold, rain, and not unfrequently with unwholesome food. If any dispute arose among them, the priests and the masters settled the difficulty, and those very men wont to tyrannize over their vassals bowed their heads cheerfully to the yoke of obedience.

When we read the history of that Masonic institution, we feel ourselves transported with admiration in view of the power of Catholic faith and divine charity which originated it and sustained it. In A. D. 1145, Aymon, Abbot of St. Peter of Dives, wrote a letter to the monks of the Abbey of Jutteburg. In this letter he gives them an account of the wonders wrought by this confraternity in the erection of St. Peter's Church. "You might see," says the Abbot, "the most powerful nobles and ladies of eminent rank, engaged heartily in this charitable work. Unmindful of their distinguished birth, the authority of their state, the delicacy of their nurture, and the charms of their princely homes, they harnessed themselves to carts and transported to the building, wood, stone, sand, and other materials. After the hard labors of the day, they watched a good portion of the night; placing lighted torches in their vehicles, and chanting hymns and pious canticles."

He then relates the origin of the Masonic fraternities at the construction of the Chartres Cathedral, and their subsequent extension over all Normandy. The Abbot of Dives here ends his interesting narrative. But we may find full details of their operations in the History of the Archbishops of Rouen, the Annals of the Order of St. Benedict, and the Continuation of Sigebert, by Robert Dumont. Spondanus, in the History of Geneva, gives a manuscript of 1213 which chronicles the institution of a Masonic corporation to build the great Cathedral of St. Peter. This noble structure was respected by the Calvinists, but sacrilegiously destroyed by modern Masons. Nowhere were these associations more wisely organized than at Strasbourg, A. D. 1450, under the architect Dotzinger. Mediæval faith and piety, as we clearly see, gave birth to the Masonic lodges under the inspiration of the Church, which won the co-operation of the faithful by the promise of indulgences granted to the Crusaders. The splendid results of this enterprise are seen in the Cathedrals of Chartres, Bourges, Cologne, Mayence, Strasbourg, Westminster; in every part of France, England, Scotland, Germany, and Switzerland. The Italian communes and republics contributed most to the admirable structures in their own country, aided, however, in an eminent degree by the confraternities.

Let us now see the two other causes in operation for the building of churches—the munificence of kings and families, and the devotion of the multitude.

"When the brave Emperor Charles," writes an old historian, "might have enjoyed some repose, he chose not to indulge in rest, but to labor for the divine service, and so he began to build the church of Aix-la-Chapelle."[*]

Earl Richard, brother of Henry III., on the vigil of St. Leonards, assisted at the consecration of the church he had built at Hales, and which cost him ten thousand marks. "Would to God," he exclaimed, after the ceremony, "that I had spent as wisely and as usefully the money which I have expended on the Castle of Wallingford."[†]

Godfrey, the bearded Duke of Lower Lorraine worked with his own hands at St. Mary's church, at Verdun; he carried the mortar like the meanest workman. This was in 1045. He did it in penance for his sins, as Lambertinus Schaffenburgensis relates.

The chapter-house and the sacristy of the convent of the Carthusians, at Paris, was built at the expense of Peter Loisel, a shoemaker, in the fourteenth century.

---

[*] Dom. Bong. Tom V. 118. [†] Matt. Paris, ad Ann. 1251.

We read in the Gospel that the Jews commended to our Lord one who had built for them a synagogue. " Now if he, on that account, deserved to be commended to our Lord, how much more is he deserving who builds a church ? " says St. Ambrose. " What shall I say of our brethren, the holy men Vitalianus and Majanus ? I know that they seek not glory from men, but from God; yet if I were not to speak their praise, these works themselves would cry out ; for they constructed this tabernacle, and at their own expense, and what great expense, considering how moderate and slight are their worldly means! Theirs was abundance of faith and the riches of simplicity, for to holy men poverty itself is always rich. Therefore, I believe that these blessed men built the church no less with their prayers than with their money ; they expended all their substance on it, and yet they wanted nothing, which shows how rich is poverty when all is expended." *

Lord Arpins and his wife made, in the year 1040, their last will in the following manner : " When we commenced to reflect that we had been conceived and born in sin, and had from our infancy committed many faults every day, and how on the day of judgment we should have to give a strict account of all our thoughts, words, and actions, and that every one would receive from the Eternal Judge what he had deserved ; and again when we reflected how sinners will be cast into fire everlasting for having neglected to redeem their sins here below, and how the elect of God will enter into everlasting bliss : then, all on a sudden, our hearts felt deeply touched by the mercy of God, and we were filled with great fear and trembling. Whilst yet reflecting about what we should do, we felt inspired to go and ask the advice of holy priests and religious men on the manner of redeeming our innumerable sins, of escaping hell, and making sure of heaven. We were told that under our circumstances we

---

* St. Ambrose, Serm. 89.

could do nothing better than to give alms and to build, out of our own means, a church and a monastery, in which monks might serve God in a holy manner, and chant His praises, according to the rule and constitutions of St. Benedict, and pray for us incessantly. With the greatest pleasure we received this advice, and went by it. We built a church in honor of our Lord Jesus Christ, and His mother, the Blessed Virgin Mary, and we made it over to the venerable Father Dominic and his monks, that they might serve and praise God therein." *

An old Chinese came one day to the missionary of his village, in order to express his ardent wish that a church should be built in the place. "Your zeal is praiseworthy," answered the father, "but at present I have not the necessary funds to meet such expenses." "I mean to build it myself," answered the villager. The missionary having known him for many years, thought him altogether incapable of accomplishing his intention. He praised anew his good will, by calling to mind that the village was large, and would consequently require a church as large as that of the neighboring city, that afterwards he might contribute to its erection according to his means, but he alone could not realize the requisite amount. "Pardon me," rejoined the countryman, "I think myself capable of doing what I propose." "But are you aware," rejoined the missionary, "that such an undertaking will cost at least two thousand crowns?" "I have them already," answered the old man, "otherwise I would assuredly have taken care not to trouble you with my request." The good father was delighted to learn that this man, whom he thought so poor, had already all the money he required, and that he wished to employ it for so good a purpose. But he was still more surprised when, having the curiosity to ask the villager, how he could save such an amount, he was told that for forty years he had been meditating this project;

---

* Baronius.

he curtailed all that was not absolutely necessary with regard to food and clothing, in order to have the consolation, before dying, of having left in his native village a church built in honor of the true God.

In the eleventh century, Bertha, the mother of St. Eberhard, Archbishop of Salzburg, carried stones on her shoulders, walking barefoot for the space of half a league, to serve in the construction of the Church of St. Mary, which then was being built in her own village of Allersdorf.

St. Victrice, Archbishop of Rouen, in the fourth century, tells us that he and his clergy labored with their own hands to build the Church of God in that city.

The Cardinal de Berulle was inflamed with such zeal that, when he had purchased ground for the Church, he used to work himself at the building, like an apostolic man, carrying the hods as if he had been a common laborer. This was in 1616.*

When the cathedral of Lincoln was being built, St. Hugh carried stones on his shoulders in a hod. Now, when a cripple who walked upon crutches, saw this, he asked permission to imitate the saint, firmly hoping that he would recover the use of his limbs. So a hod filled with stones was given to him; he carried it aided by his two crutches. A few days after he needed only one crutch to enable him to work, and a little later he threw away even that, and worked at the building without any crutch at all, being perfectly restored. "Since which cure," says Matthew Paris, "nothing can separate him from his hod." †

When the Church of St. Jacques-du-haut-pas, at Paris, was to be built, it was the piety of high and low that accomplished the undertaking. The Duchess de Longueville gave money; the owners of quarries supplied free of charge all the stone, and the workmen employed in building gave each one a day every week. ‡

---

* De St. Victor, Tableau de Paris, tom. I., 812.   † Ad ann. 1200
‡ St. Victor, Tableau de Paris, tom. III., 435.

To effect the incrustation of marble in the Church of Loretto, which alone cost about three hundred thousand crowns, the carvers gave their work gratis.

When Desiderius, the abbot of Monte Casino, was about to rebuild the church of that monastery, so great was the fervor of the faithful that the first column was borne from the base of the mountain to the summit upon the shoulders of the multitude.

After the dreadful fire which destroyed the Abbey of Crowland, in England, in the time of Ingulphus, the charity of the people far and near was excited towards the monks. They gave money and provisions, fat hogs, and beans, and corn, and oxen. Among so many good people there was a poor old woman of holy memory at Weston, named Juliana, who, out of her poverty, gave all her living, namely, some yarn and spinning-thread, to make vestments for the brethren in the monastery. Multitudes gave the labor of their hands, taking it in turn to serve one day in every month until all was finished.* Every one thought to receive a blessing from heaven if he had part in the holy work.

Fulcuin, in his history of the Abbots of Lobes, relates that there was a great assembly of people on the spot where their new church was to be built, and such was their devotion that no one can describe it. With the money then offered by the people the church is marked out and begun. To account for the sufficiency of these oblations of the people, which were either daily or weekly, it should be remembered that the laborious and simple tenor of their lives enabled them to have always some supply beyond what was required by their family wants.

Those pious confraternities of the Masons exist no longer. They have been succeeded by the so-called "Free Masons" —those diabolical confraternities, whose object is to destroy all belief in God and to assist the devil to regain dominion over mankind. Neither do we find now-a-days among em-

---
* Hist. Ingulph, p. 99.

perors, kings, nobles, and the rich, that great munificence which, in the ages of faith, erected so many magnificent temples in honor of the Lord. This want of liberality is all owing to the want of faith among the higher classes. Thousands of dollars are spent for the gratification of sinful pleasures and on frivolous objects. Nothing or but very little is given to the Lord, and what is given, is but too often given with reluctance.

Now-a-days it is the poor that build our churches. Like their ancestors in the faith, they still consider churches, in their character of Catholic sanctuaries, disposed for certain specific moral ends towards furthering the sanctification of souls and increasing the number of the elect, as having their splendor within, and as being remedies and instruments of deliverance for the wretched captives of this world. They consider them as spiritual asylums, to which men can fly at every moment to escape the death of the soul, recover the joy of salvation, and be strengthened with a perfect spirit. "This is truly the house of prayer," sings the Church in the office of the dedication. "This is the temple of the habitation of Thy glory, the seat of unchangeable truth, the sanctuary of eternal love. This is the ark which leads us from the flood of the world into the port of salvation. This is the only and beloved spouse whom Christ acquired with His blood, whom He vivifies with His spirit; in whose bosom, being regenerated by Thy grace, we are fed with the milk of the Word, we are strengthened with the Bread of Life, we are consoled with the assistance of Thy mercy Thus, He preserving, militates faithfully on earth, and He crowning, triumphs everlastingly in heaven."

This faith makes the poor contribute cheerfully, according to their ability, towards the erection of churches. They know and believe that every donation makes them share in all the Masses and prayers that are said in them; that it adds to the beauty of their souls; that it renders their prayers more powerful with Almighty God; that it multiplies their temporal goods a hundred-fold; that it cancels their sins and the temporal punishments due to them. They believe that every little contribution for the erection of a Church will avert from them God's anger; that the Sacrifice of propitiation and praise of their charitable donations will cause great joy in heaven; that it will be for them a subject of consolation in the hour of death; that it will inspire them with great confidence in Jesus Christ, their eternal Judge, and will gloriously prevail upon Him to pronounce sentence in their favor. They believe that every little contribution will give them one more claim on heaven; that it will be one more precious stone wherewith to adorn their crown of glory in Paradise; that it will bring them nearer to the delightful company of the great saints—the noble children of God in heaven; and that it will make them shine like the sun on the last day, when they will exclaim with all the saints in joyful accents: "Benediction and glory, and wisdom, and thanksgiving, honor and power, and strength to our God for ever and ever." *

As churches are built in honor of the Lord, He should have them as it were for His audience chamber, not only on Sundays, but also on the six other days of the week. In every dwelling-house the reception-room is not placed in the basement, but in the best part of the building. On the other six days of the week, then, the basement of the Church should not be assigned to the Lord of heaven and earth for His abode and audience-chamber. Love and reverence for Jesus Christ forbid it. Moreover, as churches are built chiefly by the poor and for the poor, they should have free access to their Lord in the Blessed Sacrament at any time during the day. The rich have their marble palaces where they can receive their friends and enjoy themselves; but the poor have often no other house, no other place of rest and consolation than the church, in which our Lord resides.

Is it then not strange to see so many churches closed

---

* Apocal. vii. 12.

during the whole day? One day, when blessed Balthasar Alvarez was kneeling before the altar, our dear Lord in the Blessed Sacrament manifested to him His great eagerness to distribute His graces to Christians. He showed Himself in the Sacred Host as a little child, with His hands full of precious stones, and said: "If there were only some souls here to whom I might distribute them." This complaint of our Lord is but too well founded. There are pious, faithful souls in every parish, souls that would wish to entertain themselves every day with their dear Saviour in the Blessed Sacrament—souls most desirous to follow the invitation of Jesus Christ: "Come to me all ye that labor and are heavy laden, and I will refresh you." Some of these souls are so situated that they find it convenient to go and pay a visit to our Lord in the Blessed Sacrament, almost at any hour of the day. But the greater part of them can do so only after their day's work is over; and these know that it is of no use to go to Church, because most of the churches are closed, like Protestant churches, during the whole day, with the exception of a very short time in the morning. Banks are open every day for several hours. Stores are open from morning to night. Bar-rooms are open day and night. We have access to physicians at any time in the day and night. We can pay visits even to prisoners during some hours in the day. But alas! the church, the store-house of our Lord, and the home of the poor and the afflicted, is locked for six days in the week. The people have no access to their heavenly physician, desirous, as He is, to distribute His graces to all without exception. It can only be want of faith that locks so many churches.

Faith in the Real Presence, to become quite lively, so lively as to make us exult and rejoice when before the altar, must be daily nourished. We cannot nourish and increase it better than by daily visits to our dear Saviour in the Blessed Sacrament. To lock the churches and thus prevent the people from coming to our Lord, is to keep them in a state of coldness and indifference towards Him. It is to keep them in a state of great imperfection during their whole life, for we must not expect to find much perfection where there is no lively faith. Who shall answer before Jesus Christ for this want of faith, and consequently for all the faults and evils, temporal as well as spiritual, that flow from it? It is an indispensable duty for pastors to see that their flocks should become every day stronger in faith, in order to resist the many attacks of the enemies of our holy religion. With this duty they cannot comply better than by attaching the people more and more inseparably to Jesus Christ in the Blessed Sacrament. In the great trials that soon will come upon Catholics, many will fall away for want of a lively faith in the Real Presence. Jesus Christ will hold many a pastor responsible for the loss of these souls. Let pastors, therefore, open the churches and exhort the people to visit our Lord as often as possible.

The pretext that, were the church left open, something might be stolen, is no sufficient reason for keeping it locked the whole day. Storekeepers do not lock their stores in the day-time for such a pretext. Why then should so many pastors do so? Should now and then something be stolen, our Lord and good Catholics will know how to make up for it a hundredfold. The greater the faith of the people in the Real Presence, the more liberal they will be in contributing towards the support of their good pastors and towards the embellishment of the churches.

And, after all, a little more faith, hope, and charity, an increase of which souls so easily obtain before the altar, is of unspeakably greater value before God than all the precious articles that might be taken from a church.

The greater the faith of the people is in the Real Presence, the more docile they will be to the voice of their pastor, as to the voice of the Divine Shepherd in the Blessed Sacrament, and thus they will give little or no trouble to him in guiding them in the pathway to heaven.

One who truly loves Jesus Christ in the Blessed Sacrament, ardently wishes always to stay and converse with Him; he wishes to see the hearts of his fellow-men inflamed with the same love for Jesus with which his own is burning. He does all in his power to enkindle this love in the heart of his neighbor. Nothing pains him more than to see such coldness and indifference in men towards Jesus Christ in the Blessed Sacrament. But what pains him most is to see that so many of those whose duty it is to enkindle the love of Jesus Christ in the hearts of their fellow-men, are the coldest of all towards their God and Saviour. Let this coldness towards Jesus Christ be changed into love for Him, and the churches will remain open, and our dear Saviour will always have near Him some loving souls to whom He can give His graces, and make them happy in time and for eternity.

CHAPTER XLVIII.

THE LOVE OF GOD.

Some years ago a vessel sailed from the coast of Ireland. It was filled with passengers who were coming to this country to better their fortune. The vessel set sail with a favorable wind; the sky was clear, and the sun shone gaily upon the sparkling sea. But suddenly the heavens grew dark. A fierce storm arose: the winds howled madly around the vessel, which was hurried on—on, till it was dashed against the rocks. The wild, surging waves dashed over it, and split it in twain. Part remained hanging amid the rocks, and the rest sank with those on board beneath the waves, far down into the depths of the sea. The storm continued to rage for several days. At last, when the wind had died away, some hardy fishermen who lived on the coast, took a skiff and rowed out to the wreck. They entered the part of the vessel that remained hanging amid the rocks. They broke open the cabin door. They heard distinctly the feeble wail of a child; and rushing in they found a little babe lying upon the breast of its dead mother. The child was eagerly sucking the blood which oozed from a large wound in its mother's breast. She had died of cold and hunger, but even amid her fearful sufferings did not forget her child. She took a sharp knife, and with the wonderful love of a mother's heart, made a deep gash in her breast, in order that her child might preserve its life by drinking her own heart's blood.

Now, we do not wonder at the love of this mother for her offspring. God has made the love of mothers for their children a necessary love. It is proverbial. Indeed, there is no love so pure and so thoroughly disinterested as the love of a good mother for her child. Her love knows no change. Brothers and sisters have forgotten each other; fathers have proved unforgiving to their children; husbands have been false to their wives, wives to their husbands; children too often forget their parents; but you rarely hear of a mother forgetting even her ungrateful, disobedient children, whose actions have lacerated her heart, and caused dark shadows to cross her life and enter her very soul. Still there are moments when her faithful heart yearns towards them; when the reminiscences of the happy past obliterate the present sorrow, and the poor wounded spirit is cheered for awhile, because there is still one of the fibres of the root of hope left in her forlorn breast, and a languid smile will flit over her wan and faded face. Yes, she forgives, though there is no Lethe for her to drink from in this life; showing that her love is the most pure in this world, and the nearest approach to the love that God has so graciously bestowed upon her. Who can measure the depth of the wonderful love of a mother's heart!

But what is the love of all mothers united for their children compared to that which God feels for men! "*God is love.*" This is the Gospel which the heavens and the earth are ever telling. For love of man God created the boundless universe with all its millions of stars and countless worlds; and He made the universe the temple of His endless love. The stars of heaven, as they sweep along in silent harmony, are ever singing a wondrous song, and the sweet burden of their song is "*God is love.*"

This world is the temple of God's love. The green earth, with its thousand flowers, is the carpeted floor. The clear blue sky above is the vaulted dome; its pillars are the cloud-capped mountains, white with eternal snow. The mists and vapor that are ever ascending from the earth, like the smoke of sacrifice, remind us of the thoughts of love and gratitude that should ever ascend from our hearts. The whispering of the winds, the rush of the storm, the murmuring of the brook, and roar of the cataract, are the sublime music that raise our hearts to God.

For love of man God has raised a still more wondrous temple—the temple of His Holy Church. Millions and millions of chosen souls have aided in building this wondrous temple. Its foundation was laid at the gates of Paradise. The patriarchs and prophets have labored at this temple through the long ages of hope and expectation. It was completed in the fullness of time, by the Only-Begotten of the Father, our Lord Jesus Christ. This temple of love was consecrated by the Holy Ghost on that wonderful day of love, the Feast of Pentecost. The summit of this glorious temple of love now rises to the highest heavens, and to the throne of the living God Himself. In its width it extends over all the earth, and excludes no one who is willing to enter its portals. In its depth it reaches to that region of suffering where those are detained who are to be cleansed from all stain before entering into the unutterable joys of heaven. In every part of this glorious temple you can read written, "God is love."

The Divine love for man was extreme, as it had been from all eternity. But heretofore, how great, how inconceivable it was, had not appeared. It was only when the Son of God showed Himself a little one in a stable, on a bundle of straw, that the love of God truly appeared. From the beginning of the world men had seen the power of God in the creation, and His wisdom in the government of the world; but only in the Incarnation of the Word was it seen how great was His love for man. Before God was seen made man upon earth, men could not form an idea of the Divine Goodness; therefore did He take mortal flesh, that, appearing as man, He might make plain to men the greatness of His benignity.

Alexander the Great, after he had conquered Darius and subdued Persia, wished to gain the affections of that people, and accordingly went about dressed in the Persian costume. In like manner would our dear Lord appear to act; in order to draw towards Him the affections of men, He clothed Himself completely after the human fashion, and appeared made man. By this means He wished to make known the depth of the love which He bore to man. Man does not love Me, would God seem to say, because he does not see Me; I wish to make Myself seen by him, and to converse with him, and so make Myself loved.

It was not enough for the Divine love to have made us to His own image in creating the first man Adam; He must also Himself be made to our image in redeeming us. Adam partook of the forbidden fruit, beguiled by the serpent, which suggested to Eve that if she ate of that fruit she should become like to God, acquiring the knowledge of good and evil; therefore the Lord then said: "Behold, Adam is become like one of us."* God said this ironically, and to upbraid Adam for his rash presumption. But after the Incarnation of the Word of God we can truly say—Behold, God is become like one of us. "Look, then, O man," exclaims St. Augustine, "thy God is made thy brother." He could have assumed the nature of an angel; but no, He would take on Himself thy very flesh, that thus He might give satisfaction to God with the very flesh (though sinless) of Adam the sinner. And He even gloried in this, oftentimes styling Himself the Son of Man; hence, we have every right to call Him our brother.

It was an immeasurably greater humiliation for God to become man, than if all the princes of the earth, than if all the angels and saints of heaven, with the Divine Mother herself, had been turned into a blade of grass, or into a handful of clay; yes, for grass, clay, princes, angels, saints, are all creatures; but between the creature and God there is an infinite difference.

But the more God has humbled Himself for us in becoming man, so much the more has He made His goodness

---

* Gen. iii. 22.

known to us. As the sportsman keeps in reserve the best arrow for the last shot, in order to secure his prey, so did God among all his gifts keep Jesus Christ in reserve till the fullness of time should come, and then He sent Him as a last dart to wound with His love the hearts of men.

Jesus, then, was the choice and reserved arrow of the love of God, at the discharge of which entire nations should fall vanquished. And, indeed, our Divine Redeemer drew all hearts after Him—the hearts of children, the hearts of the just, and even the hearts of sinners. Now, whence came this wondrous power? Love is the free spontaneous gift of the heart. Love cannot be forced; it cannot be bought. All the gold in the universe cannot purchase hearts. "Love me if thou wilt be loved," is the language which the human heart holds even to God Himself. You may chain the limbs, but you cannot chain the heart. How, then, has Jesus won the love of so many hearts? How has He won the love of so many souls in every age—souls who have loved Him more than wealth, more than honor, more than life itself? It is only by love. It is because Jesus has loved more than mortal man can ever love. It is because He has loved with the unutterable love of a God. The Gospel, indeed, tells us but little of the outward appearance of Jesus; but sufficient to convince us that the majesty of a sweet and winning love shone forth in all His actions. Born of a Virgin, conceived (in the chaste womb of His Blessed Mother) by the operation of the Holy Ghost, destined to be the perfect type of sinless humanity, we should have naturally expected beforehand that our Blessed Lord would be far more beautiful than even Adam was when he came forth from the hands of God in all the bloom of innocence. Indeed, the prophets foretold that He was to be "beautiful exceedingly, beautiful above the children of men." And, if we watch the effect of our Lord's appearance upon those around Him, we shall see that a majestic sweetness shone forth in His every look, word, and gesture. He chose for His emblem the Lamb, the gentlest of all creatures, and so brightly did this gentleness beam forth from His Divine countenance, that as soon as the holy Baptist beheld Him, he cried aloud: "Behold, the Lamb of God!"

Our Blessed Redeemer became a little child for the very purpose of winning our most tender love. He put on the innocent look of childhood in its most winning form. He veiled the light of intellect in His infant eyes, that there might shine through them more tenderly the playful loveliness of childhood. And at length, when He grew up and went forth into the world, the same winning sweetness accompanied Him everywhere. As He was walking one day by the Sea of Galilee, He sees some fishermen mending their nets, and, addressing them, says: "Come, follow Me," and in an instant, as soon as they see Him, their eyes gaze upon Him, and these rude fishermen are chained. They leave all to follow Him, to be His for time and for eternity.

Nor is it only pure and loving souls that follow Him. The people also follow in crowds, even into the depths of the wilderness. They left their homes, their labors, their families. When once they had gazed on the beautiful face of Jesus, when once they had heard the words of life that flowed from His sweet lips, they could not rest without Him. Without Him home was a desert, with Him the desert bloomed like a rose. Little children are generally the best judges of kindness and gentleness. The Gospel tells us how little children loved our dear Lord, and how He loved to see them around Him. When He passed through the towns and hamlets, the children flocked to Him, and mothers brought their little ones to receive His blessing. When the Apostles wished to send them away lest they should weary their Divine Master, Jesus took the part of the little ones, and said: "Let these little children come to Me, and do not send them away, for they resemble the blessed in heaven."

In order to win all hearts, Jesus made Himself all to all. Had it been left to us to decide how God should appear and act when He came on earth to live and to converse with men, we should naturally have supposed that He would come with a beautiful and glorious body, incapable of pain or weariness. We might have thought that He would shut Himself up like a king, in some gorgeous palace, to show Himself only on high festivals, surrounded by dazzling splendor, and guarded by countless myriads of bright angels. Or we might have imagined that He would live like a hermit in some wild solitude, surrounded by darkness and mystery, wrapped in perpetual prayer and contemplation. But no; Jesus is a public man. He is open to all by day and night. Rich and poor, gentle and simple, have equal access to Him. He is exposed to the unthinking rudeness of the rabble, to the importunate curiosity of the intrusive, to the refined insolence of the proud. Day after day He is subjected to the arrogance of the Pharisee, to the familiarity of the publican, even to the shameless gaze of the harlot. How great is the loving condescension of Jesus! When we consider the sanctity of God, that awful sanctity, which once by a deluge cleansed a guilty world, we naturally think that when Jesus came into personal contact with public and notorious sinners, His Divine sanctity would flash through His humanity, and crush to the earth those guilty creatures. But no. That He might banish our fears, Jesus even assures us that He "came not to judge the world, but to save the world." "I am come," He says, "not to call the just, but to call sinners to repentance." One day, the Pharisees bring before Him a woman taken in adultery, and they call on Him to judge her. Jesus risks His own life to save her's. He exposes Himself for her sake to all the taunts and calumnies of His enemies. And, when at last He is left alone with her, He releases her, and, without a word of reproach, bids her "go and sin no more."

The love of Jesus was unutterably deep, and tender, and, as is always the case with those that love, He was keenly sensitive, keenly alive to neglect and ingratitude. Witness our Blessed Lord during His agony in the Garden of Olives.

See how He rises and goes to His disciples. Listen to His melancholy wail of disappointment at finding them asleep: "Could you not watch one hour with me?" He asks three times. He goes to them to seek for sympathy, and as He emerges from the deep shade of the olive-trees, His face is ghastly pale, and on His brow there are crimson drops of blood. How well do those gory drops tell how keenly He felt the indifference of His friends. We may, perhaps, have suffered much, but we never know how long and how keenly the human heart can suffer before it breaks. There is a power of grief in it that few men ever fathom in this world. There are inward griefs that gnaw worse than the gibbet and the rack. Insult, and shame, and unrequited love, affections rudely torn, can wound and tear the heart far more than outward pain can rack the limbs; and there are times when separation or neglect can crush it, and turn its whole capacity of loving into a source of poignant grief. All this our Blessed Lord knew too well. He had created the human heart—He knew how keenly alive it is to suffering; and therefore, to show us how to suffer, to show us the greatness of His love, He endured every pang that the heart can bear. There is not a pain or grief that man has ever suffered, but Jesus suffered during His bitter Passion. There is not a pain or grief that we have ever borne but has first passed through the loving heart of Jesus. He made Himself like to us in everything except sin. Our Divine Redeemer loved us with unutterable love, and to show us how truly He suffered for us, He died for us. Had He passed through the sorrows of His Passion firm and unmoved, then, indeed, we might have worshipped Him as some ideal which we could never hope to follow. Had we seen Him bear His Passion with a calm or joyous brow, we might have worshipped the majesty of grief and turned away without a hope of ever treading in His footsteps. But when we see Him weeping and seeking sympathy, with pallid face, lying prostrate on more than mother's love. Every throb that sends the gushing blood through every pore of Jesus' Blessed Body betrays the mighty agony of love that struggles in His heart.

During His terrible agony in the garden, our Lord allowed such fear and sadness to possess His soul, that He would have died had not His Divine power upheld Him. As He kneels amid the olive-trees, in the solemn stillness of the moonlit night, He sees and feels in spirit all the pain and outrage He is to suffer on the morrow. He is to give Himself up into the hands of His enemies, and they shall glut their fiendish rage upon Him. He already feels on His cheek the cold kiss of the traitor Judas. He feels the cords upon His hands. And now, as He stands within the judgment-hall, He sees the dark scowl upon the faces of His enemies. He hears the sentence of death pronounced against Him. He feels the blows, the foul spittle upon His face, and all the while His soul is filled with unutterable horror, and He shrinks with disgust from the thought, as a modest maiden would shrink from contact with an insulting crowd. Deeper in the night another scene arises before Him. The very dignity of manhood is gone from Him, and in shame and nakedness He stands—O God! what a fearful humiliation! Tied to a pillar like a slave, while His virgin flesh is torn by the cruel lash. Farther on He sees a vast crowd deliberating on His fate, as He stands before them with the crown of thorns twining through His matted hair, and piercing His temples, while the blood is filling up His hollow eyes and coursing down His cheeks. They fix on Him a scowl of rage and hate. He hears the horrid yell ring wildly through the air: "Crucify Him! Crucify Him!"

Jesus turns away in horror from the scene; but all is not over yet. He feels the heavy Cross upon His bleeding shoulders. He sees His Mother's eyes bent upon Him, and oh! how His heart is wrung by the speechless agony of that fond look! He knows that not a pang can reach His heart but must pass through her virgin bosom. She must hear the nails crash through His tender hands and feet. She must see His tortured limbs stretched upon the Cross. How His inmost soul is racked by the thought of His Mother's compassionate grief! And now, as He struggles against the natural repugnance for suffering, the anxious question arises in His mind—the question that every one naturally asks before making a sacrifice: What shall I gain by all these sufferings? Will men profit by them? Will men use well the priceless treasures I have won for them at the cost of so much pain and labor? Will they remember Me and be grateful to Me for all I have done for them? Alas, for man's ingratitude! At that moment there arise before the soul of Jesus, all the sins, not of a single night, or of a single town only, but of the whole world, through the long course of ages, every moment of which brings forth its separate sin. The history of the world is before His mind, past, present, and to come; and now He, the Creator, shows once for all what a mighty grief its funeral deserves. Time and space are swept away from His mind, and He beholds all human beings at a glance. He knows them all by name. They are the work of His hands; but now He can only look in helpless agony upon the progress and punishment of their guilt. He looks into the inmost soul of each one, and sees it torn with horrid passions—men pale with rage and withering away with jealousy and hate. He sees the oppressor and the oppressed, the seducer and the seduced. And with boundless love for them, He is searching the while their hearts, only to find them obstinately bent on their own ruin. He wishes, He yearns to save them, but they will not be saved. He prays for them, but His very prayers only give them new graces to abuse, and all His loving favors only serve to increase their guilt in this world and their torments in the next.

Jesus looks to His Apostles, to His followers, and sees how they are hated and persecuted. He sees His priests condemned to the flames, His virgins torn with cruel scourges, and all for His name's sake. He looks forward to the time when the world shall call itself Christian, and yet even then, everywhere till the day of doom, the same sad scene comes up before Him. What He expected was a burning love of God, and He sees it feebly struggling with the love of self. What He wished for was compassion with Himself and with His blessed Mother, but He sees His sufferings forgotten, or, at best, remembered only as men think of dead relations whom they have never seen, but whose benefits they enjoy. He gave men grace enough to follow Him to the Cross with a seraph's love. He looked to them to share His glorious shame, but He sees them turn from Him in disgust because His brow is blood-stained, and his cheek is deathly pale, though all for them. He sees the truth all but dying out, and heresy triumphant. He sees whole kingdoms sold and bartered for miserable interests. He sees good men cowardly and bad men brave. He sees thousands of souls for whom He died, wandering about as sheep without a shepherd. He sees His Mother's name blasphemed by wicked men; His holy Church calumniated; His Sacraments despised and trodden under foot. Then there arises before Him the dark, dreary world of heathenism. Entire generations are swept from the earth before they hear His name; or, worse than all, whole nations are to hear it only to curse the day when Christian men came to their shores to teach them vices they never knew before.

And it is for such a world as this that He is to die? An unutterable repugnance rises within His heart as again there comes before His soul the thought of man's ingratitude, and how many would be lost in spite of all His sufferings. He looks for those who should stand foremost with Him in the battle, and there opens in the dark valley before Him the yawning gulf of hell, where He beholds some of His own chosen ones struggling in the grasp of demons—ghastly shapes with a priestly character! There, amid the devouring flames, are some of His very spouses, whom He had loved with more than a bridegroom's love! No wonder that the soul of Jesus is "sad unto death." No wonder that His soul is bowed down with despondency and repugnance—no wonder that the piercing cry is wrung from His heart: "O Father, if it be possible, let this Chalice pass from Me! But Father, not My will, but Thine be done."

Alas! His loving heart can bear no more! The cold sweat upon His brow is turned to blood, which falls in crimson drops upon the ground. O loving heart of Jesus! no scourge has touched Thy flesh, no thorn has pierced Thy brow, no nail has rent Thy hands, and see, Thy sacred Heart sends forth its precious blood! Alas! how great is the ingratitude and malice of men! They choose to be lost in spite of all God's efforts to save them. But yet Jesus at least shall do His part. Neither the crimes of sinners, nor the hatred of the wicked, the contempt of unbelievers, nor the indifference of the lukewarm, the neglect of the worldly-minded, nor the fickleness of the weak, the faithlessness of the good, nor the coldness of His spouses, shall ever lessen His love. The ingratitude, the malice of men is great, but the love of Jesus is greater. "No man hath greater love than he who layeth down his life for his friends." Jesus died upon the Cross once for all, to prove the sincerity of His love; and were it necessary, or even *expedient*, He would willingly hang upon the Cross till the day of doom. But He knows the hearts of men too well; He knows that such suffering would be useless. Nay, His continued visible presence amongst them would serve only to make them *more guilty*, more hardened in crime. Why, men were sinning at the very foot of the Cross on which He hung, dying; and by His side was a hardened wretch, blaspheming with his dying breath. No! the loving heart of Jesus has done all it could do. It can do but one thing more: it can break. There was, indeed, life enough left in the mangled form of Jesus to have lived even longer upon the Cross, but His weary heart could bear no more, and so He died of a broken heart—broken for the sins and the ingratitude of men.

And now that all is over, and that loving heart is still in death, let us come and gaze awhile upon the work of our hands. The sun has gone down upon Jerusalem; and the moon, which the night before witnessed Jesus' fearful agony in the garden, now throws its pale light upon the mournful group that prepares His Body for burial. There He lies motionless in His Mother's arms. His lips are mute. He cannot reproach us even if He would; and Mary can only point with silent finger to the wound in His side, and show us how it pierced His heart. There is a silent eloquence in that gaping wound which tells us more than words can express. It tells us that the bitter Passion—the crucifixion of Jesus—was not a mere display of God's power and justice, but that it was especially a proof of the real, hearty desire of the Creator to save His creatures. It was more, it was an earnest desire to make them forever happy. It is through the bleeding wound in His heart that Jesus now speaks to us. "Ah!" He says, "I might have passed My life on earth in the midst of ever-varying pleasures; I might have assumed a body bright and glorious, and incapable of suffering. But for love of men I chose one keenly alive to every pain, and My heart bore every woe that the human heart can ever bear. If men are lost it is no fault of Mine; I did My best to save them all. What more could I have done for them than I have done?" Did not faith assure us of it, who could ever believe that a God, out of love for such a worm as man is, should Himself become a worm like him, and die for him to save his life! A devout author says: "Suppose, by chance, that passing on your way you should have crushed to death a worm in your path, and then some one, observing your compassion for the poor worm, should say to you: Well, now, if you would restore that dead worm to life, you must first yourself become a worm like it, and then must shed all your blood and make a bath of it in which to wash the worm, and so it shall revive; what would you reply? Certainly, you would say: 'And what matters it to me whether the worm be alive or

dead, if I should have to purchase its life by my own death?'
And much more would you say so if it was not an inoffensive worm, but an ungrateful asp, which, in return for all your benefits, had made an attempt upon your life. But even should your love for that asp reach so far as to induce you to suffer death in order to restore it to life, what would men say then? And what would not that serpent do for you, whose death had saved it, supposing it were capable of reason? But this much has Jesus Christ done for you, most vile worm; and you, with the blackest ingratitude, have tried oftentimes to take away His life; and your sins would have done so, were Jesus liable to die any more. How much viler are you in the sight of God than a worm is in your own sight! What difference would it make to God had you remained dead and forever reprobate in your sins, as you well deserved? Nevertheless this God had such a love for you that to release you from eternal death, He first became a worm like you, and then, to save you, would lavish upon you His heart's blood, even to the last drop, and endure the death which you had justly deserved."

"*God is love.*" This is the language which everything speaks to us in heaven and on earth, but nothing in heaven or on earth speaks this in such burning words as the Mystery of Love, the holy Sacrifice of the Mass, the holy Sacrament of the altar, the last legacy of love. True love knows no bounds, feels no burden, cares for no hardship. It believes that it may and can do all things. Such is true love; such is the love of Jesus Christ. To gain our love He has thought that He might and could do all things. Hence the cause of those strange abasements, of those mysterious humiliations of the God-man, in presence of which reason is astounded, the senses revolt, the heart is terrified, and unbelief repeats its ceaseless question: "How is that possible?" But a voice proceeds from the altar and from the Cross, and that voice answers us: "*Sic Deus dilexit mundum.*" "It is thus that God has loved the world."

The pretended impossibilities of faith are nothing else than the ineffable condescensions of a God Who loves us as God; the height, breadth, depth of *all* the mysteries of our holy faith, is but the height, the depth of the charity of Jesus Christ. His blood, which was shed to the last drop, is His title to the most beautiful of all royalties, the royalty of love. His crown of thorns is the diadem of love. His crib, cross, and altar, are the thrones of love, and the celebration of Mass is the banquet of love.

We read in Holy Scripture that King Assuerus, to manifest the riches and glory of his kingdom, made a solemn feast which lasted a hundred and fourscore days. Jesus Christ, the King of Kings, vouchsafed also, in a feast worthy of His greatness, to manifest the riches of His treasures and the majesty of His glory; it is the heavenly banquet of Holy Communion in which He gives Himself whole and entire to us. This heavenly feast, however, is not bounded within the term of a hundred and fourscore days, as that of the King Assuerus was; it has already lasted more than eighteen hundred years; we have eaten it every day, and it will continue to the end of the world. "Come," exclaims the royal prophet, "come and behold the works of God, the prodigious things He has wrought upon earth." *

How admirable is the wisdom and depth of His counsels! And how wonderful are the means which God's love makes use of for the salvation of men!

The Incarnation was a wonder of divine Love and Wisdom, so great and so deep that human capacity shrinks from the examination of it. The Passion and Death of our Lord bring us an awful and unspeakable illustration of love. The last legacy of love combines them both in one mystery so stupendous, that the very conception of it at once presents a divine moral and an infinite affection. "Having loved His own, He loved them to the end;" and in the fullness of that love "the end was the grandest illustration."

---

* Ps. xlv. 9.

Let us place ourselves at the Last Supper in the midst of His disciples. The shadow of parting is on the festivity, and the words of our dear Lord are the words of tenderness, but of farewell: "I will not leave you orphans, I will come to you."* "And now I am not in the world, and these are in the world, and I come to Thee. Preserve them in Thy name, whom Thou hast given to Me, that like Us, they may be one." And then the solicitude of the Father of the family for the bond which thus makes the household one: "By this shall all men know that you are My disciples, if you love one another. Love one another as I have loved you." Now, at the last hour, the last time He was to behold them together, the last time He was to exhort and encourage them, until He should have gone through the dark realm of death, He thought of the perfect gift and blessing, the richest and most precious inheritance; the most inestimable of all things that love ever conceived or bestowed; and a guard, power, direction, companionship, strength, and crown that would bring His own by the hand of love, through life, to be *one* and holy; and then by death and judgment to eternal joy.

Jesus, our Father, in leaving us, would combine so much love and majesty in one single institution, that man could not look and refuse to surrender his affection. Our dear Lord said, I will unlock the barred gates of Paradise, and I will place again in the midst of it the Tree of Life, "that he who eateth of it may not die." And the angels shall minister to the being with whom I thus become one. In the souls of those who obtain this inheritance, a grand beauty, all celestial, shall be set, nay, even so that the soul itself shall shine with a brilliancy that even the Father shall admire, and that shall attract Him and the Holy Ghost to come hither and abide. And thus I will make the soul of My beloved a temple, and a throne, and a heaven, and I will be and stay there with the heir of My love for evermore.

---

* John xiv. 18.

Ponder well, my soul, this awful distinction! Union with Christ: no longer "the tabernacle of God with men," "the gate of heaven," but the Lord of heaven, your guest—yourself—made one with you as two pieces of wax melted one into the other!

We become one with God! One with the Eternal! One with the Most Holy, the Lord! Oh! how little and vain all things which can be bestowed or attained, if compared with the overwhelming dignity, power, and greatness, of becoming one with God! How can we ever withdraw our mind from the single thought: "This is life eternal, that they know Thee, and Whom Thou hast sent, Jesus Christ." It is "life eternal" to know Him "in the breaking of bread," in the Blessed Sacrament; because one with Him, we must share what He possesses, and enjoy what He makes His delight, and live His life without end! "He who eateth My flesh and drinketh My blood abideth in Me and I in him, and I will raise him up at the last-day."

So dearly has God loved the world that He has given His only-begotten Son to be the life of the world. "God is love," and this sweet Sacrament is the mystery of His love. It was on the night before His passion—that very night in which men were plotting His ruin—when they decided to condemn Him to a most shameful death, that Jesus left us this living pledge of His love as a memorial. It was not a memorial of bronze or marble, as the great ones of this world leave behind them; no, it was his own living, life-giving Body and Blood—it was Himself. Did not God tell us long ago by the mouth of His prophet, that His delight was to be with the children of men? Did He not assure us with His own blessed lips, "that He would not leave us orphans, but that He would be with us always, even to the end of the world?" "God is love." He loves us with an infinite love. He has given us this earth, He has given us heaven, but all this will not satisfy His love. He gives us Himself, His body and blood, His soul and divinity. No wonder that

God cries out complainingly: "What more could I have done for thee, beloved soul, than I have done?" Yes, in this Sacrament, God has exhausted His Omnipotence; for, though He is all-powerful, He cannot do more for us than He has done. He has exhausted his infinite Wisdom; for, though He is all-wise, He could not plan a more wonderful proof of His love. He has exhausted His infinite wealth; for in this Sacrament He has poured out all the treasures of His unfathomable love.

God is love, and He gives Himself to us in the disguise of love. What an act of charity it is to a poor weak-sighted man to hide the dazzling light from his eyes! and what loving-kindness in our dear Lord to hide His dazzling splendor from our weak, sinful souls! Were He to appear in His glory, who is there that could look upon Him and live? If we look into the sun but for a moment, we are blinded by its brightness; how then could we gaze upon the unveiled splendors of the Eternal Sun of Justice? The prophet Daniel saw only an angel, and he fainted away; how then could we bear the sight of the King of angels? When Moses came down from Mount Sinai, where he had been conversing with God, his face shone with such unearthly lustre that the people could not look upon him. He had, therefore, to veil his face so that all might see him and speak to him. Now, if people were unable to look upon the face of a man, how should we be able to look upon the face of a God? The Apostles beheld on Mount Thabor but a faint glimpse of the glory of Jesus, and they fell prostrate to the ground. St. John, in the Isle of Patmos, beheld only in a vision the glory of Jesus, and he fell to the ground as if dead. How then could we, poor, weak sinners, bear to gaze on the entire fulness of the splendors of God's Infinite Majesty? Oh, what loving goodness then in Jesus our Lord, to hide His glory behind the veils of the Sacrament, that we might approach Him and speak to Him without fear, as a child to its father as a friend to a friend! Our divine

Redeemer took many various forms to attract the love of man. That God, Who is unchangeable, would appear now as a little babe in a crib, now as an exile in Egypt, now as a docile child among the Doctors of the Law in the Temple of Jerusalem, now as an apprentice in the workshop of St. Joseph, now as a servant in the house of Nazareth, now as a good shepherd, seeking the lost sheep of Israel, as a physician of body and soul, curing the diseases of the former and forgiving the sins of the latter; as a great malefactor and the most despised of men, bleeding to death for our sins upon the Cross between two robbers; as the conqueror of death and hell, and the glorious king of heaven and earth; and lastly, as bread upon the altar.

In these varying guises Jesus chose to exhibit Himself to us; but whatever character He assumed, it was always that of a lover. It is strange that God, Who is so good, so amiable, should be forced to have recourse to so many stratagems to win our love. He commands us to love Him, He promises us heaven if we obey, and He threatens us with the flames of hell if we refuse. To win our love he has annihilated Himself. He annihilated Himself in the Incarnation, but He has gone still farther in the mystery of the Holy Eucharist.

Ah, my Lord, is there anything left for Thee to devise in order to make Thyself loved? "Make known his inventions," exclaims the prophet Isaias.* Go, O redeemed souls, go and publish everywhere the loving devices of this loving God which He has thought out and executed to make Himself loved by man; for, after lavishing so many of His gifts upon them, He was pleased to bestow Himself, and to bestow Himself upon every one everywhere. If a king speaks a confidential word to one of his vassals, if he smiles upon him, how honored and happy does that vassal consider himself! How much more so, should the king seek his friendship; should he request his company every day at table,

---

* xll. 4.

should he desire him to reside in his own palace and to abide always near him!

Ah! my great King, my beloved Jesus, as before the Redemption Thou couldst not assume man into heaven, whose gates remained closed by sin, Thou camest down and still daily comest down upon earth to be with men as Thy brothers, and to give Thyself wholly to them from the excess of the love Thou bearest them! "He loved us and delivered Himself up for us." "Yes," exclaims St. Augustine, "this most loving and most merciful God, through His love to man, chose to give him not only His goods, but even His very Self." Well, then, the affection which this sovereign Lord entertains towards us miserable worms is so immense that it induced Him to give Himself wholly to us,—being born for us, living for us, and even offering up His life and all His blood for us every day in the Mass, in order to prepare us a bath of salvation, and to cleanse us from all our sins. But, Lord, this appears an extreme prodigality of Thyself. Yes, how otherwise can we consider God than prodigal of Himself, Who, in order to recover lost man, not only gives whatever He has, but even His own Self. He gave us His blood, His life, His all in the Blessed Sacrament. After God has bestowed Himself on us, what else remains for Him to give us? He has no room to extend Himself further for the love of man.

Oh, the strength of Divine love! The greatest of all has made Himself the lowest of all! Love triumphs over God; it does not consider dignity when there is question of gaining for itself the person it loves. God, Who can never be conquered by any one, has been conquered by love.

What breast so savage as not to soften before such a God of love on the altar, what hardness which it will not subdue, what love does it not claim! Thus He would appear and stay with us, Who wished to be loved and not feared. Even the very brutes, if we do them a kindness, if we give them some trifle, are grateful for it. They come near us, they do our bidding after their own fashion, and show signs of gladness at our approach. How comes it, then, that we are so ungrateful towards God—the same God Who has bestowed His whole Self upon us, Who descends every day upon our altars to become the food of our souls!

Love is the loadstone of love. Hence, if you wish to be loved, love. There is no more effectual means to secure to yourself the affections of another than to love him and to make him aware that you love him. But, my Jesus, this rule holds good for others, holds good for all, but not for Thee. Men are grateful to all, but not to Thee. Thou art at a loss what more to do, to show men the love Thou bearest them. Thou hast positively nothing left to do, to allure the affections of men; yet, how many are there among men who really love Thee? God has not earned this at our hands; that God, so good, so tender of us.

O man, whoever thou art, thou hast witnessed the love which God has borne thee in becoming man, in suffering and dying for thee, and in giving Himself as food to thee. How long will it be before God shall know by experience and by deeds the love thou bearest Him? Truly, indeed, every man at the sight of God clothed in flesh, and choosing to lead a life of such durance, to suffer a death of such ignominy, to dwell a loving prisoner in our churches, ought to be enkindled with love towards one so loving. "Oh, that Thou wouldst rend the heavens and wouldst come down: the mountains would melt away at Thy Presence, the waters would burn with fire."* Oh, that Thou wouldst deign, my God! (thus cried out the prophet before the arrival of the Divine Word upon earth) to leave the heavens, and to descend here to become man amongst us! On beholding Thee like one of themselves, the mountains would melt away; that is, men would surmount all obstacles, all difficulties, in observing Thy laws and Thy counsels; the waters

---

* Isaias lxiv. 1, 2.

would burn with fire! Surely, Thou wouldst enkindle such a furnace in the human heart, that even the most frozen souls would catch the flame of Thy blessed love! And, in truth, after the Incarnation of the Son of God, how brilliantly has the fire of Divine love shone to many living souls! It may be asserted even, without fear of contradiction, that God was more beloved in one century after the coming of Jesus Christ, than in the entire forty centuries preceding. How many youths, how many of the nobly born, how many monarchs have abandoned wealth, honor, and their very kingdoms, to seek the desert or the cloister, that there, in poverty and obscure seclusion, they might the more unreservedly give themselves up to the love of this their Saviour! How many martyrs have gone rejoicing and making merry on their way to torments and to death! How many tender virgins have refused the proffered hands of the great ones of this world, in order to go and die for Jesus Christ, and so repay, in some measure, the affection of a God Who stooped down to become incarnate, die for love of them, and stay with them as their perpetual Victim on our altars, even to become the food and drink of their souls.

Yes, all this is most true, but now comes a tale for tears. Has this been the case with all men? Have all sought thus to correspond with this immense love of Jesus Christ? Alas, the greater part have combined to repay Him with nothing but ingratitude! And what sort of return have we ourselves made up to this time for the love our God has borne us? Have we always shown ourselves thankful? Have we ever seriously reflected what those words mean—a God to be made man, to die for us and become our food? What more could Jesus Christ have done to win our love? If the Son of God had engaged to rescue from death His own Father, to what lower humiliation could He stoop than to assume human flesh and lay down His life in sacrifice for His salvation, and to renew this Sacrifice every day, in every holy Mass? Nay, had Jesus Christ been a mere man instead of one of the Divine Persons, had He wished to gain by some token of affection, the love of His God, what more could He have done for Him? If a servant of ours had given out of love for us His very life-blood, would He not have riveted our heart to Him, and obliged us to love Him for very gratitude at least? How comes it, then, that Jesus Christ, though He has laid down His life for us and láys it down daily in Mass hundreds of times, has still failed to win our love?

To love God, how beautiful a thing it is! Man was created by love; it is on this account that he is so prone to love. On the other hand, man is so great that nothing on this earth can satisfy him. It is only when he turns to God that he feels contented and happy. Take a fish out of the water and it will die. Well! such is man without God. Oh! how blessed a thing it is that we can please God, little and low as we are! If a lost soul could but once say: 'My God, I love Thee," it would be no longer in hell. But, alas for that poor soul, it has lost the power to love which it had received, and which it refused to use! Its heart is dried up like a bunch of grapes which has passed through the winepress. There is no more happiness in that soul, no more peace, because no more love. "Unhappy souls," said St. Teresa, "they do not love." The goodness of God kindles the fire of hell. The lost will say: Oh, if God had loved us less, we should suffer less; hell would be more endurable. But to have been so much loved, what anguish!

Alas! men hold in contempt the divine love, because they do not, or rather let us say, because they will not, understand what a treasure it is to enjoy Divine Grace, an infinite treasure. Men appreciate the good graces of a prince, of a prelate, of a nobleman, of a man of letters, and yet these same persons set no value on the grace of God, but renounce it for mere smoke, for a brutal gratification, for a handful of earth, for a whim, for nothing.

Do we wish to be ranked among these ungrateful ones? Can we find ourselves something better than God? Can we find ourselves a prince more courteous, a master, a brother, a friend more amiable, who has shown us a deeper love? Can we seek for ourselves one who is better qualified than God to make us happy in the present life and in the life to come?

Whoever loves God has nothing to fear, and God cannot help loving in return one who loves Him: "I love those who love me."* And what shall he dread of, who is the beloved of God? "The Lord is my light and my salvation, whom shall I fear?"† So said David, and so said the sisters of Lazarus to our dear Lord: "He whom Thou lovest is sick."‡ It was enough for them to know that He would do everything for his recovery. But how, on the other hand, can God love those who despise His love?

Come, then, let us once for all make the resolution to give the tribute of our love to a God Who has so sincerely loved us. The kings of the earth glory in the possession of kingdoms and of wealth; Jesus Christ rests content with the sovereignty of our hearts. This He considers His principality, and this principality He sought to obtain by dying on the Cross.

Since Jesus Christ, then, has given Himself to each one, what great thing will a man do if he give himself wholly to Jesus Christ? Let us, with a good will, give our heart and our love to this God, Who, in order to gain it, has had to give His blood, His life, His whole self.

But this heart He will not have divided; He will have it whole and entire; He wishes us to love Him with our whole heart, otherwise He is not content. Aware that man, had he been redeemed by a seraph, would have had to divide his heart by partly loving his Creator and partly his redeemer, God, Who would possess the entire heart, and the entire love of man, wished, therefore, to be both our Creator and our Redeemer. And let us understand that we shall give our whole heart to God when we give Him our will entirely, not wishing anything henceforward but what God wishes, Who

---

* Prov. viii. 17.   † Ps. xxvi. 1.   ‡ John xi. 5.

certainly desires only our welfare and happiness. "To this end Christ died and rose again, that He might be Lord both of the dead and of the living. Therefore, whether we live or whether we die, we are the Lord's." * Jesus was pleased to die for us, and be our perpetual Victim upon our altars; more than this He could not have done to win all our love, and to be the sole Lord of our heart, so that from this day forward we are bound to make known to heaven and to earth, in life and in death, that we are no longer our own, but belong solely and entirely to God.

How God longs to see, and how dearly He loves a heart that is wholly His! What delicate and loving caresses does He show, what good things, what delights, what glory does He prepare in Paradise for a heart that is wholly His! Devout souls, if Jesus gain us, we shall also gain Jesus. The advantage of such an exchange is all on our side. "Teresa," said our Lord one day to this saint, "Teresa, up to this time you have not been all Mine; now that you are all Mine, be assured that I am all yours." Love is a bond which binds the lover with the loved one. God has every wish to clasp and unite us to Himself; but it is also necessary for us to strive and unite ourselves to God. If we wish God to give Himself entirely to us, it is likewise necessary for us to give ourselves entirely to Him, loving Him with our whole heart, with our whole soul, with all our strength, so that not one fibre may be left in us which does not belong to God. According to the degree of love which we bear towards God when we finish the journey of life, will be the degree of love with which we shall continue to love God for all eternity. He, then, who would love God exceedingly in heaven, must love Him very much on earth.

It is told of the Japanese that when the Gospel was being announced to them, when they were being instructed on the sublimity, the beauty, and the infinite amiability of God, and

---

* Rom. xiv. 8.

especially when they were being taught the great mysteries of religion, all that God had done for man, God born in poverty, God suffering, God dying for their love and for their salvation, they exclaimed in a transport of joy and admiration: "Oh how great, how good and amiable is the God of the Christians!" But afterward, when they heard that there was an express command of loving God and a threatened punishment for not loving Him, they were surprised, and could not conceal their astonishment. "What!" said they, "what! a command given to reasonable men to love the God Who has loved us so much! Why, is it not the greatest of all happiness to love Him, and the greatest of all misfortunes not to love Him? What! are not the Christians always at the foot of the altars of their God, penetrated with a deep sense of His goodness, and inflamed with His holy love?" And when they were given to understand that there were Christians who not only did not love God, but even offended and outraged Him, "O unworthy people! O ungrateful hearts!" exclaimed they in their indignation; "is it possible? In what accursed land dwell those men devoid of hearts and feelings?"

St. Paul exclaimed: "If any man does not love our Lord Jesus Christ, let him be anathema"—let him be accursed. Let him be accursed by God the Father, accursed by God the Son, accursed by God the Holy Ghost. Let him be accursed by angels and by men. Let him be accursed by the very demons in hell. Let him be accursed by *all creatures* for refusing to love our Lord and Redeemer, Jesus Christ.

Such is the language that the great Apostle St. Paul, the ardent lover of the Lord, uses towards all who refuse to turn upon their God the force of that ever active principle of love within them, which will never suffer them to rest, which was implanted in them by their Creator, and which they are their own greatest enemies if they do not direct to Him.

As there are none more deeply interested in the great mystery of Love of our holy religion than the priests of the

Catholic Church, it is to them in particular that these words are addressed. To the world at large, perhaps, such language will be but little understood. Surrounded with vanities, buried in spiritual sloth, and accustomed only to the language and sentiments of a profane passion, it knows not of any other, and when we attempt to raise its grovelling affections to the sublime love of an all-perfect God, and even support the exertion with all the force of the wonder of the mystery of love, it is all insensible; it hears us with indifference, if not with impatience, and coolly gives back the neglected lesson to the contemplative inmates of the cloister and the sanctuary. Let us, then, my brethren, gladly take it for ourselves. We have no ties upon the world, nor the world upon us; we have seen through and despised the emptiness of its boasted advantages, and have nothing left but to pursue with ardor that better part which we have chosen. To us, then, the impressive lessons of this tremendous mystery will be read with more effect.

Indeed, we have an additional motive to learn it well, for we are called to be the ministers and delegates of Jesus Christ—our High Priest on earth; we are the depositaries of that sacred fire which one day burned with such vehemence on Mount Calvary, and has ever since continued to burn on our altars with undiminished intensity; and we are to scatter and enkindle it through a frozen world. With what eagerness then ought we to cherish the sacred affection and light it up betimes in our own bosoms. And how shall we so effectually do it as in the contemplation of the Eucharistic Sacrifice? Yes, my brethren, it was here the Apostles grew inflamed, it was the recollection of this wonderful divine love that carried them through all their labors, and made sufferings and death their glory and their gain. And truly this is the grand compendium of all our studies. Here they centre, or are reducible to this—the knowledge and love of a crucified God in the Holy Eucharist. This sacred lesson once learned well, would supply every deficiency; it would fill us at once with true wisdom, and inspire us with genuine eloquence. Whereas, without it, though possessed of all the sciences, we should be deplorably ignorant; though adepts in human eloquence, we should be no better than sounding brass and tinkling cymbals.

If, then, my brethren, in the multiplicity and distraction of other pursuits we have too often lost sight of this grand study, let this day at least terminate the omission, and be our day of introduction to a new school.

If the love of Jesus on the altar has hitherto been to us a veiled mystery, and the holy Mass a "hidden treasure," oh! let them be so no longer, lest slighted tenderness turn to anger, and grace abused call down retributive vengeance. Let us henceforward make this mystery one of the most prominent subjects of our daily meditation and discourse to the people. Let us frequently place ourselves at the foot of the altar; let us look up with feeling affection at that sublime and expressive Host. The saints assure us that God regards with complacency even the sinner who looks devoutly upon the image of Christ. The hardest rocks are excavated by time, the coldest bodies become warm by repeated application to the fire. Though now perhaps unfeeling, we shall in time yield to the powerful impression on some destined day; the moving spectacle of an amiable God, mystically slain and expiring every day out of love for us, with expanded arms, as it were, inviting us into His embraces, will touch us with sensibility. A ray will beam from the Sacred Host upon our understandings, a spark will fall from it upon our frozen hearts. Surprised and delighted with the new sensation, we shall cherish it with ardor. Meditation will fan the flame; increasing grace will enlarge and expand it, and raise it at last into a conflagration which even the corrupt and unfriendly air of a surrounding world will thenceforth have no power to damp or extinguish.

PROTEST OF THE AUTHOR.

In obedience to the decrees of Urban VIII., of holy memory, I protest that I do not intend to attribute any other than purely human authority to all the miracles, revelations, graces and incidents contained in this book; neither to the titles, holy or blessed, applied to the servants of God not yet canonized, except in cases where these have been confirmed by the HOLY ROMAN CATHOLIC CHURCH and by the HOLY APOSTOLIC SEE, of whom I profess myself an obedient son, and, therefore, to their judgment I submit myself and whatever I have written in this book.

FATHER MICHAEL MÜLLER'S BOOKS.

PRAYER, THE KEY OF SALVATION. - - Price, $1.10.

"The Book on Prayer, Key of Salvation," writes Archbishop Spaulding, of Baltimore, "is a collection of beautiful jewels. It is a truly admirable book. In point of intrinsic merit, it is superior to its predecessor—the golden book on the Holy Eucharist,—making due allowance for the difference of subject. It is replete with interest and solid instruction, and is specially well adapted for spiritual reading in religious communities and in families. We take much pleasure in recommending to our Diocesans this excellent work of Rev. M. Müller, C. SS. R., on "*Prayer, the Key of Salvation*," which now appears in a second revised edition."

"Prayer, this daily food of the soul," writes Bishop Luers (Feb. 22, 1868), "is too much neglected even by the better sort of Christians, because its necessity is not sufficiently understood.—Your clear, solid and attractive explanations of it, will no doubt, open the eyes of many, and induce them to practise this all-important duty in earnest, and thereby save their immortal souls."

"We had scarcely laid down Fr. Müller's excellent work on the Blessed Eucharist," says the *Boston Pilot*, "when another work by the same highly gifted pen is laid on our table. A heart so fervently loving our Lord in the Sacrament of His Love must needs belong to a man of prayer, eminently so. It is the noblest, the inspiring quality of a soul enamored with Jesus in the Eucharist to know how to pray. Hence, Fr. Müller, having entertained us with loving care before the Tabernacle of our Saviour, teaches us how to tarry there by ourselves, and in sweet communing with Jesus, secure the aid we need for the eternal welfare of our soul. We allude to "Prayer, the Key of Salvation," just published by Messrs. Kelly & Piet, of Baltimore. Indeed, in reading the work, we aver that St. Alphonsus' mantle has fallen on the shoulders of his faithful disciple."

The *Catholic Mirror*, of Baltimore, speaks of this book in the following terms: "This work entitled "Prayer, the Key of Salvation" is full of unction, and cannot fail to warm up the sluggish and fortify the zealous. We have received from a friend of ours, a convert to our religion, the following interesting letter in reference to this work:

"May God bless the author of this precious book. Oh, what a most precious book! I wish I could purchase a million of copies and distribute them to the poor souls who know not the precious secret of *prayer!* What has he left unsaid? Into what secret folds of the human heart has he not penetrated, to present this dear prerogative, and what motive has he not presented! Oh, if I had had this precious book ten years ago, what a mine of untold treasure would it have been to me! For, led as I have been by prayers, fears and perplexities and doubts arose, that would all have been expelled *by the clear expositions of this book.* Strange that confessors do not enjoin and lead their penitents, particularly converts, more by prayer than they do. But in this active age, the hidden life of prayer is lost to themselves, and this is what puzzled me."

The *Catholic Telegraph* says in reference to this book : "'Prayer, the Key of Salvation' is the production of Michael Müller, C. SS. R., priest of the Congregation of the Most Holy Redeemer, author of that beautiful and universally eulogized work, 'The Blessed Eucharist.' This volume is published with the approbation of the Most Rev. Archbishop of Baltimore. In this cold, indifferent, and undevotional age, when man, in his pride, vanity, and worldliness, seldom thinks of raising his heart and mind to God for blessings, assistance, or relief, or in gratitude, but instead sees only himself, thinks only of himself and looks only to himself for assistance and success, and beholds in himself the source and cause of all his prosperity and perfection, both in spiritual and material order; *such a concise, lucid, earnest and powerful exposition of, and appeal in behalf of, that heaven-born boon to mankind, prayer, is indeed apropos and valuable.*"

"No better book," says the *New York Tablet,* "could be used for spiritual reading." "It is," adds the *Freeman's Journal,* "a needful supplement of the author's beautiful treatise on the Blessed Eucharist."

THE BLESSED EUCHARIST OUR GREATEST TREASURE. Price, $1.10.

[*Letter from Archbishop Spaulding.*]

"We have read with much pleasure and with great edification this valuable work, composed by one of our Redemptorist Fathers in Baltimore. We have found the matter solid, well digested, and instructive, and the style simple, earnest, and full of unction. The examples are, in general, appropriately selected as illustrations of the text ; and many of them are very edifying, and even touching. These are, of course, to be received, according to the author's timely protest in the beginning, with the wise reserve expressly ordered by the Church in regard to such matters, in the well-known Bull of Urban VIII. ; but, with this necessary precaution, such legends are profitable unto edification, as the way of teaching by example is much more compendious, as well as much more impressive, than that by word or writing. It is refreshing to find, in this cold utilitarian age, a work issued from the press so full of Catholic life, and so glowing with the fire of Catholic love. Believing that its extensive circulation

TESTIMONIALS.

and diligent perusal will be promotive of piety, and will be useful to all classes both within and without the Church, we earnestly recommend the work to the faithful people under our charge.

"MARTIN JOHN SPAULDING, *Archbishop of Baltimore.*

"*Baltimore, Feast of St. Francis de Sales, 1868.*"

[*Letter from Bishop Luers.*]

"Reverend and Dear Sir:—'The Blessed Eucharist,' of which you have kindly sent me a copy, is truly a charming work. It should be in every Catholic family.

"Yours truly in Christ,

"J. H. LUERS, *Bishop of Fort Wayne.*

"*Fort Wayne, January 23, 1868.*"

[*From the "Banner of the South," Augusta, Georgia.*]

"We have read this beautiful book; we have tasted the sweetness of its thoughts, and we are reading it again. There is a humility about its style so like His humility who dwells with us in the Holy Sacrament: deep thoughts in plain words—doctrinal sublimities in language so simple, that a child, without effort, may understand. It is indeed a book of piety, and it will fill many a heart with love for the Great Mystery of the Altar.

"REV. FATHER RYAN, *of Augusta, Ga.*"

[*Letter to the Editors of the "Baltimore Mirror."*]

"Messrs. Editors of the *Baltimore Mirror:*—If you have room in your columns, permit me, through them, to say a word or two about Father Müller's book, 'The Blessed Eucharist.' But how shall I begin? To say it is great, good, or grand, is not enough. The nearest I can come to expressing what I feel about it, is to say, next to receiving the Blessed Eucharist, is the perusal of this inestimable book. I wish to say to every reader of the *Mirror*, buy the book. No matter how great a sinner you are, the hope of speedy relief is pointed out to you here; no matter how weak and discouraged you are, the way to strengthen you is shown here; no matter how dear the privilege is to you of receiving the Blessed Sacrament, it will become doubly dear after reading this book. To the rich I would say, buy two copies and give one to your poor brother; his prayers and blessings will well repay you for the trifling expenditure. To the ladies I would say, spare yourself a bit of ribbon and buy the book. To the gentlemen, a few less segars or drinks, and buy the book. Every single page of it is worth the price of the volume. Could dear Father Müller have heard the prayers and seen the tears of a poor old lady who is crippled, and cannot go to church, when it was being read to her this morning, he would be rewarded as I know he wishes to be. To one and all I say, buy the book.

"CECILIA.

"*Harrisburg, Pa.*, 1868.

TESTIMONIALS.

OUR LADY OF PERPETUAL HELP, IN THE WORK OF OUR REDEMPTION AND SANCTIFICATION. With an Historical Account of the Origin and Effects of the Miraculous Picture. Price, 40 cents.

[Letter from James A. McMaster, Editor and Proprietor of "New York Freeman's Journal."]

"MY DEAR FATHER MÜLLER,—I have read the manuscript you were so kind as to leave with me, on 'Our Lady of Perpetual Help.'

"I will say, sincerely, that I think it even more valuable, and more interesting, than your book on the Blessed Eucharist, that has done so much good, and is liked so much by pious souls. More than this it cannot be needed to say; but I will add that, in my poor judgment at least, it is so desirable to have it *speedily* published, that I wish the angels may *tickle the lungs* of any one that, beyond what is necessary, delays its production.

"Affectionately and humbly yours,

"New York, May 19, 1871."   JAMES A. McMASTER.

THE GOLDEN RULE; OR, THE BOOK FOR ALL. Price, $2.00.

[From the "Boston Pilot," Nov. 25, 1871.]

"The author of this excellent work is the Rev. Michael Müller, C. SS. R.—a name deservedly held in great esteem in the Catholic community. We shall not praise the author for his eminent qualities, for we do not wish to give him pain. But of his work, which we have carefully examined, we must say that it will compare favorably with Rodriguez, Nigronius, and Cassian. True, it is written for Superiors of Religious Communities, yet it will prove eminently useful to Pastors and Directors of Souls. Father Müller exhibits a knowledge of Religious and Ascetic Economy truly wonderful. We bespeak for this work a wide circulation. It is a book of that enticing class that, once taken up, it will not be laid down until read through, from A to Z. Dry as the subject may appear, it is so handled that the *utile et dulce* must needs be felt by all readers. Again we thank Father Müller for this new addition he has given to the stock of our American Catholic Literature and profitable reading.

"REV. FATHER FINOTTI."

[From the "New York Freeman's Journal."]

"This book will be very valuable to Superiors of Religious Houses, for whom it is primarily intended. But it is the book, also, for a great many others. It is a book for Catholic Pastors of Parishes—for they have governmental responsibility of souls. It is a book for priests who sit in the Confessional, for these, too, have to deal with all sorts of temperaments and of characters. But it is a book, also, for *Catholic parents*—for these by Divine order, have the care and responsibility for the right training of their children."

[*From the "Pittsburgh Catholic."*]

"This is a work which will be very acceptable to the Superiors of Religious Orders. In a clear and forcible manner the reverend author has laid before us the awful responsibility, with its trials and consolations, which rests on the shoulders of all those who are called to rule and direct the various characters that enter the religious state.

"The art of arts, and the science of sciences, is to rule—to govern men. With this beautiful as well as profound saying of St. Gregory, the reverend author opens his first chapter. Around it he hangs all the wisdom which many years of study and experience have enabled him to collect.

"We have every hope that the work will meet with a well-merited reception. It may truly be called the 'Golden Rule,' since it embraces all the duties of Superiors."

[*From the "Baltimore Mirror," Nov. 4, 1871.*]

"This excellent work, by a talented and respected clergyman of this city, although written principally for the instruction of those who have charge of religious communities, will prove of immense benefit to all in authority, whether clerical or lay; and while the director of souls will find in it much sound advice, the parent, the teacher, will treasure it as a safe guide in the performance of duties too often little understood. If it is hard to learn to obey, still harder is it to learn how to govern. The perusal of 'THE GOLDEN RULE' will do much towards avoiding the misuse of the 'brief authority' with which one is clothed.

"This book bears the 'Imprimatur' of the Most Rev. Archbishop of Baltimore, and its typographical execution does credit to the publishers."

[*From the "New York Tablet," Nov. 11, 1871.*]

"This is truly a golden book, full of sublime instruction for the governing and the governed, not only in religious communities, for whom it seems specially intended, but amongst Christians in the world. It is a work of the highest importance, and ought to find a place in the library of every religious house."

TRIUMPH OF THE BLESSED SACRAMENT; OR, HISTORY OF NICOLA AUBRY. Price, 50 cents.

[*From the "Boston Pilot."*]

"This is a valuable work. Father Müller is a writer well-known to the Catholics; his writings have proved most acceptable for their solidity and practicalness. This is a timely production, when, by an inexplicable inconsistency, the agency of spirits is asserted, and their existence denied. The History of Nicola cannot be contradicted; and page 114 contains the clearest exposition of the nature of Spiritualism (spiritism), and the conclusive proofs of its agency.

"FATHER FINOTTI."

[From the "New York Tablet."]

"This little book is full, from beginning to end, of extraordinary and intense interest. The narrative contained in the first part of it is one that shows in a remarkable manner the dread power of Our Lord in His Sacrament of the Altar. a power which the infernal legions recognize, and before which they tremble. The second part gives a short but deeply interesting account of modern spiritualism, as the form which divination, sorcery, and devil-worship has assumed in our days. It is written in a simple, agreeable style, that makes it pleasant to read."

THE RELIGIOUS STATE. - - - - - Price, 75 cents.

[From the "Pittsburgh Catholic."]

"This is an excellent little work—one which should be read by all. It shows the origin of the religious state, and the advantages to be derived by a life solely devoted to the service of God. The many objections that are frequently put forward against religious orders are answered in a clear and brief manner."

THE CATHOLIC PRIEST. - - - - - Price, 50 cents.

[From the "New York Tablet."]

"The priest is measured in every light which the various obligations and phases of his sacred character throw around him. His mighty proportions on the world's stage are drawn with power, and thorough appreciation. Not a single grade in his ministry but is educed with a fine distinctness, from the position in which he is the dear friend and adviser of his flock, up to that awful height in which he is permitted to touch, with his consecrated hands, the Body and Blood of his Lord and God. Written in a strain of fervent enthusiasm, it is, for Catholics, a book to be read and cherished."

[From the "Pittsburgh Catholic."]

"This is a small volume of 163 pages. In it the learned author shows us how, by the institution of the Sacred Priesthood by our Divine Lord, the priest is constituted the light of the world, the salt of the earth, the guide, father, and friend of the people, and the obligations the faithful are under to hearken to his counsels. We wish the volume an extensive sale."

THE OUR FATHER. Vol. I. - - - Price, 50 cents.

PUBLIC SCHOOL EDUCATION. - - - - Price, $1.50.

[From the "Boston Congregational Quarterly," October, 1872.]

"The Roman Catholic view of our Common-School system is *frankly and ably* presented in a handsome volume, from the press of Patrick Donahoe, of this city. We hope Protestants will read the book and acquaint themselves with the principles and tactics of the Catholic Church on this great question. Too many of our speakers and writers discuss it without a clear knowledge of the real issues; the time has come when the very existence of our school-system is at stake, and it becomes us to know where we stand and why—to be able to give a reason for the faith that is in us; for the Catholics, as in the book under notice, can present an argument so plausible that it may deceive "even the very elect."

[From the "New Orleans Catholic Propagator."]

"We have read many an essay and treatise on public education, as education is understood and by law maintained in this country; but none of them has, in our opinion, hit the mark as precisely as this production of the learned Redemptorist. We bespeak for it the heartiest of receptions from the true friends of education.

"In this book the author handles his subject with scientific skill; probes down to its very marrow, rips it open and dissects it; he subjects the unsightly mass to the process of analysis, and from the watery, livid pulp which remains, extracts, like a true chemist, the original germ of the disease, which he follows up through all its stages of development, and traces out to all its disastrous effects on the religious, domestic, social, and national conditions of mankind. We thank the author for this timely contribution to our literature, and also, though the Archbishop of the Diocese is now absent, take the liberty to assure him of that learned and judicious Prelate's thanks and unqualified approbation."

Extracts from Letters.

"EPISCOPAL RESIDENCE, ALTON, Ill., July 29, 1872.

"REV. MICHAEL MÜLLER, C. SS. R.

"REV. DEAR SIR,—I have received a copy of your excellent work, 'Public School Education,' for which please accept my most sincere thanks. This book, if universally read, must be productive of much good. I am, Rev. dear sir, your obedient servant in Christ, ✠ D. P. BALTES, *Bishop*."

"COTTAGE, Monday, July 22, 1872.

"DEAR FATHER,—As to the book, 'Public School Education,' I am so entranced with it I can't lay it down. It is most capital. I shall buy up copies and circulate them among those outrageous politicians. It is your best book, best written, and contains a world of wisdom, and a right view of things, that people in general have not the most remote idea of. Just the thing that is wanted. May God reward you by opening the eyes of these people to a correct view of these things. Yours, in great haste, L. M. C."

TESTIMONIALS.

"ST. PAUL, Minn., July 5, 1872.
"REV. MICHAEL MÜLLER, C. SS. R.

"REV. AND DEAR FATHER,—I have just finished reading your admirable work on 'Public School Education,' and, though completely unknown to you, I cannot refrain from addressing you to thank you cordially for the grand work you have accomplished. Your book is so well-timed, its doctrine so correct and precise, the arguments you employ so cogent, that I am confident it will, under God's Providence, do a great deal of good. May your book be found *especially* in the hands of every priest in the land!

"Catholic education has been the dream, the great labor in my ministerial life; hence the joy with which I have welcomed your book.

"You will please excuse my liberty in writing to you, and receive my hearty wishes that God may leave you 'multos annos' to labor for His Glory. Very respectfully, JOHN IRELAND, *Pastor of Cathedral.*"

[*From the "Catholic Standard."*]

"We wish a copy of this book could be placed in the hands of every Prelate, Priest, and layman in the Church. It is a simple, clear, unpretending, but forcible exposé of the Public School System, its nature and pernicious consequences, designed and undesigned by its founders and supporters, and of the obligations of Catholics in regard to the subject of Public Education. It is not our intention to attempt to lecture American Catholics on their duty in reference to this matter. But sure we are that, as a general thing, they are neglecting it, and, to a very great extent, insensible to it. We trust Fr. Müller's work (from which we propose publishing some extracts hereafter), will lead to a more thoughtful consideration of the subject, on the part of Catholics, and more earnest and vigorous action in the establishing and supporting Catholic schools."

[*From " Brownson's Quarterly Review,"* January, 1873.]

"Father Müller, of the Congregation of the Most Holy Redeemer, well known to the Catholics as the author of several works, very highly commended by far more competent judges than we, gives us in this handsomely printed volume a very full and a very able treatise on Public-School Education from the point of view of the American citizen, deeply interested in the perpetuity and prosperity of American liberty, and also from the point of the Catholic priest intent on the spread of his religion, and the glory of his Master in the salvation of souls. The work is written in a free and energetic tone, and in an earnest and affectionate spirit, and well nigh exhausts the subject. It says all that needs be said, says the right thing, and says it well, and in the right way, etc."

CHARITY TO THE SOULS IN PURGATORY; or MANUAL FOR THE MEMBERS OF THE PURGATORIAN SOCIETY. 60 cts.

THE HOLY MASS, THE SACRIFICE OF THE LIVING AND THE DEAD. The Clean Oblation offered up among the Nations from the Rising to the Setting of the Sun.
NOW IN PRESS.

www.ingramcontent.com/pod-product-compliance
Lightning Source LLC
Chambersburg PA
CBHW021220300426
44111CB00007B/375